Pet Law and Custody

Establishing a Worthy and Equitable Jurisprudence for the Evolving Family

Barbara J. Gislason

ABA
SECTION OF FAMILY LAW

Cover design by Nick Panos/ABA Design

Printed in the United States of America.

21 20 19 18 17 5 4 3 2 1

Library of Congress Cataloging-in-Publication Data

Names: Gislason, Barbara J., author.
Title: Pet law and custody / Barbara J. Gislason.
Description: First edition. | Chicago : American Bar Association, [2017]
Identifiers: LCCN 2017032288 | ISBN 9781634258920
Subjects: LCSH: Pets—Law and legislation—United States. | Pet owners—Legal status, laws, etc.—United States. | Replevin—United States.
Classification: LCC KF390.5.A5 G57 2017 | DDC 346.7304/7—dc23
LC record available at https://lccn.loc.gov/2017032288

"Barbara Gislason, the founder of the American Bar Association's focus on animal law, has crafted a unique, well-researched, and groundbreaking book about companion animals. I recommend it to anyone with a curious mind."

—Linda Klein, ABA President 2016–2017

"This persuasive and inspiring book is the work of a lawyer who turns her passion into powerful advocacy. Barbara seeks justice for companion animals who become members of the family. This original, well-crafted, and practical book is well worth the read for lawyers around the world who care about protecting and caring for our most loyal friends who have no voice of their own."

—Laurel Bellows, ABA President 2012–2013

"Having attended the same high school and law school as Barbara Gislason, I have been intrigued by her development as a thought leader on animal subjects. She has written a fascinating book about companion animals, and it will be useful to family law practitioners and ADR professionals embroiled in pet custody disputes. This carefully crafted book is unique on the world stage and I recommend it."

—Nancy Zalusky Berg, President of the International Academy of Family Lawyers

"There was a time when women and children were considered chattels. But for the forward thinking of a few that grew into the enlightenment of multitudes, I could not have voted, become a lawyer, or had the privilege of serving as a chair of the ABA Section of Family Law. These are the thoughts that sprang to mind when Barbara Gislason outlined the labor of love she undertook when she embarked on writing the definitive book on pets in the law. *Pet Law and Custody* is a must-read for family lawyers who want to serve the interests of clients who are not content to settle for recitations that the animals in their families are property and who want to learn how to make a case for rights where none exist."

—Anita Ventrelli, Chair, ABA Section of Family Law 2008–2009

"Having long served on the board of an internationally recognized veterinary group, I observed a change in veterinary core beliefs. We recognized and adopted policies that animals are sentient. Lawyers, like health professionals, are aware of scientific breakthroughs and changing their core beliefs, too. In this seminal book by Barbara Gislason about companion animals, the ethical and moral quandaries applicable to both professions are understood and amplified. I am thrilled to recommend this indispensable resource for my colleagues, and those interested in understanding how the legal system can be improved."

—Kate Knutson, DVM; Past President, American Animal Hospital Association; Past President, Society for Veterinary Medical Ethics

"Barbara Gislason is a pioneer in the field of animal and pet law. I know because I was there early on when she faced much criticism, even derision, as she struggled to get proper recognition for this emerging discipline. But she persisted and is now internationally recognized for her efforts. She shares her experience and insights in this informative book that captures the legal aspects and emotional nuances of animal law. When representing a client with legal issues involving animals, a lawyer is well advised to have this book close at hand."

—Justice Paul H. Anderson, Minnesota Supreme Court 1994–2013

"Long aware of her national leadership in animal law, I applaud Gislason's groundbreaking and unique book. In addition to providing practical advice and intriguing case law analysis, she offers a compelling vision as to where companion animals, as family members, rightfully belong in 21st-century jurisprudence. I foresee that Barbara Gislason's book will earn its place on the world stage."

—Ellen Rosenblum, Oregon Attorney General

"A creative exploration of pet law and custody issues for a wide-ranging audience. The book is both visionary—in exploring the changing role of our pets in society and in the eyes of the law—and practical—in providing real-world advice to advocates via case summaries, practical pointers, and appendices filled with useful litigation tools."

—Daina Bray, Chair of ABA Animal Law Committee;
General Counsel of the International Fund for Animal Welfare

"A comprehensive and well-researched book on pet custody is long overdue. *Pet Law and Custody* provides readers with important practical advice about what to do if a dispute arises. I'm certain this unique book will propel much needed change in companion animal law."

—Marc Bekoff, Author of *The Animals' Agenda: Freedom, Compassion, and Coexistence in the Human Age*

"I am not familiar with any other book that unpacks the complexity of laws affecting pet custody disputes. In particular, this book offers extensive information about how ADR processes such as arbitration and mediation can be used in resolving these kinds of conflicts. I recommend this excellent book to my peers."

—Barbara Atwood, Chair, Uniform Family Law Arbitration Act Drafting Committee;
Professor Emerita, University of Arizona Rogers College of Law

"This book stands as the definitive study of the status of pet law and custody. Barbara Gislason's scholarship expands beyond that and offers cogent and compelling arguments for redefining the status given to pets within our legal system—going beyond the restrictive 'property' classification—and offers bold arguments of why companion animals should be considered as our family members legally and morally. This visionary book offers a thrilling prospect of what the future holds for us and our dog companions."

—Claudia Kawczynska, Editor-in-Chief, *The Bark*

"I applaud Barbara Gislason for writing this fascinating book about companion animals. As a family lawyer in London, I was intrigued to learn about the complexity of all the law in the States. I have invited this author to address the Family Law Commission of the Union Internationale des Avocats (UIA) at its 61st Congress. I recommend this book to family lawyers everywhere with a curious mind."

—Simon Bruce, President of the UIA Family Law Commission

"Once upon a time nonhuman animals were nearly invisible to law. No more. Today they are everywhere in law and perhaps no more often than in cases resulting from their status as family members. Barbara's book provides an excellent roadmap for those who need to know what to do when their nonhuman family member is in the middle of a legal problem."

—Steven Wise, Author of *Rattling the Cage: Toward Legal Rights for Animals*

"This thoughtfully crafted volume reveals well that grasping the significance of animal law requires a dance of partners—practicality, compassion, legal precision, and an open-hearted vision. This accessible volume should be read by anyone who hopes to make citizens in modern societies more aware that they can foster protections for many nonhuman animals who live with, among, or near us."

—Dr. Paul Waldau, Author of *Animal Studies: An Introduction*; Professor, Canisius College

"I was president of the Minnesota State Bar Association (MSBA) when Barbara Gislason historically launched the Animal Law Committee, then Section. With great respect, I applaud her achievement in writing this comprehensive and well-researched book about companion animal law. Family lawyers, judges, and ADR professionals will find this book both interesting and useful."

—Jim Baillie, MSBA President 2003–2004

"During the time I was executive director of the American Bar Association, Barbara J. Gislason sought my advice in bringing animal law to the ABA. I was pleased to assist her, knowing that with her brains, tenacity, and enthusiasm, she would be a trailblazer second to none. I am impressed by her book about companion animals and pet custody disputes and recommend it to lawyers and judges alike."

—Bob Stein, Former ABA Executive Director and Chief Operating Officer

"When Barbara spoke at Harvard Law School many years ago, I knew she was a visionary. I am honored to recommend her thoroughly researched, beautifully written, and captivating book to anyone interested in the welfare of companion animals."

—Song Wei, Dean, University of Science and Technology of China

"In 2015, I was proud to present Barbara J. Gislason with the *Outstanding Recognition Award for Laying the Foundation for the Success of the Animal Law Committee and Its Mission to Create a Just World for All* from the ABA Tort Trial & Insurance Practice Section. Now, I applaud her achievements in writing a cutting-edge book that will be useful to family lawyers, animal lawyers, and ADR professionals alike. An essential resource for anyone interested in the intersection of the legal system with the human–animal bond."

—Christopher Green, Executive Director, Harvard Law School Animal Law & Policy Program

"When animal law was in its infancy, as MSBA president elect, I sponsored Barbara Gislason in her effort to launch animal law in Minnesota. This extraordinary book will forever change the place of companion animals in American life. This is a go-to book."

—David Stowman, President, Minnesota State Bar Association 2004–2005

"I like this book because it offers extensive case analysis, practice pointers, and a vision for a better tomorrow. Family lawyers and animal lawyers alike, as well as ADR professionals, will find this book invaluable. I recommend it."

—Richard Pena, President, State Bar of Texas 1998–1999; President, American Bar Foundation 2008–2009

"Now that companion animals have become family members, it is time for lawyers, lawmakers, and bioethicists to reimagine animal welfare. I was impressed by this comprehensive and compelling work and recommend it to my bioethicist colleagues."

—Jonathan Moreno, Author of *Mind Wars: Brain Science and the Military in the 21st Century*

"Barbara J. Gislason is a trailblazer on animal welfare subjects and I am proud to be her friend. Because I know her intellectually, I was not surprised by the breadth and depth of her extraordinary book. I recommend this book to primate and companion animal enthusiasts alike."

—Sue Savage-Rumbaugh, Author of *Apes, Language, and the Human Mind*

"*Pet Law and Custody* is a groundbreaking, well-researched, and intriguing treatise on the development of custody law for the animals we love. Ms. Gislason presents a national review of pet case law, with practice pointers, and cogently analyzes past developments and discusses future trends. For both the legal practitioner and lay reader alike, this book is a must-read. You will be transformed by its contents."

—Hon. Marilyn Kaman, ABA Observer to the U.S. Mission to the United Nations and ABA Section of International Law

"Barbara Gislason's book reflects both her expertise and compassion. Her wonderful, inspiring book will help those with pet custody disputes. A groundbreaking work and treasure trove of valuable resources, this book is an important game-changer. We enthusiastically endorse and recommend it."

—Allen and Linda Anderson, *New York Times* bestselling authors of *A Dog Named Leaf* and founders of Angel Animals Network

"Barbara's passion for animals and her legal skills can clearly be seen in this comprehensive book. The subject is treated in depth and rarely does an animal law–themed book include mediation, collaborative law, and arbitration. This pioneering book, thanks to its thorough reasoning, is very useful, even for a civil law lawyer like me!"

—Jean-François Henrotte, President of Euregio Arbitration Center; Secretary-General of International Center for Collaborative Law, Belgium

"This book is a full legal handbook for the human owner of companion animals. While custody disputes about companion animals are an initial focus, the book expands into a wider circle of legal issues, with topics including family law, property law, and animal cruelty. All owners of companion animals should have this as a reference guide to legal issues."

—David Favre, Author of *Animal Welfare, Interests, and Rights*; Professor of Law, Michigan State University

"Domesticated animals and humans have a symbiotic relationship. We have bred them for thousands of years, shaping every aspect of their form for human benefit. As domesticated animals, the law has focused on animals as property. With the development of the concept of the 'companion animal,' there is a natural shift in the legal framework to acknowledge the complexity of the relationship. *Pet Law and Custody* is a substantial advance in framing these relationships in the context of ethics, laws, and symbiotic relationships between species."

—Stephen M. Hewitt and Mercedes K. Meyer, Owners/Breeders/Handlers

"Cat lovers will appreciate Barbara Gislason's comprehensive analysis of the law impacting our beloved companion animals. It is an imperative resource not only for lawyers, but laypeople and mystery fiction authors like me. I know my readers will especially value the section on wills and trusts involving animals. Thank goodness the animals have found a strong new and authoritative advocate."

—Carole Nelson Douglas, Author of *Midnight Louie Feline PI* series

I dedicate this book to my father, Robert W. Gislason, a trial lawyer who loved dogs, well. He always said, "I never met a dog I didn't like, or who didn't like me."

Contents

About the Author xvii
Acknowledgments xxi
Foreword xxiii
Introduction xxv

Chapter 1: Companion Animals and the Law **1**

Defining Pets and Companion Animals 2
American Pet Products Association 3
Pets in the Legal System 4
Legal Precedent 5
Absolute Rights 5
Animal Welfare Act 6
Animal Enterprise Terrorism Act 7
Statutes and Ordinances 7
Applying the Law to Pet Custody Disputes 8
Law and Culture 8
Conclusion 9

Chapter 2: Family Law and Replevin Actions **11**

Fictitious Standard of Value 11
Criteria for the Record 12
Joint Custody and Visitation 12
Animal/Human Bonds 13
Animal/Animal Bonds 14
Determining Family Members 14
Replevin 14
Best-Interest Factors 15
Pets and Domestic Abuse 18
Fostering Animals 20
Loss of Companionship 20
Benefits of Owning a Pet 21
Equitable Principles 21
Identifying a Pet Owner 22
Conclusion 22
Applicable Case Law 23

Chapter 3: Alternative Dispute Resolution **81**

Mediation 81
- Types of Mediation 81
- Choosing a Mediation Type 84
- Choosing a Mediator 85
- Mediator Approaches 85
- Med/Arb 85
- Final Disposition 86
- Positional and Interest-Based ADR Processes 86
- Mediation, Neuroscience, and Objectivity 87
- Records for Mediation 90
- Mediation Questions 91
- Mediators with Animal Expertise 93
- Attorney Expertise 93
- Model Standards of Practice for Family and Divorce Mediation 94
- Making Deals 102
- Client Preparation 104
- Attorney Awareness 105
- Court Action 105
- Animal-Focused Facilitation Team 106
- Collaborative Law and Uniform Collaborative Law Rules/Act 106

Arbitration 108
- Types of Arbitration 108
- Arbitration Benefits 109
- Family Law Arbitration Act 109
- Vacating Arbitration Award 111
- Binding Arbitration 111
- Single-Issue Arbitration 111
- Jurisdiction and Waivers 112
- Finality Requirement 112
- Perception of Case 113
- Co-Ownership Agreements 113
- Arbitration Controversy 113
- Private Agreements 114
- Drafting Arbitration Agreements 114
- Private and Public Justice 116

Conclusion 117

Applicable Case Law 117

Chapter 4: Estate Planning, Wills, and Trusts **141**

Estate Planning for Animals 141
- Euthanasia 142
- Oral Communications 142

Wills 143

Trusts 143
  Traditional Trusts 143
  Honorary Trusts 144
  Conditional Trusts 144
  Uniform Probate Code 144
  Pet Trust Basics 145
Estate Planning Case 147
Durable Powers of Attorney 149
Companion Animal Care through Veterinary College 150
Loved for Life Program 150
Conclusion 151

Chapter 5: Contract Law and the Uniform Commercial Code 153

Contract Concepts 153
  Statute of Frauds 154
  Equitable Principles 154
Replevin Actions 155
Contract Practice Pointers 156
  Tests, Liens, and Doctrines 158
Contract Law and Pet Custody Disputes 158
  Void and Voidable Contracts 159
  Rescue Group Contracts 159
  Breeder Contracts 161
  Standard Contract Clauses 162
  Show Dogs and Cats 162
  Reputable Breeders 162
  Foster Contracts and Bailments 163
  Indicia of Ownership 163
  Veterinarians 164
Prenuptial and Antenuptial Agreements Addressing Animals 164
Uniform Commercial Code 166
Pet Custody and Access Contracts 167
Animal Transport by Airline 169
Conclusion 169
Applicable Case Law 169

Chapter 6: Property Law and the Meaning of Things 203

Lost and Found Animals 203
  Title Passing through Operation of Law 204
  Title Not Passing through Operation of Law 204
  Owners of Lost Animals 204

Owners of Found Animals 205
Notti Legal Questions 205
Problem Solving 206
Key Research Terms 206
Microchips 206
Conclusion 207
Applicable Case Law 207

Chapter 7: Tort Law Affects Pet Law 245

Old Conceptions of Animals 245
How Animals Are Valued 246
Tort Claims 246
Economic Damages 247
Noneconomic Damages 247
Punitive Damages 250
Tort Transformation 250
Veterinary Liability and Medical Malpractice Model 251
Fundamental Interest Tort 253
Other Claims and Conceptions 254
Tort Law Impacts Family Law 255
Conclusion 256
Applicable Case Law 257

Chapter 8: Animal Cruelty, Crimes, and the Constitution 323

Human and Animal Abuse Link 324
State Animal-Related Regulations and Statutes 325
Animal Sex Offenders 325
Bestiality 326
Felony and Misdemeanor Animal Cruelty Laws 326
Animals as Victims 327
Personhood 327
Animal Mistreatment 327
Pit Bull Cruelty 328
Horse Cruelty 330
Animal Hoarders 330
Federal Laws 331
Horse Permit Requirements 331
Crush Videos 332
U.S. Constitutional Amendments 332
First Amendment 332
Fourth Amendment 333
Fifth Amendment 333
Fourteenth Amendment 334
Animal Control Officers 335

Animal Forfeitures 335
  Criminal Forfeitures 336
  Civil Forfeitures 336
Conclusion 336
Applicable Case Law 337

Chapter 9: Katrina, Katrina 365

Hurricane Katrina Sequence of Events 365
  Plight of Animals 366
  News Stories 367
Difficult Questions 367
Saving Katrina Animals 368
  Hold Periods 369
  Who Owns Katrina Animals 369
  Defining Crime 369
  Veterinary Services, Liability, and Workers' Compensation 370
  Ground Operations 370
  Lost and Found Animals 370
Development of Animal Law 371
  Hurricane Katrina Case Law 371
  Pertinent Laws 373
  American Bar Association Resolution 373
  Animal Disaster Relief Network 373
  Select Legal Panel on Emergency Management Regarding Animals 374
  Uniform Emergency Volunteer Health Practitioner's Act 374
American Red Cross 375
Food Drives 375
Blessing Animals 375
Conclusion 376
Applicable Case Law 376

Chapter 10: Dangerous Dogs and Police Powers 383

Travel Risks 384
Important Case Law 384
Constitutional Due Process Protection 388
"Shall/May" Dichotomy 389
Breed-Discriminatory Legislation 389
Potentially Dangerous Dog Labels 390
Strict Compliance 390
Declaration Consequences 391
Dangerous Dog Proceeding Consultation 391
Insurance Policies 393
Important Questions 394
Records to Obtain 395

Evidence 395
Statutes and Ordinances 395
Client Financial Commitment 396
Lower Expectations 396
Filing Pleadings 396
Lawyer Strategy 397
Hearing Officers 397
Animal Control 398
Making a Good Impression 399
Witnesses 399
Experts 399
Body Language 399
Legal Arguments 400
Mistaken Identity 400
Provocation 401
Nature or Nurture 402
Dangerous Dog Proceedings and Divorce 403
Client To-Do List 403
Owning an At-Risk Animal 404
Conclusion 406
Applicable Case Law 406

Chapter 11: Science and Technology 429

Genetic Testing 429
Conformation Standards 430
Cloning 431
Bioethics Involving Animals 432
  ART Common Law 432
  Near-Future Pet ART Issues 434
Family Values 435
Defining Patents 435
  What Is Patentable? 436
  Animal Patents 437
  Patent Case Law 437
  Tech Transfer 438
Copyrights 438
Conclusion 440

Chapter 12: Potpourri of the Predicates of Change 441

Charles Darwin 441
Freud and Jung 442
B. F. Skinner 442
Neuroscience 442

Animal Emotions 443
Sentience 444
Animals as Defendants 444
Personhood 445
Human Property 446
Carson, Singer, and Regan 447
Temple Grandin 447
Guardians 448
Council of State Governments 449
Animal Lawyer Labels 450
The 21st Century 450
The Role of the American Bar Association 451
Conclusion 452

Chapter 13: Law Office Basics, Anatomy of a Case, and Expert Testimony 453

Finding Potential Clients 454
Initial Consultation 454
Evaluating Potential Clients 455
Lack of Predictability in the Legal System 455
Learning About the Case 456
 Understanding Points of View 457
 Role-Playing 458
Fears 458
Problem Solving 458
Clients to Avoid 459
Client Financial Commitment 459
Preparing Quality Pleadings 459
Identifying Potential Experts 460
Conclusion 460

Conclusion 461
Epilogue: Life With Dogs 469
Appendix 1: Pet Custody Questionnaire 473
Appendix 2: Values Clarification Exercise 479
Appendix 3: Lost and Found Dog Pleadings 487
Appendix 4: Animal Seizure Memorandum of Law 507
Appendix 5: Companion Animal Custody and Ownership Family Law Statute Amendment: Model Language 515
Appendix 6: Pet Custody Statutory Provisions 517
Appendix 7: Joint Custody and Joint Ownership Agreement 525
Appendix 8: Characteristic Rescue Adoption Contract 531

Appendix 9: Breeder Agreement for Pet-Quality Dog 539
Appendix 10: Pet Custody Discovery 549
Appendix 11: Order Denying Replevin 579
Appendix 12: Replevin Pleadings and Analysis 587
Appendix 13: Order Regarding Motion to Dissolve Ex Parte Writ of Replevin 629
Appendix 14: Proposed Dangerous Dog Determination and Order 639
Appendix 15: Animal Law Books Published by the American Bar Association 649

Table of Cases 651
Index 655

Appendices are available for download at http://ambar.org/PetLaw

About the Author

Barbara J. Gislason is internationally known as a pioneer in the practice area of animal law; she received the Outstanding Recognition Award for Laying the Foundation for the Success of the Animal Law Committee and Its Mission to Create a Just World for All from the American Bar Association (ABA) Tort Trial & Insurance Practice Section (TIPS). Ms. Gislason earned her B.A. at Carleton College and her J.D. from William Mitchell College of Law. She has been an American Bar Foundation Fellow, a Super Lawyer, and a Leading American Attorney. She practices in the areas of family law, animal law, and intellectual property law.

After launching animal law in the professional bar of her home state of Minnesota, Ms. Gislason brought animal law to the national bar. She became the mother of animal law in the ABA. Through TIPS, she was able to found and lead the TIPS Animal Law Committee (ALC) and gather and retain the best and brightest animal lawyers from four continents. Under her leadership, the ALC flourished. She created, served as Editor-in-Chief, and contributed to the ALC newsletter, as well as *Tort Trial & Insurance Law Journal*, *The Brief*, and *TortSource*. She is now a TIPS Fellow and Uniform Law Commission Liaison.

When Hurricane Katrina devastated the Gulf Coast in 2005, Ms. Gislason created the ABA Animal Disaster Relief Network and convened the ABA Select Legal Panel on Emergency Management. She was a principal drafter and proponent of the adopted ABA Resolution titled *Model Act Governing Standards for the Care and Disposition of Disaster Animals*. She served as the ABA Section of Family Law (SFL) Liaison to the ABA Special Committee on Disaster Response and Preparedness; she also founded and chaired a related SFL task force. Ms. Gislason served as an Observer for the Uniform Law Commission Family Law Arbitration Drafting Committee. By Presidential appointment, she now serves on the ABA Special Committee on Bioethics and the Law.

Ms. Gislason also served as an ABA Advisor to the Uniform Law Commission (ULC) regarding the Uniform Emergency Volunteer Health Practitioners Act (UEVHPA) uniform law and led the effort that enabled the portability of veterinary licenses, along with medical licenses, across state lines in a disaster context. As the result of this effort, she was the subject of the feature story for *DVM Magazine*, the premier publication of the American Veterinary Medical Association (AVMA). Ms.

Gislason served on a disaster-related U.S. Department of Justice project advisory committee and participated in a U.S. Department of Homeland Security project and working group. She appeared in the documentary *Left Behind without a Choice*, and her work is described in the book *Rescued: Saving Animals from Disaster.*

The *New York Times*, *ABA Journal*, and *Maddie's Fund* newsletter have acknowledged Ms. Gislason's contributions to animal law. Following Hurricane Katrina, Dr. Phil McGraw called her the "top animal advocate attorney in the country" on his television show *Dr. Phil.*

She has held other national leadership positions, including for the ABA Intellectual Property Law Section, where she serves on Council and has led a variety of task forces. She has also served as Minnesota State Chair of the American Bar Foundation Fellows and received a distinguished national leadership award.

Ms. Gislason has lectured at a wide variety of international and national conferences and annual meetings. They include the following:

- ABA Section of Family Law Spring Meeting
- ABA Section of International Law Spring Meeting
- ABA Presidential Select Program on Freedom of Speech
- American Animal Hospital Association Annual Meeting
- American Veterinary Medical Law Association Annual Meeting
- Animal Legal Defense Fund Harvard University Animal Law Legal Conference
- Columbia Law School Joint Student Animal Legal Defense Fund and Columbia Science and Technology Organization Program
- Humane Society of the United States Disaster Conference
- Lewis & Clark Law School Animal Law Conference
- University of Quebec in Montreal (UQAM) International Animal Law Conference
- Union Internationale des Avocats Congresses in Miami, Dresden, Macau, Florence, Valencia, and Budapest
- Union Internationale des Avocats Seminars in Hefei, Budapest, and Minneapolis

With regard to international leadership positions, Ms. Gislason serves on the Board of Directors of the Paris-based Union Internationale des Avocats (UIA), is President of the UIA Biotechnology Law Commission, and is President of the UIA U.S. National Committee. She has also lectured on American democracy to prominent bar associations in Algeria.

She has presented pet-related webinars and programs sponsored by the ABA Solo, Small Firm, and General Practice Division and ABA TIPS as well as the

National Business Institute. Ms. Gislason contributed to the ABA Dispute Resolution Section Newsletter on the subject of pet custody mediation.

In addition to the above efforts, Ms. Gislason has long been active in the Minnesota State Bar Association (MSBA) Family Law Section, where she served on the Legislative Committee and chaired the Blue Ribbon Panel on the Rules of Professional Conduct. She has made CLE presentations for the MSBA Family Law Section, Animal Law Section, and the Probate and Trust Law Section. She long served on the Hennepin County Minnesota District Court Mediator and Referee Panel, where she helped resolve family law and other civil disputes at the pretrial stage. She was instrumental in the passage of the pet trust law in Minnesota.

Ms. Gislason is in private practice in Minneapolis, Minnesota. In family law, she handles custody, child support, spousal maintenance, property and business disputes, and cases involving domestic violence. For animal law, her caseload ranges from custody and ownership disputes, transactional matters, and veterinary malpractice to harassment, dangerous dog proceedings, zoning violations, and more. In intellectual property law, she represents authors, artists, entertainers, and businesses.

In her personal life, Ms. Gislason is often in the company of dogs. She is also an avid reader, world traveler, and innovator. She frequents coffee shops that attract philosophers, authors, and retired academics. For more information, go to http://www.gislasonlaw.com/.

Acknowledgments

This book would not have been possible without my steadfast editor, the Honorable Gail Baker, who has long served as the Chair of the ABA Section of Family Law Book Publishing Board. She stood by me as I first envisioned this book, then re-envisioned it, and gave me support and time to mentally process how this book, designed to contribute to the launch of a new practice area, would unfold. I was fortunate to have an editor with depth in the law and breadth in the liberal arts; she was able to rein me in when I was too far away from the assignment at hand. More than that, she stood behind me and helped me shape and polish this book. More recently, Joseph Booth was added to my editorial team and brought his valuable fresh perspective as well as his meticulous eye for detail. He was able to be frank with me about places that needed greater clarity of expression.

In addition to significant contributions from Referee Baker and Joseph Booth, this book would not have been possible without the support and commitment of my legal assistant, Stephanie Roman. When I was looking to hire a new assistant a decade ago, she made it clear that she wanted to work for me because of my devotion to, and love for, animals. She has made it possible for me to gain the private time to think while going over every word I wrote, and going through it again, to make sure that the entire text reflected my most recent analysis, as this book was many years in the making. She took care to ensure that the substantive points I made matched each footnote. Her contribution to this book is immeasurable. She is the kind of person who makes those around her better.

I express my appreciation for the fine education I received from the Edina Public Schools, Carleton College, and William Mitchell College of Law. I salute all of my teachers, professors, and fellow students, who caused me to value asking questions. I recognize my grandmother, Dr. Solvig Gislason, and Professors Joan Schaffner, Temple Grandin, and David Favre for helping me to grow intellectually, particularly on animal subjects, and young lawyer Lorelei Pacholec for her careful review of the case analysis in this book. In particular, I thank India's Raj Panjwani, who inspired me beyond measure. He sets the good example as a thought leader.

I want to extend a special thank you to all the lawyers, judges, and experts who influenced me, helped me learn about animal law, or allowed me to interview them at various stages when I was writing this book, including Barbara Atwood, Dr.

Sarah Babcock, Sir Patrick Bateson, Peter Bennett, Amy Breyer, Simon Bruce, Frances Carlisle, James Carr, Richard Cassidy, Yolanda Eisenstein, Linda Elrod, Julie Fershtman, Jennifer Finch, Julie Flaherty, Pamela Frasch, Christopher Green, Debra Hamilton, Kristina Hancock, Kathy Hessler, Rebecca Huss, Leo Jordan, Adam Karp, Linda Klein, Dr. Kate Knutson, Marcy LaHart, Nita Luis, Jill Mariani, J. Gregg Miller, the Honorable Cara Lee Neville, Martha Nussbaum, Dr. Stephanie Ostrowski, Carol Propotnik, Marilynne Roberts, Bernard Rollin, Sue Savage-Rumbaugh, Matthew Scully, Steven Snyder, Keith Streff, Joyce Tischler, Ledy VanKavage, Anita Ventrelli, Bruce Wagman, Paul Waldau, Thomas Wallen, Kim Walsh, Dean Song Wei, Jerry Weiss, Steven Wise, and Jennifer Zehr. A special thank you to Amy, Frances, Julie, Rebecca, Cara Lee, Marilynne, and Jennifer for their selected chapter critiques, together with Lungten Zangmo, Eszter Ga'l, and Floro C. Balato, Jr. from the Humphrey Fellows of the Humphrey School of Public Affairs, University of Minnesota.

I am lucky to have come from a family of lawyers, doctors, authors, inventors, social workers, teachers, and farmers that shaped my intellectual and moral foundation. This base, combined with the opportunity to accompany my trial lawyer father into the courtroom at a young age, made me confident enough to spread my wings and look at the big picture. I also learned to stay on the ground and be actively involved in problem solving; my aspiration was to become a change agent.

In addition to all the humans who have shaped me, this endeavor would have meant less to me if not for a lifetime of relationships with animals. I honor what they have given to me in ways that surpass human understanding, as I offer this effort to ensure that their futures matter in the legal system. I also owe a profound debt to Rachel Carson, the author of *Silent Spring*. Her work made my path possible.

Foreword

This book just might affect the way you see the world.

Barbara J. Gislason has made a valuable contribution to legal jurisprudence by setting forth, in meticulous detail, the progression of law that affects animal law in general, and the pet custody aspect of pet law in particular. In her inspiring and interesting book, Ms. Gislason clarifies how scientific knowledge about the cognitive abilities and emotional characteristics of other animals should lead to legal developments.

I appreciate how the author reveals the complexity of the subject of animal law while also helping the family or animal lawyer understand how to control and apply a reasoned analysis. For lawyers who want to win their cases, leave no stone unturned, and gain a foundation as to how to further advance the law, there is a wealth of information about cases combined with her own ideas about how companion animals are, and could be, treated in the legal system. Beyond that, Ms. Gislason synthesizes the information provided in many chapters with case law analysis. This is a very useful and well-crafted work for lawyers. What Ms. Gislason does well is look at the subject of pet custody disputes from many angles. For example, she helps us understand what judges do in a practical way and explores how they might think. She reminds us how cultural perspectives, cognitive biases, and points of view impact negotiations, alternative dispute resolutions, and decision-making processes. Without using the word, the author assists us in realizing and grappling with our own prejudices.

Ms. Gislason stands out for cogently building her arguments one upon another. She helps us not just to see the fabric of the law but also to see the law as a living entity, inhaling and exhaling. She is a breath of fresh air bringing a valuable new perspective through this book with intensity and fluidness. She offers concrete and practical ideas as to how to do things differently based upon a deep and multifaceted examination of the law and the liberal arts. For her, this work is neither an academic exercise nor a mere abstraction of human and animal relationships. Artfully, she has combined her knowledge and respect for the law into a vision for a better tomorrow.

Rich Cassidy[1]

1. Richard T. Cassidy is a practicing lawyer of long experience, the President of the Uniform Law Commission, the Editor of OnLawyering.com, a lover of animals, and a guardian of his own dog, Baxter.

Introduction

"Be who you are and say what you feel, because in the end those who matter don't mind and those who mind don't matter."

—Dr. Seuss

A groundbreaking book on pet law and custody, this text is a wonderful resource for a wide-ranging audience. The area of pet law and custody has grown exponentially over the years, with a variety of individuals now involved, including family lawyers, animal lawyers, alternative dispute resolution (ADR) professionals, animal advocates and owners, and those who are interested in animals. While the book discusses the law, it is accessible, useful, and interesting to nonlawyers as well. This book has something for everybody and is designed to provide practical real-world advice along with a progressive understanding of the developing area of pet law and custody as a foundation for advancing the law for the common good of all animals.

This book explores two themes that are central to a modern understanding of pet law and custody. The first is the unique position our pets hold in our culture as well as under our law. Traditionally, the law classifies entities into two categories, persons and property. Under the law, animals, including our pets, generally are classified as property. This book examines how the traditional binary classification has become obsolete and instead a continuum has developed that allows for a nuanced understanding of the role pets play in our lives and under the law. Our pets are no longer mere objects but rather are beneficiaries of trusts, companions, and family members. The book helps us see how, in the contours of a single decision, the animal's position on the continuum between classification of property and person appears malleable and can have a decisive impact on the outcome of the case. Recognizing this continuum, and capitalizing upon it, is critical to enhancing our ability to seek a just outcome for human and nonhuman animals in a variety of pet law contexts.

The second theme relates to conceptualizing animal law cases as a series of vertical and horizontal intersections. This book helps us think outside the box and develop lines of argument in one doctrinal area—for example, pet custody—from a wide variety of other doctrinal areas, such as tort, contract, criminal, and constitutional law. We learn to appreciate that these areas are not independent silos but rather a tapestry of views that can affect doctrinal outcomes across substantive areas. The author identifies how decisions across disciplines and state borders influence each other in the animal law practice area and how advocates may utilize these influences in the best interests of their human and nonhuman clients.

These two themes are evidence of changing times in our jurisprudence. While some judges are still old school, more are becoming aware that laws prohibiting animal cruelty and abuse and promoting welfare standards are the new normal and that our pets, in particular, deserve consideration. A dizzying flurry of dicta about love, affection, and friendship endorse the reality that the companion animal has entered the family unit.

In addition to exploring the changing paradigm of the companion animal within our legal system, this book provides the practical nuts and bolts necessary to advocate your case. Presented throughout the chapters and in helpful appendices are extensive case analyses and practice pointers, checklists, questions, agreements, and pleading critiques, each designed to give you the tools you need to be an effective advocate.

To accomplish these twin goals, the book is divided primarily along substantive doctrinal lines. Most chapters are devoted to a specific area of law. Each substantive chapter analyzes the basic elements of the law as they relate to pet law and custody and then summarizes and dissects the leading cases. Provided are helpful practical pointers extracted from each case explaining the key relevance of the case to the area of pet custody. In addition, there are chapters devoted to a variety of related topics, including the use of alternative dispute resolution, science and technology, law office basics, and an exploration of the Katrina catastrophe as a case study into how a natural disaster can transform law and policy. Finally, the book contains a series of appendices that provide the toolkit necessary to address pet custody cases. The following briefly summarizes each chapter to help you navigate the text.

Chapter 1 ("Companion Animals and the Law") lays the foundation for this book on pet law and custody. The chapter explores how a companion animal is defined and conceptualized under the law and includes a list of useful criteria for distinguishing companion animals from other animals. In addition, it explains how the role of the pet as a family member has evolved in our culture and how that may be reflected in the law with regard to companion animals being on a continuum between property and persons.

Chapter 2 ("Family Law and Replevin Actions") analyzes the progression of replevin cases central to the development of pet custody jurisprudence. This chapter identifies the different types of "value" humans assign to their pets, including moral, relational, sentimental, and economic. It explains animal/human and animal/animal bonds, equitable principles, and "best-interest" factors and their significance in pet custody determinations. The reader will gain appreciation as to how some jurists embrace the opportunity to render a decision with a just result in a companion animal ownership or custody dispute, while others are offended that they were assigned such a lowly case in the first place. In a way, this chapter is about the elephant in the room that is not spoken of, but it is an aspect of one's journey through this book to understand the elephant's significance.

Recognizing that, especially in the context of family law and custody, where the human and nonhuman animal "parties" may retain a relationship long after custody is determined, Chapter 3 ("Alternative Dispute Resolution") discusses how mediation, negotiation, and arbitration apply in the context of pet custody and ownership disputes. This chapter provides a primer on the various types of mediation—facilitative, evaluative, animal-centered, and transformative—and how to choose which type will best serve your goals. Further, it utilizes the Model Standards of Practice for Family and Divorce Mediation as a template for how to consider the application of these standards to pet custody disputes. The chapter then changes focus to discuss collaborative processes and the objectives of collaborative law under the Uniform Collaborative Law Rules/Act (UCLRA). It ends with a discussion of arbitration practice. At each stage, this chapter provides a variety of practical tools to facilitate the advocate's use of these ADR methods.

The passage of laws permitting pet trusts in all 50 states was a watershed event for the development of companion animal laws in the United States. While historically, property could not inherit property, the laws now allow animals to be trust beneficiaries. This development lends support to the argument advanced in this book that companion animals are something more than mere property on the continuum. Chapter 4 ("Estate Planning, Wills, and Trusts") surveys the traditional estate planning methods used to provide for pets, identifies their weaknesses, and then explores the basics of setting up a pet trust. The chapter closes with a useful checklist to share with future caregivers of a companion animal.

Chapter 5 ("Contract Law and the Uniform Commercial Code") introduces another level of complexity to pet law and custody, as our pets may be subject to, or affected by, a variety of contracts. Whether the owner adopted the animal from a rescue organization or purchased the animal from a breeder, expect a contract was involved. Moreover, prenuptial and antenuptial agreements that address pet ownership are becoming more common and raise a variety of issues for pet custody. Ideas about what could be contained in the pet custody agreement are shared, including the subjects of pet visitation and access rights. This chapter discusses the basics of contract law and equitable principles relevant to the variety of contracts involving our pets.

Chapter 6 ("Property Law and the Meaning of Things") explores the legal implications of lost and found animals and analyzes several cases that address a variety of issues, including the definition of "owner," pet restrictions in housing, and the notion of "horizontal" property rights, an important consideration in pet custody proceedings. Interestingly, cases involving animals as property evoke strong views all around and seem to represent, on one end of the spectrum, the legal fiction that pets are inanimate objects while, on the other side of the continuum, the idea that they are in a category akin to children.

Chapter 7 ("Tort Law Affects Pet Law") explores how the evolving jurisprudence of tort law affects pet law and custody. Compensatory damages awarded in tort cases could be a function of the value we place on our companion animals. For decades, advocates, the courts, and legislatures have grappled with whether to recognize and compensate for noneconomic value—the companionship value—of companion animals to their owners. This chapter details this debate and notes a common element between tort cases, where an animal dies, and a pet custody case, where companionship is lost. Both types of actions involve emotion that the legal system is ill-equipped to handle. We will see that in tort cases, the suffering of an animal is modestly addressed, if at all, whereas in family law cases, courts may at least take their maltreatment into account.

Chapter 8 ("Animal Cruelty, Crimes, and the Constitution") reminds the reader that civil law is not the only law that governs interactions with our pets. Criminal and constitutional law doctrines are significant to animal protection and have been instrumental in moving our pets along the continuum from property toward persons. This chapter notes the link between animal cruelty and abuse of human victims, which has significantly impacted the enforcement of animal cruelty laws in this country. All 50 states now have felony and misdemeanor animal cruelty laws that are independently tracked under the FBI crime reporting database. These crimes, along with arson and homicide, are tracked under Group A, as a crime against society—not property. This classification is instrumental in shifting animals along the continuum from property toward persons. Additionally, this chapter surveys a variety of criminal and constitutional topics ranging from the unique history of Pit Bulls in the legal system and the abuse directed toward them, to animal hoarding, to the 1st, 4th, 5th, and 14th Amendments of the Constitution and how these amendments apply to animal law cases, to the role of animal control officers, and to how title to an animal may be lost through criminal and civil forfeiture. Horizontal intersections among doctrinal areas of pet law are identified.

In the wake of Hurricane Katrina, humans became separated from their companion animals along the Gulf Coast. Some chose to risk their lives rather than leave their companion animals behind. In Chapter 9 ("Katrina, Katrina"), the sequence of events and plight of the animals following this hurricane are explored along with how this tragedy helped to transform pet custody dispute case law in that the courts now find this subject worthy of their time and best efforts.

Pet custody may involve the dog traveling between homes, and a pertinent question becomes whether the dog is at risk for a future dangerous dog declaration. For even a responsible owner, all it takes is one careless moment for a dog to become loose and charge another animal, or the mail carrier, passing by. Chapter 10 ("Dangerous Dogs and Police Powers") describes the laws governing dangerous dog proceedings, potential constitutional challenges to them, and the ramifications of a dangerous dog declaration. Also discussed are breed discriminatory laws that turn dogs into outlaws based solely on their breed and how these conceptions may impact a pet custody determination or agreement. This chapter emphasizes why, in pet custody disputes, the subject of who is a responsible owner deserves serious consideration.

The law is impacted by, and must respond to, advances in science and technology. For example, issues concerning cloning and artificial reproductive technology raise not only ethical issues but also important legal issues, not to mention the controversy involving conformation standards and the problems they pose for our pets. Chapter 11 ("Science and Technology") explores these topics and further addresses how patent law, copyright law, and tech transfer agreements could impact a variety of rights associated with a companion animal.

Focusing more directly on the continuum, and how our companion animals are shifting away from property and toward persons, Chapter 12 ("Potpourri of the Predicates of Change") briefly addresses animal emotions and sentience. It also surveys a few of the scientific, theoretical, and moral views espoused by key visionaries that have helped to uncover biases and transform our views of animals over time.

Chapter 13 ("Law Office Basics, Anatomy of a Case, and Expert Testimony") returns to the practical, with essential pointers on effective client advocacy. Specifically, there is useful advice on finding, interviewing, and evaluating potential clients, identifying potential experts, role-playing, problem solving, and financial considerations.

The concluding sections offer interesting insights. In the Conclusion, heroes in animal welfare are introduced, the themes of the book are revisited, and the elephant in the room is revealed. And in the Epilogue ("Life with Dogs"), the author shares her history with and love for dogs, along with her point of view. Although the reader's journey into pet law and custody is complete, significant resources for the advocate are presented in the appendices, including a pet custody questionnaire; a values clarification exercise; and sample statutes, pleadings, discovery, orders, and contracts addressing a variety of pet law and custody topics.

This pioneering book, filled with big ideas and practical real-world advice, is essential to effective advocacy in pet law and custody cases. More importantly, this book reimagines, through a creative vision guided not only by the mind but also with heart and soul, a world in which our companion animals are recognized as members of our families and given a special status in our system of justice. Enjoy!

Joan Schaffner[1]

1. Joan E. Schaffner is an associate professor of law at The George Washington University Law School; is active in the American Bar Association, Tort Trial and Insurance Practice Section, Animal Law Committee; and shares her life with many fabulous feline companions.

Chapter 1

Companion Animals and the Law

"I love a dog. He does nothing for political reasons."

—*Will Rogers*

The terminology for how animals are referred to in American case law varies widely. They may be viewed as quasi-property, a thing, sentimental property, personal property, tangible property, animal property, chattel, equipment, an invention, a product, a good, a special category of property,[1] a law enforcement professional,[2] a noncommissioned officer,[3] a best friend,[4] a companion animal, a crime victim, or a family member.[5] Hereinafter, we will call these terms "the continuum." Another

1. A police dog was buried with full police honors, including a 21-gun salute. Eun Kyung Kim, *Forever in Your Debt: K-9 Buried with Full Police Honors after Dying in Line of Duty*, TODAY, http://www.today.com/pets/police-dog-buried-full-honors-after-dying-line-duty-1D80117522 (last visited Oct. 10, 2016).

2. A police dog may be sworn in as an officer and receive a badge. *K9 Officer Career Guide*, CRIMINAL JUSTICE DEGREE SCHOOLS, http://www.criminaljusticedegreeschools.com/criminal-justice-careers/k9-officer/ (last visited Oct. 10, 2016).

3. The question of whether a military working dog has a rank in the military is illustrative of how we value, and do not value, police dogs. Although these dogs are referred to as noncommissioned officers (NCOs), by tradition, the dogs lack a rank. Even so, their abuse is prosecuted under Article 134 of the Uniform Code of Military Justice (UCMJ), not Article 91. The latter article applies to conduct involving an NCO. *Here's Why Military Working Dogs Outrank Their Human Handlers*, BARK POST, http://articles.barkpost.com/dogs-outrank-humans/ (last visited Oct. 10, 2016); Dan Rosenthal, *What's the Truth about US Military Service Dogs Being Ranked Higher Than Their Handlers?*, QUORA, https://www.quora.com/What's-the-truth-about-US-Military-service-dogs-being-ranked-higher-than-their-handlers#QRpxk (last visited Oct. 10, 2016).

4. *See* Rabideau v. City of Racine, 627 N.W.2d 795, 797 (Wis. 2001).

5. In New York, it is now legal for humans to be buried with the cremated remains of their pets. *Forever with Fido: NY to Allow People to Be Buried with Pets*, ASSOCIATED PRESS, http://mynorthwest.com/402539/forever-with-fido-ny-to-allow-people-to-be-buried-with-pets/ (last visited Oct. 10, 2016).

way this topic is explored is through the emerging idea that animals are now in an interim category between property and person.[6]

As courts wrestle with these classifications, legislators have shown their interest in animal subjects by passing a wide spectrum of animal welfare and protection laws. In this book, we will explore whether there is convergence; many threads, young and old, comprise the tapestry of our legal system. In pet law, all participate in shaping pet custody jurisprudence within a cultural context.

DEFINING PETS AND COMPANION ANIMALS

There is no universal definition for a pet or companion animal, although there is a current trend to use these nouns interchangeably.[7] The American Society for the Prevention of Cruelty to Animals (ASPCA) defines a companion animal as "domesticated" or "domestic-bred" and whose physical, emotional, and social needs are readily met.[8]

If instead the animal is used for work, research, sports, or utility, or could be classified as livestock, the animal would not be considered a pet or companion animal. It is for the above reasons that service animals, including those who serve the blind, or animals that provide law enforcement or armed forces duties, are classified differently than companion animals are.

Criteria for identifying a companion animal might include the following:

- Purchased or acquired to be a family pet
- Provides companionship
- Has a name
- Provides no significant source of income
- Receives appropriate food, water, shelter, and veterinary care
- Is bonded to a family member
- Is held out as a pet or companion animal
- Lives indoors
- Owner describes him- or herself as "mom" or "dad"
- Image appears in family photographs, including on social media
- Image is reflected on a computer or cell phone screen saver
- Name is included in family listings
- Acts like a pet

---

6. *See* Corso v. Crawford Dog & Cat Hosp., Inc., 97 Misc. 2d 530, 415 N.Y.S.2d 182, 183 (City Civ. Ct. 1979); Juelfs v. Gough, 41 P.3d 593 (Alaska 2002); and Morgan v. Kroupa, 702 A.2d 630, 167 Vt. 99 (Vt. 1997).

7. *Pet Owner or Guardian*, AVMA, https://www.avma.org/Advocacy/StateAndLocal/Pages/owner-guardian-ahi.aspx (last visited Sept. 20, 2016).

8. *Definition of Companion Animal*, ASPCA, http://www.aspca.org/about-us/aspca-policy-and-position-statements/definition-companion-animal (last visited Sept. 20, 2016).

- Brings pleasure
- Provides protection
- Has a guardian
- Is treated kindly and affectionately

Criteria for animals that might not be considered companion animals could include the following:

- Not regularly fed
- Not domesticated
- Not named
- Not bonded to a family member
- Sleeps outside
- Not properly cared for
- Used for sports, entertainment, or performance
- Used for research purposes
- Primary purpose is to breed
- Is a service animal[9]
- Performs work
- Illegal to own

American Pet Products Association

Notwithstanding the fact that there is no uniform definition for pets or companion animals, there is an abundance of statistical information about them, much of it promulgated by the American Pet Products Association. This organization offers a well-publicized annual National Pet Owners Survey. The information collected concerns dogs, cats, freshwater fish, saltwater fish, birds, small animals, reptiles, and horses.[10]

Yearly statistics provided by the American Pet Products Association reflect human dedication to animals. Sixty-five percent of American households own 207 million pets, excluding fish.[11] In recent years, more than $58 billion has been spent annually on their food, supplies, over-the-counter medicine, veterinary care,[12] animal purchases, grooming, and boarding. Thus far, the survey offers no information regarding pet cremation or burial expenses, but this may change;

---

9. Laws pertaining to equal housing rights for those with disabilities include Section 504 of the Rehabilitation Act of 1973 and the Federal Fair Housing Amendments Act of 1988. *The Fair Housing Act*, U.S. Department of Housing and Urban Development, http://portal.hud.gov/hudportal/HUD?src=/program_offices/fair_housing_equal_opp/progdesc/title8 (last visited Sept. 20, 2016).

10. *Background and Purpose*, APPA National Pet Owners Survey, http://americanpetproducts.org/Uploads/APPApubs/Background_Purpose_NPOS_2015_2016.pdf (last visited Sept. 20, 2016).

11. *Pet Industry Market Size & Ownership Statistics*, American Pet Products Association, http://www.americanpetproducts.org/press_industrytrends.asp (last visited May 12, 2016).

12. The amount spent on veterinary care includes the cost of pet insurance.

by 2013, there were already 700 pet funeral homes,[13] crematories,[14] and cemeteries. The extraordinary amount of money spent on pets suggests that their value exceeds their purchase price.

Wrestling with the definition of a pet and companion animal reminds one of the public frustration following the decision in *Jacobellis v. Ohio*,[15] a case famous for the court's inability to define the word "obscenity." In a concurring opinion, Justice Potter Stewart, rather than defining obscenity, instead said, "But I know it when I see it." In some ways, the task of sorting out who is a pet and who is not a pet has similar subjective characteristics. Even so, consider the following rule of thumb: companion animals have value beyond their economic value; they have relational value. Another way to think about this subject is that both private decisions and public policies are shaped by personal or societal preferences that are, in essence, our values.

PETS IN THE LEGAL SYSTEM

The landmark decision of *Rabideau v. City of Racine*[16] captures our collective struggle regarding which pets belong in the legal system and where. In *Rabideau*, the court said,

> At the outset, we note that we are uncomfortable with the law's cold characterization of a dog, such as Dakota, as mere "property." Labeling a dog "property" fails to describe the value human beings place upon the companionship that they enjoy with a dog. A companion dog is not a fungible item, equivalent to other items of personal property. A companion dog is not a living room sofa or dining room furniture. This term inadequately and inaccurately describes the relationship between a human and a dog.

The *Rabideau* court also expressed the concept of who can be the beneficiary of love from the human heart in a modern soliloquy. Even so, the court ultimately decided:

> Humans have an enormous capacity to form bonds with dogs, cats, birds and an infinite number of other beings that are non-human. Were we to recognize a claim for damages for the negligent loss of a dog, we can find little basis for rationally distinguishing other categories of animal companion.

---

13. Dana Macario, *Pet Funeral Business Beginning to Boom*, Today, http://www.today.com/money/pet-funeral-business-beginning-boom-998633 (last visited Oct. 10, 2016).

14. Stephen J. Dubner, *The Troubled Cremation of Stevie the Cat: A New Freakonomics Radio Podcast*, Freakonomics, http://freakonomics.com/podcast/the-troubled-cremation-of-stevie-the-cat-a-new-freakonomics-radio-podcast/ (last visited Oct. 10, 2016).

15. 378 U.S. 184 (1694) 84 S. Ct. 1676, 12 L. Ed. 2d 793.

16. 627 N.W.2d 795, 797 (Wis. 2001).

Legal Precedent

The 1897 U.S. Supreme Court decision in *Sentell v. New Orleans Carrollton Railroad Co.*[17] cast a dark shroud over all animals. There, the court said,

> Property in dogs is of an imperfect or qualified nature, and that they stand, as it were, between animals ferae naturae, in which, until killed or subdued, there is no property, and domestic animals, in which the right of property is perfect and complete. They are not considered as being upon the same plane with horses, cattle, sheep, and other domesticated animals, but rather in the category of cats, monkeys, parrots, singing birds, and similar animals, kept for pleasure, curiosity, or caprice.

The court went on to single out dogs for additional negative attention, and said,

> They have no intrinsic value, by which we understand a value common to all dogs as such, and independent of the particular breed or individual. Unlike other domestic animals, they are useful neither as beasts of burden, for draught (except to a limited extent), nor for food. They are peculiar in the fact that they differ among themselves more widely than any other class of animals, and can hardly be said to have a characteristic common to the entire race.

Later decisions rely on, rather than distinguish themselves from, this historic relic that imagined the animal kingdom in three categories. A horse, a cow, and a sheep are higher than a cat, a singing bird, or a monkey, while a dog is not even worthy of any property classification unless "dead" or "subdued." Even worse, the court described dogs in this decision as subject to "attacks of hydrophobic madness."

In addition to the above, it is notable that the court's 1897 classification ranked domestic animals with commercial value first and portrayed a point of view about the cats and singing birds kept "for pleasure, curiosity or caprice." Even though this decision is still quoted in modern jurisprudence, one can imagine that the judges relying on the *Sentell* precedent are either able to utilize an Orwellian double think ability or are ignorant about the place of pets and companion animals within our culture and within their own homes.

Absolute Rights

In searching for the roots of current jurisprudence, remember that 49 states are grounded in English common law. In the 18th century, Sir William Blackstone wrote *Commentaries on the Laws of England*,[18] a book thought to have influenced Alexan-

---

17. 166 U.S. 698, 17 S. Ct. 693, 41 L. Ed. 1169 (1897).
18. *William Blackstone, Commentaries, 1:120–41, Amendment IX*, The Founders' Constitution, http://press-pubs.uchicago.edu/founders/documents/amendIXs1.html (last visited May 12, 2016).

der Hamilton, John Marshall, and Abraham Lincoln.[19] Blackstone advocated that the English common law conferred "absolute rights of every Englishman (which, taken in a political and extensive sense, are usually called their liberties) as they are founded on nature and reason," which were "the right of personal security, the right of personal liberty, and the right of private property."[20]

The U.S. Supreme Court relied on Blackstone's correlation between legal right and remedy in *Marbury v. Madison*[21] when it held that the "very essence of civil liberty consists in the right of every individual to claim the protection of the laws, whenever he receives an injury." Blackstone also articulated the idea that "relative rights, such as those that are based on the marital relationship, are rights that are defined solely by membership in civil society."[22] Carrying his idea forward, evolving ideas about who is allowed to be a family member could be a basis for advancing animal relational interests in a family law context.

Animal Welfare Act

The Animal Welfare Act[23] is a federal law first passed in 1966 that regulates commercial dog and cat breeding,[24] animal exhibits, and research laboratories that use live animals.[25] Under Section 1.1 of this Act, animals are defined as "any live or dead dog, cat, nonhuman primate, guinea pig, hamster, rabbit, or any other warm-blooded animal, which is being used, or is intended for use for research, teaching, testing, experimentation, or exhibition purposes, or as a pet."[26] Birds and some small animals have no protection under the Animal Welfare Act.

Over the years, various efforts have been made to pass amendments to the Animal Welfare Act, including the Puppy Protection Act of 2001, the Pet Animal Welfare Statute of 2005, and the Puppy Uniform Protection Act of 2008.[27] Registries

---

19. President Abraham Lincoln owned and adored both cats and dogs. *Lincoln Pets*, National Park Service, https://www.nps.gov/abli/planyourvisit/lincoln-pets.htm (last visited Oct. 10, 2016).

20. *Id.*

21. 5 U.S. (1 Cranch) 137, 163, 2 L. Ed. 60 (1803).

22. *William Blackstone, Commentaries, 1:120–41, Amendment IX*, The Founders' Constitution, http://press-pubs.uchicago.edu/founders/documents/amendIXs1.html (last visited May 12, 2016).

23. 7 U.S.C. § 2131–59.

24. This includes buying animals for breeding and selling them to pet stores or resellers.

25. David Favre, *Overview of U.S. Animal Welfare Act*, Animal Legal & Historical Center, http://www.animallaw.info/articles/ovusawa.htm (last visited May 12, 2016).

26. *Animal Welfare Act Quick Reference Guides*, United States Department of Agriculture National Agricultural Library, https://www.nal.usda.gov/awic/animal-welfare-act-quick-reference-guides (last visited Sept. 20, 2016).

27. *Regulation of High-Volume Retailers and Importers*, Sportsmen's & Animal Owners' Voting Alliance, http://saova.org/SA3723.html (last visited May 12, 2016).

that receive substantial revenue from large commercial breeders are known to oppose these reforms.[28]

A client who searches for a lost pet or surrenders a pet to a humane society, perhaps because of a no-pets policy or zoning requirement, may have no idea that the Animal Welfare Act could impact the pet ending up in a research laboratory. This can happen if the relinquishment occurs in a state with pound seizure laws.[29] When animals become lost, there can be a very short window of time for finding them, as shelter hold period obligations typically range from three to seven days. This means that once the hold period expires, title and ownership of the animal can be transferred, or the animal can be "disposed of."

Animal Enterprise Terrorism Act

A federal law that has gained notoriety is the Animal Enterprise Terrorism Act.[30] Passed after September 11, 2001, this act defines two kinds of crimes, one grounded in economic loss and the other in fear of or actual physical injury. It also includes sanctions for co-conspirators.[31] Although seemingly aimed at terrorists, the federal law is easily applied to thwart animal rights nonviolent protesters and may have a chilling effect on free speech.[32]

Statutes and Ordinances

Pet law and pet custody disputes are impacted more by state statutes and local ordinances than by federal laws. Using the state of Minnesota as an example, key animal protection laws include these:

- Minnesota Statute § 343.21 prohibits torturing or neglecting an animal.
- Minnesota Statute § 343.24 prohibits keeping animals under inhumane conditions and cruelly transporting them.
- Minnesota Statute § 343.26 requires that animals have shelter for five months a year unless the animal has a suitable coat.

---

28. According to the Humane Society of the United States, the American Kennel Club has opposed these types of Animal Welfare Act amendments. *The American Kennel Club: No Longer "The Dog's Champion?" AKC Should Stand up for Dogs, Not Puppy Mills*, The Humane Society of the United States, http://www.humanesociety.org/assets/pdfs/pets/puppy_mills/report_akc_breeders.pdf (last visited May 12, 2016).

29. *Pound Seizure Laws*, American Anti-Vivisection Society, http://aavs.org/animals-science/laws/pound-seizure-laws/ (last visited Sept. 22, 2016).

30. 18 U.S.C. § 43.

31. Barbara J. Gislason, *Animal Enterprise Terrorism Act: Designing a Poison Pill for a Social Movement*, American Bar Association Tort Trial & Insurance Practice Section Media, Privacy & Defamation Law Committee 2007 Annual Meeting.

32. *Animal Enterprise Terrorism Act (AETA)*, Green Is the New Red, http://www.greenisthenewred.com/blog/tag/animal-enterprise-terrorism-act/page/4/ (last visited Sept. 22, 2016).

- Minnesota Statute § 343.31 prohibits dog fighting, which is considered a felony.
- Minnesota Statute § 343.40 regulates dog housing.
- Minnesota Statute § 518B.01 permits companion animals to be included in orders for protection.
- Minnesota Statute § 501C.0408 permits estate planning for companion animals through pet trusts.[33]

As reflected above, the Minnesota legislature has passed laws to protect companion animals, thereby promoting their best interests. A logical inference that could be drawn from the passage of animal welfare and protection laws in Minnesota is that the legislature is able to distinguish pets from inanimate personal property. As you will see in the case law analysis throughout this book, although Minnesota is representative of the growing trend for both legislators and courts to treat companion animals in a special way,[34] Minnesota is also representative of a state where the courts seem to be all over "the continuum."

Applying the Law to Pet Custody Disputes

A good example of how courts are reimagining how to apply the law to pet custody disputes was offered by the Honorable Regina M. Chu, a Minnesota trial court judge. She made a decision in a replevin case involving a failed nonmarital relationship where a couple jointly adopted a dog from a humane society. Although a conciliation court judge had found in favor of the plaintiff, on appeal to the district court, Judge Chu utilized four factors and found in favor of the defendant. These four factors were (1) who selected the dog and paid the initial adoption fee, (2) the extent of the care and love provided to the dog, (3) to what extent each party provided financial support, and (4) which result was in the dog's best interests.[35]

LAW AND CULTURE

The struggle with how we will fold companion animals into our rule of law takes place within the pulse of underlying institutions, routines, and norms of a society. Institutions and routines, established in the context of an organized society, influence how courts respond to contemporary problems about who should be allowed

33. With the 2016 passage of the Minnesota Pet Trust Bill, all 50 states now permit estate planning where animals, in effect, are beneficiaries. Barbara J. Gislason and Dr. Steven Barghusen played an active role in passing this bill.

34. *See* Pratt v. Pratt, N.W.2d, 1988 WL 120251 (Minn. Ct. App.). In this famous decision, the court signaled that in a divorce context, evidence of dog mistreatment could be relevant decision-making criteria.

35. This replevin order can be found in the appendix.

in the family. Norms represent our shared understanding of standards of appropriate behavior. We may be unaware of our internalized norms and simply consider them to reflect common sense. Norms affect and reveal behavior potentials for jurists, lawyers, alternative dispute resolution professionals, and clients alike. Laws exist within a cultural context; it is important to consider how law reflects culture and culture reflects law.[36]

The 1897 *Sentell* decision, discussed above, embodies the patterns of interactions between humans and animals in the 19th century, a time when animals suffering from rabies could also suffer from, to quote the *Sentell* decision, "attacks of hydrophobic madness." It is noteworthy that Louis Pasteur and Emile Roux only discovered a vaccine for rabies, formerly known as hydrophobia, the decade before the *Sentell* decision was rendered.[37] The world had changed, in part due to science, by the time the Supreme Court of Wisconsin offered its 2001 decision in *Rabideau v. City of Racine*.[38] Even so, the effect of *Sentell* continues. The entrenchment of agricultural-based norms in legal conflicts involving companion animals serves neither our citizens nor our families well.

The new cultural norm in America is reflected by the fact that more than half of U.S. states allow companion animals to be included in orders for protection. Even so, the analysis of many cases involving pet law will reveal that when it comes to pet custody disputes, we are often thrown back in time.

CONCLUSION

Now that the stage has been set, imagine yourself as an urban sleuth intent on capturing glimpses into the survival needs of the agrarian culture of the past, while at the same time noticing all the ways that the passage of time, together with scientific discoveries, suggests old perspectives might be better viewed as a curiosity rather than a precedent. Before undertaking this journey, be aware that there are biases in your own mind that you have been carefully taught. Prepare yourself to make a much-needed contribution to this fast-emerging jurisprudence.

---

36. Naomi Mezey, *Law as Culture*, Georgetown University Law Center, http://scholarship.law.georgetown.edu/cgi/viewcontent.cgi?article=1310&context=facpub (last visited Oct. 10, 2016).

37. Bill Kemp, *In 19th Century, Rabies Was Menacing*, Pantagraph, http://www.pantagraph.com/news/local/in-th-century-rabies-was-menacing/article_9e2e75de-0011-11e0-bd91-001cc4c03286.html (last visited Oct. 10, 2016).

38. 627 N.W.2d 795, 797 (Wis. 2001).

Chapter 2

Family Law and Replevin Actions

"I care not for a man's religion whose dog and cat are not the better for it."

—Abraham Lincoln

The heart of this chapter is the progression of replevin cases central to the development of pet custody jurisprudence. You may be surprised by the sheer variety of ways that pet custody disputes proceed through the courts, as well as the wide-ranging basis for legal decisions.

Claims that can be made with regard to companion animal disputes include ownership, adoption, cost, gift, conversion, lost/found, patent, and third-party rights. These claims may be affected by conditional ownership agreements, use agreements, and contractual rights, which are common in breeder sales, as well as agreements for the foster or adoption of rescue animals. Assisted reproductive technology concepts, and even patent law, may impact contractual rights now, and in the future, too.

FICTITIOUS STANDARD OF VALUE

In case law, courts investigate not only indicia of ownership but also the different types of value an animal might have, including fictitious, moral, relational, sentimental, or economic. Courts explore whether animals are cherished or sentimental property with special value, such as a family memento or heirloom.

The 1944 *Akers v. Sellers*[1] decision opened the door on this subject when the court explored what it would reject as constituting a fictitious standard of value

1. 114 Ind. App. 660, 54 N.E.2d 779 (Ind. App. 1944).

in a replevin action involving a Boston Bull Terrier who provided companionship. The court expressed its yearning to render a just and wise decision.

Important cases on how companion animals should be valued include *Raymond v. Lachmann*,[2] where a cat was viewed as having a cherished status; *Houseman v. Dare*,[3] which examined the subject of special subjective value and sentimental attachment; and *Strickland v. Medlen*,[4] a case that remains steadfast in applying what the court called a "true rule" for the purpose of circumscribing the noneconomic value of a companion animal in a tort case. *Sawh v. City of Lino Lakes*[5] is emblematic of a court that was comfortable with the application of thin due process rights in a death row case involving a yellow Labrador. To the court, the family dog was merely tangible personal property.

Criteria for the Record

When making a pet award, courts may vary as to what they say about, or how they use, the record. One judge may oppose using best-interest criteria for the award of a pet but still exercise the court's discretion that, in effect, causes the pet to receive the best home. Another court may permit significant testimony, including about the dog's daily life, which would enable the court to exercise its discretion based upon unidentified multiple factors. Beyond the trial court, appellate judges can be frustrated with their inability to place a dog where the dog yearns to be when there is a deficiency of the trial record.[6]

Joint Custody and Visitation

Courts are conflicted about whether to award joint custody or access rights, which are, in essence, horizontal property rights. In *Bennett v. Bennett*,[7] the Florida court, on appeal, reversed the lower court's visitation order because of the specter of "continued squabbling." Even so, in the New Jersey case of *Houseman v. Dare*,[8] the trial court effectively granted joint custody for a cohabiting couple in a case that garnered national attention. In contrast, some courts abhor the idea of having continuing jurisdiction over companion animals and will not enforce a care and sharing arrangement for a dog.[9]

---

2. 695 N.Y.S.2d 308 (N.Y. A.D. 1st Dept. 1999).
3. 966 A.2d 24 (N.J. Super. Ct. App. Div. 2009).
4. 397 S.W.3d 184, 185 (Tex. 2013).
5. 800 N.W.2d 663 (Minn. App. 2011) (court of appeals decision) and 823 N.W.2d 627 (Minn. 2012) (supreme court decision).
6. *See* Akers v. Sellers, 114 Ind. App. 660, 54 N.E.2d 779 (Ind. App. 1944).
7. 655 So. 2d 109 (Fla. App. 1st Dist. 1995).
8. 966 A.2d 24 (N.J. Super. Ct. App. Div. 2009).
9. *See* Desanctis v. Pritchard, 803 A.2d 230, 2002 Pa. Super. 221 (Pa. Super. Ct. 2002).

A Virginia court took a strong position against joint custody in *Whitmore v. Whitmore*.[10] While recognizing the intrinsic value of a Welsh Corgi to a childless couple who regarded the dog as a family member, the court would not permit visitation or shared custody, as the court considered this type of arrangement to be "ill-advised." From a close read of this case, it appears that the wife's devotion to the dog influenced the court's decision as to who would be awarded custody, as she had visited the dog several times a day during the dog's extended hospitalization while the husband had not.

Many cases reveal the court's long-term consternation about where animals belong in the legal system. For example, in *Arrington v. Arrington*,[11] the Texas court tolerated the lower court's award of pet visitation rights. What bothered the court was the idea of appointing a managing conservator, as this was a title reserved for human children, not canines.

In a similar vein, the *Nuzzaci v. Nuzzaci*[12] court was offended by the application of human terms to companion animals. Although a childless divorcing couple had worked out a stipulated temporary agreement for visitation given that one of them had moved to a home with pet restrictions, the court was contemptuous of their interest in sharing a Golden Retriever. The court offered a variety of definitions in the court's opinion, including definitions for "Adult," "Child," "Family," and "Relative." The court emphasized that the terms "pet," "animal," and "dog" were not included in these definitions.[13] The court continued that as "legislation reveals no mention of animal husbandry visitation rights," the court did not want to "broaden the term 'husband' in such a manner," either.

Animal/Human Bonds

Courts have become increasingly aware of the importance of human and animal relationships; some embrace pets as family members or at least recognize the animal as the family pet. Even so, courts are conflicted about whether to award joint custody or pet time, in part because of concerns about the floodgate problem. Some courts are comfortable with enforcing pet custody schedules reminiscent of child custody schedules, while others, when presented with the same topic, resort

10. Record No. 1644-10-4 (Va. App. 2011).
11. 613 S.W.2d 565 (Tex. Civ. App. Fort Worth 1981).
12. No. CN194-10771, 1995 WL 783006 (Del. Fam. Ct. Apr. 19, 1995).
13. It is interesting to note the court's choice of lowercase letters for the words "pet," "animal," and "dog," as compared to the higher court's capitalization of the human terms. The court took offense concerning the idea of bringing companion animals into the human family.

to sarcasm. Courts opposed to using animal best-interest standards may welcome minimal animal welfare standards.[14]

Animal/Animal Bonds

Examples of animal/animal bonds include the constancy of the relationship, the sharing of food and toys, or one animal sacrificing itself for another animal. The existence of an animal/animal bond is reflected in a Hurricane Katrina story[15] where a boat approached a dog left behind. Upon seeing the rescue boat, the dog first swam toward the boat and then away from safety, past the side of the house, and around to the back, where another dog was trapped. The boat followed, and both dogs were saved.

DETERMINING FAMILY MEMBERS

In the 21st century, who is loved and who is part of one's "family" is determined less by species or old definitions. In *Rabideau v. City of Racine*,[16] the Supreme Court famously said, "Humans have an enormous capacity to form bonds with dogs, cats, birds and an infinite number of other beings that are non-human. Were we to recognize a claim for damages for the negligent loss of a dog, we can find little basis for rationally distinguishing other categories of animal companion." In the same vein, there are popular books about friendships between unlikely animal species.[17]

REPLEVIN

Replevin is one of the oldest forms of actions known to common law, a type of action thought to have emerged during the reign of Henry II in 12th-century England; laws regulating animal use date back to the Babylonian Code of Hammurabi in 1754 B.C.E. Though now codified, the essence of the replevin action remains the same as it always did. It is a legal procedure to claim the right to have property returned from the possession of one who has less right to hold it.[18] This claim differs from one in trespass and trover in that it seeks the recovery of property

---

14. Recently, a new type of animal custody dispute has arisen where individuals who lack any indicia of ownership seek custody in situations where an animal, perhaps in their own neighborhood, is neglected or mistreated.

15. Allen Anderson & Linda Anderson, Rescued: Saving Animals from Disaster (New World Library 2006).

16. 627 N.W.2d 795, 797 (Wis. 2001).

17. Jennifer S. Holland, Unlikely Friendships: 47 Remarkable Stories from the Animal Kingdom (Workman Publishing 2011). A well-publicized friendship between a hippopotamus and a tortoise took place at Haller Park in Kenya. Jennifer Ludden, *A Hippo and Tortoise Tale*, NPR, Minnesota Public Radio, http://www.npr.org/templates/story/story.php?storyId=4754996 (last visited May 12, 2016).

18. Replevin actions are often used to address pet custody disputes.

rather than monetary damages. For a trover action,[19] ownership is not required, only the right to hold on to the property.[20]

Family lawyers should know that rules of court pertaining to civil replevin actions are typically different than family court rules, so get reacquainted with the civil rules. Pay particular attention to whether you have a mandatory disclosure obligation before formal discovery is allowed. Be careful to fill out whatever forms are required that detail your cooperation efforts with opposing counsel. You also need to analyze early on whether you should bring a nondispositive or dispositive motion; remember that each type of motion has a different deadline. Think about these subjects in terms of your local bench's ideas about case management.

Bringing a dispositive motion before discovery is completed may represent a wasted effort. In addition, expect the litigant out of possession to be upset, feel the passage of time is intolerable, and want the pet immediately returned, regardless of counsel's readiness to prevail in a dispositive summary judgment action.

Utilizing the theory of replevin, there are many ways to approach a pet custody case whether a party is seeking joint custody or the outright award of the pet, with or without pet time. Although courts are unlikely to replicate the wide array of best-interest standards for children in making a determination about a pet, courts now may consider a variety of interests affecting animals. In a close case, courts may favor the party willing to share the animal over the one who will not, even if the court will ultimately permit only one owner.

There are compelling public policy and equitable principles that may cause the court not to issue a replevin order based upon an ownership claim. If the court issues a replevin order, it might have the effect of the unworthy party, or bad actor, gaining possession of the pet. If the party initiating the replevin has a history of domestic abuse, animal mistreatment, or cruelty, the court may use its considerable equitable discretion, as at its roots, replevin is an equitable action. Attorneys should advance and cobble together arguments from a broad spectrum of pet law cases, including family, civil, and criminal law.

BEST-INTEREST FACTORS

Best-interest factors the court could look at in reaching a decision might include standard of living, animal/human bond, animal/animal bond, and survival. From an animal's point of view, where would the animal enjoy the best life? This subject

19. J.B. Ames, *The History of Trover. II. Replevin.*, Harv. L. Rev., Vol. 11, No. 6 (Jan. 25, 1898), at 374–86.
20. A common example of an action in trover would involve goods transported on a ship.

was addressed in *Raymond v. Lachmann*,[21] where the court effectively created a "let old, happy, sleeping cats lie" doctrine and allowed a cat named Lovey to live where she had long lived. The court recognized that Lovey had a "cherished status" and a "limited life expectancy." It is quite extraordinary that the court observed that the cat was loved and had loved. It was evident that the court utilized multiple best-interest factors in order to apply its discretion.

Some animals are more attached to a person and others to a place, such as a pasture. Some pets are costly to maintain and can have foreseeable and significant veterinary expenses. Another consideration for awarding a companion animal to one party over another is which person will properly care for and exercise the pet. This makes sense because veterinarians have found that 53 percent of adult dogs and 55 percent of cats are classified as obese or overweight.[22] Almost 94 percent of pet owners identify pet obesity as a problem, but many pet owners also believe that their own pets are of normal weight when in fact they are not. Overweight or obese pets, as with humans, are at a higher risk for high blood pressure and breathing problems and have a shortened life expectancy.

As stated above, although most courts are unlikely to replicate the wide array of children best-interest standards in making a determination about a pet, courts may consider and attorneys should advocate for the use of multiple factors. The court may want to know which party was the pet's primary caregiver and about the provision of care for the animal as evidence of a bond. In most cases, demonstrated long-term devotion to a pet would be a strong indicator of where the pet's and human's best interests lie.

The court may want to consider the age and life expectancies of both the pet and human, keeping in mind that some animals, such as birds, parrots, tortoises, and others, can survive their owners. In a situation where the pet may outlive the owner, the court could look at who has adequate estate planning in place when determining who should be awarded a long-living pet. Pet trusts are now legal throughout the country.

The ability of a party to afford a pet is also relevant. Courts might consider these costs as part of an individual's standard of living for spousal maintenance purposes. After all, when it comes to maintaining the standard of living during a marriage, if a court would consider a recreational vehicle as part of the standard of

---

21. 695 N.Y.S.2d 308 (N.Y. A.D. 1st Dept. 1999).

22. *Big Pets Get Bigger: Latest Survey Shows Dog and Cat Obesity Epidemic Expanding*, Association for Pet Obesity Prevention, http://www.petobesityprevention.com/big-pets-get-bigger-latest-survey-shows-dog-and-cat-obesity-epidemic-expanding/ (last visited May 12, 2016).

living analysis, consideration of the necessary veterinary expenses of a pet seems reasonable, too.[23]

Based upon the above preview, through a close case analysis, this chapter reveals the divergent attitudes and court decisions regarding companion animals. Even so, to the extent that there is a trend in the body of cases that could be classified as pet law, the trend seems to be leaning toward protecting animals from harm and promoting their welfare. Rather than the focus being on a companion animal's best interests, the emerging viewpoint seems to be the "best interests for all" standard advanced in *Travis v. Murray*.[24] In this decision, the court described the importance of dogs in the city of New York, described as the "collective New York psyche," and also reviewed the "progression of pet law" as distinguished from pet custody law decisions. In this replevin action, the court recognized that dogs are now family members.

Notwithstanding the above, there are still court decisions that remind us that to some courts, companion animals have the same status as a piece of furniture, even while proffering the idea that a pet can love unconditionally. A case emblematic of what we will call the "furniture approach" is the unreported case of *Conte v. Fossett*,[25] where one party purchased and gave a puppy to his live-in girlfriend. While treating the dog as furniture, the court recoiled at the idea that the puppy, like a diamond ring, was subject to a "replevy" as a conditional gift of symbolic significance made in contemplation of marriage.

Notwithstanding this decision, other courts, such as in *Ramseur v. Askins*,[26] treat companion animals differently than other property and are able to distinguish animal property from a "television set." In essence, a growing number of courts now distinguish animal property, in some way, from inanimate objects.

---

23. Cases relating to the care and custody of pets take place all over the globe, and the cost of pet upkeep is often a feature of cases in the United Kingdom, according to Simon Bruce, a partner in the firm of Farrer & Co LLP, who is also president of the Union Internationale des Avocats (UIA) Family Law Commission. A renowned English divorce case dealing with that subject involved a member of the well-known Flick family from Germany. The income request of the wife applying for a divorce award included generous provisions for the Labrador dog owned by the wife and children. The trial judge commented on the specific request for upkeep of the pet by saying, "£4000 to keep a Labrador. After all, from the dog's point of view there is not a lot of difference in being owned by a very rich family or simply a comfortably off family and I find it hard to see how a dog can cost as much as £4000 per year." F v. F (Ancillary Relief: Substantial Assets) [1995] 2 FLR 45 and following. Updated since 1994, the equivalent request for the pet would be around U.S. $10,000 per annum.

24. 2013 N.Y. Slip. Op. 23405 (N.Y. Sup. Ct. 2013).

25. 2013 WL 1143329, not reported in A.3d (2013).

26. 44 Misc. 3d 1209(A), 2014 N.Y. Slip. Op. 51068(U).

A case that carries the often-cited *Pratt v. Pratt*[27] logic a bit further, regarding the court expressing its willingness to act upon the mistreatment of a pet, is *Vargas v. Vargas*.[28] In this case, the litigants had a short marriage. Before awarding the dog to the wife, the court emphasized that the husband "spoke in loud terms to the dog." The court got the message across that the husband's violent behavior and propensities affected the court's award of Rockefeller. In other words, the court intended to reach a best interests decision.

In *Hament v. Baker*,[29] the court said that animals are in a special category of property. The family court said it was able to consider factors not set forth by statute, including animal welfare and animal emotional relationships.

The well-written decision in *Juelfs v. Gough*,[30] a case involving a post-decree pet custody modification where two parties originally had shared ownership of a chocolate Labrador, is an impressive example of this commonsense judicial approach. The court recognized that a "pet is not just a thing but occupies a special place somewhere in between a person and a piece of personal property."[31] When one party became unable to provide the dog with a stable home, and the dog became injured, the court utilized the "catch-all provision" of Rules of Civil Procedure 60(b) to apply an exception to the finality of judgments doctrine, where judicial intervention was required. Whether or not expressly stated, more and more courts are exercising their discretion to take the best interests of animals into account.

Pets and Domestic Abuse

Regardless of whether the court regards itself as making a property decision or applying a "best interests for all" standard, domestic abuse and mistreatment can also be considered in the award of pets to a party.[32] Pets can be included in domestic abuse orders in many states,[33] perhaps because an abuser could harm

27. N.W.2d, 1988 WL 120251 (Minn. App.).
28. 1999 WL 1244248 (Conn. Super. Ct. Dec. 1, 1999) (unpublished opinion).
29. 97 A.3d 461 (2014).
30. 41 P.3d 593 (Alaska 2002).
31. Other cases utilizing the concept of an "interim category" between property and person include *Litowitz v. Litowitz*, 146 Wash. 2d 514, 48 P.2d 261 (Wash. 2002), a case involving fertilizing human embryos; and *Morgan v. Kroupa*, 702 A.2d 630, 167 Vt. 99 (Vt. 1997), a case about a lost and found dog.
32. *See* Pratt v. Pratt, N.W.2d, 1988 WL 120251 (Minn. App.).
33. The following states permit domestic abuse protection orders to include animals: Arizona, Arkansas, California, Colorado, Connecticut, District of Columbia, Hawaii, Illinois, Iowa, Louisiana, Maine, Maryland, Massachusetts, Minnesota, Nevada, New Hampshire, New Jersey, New York, North Carolina, Ohio, Oklahoma, Oregon, Puerto Rico, South Carolina, Tennessee, Texas, Vermont, Virginia, Washington, and West Virginia. Rebecca F. Wisch, *Domestic Violence and Pets: List of States that Include Pets in Protection Orders*, Michigan State University, Animal Legal & Historical Center, http://www.animallaw.info/articles/ovusdomesticviolencelaws.htm (last visited May 12, 2016). On March 1, 2016, pet protection orders were signed into Wisconsin law.

the animal in order to terrorize or abuse their human target or because of concern about animal abuse. Including an animal in an order for protection may not be the same as a pet being the subject of an order for protection, so look at the statute closely. For example, if someone wants to kill a human, that person's dog can be protected, but if someone threatens to kill a dog, there may be no order issued unless the court determines that the owner was implicitly endangered by the threat to kill the pet under the statute.

Domestic abuse shelters are available for parents and their children, but few allow pets. There are a growing number of human shelters with co-location arrangements with animal shelters.[34] There are also local shelters, kennels, veterinary hospitals, and humane groups that may have foster families or temporary shelter arrangements for pets.

There can be mean-spirited aspects to family law pet custody disputes where one party may try to use the animal as a deterrent for the other party proceeding with a divorce, aware that the children may also be impacted. Some may use fighting for the animal as a payback of some kind, particularly if there is a lost love. One state has a law permitting the consideration of the well-being of a companion animal in a custody dispute.[35]

As of 2015, Oregon allows animals to be crime victims.[36] This type of cultural shift regarding animals, rather than the humans who own them, to be victims is emblematic of how companion animals are progressing in the continuum between the classification of property and person. *Corso v. Crawford Cat & Dog Hospital*,[37] a tort case involving a woman who planned an elaborate funeral for her dog and found the remains of a cat in the casket, is illustrative of how courts reject calling a dog "a piece of personal property" and instead recognize that companion animals are in an interim category on the continuum.[38]

---

34. Following Hurricane Katrina, the American Red Cross, historically a human-focused nonprofit group, recognized the need for co-location shelters to help pets during a crisis, too.

35. Gabriella Paiella, *Pets Will Be Treated Similarly to Children in Alaska Divorce Courts*, NYMAG, http://nymag.com/thecut/2017/01/pets-treated-similarly-to-children-in-alaska-divorce-courts.html (last visited Mar. 21, 2017).

36. *See* State v. Nix, 355 Or. 777, 334 P.3d 437 (2014), *vacated*, 356 Ore. 768, 345 P.3d 416 (2015); State v. Fessenden, 355 Or. 759 (Or. 2014); and State v. Hess, 359 P.3d 288 (Or. Ct. App. 2015).

37. 415 N.Y.S.2d 182, 97 Misc. 2d 530 (N.Y. City Civ. Ct. 1979).

38. LINDA & ALLEN ANDERSON, ANGEL ANIMALS, EXPLORING OUR SPIRITUAL CONNECTION WITH ANIMALS (Plume Books 1999); MATTHEW SCULLY, DOMINION: THE POWER OF MAN, THE SUFFERING OF ANIMALS, AND THE CALL TO MERCY (St. Martin's Griffin 2003).

FOSTERING ANIMALS

Custody disputes could arise in what the originating entity may regard as a temporary or conditional placement. It is wise to have formal agreements. Key ideas for these agreements in the foster context might include the following:

- The originating entity has the exclusive right of possession and ownership.[39]
- The agreement may be terminated at any time, without reservation, by the originating entity.
- The foster family has the absolute right of return.
- The foster family pays for the routine care of the foster animal, including food and veterinary care.
- The originating entity pays for emergency veterinary expenses, as well as nonroutine veterinary care, if the originating agency agrees in advance.
- The foster family is granted permission by the originating entity to obtain emergency veterinary care.
- The foster family acknowledges that the foster animal may have medical or behavioral problems.
- The foster family agrees to assume liability for any injuries caused by the foster animal while in their care and to hold the originating agency harmless from paying same.
- Foster animals shall not be permitted in dog parks.
- The originating entity may have the right to routine inspection of the foster family's home.
- Upon the return of the foster animal to the originating entity, the foster family will complete a report describing their foster experience with the foster animal as provided by the originating agency.[40]

LOSS OF COMPANIONSHIP

Loss of companionship arises differently in tort and family law cases even though the same cases are utilized in these different contexts, making it important to understand the horizontal impact of pet law cases on each other. In tort law, the loss begins with physical harm to or death of the animal, followed by an emotional

39. Originating entities should have an attorney review applicable laws to determine how this language will impact liability if the foster family or a third party becomes injured by the foster animal.

40. *See generally* Bruce Wagman, *Fostering Animals from Shelters—A Laundry List of Legal Considerations*, ABA Tort Trial and Insurance Practice Section Animal Law Committee Newsletter, Winter/Spring 2016, at 11.

reaction by the owner.[41] In family law, the loss can be reflected by lack of access or lack of a relationship with the animal, which impacts both the person's and the animal's best interests.[42]

BENEFITS OF OWNING A PET

Why might a person seek an award of an animal? More often than not, a claim for a pet is initiated when two people are strongly bonded to a pet. The companionship of beloved pets is important. Benefits for people who own a pet include lowered blood pressure, prolonged life expectancy, decreased depression, alleviated anxiety, and reduced arthritic inflammation.[43] Fish tanks can help people with Alzheimer's,[44] and owning animals provides a sense of well-being and exercise opportunities. Many pet owners believe that their pets are good for their family's health.[45]

For children, the benefits of having a companion animal can be profound. Owning a pet may be in a child's best interests because of the companionship and sense of well-being pets can provide. The dissent in *Nahrstedt v. Lakeside Village Condominium Association, Inc.*[46] elucidates this concept. Many parents believe that pets can improve their children's academic achievement, reduce stress, prevent allergy development, and alleviate attention-deficit/hyperactivity disorder (ADHD) symptoms.[47] Consider the possibility that not only do children love their companion animals, but also the companion animals love them back.

EQUITABLE PRINCIPLES

Companion animal status could be established by statute, case law, or practice. Another possibility is that the court will utilize equitable criteria, the type perhaps best articulated in a famous palimony case, *Marvin v. Marvin*.[48] This case involved a famous television actor and his significant other, a woman the actor held out

---

41. Although the emotional reaction of the pet may not be specifically considered, extreme behavior may affect the award of tort punitive damages.

42. Although an animal's best interests may be outcome determinative, the court may frame its decision to give the impression of a more legalistic and human-centered approach.

43. *Slideshow: 27 Ways Pets Can Improve Your Health*, Web MD, http://pets.webmd.com/ss/slideshow-pets-improve-your-health (last visited May 12, 2016).

44. *Study: Aquariums May Pacify Alzheimer's Patients*, Purdue News, https://news.uns.purdue.edu/html4ever/1999/990628.Edwards.fish.html (last visited May 12, 2016).

45. Rebecca J. Huss, *Re-Evaluating the Role of Companion Animals in the Era of the Aging Boomer*, Akron L. Rev. 47:497 (2012).

46. 33 Cal. Rptr. 2d 63, 8 Cal. 4th 361, 878 P.2d 1275 (Cal. 1994).

47. Bill Strickland, *The Benefits of Pets: 5 Surprising Ways Pets Are Good for Kids—And Families Too*, Parents Magazine, http://www.parents.com/parenting/pets/kids/pets-good-for-kids/ (last visited May 12, 2016).

48. 176 Cal. Rptr. 555, 122 Cal. App. 3d 871 (Cal. App. 2d Dist. 1981).

as his wife. When she later sought palimony and a division of property acquired during their relationship, the court explored all of the equitable principles that might pertain, ranging from quantum meruit to presumption of fair dealing and the use of a constructive trust.

All of these ideas could be imported into how to effectively advocate for your client in a pet custody dispute. A word of caution, though: although some courts may be receptive to including the family pet as a line item on the family budget for spousal maintenance or child support purposes, it is less likely that a court would issue an order specific to supporting the pet.

IDENTIFYING A PET OWNER

Another challenge in pet custody and ownership disputes is identifying who actually owns the pet when there are multiple indicia of ownership.[49] In one state, ownership might depend on who cares for and provides veterinary care for the pet, whereas in another, if someone feeds a stray dog for long enough, that person may be considered the dog's legal owner. In tort laws pertaining to dog bites, an owner may be synonymous with the animal's keeper.

CONCLUSION

Hopefully the information and the cases in this book will provide ideas and options for how to advance cases regarding pets and enable you to expand the analysis provided to fit clients' needs. If the case that helps you cannot be found in the discussion of applicable case law below, look at other chapters for ideas on how to prevail and advance the law. Unlike other substantive areas of the law, which are vertical, pet law can be thought of as a horizontal intersection between a wide variety of practice areas, wherein one decision impacts the outcome in a completely different substantive area.

---

49. When deciding who should receive custody or ownership of an animal, especially for poorly bred or mistreated dogs, the high cost of veterinary care and treatment may impact who can afford to care for the animal, particularly an animal with serious medical or mental health problems. In an eight-year period, veterinary costs rose 64 percent in the United States, perhaps not only because of technological advances and the availability of chemotherapy, magnetic resonance imaging scans, digital radiography, and orthopedic surgery procedures once used only in human medicine, but also because of how dogs are valued as family members. Frances Wilkerson, *Why Is Pet Health Care So Expensive?*, PET MD INSURANCE CENTER, http://www.petmd.com/centers/insurance/evr_why_is_pet_health_care_so_expensive (last visited May 12, 2016).

APPLICABLE CASE LAW

MANNING V. MITCHERSON[50]

Year: *1882*
Category: *Family Law*
Type of Action: *Replevin*
Animal: *Bird*
Pet Custody Concept: *Domestication of a wild animal constitutes a demonstration of custody.*

The court considered the issuance of a possessory warrant for the return of a canary named Sweet given to a married woman, Catherine Mitcherson, by a ship captain. This matter came before the superior court "by certiorari" following the magistrate's judgment.

At trial, evidence showed that the married woman had "tamed" Sweet during the two years the bird was in her possession. Sweet knew and responded to her name and returned home to the woman after a two-day absence. The idea that a tamed animal would belong to another simply because of the concept of dominion was at variance with the prevailing views of right and justice. Even so, the court indicated that possessing, taming, domesticating, or confining a wild animal constituted the requisite demonstration of custody or control. The court, aware that a 19th-century married woman could not assert property rights, clarified that Mrs. Mitcherson may have had the "personal care of Sweet," but the bird was clearly in "the power, custody and control of the husband."[51]

This case will be of interest to family law practitioners because the court had to determine if a property right in a canary could exist, making the subject of the bird suitable for a "possessory warrant." Once the court determined that the bird was property, the issue of the canary's return to the married woman was carefully written. This was an early example of the court coloring outside the lines in order to achieve a just and equitable result. This was a seminal case where the importance of a human relationship with a bird was recognized over other interests.

Practice Pointer: In this case, Mrs. Mitcherson was effectively awarded property named "Sweet." As vehemently as some pronounce that companion animals are property, lawyers have long told meaningful stories and advanced ideas of justice. This case was an early predicate of the New York decision *Travis v. Murray*,[52] where the court utilized the "best interests for all" doctrine.

50. 69 Ga. 447 (Ga. 1882).
51. Married women lacked property rights at this time.
52. 2013 N.Y. Slip. Op. 23405 (N.Y. Sup. Ct. 2013).

Akers v. Sellers[53]

Year: *1944*
Category: *Family Law*
Type of Action: *Post-Decree Replevin*
Animal: *Dog*
Pet Custody Concept: *If the lower court had made an adequate record of facts, the dog's custody could not tragically be awarded to one party when the love and affection of the dog lay elsewhere.*

Following a divorce, the appellant sought possession of a Boston Bull Terrier in a replevin action. Finding that the appellant left the Terrier with his wife when they separated during his "mellow years," and that the Terrier had not been named in the divorce decree, the court determined that although a veterinarian gave the Terrier to the appellant, the appellant gave the Terrier to the appellee. The court not only denied the appellant's replevin action but also determined that the appellee possessed and owned the dog.

This groundbreaking case is often quoted in pet custody jurisprudence. Some of the principles and ideas that the court grappled with, together with quotable commentary, include the following:

- The appellant rightfully sought the companionship of "man's best friend." This was an early expression of the human's best interests.
- The court questioned if economic value was the correct kind of value for the dog rather than moral and social value.
- The court said it did not suffer any "injured dignity" by listening to this kind of dispute wherein the parties utilized a "fictitious standard of value."[54]
- The appellate court complained that it lacked an adequate record of the facts regarding the Terrier from the lower court. The court said that if it had sufficient records, it could have made a "just and wise decision." The court continued with its often-quoted "polar star" oration, "Whether the interests and desires of the dog, in such a situation, should be the polar star pointing the way to a just and wise decision, or whether the matter should be determined on the brutal and unfeeling basis of legal title, is a problem concerning which we express no opinion."
- The court comfortably used the phrase "care and custody" regarding the award of the Terrier. This was an early exemplar of the court interchangeably using the word "custody" in the same decision where the court made an ownership and possession decision about a pet.
- The court said it would be a "tragedy" to award the dog to the appellee if "his love, affection and loyalty are for appellant."

---

53. 114 Ind. App. 660, 54 N.E.2d 779 (Ind. App. 1944).

54. This is a welcome comment for practitioners who tire of judges indicating that the subject of pet custody is frivolous or a judicial resource that somehow has been stolen from more deserving ubiquitous children.

The *Akers* court plainly stated that if it had been aware of the best interests of the Terrier, it would have taken them into account. The court did not shy away from the bold idea that a dog can love.

Practice Pointer: Everything about this decision reflects the court's sensitivity to moral decision making and the best interests of animals. The court clearly signaled the need for adequate records to be made so that courts are able to make wise and just decisions. Be sure to make the record in the lower court that the appellate court needs.

Ballas v. Ballas[55]

Year: *1960*
Category: *Family Law*
Type of Action: *Appeal of Interlocutory Decree in Dissolution of Marriage*
Animal: *Dog*
Pet Custody Concept: *Regardless of a separate property claim, the court may award a dog to the party who cared for the animal.*

A district court of appeals reviewed a type of temporary order known as an interlocutory decree in a divorce action. At issue was whether the lower court erred in awarding both a Pekingese dog and a Volkswagen vehicle to the husband. The higher court had the authority to "review the action of the lower court in awarding property in actions for divorce" and "to make such order thereupon as it may deem proper, independent of the question of discretion." The civil code granted authority to the court to award distribution of community property in order to "render justice" pursuant to a statutory provision.

The wife asserted that because the Pekingese was her separate property, the law required that she be awarded the dog. To prove the dog was her separate property, she offered evidence that her own personal funds were used to acquire the dog, the dog was registered in her name, and the dog was in her possession following the parties' separation.

The district court modified the interlocutory order in the wife's favor, finding it "immaterial whether the dog was community property or the separate property of the plaintiff." The higher court observed that the husband had not mentioned the Pekingese in his answer or his cross-complaint, although he did seek the Volkswagen. The *Ballas* court appeared to have scoured the records trying to discern whether the husband had placed importance on the dog and stated, "It appears probable that the item 'Dog' was inserted as an afterthought." Rather than discussing the dog's commercial value, the court wanted to know who cared about the dog and, seeing lack of evidence that the defendant did, awarded the dog to the wife.

55. 3 Cal. Rptr. 11, 178 Cal. App. 2d 570 (Cal. App. 2d Dist. 1960).

Practice Pointer: If in California, or a jurisdiction where the district court has equitable and discretionary authority to "render justice," point to evidence in the pleadings and the record that the subject of the pet was an afterthought.

Sullivan v. Ringland[56]

Year: *1977*
Category: *Family Law*
Type of Action: *Replevin*
Animal: *Dog*
Pet Custody Concept: *When one party to a divorce transfers title of a dog to another with a child, the spouse of the transferee may be unable to recover the dog through a replevin action against the new owner.*

This case was heard before the Supreme Court of New Hampshire without the benefit of a transcript from the district court. It is uniquely challenging to review this decision, as it appears that the court considered far more than what was offered in the decision itself.

When the plaintiff and her husband separated, the plaintiff left a jointly owned dog named Gun with her husband, saying she would make arrangements to take him once she had relocated. Almost immediately thereafter, the trial court determined that her husband "made a gift of Gun to the defendant, thereby undoubtedly delighting the defendant's young son." When the plaintiff learned of this development, she initiated legal action. Because the husband had transferred his interest in the dog to the defendant, the civil court denied the plaintiff's action in replevin.

It is difficult to identify to what extent the relationship between Gun and the boy impacted the supreme court's decision. Although this case was pled as a replevin action, or as the court put it, a "replevy," the supreme court's decision may have been influenced by the best interests of the boy, or even the dog. The court stated, "The gift was effective to transfer the husband's interest" in Gun.

Practice Pointer: The court offered no analysis as to why one of two dog owners would be able to transfer title of what was presumably a jointly owned marital dog to another, particularly when the receiving party may have been well aware of the wife's ownership interest in a divorce action. This case represents how arbitrary an award can be. Prepare your client for the lack of predictability in these types of procedures. It is also a good rule of thumb not to "temporarily" leave a pet with an opposing party.

56. 376 A.2d 130, 117 N.H. 596 (N.H. 1977).

ARRINGTON V. ARRINGTON[57]

Year: *1981*
Category: *Family Law, Probate Law*
Type of Action: *Dissolution of Marriage Appeal Regarding a Managing Conservator for a Pet*
Animal: *Dog*
Pet Custody Concept: *While emphasizing that the role of a managing conservator was for humans only, the court did not disturb the award of pet visitation rights.*

This case stood out because the family court grappled with a dog's property status, love, and whether the court could permit dog visitation. It was unusual because the trial court recognized that in addition to dividing property between the divorcing parties, Bonnie Lou, the dog, would have a managing conservator.

The parties married later in life and each owned considerable "separate property." After 16 years of marriage, they commenced a dissolution proceeding. On appeal, there was no issue with regard to the division of property, except for two dressers. There was, however, a dispute about the division of community property. The trial court, without making any findings of fact or conclusions of law, decided that the appellee would be Bonnie Lou's managing conservator.

Prior to this case coming on before the court of appeals, the appellant made a motion on a limited basis for a new trial. The motion was overruled when the court entered a *nunc pro tunc*[58] judgment, which was a condition precedent for the defendant's right to appeal.

Family lawyers may find two of the higher court's points of error worthy of attention. In point of error number five, the appellant did not disagree with the dog being awarded to the appellee or claim that the appellee was not cooperating with the appellant's visitation rights, but the appellant did complain that the appellee was appointed as the "managing conservator."

The higher court seemed infuriated when it said, "The office of 'managing conservator' was created for the benefit of human children, not canine." In looking closely at the court's statement, there was a Freudian slip, where it almost seemed as if the court used the words "canine children." The court had already stated that "Bonnie Lou is a very fortunate little dog with two humans to shower upon her attentions and genuine love frequently not received by human children from their divorced parents."

For some courts, whatever an animal receives is viewed as a loss for humans and, if not the children of the parties, such as in *Arrington*, the ubiquitous human children. In pet law cases, there is a continuing specter of this type of jealousy. Thus, it was not surprising that the court said, "All too often children of broken homes are used by their parents to vent spite on each other or they use them as human ropes in a post divorce tug-of-war. In trying to hurt each other they often wreak immeasurable

---

57. 613 S.W.2d 565 (Tex. Civ. App. Fort Worth 1981).
58. *Nunc pro tunc* is Latin for "now for then," which refers to changing back to an earlier date of an order, judgment, or filing of a document.

damage on the innocent pawns they profess to love. Dogs involved in divorce cases are luckier than children in divorce cases [that] do not have to be treated as humans."

The court further stated, "A dog, for all its admirable and unique qualities, is not a human being and is not treated in the law as such. A dog is personal property, ownership of which is recognized under the law." Furthermore, the court said, "We are sure there is enough love in that little canine heart to 'go around.' Love is not a commodity that can be bought and sold or decreed. It should be shared and not argued about."

The court overruled point of error number seven "with the hope that both Arringtons will continue to enjoy the companionship of Bonnie Lou for years to come within the guidelines set by the trial court." It appeared that the appellee still had custody of Bonnie Lou, subject to the appellant's visitation rights, and that the role of managing conservator was reserved for humans only.

To this court, Bonnie Lou was a commodity even though the "love in that little canine heart is not a commodity." *Arrington*, as much as any decision in family law pertaining to dogs, demonstrated that at some level, the court knew it was in the best interests of the humans and the dog to share this love. The court searched for where a dog belongs in American jurisprudence.

Practice Pointer: Be prepared for jurists to be conflicted on how they think about companion animals and where canines belong in human-based jurisprudence.

Marvin v. Marvin[59]

Year: *1981*
Category: *Family Law*
Type of Action: *Palimony and Property Division*
Animal: *None*
Pet Custody Concept: *When making a property determination, the court may consider independent factors, such as the provision of services, as well as equitable principles.*

Although this case did not involve a companion animal, it is included here, as the ideas and legal theory concepts expressed and explored are particularly useful for a variety of pet custody dispute arguments.

Famous attorney Marvin Mitchelson represented unmarried Michelle Triola Marvin in a palimony action against well-known television actor Lee Marvin. Mitchelson invented the word "palimony" based upon the words "alimony" and "pal."[60] The word "petimony," which sometimes comes up in pet custody disputes (perhaps sarcastically), is derivative of the word "palimony."

The trial court granted Lee Marvin a judgment on the pleadings and denied Michelle Triola Marvin a trial on the merits. The legal issues included whether an

59. 176 Cal. Rptr. 555, 122 Cal. App. 3d 871 (Cal. App. 2d Dist. 1981).
60. Mimi Avins, *On Mitchelson, Palimony and Contractual Obligations*, Los Angeles Times, http://articles.latimes.com/2004/sep/21/entertainment/et-avins21 (last visited May 12, 2016).

express contract could be enforced when sexual services were involved, whether an implied contract could be determined based upon conduct, and whether the parties' relationship was a partnership or joint venture. The higher court also considered equitable principles, including the doctrine of quantum meruit, and whether the court could establish a constructive trust as an equitable remedy.

The discussion below focuses on the parallels between claims in this case and those that could arise in the context of a pet custody dispute. Here are some factors the California court used in reaching a determination, followed by some possible legal implications in a pet context:

Marvin Factor: They agreed to "hold themselves out to the general public as husband and wife." The plaintiff also agreed to take the defendant's last name.

Pet Custody Comment: In a pet custody context, look for evidence on how the pet was routinely referred to, both in private and in public. For example, was the cat referred to as "his cat" or "her cat" or "our cat"? Look for holiday cards, voicemail greetings, veterinary records, and licensure records as evidence that the pet was held out as a family member.

Marvin Factor: The defendant argued that because of the immoral character of his unmarried relationship with the plaintiff for seven years, the court should not enforce the contract between them for public policy reasons. He further asserted that the contract's lack of enforceability stemmed from his own immoral behavior of engaging in his relationship with the plaintiff while he was still married for a portion of this relationship.

Pet Custody Comment: This public policy assertion had an equitable counterpoint, as one should not come into the court of equity unless one has clean hands. In pet custody disputes, public policy and equitable remedy arguments should be asserted. The court may utilize equitable principles in the court's exercise of discretion.

Marvin Factor: The court stated, "The fact that a man and woman live together without marriage, and engage in a sexual relationship, does not in itself invalidate agreements between them relating to their earnings, property, or expenses." In the context of a relationship that contains sexual services as an aspect of contractual consideration, the court emphasized that it could enforce "any severable portion of the contract supported by independent consideration."

Pet Custody Comment: The court was aware that the parties enjoyed the benefit of appearing married. Imagine that during this seven-year relationship, Lee Marvin bought a dog and held the dog out as "our dog." The court held in *Marvin* that all property acquired during those seven years was joint property. Look carefully at the words "independent consideration." One could speculate that independent services in *Marvin* could include a cook, cleaner, interior decorator, personal assistant, acting coach, party host, chauffer, or publicist, and if they had a dog, a dog walker, dog sitter, or dog groomer.

Marvin Factor: The court stated that "defendant's proposed standards, if taken literally, might invalidate all agreements between non-marital partners, a result no one favors. Moreover, those standards offer no basis to distinguish between valid and invalid agreements. By looking not to such uncertain tests, but only to the consideration underlying the agreement, we provide the parties and the courts with a practical guide to determine when an agreement between non-marital partners should be enforced."

Pet Custody Comment: The court discussed what kind of consideration was enough to make a contract enforceable. This sufficiency of consideration issue could be addressed if there was an agreement with regard to pet ownership, possession, or access. Beyond that, if arguing the opposite side, look for case law related to when an agreement should be considered invalid for public policy reasons. For example, an agreement might have been made between two adults before the dog was mistreated or before a child with a disability became bonded to the companion animal.

Marvin Factor: The court addressed the claims of a putative spouse before the passage of California's Family Law Act of 1970. By judicial decision, the court permitted recovery of half the property on theories ranging from partnership agreements to joint ventures and permitted awards based upon quantum meruit and other equitable principles to achieve a fair division. The court applied common law principles to express contracts but not implied contracts. As the supreme court put it, "Refusing to enforce such contracts, the courts spoke of leaving the parties 'in the position in which they had placed themselves' just as if they were guilty parties *in pari delicto*."[61]

The supreme court was troubled by the double standard used with regard to express versus implied contracts in their review of common law principles influenced by prejudices about sexual behavior. The court noted a dissent in an earlier case where it was pointed out that if the couple had not been illegally living together, "it would be a plain business relationship and a contract would be implied."

Pet Custody Comment: These kinds of distinctions may be relevant in pet custody disputes. Contracts between two parties might be implied even when one party bought the animal. Evidence for an implied contract and the utilization of equitable principles might arise based upon conduct, such as holding the animal out as "ours" or sending out holiday cards describing "our family." Quantum meruit and other equitable arguments can also be made to show that the award of animal property to a party represents a "fair division."

Marvin Factor: The court described how the bench historically emphasized express contracts and the contribution of funds or property in a relationship, rather than the contribution of services as a basis for measuring what property was accumulated through joint effort. The court emphasized how unfair this was.

Pet Custody Comment: When it comes to the subject of pets, cohabiting parties may not treat the companion animal as one person's property. It may be the nonowner who looks after the animal and provides primary care while the other is on the road. Rather than focusing on only behaviors at the point of purchase, the contribution of

61. *In pari delicto*, Latin for "in equal fault," means that two or more people are at fault or guilty of a crime. *In pari delicto*, LAW.COM, http://dictionary.law.com/Default.aspx?selected=971 (last visited May 12, 2016).

services for the animal could be given weight. As the *Marvin* court pointed out, focusing on economic contributions to the exclusion of service contributions is unfair.

Marvin Factor. The court stated that the Family Law Act was designed to "eliminate fault or guilt as a basis for dividing marital property" and to get away from the "policy of punishing persons guilty of cohabitation without marriage."

Pet Custody Comment: This comment is perhaps more tangential, as it addresses more of the collective guilt of humans about affection between the unmarried or between a human and a companion animal. Some courts belittle parties who have emotional bonds with animals, as well as the bonds between animals themselves, finding a controversy involving a pet to be an opportunity for hilarity and mirth. The courts' way of shaming these individuals is to imply that it is frivolous or beneath the courts' dignity to address the division of property lacking economic value. Recall that in *Akers v. Sellers*,[62] the court had no injured dignity in making a decision regarding a Boston Terrier.

One or both of the attorneys for the parties may also share the viewpoint that economic value, rather than sentimental value or other types of noneconomic value, matter within the pet law context. It is as if the court does not understand that what people often value most is who they love. Pet owners and even their neighbors, as well as firefighters, risk their lives to save dogs and cats, not jewelry, in fires. Likewise, pets have been known to save their owners, too, or stand by their graves after their owners pass away.[63]

Marvin Factor. The court, looking at its own precedent, concluded, "We have examined the reasons advanced to justify this denial of relief, and find that none have merit." More specifically, the court stated, "Concepts of 'guilt' thus cannot justify an unequal division of property between two equally 'guilty' persons." In the first paragraph of its decision, the court said, "During the past 15 years, there has been a substantial increase in the number of couples living together without marrying." The court recognized a cultural shift and explained why sexual attitudes of a prior time need no longer apply.

Pet Custody Comment: Although not mentioned in *Marvin*, another aspect of the cultural shift is the changing nature of the American modern family to include companion animals within the family circle. Courts going back to at least the 1940s[64] began making custody rather than property awards for companion animals.

Marvin Factor. The court said, "There is no more reason to presume that services are contributed as a gift than to presume that funds are contributed as a gift; in any event the better approach is to presume, as Justice Peter suggested, 'that the parties intend to deal fairly with each other.'"

Pet Custody Comment: In a pet custody dispute, considering only money paid at the point of purchase seems to invite the *Marvin* compelling principle of the presumption

62. 114 Ind. App. 660, 54 N.E.2d 779 (Ind. App. 1944).

63. Lauren Hansen, *The Phenomenon of Grieving Dogs: The Ultimate Loyalty [Updated]*, The Week, http://theweek.com/articles/482840/phenomenon-grieving-dogs-ultimate-loyalty-updated (last visited May 12, 2016).

64. *See* Akers v. Sellers, 114 Ind. App. 660, 54 N.E.2d 779 (Ind. App. 1944).

of fair dealing. When a duty of loyalty and other fiduciary duties are expected in a business setting, why would less be expected in significant nonbusiness human interactions?

Marvin Factor: The court said, "The mores of the society have indeed changed so radically in regard to cohabitation that we cannot impose a standard based on alleged moral considerations that have apparently been so widely abandoned by so many."

Pet Custody Comment: With regard to pet custody, social mores have radically changed, not to abandon moral considerations, but to embrace them. In a moral way, it is appropriate to look at the primary caregiver of a companion animal, as well as to appreciate bonds and best-interest factors, in the decision-making process.

Marvin Factor: In a vigorous dissent, complaint was made about recovery based upon equitable principles and quantum meruit. The dissent said that the "majority fail to advise us of the circumstances permitting recovery, limitations on recovery, or whether their numerous remedies are cumulative or exclusive." The dissent characterized the majority's overreaching by saying, "The majority perform a nunc pro tunc marriage, dissolve it, and distribute its property on terms never contemplated by the parties, case law or the Legislature."

Pet Custody Comment: The dissent well captured the need for both the legislature and the judicial branches to develop standards that can be applied fairly in pet custody disputes.

Practice Pointer: *Marvin*, though not about pet law, is a significant case to analyze and shepardize because the types of issues, analyses, and groundbreaking legal reasoning that arise could influence the evolution of both pet law and pet custody disputes. As people move toward more contract-based marital relationships, will the courts strictly enforce these types of agreements if one of the parties gives primary care to an animal and the other is indifferent to the animal's needs? The court might grant the meritorious caregiver a constructive trust or offer other types of equitable relief. Be careful not to promise your client anything.

STEWART V. WILSON[65]

Year: *1984*
Category: *Family Law*
Type of Action: *Dissolution of Marriage*
Animal: *Dog*
Pet Custody Concept: *When one party routinely took the dog to work, the lower court found no reason to disturb the award of the lower court, notwithstanding a gift claim.*

Joan Wilson appealed the trial court's allocation of spousal maintenance and marital property; the subject of marital property included who had the right of possession of a dog. Although Jay Stewart gave the dog to Wilson as a Christmas gift, the dog remained with Stewart after the parties' separation. The marital property awarded to

65. 356 N.W.2d 611 (Iowa App. 1984).

each party was almost equal, and the marriage had been of a short duration. In its brief discussion of the dog, the court found that the dog accompanied Stewart to his veterinary office and spent a "substantial portion of the day" with him.

The court of appeals said, "The trial court found that custody of the dog should be with Jay. A dog is personal property and while courts should not put a family pet in a position of being abused or uncared for, we do not have to determine the best interests of a pet. We have considered the property division as a whole. We find no reason to disturb the trial court's decision on the award of the dog to Jay. We affirm the decision of the trial court."

Practice Pointer: Courts seem to favor awarding an animal to a person who routinely takes the animal to work, and more so if that person is a veterinarian, notwithstanding the ownership "gift" claim. In dicta, the court emphasized that the best interests of animals matter, particularly if an animal is mistreated, while claiming that the court was making a property award. Prepare your client that the true basis for how a court exercises its discretion may not be revealed. For this reason, it is important to provide the court with a compelling narrative.

Pratt v. Pratt[66]

Year: *1988*
Category: *Family Law*
Type of Action: *Dissolution of Marriage*
Animal: *Dog*
Pet Custody Concept: *The lower court was afforded the discretion to define the meaning of acceptable basis in fact, while the higher court signaled that if a dog was mistreated or abused, the best-interest standard for the dog would apply.*

Though unpublished, this compact decision from the Minnesota Court of Appeals is often quoted and is of great importance and interest around the country because the court recognized that a custody award of the parties' two dogs could be premised upon "evidence of mistreatment." This decision was made long before more than half of the states in the United States allowed family pets to be included in orders for protection.

The parties were married for 14 years, in their mid-thirties, and childless.[67] They owned two registered St. Bernard dogs. After the parties separated, the appellant lived alone in the parties' joint home for 14 months without contributing to the mortgage and then filed a separate tax return to reduce his tax obligation. When the trial court awarded the dogs to his wife in the dissolution of marriage action, the appellant claimed that the court erred when it based its decision on the statutory best-interest standard used for child custody cases. Even so, the appellate court emphasized the trial

66. N.W.2d, 1988 WL 120251 (Minn. App.).
67. As is common in other disputes in the marriage context, the court observed the "childless" context of this dispute.

court's "broad discretion in the division of property" and found that the court's determination only needed to be reasonable and have an "acceptable basis in fact." The trial court's decision was affirmed because there was no abuse of discretion.

Although the St. Bernard dogs were registered, and perhaps had economic value, there was no discussion of their economic value. While the court specifically agreed with the appellant that the use of a child custody best-interest analysis did not pertain to a pet custody dispute, the court did not limit how it could exercise its broad discretion or define the meaning of an acceptable basis in fact.[68]

Practice Pointer: Always let the court know if there is evidence that a companion animal has been mistreated or abused. Although a court may not state what criteria it will use when exercising its broad discretion, again, it matters that lawyers provide the court with a compelling narrative.

S.L.J. v. R.J. v. Kahn[69]

Year: *1989*
Category: *Family Law*
Type of Action: *Dissolution of Marriage*
Animal: *Dog*
Pet Custody Concept: *When a dog is gifted to a teenage child living with the other parent, the child's interest in having the dog accompany her to both parents' homes is a worthy consideration by the court.*

A well-educated woman, her attorney spouse, and their two children lived in Missouri when they became embroiled in a divorce. The wife sought spousal maintenance; the husband gave up his attorney license in Missouri and claimed to be unemployed. As the conflict between the parties escalated, the husband brought an alienation of affection lawsuit against his wife. The family court required the parties and their children to participate in psychological examinations and appointed a guardian ad litem for the children.

68. In a replevin order issued by District Court Judge Regina Chu in Minnesota 21 years later, which can be found in the appendix, Judge Chu referenced *Pratt* in her decision. Consistent with the broad discretion approach articulated there, she utilized the following criteria in making a pet custody award: which party selected the animal for adoption and paid the initial adoption fee, the extent to which each party provided care and love for the animal, the extent to which each party provided financial support for the animal, and which result was in the animal's best interest. Judge Chu's decision was consistent with a more modern hybrid approach where the court considers both traditional and best-interest criteria.

69. 778 S.W.2d 239 (Mo. App. E.D. 1989).

In this highly contested divorce, child custody, child support, spousal maintenance, and property division were all disputed.[70] The issue with the dog arose when one of the children refused to go to his mother's home unless the family dog went, too. The court said that the dog was a gift to the boy. An interesting aspect of this case was that the 13-year-old child "filed various post-trial motions that were denied."[71]

Another issue that arose, which could have implications for a pet custody dispute, was whether an intervention was permissible in a post-dissolution proceeding. After the minor child initiated a motion seeking the appointment of another guardian ad litem, the question then arose as to who had standing to appeal the court's denial of this intervention. The father claimed he had standing per *In re Estate of McCahon*.[72] Although a parent is considered a "natural guardian" under Missouri law, the court's appointment of a guardian ad litem superseded the father having standing as a natural guardian for the duration of this appointment. Accordingly, the court refused to grant the father standing.

The court did not explain why the minor child wanting to bring his dog to his mother's home was so important. The only information the court offered was that it affirmed the trial court's orders finding the father in contempt. One of the instances shared involved the day the minor child refused to go to his mother's house unless she would take the family dog, too. The court found evidence that the husband failed to encourage the child to go home with his mother and instead "supported Robbie's use of the dog to manipulate his mother and used the situation to 'poison' Robbie's mind against his wife."

No information was offered as to why the mother objected to the dog being at her home. For example, it was not said if the mother was allergic to, or afraid of, the dog. It was not said if she lived in housing that did not allow dogs, if the dog fought with other animals in her household, or if the issue was that she was reluctant to give in to her husband's plot to cause an unwanted dog to live in her home. Ultimately, the court simply affirmed the decree of the trial court as amended.

Practice Pointer: Although this case is not particularly illuminating, it is useful for lawyers handling pet custody disputes to see that courts may consider a child's relationship with a pet if it is brought to their attention.

---

70. Although not raised in the trial court as a constitutional issue, on appeal, the husband claimed that the award of the children to a non-Jewish person violated Article I, Section 7 of the Missouri Constitution based upon a separation of church and state theory. The court stated that this issue was not "passed upon" by the trial court and thus was not preserved for appeal. The court said that even if the issue was available for appeal, the trial court's order was curable by deleting a few words from the existing decree given that the mother had agreed to raise the children in the father's faith. The constitutional issue was included in this decision as a 14th Amendment due process claim, which is common in a variety of animal law actions. Lawyers may want to raise a constitutional issue, such as procedural due process claims, common in pet law. If due process claims are brought up in your case, make sure a good record is made, complete with objections, before the trial court.

71. It is unusual for courts to articulate what a minor child owns in a family law decision. Would this minor, who owned the dog, have the right to make decisions about veterinary care? If a dog is given to a child, does this mean the primary custodial parent of that child owns the dog? In a footnote, the court explained that in some instances, when a child seeking the child's own welfare appears before the court, said child can become a ward of the court, as established in *State ex rel. Catholic Charities of St. Louis v. Hoester*, 494 S.W.2d 70, 73 (Mo. banc 1973). The court also referenced the decision in *C.J. (S) R. v. G.D.S.*, 701 S.W.2d 165, 169 (Mo. App. 1985) with regard to the court having a guardian role.

72. 729 S.W.2d 67 (Mo. App. 1987).

BOLAN V. BOLAN[73]

Year: *1990*
Category: *Family Law*
Type of Action: *Dissolution of Marriage*
Animal: *Cat, Dog*
Pet Custody Concept: *A court can arbitrarily award a cat to one party and a dog to the other.*

In this bifurcated divorce, the chancellor deferred rendering a decision about marital property. When the appellant wife raised issues on appeal, one of her claims was that the chancellor erred in awarding the parties' dog to the appellee. The court of appeals reiterated that the chancellor, aware that the parties had a cat and a dog, awarded the dog to the appellee. Without findings, the court simply affirmed the chancellor's decision, saying, "appellant received the cat, and we cannot conclude that the chancellor's decision as to the dog is clearly erroneous."[74]

Typically, lower court determinations are honored on fact questions, unless clearly erroneous. When there is a question of law, the matter may be revisited de novo, which is as if the higher court was considering the matter for the first time and the trial court's view ignored.[75]

The subject of what is "clearly erroneous" is worthy of attention.[76] As one law professor put it, "Should an issue be treated as a unit, or should it be analyzed, layer after layer, until the component parts are reduced to absurdity? Should the overarching philosophy concentrate on the effects of review on the outcome, or should the reviewing court try to invoke the standards as pure theory?"[77] One might ask if the clearly erroneous standard should be applied differently to pet awards than to the division of inanimate property.

Practice Pointer: A lawyer could assert that because companion animals have been distinguished from other personal property in both case law and state statutes, the clear and convincing standards should apply rather than a clearly erroneous standard. Warn clients that courts may lack diligence and be thoughtless in their decision-making process about a companion animal's life. Perhaps the best thing to do is make a record that the court did not consider evidence, and therefore, violated your client's 14th Amendment due process rights.

---

73. 796 S.W.2d 358, 32 Ark. App. 65 (Ark. App. 1990).

74. What might a clearly erroneous standard be with regard to the award of the dog? What facts should a court know about an animal and the parties before making a determination? Should the chancellor have made any determination as to whether one of the parties had been the primary caretaker of the dog? Was the dog uniquely bonded to one of the parties or the cat? Other than the fact that the dog and cat existed, had the court received any testimony or evidence regarding their lives? Could the clearly erroneous standard be applied if the dog had been harmed in the past by the person awarded the dog? Should the clearly erroneous standard be different when applied to a mistreated family pet than for other thoughtless inanimate property award decisions?

75. Professor C.M.A. McCauliff in C.M.A. McCauliff, *Burdens of Proof: Degrees of Belief, Quanta of Evidence, or Constitutional Guarantees?*, 35 VAND. L. REV. 1293, 1328 (1982).

76. Martha S. Davis, *A Basic Guide to Standards of Judicial Review*, 33 S.D. L. REV. 469 (1988).

77. *Id.*

Bennett v. Bennett[78]

Year: *1995*
Category: *Family Law*
Type of Action: *Dissolution of Marriage*
Animal: *Dog*
Pet Custody Concept: *While the court recognized that pets have a special status, the court would not permit a visitation schedule because of the risk of continued squabbling.*

Reversing the trial court's ruling that the husband was awarded custody of the dog, Roddy, and his wife granted visitation every other month, the higher court awarded all right to Roddy to the husband. The explanation offered was that to do otherwise would result in "continued squabbling."

The focus in *Bennett* was on strict construction of the equitable distribution statute and whether an award of custody to one party with visitation rights to the other would result in a floodgate problem. Acknowledging that some states give family pets a special status within dissolution proceedings, the court characterized this approach as "unwise." It reasoned that the courts, "overwhelmed with the supervision of custody, visitation, and support matters related to the protection of our children," could not "undertake the same responsibility as to animals." This was the classical analysis that time given to animals is time taken away from children. Courts make no similar analogy when time is devoted to motor vehicles or boats or the analysis of a footnote on a balance sheet.

Perhaps if *Bennett* had been decided two decades later, the court might have permitted more flexibility and dog visitation if the court knew the litigants could cooperate. If the court could have put a mediation mechanism (or something akin to a pet consultant) in place to address the "continued squabbling" concern, the result might have been different. Without the reduced specter of a floodgate problem, the court might have perceived the family dog as deserving of at least some modest attention. If the parties had agreed to a waiver of the family court's jurisdiction on any further disputes and also agreed to maintain funds for a fixed period of time in a trust account to be used for binding arbitration (perhaps with the court retaining limited jurisdiction[79] if claims of endangerment or cruelty arose), maybe the court would have been able to justify a path around strict allegiance to an equitable distribution statute.

Practice Pointer: Lawyers should enter into agreements or offer solutions that minimize further use of judicial resources. If there is to be joint custody or an award of custody to one party and visitation or pet time to the other, it is important that both lawyers convey to the court that the parties will be able to cooperate rather than squabble. Perhaps the court would permit this type of arrangement if further conflicts were stipulated to be addressed in a mediation or arbitration context.

78. 655 So. 2d 109 (Fla. App. 1st Dist. 1995).
79. A question that needs to be addressed as this practice area unfolds is when the courthouse doors should be reopened for public policy reasons.

Mongelli v. Cabral[80]

Year: *1995*
Category: *Family Law*
Type of Action: *Replevin*
Animal: *Bird*
Pet Custody Concept: *When there is a bad actor in possession of a pet bird, the court may determine that the bird came into that party's possession without donative intent.*

A five-year-old white Cockatoo named Peaches was purchased for $2,700. The plaintiff owners transferred possession of the bird to a relative's friends while one of the owners underwent medical testing. The plaintiffs, who had well cared for Peaches, understood the defendants would be caretakers.

When the plaintiffs sought Peaches's return, the defendants refused, claiming that the plaintiffs had donated the bird to them as a gift. The plaintiffs brought an action in replevin and sought recovery of a chattel. The defendants counterclaimed for the intentional and/or negligent infliction of emotional distress, slander, and breach of a quasi-contract.

The defendants had the burden of proving that Peaches was a gift, and they failed to meet this burden. Although the plaintiffs sought $3,000 or the return of Peaches, the court appreciated that they preferred to have Peaches returned because "Peaches is unique and the Mongellis love her and no amount of money is capable of replacing this particular animal."

The court was aware that it might lack subject matter jurisdiction over Peaches because in small claims court, the limit for a cause of action when this case was decided was $3,000. Even so, the court found that it had authority that was equitable in nature. Aware that another court had ordered a parrot to be returned in a replevin action, the court in the instant case considered dismissing the current action so the parties could commence a new action in the higher court.

In a surprising turn, the court awarded the plaintiffs damages of $3,000 and said that the defendants could avoid a judgment by returning Peaches "in good health, along with her cage, her bowls and her toys to the Mongellis." The tone of the decision indicated that the court did not expect the defendants, who were in the bird business, to want to pay $3,000 for a bird known to be a screamer.

This case will be of interest to family lawyers who handle pet custody disputes in civil court. The court came up with a remedy likely to result in Peaches's speedy homecoming. Family lawyers, too, can be as ingenious.

Practice Pointer: Consider helping the court devise a practical solution that is likely to lead to a favorable result. Think outside the box.

---

80. 632 N.Y.S.2d 927, 166 Misc. 2d 240 (N.Y. City Ct. 1995).

NUZZACI V. NUZZACI[81]

Year: *1995*
Category: *Family Law*
Type of Action: *Dissolution of Marriage*
Animal: *Dog*
Pet Custody Concept: *When childless divorcing parties reach a detailed stipulated agreement about visitation for a dog, the court may not only reject their agreement but also make fun of them.*

In this unpublished decision, the court observed that the parties had a childless marriage and disdainfully declined to "get into the flora or fauna visitation business." The subject of the court's personal property decision was a Golden Retriever named Zach.

There was no factual recitation to suggest that the parties were in any way difficult. To the contrary, this matter came before the court when the judge was asked to sign an interim stipulation and order on the subject of visitation. The reason the parties sought this arrangement was because the wife, conscientious about the explicit terms of her rental lease agreement, could not have Zach stay with her "more than one weekend per month and one afternoon per week." Their agreement was detailed as to when the wife would have visitation and even stated that the "specific weeknight to be chosen for visitation" was flexible.

The court's contempt for the parties' interest in sharing their Golden Retriever was revealed when the court included a variety of definitions in the court's opinion, including definitions for "Adult," "Child," "Family," and "Relative." The court emphasized that the terms "pet," "animal," and "dog" were not included in these definitions.[82] The court continued that as "legislation reveals no mention of animal husbandry visitation rights," it did not want to "broaden the term 'husband' in such a manner."

In addition to sarcasm, the court offered a traditional analysis regarding its obligation to divide, dispose of, or assign property. On the subject of property, the court said, "The term is said to extend to every species of valuable right and interest." The court then declared, "I decline to sign an order which is in essence a visitation order in every respect, except as to the biological classification of the 'objet d'etre.'"

Continuing in the same vein, the court referred to a statute pertaining to child visitation and exclaimed, "Nowhere does it mention what factors would have to be considered in the best interests of a non-human genus, should the parties not be able to agree on visitation." The court speculated on what might occur if the behavior contemplated by the parties was permissible. The parties might not agree on how to clean the Golden Retriever's bowl, get the dog groomed, or "be forced to decide such issues as which dog training school, if any, is better for Zach's personality type

81. No. CN194-10771, 1995 WL 783006 (Del. Fam. Ct. Apr. 19, 1995).
82. It is interesting to note the choice of lowercase letters of the words "pet," "animal," and "dog," as compared to the higher court's capitalization of the human terms.

and whether he should be clipped during the summer solstice or allowed to romp 'au naturel.'"[83]

The least sincere aspect of this decision was the declaration, "I do not in any way intend to offend Husband and Wife in the present action." This statement was quickly followed by the court's analysis of the limits of judicial authority as being "powerless to come to their aid, except to award the entire dog to one spouse or the other."

This decision stands out among all published and unpublished decisions involving pets for lacking respect and compassion for the parties. The level of contempt conveyed by the way the judge framed his arguments and how important it was to emphasize that a human is not a dog was curious. Because of the way the decision was written, it is challenging to get past the rhetoric to understand what concerns the court actually had.

Practice Pointer: Clients should be aware that some judges think about companion animals as family members and others do not. Beware of pompous judges quoting French expressions.

TEVIS-BLEICH V. BLEICH[84]

Year: *1997*
Category: *Family Law*
Type of Action: *Dissolution of Marriage*
Animal: *Dog*
Pet Custody Concept: *Following a divorce, if one of the parties seeks to terminate the other party's visitation rights, that party better not only bring the right motion but also provide sufficient grounds.*

In Kansas, the statute requires that once an agreement is incorporated into a decree, the only matters subject to modification are custody, support, and child education, unless the agreement permits a later modification. When the appellant brought a motion for judgment to terminate visitation rights for a dog, the court interpreted her action as seeking relief from judgment rather than as a modification of the judgment per statute. Not only did the appellant bring the wrong motion, but also she failed to provide sufficient grounds in her narrative, which lacked a factual proffer, and also neglected to file the required memorandum pursuant to a supreme court rule.

The appellant did not allege fraud, misconduct, or that the separation agreement she signed was "ambiguous or the result of mutual mistake." The appellate court found that the appellant "did intend for visitation to occur in accordance with the agreement when it was executed." Based upon the substantive and procedural inadequacies of

83. This comment suggested that the judge had spent some time in New York City, where quality-of-life issues about dogs are legendary. *See* Travis v. Murray, 2013 N.Y. Slip. Op. 23405 (N.Y. Sup. Ct. 2013).

84. 939 P.2d 966, 23 Kan. App. 2d 982 (Kan. App. 1997).

the appellant's effort, as well as her failure to request reconsideration, the court determined it lacked subject matter jurisdiction to grant her relief.

Apart from the analysis itself, the court expressed no difficulty with the idea that the appellee could have visitation rights with the family dog or that the appellant, if she had properly captioned her case to obtain relief from the judgment, would have had a claim upon which relief could have been granted. The court might have asserted its limited post-decree jurisdiction in a matter involving a companion animal.

Practice Pointer: Be very careful to make sure that you are properly framing your appeal. Always think about how to present a case effectively while being conservative with the use of the court's time. When constructing an agreement, think ahead about remedies if the shared access does not work out. Do you have a decision maker that would permit a periodic review in a companion animal case? Think about ways to utilize mediation processes for future disputes if custody with a visitation schedule or joint custody is contemplated and address how future proceedings in front of the court could be efficiently addressed.

Patchett v. Patchett[85]

Year: *1998*
Category: *Family Law*
Type of Action: *Dissolution of Marriage*
Animal: *Wallaby*
Pet Custody Concept: *A contempt of judgment can be vacated when inadequate proof is proferred.*

The court of appeals reversed the trial court on the sufficiency of a stock pledge and with regard to a contempt judgment.[86] The latter pertained to compensatory damages and attorney's fees owed following the disappearance of a wallaby[87] named Skippy who was characterized as a corporate asset. Although the lower court had resolved an "ambiguity" about the stock pledge in the husband's favor, the higher court found the writing was not ambiguous as a matter of law.

On the matter of the wallaby, the trial court said that the wife had "moved away from the property and apparently left Skippy there in an unsecured cage." She claimed that even though she had moved, she checked on the wallaby every day. The court opined that at the contempt hearing, the husband failed to produce testimony as to why his attempts to recover the wallaby were unsuccessful. Since there was no

85. 964 P.2d 1114, 156 Or. App. 69 (Or. App. 1998).

86. The court comfortably compelled the ex-husband to give the wife a stock pledge until he paid her "an equalizing judgment of $850,000."

87. States vary on what wildlife can be maintained as pets. A useful summary can be found at www.bornfreeusa.org. As an ethical matter, if your client owns wildlife in a state where this is allowed, encourage animal enrichment and exercise opportunities needed to promote both physical and mental health. Zoos with conservation programs could be utilized to appreciate what humane standards would be appropriate.

evidence that the wife "willfully prevented husband's recovery of Skippy," the contempt holding was reversed.

This case showed a different way that an animal could be owned. Even though Skippy seemed to have lived for a long time at a private residence with a married couple, he was legally considered to be a corporate asset.

Practice Pointer: Find out if there is any claim that the companion animal is owned by a business. Although the trial and appellate courts did not address the legal issue about Skippy as a pet custody dispute, how might this case have been handled had the wife been closely bonded to and provided primary care for Skippy? Courts seem to ignore third-party rights when they want to.

FRAUENSHUH V. GIESE[88]

Year: *1999*
Category: *Family Law*
Type of Action: *Dissolution of Marriage*
Animal: *None*
Pet Custody Concept: *Even if the parties can stipulate to a standard of review for modification of sole physical custody, this does not mean they can stipulate to the standard of review for modification of joint custody unless the legislature permits it.*

This case addressed whether the parties could stipulate to different standards of review than would otherwise be available under the state statute on the subject of a future modification of a child custody award. Although this case only addressed the subject of child custody, it is included in this book because which standard of review applies is foreseeable in a pet custody dispute that could involve sole custody without visitation, sole custody with visitation, or joint custody.

The parties agreed that if either moved a distance greater than 50 miles, the court could utilize a best-interest standard in a modification order rather than an endangerment standard.[89] When his former wife, who had sole physical custody of the children, wanted to move 150 miles away, the children's father asked the court to modify custody and to utilize this best-interest standard. The family court allowed the former wife to move and applied the endangerment standard as the standard for review. The court indicated that "dissolution is a statutory action and the authority of the trial court is limited to that provided for by statute."

Notwithstanding the power to stipulate to a standard of review in a sole physical custody case, the court observed that the legislature had not allowed parties with a joint physical custody arrangement to stipulate to a modification standard. The court said, "The determination by the legislature to provide different standards for modification of sole physical and joint physical custody awards 'is indicative of a legislative intent

88. 599 N.W.2d 153 (Minn. 1999).

89. Although the Supreme Court of Minnesota declined to utilize this stipulated standard in 1999, now, due to legislative changes, this type of provision is permissible by statute.

to impart a measure of stability to custody determinations in most circumstances.'" Somewhat apologetically, the court acknowledged the "importance of stipulations as a means for resolving marital dissolutions" and that the court did not seek "to discourage creative and amicable resolution of those cases within the confines of the law."

The higher court emphasized that its paramount duty was to promote the welfare and best interests of children, saying, "We cannot equate decisions regarding child custody to decisions regarding property. It is one thing to hold for another day issues related to money or property of a party; it is quite another to permit a stipulation which effectively holds for another day the decision of who has custody of a child." The dissent opposed setting aside a five-year-old court-approved custody agreement.

Practice Pointer: As companion animals may be leaving the strict category of only property or personal property and moving in the direction of at least special property, if not in the interim category between property and personhood, the court might be willing to maintain subject matter jurisdiction within certain, well-defined parameters. Think outside the box and construct solutions with which the court might be receptive. Most courts are against the cruel treatment of companion animals.

Raymond v. Lachmann[90]

Year: *1999*
Category: *Family Law*
Type of Action: *Civil Property Dispute*
Animal: *Cat*
Pet Custody Concept: *Let old, happy, sleeping cats lie. The best interests of a cat with a limited life expectancy are pertinent to an ownership award.*

In this famous short decision by the New York Supreme Court Appellate Division, the court awarded ownership of a cat named Lovey based solely upon Lovey's best interests. The court framed its holding as follows:

> Cognizant of the cherished status accorded to pets in our society, the strong emotions engendered by disputes of this nature, and the limited ability of the courts to resolve them satisfactorily, on the record presented, we think it best for all concerned that, given his limited life expectancy, Lovey, who is now almost ten years old, remain where he has lived, prospered, loved and been loved for the past four years.

It could be said that the court offered a "let old, happy, sleeping cats lie" doctrine. This decision represented a reversal of the trial court's decision, wherein Lovey was awarded to the nonpossessory party. Although the basis for the trial court's earlier grant of summary judgment to the nonpossessory party was unknown, it could be speculated that said party was able to demonstrate ownership based upon traditional, rather than possessory or best-interests, criteria.

90. 695 N.Y.S.2d 308 (N.Y. A.D. 1st Dept. 1999).

An aspect of this decision that stood out was the concept that not only was Lovey loved by his owner, but also that Lovey the cat had "loved." The court also looked at how Lovey was doing in his current surroundings and observed that he had prospered there for four years. This was a standard-of-living concept. The court emphasized that Lovey's limited life expectancy was an important factor for why he should not be transferred to a new home. The plaintiff was entitled to possession and ownership of Lovey "conditioned upon plaintiff's payment for all veterinary expenses incurred by the cat" for a number of years.

Practice Pointer: It is a good idea, no matter how conservative or traditional the court, to present compelling facts about where the animal should live. The court may make a decision based upon a cat's best interests even if the court does not tell you so.

Vargas v. Vargas[91]

Year: *1999*
Category: *Family Law*
Type of Action: *Dissolution of Marriage*
Animal: *Dog*
Pet Custody Concept: *Notwithstanding a claim that the dog was a gift, the court may use its discretion to consider overall circumstances before making the award.*

The defendant/wife gave her plaintiff/husband a Rottweiler named Rockefeller. The dog was registered in the plaintiff's name with the American Kennel Club. During their 20-month marriage, the plaintiff lost his job following problems with his employer and his employer's son. Both the plaintiff and the defendant had challenges with the plaintiff's adult children from a previous marriage. As the court put it, "The marital union apparently was beset with problems from the very beginning mindful of a dispute that arose even during the honeymoon. In addition, apparently problems with adult children of the parties by virtue of former marital unions created stresses or problems which led to difficulties between the plaintiff and the defendant."

The court focused on evidence suggesting that the plaintiff had violent propensities. Although the plaintiff accused the defendant of tearing up pictures of his grandchildren and doing something to his "animal trophies," the court was aware of disorderly conduct charges against the plaintiff for pushing the defendant down the stairs, causing her to suffer a sprained shoulder, multiple contusions, and abrasions. The court mentioned that the plaintiff was a truck driver and mechanic and that the defendant was a registered nurse.

The plaintiff admitted that he occasionally "spoke in loud terms to the dog" and was very strict. It was also reported that when the defendant came home one night

91. 1999 WL 1244248 (Conn. Super. Ct. Dec. 1, 1999) (unpublished opinion).

after working a midnight shift, the plaintiff "spoke about shooting the dog Rockefeller, and burning down a shed that was on the premises."

Although the plaintiff asked to be awarded Rockefeller, claiming to have trained him, the court said, "The court should award possession of the Rottweiler dog Rockefeller to her on the basis of the overall circumstances." Rockefeller's economic value was not mentioned.

This decision went into great detail about facts related to claims by both parties before and after their marriage. Because Rockefeller had originally been a gift to the plaintiff, the court was careful to make a record that justified its award of Rockefeller to the defendant. The court was affected by the plaintiff's violent behaviors and made a decision regarding the dog's best interests.

Practice Pointer: Always let the court know if one of the parties is violent and has yelled at a family pet. Threats to kill or harm the family pet, even in jest, can be outcome determinative in this type of case. Courts may be influenced by the occupation or profession of a party. The court seems to favor veterinary and other medically trained animal owners, as well as health care professional animal owners, and disfavors those with violent histories.

Fitch v. Eiseman[92]

Year: *2000*
Category: *Family Law*
Type of Action: *Post-Decree Pet Visitation Enforcement*
Animal: *Dog*
Pet Custody Concept: *When a custody and visitation arrangement becomes unfeasible, the trial court has the authority to issue a sole ownership award.*

The parents of two children separated while disagreeing about the custody and visitation of their children, as well as about the custody of two family dogs.[93] Following their separation, the father moved to a cabin without running water and the mother remained in the family house with the children.

At trial, the father,[94] who had earlier advocated that each party be awarded one of the two dogs, listened to the mother's argument that the "dogs were really the children's dogs and should not be separated." He accepted the court's idea that the children could bring the dogs to his house when he had access if they wanted to.

The issue raised on appeal was the discrepancy between the "oral agreements made at trial regarding the ownership of the dogs" and the written order that followed. The father asserted that the mother did not allow the dogs to travel back and

92. 2000 WL 34545801 (Alaska 2000) (unpublished opinion).

93. Although unpublished, this case requires a little reading between the lines to get the gist of the court's analysis.

94. The father represented himself as a pro-se litigant but retained legal counsel later in the process.

forth as the children wanted. The higher court remanded the issue to the trial court so that a determination could be made concerning sole ownership of the dogs.

Practice Pointer: The best interests of children may be taken into account by the court when the award of an animal is made.

C.R.S. v. T.K.S.[95]

Year: *2002*
Category: *Family Law*
Type of Action: *Dissolution of Marriage Temporary Order*
Animal: *Dog*
Pet Custody Concept: *When a dog is secreted during the pending action, the court may award temporary possession of the dog to the other party.*

The defendant, who suffered from mental illness, was awarded temporary possession of a dog. Although the dog was a gift from the plaintiff to the defendant for her birthday, the court characterized this gift as "an inter-spousal gift" and, therefore, the dog was marital property. In issuing its temporary order, the court stated, "Plaintiff is directed to make the location and circumstances of the parties' Chocolate Labrador Retriever dog known to defendant's attorneys forthwith upon receipt of this decision and order and to make the dog, with his license tags, leash and collar, available for retrieval by defendant within five days of defendant's written demand."

The court took into account evidence that the defendant was the primary caregiver of the dog, as the plaintiff worked and traveled while the defendant remained at home. The court was aware that the defendant was forced to leave New York City without the dog because the plaintiff, who had denied her access to their residence, told her the dog was in a boarding kennel. She alleged the defendant was "using possession of the dog as punishment."

The court observed that neither party asserted a monetary value for the dog nor that the dog was "income producing property" or a "durable asset that will increase in value." The court, in giving possession of the dog to the defendant, offered that a credit would be forthcoming if the value of the dog could be proven.

Practice Pointer: When a party is a bad actor, an otherwise valid claim may be lost. Even when courts do the right thing, they still want to appear traditional in the opinion offered. Find out what the law in the applicable state has to say about whether title passes in "inter-spousal gifts."

95. 192 Misc. 2d 547 (2002), 746 N.Y.S.2d 568, 2002 N.Y. Slip. Op. 22625.

DESANCTIS V. PRITCHARD[96]

Year: *2002*
Category: *Family Law*
Type of Action: *Post-Decree Complaint in Equity*
Animal: *Dog*
Pet Custody Concept: *When the parties reached a supplemental visitation agreement outside of the divorce decree, the higher court decided that the appellant's complaint in equity for enforcement was null and void. This had the effect of making the visitation agreement unenforceable.*

This well-known case negatively impacted flexibility in pet custody jurisprudence. A couple acquired a dog named Barney during their short marriage. When they entered into a written agreement wherein one would have full custody of the dog and the other visitation, they chose not to incorporate the supplementary agreement into their divorce decree. Following their divorce, when the former husband sought to enforce his visitation rights through a "Complaint in Equity," the higher court explored whether this dispute should have been on "the law side of the Court."

The superior court found the appellant's complaint seeking injunctive relief to be analogous to a mandate for shared custody. It was determined that the trial court was correct in not certifying this dispute on the "law side of the Court," per statute. The court also scoffed at the parties' written agreement, stating that it was "analogous, in law, to a visitation schedule for a table or a lamp."[97]

The court ultimately determined that a supplementary agreement to a divorce decree regarding shared custody or visitation was void and unenforceable. Although the court quoted provisions from Pennsylvania codes, its rationale for why "Barney and his social schedule belong exclusively to appellee" was proffered as self-evident. *Desanctis* lacked the depth of analysis that the neighboring state of New Jersey exemplified a decade later in *Houseman v. Dare*.[98]

If this case came before this court at the same time, would the court have reached the same result? The popularity of mediation processes has increased, and the family law system has been granted more contractual freedom, including freedom with regard to the disposition of both real and personal property. Advances in science have shown that unlike a table or lamp, companion animals are sentient.[99]

For commercially valuable show dogs and racehorses traveling back and forth between co-owners that have written agreements about possession and breeding rights, why might a court permit an enforceable possessory right for commercially valuable animals that the court would not permit when the value of the dog is unrelated to

---

96. 803 A.2d 230, 2002 Pa. Super. 221 (Pa. Super. Ct. 2002).

97. The law is all over the map with regard to the subject of companion animals but offers animal protection laws for animals that are not extended to inanimate objects. These laws, as well as the common law, affect the status of companion animals in American jurisprudence.

98. 966 A.2d 24 (N.J. Super. Ct. App. Div. 2009).

99. Seth Davis, *AAHA Position Statement Classifies Animals as Sentient Beings*, NEWSTAT, http://www.aahanet.org/blog/NewStat/post/2012/10/17/521946/AAHA-position-statement-classifies-animals-as-sentient-beings.aspx (last visited May 12, 2016).

the animal's fair market value? Remember *Akers v. Sellers,*[100] where the court explored the concept of "no injured dignity" and how it utilized a "fictitious standard of value." The real issue may not be about companion animals being personal property but actually about the values held by the court.

Mediation processes are utilized to resolve nontraditional legal challenges that arise when valuable homes have negative equity. Courts may give up jurisdiction based upon contractual waivers involving spousal maintenance payments or retain jurisdiction to enforce the division of retirement assets through qualified domestic relations orders.

Desanctis represents 20th-century views even though it was decided in 2002. Courts across the country that previously only gave their best judicial efforts to cases involving pedigree animals and animals subject to warranties, or whether pets are products under the New York doctrine or goods under the Illinois doctrine, were beginning to look at how animals entering the family circle belonged in the legal system.[101]

Practice Pointer: Pay attention to whether the court utilizes 20th- or 21st-century thinking as to how companion animals should be treated in the family. If the court is focused on 20th-century logic, with notable exceptions, the concept of ownership is cost-based and the subject of emotional bonds and best interests of little interest to the court. Not only were 20th-century courts adversely affected by using human language when referring to animals, but some of these courts also emphasized how the law is unable to distinguish between inanimate and animate property. The common law changed in the 21st century, where courts became more comfortable traversing between 20th-century traditional thinking and 21st-century relational value, standard-of-living, and best-interest reasoning. In the 21st century, there is growing evidence that companion animals are being viewed as family members, and the judicial decisions are more often in concert with our cultural shift.

In addition to the above, lawyers should be cautious about side agreements or supplemental agreements. It is a good idea, if possible, to test the waters in advance to see if the trial court will sign an order or judgment that permits freedom of contract. Even if the trial court agrees to enter a decree with some type of shared ownership, possession, or access, it is foreseeable that another judge or the higher court might not enforce this type of provision because of the finality rule. As current jurisprudence moves toward the use of private mediation processes, as well as binding arbitration in family court matters, the terms of an agreement or award being enforced may be directly related to the court's valid expectation that most cases are unlikely to come back on the court's docket.

100. 114 Ind. App. 660, 54 N.E.2d 779 (Ind. App. 1944).

101. Strickland v. Medlen, 397 S.W.3d 184, 185 (Tex. 2013), is a famous tort decision illustrative of how courts are very aware of a pet's relational value, even when the court would not permit damages for noneconomic loss. In *Strickland*, the court was effusive about its love for animals.

JUELFS V. GOUGH[102]

Year: *2002*
Category: *Family Law*
Type of Action: *Post-Decree Pet Custody Modification*
Animal: *Dog*
Pet Custody Concept: *Recognizing that a pet is in a special place between a person and property, and not just a thing, the court modified a seven-year-old shared custody award and granted sole custody to one party.*

The *Juelfs* decision squares with the 21st century. Julie Juelfs and Stephen Gough were awarded "shared ownership" of Coho, a chocolate Labrador. Seven years after the entry of the judgment and decree, Juelfs initiated a post-decree action alleging that Gough had not given her access to the dog. Gough's explanation was that two other dogs at Juelfs's residence "threatened Coho's life," and as a result, Coho suffered a dislocated elbow. Coho's injury was serious enough to require Gough's constant care. Gough effectively made a dog's best-interests argument.

The trial court awarded "legal and physical custody of Coho to Stephen" subject to Juelfs's reasonable visitation rights, as determined by Gough, who was responsible for paying Coho's medical bills. The court also said that a "pet is not just a thing but occupies a special place somewhere in between a person and a piece of personal property."

The higher court used the following words and phrases in its opening: "grant sole custody," "award Stephen full custody of Coho," "he is awarded legal and physical custody to Coho," "Julie is allowed reasonable visitation rights," and "all of Coho's medical bills." The court described the dog using traditional child custody language.[103] These word choices are reflective of a 21st-century human terminology trend.

When this matter came before the supreme court based upon an appeal of the denial of a Rule 60(b) motion under the Rules of Civil Procedure, the court expressed its position on the finality of judgments, saying, "A property division incorporated within a divorce decree is a final judgment and is modifiable to the same extent as any equitable decree of the court."

The court considered whether the "catch-all provision" of Rules of Civil Procedure 60(b) applied, a provision only available if "none of the other five clauses apply and extraordinary circumstances exist." Deciding that it would "balance the interest in the finality of judgments against the interest in granting relief from judgment when justice so requires," the court turned to the three factors of the "catch-all provision,"

102. 41 P.3d 593 (Alaska 2002).

103. Following the family court's award of sole custody to Gough, Juelfs brought numerous motions as the relationship between the parties further deteriorated. Both parties sought restraining orders against each other. This matter came back before the trial court after the superior court reaffirmed its earlier ruling that Gough would get full physical and legal custody of Coho and also clarified that Juelfs would not need to be consulted about "any medical decisions." Again, the court utilized the word "medical" rather than "veterinary" when it referred to how decisions about Coho's physical well-being would be made.

which were (1) prejudice, if any, to the nonmoving party if relief from the judgment was granted, (2) whether any intervening equities made the grant of relief inappropriate, and (3) any other circumstances relevant to consideration of the equities of the case.

Looking at the plain meaning of the finality of judgment doctrine, the court said, "Although there is an interest in the finality of judgments, it is clear the judgment would never have been final under the circumstances that faced the court" because in this case, "the parties were unable to share custody of Coho without severe contention." The court utilized the Rule 60(b)(6) equitable "catch-all provision" because the other provisions did not apply[104] and because judicial intervention was required.

Although some may argue that *Juelfs* represents a floodgate problem wherein shared ownership was allowed in the first place, seven years had passed from the entry of the judgment and decree before any motion was made. The supreme court was not concerned about the parties' freedom to contract, or even a shared custody arrangement, but rather, that the parties were unable to share custody without "severe contention," which resulted in judicial intervention.[105] Ultimately, the supreme court determined that the superior court "did not abuse its discretion in modifying the property settlement incorporated into Julie and Stephen's dissolution decree in awarding Coho to Stephen."[106]

Practice Pointer: In both negotiations and mediation processes, lawyers should be aware of how the finality of judgment rule may be applied if the parties' agreement does not work out as planned. Carefully review Rule 60 of the Rules of Civil Procedure. If representing a party seeking modification based upon animal cruelty, look at cases out of the states of Alaska and Oregon, including *State v. Nix*[107] and *State v. Fessenden.*[108]

---

104. *See* Clauson v. Clauson, 831 P.2d 1257, 1261 (Alaska 1992).

105. More of the court's rationale is revealed in note ten, where the court incorporated by reference a one-year deadline as defined under Civil Rule 58.1(c), stating, "This rule does not limit the power of a court to entertain an independent action to relieve a party from a judgment, order or proceeding, or to grant relief to a Defendant not personally served, or to set aside a judgment for fraud upon the court."

106. The court said that certain writs were abolished in the state of Alaska. Because these writs may not be abolished in other states, they are briefly set forth here, together with a definition. Writ of coram nobis is a remedy for setting aside an erroneous judgment in an action that resulted from an error of fact. A writ of audita querela is applicable when a defendant is in danger of execution on judgment based on some matter of discharge which occurred after the judgment, while excluding any matter which the defendant could have pled. Although the writ of audita querela was abolished, it seems that the court utilized similar reasoning and employed an equitable remedy.

107. 355 Or. 777, 334 P.3d 437 (2014), *vacated*, 356 Ore. 768, 345 P.3d 416 (2015).

108. 355 Or. 759 (Or. 2014).

Conahan-Baltzelle v. Baltzelle[109]

Year: *2004*
Category: *Family Law*
Type of Action: *Dissolution of Marriage*
Animal: *Dog*
Pet Custody Concept: *In exercising its broad discretion, the court may consider who found the dog at a shelter, who adopted the dog, and who had a close relationship with the dog.*

The trial court exercised its discretion when it awarded a couple's dog to the husband. In his pleadings, the husband accused his wife of "extreme mental cruelty and constructive desertion," and she in turn cross-billed him for a "divorce *a vinculo matrimonii* on the ground of adultery." The parties were married for almost six years when the husband temporarily moved out of the marital residence with the expectation that he would soon move back in and buy out his wife's interest in the homestead equity.

The husband thought it would be easier to leave the dog in the house during this brief time period. When the wife decided she wanted to buy out her husband's interest in the homestead, the husband worked out a visitation schedule with the dog. He was able to give the dog extensive exercise, including "hikes in the mountains, runs in the park and walks." The husband's primary complaint about his wife was that she did not adequately exercise the dog.

The husband had found the dog at an animal shelter, instantly bonded with the dog, and visited the dog daily until the adoption was completed. The husband said the dog was "like a child that I don't have." He said he "took the dog with him everywhere he went" and claimed that the dog meant "everything to him." The wife said she was the one who took the dog to the veterinarian and paid the costs associated with his care. The wife also arranged for the dog's licenses. Like her husband, she said that the dog was like "a child to me."

The higher court reiterated how "equitable distribution does not mean equal distribution." Instead, the higher court said the trial court's award was within its sound discretion, subject to statutory mandates. Relevant factors per statute included monetary contributions, duration of marriage, and circumstances of the dissolution.

Acknowledging that even though "both parties clearly have affection for the family dog, only one party could be awarded the dog," the higher court said the husband "presented evidence that he located the dog at the animal shelter, he adopted the dog, and he has a close bond with the dog. Under these circumstances, we cannot say the trial court abused its discretion by awarding the dog to husband." The judgment of the trial court was affirmed. There was no discussion about the economic value of the dog.

Practice Pointer: Courts seem to value certain behaviors more than others, and behaviors may be outcome determinative. Giving a large dog adequate exercise is one of them. This is a dog's best-interests factor. It is important to many courts that the parties convey the bond between the human and the dog, too.

109. Record No. 0830-04-3 (VA 9/7/2004) (Va. 2004).

Beardsley v. Garcia[110]

Year: *2008*
Category: *Family Law*
Type of Action: *Order for Protection*
Animal: *None*
Pet Custody Concept: *Regardless of other statutes with visitation provisions, the court can grant visitation in a domestic abuse proceeding.*

Although this case did not involve a pet, the fact sequence may have parallels to how an order for protection involving a pet could be analyzed.[111] A woman was granted an ex parte order for protection following serious death threats. She argued that the recognition of parentage she and the biological father signed did not result in his having the status of an adjudicated father.

On appeal, the higher court interpreted the governing law as giving the court authority to grant "a wide array of relief" in the domestic abuse context as long as the court gave "primary consideration to the safety of the victim and the children." The court further reasoned that the ability of a father to seek parenting time under one statute[112] did not preclude that individual from seeking parenting time in a domestic abuse proceeding. The court refused to apply the "ambiguity-created-by-silence principle with regard to statutory interpretation," particularly where "statutory authority to award parenting time already exists."

The higher court took issue with the contention of the dissent, as described below, that this access had "the perverse consequence of rewarding acts of domestic violence" in a case where no finding was made that domestic abuse had occurred.[113] Paying homage to the broad discretion of the trial court, the higher court reiterated that the trial court had the duty to consider the safety of the children.[114]

The dissent began with how legislative intent could be understood in the context of three statutes, the Domestic Abuse Act, the Parentage Act, and the Recognition-of-Parentage Statute. To discern legislative intent, the dissent emphasized that in two of the three statutes, the legislators "made the decision to treat unmarried fathers differently than married fathers when it comes to the issues of custody and parenting time." Thus, it was a "policy decision" of the legislature that "unmarried mothers have sole custody of their children absent a court order granting custody or parenting time rights to the father." Accordingly, an unmarried father lacks any custody rights "until a court becomes involved and determines those rights."

---

110. 753 N.W.2d 735 (Minn. 2008).

111. Rebecca F. Wisch, *Domestic Violence and Pets: List of States that Include Pets in Protection Orders*, http://www.animallaw.info/articles/ovusdomesticviolencelaws.htm (last visited May 12, 2016).

112. In the state of Minnesota, when paternity is established, parental access is governed under Minnesota Chapter 518, which is the same statute as dissolution of marriage.

113. An alleged domestic abuser may avoid findings by agreeing to the entry of an order.

114. In Minnesota, the court will permit the entry of an order for protection without a finding of domestic abuse if the alleged perpetrator, but not the person claiming to be the victim of domestic abuse, agrees to it. For that reason, the higher court, pointing out that there were "no findings," was a bit disingenuous.

Perhaps more importantly, the dissent asserted that the majority failed to properly interpret the purpose of the Domestic Abuse Act, which was to "provide victims of domestic abuse and their children with quick relief from the courts to help protect them from acts of family violence." Pointing out that the court was effectively allowing a recognition of parentage father to avoid the best-interest scrutiny that he would have otherwise been subjected to in family court, the dissent also described the legislative history of the act and how the definition of a "family or household member" was broadened.

The analysis of the majority and dissent could pertain to a pet in an order for protection type of action. For example, if the recognition of parentage father was in and out of the mother's home and at some point brought a dog with him, there could be an issue of whether the dog was a gift, abandoned, or even co-owned. There might also be an issue as to whether there was legislative intent to protect the animal, without getting into outcome-determinative ownership claims, in a situation where a domestic abuse order was issued.

Practice Pointer: While courts are trying to prevent floodgate problems in domestic abuse cases by allowing stipulated orders without findings, if either child or companion animal access questions arise, the court lacks relevant information on the extent of the dangerousness of the person subject to the domestic abuse order. If there is information relevant to the subject of this dangerousness that is not included in the domestic abuse petition filed with the court, perhaps because the petitioner was pro se, consider preparing and filing an amended petition or making an offer of proof on the record. For example, the court may not be aware that in addition to a recent threat to kill the dog, there had been too many unexplained "accidents" involving the pet.

If your state does not specifically cover companion animals in orders for protection, seek the award of the pet under a catch-all type of provision, such as "any other property type." Perhaps you might carefully inform the court that although a pet is not a person, in *Rabideau v. City of Racine*,[115] the court granted a dog the status of "best friend." Be light on your feet.

Wolf v. Taylor[116]

Year: *2008*
Category: *Family Law*
Type of Action: *Domestic Partnership Dispute*
Animal: *Dog*
Pet Custody Concept: *When the court viewed the challenge to the legality of a stipulated visitation arrangement as a challenge to the entire settlement agreement, the claim concerning visitation was implicitly denied.*

After 15 years in a domestic partnership, a couple who owned a dog named Mike reached a settlement in their dissolution action. In their agreement, the defendant was

115. 627 N.W.2d 795, 797 (Wis. 2001).
116. 197 P.3d 585, 224 Or. App. 245 (Or. App. 2008).

awarded the exclusive ownership of Mike and the plaintiff was awarded conditional visitation. The plaintiff was required to keep Mike away from other dogs and in an enclosed area where he could not get loose. The full agreement, which included a severability clause, was placed on the record.

Later, the plaintiff sought to rescind the entire agreement based upon "unlawfulness" because personal property was not subject to visitation rights and no common law authorized "custody" or "visitation" to personal property. She argued that the agreement was impossible to perform, as visitation with a dog was "incompatible with principles of ownership" and because "there is no reasonable or legal way for them to succeed in accomplishing" the purposes of the agreement. The defendant countered that Oregon law did not prevent a private settlement that included a visitation arrangement.

Notwithstanding the severability clause, the higher court denied the plaintiff's motion and referenced *DeSanctis v. Pritchard.*[117] Although in *DeSanctis*, the higher court declined to enforce pet visitation rights, the Oregon court determined that there was no need to determine whether the dog visitation provision was valid, as the plaintiff's motion pertained to the entire settlement agreement, an agreement that was upheld.

Practice Pointer: At a time when courts hope to have more cases settled through mediation processes, the likelihood increases that courts will reinforce the validity of private agreements, including those with visitation clauses. Courts can use their influence to cause parties to utilize alternative dispute resolution processes before having access to the court.

Houseman v. Dare[118]

Year: *2009*
Category: *Family Law*
Type of Action: *Replevin*
Animal: *Dog*
Pet Custody Concept: *The award of joint pet ownership is permissible, even if called a "shared caregiving agreement."*

At the center of this seminal case that garnered national attention was the jaw-dropping joint custody award of a Pug named Dexter to two estranged parties who once cohabited. Although this case involved a property-based action in replevin, the appellate decisions focused more on contract law and equitable principles.

While engaged and joint homeowners, Doreen Houseman and Eric Dare searched for a dog and chose a Pug they named Dexter. Dare paid $1,500 for Dexter and registered him with the American Kennel Club under his name. Houseman's name also appeared on the American Kennel Club registry.

117. 803 A.2d 230 (Pa. Super. Ct. 2002).
118. 966 A.2d 24 (N.J. Super. Ct. App. Div. 2009).

Shortly after Dexter was purchased, the parties' relationship ended. According to Houseman's attorney,[119] when Dare asked Houseman to leave, he kept possession of the house and Houseman received possession of Dexter and most of Dexter's things. Later, upon Dare's request, Houseman worked out a visitation schedule so Dare could have access to Dexter.

Dare's attorney offered a different history, saying that Dare considered Dexter to be "his dog," and he paid all the dog's expenses, including veterinary bills. Dare gave Houseman visitation rights for a period of time. When his client "moved on" with another woman and Houseman would not let go, he stopped Houseman's visitation with Dexter.

For months, the parties regularly exchanged Dexter, with one party having Dexter on the weekends and the other on weekdays. After this action was commenced, it was more than two years before Houseman saw Dexter again, as the trial court granted no interim relief.

At pretrial, the court declined to hear evidence on Houseman's claim for specific performance to enforce the parties' oral agreement. Following trial, the trial court made findings describing Houseman as particularly credible as she avoided self-serving testimony. The court learned that while Dare had underpaid Houseman's share of the homestead equity and overlooked giving her half of the money from a joint banking account, Houseman offered to withdraw her financial claims and pay Dare $500 if she was awarded Dexter.

Even though Houseman testified that she relied on Dare's promise to abide by their oral agreement, the court decided that Dexter would remain where he was, with Dare. This decision was consistent with the well-known legal axiom that "possession is nine-tenths of the law." The court resolved the financial issues in favor of Houseman.

The appellate court focused on whether the parties had an enforceable oral contract to share custody of Dexter, and, if so, whether it was subject to enforcement by specific performance. The higher court used groundbreaking language with regard to special subjective value, saying, "The special subjective value of personal property worthy of recognition by a court of equity is sentiment explained by facts and circumstances—such as the party's relationship with the donor or prior associations with the property—that give rise to the special affection. In a different context, this court has recognized that pets have special 'subjective value' to their owners."

From an equitable perspective, the court further determined that each party's claim for the dog "property" was in good faith. The court described its power of equity with regard to sentimental attachment when it said, "There is no reason for a court of equity to be more wary in resolving competing claims for possession of a pet based on one party's sincere affection for and attachment to it than in resolving competing claims based on one party's sincere sentiment for an inanimate object based upon a relationship with the donor."

The court further found that when joint owners of a dog entered into an oral agreement and that agreement was breached, specific performance was an available remedy. This is because the remedy of specific performance addresses the breach of an enforceable agreement "when money damages are not adequate to protect

119. Barbara J. Gislason interviewed the attorney for each party in this case.

the expectation interest of the injured party and an order requiring performance of the contract will not result in inequity to the offending party."[120] On the subject of whether an oral agreement considering a pet should be treated differently than other oral agreements, the higher court said, "We conclude that the trial court erred by declining to consider the relevance of the oral agreement alleged on the ground that a pet is property. Agreements about property jointly held by cohabitants are material in actions concerning its division. They may be specifically enforced when that remedy is appropriate."

Establishing that it was the trial court's responsibility to give the parties the opportunity to present evidence so that competing equities could be evaluated, the court said,

> Recognizing that the trial court is in the best position to evaluate the equities implicated by Houseman's request for possession of the dog, and that Dare had no reason to present relevant evidence because he had possession of the dog when the trial court made its improvident pretrial ruling on specific performance, we remand for further proceedings on the existence of an oral agreement about ownership and possession of the dog and the propriety of specific performance.

In this carefully worded and historic decision, the court declared that Houseman's sentiments about Dexter were as worthy as a person having a sincere sentiment about a family heirloom. Although the higher court ultimately rendered its decision using a more traditional legal standard and vocabulary, this decision was significant with regard to property law and companion animals. An opening in the law was created for a joint pet custody award.

As stated above, the case was remanded to the trial court for further proceedings with respect to the existence of an oral agreement about ownership and possession and to address Houseman's claim of specific performance. Upon remand, the parties returned for another trial court proceeding, again with national media attention. There was consensus by both attorneys that at the second trial, an expert witness would be required on the subject of human/animal bonds as a predicate for offering bonding evidence.[121] No expert was called.

At the conclusion of the proceeding, the trial court issued a decision that Houseman had failed to meet her burden of proof that specific performance was warranted. Even so, the court reinstated the parties' dog sharing agreement, wherein Dexter would be exchanged between the parties every five days. Following a bench discussion, the judge said that the joint owners would each have sole possession of Dexter at specified times during the calendar year. While declaring that the court had not

---

120. *New Jersey Court Rules that Formerly Engaged Couple Must Share Custody of Pet Dog*, Animal Legal Defense Fund Update, http://aldf.org/downloads/Update_Winter_2010.pdf (last visited May 12, 2016).

121. Two nonprofits filed amicus briefs in this case, the Animal Legal Defense Fund and Lawyers in Defense of Animals. Both advocated that the court should utilize a best interest of the animal standard in rendering its decision. Although the higher court did not apply the best interest of the animal standard advocated in the two amicus curiae briefs, the court said that the best-interest standard could be applied if there was evidence of animal abuse and neglect.

made a "custody arrangement," but rather a "shared care-giving agreement," and that Dexter was "still property," the judge still awarded joint pet ownership with alternating rights of possession.[122]

The judge added the salvo that the shared caregiving arrangement should continue until Dexter "goes to the Great Kennel in the Sky"[123] and that "when Dexter dies, Houseman and Dare should amicably split the ashes and not turn the issue into a court battle. 'Hopefully I won't be here at that point,' he said right before leaving the bench with his robe flying."[124]

Dare appealed the trial judge's decision as arbitrary and capricious. The higher court, per curiam, affirmed the trial court's decision by saying, "On a prior appeal, we remanded for further proceedings. Specifically, the trial judge was asked to determine whether the parties, joint owners of a dog, had an oral agreement about the dog's ownership and possession following their separation and, if they did, whether that agreement should be enforced."[125] The higher court also said Dare's arguments were without sufficient merit to warrant discussion in a written opinion.[126]

Practice Pointer: It is important for lawyers to properly prepare clients in mock settings on how to be effective in presenting their testimony. Although telling your client to tell the truth is a good place to begin, many clients have difficulty keeping their stories straight, so preparation is vital. An important aspect of preparation is the timeline.

Although media attention can be counterproductive, sometimes the legal system is at its very best when a subject is of great public interest, such as the right of access to a beloved dog. If a case gains media attention, be sure to give the court the in-depth analysis that hopefully this book will make possible.

Although an expert on human/animal bonds was not called in *Houseman*, it is foreseeable that some courts will resist permitting this type of testimony, so be sure to assert due process rights utilizing a well-written brief. Have careful discussions with your client early and often about the expense of this litigation, too. In your practice, you may find that cohabiting or engaged couples that split up, as was the issue in *Houseman*, are the most common types of clients to walk through your door with pet custody dispute issues. Know this case well.

---

122. *Couple Who Split Up Must Share Dexter the Pug*, Today, http://today.msnbc.msn.com/id/32985480/ns/today-today_pets_and_animals/t/couple-who-split-must-share-dexter-pug/ (last visited July 1, 2015).

123. *Id.*

124. *Id.*

125. Houseman v. Dare, 405 N.J. Super. 538, 545–46 (App. Div. 2009).

126. R. 2:11-3(e)(1)(E). Affirmed. N.J. Super. A.D., 2010. Houseman v. Dare not reported in A.3d, 2010 WL 4025584 (N.J. Super. A.D.)

Prim v. Fisher[127]

Year: *2009*
Category: *Family Law*
Type of Action: *Conversion*
Animal: *Dog*
Pet Custody Concept: *An action for pet custody, framed as a conversion action, must meet the requirements of the Restatement (Second) of Torts in some states.*

A Golden Retriever named Kaos was the subject of a pet custody dispute. The dog was purchased when the parties cohabited, and when they separated, the defendant kept the dog and would not allow the plaintiff to see him. The plaintiff sought joint custody of Kaos, framed in a conversion action, a disposition the court found unsupported by the Restatement (Second) of Torts.

Although the court could have contemplated a remedy such as a forced sale or an award of money, it was at a loss for how to utilize its equitable powers, particularly when the defendant opposed any contact with the plaintiff. The court also stated that a pet's value was not primarily financial and was instead derived from the animal's relationship with human companions. It bears repeating that this court used the concept of relationship value.

The court denied the plaintiff's motion for a preliminary injunction for the Golden Retriever because she was unable to establish irreparable harm and because the court doubted the likelihood of her success on the merits, as she essentially sought a joint custody disposition. The court also rejected the plaintiff's claim for conversion because the parties were co-owners and because the normal remedy when a conversion claim is brought is an award of monetary damages.

Practice Pointer: When bringing a conversion action, make sure your client is aware that a positive award may only be monetary. When entering uncharted areas in the law, be sure your client understands that the court may scoff at the relief sought, such as a joint custody disposition. Do not promise an outcome the court might reject for a variety of reasons, and be aware that courts around the country are reaching different determinations based upon wide-ranging types of legal analyses.

127. No. S1464-09 CnC (Toor, J., Dec. 22, 2009).

DECORSO V. SAKSA[128]

Year: *2011*
Category: *Property Law*
Type of Action: *Replevin, Conversion*
Animal: *Dog*
Pet Custody Concept: *To succeed in a writ of replevin, the party seeking the writ must establish by probable cause that that party would succeed on the merits.*

Kathleen Saksa purchased a Pit Bull Terrier named Anna and provided her with food, shelter, medical treatment, leashes, a muzzle, and a crate. She also paid to have the dog bathed and trained. Saksa's roommate, Gail Decorso, took care of Anna, too, and occasionally brought Anna with her to the market.

When the two had difficulties, Decorso surreptitiously recorded a conversation wherein Saksa told Decorso she could have Anna if certain conditions were met. Even so, Saksa removed the dog from the home under false pretenses. After the dog was gone, Decorso obtained a dog license that listed her as the dog's owner, gained access to Anna's veterinary records, and brought an action in replevin and for conversion.

The court held that to proceed with the writ of replevin, Decorso needed to establish probable cause that she had "a general or special property interest with a right to immediate possession" of the dog and that the dog was being "wrongfully detained." The probable cause standard was defined as "a bona fide belief in the existence of the facts essential under the law for the action and such as would warrant a man of ordinary caution, prudence and judgment, under the circumstances, in entertaining it." The court explained that "Probable cause is a flexible common sense standard. It does not demand that a belief be correct or more likely true than false."

While Decorso failed to establish "any general or special property interest superior to that of Saksa," and did not prevail in her claim, the court observed that Decorso discovered Anna, assisted her, and loved her. The court carefully reviewed the facts and the law while comfortably acknowledging the idea that the losing party loved the dog, too.

Practice Pointer: If a case is won, be nice about the plight of the losing party. Here, the court was kind in acknowledging that when two people are responsible for the care of a dog, both will have bonds. In this particular case, it is possible that an expert witness testifying about bonds would have advanced an otherwise thin claim.

128. 2011 WL 2611801, not reported in A.3d (2011).

LeConte v. Lee[129]

Year: *2011*
Category: *Family Law*
Type of Action: *Replevin*
Animal: *Dog*
Pet Custody Concept: *The original owner prevailed on a replevin claim in the parties' relationship of short duration, notwithstanding caregiver claims.*

In a replevin action for a Maltese dog named Bubkas, who was in the possession of the plaintiff's ex-girlfriend, the plaintiff sought summary judgment. The parties stipulated that Bubkas was a gift to the plaintiff by his parents when the parties were residing together, and the plaintiff was the dog's original owner. The court considered whether a material issue of fact was in dispute.

The defendant argued that she was the primary caregiver of the dog even though both parties shared the care and custody of Bubkas when they cohabited. The parties disputed whether the plaintiff surrendered, conveyed, or abandoned Bubkas when they separated and he searched for a new residence. The defendant advocated that it was in Bubkas's best interests for him to live with her. While this matter was pending, the court issued a temporary order saying that Bubkas would be exchanged between the parties on alternate weekends.

In rendering its decision on the issue of superior possessory right to chattel, the court stated that abandonment was not a defense.[130] The court recalled that in *Raymond v. Lachmann,*[131] it had considered the best interests of a cat when rendering its decision, as the ten-year-old cat had been in the custody of the defendant for four years. The *Raymond* court, recognizing the "cherished status accorded to pets in our society," allowed the cat to stay with the defendant, where the cat had long lived. The court then distinguished between the best interests of the cat standard articulated in *Raymond* from the instant case based upon the short time period that Bubkas resided with the defendant. The court undertook a primary caregiver analysis, too.

This diligent court also considered the effect of New York's Family Court § 842, wherein pets are granted protection as family members in orders for protection. Even so, the court found that the plaintiff had failed to demonstrate the same type of compelling scenario as found in *Raymond,* where the cat had "lived, prospered, loved and been loved" by one party.

The court was unimpressed by the defendant's criticism that the plaintiff crated Bubkas. The court wanted the parties to "find a way for Bubkas to continue to spend time with both parties." Even so, as the plaintiff had superior possessory rights, he was awarded Bubkas effective on the next transfer date established per the temporary order.

LeConte showed that the court would welcome a best interests of the pet analysis and would give weight to a primary caregiver factor if the facts were compelling.

---

129. 35 Misc. 3d 286, 935 N.Y.S.2d 842, 2011 N.Y. Slip. Op. 21452 (N.Y. Civ. Ct. 2011).
130. *See* Valenza v. Valenza, 67 A.D.2d 879, 413 N.Y.S.2d 680 (1st Dept. 1979).
131. 264 A.D.2d 340, 695 N.Y.S.2d 308 (1st Dept. 1999).

Because the facts in *LeConte* lacked this type of persuasive narrative, the court awarded Bubkas based upon the traditional replevin action analysis.

Practice Pointer: The court signaled that with more powerful facts, it would have given consideration to the dog's primary caregiver and the dog's best interests. Always make the court aware of facts that help you.

Walash v. Kilgour[132]

Year: *2011*
Category: *Family Law*
Type of Action: *Replevin*
Animal: *Dog*
Pet Custody Concept: *The question of whether the new owner of a dog was complicit with one of the divorcing parties in the two-step transfer of title to the dog was likely to be outcome determinative as to the issuance of a writ of replevin.*

In this unreported decision, a replevin action was initiated by the plaintiff/husband against the defendant, who adopted a marital English Bulldog named Mo while the plaintiff's divorce action was pending. The dog was surreptitiously placed for adoption by the plaintiff's wife, Samantha Walash, with the Pet Spa and Resort. She hid the Bulldog's whereabouts from her husband.[133]

The defendant adopted Mo through a spa where Samantha's affidavit was on file. In this affidavit, Samantha represented that she was Mo's sole owner. The defendant claimed that the plaintiff himself knew the dog was at the spa because of an early text message between the plaintiff and his then-wife, Samantha, and that the plaintiff had no standing to sue her because he had "no privity of relationship, contractual or otherwise." The defendant further argued that the plaintiff had economic recourse against his wife for the value of the English Bulldog because of "equitable distribution in the divorce action."

It was further asserted that because the plaintiff's wife had relinquished "title and possession" of the dog before the divorce was commenced, the automatic orders regarding disposition of property during the plaintiff's divorce did not apply regarding Mo's transfer. She said good title was conveyed to her as a third party and that the plaintiff had "no superior possessory right to the chattel over the possessory right of the defendant."

The court decided that Mo was a unique chattel, and therefore, a replevin action was appropriate. The court also pointed out that the plaintiff was timely in all his efforts and that they were "met with deception and resistance" by his wife.

With regard to whether the dog should be returned to the plaintiff, the court concluded that the record was not sufficient for a ruling, particularly as it was unknown whether the adoptive owner was "blameless." The issue of the superior right of

---

132. 32 Misc. 3d 1244(A) (2011), 938 N.Y.S.2d 230, 2011 N.Y. Slip. Op. 51700(U).
133. There was no mention of concern about mistreatment of the dog by either party.

possession seemed to depend on whether the defendant was "non-complicit" with regard to Samantha's actions. The court said there was a need for "a full and complete presentation of the facts" and ordered that the plaintiff have access to Mo pending the outcome of the proceeding.

Practice Pointer: If a person is a bad actor in the acquisition of a pet, it is foreseeable that he or she will not only pay high legal fees but may also lose in the end. A difficulty in these types of cases is that an apparent bad actor might have a worthy motive to protect the dog, including if a pet was neglected or mistreated. It is also a good idea to ask whether any aspect of the case is impacted by payback, perhaps from a jilted lover.

Whitmore v. Whitmore[134]

Year: *2011*
Category: *Family Law*
Type of Action: *Dissolution of Marriage*
Animal: *Dog*
Pet Custody Concept: *Even though both parties had a strong claim to the dog, the court denied visitation or shared custody because the court regarded this type of arrangement to be ill advised.*

This case represents the difficulties a family court can face in awarding a dog to a couple dissolving their marriage when each party has a good claim, is devoted to the dog, and regards the dog as a family member.

The husband initially found the Welsh Corgi in a pet shop four years after the parties' marriage. Like other courts before them, this court attached some significance to the fact that the parties did not have any children. While it was known that both parties were at the pet shop at the point of purchase, they disagreed about whether the husband was buying the dog as a gift for his wife. Both parties' names appeared on the Corgi's American Kennel Club registration. The court found that the dog was jointly purchased and represented a mutual gift.

The higher court recognized that old economic ideas about the value of a dog differed from the more modern concept of a dog's "intrinsic value" to the dog's owners. The higher court observed that the trial court had not minimized the significance of a pet.

In Virginia, issues that go up on appeal are framed in terms of "errors." In *Whitmore*, the court addressed eight "Assignments of Error." The first issue, which is inherently thorny in divorce pet custody disputes, is how to value the companion animal. The husband, who was not awarded the dog but instead was given compensation for the dog's purchase price of $750, argued that the trial court put "too much emphasis on the monetary award of the dog." The higher court's reaction to this, and to most

134. Record No. 1644-10-4 (Va. App. 2011).

of the errors alleged by the husband, was that if a party wants to have a sufficient basis for reversal on appeal, then the party must state its objection "with reasonable certainty at the time of the ruling."

Although the court seemed dismissive of the husband's objection to the court's economic valuation method, in the court's analysis of errors, the court offered a conscientious background analysis of the case. It seemed that the trial court extensively considered claims related to the care of the dog and knew who was by the Corgi's side during an extended hospitalization.

The court considered the fact that except for four to six days per month, the wife worked in her "separate property" home office, a home where the dog had always lived. The husband left the dog in her care when he moved out, and she paid $350 each month for a pet service during the several days each month she traveled. The court said that the wife did not want to share the dog because her husband "destroyed our marriage by having an affair and she did not want him in her life."

The wife said she paid $4,000 for the Corgi's veterinary bills during an extended hospitalization, and the husband testified that he paid for veterinary expenses, too. The court found that both parties "contributed to the care, training and maintenance of the dog." The court seemed impressed by the wife's devotion to the dog in a time of need when it said, "When the dog was hospitalized for five days, wife visited the dog several times per day" and that the husband "did not visit the dog in the hospital." The court specifically stated, "Both husband and wife testified they love the dog and they considered her to be a family member." Both presented evidence of a "strong bond with the dog."

Throughout this decision, there were indications that the court considered more than the dog's economic value and that the court was affected by the best interests of the parties and the dog. Even so, the court said it utilized the state's equitable distribution statute, as the dog was both "a marital asset and marital property." The reason the court denied visitation or shared custody of the dog to the husband was not based on any identified rule of law. The trial court's conclusion that such an arrangement would be "ill-advised" seemed to be a satisfactory analysis.

With regard to other errors, the court based its decision on the rules it needed to follow for the division of property. First, the court had to determine if the property was marital, separate, or "a hybrid." Here, the dog was marital property. The trial court, exercising its sound discretion, then had to make a decision "based upon the equities and the rights and interests of each party."

The husband complained that the court failed to properly consider and weigh his monetary and nonmonetary contributions to the "acquisition, care, and maintenance of the dog." He alleged that the court placed "undue emphasis on the current location of the dog" and that the court should have focused on the Corgi's best interests. He made contradictory arguments too, and claimed that the court paid too little attention to the facts surrounding the dog's acquisition and also criticized the court for treating the dog as an "inanimate object" rather than a "living, sentient being."

The higher court stated that the trial court "need not quantify or elaborate exactly what weight was given to each of the factors." In that vein, the court found that the award of $750 to the husband to "acquire a similar dog" was not an abuse of discretion. Although the higher court contemplated the idea of the intrinsic value of the Corgi, it utilized the replacement value for balance sheet purposes.[135]

Practice Pointer: Because courts have broad discretion as to what factors to use and how to weigh the factors selected, help the court consider the factors most advantageous to your position and advocate that those factors should be weighed the most heavily. The court may have awarded the parties joint custody if not for the husband's infidelity and the wife's abhorrence in dealing with him. While infidelity is not normally outcome determinative in no-fault cases, it seems to be given some weight with regard to whether the parties can cooperate in sharing joint custody of a dog.

Aho v. Aho[136]

Year: *2012*
Category: *Family Law*
Type of Action: *Dissolution of Marriage Post-Decree*
Animal: *Dog*
Pet Custody Concept: *When awarding the disputed dog, the court emphasized the importance of keeping all of the parties' animals together.*

In an unpublished post-decree decision following the parties' dissolution of marriage, the defendant contested the award of the family dog, Finn, to the plaintiff. The plaintiff argued that rather than applying a best-interest standard, the court should have instead treated Finn as a chattel for division purposes.

Noting that the defendant did not seek the award of the parties' other animals, the higher court found that "awarding Finn to plaintiff was proper in order to keep all of the animals together. We find nothing unfair or inequitable about the court's ruling." The higher court also said that it was the defendant who had used "custody-like terms" regarding Finn. The court seemed to take into account the dog's best interests in terms of the dog's relationship with the parties' other animals.

Practice Pointer: When telling a compelling story, consider including animal bonds as an argument.

135. The husband brought to the court's attention an unpublished en banc 1999 decision of the Virginia court. Although the court mentioned the case, it dismissed the opinion, as it "was unpublished and carries no precedential value." *See, e.g.*, Fairfax County Sch. Bd. v. Rose, 29 Va. App. 32, 39 n.3, 509 S.E.2d 525, 528 n.3 (1999) (en banc).

136. Not reported in N.W.2d (2012).

Dubin v. Pelletier[137]

Year: *2012*
Category: *Family Law*
Type of Action: *Replevin*
Animal: *Dog*
Pet Custody Concept: *While the court recognized there was no single indicium of ownership, in this dispute about a famous show dog, the court found the woman in possession of the dog had the burden of proving she had a superior claim to the original owner.*

This was an important case with regard to what constitutes animal ownership; the case looked at a variety of indicia of ownership. The plaintiff, Jayne Dubin, purchased a dog officially named Ch Final Lea Big Ticket Item, also known as Mr. Big. She registered him with the American Kennel Club, and her name appeared on Mr. Big's microchip registration form. She received stud fees for Mr. Big's progeny.

The plaintiff was in regular contact with the defendant, Lori Ann Pelletier, who maintained a kennel for "show dogs as a hobby," and communicated with her about breeding decisions for Mr. Big. As was common in the industry, the defendant's billing for handling, showing, and boarding show dogs was based upon an oral agreement. Payments by the plaintiff to the defendant were often in cash, and the plaintiff admitted that she did not record all her payments to the defendant in her ledgers. Beyond paying the defendant for services rendered, there seemed to be an agreement that some of the monies due the defendant would come from Mr. Big's stud services.

The parties usually held the plaintiff out as the owner of Mr. Big, although both parties' names appeared as co-owners for the American Norfolk Terrier Association Fall Festival. At Mr. Big's retirement dinner, the plaintiff proclaimed that Mr. Big would stay with the defendant, where Mr. Big had long lived. To the defendant, the plaintiff's statement was a promise to transfer ownership and possession of Mr. Big to the defendant.

Even when the plaintiff and the defendant began having conflicts about monies due for the defendant's services, the plaintiff continued to hire the defendant to show additional dogs and maintained a relationship with her. While they had an on-again, off-again friendly relationship, there was finally an impasse with regard to monies the defendant claimed the plaintiff owed her for services rendered for show dogs Iffy and Wilma. The plaintiff then "refused to register the last three litters sired by Mr. Big" and also would not verify the American Kennel Club litter registrations.

The plaintiff initiated legal action and sought a declaratory judgment that she was Mr. Big's owner. She also initiated a writ of replevin for the return of Mr. Big, sought to recover stud fees paid to the defendant for Mr. Big based upon a theory of unjust enrichment, and sought damages based upon conversion. In her counterclaim, the defendant sought to establish her right to ownership and possession of Mr. Big and advanced the legal theories of "gift, breach of implied contract, guardianship under R.I. Gen. Laws §§4-13-1.2 and 3-14-41, and best interest of the dog." In addition, she

137. 2012 WL 5983184 (2012).

alleged fraudulent inducement and fraudulent misrepresentation. Another issue was how much was still due the defendant for her services, and contribution to Mr. Big's three-year, expensive "specials campaigns," all of which were necessary for Mr. Big to achieve valuable ranking.

The standard of review on appeal was established by a ruling that required that "in all actions tried upon the facts without a jury . . . the court shall find the facts specifically and state separately its conclusions of law thereon." In addition, the state Uniform Declaratory Judgments Act granted the court "the power to declare rights, status, and other legal relations whether or not further relief is or could be claimed."

The plaintiff had the burden of proof concerning her claim for a declaratory judgment of ownership. If the plaintiff could establish a prima facie case of ownership, then "it falls to the party opposing the declaratory judgment to establish the invalidity of that ownership by clear and convincing evidence." Although Mr. Big's certification of registration was sufficient to meet the plaintiff's prima facie burden of proof, the court determined that there were indicia of ownership, including ownership of the mother, exclusive possession, and the exercise of control.[138]

More importantly, the court declared, "No single indicium of ownership is dispositive, however, and often courts determine ownership based on the intent of the parties."[139] The court cited its earlier decision wherein the court relied heavily on the "intent of the original owner." The court also observed that when there was no intention to divest ownership to another, the original owner retained sole ownership.

The court then considered the defendant's rebuttal evidence, including her claim that Mr. Big was a gift to her at the end of his show career. To prevail on her theory of gift, the defendant was required to demonstrate "donative intent" by clear and satisfactory evidence and also to prove delivery. The trial court determined that the defendant failed to meet her burden of proof in this regard, in part because the defendant testified that the plaintiff "could have taken Mr. Big back at any time."

The defendant's claim that there was an implied-in-fact oral agreement was also rejected by the court, even though the defendant asserted that the statute of frauds did not pertain based upon "part performance." In weighing this evidence, the court considered not only the course of dealings between the parties[140] but also how these dealings were "consistent with the industry practice regarding billing in the dog show world."

The court found no mutual agreement between the parties regarding ownership, as the defendant sought the plaintiff's permission to withdraw Mr. Big from a particular dog show. The court observed how the defendant listed the plaintiff as Mr. Big's owner for a Westminster dog show. The court stated that not only did the plaintiff have possession and control over some of Mr. Big's frozen sperm, but also the defendant had

138. *See, e.g.*, Jones v. Office of Fin. of Baltimore County, 451 A.2d 926, 928 (Md. 1982) (noting that "offspring or increase of tame or domestic animals belongs to the owner of the dam or mother"); Buczkowicz v. Lubin, 399 N.E.2d 680, 682 (Ill. Ct. App. 1980) (concluding that certificate of registration created prima facie presumption of title, and considering the payment of stud fees as evidence of ownership); and Beard v. Mossman, 19 A.2d 850, 851 (Pa. Super. Ct. 1941) (reasoning that one-year possession of a dog was presumptive evidence of ownership).

139. *See* Servel v. Corbett, 290 P. 200, 203 (Idaho 1930).

140. It seems that the court was thinking about the Uniform Commercial Code while not actually referencing it.

"continued to credit Dubin for his stud fees, even after his retirement dinner." The court emphasized that strong evidence of ownership, as established through possession, "does not stand up when in conflict with direct evidence of ownership."[141] The court rejected the defendant's counterclaim based on implied contract.

The court then focused on the replevin action. The defendant countered that she had a superior ownership interest as Mr. Big's guardian, while advancing a best-interests claim. To prevail, the defendant was required to prove by clear and convincing evidence that her right to possession was superior to the plaintiff's presumptive right.

According to the statute, the "owner keeper" of a dog is "any person or agency keeping, harboring or having charge or control of or responsibility for control of an animal or any person or agency which permits any dog . . . to habitually be fed within that person's yard or premises. This term shall not apply to veterinary facilities, any licensed boarding kennel, municipal pound, pet shop, or animal shelter." The guardian of a dog is defined as "a person having the same rights and responsibilities of an owner, keeper and both terms shall be used interchangeably. A guardian shall also mean a person who possesses, has title to, or an interest in, harbors or has control, custody or possession of an animal and is responsible for an animal's safety and well-being."

The court determined that the defendant's services constituted "those of a kennel" under the applicable statute and that the defendant's own business card described her services consistent with this interpretation. In addition to the plain meaning of the statute, the court said, "[T]he primary purpose of this statutory scheme is to provide guidance with respect to the imposition of liability for damages caused by dogs and the right of private citizens to defend themselves against dog attacks." The court also dismissed the defendant's guardian claim as not applicable based upon legislative purpose.

The court found the defendant had failed to meet her burden of proof that there was an implied-in-fact contract regarding Mr. Big's possession. On the subject of the law advanced by the defendant to support her best-interests claim of Mr. Big, the court said, "Those courts were either acting with specific legislative approval to engage in a best interests of the dog analysis, were interpreting statutes broadly to include the power to engage in property disposition, or did not engage in a best interests of the dog analysis."[142]

The court addressed the plaintiff's claim against the defendant for conversion, a claim that required the plaintiff to "establish an intentional, un-consented-to exercise of dominion or control over a chattel that so seriously interferes with the right of another to control it that the actor may justly be required to pay the other the full value of the chattel." The court was "hard-pressed to find conversion," as the plaintiff had not established evidence of harm.

---

141. *See, e.g.*, Terral v. La. Farm Bureau Cas. Ins. Co., 892 So. 2d 732 (La. Ct. App. 2005) (explaining that a possessor of a lost animal is presumed to be the owner until the right of the true owner is established); Schutzman v. Munson, 51 So. 2d 125 (La. Ct. App. 1951) (finding the plaintiff's ownership of cows trumped the defendant's claim of ownership when the defendant was a mere possessor and could not provide clear and definite proof of ownership); and Sandefur v. Jeansonne, 9 So. 2d 80, 81 (La. Ct. App. 1942) (holding that the plaintiff's possession of mules for many years was not sufficient to establish ownership when there was no evidence that the defendant sold them or gave them to the plaintiff).

142. While the court seemed unruffled by the defendant's "novel best interest of the dog theory," and acknowledged the wonderful care the defendant had given Mr. Big, the court stated the defendant's argument would be more appropriately addressed to the general assembly. The court also expressed concerns about a floodgate problem.

The defendant argued that the plaintiff misrepresented that she could "keep Mr. Big to induce Pelletier to provide services during Mr. Big's specials campaign." The defendant failed to meet the state's burden of proof, which required "the fraudulent intent at the time he or she made the promise to do something in the future."

The defendant asserted that if she was not the owner of Mr. Big, then the plaintiff owed her $80,261.86 for the "care, custody, training, and show career of Mr. Big" over seven years. The court said unjust enrichment was an action in quantum meruit and that "To recover damages under a theory of quantum meruit, a party must satisfy the following elements of unjust enrichment: '(1) the defendant conferred a benefit upon the plaintiff; (2) the plaintiff appreciated the benefit; and (3) under the circumstances it would be inequitable for the plaintiff to retain such benefit without payment of the value thereof.'"

The court looked at evidence regarding entry fees, handling fees, show fees, boarding fees, breeding fees, post-show career grooming fees, and veterinary fees, and then it rejected the defendant's claims for boarding, breeding, and grooming fees, as well as special trip costs and for what the defendant called "kennel help" while traveling when the dog lived with the defendant as her pet. The court also denied expenditures where the defendant lacked adequate documentation or made "bare statements."

Based upon the above, the plaintiff's ledgers, and evidence that the plaintiff made a partial payment to the defendant of $10,000 in cash, the court determined that the plaintiff owed the defendant $16,411.51. The court said the common law doctrine of accord and satisfaction advanced by the plaintiff would not apply unless the creditor understood that the performance was offered as a full satisfaction of the claim. The court said, "Testimony about Pelletier and Dubin's course of dealings and testimony by Pelletier's other clients show, however, that it was common for Pelletier to accept partial payment during the dog's show career and then provide an invoice with the remaining balance when the dog was returned."

The court concluded that there was no evidence that the defendant's right to compensation for expenses associated with Mr. Big was extinguished by partial payment. The court found that the defendant received $16,000 for stud fees that the plaintiff was entitled to recover. Thus, when the amounts due the plaintiff and the defendant were netted out, the plaintiff only owed the defendant $411.51 and the defendant was required to transfer possession of Mr. Big to the plaintiff. The court declined to grant either party attorney's fees.

In this dispute about show dogs, the court was more than willing to permit extensive testimony and comb through voluminous exhibits. The court also allowed the trial record to consider numerous depositions of witnesses who did not even testify at trial. The court accepted post-trial memorandums.

Practice Pointer: No single indicium of ownership is dispositive. Here, the court was willing to exhaustively and intensively review legal claims involving show dog ownership that the court might not bestow on a claim about a less economically valuable companion animal. This case also reviewed the many ways a human might be considered an animal's owner and how the definition of ownership differs when applied to a tort claim rather than in other contexts.

Aronson v. Aronson[143]

Year: *2013*
Category: *Family Law*
Type of Action: *Conversion*
Animal: *Dog*
Pet Custody Concept: *Once the court determined that the teenage girl living with her mother was the co-owner of a dog, the father could not pursue a conversion claim unless he could establish his unconditional right to possession.*

Following a divorce, the plaintiff/father and his daughter purchased a dog for $100 and received a statement of ownership in the plaintiff's name. Although the plaintiff did not state that the dog was a gift to his 13-year-old daughter, the dog's primary residence was with the plaintiff's daughter and the defendant, the plaintiff's ex-wife. When the parties' daughter had visitation with the plaintiff, which was not overnight, the dog went with her.

While the dog lived with the defendant, the defendant paid for the dog's veterinary care, regular grooming, and obedience classes. The dog wore a tag with the defendant's telephone number and address, although the defendant failed to license the dog.

During one of his daughter's visits to his house, the plaintiff took the dog and would not let the dog return to the dog's primary residence with the defendant and his daughter. Several months later, when the defendant returned a piano to the plaintiff, the defendant took the dog back.

Three years later, the plaintiff brought a claim for trover and conversion. The proof for a tort action of conversion required him to prove that he had a right to the property, had an absolute and unconditional right to the immediate possession of the property, and made a demand for possession. The plaintiff was also required to prove that the defendant wrongfully and without his authorization had assumed control, dominion, or ownership over his property.[144]

The trial court determined that although the plaintiff had not gifted the dog to his daughter, the plaintiff had abandoned the dog. Without reaching the abandonment question, the higher court said the record established that the parties' daughter was "at least a co-owner of the dog." The court further said that "the owner of an animal is someone who exercises some level of care, custody, or control over the animal," and because the parties' daughter was an owner of the dog, the plaintiff could not "show the unconditional right to possession required for conversion," thereby affirming the judgment of the circuit court.

Practice Pointer: This is a good example of why lawyers should consider utilizing more than one theory of a case in a pet custody dispute. It is hard to determine which type of argument the court may prefer. When in doubt, offer the court compelling facts and a variety of claims. Notwithstanding the above, find out if a replevin action can only be brought as a stand-alone action in your state.

143. 2013 Ill. App. (3d) 120715-U, not reported in N.E.2d (2013).
144. *See* Loman v. Freeman, 229 Ill. 2d 104 (2008).

BAGGETT V. BAGGETT[145]

Year: *2013*
Category: *Property Law*
Type of Action: *Post-Decree*
Animal: *Dog*
Pet Custody Concept: *Credibility matters.*

Following a divorce, the husband challenged the property division. Both parties sought the award of the marital house and possession of the two dogs. This case was decided in a state that made a distinction between marital and separate property. The practice was to first award each party his or her separate property and then to equitably divide marital property.

The court noted that at the time of trial, the husband was nearly 70 and the wife 52. The court set forth relevant factors in both considering and determining that the wife received $56,931.86 in marital property and the husband $34,008.22. These figures were in sharp contrast to the husband's claim that the wife received "$367,842.60 + dogs + $1,000 death benefit" while he got $25,620.

While not agreeing with the husband's figures, the court commented on the husband's credibility and said that 50/50 division of marital property was not required. The court explained, "The division of the estate is not rendered inequitable simply because it is not mathematically equal, or because each party did not receive a share of every item of marital property. In the final analysis, the justness of a particular division of the marital property and allocation of marital debt depends on its final results." Although the dogs did not appear on the wife's balance sheet offered by the court, it seemed that the wife received the dogs based upon the husband's complaint about marital property allocation.

Practice Pointer: The trial court has considerable discretion.

BANKEN V. BANKEN[146]

Year: *2013*
Category: *Family Law*
Type of Action: *Parental Access Modification*
Animal: *Dog*
Pet Custody Concept: *Keep cruel children away from pets.*

A couple's son mutilated a dog with a gardening tool by either cutting off its tail or severing its spine while in the appellant's care. The trial court modified the parties' current parenting plan after this mutilation occurred. An order was issued wherein the

145. 2013 WL 4606383 (Tenn. App. 2013).
146. State of Minnesota in Court of Appeals, A11-2156, Minn. App. 2013.

appellant was only allowed supervised parenting time and was required to undergo a complete psychological evaluation.

Practice Pointer: Any child's mutilation of an animal should raise a red flag. Courts and behavioral experts are aware that serial killers usually have the following three common childhood behaviors, known as the Macdonald triad: (1) animal cruelty, (2) enuresis (bed wetting), and (3) fire starting.[147] In a case involving a pet, generally speaking, courts ask questions about the child's bond with the pet, not whether the child is prone to harming an animal, such as in the instant case. Children with a history of animal abuse should not have pets, and any access to an animal should be carefully supervised.

Clark v. McGinnis[148]

Year: *2013*
Category: *Family Law*
Type of Action: *Civil Property Division*
Animal: *Dogs*
Pet Custody Concept: *The concept of splitting up children was not equivalent to the concept of splitting up dogs.*

When two co-habitants split up, they disagreed about whether the three dogs they acquired should be kept together or equitably divided. While the appellant advocated that the court should follow the child custody approach and emphasized that divided custody rarely works and is detrimental to a dog's health, the court disagreed. In a memorandum of law, the court pronounced, "Children are not relatively similar to dogs to justify applying the child custody law to this situation."

Practice Pointer: Avoid having clients make companion animal and human children analogies, as the court may take offense. It is not easy to win a best interest of an animal argument. Consider utilizing an expert witness when making an argument about animal bonds or presenting a compelling story where the court feels comfortable with multiple factors so that it can make a just and wise decision in exercising its discretion. Courts seem to like friendly veterinarian experts on animal subjects, although there are a variety of other types of experts, too, including behaviorists. If you are bringing in an expert, advise him or her to be aware that some courts abhor dog and child comparisons, even when the court makes a point of stating that the parties are "childless."

---

147. Makini Brice, *The Macdonald Triad: Do Three Common Childhood Behaviors Predict a Serial Killer?*, Medical Daily, http://www.medicaldaily.com/macdonald-triad-do-three-common-childhood-behaviors-predict-serial-killer-243106 (last visited May 12, 2016).

148. 298 P.3d 1137 (2013).

Conte v. Fossett[149]

Year: *2013*
Category: *Family Law*
Type of Action: *Replevin*
Animal: *Dog*
Pet Custody Concept: *When a dog is given as a gift to a girlfriend, a writ of replevin will not be granted to the donor.*

While the plaintiff cohabited with his defendant girlfriend, she wanted a dog. The plaintiff purchased a puppy, brought the puppy home to the defendant, and said "Surprise!" The plaintiff later asserted that the gift of the puppy, named Dennis Hopper, was made "in contemplation of the couple's relationship." If it was, the plaintiff asserted that this made the dog a conditional gift to her. The plaintiff argued that the court should extend the idea earlier articulated in *Elliott v. Hunter*[150] that it was possible for a gift donor to replevy property given in contemplation of marriage when the gift had "symbolic significance."

Here, the court not only rejected the idea of extending the *Elliott* revocable gift category to cohabiting couples but also went out of its way to use insincere language that characterized a handful of cases where ownership of dogs was in dispute. At the beginning of this unpublished opinion, the court said, "For many, 'happiness is a warm puppy.' To some, a dog is a 'minor angel,' because it can 'love unconditionally, forgive immediately, [and is] the truest [friend], willing to do anything that makes us happy.'"

Although the court recognized that after the breakup, the parties had "a fluid shared-custody agreement," the court held that the trial court had erred as a matter of law when it determined that the plaintiff's gift of the dog to the defendant had "symbolic significance." The higher court also added that under Delaware law, the dog had "the same legal status as a piece of furniture," and that "It is 'nothing personal,' but Dennis has no symbolic significance." The court determined that because the dog was a gift to the plaintiff's then-girlfriend, there could be no writ of replevin.

Practice Pointer: Do not be surprised if the court is affronted by the indignity of hearing a pet custody dispute case. Some courts reiterate and even relish in how dogs are so lowly in the law that they are equivalent to inanimate objects. Remind your client not to be surprised if on one hand, the court can imagine a puppy as a minor angel, as the *Conte* court did, while on the other, treat the puppy as having the same legal status as an inanimate object.

149. 2013 WL 1143329, not reported in A.3d (2013).
150. 1967 WL 90379 (Del. Super. June 14, 1967).

Travis v. Murray[151]

Year: *2013*
Category: *Family Law*
Type of Action: *Replevin*
Animal: *Dog*
Pet Custody Concept: *Before awarding a dog, the lower court should conduct a hearing and utilize a "best interests for all concerned" standard.*

This case garnered national attention, in part because the court did a good job of summarizing the progression of decisions affecting pet custody disputes, and also because it weaved in cases outside of family law with regard to how ideas about pets as property are shifting.

The court, puzzled by the "collective New York psyche" with regard to a "canine-centric city," began its decision by saying, "People who love their dogs almost always love them forever" and "What is even more surprising, considering New Yorkers' dedication to their dogs and their propensity for litigation, is that there are so few reported cases from the courts of this state dealing with pet custody in general and no cases at all making a final award of a pet to either side in the context of a divorce."

The parties, a lesbian, gay, bisexual, and transgender couple, cohabited before they married. During this time, the plaintiff bought Joey, a ten-week-old puppy, from a pet store. When the plaintiff and the defendant split up, the defendant took Joey and briefly pretended that Joey was lost in Central Park. The plaintiff brought a motion seeking the care and sole residential custody of Joey. In the meantime, the defendant relocated the dog to her mother's home in Maine.

The plaintiff argued that not only had she paid for Joey, but also that it was in the dog's best interests for Joey to be returned to her. The defendant countered that the plaintiff gave Joey to her as a gift, that she provided for the dog's "emotional, practical, and logistical needs," and that it was in the dog's best interests to be "healthy, safe and happy" with her mother in Maine.

The court portrayed the purchase-versus-gift argument as a traditional property analysis and the second aspect of each party's claims as a custody-type analysis. In a lively discussion, the court stated, "Where once a dog was considered a nice accompaniment to a family unit, it is now seen as an actual member of that family, vying for importance alongside children."

The court proceeded with an affirmation, stating, "When those litigants own a dog, matrimonial judges are called upon more and more to decide what happens to the pet that each of the parties still loves and each of them still wants." The court also cited a Gallup Poll that reflected that "most pet owners would not trade their pets for even $1 million in cash." Notwithstanding the court's articulation of the New York state of mind, the court emphasized the prevailing law that "a dog is in fact personal property."

151. 2013 N.Y. Slip. Op. 23405 (N.Y. Sup. Ct. 2013).

Next, the court cited *C.R.S. v. T.K.S.*,[152] where a New York court decided to award a chocolate Labrador to one party based upon the concept of an interspousal gift, without consideration of the dog's best interests, notwithstanding *Corso v. Crawford Dog and Cat Hospital, Inc.*[153] There, the court alleged that damages beyond fair market value were appropriate with regard to the misplaced remains of an animal because "a pet is not just a thing but occupies a special place somewhere in between a person and a personal piece of property."

Citing *Feger v. Warwick Animal Shelter*,[154] the court observed that the "reach of our laws has been extended to animals in areas which were once reserved only for people" and that "these laws indicate that companion animals are treated differently from other forms of property. Recognizing companion animals as a special category of property is consistent with the laws of the state."

The court then cited *Goodby v. Vetpharm, Inc.*[155] for the proposition that "Pets may be distinguished from other chattel by the mutual relationship: Pet owners love their pets and their pets love them back." Here, the court reviewed the "progression of the law" in both New York and other states and reached the conclusion that "a strict property analysis is neither desirable nor appropriate."

Next, the court addressed whether the plaintiff purchased Joey or whether the defendant received Joey as a gift and determined that it was only one factor to consider in the determination of "what becomes of him." While the court acknowledged a floodgate problem if a full-blown pet ownership dispute was allowed, the court reasoned that this did not mean it would not give any consideration to a dog that the parties regarded as a family member.

The court said, "If judicial resources can be devoted to such matters as which party gets to use the Escalade as opposed to the Ferrari, or who gets to stay in the Hamptons house instead of the Aspen chalet, there is certainly room to give real consideration to a case involving a treasured pet." The court then determined that a one-day hearing should proceed with the court applying the "best for all concerned" standard.[156] In granting this opportunity for a hearing, the court emphasized that this would be the final hearing, with the resulting award being sole possession.

Practice Pointer: Be aware of the cultural context in which your case arises, as a New York City judge, aware that he lives in a canine-centric city, may be unlike a judge who grew up on a farm with outdoor animals. Consider the personal viewpoint of the court, not just the facts and the progression of pet law and the subset of pet law that impacts pet custody disputes.

---

152. 192 Misc. 2d 547 (Sup. Ct., N.Y. Cnty. 2002).
153. 97 Misc. 2d 530 (Civ. Ct., Queens Cnty. 1979).
154. 59 A.D.3d 68 (2d Dept. 2008).
155. 182 Vt. 648, 927 A.2d 792 (2007).
156. This standard was first described in Raymond v. Lachmann, 264 A.D.2d 340, 341 (1st Dept. 1999).

Van Arsdale v. Van Arsdale[157]

Year: *2013*
Category: *Family Law*
Type of Action: *Property Division*
Animal: *Dog*
Pet Custody Concept: *Although the parties were granted joint custody, the Labrador retrievers' principal residence would be with one party.*

Both parties appeared pro se in this limited contested trial. An aspect of the court's order, under the heading "personal property," was, "The parties shall have joint legal custody of the Labrador retrievers but the Labrador retrievers' principal place of residence shall be with the plaintiff. The parties equally share the reasonable costs associated with feeding and grooming the dogs as well as their veterinary care."

Practice Pointer: This unpublished decision is consistent with the variety of ways courts fumble with the ownership issue. Here, the dogs had a principal place of residence, but the other party, who shared joint legal custody, had financial obligations, too. The question of who would be responsible if there were liability or insurance issues was not addressed.

Hament v. Baker[158]

Year: *2014*
Category: *Family Law*
Type of Action: *Dissolution of Marriage*
Animal: *Dog*
Pet Custody Concept: *While rejecting a shared custody arrangement, the court stated that in rendering its decision, the court could consider criteria not set forth in the statute, including the animal's welfare and the animal's emotional relationships.*

Both parties were emotionally bonded to an 11-year-old German Wirehaired Pointer named Belle. Before the trial, which was held solely on the subject of the award of Belle, both parties were advised that the court would not entertain a shared visitation schedule. Although the parties were warned that the trial court was unconcerned about the dog's primary caregiver, the court listened to fully developed testimony about the dog's welfare, emotional connection to each party, typical day, and present and future veterinary needs.

The court granted ownership of the dog to the husband veterinarian. He had a long-standing habit of bringing Belle to work with him, where she had "the run of the place," and he "showed the right 'balance' while wife treated the dog like a child."

157. 2013 WL 1365358, not reported in A.3d (2013).
158. 97 A.3d 461 (2014).

The record showed that the parties were childless and that the wife was awarded the house where the dog had long lived.

The supreme court, reviewing the well-developed history in Vermont where pets are considered as a special category of property, rejected the idea that the best interests of a pet should apply in a pet custody dispute. However, the court set the stage for making a best-interests determination another way, based upon animal welfare and bonds. The high court pointed out that the family court was not limited to factors enumerated in the statute but could instead consider all relevant factors.

More specifically, the court said, "In the case of pets, we hold that the family division may consider other factors not set out in the statute: the welfare of the animal and the emotional connection between the animal and each spouse. These factors underlie our animal welfare laws and our case law, which recognizes the value of the bond between the animal and its owner." The court further added, "Evidence concerning welfare of the animal includes evidence about its daily routine, comfort, and care. Evidence concerning the emotional connection may include testimony about the role of the animal in the lives of the spouses."

In the end, the supreme court agreed that the factors the trial court considered, "the dog's welfare and its emotional relationship with the parties," were not only appropriate but also "appropriate for the resolution of similar questions in the future." The court explained why it would not impose an enforceable visitation schedule, saying,

> In contrast to enforcement of other kinds of property division orders, enforcement of an order requiring ongoing sharing of a family companion animal would require the power of modification, since the animal's well-being in the context of changing circumstances could be a substantial factor in the analysis. Unlike child custody matters, there is no legislative authority for the court to play a continuing role in the supervision of the parties with respect to the care and sharing of a companion animal. Divorce has few concrete advantages for the parties, but one of the greatest is that they are no longer compelled to be in contact over the care and use of their property or the way they spend their time.

The court also offered that a voluntary visitation schedule was always possible. An issue not addressed in this case was whether the court would have entertained the possibility that one of the parties could have visitation only if any further conflict could be resolved exclusively in an alternative dispute resolution process, such as mediation. Although some courts will not allow private agreements to circumvent the finality of judgment rule, the trend seems to be moving toward freedom of contracts. Building mediation and arbitration into an agreement will probably result in courts being far less concerned about continuing jurisdiction and floodgate problems.

Practice Pointer: You may be able to get the result you like by using the language the court prefers. If the court does not like to hear the words "best interests," perhaps the court will prefer the utilization of daily routine or comfort and care, as this court did. Courts may prefer a party engaging with an animal in what the court considers to be normal ways. Unless you are in a city like New York, where dressing up pets in a myriad of outfits is common, you might want to emphasize traditional aspects of the companion animal's care. Some courts will not award a pet to a person they regard as having species-inappropriate behavior.

RAMSEUR V. ASKINS[159]

Year: *2014*
Category: *Family Law*
Type of Action: *Replevin*
Animal: *Dog*
Pet Custody Concept: *As pets are a special category of property, the court applied the "best for all concerned" standard for the award of the dog and thereby awarded the pet to the original owner's aunt.*

This case involved a dispute between the purchaser of a Shih Tzu puppy named Deva and the purchaser's aunt. Although initially, the plaintiff took the puppy to a veterinarian and regularly walked her, he soon left Deva with his mother. His mother then transferred Deva to the plaintiff's aunt, who purchased Deva's food, paid to have her groomed, and walked her daily. All of the members of the plaintiff's aunt's household were closely bonded to Deva.

Eventually, the plaintiff wanted Deva back so he could breed her. In court, the plaintiff made no record as to how his new wife or her son felt "about Deva joining the household." In contrast, the plaintiff's aunt offered many photographs of Deva interacting with her family. There was credible testimony that Deva became anxious when the defendant was absent. The court concluded that "Deva is loved by defendant and her family and they are in turn loved by Deva." The court also observed that Deva had grown and thrived during her two years with the defendant, and that it might be stressful to re-home Deva.

The court provided a distinct review of the emerging standards for pets, particularly that companion animals fall within a special category of property and, for that reason, are treated differently than other property, including a television set.[160] The court questioned "what standard to apply when determining ownership of this special category of personal property." The court indicated that the "best for all concerned" standard applied in *Raymond v. Lachmann*[161] could be applied to the dispute about Deva. The court determined it was best for all concerned that the defendant be awarded possession of Deva.

Practice Pointer: Remember to argue for the emerging "best for all concerned" standard if it advances a client's claim. Remember, too, that bad actors often lose.

159. 44 Misc. 3d 1209(A), 2014 N.Y. Slip. Op. 51068(U).
160. *See* Feger v. Warwick Animal Shelter, 59 A.D.3d 68 (2d Dept. 2008).
161. 264 A.D.2d 340, 341 (1st Dept. 1999).

In re Marriage of Enders and Baker[162]

Year: *2015*
Category: *Family Law*
Type of Action: *Dissolution of Marriage*
Animal: *Dog*
Pet Custody Concept: *When a bad actor deceives the court about a marital asset, the court may be resourceful in awarding the dog to the other party, particularly if the court can hang its hat on a useful definition of ownership.*

In 2015, in an unpublished decision, the Illinois Court of Appeals offered its opinion on a case of first impression regarding whether pet visitation would be permissible. It is important to read this case in its entirety, not just the pet custody aspects. Although the court's opinion lacked detail in many important aspects, the court signaled, more than once, that the respondent/husband lacked credibility, in particular because of his testimony about a retirement asset.

The marriage at issue was a second marriage for each. The petitioner, a lawyer, and the respondent, a CPA, married shortly after they signed a premarital agreement. Both parties had children. All we learned about their two marital dogs was that Grace was 11 years old and had a shoulder injury and cataracts, and Roxy was seven. The court offered nothing about how the dogs were acquired, who provided primary care, or to whom the dogs were bonded. All we know about the dogs' standard of living was that the petitioner had a home with a yard, and the respondent lived in an apartment that did not allow pets; he had a side deal with his landlord that would enable him to have visitation.

The respondent moved out of the petitioner's home in 2011 and several months later sought temporary visitation rights. He claimed that when he moved out, the parties had agreed to joint custody of the dogs. Because we learned so little from the court's opinion about the underlying facts to this dispute, an analysis of the wisdom of the court's decision is accordingly circumscribed. Reading between the lines of this decision, there is an implication that the court could understand why the petitioner wanted nothing more to do with her husband.

It was curious that from a legal analysis perspective, the court seemed to hang its hat on only one out-of-state precedent, as well as an animal control ownership definition from section 2.16 of the Animal Control Act that defined ownership very broadly[163] as "any person having a right of property in an animal, or who keeps or harbors an animal, or who has it in his care, or acts as its custodian."[164]

---

162. 2015 Ill. App. (1st) 142435 (Ill. App. 2015).

163. Consider why animal control ownership definitions are broad. They are not broad to help the court in pet custody disputes; they are broad because of the need for the government to assert its police powers. Broad animal definitions under state laws or local ordinances may prove useful in tort litigation, too. This is why a person who feeds a stray dog on a regular basis may be subject to liability if that dog causes a car accident. *See* Terral v. Louisiana Farm Bureau Casualty Insurance Company, 892 So. 2d 732 (La. 2005).

164. Animal Control Act, 510 ILCS 5/2.16 (West 2014).

One may wonder about the court's goal in utilizing what seemed to be an animal control definition of ownership in a context where the court already had discretion to award the dogs the way it preferred. Perhaps the court wanted to set the stage for adopting the progressive "best interests for all" standard in *Travis v. Murray*,[165] while framing its decision in definitional language. It would have been interesting, if the court had not used the animal control definition, how it would have applied the "best interests for all" analysis. Maybe the court preferred not to use it because the respondent was at home for a year with the dogs when he was out of work. If the real reason behind the court's decision was that giving the dogs to the petitioner was the right thing to do, the legal analysis here should not be broadly construed. As stated before, the court found the respondent not to be a credible witness on the subject of a retirement account.

What is confusing about this decision is that the court seemed to reject the old idea that "dogs do not rise to the same level of importance as children." Yet, the court clearly saw the dogs as having enough importance and status to utilize what ultimately was judicial time and resources to achieve a "best interests for all" result. Given this progress, it seems illogical to then embrace the conclusion that joint ownership or visitation would result in "endless post-divorce litigation." The counter to this position is that the court is selective about which parties would be successful. In reaching its decision, the court could take into account the history of the parties' cooperative behavior and the likelihood that they would follow a court order.

Practice Pointer: The court could have said, "While the parties to this litigation exhibited qualities that made it seem likely that joint custody or sole custody with access would cause a floodgate problem, the court entertains the idea that for those committed to this type of arrangement, the court would consider it if the parties stipulated to reasonable terms that enhanced the utilization of alternative dispute resolution processes if problems arose." It would be a mistake to broadly apply this unpublished decision wherein the court revealed that one of the parties was a bad actor.

165. 977 N.Y.S.2d 621 (Sup. Ct. 2013).

Chapter 3

Alternative Dispute Resolution

"The human spirit is not dead. It lives on in secret. . . . It has come to believe that compassion, in which all ethics must take root, can only attain its full breadth and depth if it embraces all living creatures and does not limit itself to mankind."

—*Albert Schweitzer*

In this chapter, both alternative dispute resolution (ADR) processes and negotiation basics will be discussed, as well as how they might apply differently to a pet custody or ownership dispute than to other types of disputes. The perspective in this chapter will be useful to both lawyers and ADR professionals.

MEDIATION

Types of Mediation

We will begin with the subject of mediation. There are several different types of mediation, including facilitative, evaluative, and transformative,[1] although we will also discuss some variations on those themes for animal-centered mediation.

1. Zena Zumeta, *Styles of Mediation: Facilitative, Evaluative, and Transformative Mediation*, MEDIATE.COM, http://www.mediate.com/articles/zumeta.cfm (last visited May 12, 2016).

Facilitative Mediation

In facilitative mediation, the parties' individual interests are stressed rather than their legal positions. The mediator's role is process-based, meaning the mediator leads the discussion and validates conflicting points of view which are not contrary to public policy.[2] Facilitative mediation may occur in a joint session or may take place in separate rooms or "caucuses" if the parties agree. The parties are the decision makers while their attorneys, if present, offer legal advice and help shape the agreement.[3]

In facilitative mediation, lawyer and nonlawyer mediators have a goal of facilitating a mutually agreeable settlement offer. Some may discount the utilization of substantive legal expertise. There is a risk, however, of wasting time if the mediator is not conversant with pet law and what types of mediated agreements courts might allow and enforce or under what circumstances post-decree modifications could arise.[4] For example, a joint custody agreement, or an agreement wherein physical custody is awarded to one party subject to another party's visitation with the animal—a schedule that could be called "pet time"—might not be enforceable but may work out fine if the parties' word is their bond.[5] A good mediator should be fully aware of the local legal cultural context from which the dispute arises, pet law court decisions across the country impacting the enforceability of these types of agreements, and under what circumstances, if any, post-decree modifications will be permitted when a dispute arises.[6] In a facilitative process, it is important to know that a mediator who is more sensitive to the best interests of the pet may approach the process differently than a mediator who is more mechanistic and even dismissive about personal property division.

Evaluative Mediation

In evaluative mediation, the mediator typically offers an evaluative opinion on how the bench might perceive the strengths and weaknesses of each party's claims. This

---

2. Determining what would be against public policy presents its own challenges.

3. Good lawyers often prepare their clients for the mediation process by helping them get their story straight, exploring the other side's point of view, and making sure they are prepared not to be derailed if negative statements are said about them.

4. There are a variety of post-decree modification challenges. For instance, if the family pet is awarded to one party and not the other, and the animal is later mistreated by a new member of the owner's household, can the former owner seek a change of custody based upon an endangerment standard? This might depend on whether the finality rule applies to living property differently than if applied to other types of property, or whether courts are more interested in upholding private agreements, finality rules, or promoting public policy. If animal cruelty takes place, criminal charges may follow. Another aspect of post-decree modifications is whether courts will treat this topic differently in states where companion animals are in the interim category between property and person.

5. In various substantive orders, including in pet custody cases, the parties enter into side agreements that are, in effect, what the parties promise to do regardless of what the legal system may support, including in an order entered by the court. Lawyers should be aware that unenforceable side agreements could pose a legal malpractice problem, particularly in a divorce agreement where the parties represent that their stipulation is their entire agreement. There is also potential for a professional misconduct issue if the court is deceived by an officer of the court.

6. Appellate courts may have a different perspective than family courts do on the enforceability of a joint custody or access sharing agreement.

type of mediation is typically law- and rule-based and dominated by legal rights and the concept of fairness. This type of mediation could be impacted by well-presented arguments on issues emerging in case law, such as property, with its traditional arguments, and custody, with its best interest and bonding arguments. The mediation discussion might also involve legal presumptions and concepts such as superior title after exploring the myriad indicia of ownership. The mediator might not address those subjects and instead examine other decision-making criteria.

Separate caucuses are common and individual interests may be addressed in evaluative mediation. An evaluative mediator often influences the outcome of mediation and should have subject matter expertise.[7] It is helpful if the mediator is well-versed on whether courts in the jurisdiction are strict constructionists on the subject of finality of judgment,[8] what the typical exceptions are, and if the trial courts and appellate courts lean toward freedom to contract in private agreements. It is possible that as courts become more accustomed to flexible provisions with mediated agreements, they may also become more comfortable with a broader spectrum of private agreements.

The parties can authorize an evaluative mediator to utilize best-interest principles through a signed mediation agreement. Best-interest criteria could include the best interests of the companion animal, the best interests of the parties, the best interests of a child, the best interests of a disabled or elderly family member, or even the best interests for all concerned.[9] The agreement could also enable the mediator to consider bonds, including animal/human bonds and animal/animal bonds.[10]

Animal-Centered Mediation

Imagine an animal-centered mediation. Indispensable third parties, such as a breeder or rescue group, could be participants. In the animal-centered approach, the mediator would keep the focus on the best interests of the animal, not what a particular person wants. The conversation would not be, "I consider the dog to be like a child," but instead something like, "When I got Baxter at the shelter and I brought him home, he would hide behind the furniture on the patio. I worked closely with a behaviorist for two years, and now when we go out on the patio, Baxter is able to comfortably lie at my feet."

Another illustration of an animal-centered statement would be, "I should be awarded Lucas the cat because I have taken care of cats most of my life, and my

7. Both family law and animal law expertise would be valuable.

8. Even if the bench has a reputation for having strict constructionists, as more and more judges and their law clerks develop expertise and knowledge about animal law, it is foreseeable that there will be evolving positions on these benches.

9. *See* Travis v. Murray, 42 Misc. 3d 447, 977 N.Y.S.2d 621 (2013).

10. For animals who have spent their lives together, separating them may be cruel. You can get a sense of this from photographs and videos about animal friendships.

spouse knows little about them." A cat's best-interest focus is better described as "Lucas is a solitary cat and spends most of his day lying in the sunlight by a window on the third floor. We have agreed that I should keep the house, and I think staying in the house is in Lucas's best interests."

An animal-centered discussion would explore whether the animal would benefit from going back and forth between the two parties. There, the discussion would not be, "I think a 5/2/2/5 schedule should work for Francis the ferret, the same schedule we use for our teenage daughter." If the mediation were more pet-focused, then you would expect the person might instead say, "I think Francis should live with me because ferrets are legal where I live."[11]

Another example would be, "You know that Francis is not good with small children, and your significant other has two toddlers. I am really concerned that Francis will bite one of them. If he does, animal control might put him down." A third approach, using a pet-centered statement, could be, "I think it would work out if Francis was with you at a time that your significant other's children are with their grandparents, which is practically every Sunday. This way, Francis gets to snuggle with you without running the risk that he will get into trouble for hurting someone."

When having an animal-centered mediation, the challenge is not only to keep the focus off the parties and on the pet but also to advance a conversation about the animal and the animal's unique needs and preferences. Beyond the above, a hybrid approach could be used by combining any of the traditional mediation techniques with an animal-centered method.

Transformative Mediation

Transformative mediation is dominated by ideas such as empowerment and recognition; it is considered an outgrowth of facilitative mediation. Each party's needs, interests, and values are identified, and each party's point of view is validated. The mediator takes more of a back seat, allowing the parties to structure the process and outcome as a peacemaking technique. Over time, mediators often develop a personal style, which makes categorizing them as facilitative or transformative more difficult. The animal-centered version of this approach would be on the animal's needs, interests (including standard of living), and emotional bonds.

Choosing a Mediation Type

When choosing which type of mediation is best, consider whether the parties need an enforceable court order or if there is good reason to believe that their word will serve as their bond. Although enforceability of a mediated agreement may not be an issue

11. Ferrets and other animals may be prohibited as companion animals per a state statute or local ordinance.

at the time the parties enter mediation, the original cooperative spirit could change once new family units are established or if one of the parties believes that a joint custody arrangement is no longer feasible. Thus, it is worth discussing how the schedule would be revisited or revised or how decisions would be made in the future. For example, the parties could agree to mandatory mediation on an annual basis unless both parties waive the mediation requirement in writing 30 days in advance.

If enforceability of the agreement is crucial, and the agreement needs to be incorporated into a judicial order in a divorce or civil proceeding, the use of lawyers and mediators with subject matter expertise becomes essential. The agreement should be structured so that the court is more likely to sign and enforce it.

Choosing a Mediator

Mediation is both a confidential and voluntary process. If the mediator seems to be working for the court in a quasi-judicial role, where confidentiality might be compromised, it might be better to find a more independent neutral. When attempting to mediate a case that could result in some type of shared custody agreement, utilizing a respected mediator such as a retired judge or referee could make it more likely that the court would enforce a private mediated agreement.

Mediator Approaches

Regardless of what name we give to the type of mediation selected, there are a variety of mediator approaches. Some mediators will emphasize problem solving and right or wrong concepts, while others are more caring, contextual, and relationship-focused. A mediator might be good at using noncompensatory methods to advance goodwill during the negotiation.

One illustration would be to acknowledge another party's positive contributions toward caring for the companion animal or to show empathy toward a person who will suffer because he or she will no longer see the companion animal because of an across-country move. In the same vein, if one party lacks the health and physical ability to continue to care for an animal, acknowledgment by the other party that the companion animal is strongly bonded to that person may help move the discussion in a positive direction.

Med/Arb

If a private agreement is reached but is not approved by the court, perhaps because the family court is against co-ownership or a joint custody agreement,[12] the parties

12. Co-ownership agreements are common not only among breeders but also between a breeder and the co-owner in possession of the dog. The latter arrangement typically arises in situations where the animal is perceived to have commercial value or is involved in competitions.

could return to mediation for "med/arb" if permitted by statute and the written agreement of the parties.[13] This is the term used for a mediation/arbitration hybrid approach. The mediator could thereby change hats and become the arbitrator with decision-making authority.[14] Different questions may arise than those that pertain only to mediation. The arbitrator acts like a judge, listens to the evidence, and makes a legal decision. There should be agreement ahead of time between the parties as to whether the arbitrator's decision is binding or nonbinding. Another important issue to decide is which state's law to apply, also known as the choice of law approach.

Final Disposition

Some courts may require a final disposition on pet property ownership, with no co-ownership or visitation allowed, whereas other judicial officers will allow and even encourage an award subject to a provision where pets travel back and forth with the parties' children. Family courts may be more rule-based and against joint ownership than judges who serve on the civil docket, where co-ownership of an animal is common, especially when economically valuable animals or animals regarded as prestigious are concerned.[15]

Positional and Interest-Based ADR Processes

Another challenge with pet custody disputes is the difference between two types of ADR processes, "positional" and "interest-based." The difficulty with the positional approach is that neutrals might be expected to use law based upon external norms, such as a system wherein the family pet may be classified as personal property. A positional negotiation therefore might focus on purchase price, title, and registration, whereas the "interest-based" human-centered approach might focus on which party is suffering from a chronic condition and receives comfort from an animal's companionship. However, this interest-based human-centered model is distinguishable from an animal-centered model. For instance, the animal-centered method would focus on the best outcome for the pet. For a cat, the best outcome may be to stay in the same house where the cat has long lived.

What is interesting about comparing one type of problem solving, such as positional or interest-based, to the other is that there can be lack of awareness with regard to how perceptions of power affect neurobiology. If a party, lawyer, or

13. Check to see if the Family Law Arbitration Act has been enacted and adopted in your state, and learn if any other uniform laws or state arbitration statutes may apply.

14. In this regard, determine if the arbitration award is binding. The attorney should know how binding arbitrations are viewed in the applicable state, including the criteria for the appeal of an arbitration award. For example, an arbitrator's failure to disclose a conflict of interest may be grounds for appeal.

15. Courts are more likely to permit co-ownership when animals have commercial value rather than primarily relational value.

mediator is perceived as powerful, there could be more complex dynamics in the negotiation process.[16]

Mediation, Neuroscience, and Objectivity

Very little is known about how our brains work,[17] including inside or outside of mediation processes. While there may be a scientific basis that people behave differently and make better decisions in calm mediation processes, there seems to be a dearth of information about how interest-based systems are more cerebral and less "animal" than the positional approach.[18] There is no such thing as the brain thinking logically devoid of emotional influences. To the contrary, they function together.[19]

Implicit Bias

We are hardly objective when referring to a living creature as "it" any more than in calling all humans "he." Words reflect implicit bias. Notice the presence or absence of the word "it" in animal-related case law, even case law that negates the noneconomic value of animals.[20] In more recent case law, instead of jurists using the word "it," the actual name of the animal is used and many courts refer to the animal by species. These emerging practices will impact mediation, too.

Animal Classifications

When leaving the courtroom and entering a mediation process, lawyers, mediators, and even the parties involved may consciously or unconsciously be affected by a perception of the subject of the dispute. Some may classify the dispute as "silly." Not only do most family pets have uncertain value, but they may be classified according to a continuum ranging from quasi-property, to things, to sentimental property, to personal property, to products, to goods, to a special category of property, to best friends, to companion animals, to being in an interim category between property and person, if not as a family member. What is in part ironic about our sensitivity to word use is that we are on the verge of being less human as we utilize scientific advances to fundamentally change ourselves into an entity that may be more humanoid than human.[21]

---

16. Mark Turrell, *Sex and the Brain: How Neuroscience May Soon Change All Our Relationships*, https://markturrell.wordpress.com/2012/03/18/sex-and-the-brain-how-neuroscience-may-soon-change-all-our-relationships-6/ (last visited May 12, 2016).

17. In 2013, the European Commission committed to invest more than $1 billion into the creation of a simulated human brain called the Human Brain Project (HBP).

18. Although we believe the fight or flight response is real, research may show that there is more complex neuro-circuitry involved.

19. Antonio Damasio, Descartes' Error: Emotion, Reason, and the Human Brain (Penguin Books 2005).

20. *See* Strickland v. Medlen, 397 S.W.3d 184, 185 (Tex. 2013).

21. Given developments in neuroscience and nanotechnology, medical devices or nanobot drug systems may be utilized to promote cognitive enhancement. Barbara J. Gislason, *Influencing Young Minds through Cognitive Enhancement: The Power, the Glory, and the Loss of Self*, American Bar Association Section of International Law 2016 Spring Meeting.

Mediator Cognitive Biases

Seek a neutral mediator who is professional and competent. Education, preparation, training, and experience are all important, as is the mediator's ability to communicate with those of the same or differing race, gender, economic class, ethnicity, and the neutral's awareness of stereotypes.[22] In disputes about companion animals, neutrals should be aware of their own cognitive biases about nonhuman animals and the limits of their personal knowledge about animals. Mediators who are not "animal people" may be less able to follow the implications of what is said or meant by those who self-identify that way.

An animal person may recognize that if two animals have long lived paw to paw, separating the animals may be cruel. An animal person might find this to be similar to when a person loses a loved one or when a mate dies shortly after the other. A horse person may know about the unique nutrition requirements of a particular breed of horse and that not all horses can graze well in the same pasture.

Client Perception

It is important to realize that how a client feels about the mediation result may be impacted by whether his or her goals and purposes were satisfied within the process itself. Carrie Menkel-Meadow has well explained how process can matter "independent of outcome."[23] This is, in part, because a client may value a noncompensatory behavior, such as an apology, as well as other behaviors classified as "exta-legal."[24]

Gendered Communications

Upon entering the mediation process, consider the possibility that there are gendered communications.[25] Women clients may be more effective in expressing themselves in the mediation process because they have a superior ability to use the language of psychological needs and demonstrate greater problem-solving ability.

In verbal communication, language can reflect a descriptive function, such as a description of an animal, or an expressive function wherein special words or phrases are utilized for emphasis, as well as a social function, such as expressing a request or offering help. The use of language in our communication codes involves a level of complexity because communication may embody signals within signals within signals.[26]

---

22. Carrie Menkel-Meadow, *Women in Dispute Resolution: Parties, Lawyers and Dispute Resolvers What Difference Does "Gender Difference" Make*, Dispute Resolution Magazine, Spring 2012.

23. *Id.*

24. *Id.*

25. *Id.*

26. José Fernando Fontanari & Leonid I. Perlovsky, *Evolving Compositionality in Evolutionary Language Games*, IEEE Transactions on Evolutionary Computation, Vol. 11, No. 6, December 2007, http://leonid-perlovsky.com/new-materials/35%202007%20IEEE_TEVC%20FF,%20LP.pdf (last visited Oct. 4, 2016).

Some contend that women can be less rule-based and perceive the world in a more relational context, whereas men may be less patient or resourceful, more rule-based, seek a quicker resolution, and desire a clear win. If accurate, one way these gender-based differences could manifest in the pet custody dispute context is if one party places more importance on who cared for and had a close bond with an animal, whereas the other party's perspective could be based upon a mathematical calculation with regard to each party's economic contribution, with particular significance attached to who paid the animal's purchase price.

Speaking in general terms, some claim that females may lack the ability to hold their power. Research findings show that nonlawyer female mediators can be overpowered by aggressive male lawyers, and unrepresented female parties can be overpowered by male mediators.[27] According to Menkel-Meadow, gender is more important in certain substantive areas, including family law, domestic violence, civil rights, and criminal law.[28] Thus far, it is not known if or how gender will impact animal-centered processes. Mediation could also be affected by a desire to focus on the emotional aspect of a human and pet relationship, something courts are shy to do.

Another argument advanced by Menkel-Meadow is that in the above-described subject areas, a judge's political party, background, and demographic factors could also impact the outcome. According to Menkel-Meadow, female judges may give a female criminal defendant a worse sentence than a male judge may.[29] Extending this idea to pet custody disputes, a female judge might be more rule-based and reject a private agreement allowing one party to have custody of a pet and the other party pet time than a male judge might. Even so, these are stereotypes and even if correct, there are always exceptions to these generalizations. It is more important to know about the actual jurists involved.

When thinking about what kind of mediator to select in a case, Menkel-Meadow says research results indicate that parties to an action might prefer the facilitative mediation approach while their lawyers might prefer evaluative mediation,[30] female lawyers prefer mediation more than males do, men are more vulnerable to being manipulated in the mediation process, and a party's goals and purposes in mediation might be different from those of the party's lawyer.[31] In family law, some mediators prefer to work with co-mediators with subject matter expertise. If a pet

27. Menkel-Meadow, *supra* note 22.

28. *Id.* It seems probable based upon these findings that gender would matter more in pet custody and ownership disputes, too.

29. *Id.*

30. *Id.*

31. *Id.*

custody issue is involved, a family law mediator might seek a co-mediator with appropriate animal credentials, such as an animal lawyer or an animal expert. This may depend on what the parties can afford.

Records for Mediation

Depending on what type of mediation is contemplated, in preparing for mediation, it may be a good idea for your client to provide you with the following types of records:

- Ownership records
- Application to breeder
- Breeder contract
- Application to rescue group
- Rescue contract
- Purchase or adoption payment records
- Foster application
- Foster agreement
- Registration records
- Pet license records
- Photographs
- Veterinary records
- Pet insurance records
- Dental records
- Ferrier or teeth floating records, if hoofed animals are involved
- Police and animal control reports and records
- Administrative proceeding records, such as for a dangerous dog
- Criminal or domestic abuse records regarding litigants or significant others
- Training records
- Text messages, emails, and letters
- Social media communications
- Video or audio recordings
- Training records
- Certificates and awards
- Financial records directly or indirectly related to the animal
- Homeowner's insurance records related to the animal
- Automobile insurance records related to the animal
- Other important written or electronic communications or postings

Mediation Questions

Positional-Based Questions

Lawyers can help their clients be prepared to answer the following questions in mediation:

- Who found the pet?
- Who first owned the pet?
- Who purchased the pet?
- Did the money to purchase the pet come from a joint account or joint credit card?
- Was the pet a gift?
- How was donative intent demonstrated?
- How long did someone have sole possession of the pet?
- Was there a prenuptial agreement, antenuptial agreement, post-marital agreement, partnership agreement, or other contract?
- Is there an argument for one party to have an equitable interest in the pet, such as a constructive trust?
- Who paid for the pet's veterinary care, dental surgery, emergency services, training, grooming, medications, boarding, food, day care, and other significant expenditures?
- Whose name is reflected on veterinary, specialty store, and city records?

Human Best-Interest Topics

Topics covered in mediation with a human best-interest focus might instead come from this list:

- Does someone have a condition the pet is thought to help, such as high blood pressure, anxiety, or depression?
- Does the pet go to the office regularly with one of the parties?
- Does the pet spend the day with one of the parties in a home office?
- Who spends more available free time with the pet?
- Who does the pet hang around with or sit near at home in the evening?
- Where does the pet sleep?
- Who has a photograph of the pet on his or her cell phone, as a screen saver, or on his or her desk?
- Did one party stay at the veterinary hospital while the pet had surgery and remain with the pet for hours while the pet was in recovery?
- Do any of the individuals or significant others in either party's life have a criminal record or a history of mental health problems or domestic abuse?

- Have there been any incidents where a pet, or even a former pet, in the household was harmed by a human or another companion animal?
- Are there issues with regard to neighbors or other animals either inside the home or in the neighborhood who might bring a nuisance, zoning, pet weight restriction, or other type of complaint about the animal?
- Are there foreseeable problems in a new blended household where there are other animals, boisterous children, or lack of space?
- Is there any evidence that one of the owners yells at, hits, or physically hurts the pet, or has threatened to give the pet away or kill the pet?
- Who is able to pay for pet health insurance and the pet's uninsured health and dental expenses, including medications?
- Who wants to bring the pet along on vacation?
- Can the parties cooperate on quality of veterinary care decisions, as well as life and death and euthanasia decisions?
- Will homeowner's insurance, renter's insurance, automobile insurance, or other liability policies cover the animal in case the animal causes an injury?
- What is the likelihood the animal would cause injury if loose?

Animal Best-Interest Topics

Topics covered in mediation with a best interest of the animal focus might instead come from this list:

- Are the pet's best interests each party's primary concern?
- How have the pet's needs been prioritized?
- How would each party meet the pet's needs now?
- Is there a plan for the pet in case of an emergency?
- Is the pet clearly emotionally bonded to a particular human?
- Is the pet clearly emotionally bonded to a particular animal?
- What is the evidence of the bond?
- Where does the pet sleep?
- What standard of living is the pet used to with regard to quality and amount of food, indoor space, outdoor space, exercise, and day care, as well as veterinary, dental, and other care?
- Which party is better able to maintain the pet's standard of living?
- Is the pet close to other animals or people who should be considered, such as a dog trainer, dog walker, horse trainer, or day care provider?
- Who takes care of the pet when frightened during a thunderstorm or fireworks or when the pet is sick?
- Who gives the animal necessary shots or medication?

- Who takes the pet to obedience or other training or behavioral classes?
- Who makes sure the animal is properly groomed and nails clipped or hooves trimmed?
- Which party is aware of risks to the animal from cleaning products, furniture, rugs, plants, and chemical yard or field products?
- Who is careful with regard to keeping doors or fences closed or locked?
- Who would give the pet necessary vaccines for a chronic medical condition?
- Who would open his or her wallet to pay for expensive veterinary services?

Mediators with Animal Expertise

Mediators with animal expertise are few and far between. New York attorney Debra Hamilton has been influential in advocating animal mediation.[32] Hamilton offers what she calls a hybrid of evaluative and transformative mediation, and her technique was influenced by the work of Gary Friedman and Jack Himmelstein.[33] She argues that mediators can uniquely take into account the best interest of pets; benefits of mediation can be realized if the mediator listens and values each party's position, and if the parties are amenable to exploring solutions and are committed to hard work. In her practice, she has found that co-ownership is common for animals that compete in the show world. The people who most often seek her mediation services are co-owners of animals.[34]

Attorney Expertise

Since most attorneys know little about this practice area, a lawyer who is well-versed in animal law has an advantage; there may be unintended deference to someone with expertise. If you can comfortably talk about five pet law cases during negotiations, you will likely know five more cases than anybody else in the room. Lawyers want to sound like experts.

It is time consuming to prepare for mediation, and more so because of how animal law cases now seem to be subject to a rapid progression past old norms. Keep clients in the loop. When in a new terrain, evaluate whether to pass all or some of the costs of preparation on to a client. Nothing forces an attorney to put five hours of actual time on a client's bill or to work without compensation.

---

32. *Hamilton Law and Mediation PLLC*, http://hamiltonlawandmediation.com/ (last visited May 12, 2016).

33. Gary Friedman & Jack Himmelstein, *Challenging Conflict: Mediation through Understanding* (American Bar Association 2009).

34. Barbara J. Gislason interviewed Debra Hamilton.

Model Standards of Practice for Family and Divorce Mediation

Following almost a decade of effort, the Model Standards of Practice for Family and Divorce Mediation[35] were developed for family law facilitative mediation.[36] While these standards were not designed for pet custody disputes, there is value to reviewing these standards from a pet custody dispute perspective. Selected aspects of these standards will be discussed here.

Self-Determination

Standard I of the Model Standards of Practice for Family and Divorce Mediation emphasizes the parties' right to self-determination.[37] What is problematic in a pet custody dispute is that not all private agreements reached in mediation may be enforceable because of statutory finality requirements in the divorce context. Even so, courts encourage parties to come up with private solutions.

Mediator Education and Training

Standard II discusses the proper education and training of a mediator. This concept is in the very early stages of development for mediators involved in a pet custody dispute.[38] Other than veterinarians, behaviorists, animal lawyers, and perhaps family lawyers familiar with child custody disputes, appropriate credentials are determined on a case-by-case basis. Mediators should be comfortable with how clients communicate about their companion animals, as some mediators may not only find expression of love for animals offensive but also regard attention to animals as taking away necessary time and resources better devoted to children or another worthier purpose. Mediators should realize that attachment to an animal, regardless of how unusual it may seem to them,[39] constitutes a legitimate point of view.

Mediators should be comfortable with the following scenarios:

- Is the objective to place the animal in a home where the animal will have a good standard of living, such as a home with a large yard?

---

35. *Model Standards of Practice for Family and Divorce Mediation*, Mediate.com, http://www.mediate.com/articles/afccstds.cfm (last visited May 12, 2016).

36. Mediators might want to repurpose some of these standards in a pet custody context.

37. "Standard I: A family mediator shall recognize that mediation is based on the principle of self-determination by the participants."

38. "Standard II: A family mediator shall be qualified by education and training to undertake the mediation."

39. This is said with the exception of bestiality. When this issue presents itself, even if there is no law against this practice, the mediator could promote the best interests of the animal based upon public policy.

- Is the objective to allow the animal to continue a relationship with another animal, such as a littermate or long-term companion? Companion animals, like humans, are impacted by grief and depression.[40]
- Do the parties want to avoid placing the animal in a blended family where the animal may be in conflict with other animals? Some animals cannot live with other animals, and it might be advisable to utilize a trial period in a new household first.
- Do the parties want the animal to continue in training and activities the animal is accustomed to and enjoys? If so, who would be willing to contribute to these out-of-pocket costs if the primary home of the animal was with another person?
- Do the parties want the animal to continue to have access to a stepchild or perhaps an older disabled adult?
- Do the parties want the animal to have access to quality veterinary care, particularly if the animal has serious medical or behavioral challenges?[41]
- Is the pet being used as an excuse for one party to have continuing contact with the other party?
- What if a non-animal issue is at the heart of the conflict, such as payback or revenge?

Capacity to Mediate[42]

With regard to Standard III, the mediator must assess the participants' capacity to mediate. Clients should be educated about this. When it comes to an individual's capacity to mediate, presume that "capacity to mediate" is a synonym for "ability to mediate." If a client has a mental health issue or is not sober, they may be unable to be fully attentive in the negotiation process.

The way a facilitative mediator approaches a pet custody dispute may differ from mediator to mediator. A mediator who self-identifies as a "dog person" or "cat person" or "animal person" would likely be different from a mediator who starts out the mediation with the disclosure, "I am not an animal person."

---

40. Linda Carroll, *Died of a Broken Heart? The Science behind Close Couple Deaths*, TODAY HEALTH, http://www.today.com/health/died-broken-heart-science-behind-close-couple-deaths-8C11018276 (last visited May 12, 2016); Cesar Milan, *Dog in Mourning: Helping Our Pets Cope with Loss*, CESAR'S WAY, http://www.cesarsway.com/dog-training/socialization/A-Dog-In-Mourning-Helping-Our-Pets-Cope (last visited May 12, 2016).

41. Some breeds are known to have very expensive veterinary needs because of a genetic propensity to develop cancer or hip dysplasia. Animals from rescues may have costly dental needs or require behavioral training.

42. "Standard III: A family mediator shall facilitate the participants' understanding of what mediation is and assess their capacity to mediate before the participants reach an agreement to mediate."

Mediator Impartiality, Values, and Legal Perspective

Under Standard IV, if there is anything improper about a mediator's relationship with another party or attorney, it must be addressed.[43] Determining mediator potential bias in a pet custody dispute presents itself as both a challenging and important matter; the decision-making criteria and framing of interests that could be applied in pet-related mediation could differ enormously. Mediators who favor a traditional property division rather than a best-interest and custody approach may not be perceived as impartial by clients, or vice versa. A mediator experienced with equine or show animal disputes where co-ownership agreements are common and the purpose of the animal is more use-based than relational-based might approach a pet custody dispute quite differently than a vegan attorney. The latter may only accept mediation cases where the parties agree to use the sole criteria of the animal's best interests.

When selecting a mediator, the lawyer should find out if the mediator emphasizes the property-based method effectively settled law, or if the mediator views a companion animal as both a sentient being[44] and a family member whose interests should be considered and protected. Perhaps the mediator perceives the animal in an interim category between property and person. A mediator may reveal his or her perspective by describing the animal as property or by using vernacular about trying to do the right thing. Even though all mediators may present themselves as neutral, and even intend to be so, a mediator who is not an animal person and who does not understand the significance of relationships between humans and animals, or have any knowledge of how costly animals' veterinary and other expenses can be,[45] may lack the necessary skills to facilitate a comprehensive discussion.

As pet mediation expertise evolves, it is likely that mediators will utilize an increasingly broader variety of criteria or factors to reach an outcome. A facilitative animal-centered mediation may be the best option in cases with a relational focus, as evaluative mediators may not appreciate the dearth of statutes and common laws in the applicable state.

---

43. "Standard IV: A family mediator shall conduct the mediation process in an impartial manner. A family mediator shall disclose all actual and potential grounds of bias and conflicts of interest reasonably known to the mediator. The participants shall be free to retain the mediator by an informed, written waiver of the conflict of interest. However, if a bias or conflict of interest clearly impairs a mediator's impartiality, the mediator shall withdraw regardless of the express agreement of the participants."

44. Sentient being means a conscious ability to sense, perceive, or feel. The court referred to animals as being sentient in *State v. Nix*, 355 Or. 777, 334 P.3d 437 (2014), *vacated*, 356 Ore. 768, 345 P.3d 416 (2015). The *Nix* holding was reaffirmed in State v. Hess, 359 P.3d 288 (Or. Ct. App. 2015).

45. A companion animal that comes from a breed with genetic problems that will require surgery can be particularly expensive.

Mediator Compensation and Attitude about Pets

With regard to Standard V, it is important that the mediator disclose his or her compensation and fees.[46] From a due diligence perspective, it is a good idea to seek information about this, perhaps in a disclosure form.

While most mediators are sensitive to child welfare and that personal value influences the mediator's evolving personal style, there could be a much more significant disparity between mediators if the dispute is about animals. Some may not even think about nor consider animal welfare, may be against animal rights, or may be unaware of minimal care legal statutory requirements. Rather than taking the dispute seriously, a mediator may make puns with a staff member about whether one of the parties is "barking up the wrong tree." Hearing quips like these in the context of a dispute about a companion animal is either a signal that the person is very uncomfortable in his or her role or that he or she finds the subject of the dispute to be frivolous and not meriting serious attention.

Making Informed Decisions

Standard VI involves the mediator structuring the mediation process so that the participants can make decisions based upon sufficient information and knowledge.

One aspect of Standard VI that is important in a pet custody dispute is to think ahead about the parties' ability to meet a companion animal's foreseeable veterinary expenses.[47] Pet insurance is now widely available, and if purchased early, there are no preexisting condition exceptions.[48] Many veterinarians will identify insurance carriers with whom they prefer to work.

Another option for paying veterinary expenses is using a credit card called Care Credit.[49] Owners can also seek help from financial aid or Give Forward,[50] where, for a small fee, a personal fundraising page can be created. There are also veterinary assistance programs specific to an owner's needs. For example, Labrador owners could utilize Labrador Harbor,[51] LabMed,[52] or Labrador Life Line.[53]

---

46. "Standard V: A family mediator shall fully disclose and explain the basis of any compensation, fees and charges to the participants."

47. "Standard VI: A family mediator shall structure the mediation process so that the participants make decisions based on sufficient information and knowledge."

48. *Having Trouble Affording Veterinary Care? Help Is out There*, THE HUMANE SOCIETY OF THE UNITED STATES, http://m.humanesociety.org/animals/resources/tips/trouble_affording_veterinary_care.html (last visited May 12, 2016).

49. *Care Credit*, http://www.carecredit.com/ (last visited May 12, 2016).

50. *Give Forward*, http://www.giveforward.com/ (last visited May 12, 2016).

51. *Labrador Harbor*, http://www.labradorharbor.org/ (last visited May 12, 2016).

52. *LabMed*, http://www.labmed.org/ (last visited May 12, 2016).

53. *Labrador Life Line*, http://www.labradorlifeline.org/ (last visited May 12, 2016).

Domestic Abuse

Because of growing awareness that many domestic violence victims are afraid to leave their pets behind, more than half of the United States has enacted legislation that contains a pet provision in an order for protection.[54] According to the National Coalition Against Domestic Violence, 71 percent of pet owners entering shelters report that their abuser threatened, injured, or killed a family pet.[55] It is also well-understood that animals may be hurt in the presence of a partner for the purpose of exacting revenge or maintaining control.[56] Children are present in 76 percent of these incidents.[57] Mediators should always be aware of expressed or unexpressed violence concerns and control methods.

Topics for Discussion

In addition to the variety of questions posed earlier in this chapter, mediators helping parties make decisions based upon sufficient information and knowledge might direct the conversation so that the participants consider the following:

- Can the animal travel well?[58]
- Does the animal have special needs during transport, such as the need for temperature control?
- Has consideration been given to avoiding transporting animals with predator/prey relationships? For example, a parrot should not be transported next to a snake.
- Does the animal have anxiety problems, including upon separation or during a thunderstorm, or because of past neglect or abuse? How could the proposed schedule impact the animal's need for stability? Should there be a step-by-step process?
- Is the animal known to be anxious? If so, it might be wise to obtain veterinary or behavioral advice to evaluate whether the animal has a medical problem that contributes to the animal's presenting behaviors. Holistic options could be explored, such as the use of over-the-counter products like Rescue Remedy, to help animals deal with travel anxiety. There are

---

54. Rebecca F. Wisch, *Domestic Violence and Pets: List of States that Include Pets in Protection Orders*, Michigan State University, Animal Legal & Historical Center, http://www.animallaw.info/articles/ovusdomesticviolencelaws.htm (last visited May 12, 2016).

55. *Pets and Domestic Violence*, National Coalition against Domestic Violence, http://www.hope-eci.org/_documents/petsanddv.pdf (last visited May 12, 2016).

56. *Id.*; Joni E. Johnston, *Children Who Are Cruel to Animals: When to Worry*, Psychology Today, https://www.psychologytoday.com/blog/the-human-equation/201104/children-who-are-cruel-animals-when-worry (last visited May 12, 2016).

57. *Id.*

58. Karen Becker, *The New Rules about Who Gets Your Family Pet in a Divorce*, Healthy Pets Mercola, http://healthypets.mercola.com/sites/healthypets/archive/2013/10/04/pet-custody-during-divorce.aspx (last visited May 12, 2016).

also prescription medications that may help, particularly for animals sensitive to thunderstorms. Consider purchasing a Thunder Shirt.

- Has the animal been exposed to stress or anger and is urinating or defecating in inappropriate places? When an experienced mediator hears this, he or she should know that the parties could be missing something obvious. If talking about a cat, ask questions about the cat's litter box, including the brand and scent of litter and where the box is located. Is another cat now using the same litter box? Is there a new family member? Is there a potential medical or dental problem? Could the cat be aging and have poor vision? Is another cat outside? Has there been an illness, injury, diet change, or medication change?
- Is the animal suffering from depression? There is growing scientific evidence that dogs are aware of their owners' emotions and moods, including depression. Animals can become frightened or depressed when their owners are frightened or depressed. Moving to a different environment may cause confusion and separation anxiety. This pertains to loss of not only human relationships but also relationships with other animals. The animal may also be affected by a new routine.[59]
- Would the animal prefer to live where the animal has always lived? The parties may know.
- Is one of the parties unable to afford the animal's expensive veterinary bills? What resources do they have to change this?
- Are the owners of long-living animals, such as parrots, aware of the need for estate planning once custody is determined? Would it be prudent to have a pet trust and estate planning discussion?
- Is the animal being used as a threat to the other party, including in a domestic abuse situation? Take into account whether either party has a violent history of any kind, including a history of harming animals.

Child-Focused Considerations

The best interests emphasized in Standard VIII[60] are critical because mediators should be aware that animal abuse occurs 76 percent of the time in the presence of children.[61] Should children be in a home where they continue to witness animal

---

59. Tom Ryan, *Does Divorce Affect Dogs*, The Nest, http://pets.thenest.com/divorce-affect-dogs-11622.html (last visited May 12, 2016).

60. "Standard VIII: A family mediator shall assist participants in determining how to promote the best interests of children."

61. *Pets and Domestic Violence*, National Coalition against Domestic Violence, http://www.hope-eci.org/_documents/petsanddv.pdf (last visited May 12, 2016).

abuse and are helpless to prevent it?[62] In the same respect, the best interests of children are promoted when children are around well-cared for animals.

Another aspect is whether any children in the household exhibit cruelty to the pet in question, perhaps having learned to abuse others by a parent. If the parties involved in mediation are concerned about mistreatment of the animal, the mediator can explain that cruelty to animals by children is widely viewed as a precursor to delinquency, violence, and criminal behavior.[63] It is also believed that children, who feel powerless when they are abused, may find victims such as pets to exercise control over to gain power. According to anthropologist Margaret Mead, "One of the most dangerous things that can happen to a child is to kill or torture an animal and get away with it."[64]

The Link

Child abuse and neglect are discussed under Standard IX.[65] When children are abused, pets may also be abused, and it could be the child doing the abusing, as described above. Many now believe there is a link between human and animal abuse.[66] When mediating a pet custody dispute involving an abused pet, the mediator could help the parties explore relinquishing the abused pet to an animal rescue, or better yet, a new owner, to prevent the animal from being further harmed if an abusing child is traveling between households.

Rather than the mediator just being in a facilitative role, the mediator could be proactive in helping the parties obtain therapy or counseling for a child involved in animal cruelty. Professionals can help an endangered human or animal. Although this type of advocacy does not fit into the idea of a neutral's role, when violence has already occurred, perhaps the neutral can make it clear that he or she will cease services unless issues regarding violence are addressed.

Regardless of what mediators are told at the onset of mediation, they should pay attention to the dynamics between the parties and watch for signs of domestic abuse, per Standard X.[67] For example, does one partner appear to be helpless, scared, or otherwise submissive or small? What does each party's clothing tell you? Does one party seem powerful and condescending, with his or her chin

62. If the perpetrator vents anger at the pet rather than the children, once the pet is removed, the anger may be physically directed at the children. This is a difficult subject for mediators to navigate.

63. Johnston, *supra* note 56.

64. *The Animal Abuse-Human Violence Connection*, PAWS, http://www.paws.org/get-involved/take-action/explore-the-issues/animal-abuse-connection/ (last visited May 12, 2016).

65. "Standard IX: A family mediator shall recognize a family situation involving child abuse or neglect and take appropriate steps to shape the mediation process accordingly."

66. Allie Phillips, *Understanding the Link between Violence to Animals and People*, ASPCA, http://www.ndaa.org/pdf/The%20Link%20Monograph-2014.pdf (last visited Oct. 4, 2016).

67. "Standard X: A family mediator shall recognize a family situation involving domestic abuse and take appropriate steps to shape the mediation process accordingly."

jutting out or shoulders square? Is one party staring and tone loud or steely, or making false allegations to gain control?

If an abuser is in the room, at the very least, the mediator should divide the parties and then interview them individually to see if the mediation can continue and, if so, in what form. Mediators should also take care of their own personal safety.

Mediator Promotion

Standard XII pertains to advertisements for mediation.[68] When preparing ads and solicitations for pet ownership and custody mediation, mediators should consider some of the following questions:

- What terminology will be used? Choices include pet, companion animal, or the specific type of animal. Dogs are the most common animals in pet custody disputes, although there is plenty of litigation related to horses, too.
- How will the advertising and solicitation message factor in traditional property, blended property, custody tracts, and approaches? Will the mediation simply be animal-centered?
- How does the mediator address the problem of judicial cooperation with private mediation agreements that do not meet finality requirements?
- Will the mediator have mediation/arbitration authority from the parties if mediation is unsuccessful? Is the prospective arbitration subject to a negotiated written agreement? Is the court more likely to respect and enforce a mediated private agreement or a binding arbitration award?
- In divorce agreements, courts may expect lawyers and parties to put the terms of their agreement into what becomes the judgment and decree or final decree, or in some contexts, the court order. An ethical question may arise as to whether the mediator should participate in negotiating a side agreement on a pet issue.[69] Would the pet be hidden from the court if the parties to the mediated agreement stipulated that the animal was not property? As animals move away from being categorized as personal property and into the human family, an interim category may impact mediation and other ADR processes in unexpected ways.
- If the mediator uses only one type of mediation method, such as facilitative and not transformative, should this be disclosed?

68. "Standard XII: A family mediator shall be truthful in the advertisement and solicitation for mediation."

69. Because some mediators are not attorneys, they may not fully appreciate the risks inherent in unenforceable side agreements.

Mediator Competence

Standard XIII discusses a family mediator's professional competence.[70] In pet-centered mediation, competence can be facilitated by both the mediator's curiosity and knowledge about pets in a family system. This book is also designed to give mediators a strong baseline of working knowledge for serving mediation participants.

Attorney/Client Mediation Preparation

It may be helpful, before entering negotiations, to have a rough draft of the desired agreement, a detailed recital of facts, a good outline of pertinent cases and statutes, and all the vital facts literally on the same page. Work with your client to gather, identify, and distinguish between important verifiable facts and beliefs.

If your client presents the facts in an unusual way, help him or her understand what facts will be important to others as opposed to what facts the client keeps repeating. For example, a client may think it is significant who paid for the animal with a check but may not think about the fact that the check was issued from a joint account or that the other party will claim there was a cash reimbursement for half the cost. There could be other complicating facts, too, such as if the nonpurchasing party was the animal's foster, or if there is a claim of abandonment or gift.

Having a pre-mediation proposal ready will give your client confidence that you are on top of the case and will also help you feel that you can close the deal if there is an opportunity. Lawyers do not want to lose a precious hour covering the basics in the midst of negotiations. It is advisable to have smart technology available so that the draft agreement can be revised, printed, and signed during the session. A good lawyer should also be prepared to give up on preconceived notions of what should happen, including as reflected in the prepared proposal, if superior ideas arise in the mediation process.[71]

Making Deals

Next, we will consider client and attorney strategy in the mediation and ADR context and the concept of deal points, secondary points, and trade points in a negotiation.[72] In the context of a pet custody or ownership dispute, the deal point might

70. "Standard XIII: A family mediator shall acquire and maintain professional competence in mediation."

71. To some, the preparation techniques discussed herein could be viewed as incompatible with the frank and deep discussion the mediator can facilitate. Your client should be advised about the pros and cons of this preparation process.

72. H. Lee Hetherington, *Planning for Settlement Negotiations: The Big Picture*, ABA Section of Family Law Family Advocate, Winter 2015, Vol. 37, No. 3, at 10–11.

be where the dog will live and the secondary point might be access to the dog on alternate weekends. If the access subject is vital to one party, then it is a deal point. The trade point may be important to both parties, or to one party and not the other. One party might want the prized antique rocking chair inherited by the other party, and the party who inherited the chair might be indifferent about it. Giving up this family heirloom might be considered a trade point for the companion animal.

In pet custody disputes, a strategy could be developed long before entering into the negotiation, for example, train clients to advance a deal point by talking in a kind manner about the other party and being factual about the advantages for the animal in the client's care.

Deal Points

While in mediation, be careful about the final push near the end of the session when a client insists he or she has no more money to spend or just wants it over. Regardless of what a client says in order to gain closure, he or she does not want a poorly conceived and confusing deal that costs more money or upsets him or her later. It is better to sign off on five well-conceived deal points, which will have to be filled in by one of the lawyers, than one page of language that no one knows how to interpret. Explain to your client before mediation about what happens when the clock is running out, and make sure your client watches the clock throughout the process so that no one is caught off guard when there are only ten minutes left.

Anticipating Negotiation Dynamics

Do everything possible to analyze what strategy the other side will utilize, including what insults may be hurled. Your client will have insight into the other side's strengths and weaknesses. Sometimes this insight is gained when family or friends are made aware of careless social media posts by the other party. In advance of the mediation, imagine and role-play the other side being pleasant, angry, and condescending.

It is helpful to know if either party holds opposing counsel in a high regard and for what reason. Did that attorney represent one of the parties successfully before? You want to know how much power the other attorney has in this respect and consider how you might change the dynamic. If both you and your client are well prepared, imagine quickly shifting any power imbalance in your favor.

Exchanging Discovery

It is sometimes desirable to exchange discovery information in advance of negotiations. Relevant information to exchange might include contracts, veterinary records, dangerous dog declarations, and evidence of the quality of the relationship, including photographs, videos, social media posts, copies of holiday greeting cards, and recordings of voicemail messages. It is also possible that the better strategy is not to pursue discovery simply because you and your client are prepared and it is probable that the other side is not. Bringing up the subject of discovery might cause the other side to step up their preparation.

Best Interests for all Concerned

Consider, in advance of negotiations, whether everyone involved is willing to explore a "best interests for all concerned" standard. If you go into negotiations advocating this approach, but the other side is only willing to have a traditional property and rule-based discussion, have a few cases ready that support that this best-interest approach reflects emerging jurisprudence.[73] The hidden elephant in the room may be that the mediation matters more from a process perspective, as a party may need to express emotions or deal with grief even when aware he or she is going to "lose." Know, too, that either party's objective could change during the negotiation process.

Client Preparation

Prepare your client about how to express him- or herself in mediation through a series of rehearsals or training sessions. Rehearsals, even if short, may reduce your client's anger or anxiety and help with mental preparation for what the process will be like. You may be surprised to see how much your client improves from rehearsal to rehearsal. In the first rehearsal, have your client focus on his or her best attributes and history of caring for the pet. In the second rehearsal, focus on the defects of the other party and his or her own flaws.

Even if your client is prepared to present information to the mediator, he or she also needs to be prepared about how to react to unexpected statements. Part of the preparation should include your client imagining negative things that the other party might say. Have your client role-play by pretending to be the other party and make denigrating statements about him or her. The more the client practices, the more he or she will be able to handle critical comments in the mediation process.[74] Let your client know that when emotions run too high in the mediation process, a time-out is advisable.

73. *See* Travis v. Murray, 2013 NY Slip. Op. 23405 (N.Y. Sup. Ct. 2013).
74. This may also help your client identify what records he or she should gather.

Attorney Awareness

A popular idea in mediation is to not trigger a fight or flight reaction from the participants. Consider the many ways your client may be in fear in a pet custody dispute. Your client may be afraid of being alone, of losing the only dependable love relationship he or she has, of the animal being hurt, of the animal not being given proper veterinary care, of the animal being underfed or overfed, of the animal being left alone, of the other party not paying for the animal's heartworm prevention medication, or of the other party being lazy about exercising the animal. Another aspect to your client's feelings may simply be sadness. Realize, too, that payback or retaliation may influence a party to participate in this type of dispute.

It is difficult, even for an experienced lawyer, to handle a pet custody or ownership dispute in an area where the law seems to be in its infancy. You may despair that all is lost when you perform research and find an adverse appellate decision. Do not feel hopeless. Utilizing this book as a tool, you will appreciate that not only is the common law dynamic, but also injustice can lead to much needed legislation.

Court Action

An inherent problem in mediation is whether the court will sign off on an agreement reached in a negotiation or ADR process, and also whether the court will enforce a binding arbitration award. There are more unknowns in the realm of pet custody disputes than in many areas of the law. It is important that your client be aware of this.

It still matters, given provable facts and rapidly changing animal jurisprudence, where ownership lies. If the animal was co-owned or was marital property, the court may apply more than one decision-making criterion. You may need to bring a court action before the other party will participate in an ADR process. If you appear before the court only to listen to the court's admonition to utilize an ADR process, learn whether the court will hold an evidentiary hearing if an agreement is not reached, and if so, whether the court will look at only property and contract law, only custody issues, or a mixture of both. Sometimes, the court will give you a hint about its value system. An example would be one lawyer's jests to the court, "Maybe we should just split the animal in half," to which the court responds with easy-to-understand body language, such as a hand over the mouth or crossed arms. It is important to learn early about the judge's viewpoint, if you can, in order to learn if a private agreement or arbitration award will be enforceable.

Although the family court has considerable discretion and leeway in achieving the result it desires, it is unpredictable when a jurist may exercise restraint when the court believes the finality rule is impacted.

Animal-Focused Facilitation Team

Be imaginative about resources that could be incorporated into the mediation process. You could borrow from the concept of a child-focused facilitation team (CFFT), where experts are put together to help children,[75] and implement a variation of this theme. You could call it an animal-focused facilitation team (AFFT). Individuals serving on this team could include a retired judge, an experienced animal law attorney, or an animal expert, preferably a behavioral expert or someone the participants deem has relevant experience or expertise. The focus of the AFFT would be to determine the best interests of the companion animal and to issue a report. You would need to decide if this report would be confidential and only for use in the ADR process, or whether the report could be used in court if the ADR process is not successful.

Collaborative Law and Uniform Collaborative Law Rules/Act

Collaborative law came of age when the Uniform Law Commission created the Uniform Collaborative Law Rules/Act (UCLRA).[76] Originally passed in 2009, the act was amended in 2010.[77] According to the Uniform Law Commission, the purpose of the UCLRA is to standardize important practice features in the context of ethical concerns and evidentiary privileges. States may differ on how to apply the UCLRA to family law matters. Key collaborative ideas include that the process is voluntary; lawyers only represent individuals for purposes of settlement; if a case is litigated, the parties must find new counsel; the parties seek an equitable solution; the parties retain experts as needed; and the parties may terminate their participation at any time.

Collaborative Rules Selected for Discussion

There are 24 rules/sections in this act.[78] Only selected rules will be discussed here. Collaborative lawyers should be conversant with the evolving jurisprudence of pet law and how it impacts pet ownership and custody disputes, as discussed throughout this book. Many of the questions, ideas, and techniques addressed earlier in this chapter will also be beneficial in collaborative law processes.

---

75. Hugh E. Starnes & Sheldon E. Finman, *The Court's Role in Settlement Negotiations*, ABA Section of Family Law Family Advocate, Winter 2015, Vol. 37, No. 3, at 30–35.

76. States that have enacted this act include Alabama, Arizona, Florida, Hawaii, Maryland, Michigan, Montana, Nevada, New Jersey, Ohio, Texas, Utah, Washington, and Washington, D.C. *Collaborative Law Acts*, Uniform Law Commission, http://uniformlaws.org/Act.aspx?title=Collaborative Law Act (last visited May 12, 2016).

77. *Id.*

78. *Collaborative Law Act Summary*, Uniform Law Commission, http://uniformlaws.org/ActSummary.aspx?title=Collaborative Law Act (last visited May 12, 2016).

Decision-Making Criteria

One of the more important rules/sections, from an animal law perspective, is rule/section 4, which requires a signed agreement containing a description of the matter. It is significant for those entering into a pet custody dispute collaborative law practice to clarify what, if any, best-interest standards will be utilized. For example, they could include best interests for humans, best interests for animals, or best interests for all concerned. The parties might agree on which factors to explore to achieve an equitable result.

Court Approval

Rule/section 8 is important because it authorizes the tribunal to approve an agreement resulting from a collaborative law process. The same issue arises with collaborative law as with mediated agreements or arbitration awards—whether the court will approve certain types of private agreements in mediation, arbitration awards in arbitration, or collaborative agreements in collaborative law. Essentially, the question is whether the court will agree, implicitly or otherwise, to retain jurisdiction after the entry of a judgment and decree when there is no final disposition of animal property.

Might the court be willing to embrace the private agreement utilizing the legal analysis of other courts detailed in this book that animals are not just property anymore but have another status? In fact, companion animals may already be in an interim category between property and person given the growing number of animal protection laws and because their interests are being protected in domestic abuse orders. Some courts may perceive joint custody or pet time agreements as problematic and refuse to sign orders implementing the agreements, especially if the court views it as violating the finality requirement.

If the court respects the collaborative lawyers involved, the court may be more likely to sign orders and judgments based upon agreements achieved in the collaborative process. Collaborators may need to suggest that the parties draft their agreement as they want it, and if unsuccessful, they can hope the court signals what revisions might be acceptable.

Party Disclosures

Rule/section 12, which addresses disclosure of information, may have unique applications with regard to pet custody disputes. The parties are able to define the scope of disclosure and utilize informal methods. This rule/section is important and should be carefully thought through because the disclosure sought may affect whether the collaborative focus is on a rule-based type of analysis or whether the collaborative process will emphasize best interests or other decision-making criteria.

Abuse Reports

Rule/section 13 addresses the obligation of lawyers to report abuse. It does not define whether the abuse could be directed toward an animal. A child abusing an animal may be a child subjected to abuse. If for no other reason than there is a known link between animal and human abuse, due consideration of this reporting obligation is important.[79]

Collaborative Lawyer Disclosures

Disclosure obligations are described in rule/section 14 and are relevant because the parties should be made aware that even if they work out a joint custody or sole custody and pet time agreement in a collaborative process, a judge or referee may not be willing to sign or enforce an order or judgment based upon the agreement. Courts may be less concerned about the finality requirement if there is a mandatory requirement to return to a collaborative or other ADR process in advance of a court motion, except under exigent circumstances. Empower yourself to offer methods that will allay the courts' fear of the floodgate problem.

Duress

Rule/section 15 addresses a collaborative lawyer's obligation to establish safeguards within the collaborative law process regarding the lawyer's client, who may have a history of being subject to coercive or violent behaviors. A dispute over a companion animal may be the mechanism through which an individual seeks to manipulate, control, and scare another party when domestic abuse has occurred. Lawyers engaged in collaborative processes are encouraged to learn the laws and ethical rules in the applicable state.[80]

ARBITRATION

Types of Arbitration

There are three basic types of arbitration: standard arbitration, where an arbitrator renders an award; high/low arbitration, where the arbitrator is not told what the upper or lower limits for the award will be;[81] and last best offer arbitration, where the last best offer closest to what the arbitrator determined is the one

79. This rule/section should be expanded to include animal abuse the next time the act is amended.

80. Ethical rules should be revised so that ADR professionals can help fashion agreements consistent with new conceptions of the modern family where animal cruelty is not tolerated.

81. If the arbitration award is higher or lower than these parameters, the award would be adjusted within these parameters. This idea could be expanded to nonmonetary high/low arbitration in family law. The high could be that the other party is awarded the dog, subject to alternate weekend visitation, and the low could be just the opposite.

accepted. An alternative to these methods is for the arbitrator simply to choose between both parties' final offers.

Arbitration Benefits

The typical benefits of arbitration include

- Less costly than litigation;
- Less delays than in litigation;
- Relaxed application of rules of evidence;
- Relaxed application of other civil rules;
- Less strict application of law;
- Greater expertise available;
- Easier to utilize experts at a specific time;
- Affidavits or reports can be stipulated;
- The award can be binding;[82]
- Can be used for the whole dispute or part of a dispute;
- Rather than in a public courtroom, arbitrations are conducted in a private setting;
- If permissible, the arbitrator could be a nonlawyer veterinarian, animal trainer, or behavioral specialist;
- Less impacted by the crowded court docket, where you might be bumped; and
- Difficult issues could be addressed on separate dates.[83]

Family Law Arbitration Act

Most states allow family law arbitration through statute, court rule, or case law. State laws may differ as to whether disputes may be arbitrated, which arbitration rules apply, the nature of judicial review, the subject of ongoing jurisdiction, and what role the court will play in enforcing the award.

The Uniform Law Commission Family Law Arbitration Act[84] has been developed for use by family lawyers. The act's definition of person is "an individual, estate, business or nonprofit entity, public corporation, government or governmental

82. Arbitrations are typically nonbinding on custody, visitation, and child support issues. For pet custody arbitrations, an important question is whether the arbitration should be binding. For example, should there be an exception for animal neglect, endangerment, or animal cruelty?

83. The subject of a pet custody dispute could be scheduled for one day and the subject of valuation and division of retirement benefits on another.

84. *Family Law Arbitration*, Uniform Law Commission, http://www.uniformlaws.org/Committee.aspx?title=Family%20Law%20Arbitration%20 (last visited May 12, 2016).

subdivision, agency, or instrumentality, or any other legal entity."[85] Issues of importance in the arbitration process with regard to a pet custody dispute might include

- Scope of arbitration;
- Definition of partiality or bias;
- Whether alternative law in private agreements is permissible;
- Continuing jurisdiction;
- Modification criteria, if any;[86]
- Obligation of fact finding;
- Judicial enforcement of joint custody awards;
- Judicial enforcement of pet time or access;
- Conditions for removal of an arbitrator;
- Post-decree jurisdiction of the case;
- Animal endangerment considerations;
- Factors for indicia of ownership;
- Use of best-interest criteria for humans;
- Use of best-interest criteria for animals;
- Use of best-interest criteria for all concerned;
- Use of rebuttable presumptions, such as based upon a prenuptial agreement, evidence of purchase, or evidence of possessory right;
- Which evidentiary standard applies to a rebuttable presumption;
- Exceptions to the finality of a judgment and decree based upon ADR contractual provisions;
- Finality exceptions to a binding arbitration award based upon public policy;
- Enforceability of duty to mediate before arbitration when a post-judgment companion animal conflict arises, and the scope of the issues subject to mediation;
- The effect of a liability waiver;[87]
- Endangerment and public policy exceptions to finality awards;
- Standard for judicial review;

85. This definition is of interest given that the progression of laws in the United States reflects that companion animals are moving to an interim category between property and person.

86. Of particular concern would be an inability to modify the award when there is evidence of abuse or neglect, such as lack of veterinary care for an animal with a chronic condition or evidence of dramatic weight loss.

87. An interesting question is whether both parties would release, waive, and discharge an arbitrator of liability in the arbitration agreement if this waiver was binding. If the lawyer is subject to liability, then the question arises as to whether lawyers serving as arbitrators would have coverage under typical state lawyer liability coverage policies if no exclusion is indicated.

- Whether the companion animal will be treated as personal property, a subset of personal property called living property, a new property category of living property, or in one of the evolving categories, such as an interim category or a new type of personhood; and
- The impact of an ethical violation.[88]

Vacating Arbitration Award

The grounds for vacating an arbitration or property award are narrow and generally focus on the partiality or lack of disclosure of the arbitrator; whether a failing of the underlying contract concerning arbitration made the arbitration agreement unenforceable; whether the award is compliant with the terms of the arbitration agreement, including the scope of the agreement; and whether the process conforms to statutory requirements. Because someone who is unhappy with an arbitration award may aggressively seek to vacate the award, arbitrators should run a tight ship, beginning with a well-crafted arbitration agreement.[89]

Binding Arbitration

While binding arbitration should apply to matters related to inanimate property division, the application of binding arbitration to living animals who have achieved companion animal status is problematic. For example, if one party is awarded an animal and is then deployed for two years in the military, perhaps the other party should have something akin to a right of first refusal. If there is post-decree evidence of animal cruelty by the party awarded the dog, would this behavior be grounds for modification of a binding award subject to public policy exceptions? When could a person in a role akin to a private attorney general advocate for the removal of a mistreated pet? Another question that arises is what the scope of judicial review of an arbitration award would be.

Single-Issue Arbitration

In the family law context, a single-issue arbitration on the subject of pet custody could prove useful. The conundrum for lawyers handling pet custody disputes is which standards, burdens of proof, and factors the arbitrator would consider, including from an animal welfare standpoint. Should the arbitrator utilize the rule

88. If an arbitrator violates an applicable code of ethics, a question could arise as to whether this violation would cause a valid arbitration to be set aside, and whether this violation would impact an arbitrator's statutory immunity. Thus far, it seems that there is little known about arbitrators and ethical violations, and whether the latter impacts insurance coverage.

89. If the arbitrator has a signed agreement from the parties agreeing to a departure from earlier legal precedents, this could provide the arbitrator with an effective shield if later complaints or appeals arise about partiality, bias, or the duty to follow the law.

of law or instead enforce a contract devised by the parties as to the legal standard and applicable criteria or factors stipulated? Should the arbitrator offer a comprehensive checklist as to what these criteria might be? If so, should the arbitrator offer a broad-spectrum checklist for the parties to use? An immediate challenge is what criteria, factors, presumptions, and balancing tests an arbitrator would use.

Jurisdiction and Waivers

Post-decree motions to modify the duration or amount of spousal maintenance are common. Many jurisdictions have devised new schemes, some by statute and others through case law, in order to achieve finality. The court could be divested of jurisdiction by a mutual agreement utilizing a waiver. With these extra safeguards, agreements about spousal maintenance were to be set in stone.

How might the concept of mutual waivers apply in a pet custody dispute? If the parties can agree to a mutual waiver of spousal maintenance, how many types of other mutual waivers might there be? There could be a waiver of jurisdiction or a waiver related to preclusion, such as collateral estoppel or *res judicata*. The parties might be able to waive preclusion for modification.[90] In a case involving a pet, could the parties mutually waive recourse in the court, with their only remedy being binding arbitration?[91]

Finality Requirement

It will be determined on a state-by-state basis whether arbitration awards for shared pet custody circumvent the finality requirement of a judgment and decree. Lawyers and judges differ in how they interpret the concept of finality. Courts can assent to private agreements that reach a result contrary to what the court would have ordered.[92]

In the family court context, some jurists, for public policy reasons, have failed to enter judgments based upon stipulated agreements where low-income earning spouses in long-term marriages lack adequate funds or assets or when child support obligations are too low. Find out if a statement like this resonates in your own state: "Courts favor stipulations in dissolution cases as a means of simplifying and expediting litigation, and to bring resolution to what frequently has become an acrimonious relationship between the parties."[93]

---

90. *See* Bowman v. Brooklyn Pet Hospital, 247 N.W.2d 424 (Minn. 1976).

91. How binding would the arbitration award be when public policy questions such as pet endangerment or cruelty arise? Can waivers be precluded based upon unconscionability? Is a binding arbitration agreement for living property subject to modification differently than other property awards are?

92. The answer may depend where on the continuum between property and person a companion animal is in a particular state.

93. *See* Shirk v. Shirk, 561 N.W.2d 519 (Minn. 1997).

If your state emphasizes the value of freedom of contract, it would follow that the court would be receptive to a more lenient application of the finality rule. Look at the spousal maintenance cases in your state to get a sense of how courts treat private contracts and the court's jurisdiction, including from a public policy perspective.

Perception of Case

It is important for arbitrators and attorneys to understand the people involved in the dispute and to learn whether they perceive the case as a property dispute, custody dispute, or a hybrid of both. An individual seeking the award of a companion animal may have claim to the animal but may be unsure of the strength of that claim. Is the act of paying for the animal outcome determinative, or does possession for more than six months establish possessory rights? The advocate should educate the arbitrator and other attorney about the emerging jurisprudence and make sure the arbitrator understands the scope of his or her authority for decision making.[94]

Co-Ownership Agreements

When thinking about pet custody, consider that what is permissible in family court may be different from what is permissible in the rest of the civil calendar. Outside of family court, co-ownership agreements are common when animals are acquired for a commercially useful purpose, such as a show cat or racehorse. Contracts regarding rights of co-owned animals can be very detailed and include breeding, performance, and possessory rights. Why would courts grant more rights to co-owners of agility dogs who might get into a dispute about which shows to compete in? Why would they be more deserving of the court's time than a couple who gets along but simply wants an enforceable access schedule for their pet as part of their decree? There is a double standard in how the law is applied.

Arbitration Controversy

Arbitration standards and codes of ethics were developed by the American Bar Association and the American Arbitration Association. Since the adoption of the Code of Ethics for Arbitrators in Commercial Disputes, a highly charged debate has emerged about "Islamic law, women, and the limits of pluralism in a liberal polity."[95]

94. Case law seems to interpret scope broadly.

95. Mohammad H. Fadel, *Religious Law, Family Law and Arbitration: Shari'a and Halakha in America*, Chicago-Kent Law Review, 90 Chi.-Kent L. Rev. 163 (2015).

In Ontario, Canada, arbitrators were prohibited from utilizing non-Canadian law in family law disputes.[96] According to Canadian Professor Mohammad H. Fadel, "The debates surrounding whether to permit binding family law arbitration, particularly when such arbitrations are based on religious or otherwise non-liberal legal systems, raise many important and difficult questions from the perspective of liberal political theory." He explained that this arbitration practice impacts the subjects of gender equality and religious freedom. Fadel emphasized how there could be a conflict or potential conflict between "liberalism's egalitarian commitments and its commitments to personal and associational autonomy."[97]

Private Agreements

The same difficulties that apply to this religious controversy in the arbitration context also affect pet custody dispute arbitrations. How far can the parties go in utilizing a process with a private agreement that may lead to a different result than permitted under state law? If the state law treats animals as property, and the arbitration agreement permits consideration of a broad range of factors for making a determination and also permits the arbitrator to award joint custody, co-ownership, or pet time, is the underlying arbitration agreement so at odds with the state law that the arbitration agreement could be voided based upon public policy consideration?

Is the arbitration award impacted by whether companion animals are, in some way, treated differently under the law than inanimate objects are? Would the arbitrator have more authority if the dog or horse did not qualify as a companion animal because the animal's primary purpose was commercial use? Although it seems that courts would welcome transferring pet custody disputes to an ADR process that permits binding arbitrations, the interest of the parties in doing so may be affected by how freedom of contract in private agreements is impacted by this state versus religion controversy.[98]

Drafting Arbitration Agreements

When drafting an arbitration agreement or a broader agreement, such as a premarital agreement with an arbitration clause, some principles you may want to consider include the following:

96. *Id.*
97. *Id.*
98. How the court construes private law for a religious group may also impact how the court generally construes what can be the subject of a private agreement.

- Will the validity of the underlying agreement impact the enforceability of an arbitration provision?[99]
- Is the arbitration clause in the antenuptial agreement in concert with public policy?[100] If not, is the provision of the arbitration agreement pertaining to companion animals severable?
- If an agreement is subject to binding arbitration, which arbitration rules will apply?[101]

Arbitration Acts and Common Law

Look at whether your state has adopted the Uniform Law Commission Family Law Arbitration Act or any other arbitration act. If so, learn which provisions apply or are unique to your state. If your state has not adopted any uniform act, most states do recognize and enforce some type of common law arbitration, so learn more about yours.[102]

Judicial Arbitration and Mediation Services

A useful resource to consult is the Judicial Arbitration and Mediation Services (JAMS) checklist for all arbitrators.[103] This is a well-known arbitration and mediation group that utilizes its own "Comprehensive Arbitration Rules and Procedures." The JAMS website is a good starting point if you want to use their services or utilize a well-conceived example of how the arbitration system should work.[104]

An interesting aspect of the JAMS Rules and Procedures is Rule 34, titled "Optimal Arbitration Procedures." If the parties' arbitration agreement allows for this option, in a situation where a companion animal was mistreated or harmed, it seems that the ADR process would allow for continuing jurisdiction through the mechanism of an appeal procedure. It is possible, of course, that JAMS will further refine the meaning of the Rule 34 option.[105]

---

99. Linda J. Ravdin, *Premarital Agreements: Drafting and Negotiation* (American Bar Association 2013).

100. Laura W. Morgan & Brett R. Turner, *Attacking and Defending Marital Agreements* (American Bar Association 2014).

101. Gary N. Skoloff, Richard H. Singer, Jr., & Ronald L. Brown, *Drafting Prenuptial Agreements* (Aspen Publishers 1995).

102. It might be prudent to learn if your state passed a law abolishing common law arbitrations.

103. *JAMS*, http://www.jamsadr.com/ (last visited May 12, 2016).

104. *Id.*

105. *JAMS Comprehensive Arbitration Rules & Procedures*, JAMS, http://www.jamsadr.com/rules-comprehensive-arbitration/#Rule%2016.1 (last visited May 12, 2016).

American Arbitration Association

It is wise to be conversant with the American Arbitration Association (AAA) Commercial Arbitration Rules and Mediation Procedures.[106] Under the AAA rules, an arbitrator has the authority to order discovery and issue enforcement orders. If you want a record of the proceeding, make arrangements with the AAA for a stenographic record. Under AAA rules, if the arbitrator deems it necessary, the arbitrator has the power to make an inspection or investigation; each of the parties may be present if this investigation should occur. In cases where allegations are made about one party's residence in a pet custody dispute, the flexibility wherein the arbitrator may inspect or investigate should be noted and, in the right circumstances, advocated.

The arbitrator also has the authority to nominate a special master to consider and report on an application for emergency relief. This power could be utilized in an arbitration situation when mistreatment or cruelty toward a companion animal is alleged. Notwithstanding the above, the scope of the arbitration award must be within the scope of the parties' arbitration agreement. Usually, an arbitrator is granted broad powers, including the power to make interim rulings or assess fees.

The AAA time period for modifying the award is limited, and the rules do not offer anything equivalent to the arbitrator maintaining jurisdiction. Thus, it is not known if under the AAA rules, the parties could contractually agree to utilize the same arbitrator if there is a need for future modification or the imposition of sanctions for not complying with a long-term pet time award. The AAA Commercial Arbitration Rules and Mediation Procedures currently lack structure on how an arbitration agreement would apply when problem solving involving companion animals could be long term.

Private and Public Justice

An important public policy issue that needs to be addressed is the difference between private and public justice.[107] Private justice is when "the parties take into account the costs of public justice, balanced agreement or power, personally tailored agreements, and choose what they decide to be appropriate for their own situation."[108] When there is private justice, there is no opportunity for the development of legal precedents or growth of the common law. The public has a stake in

106. *Commercial Arbitration Rules and Mediation Procedures*, American Arbitration Association, https://www.adr.org/aaa/ShowProperty?nodeId=/UCM/ADRSTG_004103 (last visited May 12, 2016).

107. Kathy M. Hessler, *Mediating Animal Law Matters*, Bepress Legal Repository, http://law.bepress.com/expresso/eps/1533/ (last visited May 12, 2016).

108. *Id.*

the resolution of questions pertaining to animals, as well as knowledge about how these disputes can be resolved.

CONCLUSION

In the future, it is foreseeable that a majority of pet custody conflicts will be addressed in ADR contexts. The dynamics of these processes are complex. At the onset, it is important for those engaging in an ADR process to know whether the best interests of the animal, both short term and long term, should be taken into account.

APPLICABLE CASE LAW

EDWARD ELEC. CO. V. AUTOMATION, INC.[109]

Year: *1992*
Category: *Arbitration*
Type of Action: *Punitive Damages*
Animal: *None*
Pet Custody Concept: *Unless the provisions of an arbitration award are dependent upon each other, if one portion of the award is vacated, the rest of the award stands.*

The parties to this action were a general contractor and a subcontractor. Pursuant to their arbitration agreement, they were required to submit their dispute to the AAA. When the parties could not agree on arbitrators, three arbitrators were selected for them in compliance with the state's AAA Construction Industry Rule. The award of the arbitration was subject to the AAA rules and the requirements of the Illinois Uniform Arbitration Act. The latter provides very limited grounds for challenging an award.

When the arbitrator awarded the subcontractor $119,633.50, the subcontractor filed a motion to confirm the arbitration award and the general contractor filed a petition to vacate it. When the trial court vacated the arbitrators' award, this matter went up on appeal.

The appellate court acknowledged its obligation to construe awards to uphold their validity. The court also said, "It is well settled that an arbitration award will not be vacated on the ground that the arbitrators misinterpreted the applicable law." This was because the arbitrators, by agreement of the parties, "become the judges of both the law and the facts" unless "a gross mistake of law or fact" appears on the "face" of the award. Even if there was an error of this nature, the court said, "a party will not be heard to complain of an error that works him no injury."

---

109. 593 N.E.2d 833, 229 Ill. App. 3d 89, 171 Ill. Dec. 13 (Ill. App. 1st Dist. 1992).

In analyzing the general contractor's complaints, the court observed that when a case involved interrelated claims and cross claims for money damages, as this matter did, the arbitrator had no duty to "show how each item of the parties' respective demands was resolved." Even with the absence of detailed findings as to how the award was determined, the court emphasized that its scope of review was still limited and should not be an "invasive review of the facts." The court perceived the general contractor's allegations of arbitrator partiality as their effort to overturn an unfavorable award.

The general contractor alleged that because the arbitrators accepted affidavits in lieu of testimony, this had the effect of denying the general contractor the due process right to cross-examination. Because of the specific arbitration rules for the construction industry, the court was not persuaded by this claim. Despite the general contractor's claim that the arbitrators exceeded their powers arising from the arbitration agreement, the court also found that the arbitrators' powers were broad enough to consider both the law and facts necessary to reach "an ultimate decision." If the parties wanted less than this, there should have been an express reservation in their arbitration agreement.

As a matter of first impression in Illinois, the issue arose as to whether the arbitrators had the power to award punitive damages against the general contractor. The court compared and contrasted prevailing punitive damage practices. Federal arbitrators have the power to award punitive damages; in contrast, for the state, only judges have the authority to award punitive damages as a sanction unless (1) the state permits arbitrators to issue sanctions, and (2) the parties agree that the arbitrator can award sanctions in their arbitration agreement.

The appellate court admitted that under the state's case law, punitive damages were not favored and should be closely scrutinized. Since the parties did not have a written agreement giving the arbitrators the power to grant punitive damages in this case, none could be granted even if, from a public policy standpoint, giving the arbitrators more freedom to fashion remedies was desirable. The court also determined that the arbitrators' determination of punitive damages, when not permitted, did not require that the entire award be vacated. To the contrary, as the punitive damages award was not dependent upon any other part of the award, the entire award was severable and the remainder of the award in favor of the subcontractor was enshrined.

Practice Pointer: If handling an arbitration case, be conversant with the arbitration laws in your state, as well as decisions under the Federal Arbitration Act. In particular, the Uniform Law Commission is in the process of promulgating a Family Law Arbitration Act, and you should be familiar with whether it passed in your state, as well as follow cases in other states that construe its provisions. It seems that courts give a lot of power to the written arbitration agreement and that the standards for due process in the arbitration context are quite relaxed. Make sure your client knows this. If your state permits punitive damages clauses by arbitrators and the parties stipulate that an arbitrator can award punitive damages, then perhaps an arbitrator could award punitive damages resulting from lack of compliance with joint custody or a pet visitation schedule.

Flexible Mfg. Systems Pty. Ltd. v. Super Products Corp.[110]

Year: *1996*
Category: *Arbitration*
Type of Action: *Breach of Contract*
Animal: *None*
Pet Custody Concept: *The court is reluctant to set aside an arbitration award based upon mere errors of fact or law and might impose sanctions if the appeal of an arbitration award appears frivolous.*

The parties to this suit had a licensing agreement pertaining to the manufacture of vacuum loading equipment. The agreement required that any dispute between the licensor and licensee be resolved through the Commercial Arbitration Association. The district court entered an order to compel arbitration pursuant to the terms of the licensing agreement. More specifically, the district court required arbitration before the AAA because "there is no entity known as the Commercial Arbitration Association."

The arbitration panel heard testimony and counterclaims regarding each party's claims of breach of contract. Following the arbitration award, the appellant sought to vacate the award and the court observed that both the Federal Arbitration Act and the Wisconsin Arbitration Act listed very limited and specific grounds upon which an arbitration award could be vacated. For example, an arbitration award could not be overturned for mere errors of law or fact. The standard is more one of either "perverse misconstruction or positive misconduct."

The court then reviewed how arbitration principles have been addressed in four U.S. Supreme Court decisions: (1) *Allied-Bruce Terminix Companies, Inc. v. Dobson,*[111] (2) *Mastrobuono v. Shearson Lehman Hutton, Inc.,*[112] (3) *First Options of Chicago, Inc. v. Kaplan,*[113] and (4) *Vimar Seguros y Reaseguros, S.A. v. M/V Sky Reefer.*[114] The prevailing themes of these opinions were as follows:

- Bona fide agreements to arbitrate must be respected.
- When selecting a choice of law, the choice pertains to substance, not procedural law.[115]

110. 86 F.3d 96 (C.A. 7 (Wis.) 1996).
111. 513 U.S. 265, 115 S. Ct. 834, 130 L. Ed. 2d 753 (1995).
112. 514 U.S. 52, 115 S. Ct. 1212, 131 L. Ed. 2d 76 (1995).
113. 514 U.S. 938, 115 S. Ct. 1920, 131 L. Ed. 2d 985 (1995).
114. 515 U.S. 528, 115 S. Ct. 2322, 132 L. Ed. 2d 462 (1995).
115. The choice of New York law does not mean that the procedural rule in New York forbidding arbitrators from awarding punitive damages applies.

- Unless the duty to arbitrate is clear from the agreement, the court determines the arbitrability issue.
- When the scope of the arbitration is unclear, any doubts are resolved in favor of a broader arbitration scope.
- If a state's arbitration law is not favorable to arbitrability, the Federal Arbitration Act should be used pursuant to the U.S. Commerce Clause.
- Disagreements about the law used by the arbitrator could be considered at the enforcement stage.

The court then turned its attention to arbitration awards in the state. Awards are only to be overturned on narrow grounds, including,

> (1) the award was procured by corruption, fraud, or undue means; (2) there was evident partiality or corruption in the arbitrator(s); (3) the arbitrators were guilty of certain kinds of procedural misconduct; and (4) "the arbitrators exceeded their powers, or so imperfectly executed them that a mutual, final, and definite award" was not made.

In the instant case, the appellant did not present clear and convincing evidence sufficient to overcome the validity of the arbitration award; awards are not vacated because of "mere errors of judgment as to law or fact." Deliberately disregarding the law could serve as grounds for vacating an award.[116] The court of appeals also upheld the lower court's imposition of sanctions against the appellant for a frivolous appeal.

Practice Pointer: As pet law is far from settled, which arbitration awards are mere errors of judgment as to law or fact compared to a deliberate disregard of the law may be a subject on the front lines. The best practice is to have an arbitration agreement crafted to give the arbitrator the authority, for example, to have the best interests of the companion animal be the prevailing decision-making criteria. In federal court, damages sanctions are available under Fed. R. App. P 27 and 38. Be aware that if you appeal a disappointing arbitration award on behalf of a client, the client should be forewarned if sanctions are possible. The pendulum seems to be swinging in favor of awarding sanctions against parties who frivolously appeal arbitration awards.

---

116. *See* Eljer Mfg. Inc. v. Kowin Development Corp., 14 F.3d 1250, 1255 (7th Cir.), *cert. denied*, 512 U.S. 1205, 114 S. Ct. 2675, 129 L. Ed. 2d 810 (1994) (interpreting the Federal Arbitration Act's counterpart to WIS. STAT. § 788.10(1)(d)).

In re Marriage of Bereznak and Heminger[117]

Year: *2003*
Category: *Arbitration*
Type of Action: *Void as to Public Policy*
Animal: *None*
Pet Custody Concept: *Child support is not delegable even when arbitration agreements on this subject are involved.*

Following their divorce, two parties continued to have disputes about child support. They returned to court, and one aspect of the forthcoming court order was that the parties agreed to binding arbitration on future child support modification issues.

When a dispute came before the arbitrator, an award was issued on the subject of child support arrearages and on the subject of the appellant's earning capacity. When the appellant wanted the arbitrator to reconsider and modify her award by letter, the appellant also sought to initiate a second arbitration with the same arbitrator on the subject of his change of income.

When this matter came before the court of appeals, the appellant's "principal contention" was that submitting issues to an arbitrator on child support was void as against public policy. As the appellant did not seek independent review of the arbitration award by the appellate court, the court's role in reviewing the arbitration award itself was limited.

The court observed that the appellant was trying to game the system and essentially get two bites of the apple. Requiring that the appellant pay the costs of appeal "in the interests of justice," the court of appeals agreed with the appellant that arbitration awards concerning child support were void as against public policy. The case was remanded to the trial court.

Practice Pointer: It is likely that public policy issues will arise in cases referred to binding arbitration. One party may assert that companion animals are no longer "just" property, or are in an interim category between property and person, and are protected by a variety of state laws in ways that property is not. If companion animal classifications change, delegation to arbitrators on certain topics may be impacted. If credible evidence was presented on the subject of pet endangerment, public policy issues would be even more compelling.

117. 2 Cal. Rptr. 3d 351, 110 Cal. App. 4th 1062 (Cal. App. 2003).

VUE V. VUE[118]

Year: *2006*
Category: *Arbitration*
Type of Action: *Public Policy*
Animal: *None*
Pet Custody Concept: *An arbitration award will not be vacated when the parties entered into a written arbitration agreement that the arbitration process would be governed by Hmong tradition and culture rather than the state statute.*

The parties to a divorce agreed to bifurcate their action. While agreeing to dissolve their marriage and to the division of automobiles and retirement accounts, the subjects of custody, child support, and the division of other property would be addressed pursuant to an arbitration agreement where seven Hmong elders would serve as arbitrators. The award would be subject to the provisions of the state statute.

Pursuant to state statute, the court could vacate an award when there was (1) corruption, fraud, or other undue means; (2) evident partiality, corruption, or prejudicing misconduct; (3) a decision beyond the scope of the arbitrators' powers; (4) a refusal to postpone the hearing upon sufficient cause being shown or refusal to hear evidence material to the controversy, or the hearing was contrary to a state arbitration statute, thereby prejudicing a party; or (5) timely objection to the lack of an arbitration agreement. An arbitration award will not be set aside because the court prefers a different decision on the merits.

When the court approved the arbitrators' award, the appellant sought to vacate it. She alleged that the arbitrators were not impartial and also claimed that the arbitration agreement itself was void, as it violated public policy because it was based upon Hmong culture and traditions and not the state law.

The court of appeals reiterated the following guiding arbitration principles:

- Arbitration proceedings are favored in the law.
- Unless there are express terms limiting an arbitrator's authority, the arbitrator is the final judge on matters of law and fact.
- The arbitrator interprets the terms of the arbitration agreement.
- Reasons to vacate an award include fraud, mistake in applying the arbitrator's own theory, misconduct, or other disregard of duty, as well as pursuant to limited public policy exceptions.[119]

118. No. A05-728 (MN 2/7/2006) (Minn. 2006).

119. *See* City of Minneapolis v. Police Officers' Fed'n, 566 N.W.2d 83, 89 (Minn. App. 1997). On the subject of a public policy exception to arbitrators' powers, the court of appeals said,

> No court will lend its aid to one who founds a cause of action upon an immoral or illegal act, and is further justified by the observation that the public's interests in confining the scope of private agreements to which it is not a party will go unrepresented unless the judiciary takes account of those interests when it considers whether to enforce such agreements.

Nothing in this doctrine restricted utilizing an arbitration panel that reflected Hmong culture and traditions.

Next, the court addressed arbitration basics from a procedural due process aspect, saying that awards are subject to limited review, an award's finality and validity is presumed, and the award challenger has the burden of proof.[120]

Observing that both parties were represented by legal counsel when the arbitration agreement was executed and that no evidence was presented on appeal as to how the arbitration agreement violated public policy, the arbitration agreement was upheld. Notwithstanding the appellant's complaints about due process and the failure of the arbitrators to comply with the state statute, the arbitration agreement itself permitted that Hmong traditions and accepted practices could be used to modify or nullify the consideration of evidence and testimony. More specifically, the court said, "Arbitration, by its very nature, frequently and necessarily entails that the parties forfeit certain rights normally afforded to them in state court."

Another complaint made by the appellant was that even though there were six hearings, during one of them, there were five rather than seven arbitrators. The court interpreted the concept of "conduct the hearing" to mean "manage or control the hearing."

Practice Pointer: This case suggests that there can be a departure from the traditional rule of law when the parties agree to another method in their arbitration agreement that explicitly waives other rights. Given disputes arising since this decision about the use of Sharia law in private agreements, the subject of how much leeway the parties will be permitted in private agreements should be considered.

IN THE INTEREST OF T.B., A CHILD[121]

Year: *2009*
Category: *Arbitration*
Type of Action: *Verbal Arbitration Agreement*
Animal: *None*
Pet Custody Concept: *Unless there is an exception on the subject of the best interests of the child, arbitration awards are binding and enforceable.*

Even though the parties entered into a mediated settlement agreement related to a parent-child relationship, there were issues as to how to interpret and enforce the agreement. Instead of returning to mediation to solve this problem, the parties verbally agreed to arbitration. According to the court, "No written guidelines or instructions were provided to the arbitrator."

120. The court reiterated the statutory provision in MINN. STAT. § 572.19, subd. 1, which addresses corruption, fraud, partiality, arbitrators exceeding their powers, failure to provide fair hearing processes, and lack of arbitration agreement.
121. 2009 WL 891882 (Tex. App. San Antonio).

At the conclusion of arbitration, the arbitrator signed a handwritten document that addressed conservatorship issues related to the child, as well as the division of assets. Neither party signed the document. The entry of an order based upon this award was delayed for two years. On appeal, it was asserted that the court's order (1) conflicted with the valid and enforceable mediated settlement agreement, (2) exceeded the scope of the arbitration agreement, (3) exceeded the arbitration award, and (4) was derived from an invalid mediation settlement "wrongfully characterized as an arbitration award." The appellant's rationale for the last assertion was that "the agreed arbitration developed into a mediation and that the document entitled 'Arbitration' is, in effect, a mediated settlement agreement" that was unenforceable as not signed by the parties.

The appellant's complaints about the arbitration process included that (1) sessions were informal, (2) there was "little" examination of witnesses, (3) documents were not submitted for review and records were not kept, and (4) the process was not done by agreement. The appellant did not contemporaneously complain about the absence of a written arbitration agreement.

With regard to the standard of review for an arbitration award, the court emphasized that the scope of review was "extraordinarily narrow," the validity of the arbitration award was presumed, an award would be upheld even if there was a mistake of law or fact, and the trial court could not substitute its authority for that of the arbitrator when the court made a determination that the arbitrator's judgment was in the best interests of the child. Based upon the above principles, governed by the state's arbitration act and the family code, the appellate court determined that the aspect of the court order based upon the arbitration award was valid. Neither party had failed to timely object to its terms; the aspect of the court order that modified the arbitration award constituted an abuse of discretion. The matter was remanded to the trial court for further provisions consistent with its opinion.

Practice Pointer: Always use well-drafted arbitration agreements, and, to the extent that any issues have already been resolved in mediation, make those areas of settlement clear in a written document. If an arbitrator has made an error, such as failed to address an issue, bring this to the arbitrator's attention in a timely way. With regard to the subject of best-interest standards in your state, it is the court, not the arbitrator, who has final say on child matters. Perhaps this standard will evolve to apply when companion animals are involved, too.

The presenting difficulty in a companion animal arbitration is under what circumstances the arbitrator might not have had final say. One method would be to have the arbitrator be the fact finder, based upon narrow terms of the arbitration agreement, while the trial court would have the decision-making authority and could utilize a variety of stipulated factors in rendering its decision. Another option is to have the arbitrator make a decision based upon the presumptions or factors the parties agree to. Extending the logic of this case, you might assert that, absent a determination that the arbitration award was not in the best interests of the companion animal because of mistreatment or cruelty, or other public policy criteria, the arbitration award is enforceable.

In re Mabray[122]

Year: *2010*
Category: *Arbitration*
Type of Action: *Writ of Mandamus*
Animal: *None*
Pet Custody Concept: *Private cooperative alternative dispute resolution agreements are valid and do not conflict with a state's collaborative law statute.*

When divorce was inevitable following a 35-year marriage where infidelity was involved, the parties entered into a four-page "Cooperative Law Dispute Resolution Agreement." According to the terms of their agreement, if the case was not settled by a particular date, the matter would proceed by binding arbitration. When settlement was not achieved by the deadline, the trial court said that "the cooperative law process ceased by its own terms."

After the appellant substituted counsel, as there was need to substitute the first arbitrator based upon a conflict of interest, a new arbitration order was signed pursuant to a signed agreement of the parties. The appellant then petitioned for a writ of mandamus, asked to have her husband's lawyer disqualified on public policy grounds, and also sought to revoke her consent to arbitration. She claimed her former lawyer had coerced her into signing the arbitration agreement when she was both emotionally distraught and "under the influence of tranquilizers." She asserted that the "Cooperative Agreement" was an effort to "contract around" the state's "Collaborative Law" statute, a statute that would have had the effect of disqualifying her husband's attorney from continuing to represent him. She alleged that her husband had also not participated in the "Cooperative Law" aspect of their dispute in that he had concealed assets. The trial court found that the parties had "eschewed formal, sworn discovery" in their cooperative law agreement and had entered into a private cooperative law agreement, and that neither violated the collaborative law statute nor public policy.

The court of appeals addressed the subject of standard of review for a writ of mandamus. The court conceded that when a trial court improperly denies a motion to disqualify opposing counsel, there would be no adequate remedy by appeal and mandamus relief would be appropriate; mandamus review was appropriate when the issue was whether an order could compel arbitration because of the important substantive and procedural rights involved. The court's consideration of a writ of mandamus must be distinguished from whether the appellant could prevail, as the parameters of this type of writ are narrow and the process is controlled by equitable principles.[123] Furthermore, to succeed, the appellant needed to prove that the arbitrator clearly abused the arbitrator's discretion.

On the subject of a cooperative law agreement, the court first considered the fact that for collaborative law, the "presence of a disqualification agreement is widely held to be the minimum qualification." Even so, the court recognized that in some

122. 355 S.W.3d 16 (2010).
123. *See* Rivercenter Assocs. v. Rivera, 858 S.W.2d 366, 367 (Tex. 1993).

jurisdictions, collaborative lawyers could enter into a collaborative law agreement where they could continue as the lawyer in any alternative dispute resolution process, including arbitration. Texas was not one of those jurisdictions.

The court characterized cooperative law as having many of the "hallmarks" of collaborative law without the requirement of a lawyer's disqualification. More specifically, the court described cooperative law as "A written agreement to make full, voluntary disclosure of all financial information, avoid formal discovery procedures, utilize joint rather than unilateral appraisals, and use interest-based negotiation." The court observed that to the best of its knowledge, cooperative law had been neither codified nor prohibited. In considering the subject of whether any argument could be made that the collaborative law statute was controlling, the court pointed out that "the collaborative law statute is elective, not mandatory."

The court specifically found that cooperative law was not prohibited by the state's collaborative law statute and that a Colorado Bar Association Ethics Committee had determined the cooperative process "passes ethical muster while collaborative law does not." An advantage to the competing processes was that "cooperative law clients are less likely to feel mired in the cooperative process because they need not hire and educate new lawyers should litigation ensue." Even so, the court could see how the cooperative law had a less compelling problem-solving atmosphere than collaborative law had.

The court pointed out that the state legislature encourages four processes: arbitration, mediation, collaborative law, and informal settlement conferences but does not make any of them exclusive. The legislature had not limited or constricted how informal settlement conferences would be conducted but instead gave broad approval of other approaches. Finding no reason to determine that the legislature meant to prohibit parties from entering into cooperative law agreements, the appellate court overruled the appellant's first point of error.

The next subject the court considered in the second point of error was whether the appellant could revoke her consent to arbitrate based upon the following claims: (1) the agreement violated public policy, (2) the opposing lawyer's dishonesty in the cooperative law process breached and invalidated their agreement, (3) she lacked the mental capacity to enter into the agreement and/or it was "obtained fraudulently," and (4) she properly revoked her consent. When the court reviewed the underlying agreement of the parties, which had four sections, the court said that it was reasonable to treat the detailed arbitration section as an independent agreement; the court emphasized that the state public policy favored the freedom to contract.

The court discussed how both collaborative law and cooperative law have no good mechanisms for preventing the disclosure of privileged information to the opposing counsel or party in what the court characterized as a "four-way" meeting. While the collaborative process disqualifies an attorney from acting as counsel if the attorney may have had access to privileged information, if the process proved unsuccessful, nothing prevented the opposing party from imparting confidential information to new litigation counsel.

Based upon the above rationale, the court determined that the appellant had failed to prove that her husband continuing with the same legal counsel had the effect of violating public policy. The court was unimpressed by the appellant's claim that her husband failed to act honestly and thereby breached the cooperative law agreement. Not only did the court not find the argument to be what the court dismissively called a "gateway matter," but also it found that this issue was one to be determined by the arbitrator. Although the court appreciated the appellant's claims that she lacked mental capacity and that her husband committing fraud were also "gateway matters," the trial court found these claims not to be meritorious.

While the appellant asserted that a party can withdraw consent to a Rule 11 settlement agreement prior to judgment, the court found the appellant to be misinformed, saying, "This rule only allows parties to revoke their consent to the entry of an agreed judgment, not the process that could lead to such a judgment." Accordingly, Rule 11 did not apply. The court observed that the appellant had not attempted to revoke her consent to arbitrate until a court had signed an order at the behest of both parties. With regard to the doctrine of laches, the court said, "Delay alone will not constitute laches; injury or prejudice must also be established." The appeals court made a factual determination that the doctrine of laches did not apply. The court of appeals held that the parties' cooperative law agreement was valid, the provision in the cooperative law agreement to retain counsel if the process was unsuccessful did not violate public policy, and the issue of whether the other party breached the terms of the agreement was a decision for the arbitrator.

There was a forceful dissent in this case wherein the court extolled on the virtues of collaborative law and went into detail about the benefits of the collaborative law process. The court said that a "full and candid exchange of information between the parties and their attorneys" was necessary to properly evaluate the case, court intervention was suspended while the parties used collaborative law procedures wherein jointly agreed experts could be hired, all counsel would withdraw if the dispute could not be settled in the collaborative law procedure, and where other provisions could be agreed to by the parties "consistent with a good faith effort to collaboratively settle the matter." The dissent reiterated how a party is entitled to judgment on a collaborative law agreement if the agreement "(1) provides, in a prominently displayed statement that is boldfaced, capitalized, or underlined, that the agreement is not subject to revocation; and (2) is signed by each party to the agreement and the attorney of each party."

In the instant case, the dissent characterized the central issue as when "the public policy of the State of Texas permits marriages to be dissolved pursuant to private 'cooperative law' agreements, unauthorized by statute, whose provisions track and conflict with the provisions of Texas's collaborative law statute." The dissent described cooperative law as an illegal contract contrary to public policy, particularly on the subject of lawyer disqualification. The dissent also emphasized why the cooperative law agreement was similar to the collaborative law statute, saying that the former "expressly contravene[s] its protections while taking advantage of its benefits."

Explaining how attorneys have unique roles when representing clients in contexts where there is to be a full and candid exchange of information, and that they are expected to produce information that otherwise might be protected by attorney-client privilege, the dissenter further addressed his public policy concerns, saying, "The different roles of the attorney representing parties in settlement negotiations based on 'full and candid' disclosure of information and of the attorney representing his client in court set up the potential for a conflict of interest or waiver of the client's privilege."

The dissenter was also concerned that a binding agreement for arbitration should not be made in advance of settlement negotiations, consistent with the approach in collaborative law, and that the cooperative approach lacked the safeguards of having a case set for trial if an agreement was not reached. He complained that the cooperative agreement "intentionally avoids the provisions for court supervision of settlement negotiations and denies recourse to the courts to a party to the Agreement if the other party fails to participate in the negotiations in good faith." He emphasized that the two types of agreements differed with regard to how a trial court would be put on notice that an agreement had been reached, as required by Rule 11.

Practice Pointer: This decision should be on your recommended reading list, as it focuses on public policy and how cooperative law agreements and collaborative law agreements might be attacked. Although in this case, the public policy dispute had nothing to do with companion animals, it illustrates how public policy arguments can be made.

RACHAL V. REITZ[124]

Year: *2011*
Category: *Arbitration*
Type of Action: *Application of Arbitration Principle to Trust Beneficiary*
Animal: *None*
Pet Custody Concept: *When a settlor attaches arbitration conditions to an inter vivos trust, this condition is binding on beneficiaries who are not signatories to an arbitration agreement, as otherwise the doctrine of direct benefits estoppel would apply to them.*

This matter came on before the court following an interlocutory appeal regarding a binding arbitration provision in an inter vivos trust. A divided court of appeals found that this trust provision was an unenforceable contract, in part because there was no consideration, and in part because there was no contractual obligation to arbitrate. The dissenting court of appeals justice stated that under the Texas Arbitration Act, a trust could be a written agreement to arbitrate even without the signature of beneficiaries or successor trustees.

When this matter came on before the Texas Supreme Court, the question was whether an arbitration provision under the Texas Arbitration Act in an inter vivos trust would be enforceable against trust beneficiaries. The threshold question was whether there was a binding arbitration agreement. To reach this determination, the court determined that it must ascertain statutory legislative intent. The principles the court preferred were as follows:

124. 403 S.W.3d 840 (Tex. 2013).

- Utilize the plain meaning of a statute, if possible.
- Determine legislative intent for the entire act.
- The Texas Arbitration Act only requires an agreement to arbitrate a future dispute.
- Trusts should be enforced consistent with the settlor's intent.
- The express language of a trust is revelatory about a settlor's intent.
- The term "agreement" is not a synonym for the word "contract."
- Not every agreement is a contract.
- An agreement must be supported by mutual assent.
- Mutual assent does not require the formality of a signed contract.
- The doctrine of direct benefits estoppel is a type of equitable estoppel.[125]
- Mutual assent can be established by behaviors.

In the instant case, the Texas Supreme Court said that in *In re Kellogg Brown & Root, Inc.*,[126] the court had already established that when a nonsignatory to a contract seeks the contract benefits, or to enforce the contract, that party is estopped from attempting to avoid the burdens of the contract, including the duty to arbitrate contractual disputes. The court then considered whether the direct benefits estoppel doctrine would apply to a trust arbitration provision. In this case, the beneficiary of the trust claimed the successor trustee had breached fiduciary duties. Holding that the doctrine of direct benefits estoppel applied to the beneficiary's claim that the trust was invalid, the court emphasized how the doctrines of direct benefits estoppel and promissory estoppel "promote[d] fairness by holding a party to its position in the performance of an agreement or in bringing litigation."

On the subject of whether the dispute was within the scope of the arbitration agreement, the court said all doubts should be resolved as to the agreement's scope "in favor of arbitration." The court determined that the arbitration agreement covered the claims at issue, reversed the judgment of the court of appeals, and remanded the case to the trial court for the issuance of a continuing order.

Practice Pointer: Like the *Marvin v. Marvin*[127] decision, this case is a good example of how the court may employ equitable doctrines to achieve what the court regards as a fair result. Learn everything you can about how your state utilizes equitable principles.

---

125. There are at least six theories in contract and agency law that may bind nonsignatories to arbitration agreements: incorporation by reference, assumption, agency, alter ego, equitable estoppel, and third-party beneficiary. *See In re* Kellogg Brown & Root, Inc., 166 S.W.3d 732, 739 (Tex. 2005).

126. 166 S.W.3d 732, 739 (Tex. 2005).

127. 176 Cal. Rptr. 555, 122 Cal. App. 3d 871 (Cal. App. 2d Dist. 1981).

Hanson v. Belveal[128]

Year: *2012*
Category: *Family Law*
Type of Action: *Material Change*
Animal: *Dog, Cat*
Pet Custody Concept: *Once custody has been established, the court need not set aside the award based upon one party's relocation, as this is not a material change.*

Although this case is about a family court's decision about relocation affecting children, imagine that the same problems could arise following a pet custody agreement. The state supreme court determined that notwithstanding express language in the underlying divorce decree, a mother's relocation with her children to another state was not by itself a material change in circumstances sufficient to enable the father to seek a child custody modification. Even though the district court had the authority to modify a divorce decree where there was a material change in circumstances, the parties could not substitute an agreement for the court's independent evaluation of facts determining whether a material change in circumstances occurred.

The court explained that the parties' underlying agreement was invalid, as previous jurisprudence opposed a "purely speculative" outcome "without consideration of the surrounding facts." An "anticipatory conclusion" did not constitute a material change. In reaching this decision, the court stated that it recognized the constitutional right of a parent to travel or relocate and that the constitutional concern of relocation by itself was not evidence of a material change.

Emphasizing the importance of proving an "independent" change in circumstances, the court said it lacked subject matter jurisdiction for a modification, as the court would not uphold a jurisdictional waiver or consent to subject matter jurisdiction when that jurisdiction would not otherwise exist. The court distinguished the standard for modification in cases, where one parent had physical custody of the children from joint physical custody cases, wherein a lesser modification standard was permitted.

One of the more tangential allegations made by the father was that "the district court erred in not finding a material change of circumstances" because the mother kept two dogs and a cat even though one of the children had allergies to pets and used an allergy medication. The district court, though not considering the mother's hearsay statement about an allergist's opinion, said she could have the pets as long as the child was not "unduly exposed" to the cat. The claim about the pet allergy was insufficient in helping the father meet his burden of proof that a material change had occurred. The court described the father's case as a "generalized attack on Mother's judgment and quality as a parent."

When reading this case, one could imagine that similar problems could arise if there was a relocation following the award of an animal by an arbitrator. Would the concept of binding arbitration cause this topic to come back on before an arbitrator? As this case illustrated, courts are good at establishing doctrines to control the floodgate problem. Be resourceful in helping the court craft new doctrines.

128. 2012 WY 98, 280 P.3d 1186 (Wyo. 2012).

Practice Pointer: Because of the limits of statutes and case law with regard to cases with animal subjects, be resourceful in making a claim. Consider that there is a cultural shift from talking only about companion animals as property to perceiving of them as only property and family members at the same time. A concept such as an "independent" change in circumstances might apply to your pet custody dispute. Consider what modification standards should apply if one of the parties to a joint pet custody agreement moves.

In re Marriage of Golden and Friedman[129]

Year: *2012*
Category: *Arbitration*
Type of Action: *Injunction*
Animal: *None*
Pet Custody Concept: *Once parties agree to arbitration, courts are likely to broadly construe this duty.*

Pursuant to the terms of a divorce decree, the petitioner would be the primary residential custodian within the context of a detailed joint parenting agreement. The parenting schedule was later amended to give the petitioner sole physical custody and for the parties to primarily utilize a parenting coordinator to facilitate nonemergency communications. The amendments to the parenting time schedule included (1) the utilization of "our family wizard" for communications between the parties, and (2) that each party would have the right of first refusal regarding "parenting time that the other parent was willing to relinquish." The agreement contained an arbitration provision saying, "The matters of camp, medical decisions and the regular parenting time schedule are the only matters which shall be arbitrated."

When the petitioner forfeited a significant amount of her parenting time that became available to the respondent under his right of first refusal, the respondent complained that the petitioner's absence placed a burden on him of having extensive additional time with his children. If the petitioner, as the sole custodial parent, was not making the children's welfare her first priority, the respondent alleged that her lack of regularity was "not good for our children."

While the respondent sought arbitration pursuant to the terms of the arbitration agreement, the petitioner asserted that a motion for arbitration required specificity and that the respondent's desire to discuss the regular parenting schedule did not fall within the scope of their arbitration agreement. From the petitioner's point of view, if the respondent wanted a specific proposed change, he should have proposed it. It was also her position that if she agreed to the change, there would be no need for arbitration. The trial court not only denied the respondent's request for arbitration but also imposed a three-stage protocol that would be applied to future modification requests: (1) set forth the issue to be arbitrated and the resolution of the issue sought; (2) the other party shall respond to the statement of the issue within 14 days; and (3) if the parties cannot agree within 14 days, the parties shall arbitrate the issue.

129. 974 N.E.2d 927, 363 Ill. Dec. 130, 2012 Ill. App (2d) 120513 (2012).

Because the impact of an order compelling arbitration is the grant of injunctive relief, it is permissible for a party to appeal "an order of the trial court 'granting, modifying, refusing, dissolving, or refusing to dissolve or modify an injunction.'" The court of appeals disagreed with the trial court that only a specific disagreement, or an arbitration controversy, would trigger the duty to arbitrate, as the arbitration clause was broad. In contrast, the subject of the scope of an arbitration agreement should be resolved by the arbitrator. While the petitioner asserted that her duty to arbitrate was conditional, the appellate court saw no legal authority to support a "narrow concept of controversy or dispute."

As the Illinois statute lacked clarity on the definition of an arbitration controversy, the court looked to case law to better evaluate where the grounds for arbitration would be. They concluded the grounds would be (1) a dispute or honest difference of opinion regarding a subject in which both parties were interested or (2) less than a legal cause of action. The court declined to impose exceptions, limitations, and conditions on the arbitration statute.

When the court reviewed the history of conflict between the parties, it observed that the petitioner was well aware that the continuation of her conduct wherein she forfeited substantial time with the children was of concern. Accordingly, the petitioner's denial that there was no clearly defined conflict was not credible. The court determined that as the parties had a dispute related to the regular parenting time schedule, the conflict fell within the subject matter of the arbitration clause. The trial court's order denying arbitration was reversed, and the matter was remanded to the trial court for future processes consistent with enforcement of the arbitration agreement.

Practice Pointer: This is the type of case that one could foresee coming up in a pet custody dispute if the settlement agreement contained an arbitration clause and one of the parties wanted to get out of using it. As courts seem to respect written arbitration agreements, be sure to address which future disputes are not subject to arbitration, as otherwise courts give agreements to arbitrate broad construction.

PRESTON V. DYER[130]

Year: *2012*
Category: *Arbitration*
Type of Action: *Scope of Arbitration Clause*
Animal: *None*
Pet Custody Concept: *In interpreting a premarital contract with an arbitration agreement, if one of the parties seeks an outcome that is contrary to public policy, the court may withhold an arbitrator's broad power to award attorney's fees.*

Before they married and had a child, the parties entered into a premarital agreement subject to the Texas Arbitration Act. The parties were granted 50/50 custody under the time-sharing provisions of a Kentucky order. As required by their premarital

130. 2012 WL 5960193 (Tex. App. 2012).

agreement, the parties participated in an arbitration process pursuant to the Texas Arbitration Act. Although the arbitration award was not timely, objections as to limitations made after an award were treated as a waiver.

The appellant contended that the arbitration award exceeded the scope of the arbitrator's authority and that aspects of the award were contrary to express terms in the executed premarital agreement. He asserted that the premarital agreement gave the arbitrator no authority to award spousal maintenance and that the arbitration award of attorney's fees exceeded the permissible terms of the underlying agreement. He further asserted that because his child support obligation was contractual, his obligation to pay child support was not enforceable by a contempt action.

Dissatisfied with the arbitrator's rulings, the appellant filed his appeal. The guiding principle for the standard of review on appeal is whether the arbitration award exceeds the arbitrator's authority, as set forth in the controlling arbitration clause. If the award exceeds this authority, then the award is void. Judicial review is narrow absent a written agreement for expanded judicial review, which was not applicable here. The issue before the court of appeals was whether the arbitrator's decision exceeded the scope of the parties' agreement to arbitrate.

Because the question of the scope of arbitration is a contract question, this is a question reviewed by the court de novo. When interpreting an arbitration agreement, the court looks at either express terms or the necessary implications of those express terms. All doubts about the scope of the arbitrator's powers are resolved in favor of arbitration.

The appellant specifically complained that the arbitrator had required him to pay the appellee $25,000 in attorney's fees even though the underlying agreement restricted the payment of attorney's fees to specific circumstances. Notwithstanding this limitation in the agreement, the court of appeals approved the arbitrator's authority to award attorney's fees under the Texas Arbitration Act and referenced state laws allowing for this type of recourse on a claim for child support and for recovery upon a breach of contract. The court concluded that the arbitrator's award of fees was authorized under the law.

Practice Pointer: This case illustrates that when a premarital agreement is unfair or overreaches, and the matter is subject to arbitration, unless the parties expressly limit the arbitrator's powers or broaden the scope of judicial review to cover subjects such as reversible errors, the arbitration award is likely to be withheld. It was surprising that even though the arbitration award restricted the issuance of attorney's fees, the court seemed comfortable with the arbitrator broadly using statutes, including the state's arbitration act, to justify an award of attorney's fees. The court gave the arbitrator powers beyond the scope of the written arbitration agreement, presumptively on public policy grounds.

This case will be of interest to a lawyer handling a pet custody dispute because it is a good example of how arbitrators, just like the courts, will do what they can to achieve justice when it seems a bad actor is involved. Thus, if your client believes he or she will win based upon the terms of a premarital agreement and even a tightly crafted arbitration agreement, there is always a risk that if your client is involved in unfair dealing, an unexpected award may be on the horizon. Although agreeing to binding arbitration may have curb appeal, inform your client that if he or she is unhappy with the arbitration award, it will be difficult to challenge it.

Chang v. Siu[131]

Year: *2014*
Category: *Arbitration*
Type of Action: *Community Property*
Animal: *None*
Pet Custody Concept: *If a pre-arbitration agreement is clear, the court will give it great weight if the arbitration award is later disputed.*

In Arizona, the judiciary is organized as follows: (1) the superior court, with 180 judges, (2) the court of appeals, with Division I from Phoenix and Division II from Tucson, and (3) the supreme court. This information is necessary to understand the parties' dispute.

The parties were married for about ten years when the wife filed a petition for dissolution of marriage. The appellant had made security deposits into a new brokerage account that contained community property funds. The parties later disputed whether this brokerage account could now be characterized as community property. They entered into a binding arbitration agreement with a retired superior court judge, and pursuant to the parties' arbitration agreement, the arbitrator was to hold hearings and require the production of evidence, rule on the admissibility of evidence, examine witnesses, utilize the state's rules of evidence, make an award based upon submitted issues, provide findings of fact and conclusions of law on disputed issues, and issue a binding arbitration award order. In addition to the above, pursuant to the arbitration agreement, each party preserved his or her right to appeal the award to the court of appeals and specifically not the superior court.

Following a nine-day hearing, the arbitrator issued a 34-page ruling. Finding all of the brokerage accounts were community property, the arbitrator divided the brokerage accounts evenly. After the arbitration award, the husband brought a motion before the arbitrator seeking to "amend" or "correct" characterizations of the disputed accounts as community property. The wife sought enforcement of the award through the superior court, and a judgment and decree was entered that incorporated the arbitrator's findings and conclusions.

The court of appeals considered the merits of arbitration processes, including that arbitration is a favored means to resolve controversy, is an inexpensive dispute resolution method, and allows for speedier dispositions. The question before the court of appeals was whether, by agreement, the parties could "avoid the procedural and substantive limitations our statutes and common law impose on the review of a private arbitration award." This meant, in effect, could the parties affect the scope of the court's review by their agreement?

An unusual aspect of the case was that when the superior court confirmed the arbitration award, the husband made no appeal to the superior court. The court said, "In fact, he did not ask the Superior Court to rule on any of the legal and factual issues he raises on appeal." While recognizing that the appellate court would not normally address arguments unless raised in the superior court, the court could do so when

131. 234 Ariz. 442, 323 P.3d 725, 685 Ariz. Adv. Rep. 18 (Ariz. App. 2014).

there "is no question of notice and the issue is a matter of law." The court then clarified the difference between the concepts of waiver and jurisdiction. The appellate court's jurisdiction arose not from the parties' agreement, but from the superior court's final order and judgment.

The court reviewed a decision under the Federal Arbitration Act in *Hall Street Associates, L.L.C. v. Mattel, Inc.*[132] There, the court was not persuaded by the husband's contention that by contract, the scope of review could be expanded beyond what the statute provided. Even so, it did not address whether an arbitration governed by state law could have a more expansive judicial review. From there, the court considered the revision to the Uniform Arbitration Act in 2000, which was adopted in Arizona. Under this uniform law, the court emphasized that the state of Arizona chose not to adopt a provision that would have permitted judicial review if there was an error of law or fact.[133]

Ultimately, the court appreciated that "arbitration is a creature of contract law" and should be understood within the principles of contract law. The key concept with regard to that interpretation of a contract was the parties' intent. Because the parties had agreed to binding arbitration, which is subject to very limited review by the court, it did not follow that a right to appeal meant a review on the merits. In this case, where the parties made an express reference to an arbitration act, which provided for narrow judicial review, it was illogical to assert that the parties had agreed to substantive judicial review.

The court then reviewed the grant of the arbitrator's authority in the parties' joint pre-arbitration statement. This statement asked that the arbitrator determine if the brokerage sub-accounts had been "commingled to an extent that transmutes Husband's sole and separate funds into community property." Because this joint pre-arbitration statement demonstrated that the arbitration award was "squarely within the arbitrator's authority," the superior court confirmed the arbitration award and the decree of dissolution was upheld.

Although this case did not address the subject of commingling an asset to the extent that the commingling "transmuted" sole and separate assets into community property, the concept is worthy of exploration in a pet custody dispute. Although here, "commingling" applied to putting together nonmarital money or funds with community property, it is irrational that the same concept cannot apply to the transformative aspect of a solely owned pet becoming a marital or a community pet. Consider these words of William Wordsworth:

> Say, when the "moving" creatures saw
> All kinds commingled without fear,
> Prevailed a like indulgent law
> For the still growths that prosper here?
>   Did wanton fawn and kid forbear
>   The half-blown rose, the lily spare?

We, too, could conceptualize a more indulgent law.

---

132. 552 U.S. 576 (2008).

133. The husband preferred that the court apply the case law from California and Texas, where substantial appellate review was broader.

Practice Pointer: This is another case that suggests that an arbitration award will be upheld as long as the award is consistent with the arbitrator's authority. Thus, the authority given to the arbitrator becomes outcome determinative.

Gossman v. Gossman[134]

Year: *2014*
Category: *Family Law*
Type of Action: *Jurisdiction*
Animal: *None*
Pet Custody Concept: *When parties waive the jurisdiction of the court, they cannot contractually reclaim the jurisdiction of the court.*

Although not about pets and not about ADR processes, this case represents a cautionary tale in many respects, including on the subjects of private contracts, jurisdiction, and waivers, and is therefore included in this chapter. If the parties to a private pet custody agreement decide what jurisdiction a court will retain, including in an ADR process, their written agreement is not necessarily binding on the court.

In *Gossman*, the husband agreed to pay his wife the sum of $5,000 per month in spousal maintenance for five years, utilizing a provision wherein the court was divested of jurisdiction following the entry of the judgment and decree. The parties entered into a few post-decree stipulations from which post-decree orders were issued. Later, the party who was due the spousal maintenance sought to revoke the modification orders based upon her claim that subsequent orders to modify spousal maintenance were void and unenforceable because the district court lacked the jurisdiction to modify the original maintenance award.

Because this case involved the question of both jurisdiction and statutory interpretation, the court applied the de novo standard. The former husband argued that he and his former wife could enter into a subsequent agreement to modify the maintenance award by a mutual agreement, as other agreements could.

After considering extensive legislative history and relevant case law, the court of appeals determined that the waiver was a "matter of jurisdiction, not a matter of contract." When the waiver was incorporated into the judgment and decree, there was a transformative effect and there was no longer "simply an agreement between the parties." The court stated,

> After a district court issues a final judgment and decree that divests the district court of jurisdiction over the issue of maintenance, that issue is not subject to modification merely because the parties subsequently enter into another agreement that seeks to modify the original maintenance award. Both before and after *Karon,* the Supreme Court has stated that parties may not confer jurisdiction upon a district court by stipulation or agreement.

134. 847 N.W.2d 718 (Minn. App. 2014).

Simply put, the parties could not, "by mutual agreement, restore the jurisdiction that the district court itself has relinquished."

The district court described the cases relied upon by the husband as "concerned only with private contracts between parties; they say nothing about a district court's assertion or divestiture of jurisdiction over a case or issue." The court stated,

> Mr. Gossman also cites cases holding that parties to an arbitration agreement may, by mutual agreement or waiver, litigate a dispute in a district court despite their prior agreement to arbitrate the dispute. But these cases also are not on point, for essentially the same reason. In each case, the district court was not party to the arbitration agreement and never issued an order that divested itself of jurisdiction over the matter governed by the arbitration agreement.

Practice Pointer: This case is here to remind you that once the court's jurisdiction is waived, it is unknown whether you can ever get it back. Thus, if a party wants to modify a binding arbitration award of joint custody based upon a pet endangerment claim because of a dangerous dog in one party's household, the party may not be able to have the matter heard before the court again.

TENASKA ENERGY, INC. V. PONDEROSA PINE ENERGY, LLC[135]

Year: *2014*
Category: *Arbitration*
Type of Action: *Arbitration Partiality*
Animal: *None*
Pet Custody Concept: *When an arbitrator fails to disclose facts that would cause a reasonable person to have the impression of partiality, the fact of partiality will require the vacating of an arbitration award.*

This case involved the sale of one party's interests to a power plant. The executed purchase agreement contained a broad arbitration clause. The clause required arbitration under the rules of the AAA but did not require an AAA arbitrator. According to the AAA Commercial Arbitration Rules,

> Any person appointed or to be appointed as an arbitrator shall disclose . . . any circumstance likely to give rise to justifiable doubt as to the arbitrator's impartiality or independence, including any bias or any financial or personal interest in the result of the arbitration or any past or present relationship with the parties or their representatives. Such obligation shall remain in effect throughout the arbitration.

135. 437 S.W.3d 518 (Tex. 2014).

In the instant case, although one of the arbitrators, Samuel Stern, had disclosed that he had served as an arbitrator for the law firm of Nixon Peabody three times, and had an outsourcing deal with LexSite, the extent of his business relationship with Nixon Peabody was hidden. Stern was still involved in active negotiations with Nixon Peabody when the opposing parties in the arbitration had alternately proposed either a $125-million or $1.25-million settlement figure. Stern was one of two arbitrators on a divided panel that awarded the Nixon Peabody client the better $125-million settlement.[136]

When this award favoring Nixon Peabody's client was challenged, the trial court determined that arbitrator Stern had not disclosed

> that his contact[s] with Nixon Peabody were all with Mr. Penski or Ms. Boland, failed to disclose additional meetings or contacts regarding LexSite with Ponderosa[ ]'s counsel, failed to disclose the true extent of his ties to LexSite and his activities for LexSite, and allowed Ponderosa[ ]'s counsel to modify his disclosures in a way that minimized the contact. . . . Stern's disclosures were intentionally incomplete and inaccurate.

The court of appeals reversed the trial court's determination and found that Stern's partial disclosure of his business ties with Nixon Peabody was sufficient to put the other party on notice.

When this matter went up to the Texas Supreme Court, the high court looked to the express language of the FAA governing the vacating of arbitration awards when there is evident partiality. The Texas Supreme Court looked to the U.S. Supreme Court decision in *Commonwealth Coatings Corp. v. Continental Casualty Co.*,[137] a case where an arbitrator failed to disclose $12,000 in business from the prime contractor over four to five years, but not in the past year. In *Commonwealth*, because the arbitrator had failed to disclose his relationship with the prime contractor, the arbitration award was set aside even though there was no evidence of bias. The U.S. Supreme Court found that "even the slightest pecuniary interest in an arbitration could be grounds to set aside the award." Ultimately, the Texas Supreme Court said, "When we examine this undisclosed information together against what Stern actually disclosed, we conclude the information is not trivial and might have conveyed an impression of Stern's partiality . . . to a reasonable person."

Revisiting its earlier holdings, the court also said that evident partiality was established from nondisclosure itself, regardless of the arbitrator's intent or proof of actual bias. While recognizing that its full disclosure requirement might lead to the vacating of some awards, and that the losing party might seize on every undisclosed detail as a material omission, the supreme court thought the better view was to require full disclosure by the arbitrator. The court also emphasized that it was unimpressed by the

136. While this matter was pending, Nixon Peabody changed how it was compensated for its services. Rather than billing clients at their hourly rate, the firm would receive 15 percent of the first $50 million of an award and 12.5 percent of any amount over $50 million.

137. 393 U.S. 145, 147, 89 S. Ct. 337, 21 L. Ed. 2d 301 (1968).

argument that a party waives a partiality challenge by "proceeding to arbitration based upon information it was unaware of at that time." If the court were to pursue that line of reasoning, the court would place a premium on concealment. The supreme court reversed the judgment of the court of appeals and reinstated the trial court's order, an order that vacated the arbitration award and required a new arbitrator.

Practice Pointer: In this case, the partiality had to do with the arbitrator's financial interest. In a pet custody dispute, it is possible that this subject could arise based upon partiality toward, or away from, a property analysis regarding the companion animal. The subject of what constitutes partiality, as well as bias, is important in pet custody disputes. A well-crafted arbitration agreement may help.

Chapter 4

Estate Planning, Wills, and Trusts

"Happiness is a warm puppy."

—*Charles Schulz*

The passage of pet trust laws in all 50 states has served as an important indicator for courts of a cultural shift about the status of animals. Where once, an animal as property could not be a beneficiary of a trust, now, an exception under the law has been made for the family pet.

ESTATE PLANNING FOR ANIMALS

Estate planning for animals is particularly important for aging animal owners, animal owners with health problems, people who own animals that may outlive them, and animal owners who want the peace of mind that comes from having a plan in place. After all, if a client cares enough to pay for pet custody legal services, that client would likely value the importance of estate planning for pets.[1] Having a pet trust in place when contemplating flexible ownership, custody, and access means that monies are already in place should challenging circumstances arise, including an owner or co-owner's disability, incapacity, or death.

Companion animal estate planning took root more quickly than pet custody laws did and reflects animal welfare values. The traditional main instruments of estate planning include wills, trusts, health care directives, and durable powers of attorney, all of which will be discussed below. Although estate planning for companion animals is a well-developed area, from a statutory standpoint, there

1. While probate laws protect children upon the death of their parents, there is no law to protect pets.

are significant differences between states as to the types and effectiveness of the instruments used.

Important aspects of estate planning for companion animals include estimating the animal's life expectancy; identifying suitable executors, caregivers, and trustees; and calculating sufficient veterinary and homeowner's insurance to include animals when ascertaining their reasonable living expenses. The idea is that funds will be dedicated so that the animal's lifelong needs will be met upon the animal owner's incapacitation or death.[2] Proper estate planning assures that the animal "property" is transferred to the designated person or trust at the right time for the animal's protection. There is a growing national trend for states to have look-back provisions to invade trusts according to certain parameters, so be up to date on your state's practices.

Euthanasia

Without estate planning by an owner, a companion animal's future could be in jeopardy. According to the American Society for the Prevention of Cruelty to Animals (ASPCA), only 17 percent of pet owners safeguard their pets' future; three to four million animals are euthanized each year.[3] Euthanasia rates for companion animals following an owner becoming disabled or deceased are between 12 and 27 percent.[4] The ASPCA estimates that every year, more than 100,000 animals enter shelters following the death or incapacity of their owner.[5]

Oral Communications

Before delving further into the basics of estate planning, a good place to begin is to have your client inform others of his or her individual goals, ideas, and intentions. Oral communications have the effect of reinforcing compliance with your client's written instruments. More specifically, explain this to your client in plain language, such as, "Be sure, Jessica, to tell Robert that you want your twin sister to get your cat."

---

2. A power of attorney for an animal owner should include a provision that authorizes the use of funds for the care of his or her companion animals.

3. Jacoba Urist, *Superstorm Showed Need for Estate Planning for Pets*, Today, http://www.today.com/money/superstorm-showed-need-estate-planning-pets-1C7000569?franchiseSlug=todaymoneymain (last visited May 12, 2016).

4. Gerry W. Beyer, *Pet Animals: What Happens When Their Humans Die?*, Michigan State University Animal Legal & Historical Center, https://www.animallaw.info/article/wills-trusts-pet-animals-what-happens-when-their-humans-die?goback=.gde_77136_member_97694611 (last visited May 12, 2016).

5. Of 7.6 million companion animals that enter animal shelters annually, 2.7 million are euthanized. *Pet Statistics*, ASPCA, http://www.aspca.org/about-us/faq/pet-statistics (last visited May 12, 2016). Twenty-five percent of euthanized dogs in shelters are purebred; 60 percent of dogs in shelters are euthanized. Seventy percent of cats at shelters are euthanized. Twenty-five percent of cats and dogs are adopted from shelters. *Animal Shelter Statistics*, Statistic Brain, http://www.statisticbrain.com/animal-shelter-statistics/ (last visited May 12, 2016).

WILLS

For estate planning purposes, lawyers are usually most familiar with the creation of a will. A will has a testator and one or more beneficiaries. A beneficiary must be a natural person or a legal entity. Because animals as property cannot own property, dispositions to animals are not enforceable; a companion animal has no standing to enforce a bequest. Wills are public documents that may be subject to probate.

Lawyers often discourage clients from using bequests under wills for companion animal estate planning purposes because of their unenforceability. For example, if a testator leaves his or her cat and $10,000 to his or her sister, the sister has no obligation to use the money for the cat's care. If the sister becomes inconvenienced by the cat and drops the animal off at a public access shelter, the sister would still be able to keep the $10,000.

A seminal case that influenced the development of uniform estate planning laws was *In Re Estate of Russell*,[6] where Thelma Russell left half of her estate to a man and the other half to her dog in her will. The court determined that an animal could not be the beneficiary of a will and did not award anything to the dog. The court also determined that the man had no enforceable duty to the dog. Even though bequests under wills are not the best way to protect the future of pets, lawyers may still utilize them when it is believed that the person named to receive the bequest for the animal will respect that intent.

TRUSTS

All 50 states, as well as the District of Columbia, have enacted one of several versions of pet trust laws.[7] Although there are variations between states about trust provisions, most reflect or are derivative from uniform laws. The best-known types of trusts are traditional trusts, honorary trusts, conditional trusts, and, more recently, pet trusts.

Traditional Trusts

In a traditional trust, three parties are involved: a settlor/trustor/grantor, a trustee, and a beneficiary. Fiduciary, equitable, and enforceable property interests are advanced. Traditional trusts are private documents not subject to probate; they

6. 70 Cal. Rptr. 561, 69 Cal. 2d 200, 444 P.2d 353 (Cal. 1968).

7. Following the death of attorney Vicki McIntyre, attorney Barbara J. Gislason and veterinarian Steven Barghusen spearheaded efforts to secure passage of a Pet Trust Bill in Minnesota in concert with the Minnesota State Bar Association Probate and Trust Law Section. The Pet Trust Bill passed and was signed by Minnesota Governor Mark Dayton on May 22, 2016.

can be effective even while the person is still alive. The beneficiary should be a person, not property, even if the property is a companion animal considered to be a family member. If an animal is named as a beneficiary of a traditional trust, the trust may be deemed void.[8]

Honorary Trusts

Honorary trusts are rooted in the American Law Institute Restatement of Trusts (First), (Second), and (Third). A trustee of an honorary trust may apply property to a designated purpose. In common law, honorary trusts for the benefit of an animal, though valid, are not enforceable. Like traditional trusts, honorary trusts are subject to the Rule Against Perpetuities (RAP).[9]

Conditional Trusts

A conditional trust is the best alternative to a pet trust. The settlor leaves the companion animal and monies to a trustee, and the settlor names a caretaker as a beneficiary, conditioned upon the caretaker providing for the companion animal in accordance with the terms of the trust. If the caretaker does not perform these duties, the trustee may replace the caretaker with an alternate caretaker specified in the trust. If the trustee does not provide the funds as required, the caretaker has standing to enforce the trust.[10] The human beneficiary avoids the problem of the animal beneficiary having no standing to enforce the trust and the RAP, which can link the duration of the trust to the life of the caretaker. A successor or alternate trustee and caretaker need to be named, and the trustee cannot be the same person as the caretaker.[11] An inter vivos trust should include a residual clause.

Uniform Probate Code

In 1990, the National Conference of Commissioners on Uniform State Laws (NCCUSL), now known as the Uniform Law Commission (ULC), adopted a provision of the Uniform Probate Code (UPC) that provides for "enforceable trusts for the care of a designated domestic animal and the animal's offspring."[12] UPC section

8. Traditional trusts are subject to the Rule Against Perpetuities (RAP), which says that "no interest is good unless it must vest, if at all, not later than twenty-one years after some life in being at the creation of the interest." Vicki M. McIntyre, *Estate Planning for Companion Animals*, William Mitchell College of Law Animal Law Class, April 9, 2009.

9. *Id.*

10. *Id.*

11. *Id.*

12. *Pet Trusts: Caring for a Pet that Outlives Its Owner*, American Veterinary Medical Association, https://www.avma.org/Advocacy/StateAndLocal/Pages/sr-pet-trusts.aspx (last visited May 12, 2016).

2-907 was enacted in 1990 and amended in 1993. For states that have adopted UPC section 2-907, a trust for a companion animal is valid and the RAP is eliminated.

Uniform Trust Code

While some states have enacted UPC section 2-907, others utilize Uniform Trust Code (UTC) section 408; others fashion a hybrid of both. The main idea of a pet trust is that the testator leaves money in the trust for the animal beneficiary, and a trust protector makes sure the trustee enforces the trustee's obligation to ensure that the caregiver is paid only if the animal is still living and properly cared for.

UTC section 408, which permits the creation of trusts for the benefit of companion animals with animal beneficiaries, was implemented in 2000. An important aspect of UTC section 408 is, "A person having an interest in the welfare of the animal may request the court to appoint a person to enforce the trust or to remove a person appointed."[13] Accordingly, third parties can be appointed as enforcers to assist the trustee in fulfilling his or her obligations.

Uniform Statutory Rule Against Perpetuities

Learn if the law in your state has adopted the Uniform Statutory Rule Against Perpetuities (USRAP).[14] The ULC enacted the USRAP in 1986 and amended it in 1990. It supersedes the common law RAP; under the USRAP, the interest either vests or terminates within 90 years after the creation of the interest.[15] Although the RAP should not impact estate planning for most companion animals, it could impact long-living companion animals such as horses and birds.

Pet Trust Basics

A pet trust should be drafted so that at the time of the testator's death, the testator's living animals are encompassed in the instrument. Pet trusts may be testamentary trusts (created under a will), or inter vivos trusts (created while the settlor is alive). Inter vivos pet trusts have the advantage of allowing a pet to be cared for while the owner is still alive but unable to care for the animal. Inter vivos pet trusts do not go through probate, so money is immediately available for the animal's care. It is good practice not to overfund a trust; assets should be put in the trust that reasonably relate to the pet's expenses and life expectancy.

Pet trusts should include the following:

13. *Model Laws, Pet Trust*, ANIMAL LAW RESOURCE CENTER, http://www.animallaw.com/PetTrust.htm (last visited May 12, 2016).

14. The purpose of the USRAP is to prevent legal instruments from establishing future interests that do not vest within a proscribed time, thereby preventing a "dead hand" from controlling property interests.

15. McIntyre, *supra* note 8.

- The animal or animals named as the beneficiary (after naming the pet beneficiary, some attorneys add a statement that the trust is to cover all other pets that might be owned at the time of the pet owner's death. In this way, new pet trusts do not have to be drafted every time a new pet is acquired),
- A detailed description of the beneficiary,
- The beneficiary's microchip number,
- A caregiver appointed with authority to make animal care decisions,
- A trustee named and duties listed, including the task of caregiver payment,
- A trust protector named, and
- Remainder clause about disposition of funds upon termination of the trust.

Leona Helmsley Pet Trust

A pet trust story that garnered significant media attention was when hotel tycoon Leona Helmsley left $12 million in a pet trust for her Maltese dog named Trouble, a dog known for enjoying a lavish lifestyle.[16] The court reduced the monies in this trust from $12 million to $2 million. There was public outrage about this pet trust, as well as death threats against the Maltese; Trouble's monthly expenses included a security detail. The dog achieved such notoriety that Trouble's death in 2010 was reported in the *New York Times*.[17]

The balance of the $12 million was poured over to a Helmsley trust for charitable purposes that was not distributed consistent with the trustor's intent.[18] The lawyer who drafted the Helmsley trust failed to reconcile her mission statement with later contradictory verbiage, which had the effect of negating the enforceability of the mission statement. According to the *New York Times*, her mission statement said that her entire trust, valued between $5 and $8 billion, would be applied to the care and welfare of dogs.[19] The trustees petitioned the court to be able to use discretion and succeeded. News stories have reported that Helmsley trustees did not give Helmsley's money to the dogs.[20]

---

16. *See* Matter of Helmsley, 31 Misc. 3d1233(A).
17. Cara Buckley, *Cosseted Life and Secret End of a Millionaire Maltese: Leona Helmsley's Millionaire Dog, Trouble, Is Dead*, NY Times, http://mobile.nytimes.com/2011/06/10/nyregion/leona-helmsleys-millionaire-dog-trouble-is-dead.html (last visited Oct. 10, 2016).
18. *Id.*
19. Stephanie Strom, *Helmsley Left Dogs Billions in Her Will: Leona Helmsley's Fortune May Go to Benefit Dogs*, NY Times, http://mobile.nytimes.com/2008/07/02/us/02gift.html (last visited Oct. 10, 2016).
20. Nathan Guttman, *Where Does Leona Helmsley's Money Go? Hint: Not to the Dogs*, Forward, http://forward.com/news/israel/212349/where-does-leona-helmsley-s-money-go-hint-not/ (last visited Oct. 10, 2016).

ESTATE PLANNING CASE

The estate planning case of *Mittasch v. Reviczky*[21] reflects legal resourcefulness, notwithstanding the result. It is offered to demonstrate the many ways that solving legal issues in the pet law context may manifest. Although unreported, this case involved a lawyer who advanced a novel argument. Two Rottweilers, Stella Blue and Tazzy, were in a home with their owner when a police officer opened the screen door, causing the dogs to get loose. While the officer sought to arrest the dogs' owner, Stella Blue "nipped" the officer. A disposal order was later issued for Stella Blue, who was taken, quarantined, and held by the local municipality.

Although the owner requested a hearing to appeal the disposal order, a hearing was not scheduled until more than six months had passed, while Stella Blue remained at the pound. While the hearing was pending, the owner created a companion animal trust for the benefit of Stella Blue and Tazzy. The owner named the plaintiff, who was president of the Lexus Project, Inc.,[22] as the trustee; the general counsel of the Lexus Project, Inc. was named as the trust protector. The trust was funded with $100 in cash property, and the dogs were named as beneficiaries. The trustee's duties included the right to determine if it would be in the best interests of the beneficiaries to place them in an adoptive home, the right to defend or prosecute claims or causes of action on behalf of the beneficiaries, and the authorization to use funds from the trust to protect and defend the dogs if an action arose that could jeopardize the dogs' lives or freedom.

At the time of the trust's creation, Stella Blue was impounded and Tazzy was living with a third party. The trustee initiated a lawsuit against a variety of governmental officers, animal control officers, and employees. The plaintiff alleged a variety of constitutional violations and sought to declare a statute invalid because it was overbroad, vague, and unconstitutional on its face because the dogs were "deprived from the trust." The trustee also sought the return of Stella Blue and an injunction against the state to prevent a hearing.

The defendants asserted that the plaintiff lacked standing under Rule 12 of the Federal Rules of Civil Procedure. This was the sole issue addressed by the federal district court. When a Rule 12(b)(1) motion to dismiss was initiated, the plaintiff was obligated to affirmatively and plausibly demonstrate standing to sue based upon the conditions precedent of injury-in-fact, causation, and redressability. The court looked to the adequacy of the trust's property interests. Aware that property interests are constitutionally protected, the court said, "[T]hey are created

21. 2013 WL 2948344, not reported in F. Supp. 2d (2013).

22. The Lexus Project is a 501(c)(3) organization that is now known as the Lexus Project, Legal Defense for All Breeds, http://www.thelexusproject.org/ (last visited Oct. 10, 2016).

and their dimensions are defined by existing rules or understandings that stem from an independent source such as state law."

The court found that the trustee did not own the trust beneficiaries, the beneficiaries were equitable owners of the trust property that was subject to enforcement by a trust protector, the trustee's claim of possessory interest in the beneficiaries was diminished by the fact that the trustee never had possession of the beneficiaries, and the trustee, who never had possession of the dogs or attempted to take possession of Tazzy, did not qualify as a "keeper" of the dogs under constitutional law.

Further determining that the trust had not expended money for the care of the dogs, but merely complained about the costs of care for the impounded dog, the court said that since the trustee was never the owner or keeper of the dogs, the trustee had no obligation to pay these costs. The court complained that the plaintiff trustee had "never even laid eyes on the dogs" and never sought to exercise dominion or control over them. Without this exercise, a possessory interest was without merit; the court relied on *Andrus v. Allard*.[23]

The court said that an individual is a keeper of a dog, for liability purposes, "where the plaintiff had sole possession of dog, allowed it to live at his residence, fed and sheltered the dog, and accepted full responsibility for its care."[24] Explaining that the powers granted to the trustee were not powers that created "a possessory interest to create standing," the court focused on how the trustee was not expected to care for the dogs, did not find a caretaker for the dogs, and did not appoint a guardian for the dogs. The court summed up its position by saying, "In short, nothing in the Trust requires the Plaintiff to do anything that would actually entail taking possession of the dogs."

The court was not persuaded by the assertion that the trustee had a property interest in the dogs, as demonstrated by the right of the trustee to put the dogs up for adoption. As the trustee was not the guardian of the dogs and lacked the duty as a trustee to care for them or take custody of them, the court said it was "doubtful that the Trust vests her with a right to place the dogs for adoption."

Of particular interest is that the court seemed comfortable applying the state's Uniform Guardianship and Protective Proceedings Act to the situation of the dog beneficiaries. It seemed that but for defects in the trustee's powers and the trustee's failure to actively seek a possessory interest, the trustee might have been granted standing. The court concluded, "Standing is not a matter of the parties'

---

23. 444 U.S. 51, 65 N. 21, 100 S. Ct. 318, 62 L. Ed. 2d 210 (1979).
24. *See* Murphy v. Buonato, 42 Conn. App. 239, 244, 679 A.2d 411 (1996).

intent, and it does not arise by *ipse dixit*." Thus, the federal court lacked jurisdiction when a party had no "legally cognizable injury."[25]

The *Mittasch* court very carefully examined the New York pet trust statute that passed in 1996. It determined that unlike statutes that expressly permitted both testamentary and inter vivos trusts, the New York statute was premised upon the presumption that the grantor would be dead upon the termination of the trust. It was also emphasized that the court would not construe a statute to abolish a common law right unless there was clear legislative intent.[26] Looking at the legislative history of the New York pet trust law, including the Sponsor's Memorandum attached to the bill, the court surmised that the legislative interest specific to the care of the animal meant following the owner's death.

After searching the case law on the subject of inter vivos trusts, the court selected *Feger v. Warwick Animal Shelter*,[27] which addressed whether the identity of a person adopting a pet could be revealed to a putative prior owner. The *Mittasch* court interpreted this decision as banning inter vivos trusts, at least when the owner was not incapacitated.[28]

In conclusion, the *Mittasch* court determined that the New York statute did not permit an inter vivos trust for the care of animals, and because the trust was not a recognizable legal entity, the trustee lacked standing to initiate this claim. This case signals that in some states, there may be litigation over the enforceability of inter vivos trusts.

DURABLE POWERS OF ATTORNEY

Another type of estate planning instrument is a durable power of attorney, where a companion animal owner can authorize an agent to make payments for the care of an animal, including veterinary care, during the owner's absence or incapacity.

25. Still focused on the subject of standing, the court explored whether the applicable trust was valid under New York law. Under common law, trusts for animals are not valid as they cannot be enforced based upon the RAP. An early distinction described was that the trust empowered, but did not require, care for the animal because property could only be left to a human, together with a request for pet care. The court also reviewed the history of New York's common laws on testamentary trusts. One of the concerns the court had in the past about this subject was that the measuring life was the life of the animal, not the life of the human, thereby violating this rule.

26. *See* Ellington Constr. Corp. v. Zoning Bd. of Appeals, 77 N.Y.2d 114, 123, 564 N.Y.S.2d 1001, 566 N.E.2d 128 (1990).

27. 59 A.D.3d 68, 870 N.Y.S.2d 124 (N.Y. App. Div. 2008).

28. Given the prominence of chimpanzee habeas corpus cases in New York in 2013, the year that this decision was issued, it was interesting that the *Mittasch* court said,

> In *In re Fouts*, 176 Misc.2d 521, 677 N.Y.S.2d 699 (N.Y.Sur.Ct.1998), the New York Surrogate's Court in Nassau County considered a petition to transfer the situs of an *inter vivos* trust, which was created under EPTL § 7-6.1 to provide for the care of five chimpanzees. Although that case involved an *inter vivos* animal trust, the Court did not address whether the statute authorizes such a trust, because the issue was not raised.

An agent can also facilitate arrangements for the owner to have access to the companion animal if the owner must go to a care facility that does not allow animals. A durable power of attorney remains in effect through the owner's incapacity but terminates upon the owner's death. Special limited durable powers of attorney can be authorized for one purpose, such as veterinary care for the animal while the owner is away or on vacation.[29]

COMPANION ANIMAL CARE THROUGH VETERINARY COLLEGE

Another option for estate planning for a companion animal is through a care facility or veterinary college. Some facilities will pledge to care for a companion animal for the animal's lifetime in exchange for a fee, which is sometimes quite substantial. Some veterinary colleges allow owners to set up endowed scholarships, where the student receiving the scholarship will care for the companion animal. If your client is leaving his or her animal to an institution, he or she should give the institution his or her specific views on what will make the animal healthy and happy. For example, it is important to identify the animal's veterinarian, preferred brand of food, favorite treats, and details about activities the animal enjoys. Share information about the animal's sensitivities or fears. Be sure to do due diligence if an institution or nonprofit is involved. Make sure the entity is sound and likely to still exist at the end of the beneficiaries' lives.

LOVED FOR LIFE PROGRAM

Another estate planning option for companion animals is a program called Loved for Life, offered in Minnesota through the Animal Humane Society.[30] This program provides wallet cards and tags for pets so that people are aware that the pet is a part of the program. Once an owner becomes incapacitated or passes away, the person in possession of the animal contacts Loved for Life and the group will pick up the pet. Upon arrival, the pet is examined by the Animal Humane Society staff veterinarians and behavior experts and receives medical care and vaccinations. Animals in this program are quickly placed and will be cared for in a vetted foster

---

29. Those with powers of attorney should be conversant with the Federal Fair Housing Act and the Americans with Disabilities Act.

30. *Loved for Life*, Animal Humane Society, http://www.animalhumanesociety.org/donate/loved-life (last visited May 12, 2016).

care home until a permanent home can be found. The animals in this program are reported to spend little or no time in the Society's shelter.[31]

CONCLUSION

All animal owners should be proactive about having a plan in place in case of an accident, illness, disease, or death. Information and records about each animal should be kept in a safe place where it can be easily found. A good checklist includes the following:

- The location of the pet trust instrument;
- The animal's name, date of birth, and physical description;
- The animal's microchip information;
- The animal's photograph;
- A description of the animal's daily routine, including meals, exercise, medications, and so on;
- A description of anything the animal enjoys or dislikes;
- A description of the animal's special needs and fears and how to address them;
- Contact information for family, friends, and neighbors;
- Contact information for the animal's veterinarian and emergency clinic;
- The animal's vaccination history; and
- A detailed plan in case of a disaster, including alternative caregivers and their contact information.

Pet trusts are the best estate planning instrument, as they are the most reliable way for an owner to create a plan for the care of his or her companion animal after a disability or death. Even so, there is a place for specified facilities, programs, durable powers of attorney, and wills, too. In a pet custody dispute, an estate planning discussion should be considered.

31. The Loved for Life program offers a Legacy Circle, where members have an opportunity to fill out a pet profile to guide the Animal Humane Society staff in finding an ideal placement for his or her pet, as well as write a letter to the new caregiver to be given to the pet's new family. The Animal Humane Society staff uses a one-on-one counseling process to screen potential adopters using information from the pet profile and also follows up after the adoption to ensure the placement is working well. The adoptive family has access to Animal Humane Society behavior experts throughout the pet's lifetime for assistance with issues that may arise.

Chapter 5

Contract Law and the Uniform Commercial Code

"The assumption that animals are without rights and the illusion that our treatment of them has no moral significance is a positively outrageous example of Western crudity and barbarity. Universal compassion is the only guarantee of morality."

—*Schopenhauer*

In this chapter, we will discuss many of the finer points of how contract law and the Uniform Commercial Code (UCC),[1] as well as state business laws and equitable maxims, impact companion animal commercial transactions. We will begin with some basic concepts. Significant case law will also be reviewed.

CONTRACT CONCEPTS

In order for a contract to occur, there is the requisite offer and acceptance with consideration, which could include a promise for a promise. Contracts cannot involve minor parties; they do not actually form if one of the parties lacks the capacity to enter into the contract or if the contract was formed under duress or the signor was subject to undue influence. Other applicable concepts include

1. The United Nations has a Convention on Contracts for the International Sale of Goods (CISG).

mutual mistake, fraud and misrepresentation, unconscionability, supervening illegality, and frustration of purpose.

Statute of Frauds

There is an expectation that contracts will be entered into with an implied covenant of good faith and represent a fair deal.[2] When contracts are not in writing, they are more vulnerable to attack, such as under the statute of frauds. Advancing part performance as a formation argument may be effective. In *Andersen v. Koss*,[3] the court addressed the effort of a Skye Terrier breeder to regain possession of a dog. After the other party paid the dog's transit costs and sent the breeder $500, the breeder sought to force a co-ownership agreement upon the buyer in possession, asserting that their oral contract was subject to the statute of frauds. The purchaser prevailed as the court emphasized the part performance aspect of this transaction.

Another important case where the court explored the contours of part performance was *Scruggs v. Caba*.[4] When a woman asserted co-ownership of a Poodle, the court found that she failed to meet her burden of proof to establish part performance.

Contracts that are subject to the statute of frauds in family law include prenuptial and marital agreements. Another type of contract that could be subject to the statute of frauds is one where a party offers to pay the bill of another, such as a legal bill.[5]

Equitable Principles

It is well known that the laws of 49 of our 50 states stem from English common law. Equitable principles pertinent to contractual legal disputes have jurisprudential roots traceable to the rule of Henry VII in England, who reigned from 1485 to 1509. The judicial powers of chancellors were recognized when Sir Thomas More was a chancellor under Henry VIII. By the 17th century, English jurist John Selden said, "Equity is a roguish thing. For law we have a measure, know what to trust to; equity is according to the conscience of him that is chancellor, and as that is larger or narrower, so is equity."[6] Equitable principles impact how fair-minded

2. See the order addressing the good faith and fair deal covenant in the appendix.
3. 527 N.E.2d 1098, 173 Ill. App. 3d 872 (Ill. App. 1st Dist. 1988).
4. 2007 WL 866068 (Conn. Super.).
5. A contract may not be enforceable if there is a mistake or misrepresentation, as reflected in Rule 60 of the Rules of Civil Procedure, as well as in state common laws.
6. *Equity Definition*, Duhaime's Law Dictionary, http://www.duhaime.org/LegalDictionary/E/Equity.aspx (last visited May 12, 2016).

people perceive a dispute should be resolved;[7] they may be applied by the court in contract disputes.

Equitable principles reflect, if not advance, the ideas of laches, waiver, equitable trust, unjust enrichment, judicial estoppel, unconscionability, res judicata, license estoppel, promissory estoppel, equitable estoppel (also known as estoppel in pais), changed conditions or frustration of purpose doctrine, not slumbering on rights, not sitting on the breach, and estoppel by acquiescence and silence. Quantum meruit for services rendered is a type of unjust enrichment claim.[8] One who seeks equity must do equity, and equity will not assist a volunteer. Equitable remedies may not be applicable when there is a bona fide purchaser. Equity will not suffer a wrong to be without a remedy. Perhaps as a reflection of these equitable ideas, courts emphasize contract flexibility and elasticity.

One who comes into the court of equity must come with clean hands. The law will prevail when equities are equal. Equity will not compel an imperfect gift and will not allow a statute to be used as a cloak for fraud. The first in order shall prevail unless equities are equal. Make it your habit to collect equitable maxims.

Whether we are conscious of the application of these equitable principles in the current day, they permeate our beliefs about fairness and justice and, to a certain degree, form the spine of the rule of law, to the extent that it has a moral center. When applying equitable doctrines, it is possible to get a bit tangled in their applications. For example, courts differ as to whether there can be an equitable defense to a common law claim, or when the equitable defense can only be paired with an equitable claim. Equitable arguments have a moral or public policy component in that unconscionability is abhorred. When the court has the power to exercise discretion, equitable principles may affect that exercise.

REPLEVIN ACTIONS

Equitable relief may be obtained in pet ownership disputes through replevin actions[9] that result in temporary or permanent injunctions that can be preventative, as in a cat cannot be removed from New Jersey, or mandatory, as in a dog should be delivered by high noon. The latter is an example of a specific performance action used to regain possession of a unique good, or in this case,

7. *Social Contract Theory*, Internet Encyclopedia of Philosophy, http://www.iep.utm.edu/soc-cont/ (last visited May 12, 2016).

8. A great case for reviewing how to apply equitable principles is *Marvin v. Marvin*, 176 Cal. Rptr. 555, 122 Cal. App. 3d 871 (Cal. App. 2d Dist. 1981). Be aware of the Restatement (Third) of Restitution and Unjust Enrichment.

9. These actions may arise based upon either a statute or common law.

a companion animal. In some states, replevin actions must be independent from other claims. Other states allow multiple causes of action, including a replevin action.

When specific performance is sought in a replevin action, determine if the claimant is bringing more claims than allowed. Determine also whether the action is based upon an equitable principle rather than a statutory claim. In the common law court of equity, you must enter with clean hands.

Case Law with Equitable Aspects

In the small claims case of *Nuijens v. Novy*,[10] the court found that because the seller was not a merchant under the UCC, the buyer, who had neither produced a licensed veterinary certificate nor returned the dog in a timely manner, was not entitled to relief for a very sick dog.

In stark contrast, and employing equitable principles, the court in *Maguire v. Mohrmann*,[11] upon the sale of a sick English Springer Spaniel puppy with hidden health problems to the buyer, determined that the buyer had "substantially," if not exactly, complied with similar applicable laws. The buyer was awarded the purchase price of the dog, together with veterinary costs for the dead dog.

Another case where the court utilized equitable principles was *Appell v. Rodriguez*.[12] There, the court, upon rendering a decision representing substantial justice when a buyer purchased a sick Great Dane puppy, decided to overlook the buyer's tardiness for getting a veterinary opinion in this action subject to the Uniform Commercial Code.

CONTRACT PRACTICE POINTERS

The following practice pointers can be utilized to help you think about contracts and what evidence to gather. Construct the claim following an in-depth inquiry, as this thorough investigation can result in gathering evidence that could be outcome determinative. Find out what contracts a client has with others and how the contracts were prepared. If applicable, find out who drafted the contract and obtain copies of every contract the client has signed or might be impacted by.[13] Gather communications that address, and may constitute, contractual terms, including through social media, text messages, e-mails, faxes, and snail mail.

10. 543 N.Y.S.2d 887, 144 Misc. 2d 453 (N.Y. Just. Ct. 1989).
11. 935 A.2d 1259, 397 N.J. Super. 103 (N.J. Super. 2007).
12. 2007 N.Y. Slip. Op. 50051(U) (N.Y. App. Term 1/8/2007), 2007 NY Slip. Op. 50051 (N.Y. App. Term 2007).
13. There has been an increased tendency for a party to use an inadequate contract purchased off a commercial social media site.

Contracts that might apply to your case could involve co-owners, breeders, fosters, rescues, trainers, instructors, dog walkers, veterinarians, pet sitters, and boarding facilities. Analyze how each contract relates to the topic of indicia of ownership or represents third-party rights that might impact ownership or a pet custody dispute, including with regard to a conditional sale or breeding rights. Consider the likelihood of a third-party intervener making a tortious interference of contract rights claim, too.

Never assume that just because the parties have a written contract, the contract was properly drafted, was properly executed, is enforceable, or passes title. Determine if there are contractual limitations or conditions on leasing or assigning rights to the animal. A rescue group or breeder may require that the animal be returned or relinquished if the adopter can no longer care for the animal, or if a spay or neuter requirement is violated. If contractual violations have occurred, analyze the range of remedies. Pay attention to details, including which party's name is listed on the contract, whether the animal is correctly identified, and whether the registration numbers are accurate. Analyze any warranties, representations, waivers, or problems that occurred during the formation of the contract. See if the contract contains "no modification unless in writing" or merger language. Learn if there are exceptions to the merger doctrine. Look at your state's case law.

Determine whether all signatories to the contract were at the age of majority at the time of execution and if all necessary parties were signatories, including a co-owning spouse. If someone involved claims to have power of attorney or is acting as an agent, verify that the individual has proper authority. Make sure that the companion animal is not owned by one party's business.

Identify all applicable state laws, including under the UCC, particularly sections 2, 2A, and 9, as well as other applicable state laws, the Restatement (Second) of Contracts, and local laws. For example, the UCC might be one of several state laws impacting the sale of sick animals. Consumer or general business laws and lemon laws[14] may impact the sale and establish remedies, too. Lemon laws in the applicable state typically expire between 10 and 14 days after pet acquisition. Remedies may not be exclusive. Equitable principles, again, may also apply. You may find that equitable remedies are better understood and applied in small claims court or other courts focused on the subject of substantive justice.

14. Lemon laws provide incomplete remedies to buyers. Unless an individual regards an animal brought home for companionship purposes as equivalent to nonliving property, wherein a refund upon the return of the property is sufficient, the remedies available under lemon laws that are dependent upon the return of the pet to the seller are troubling. The new owner's wallet is refurbished, and the animal, if returned, will likely be killed. Rebecca F. Wisch, *Pet Purchaser Protection/Puppy "Lemon Laws" Brief Summary of Pet Sales*, Animal Legal & Historical Center, https://www.animallaw.info/intro/pet-purchaser-protectionpuppy-lemon-laws (last visited May 12, 2016).

Learn when releases of liability are permitted in the applicable state, and more importantly, learn what risks cannot be waived or released.[15] Keep current with the case law on this. Joint and severable liability is an important concern if the parties are awarded joint custody or co-ownership or if one party receives visitation or pet time and is in the status of keeper of the animal if an incident occurs. Learn when "as is" language pertaining to an animal can be challenged in a legal proceeding in the applicable state. For example, if the sale is by a merchant, including a nonprofit, there may be specific requirements for waivers of the implied warranties of merchantability and fitness for a particular purpose to be effective.

Tests, Liens, and Doctrines

When representing a client buying an animal, it is a good practice to first review the animal's medical and dental history, including vaccination history and, if applicable, performance record. It is always wise for the buyer to have a veterinary examination, which may include x-rays and blood tests; buyers should also be aware of the potential for pre-sale drug enhancements.

Learn about any lien that might affect the transaction, such as an agister's lien, veterinary lien, farrier lien, or breeder lien. Horse leases may be governed under section 2A of the UCC; the UCC does not apply to personal service contracts. Find out if the applicable state has adopted a specific provision on services or adopted the Restatement (Second) of Torts, the Restatement (Third) of Torts, or the Restatement (Second) of Contract.[16]

Under the UCC, a companion animal is referred to as a product under the New York doctrine[17] or a good under the Illinois doctrine. Research the implications of the pertinent classification. An animal could be subject to a security agreement under UCC section 9, making the companion animal collateral subject to a replevin action by a stranger. Consumer and general business remedies may be broader or narrower than UCC remedies. Look at the scope of the applicable state's consumer fraud laws. They may be included with business laws and in the statutory framework.

CONTRACT LAW AND PET CUSTODY DISPUTES

In terms of how to apply contract law to a pet custody dispute, it is wise to dissect all applicable contracts before planning your strategy. If the contract is hard to

15. A well-appreciated concept in equine law is that, limited liability laws, provisions, and waivers may be challenged.

16. Research any Restatements that might apply.

17. In New York, animals are products under the New York doctrine, as set forth in Beyer v. Aquarium Supply Co., 94 Misc. 2d 336, 404 N.Y.S.2d 778 (N.Y. Sup. Ct. 1977).

understand or follow, realize that with technological innovation, there is ease in cutting and pasting lengthy provisions from different sources, thereby increasing inconsistent wording and use of terms. Ask your client for the contract, amended contract, and any addendums, together with any evidence related to the contract, including snail mail, text messages, social media postings, and e-mails. Recapture the details of parole evidence; this could be particularly useful in a mediation or alternative dispute resolution context.

Thoroughly read any contract involving a companion animal who is the subject of controversy. Although problems might be found while reading a contract the first time, it is wise to pick up the contract and read it word for word, preferably out loud. Read the contract in separate sittings, as standard boilerplate language may not reveal itself as problematic until the third read through. Consider that when contract drafters cut and paste language, they may reverse and contradict concepts by not paying attention to positive or negative qualifiers, as well as headings. If this kind of discrepancy is found, the lawyer might advance to a better bargaining position. Many contracts reveal amateur drafting efforts that infuse vague, lofty, overreaching, and—again—contradictory provisions that in some cases may mean the failure of a meeting of the minds.

Void and Voidable Contracts

It is important to understand the difference between a void contract and a voidable contract. A void contract cannot be enforced by either party and might include the requirement of a person subject to the contract to perform an illegal or impossible act, contrary to public policy. In contrast, a voidable contract could be performed or voided by one or more parties. Voidable contracts include contracts that are based upon misrepresentation or fraud.

Rescue Group Contracts

Dedicated rescue groups follow up to make sure material contractual terms between the group and forever families are satisfied through correspondence, phone calls, and sometimes unannounced visits. Rescue groups often try to advance an animal's best interests by using provisions that impact and condition the permanency of an animal placement with a new owner if a material contractual obligation is violated.

A rescue group might seek to rescind the adoption or sale of an animal or otherwise have the transaction invalidated for several reasons, including if the animal was not timely neutered, if more animals live at the residence than permitted by contract or disclosed in the pre-purchase application, if reasonable access to inspect the premises is denied, or if the animal's ears or tails are docked contrary to a contractual prohibition. There are other behaviors offensive to rescue groups that indicate the adopter lacks stability, as reflected by frequent changes of address or reports to the rescue of chemical abuse. In these situations, the rescue group fears that an animal is being mistreated, often for good reason. Neighbors are often aware of animal endangerment but are reluctant witnesses if litigation ensues.

Merchants

Rescue groups may unwittingly find themselves merchants subject to the UCC and may not realize that sales transactions, including those called adoptions, are subject to an implied warranty of merchantability under UCC section 2-314. This provision applies to the sale of goods for "personal, family or household use," unless qualities and characteristics not subject to warranty are properly particularized.[18] These groups, just like for-profit businesses, can be liable under a state's common law or other statute if they engage in fraud or misrepresentation.[19]

Passing Title

Rescue groups often have high ideals and are adamant about retaining significant dominion and control over the animals they adopt out. If transfer of ownership is too conditional, title may not pass. Rescue groups would benefit from the help of lawyers with contract experience, as they do not want to be deemed the animal owner should a post-adoption injury occur and liability arise. A rescue group's options following a violation of contractual terms are impacted by whether material terms of the contract were violated. Under some circumstances, the rescue group may be able to regain possession and ownership of the animal through a replevin action.

Another issue that may arise with a rescue group involves the relinquishment or surrender of an abused animal by someone who does not own the animal. The best practice for the rescue is to place the animal with the proper entity able to satisfy the statutory hold period so that the rescue can then pass good title to a new owner.

Third-Party Rights

Rescue groups may be subject to contractual obligations, too. For instance, the group could have a contractual obligation to animal control not to sell or adopt out animals unless they have been spayed or neutered as a condition of operation,

18. *U.C.C. Article 2 – Sales*, Legal Information Institute, http://www.law.cornell.edu/ucc/2/article2 (last visited May 12, 2016).

19. There should be disclosures about an animal's health and violent propensities.

a requirement that was important in *Take Me Home Rescue v. Luri*.[20] There, the court permitted a rescue to enforce a mandatory neuter clause against the preferences of an adopting foster to have an intact dog who would be a better agility competitor. There is also a possibility that a rescue could have a third-party interest in a pet ownership dispute if an animal has been lost or found.

Lines can be difficult to draw, from an ownership perspective, between an adopter and a rescue group. For example, is the rescue group making a conditional gift or donation of the animal to the adopter? Is the group making a conditional transfer while retaining a reversionary contractual right to regain possession? Is there a conditional sale? When is a future right of conversion enforceable through a future right of entry? Who has fee simple ownership? The answers to these questions may depend on the state's common law or statutory framework. In addition to case law, review sections 2, 2A, and 9 of the UCC in the applicable state, as well as the Restatement (Second) of Contracts and other Restatements.[21] Judicial opinions may also change as companion animals continue to advance into the interim category between property and person.

Breeder Contracts

There are many terms and concepts that could arise in a contract with a breeder involving a show animal, working animal, or pet-quality companion animal. A contract may state that the animal will be co-owned by the breeder and purchaser subject to general or very specific terms and conditions.

Breeder Contract Provisions

The law of the breeder's state may be applied in the event of a dispute. There may be an obligation to cooperate with a breeding program. Specific language may be included about rights to the offspring[22] or obligations to spay and neuter. The breeder may require that the breeder's name appear on registrations[23] and pedigrees. A list of the co-purchaser's duties regarding animal welfare may be included, together with other health-related provisions. Kennel club or similar requirements may be incorporated by reference. Prohibitions, such as no sleeve work on train-

20. 208 Cal. App. 4th 1342, 146 Cal. Rptr. 3d 461 (Cal. App. 2012).

21. *Uniform Commercial Code*, Legal Information Institute, http://www.law.cornell.edu/ucc (last visited May 12, 2016).

22. These contracts may involve artificial reproductive technology and intellectual property rights.

23. There are a variety of registries for dogs, including the American Kennel Club, the Dog Registry of America, the National Kennel Club, the North American Mixed Breed Registry, the United Kennel Club, the American Rare Breed Association, and the American Mixed Breed Obedience Registration. Cat registries and organizations include the Cat Fanciers' Association, the Fédération Internationale Féline, the International Cat Association, the American Cat Fanciers Association, and the North American Purebred Registry, Inc.

ing, can be general or detailed. Usually, a contract lists a description of any defects specific to the breed. The contract may address how the soundness of the animal will be determined; statutes may apply, too.

Standard Contract Clauses

Most contracts include a severability clause, an heirs and assigns clause, and a no contract modification unless in writing clause. There may be an assignment of ownership or possession prohibition or language about the payment of attorney's fees and court costs if there is a dispute, including how much, when, and by whom. A provision about alternative dispute resolution is typically utilized. The execution of multiple original copies of a contract is often required. A waiver of an adverse inference against the contract drafter on the subject of contract construction may be included.

A useful decision on the subject of breeder contracts was *Schneider v. Green*.[24] This case almost represents a tutorial on the myriad of claims that might arise between two co-owners.

Show Dogs and Cats

For show dogs or cats, a contract may include obligations related to points for championship or title, or address other expected achievements. Breed standards may be described and incorporated by reference, pointing to a breed standard source. If the animal is acquired for show purposes, the seller may provide a warranty of no disqualifying fault. If the animal will be in a breeding program, the right to select the bitch or stud should be addressed. Expectations about training and handling can be general or specific. When a show animal is involved, the contract may describe under what circumstances additional monies[25] are owed or contributed, including how much, when, and by whom.

Reputable Breeders

Two types of animals are sold by reputable breeders: animals expected to be available for competitions and championships, perhaps through a co-ownership arrangement, and pet animals. The second type may be referred to as a pet-quality animal. Prior to sale, for example, a dog might be spayed or neutered, or subject to contractual requirements to have this procedure done by a certain age, perhaps six months for females and one year for males. This delay in surgery may be required if a breeder believes that an early surgery may affect the dog's hormones

24. 1990 WL 151142 (S.D.N.Y.).
25. Because showing animals can be expensive, there can be provisions on who will pay what costs.

and bone growth. Other breeders may want an early spay or neuter so that the probability of unplanned offspring is decreased and to prevent offspring with genetic problems.[26]

You should know whether your client received all right, title, and interest to the dog, or only co-ownership rights, or whether there was a conditional sale. Consider privity of contract issues between your client and the breeder, as the acquiring party whose name appears on the breeder contract may have legal importance in a future ownership dispute. Read the contract fine print carefully, particularly with regard to breeding rights.

Foster Contracts and Bailments

Foster contracts differ as to whether the foster is permitted, encouraged, or prohibited from adopting the animal. The legal relationship between a rescue group and a foster is typically a bailment, wherein property is delivered for a contractual purpose and the bailee agrees to meet certain obligations, including the obligation to return the property when the bailment is fulfilled. Unless the foster has the right to adopt the property subject to the bailment agreement, the bailee is obligated to deliver the animal property to the rescue group bailor upon a rescission demand. Even so, pet custody disputes between fosters and rescue groups can and do arise.

Indicia of Ownership

The idea of who owns an animal may be subject to challenge in a cohabitation, roommate, or familial context for a variety of reasons. One party may have searched for and then found the animal to be purchased and negotiated the sale. The cash used to purchase the animal could have been withdrawn from the other party's bank account. The animal may have been purchased using a joint bank account, or paid for on a joint credit card that only one party made payments on. Both parties may have contributed to the animal's insured and uninsured veterinary care expenses.

One party may have provided care for the animal while the purchaser traveled, which could be viewed as a contribution based upon quantum meruit theory. The intended owner may have been medically unable to travel or on a business trip at the time the animal was purchased and a significant other may have served as that person's agent and signed the acquisition papers. The animal may have been purchased as a gift for the other party. Perhaps both parties were present at the time of purchase, although only one party's name appears on the sales contract

26. Laura J. Sanborn, *Long-Term Health Risks and Benefits Associated with Spay/Neuter in Dogs*, http://www.2ndchance.info/cruciatelongtermneuter.htm (last visited May 12, 2016).

because there was only space for one signature. In addition to these types of contractual arguments, there are a wide variety of legal theories that could be utilized that are not contract-based, as other chapters in this book reveal.

Interview your client extensively about all the facts related to how the animal in a dispute was acquired and what happened thereafter. Advise your client that the issue of ownership from a contractual standpoint can be up for debate, particularly when there are compelling circumstances, including when a long-term spouse or partner was the primary caretaker of the animal, or if the case arose in a jurisdiction where the courts are inclined to consider best-interest standards. If advocating for the nonpurchasing party, identify all the gray areas and argue them forcefully.

Veterinarians

Veterinarians can be impacted by ownership and possession disputes. When animals are provided veterinary care, veterinarians have limited ability to ascertain who owns the animal or who has the authority to consent to costly services, including for emergency surgery. A veterinarian may be unsure about who has the authority to make a euthanasia decision. Information the veterinarian has typically includes representations made on client forms, statements by the client, information on the animal's tags or licenses, or information that can be gleaned from a microchip.

Although a veterinarian might be able to contractually pinpoint who originally bought or adopted the animal, and who registered, licensed, or microchipped the animal, this evidence might not be dispositive as to who owns the animal or who has the authority to make a decision given that there may be more than one indicia of ownership. Ownership of an animal could have been transferred through a gift, or another owner could have moved out and abandoned the animal.[27] The animal may have been lost and found. There could be two co-owners.

PRENUPTIAL AND ANTENUPTIAL AGREEMENTS ADDRESSING ANIMALS

In recent years, prenuptial and antenuptial agreements addressing animals have become more common, as animal lawyers sometimes offer this service as a way to protect the original owner from losing a companion animal in the event of a

27. Animal abandonment and lack of lifetime commitment when an animal is obtained through an impulse purchase or gift or unplanned offspring contribute to companion animals being at risk for euthanasia. They are also impacted by their owners' lack of financial means to provide adequate veterinary care or pay for basic training. Pets' lives are also affected by zoning restrictions, no-pets policies, and an owner's incapacity or death.

breakup. While this is understandable, it does not necessarily mean that treating companion animals as personal property in prenuptial agreements is commensurate with the place companion animals are gaining in American families. Even so, if one of the parties has creditors, a prenuptial agreement might protect the other party from collection efforts, which could be directed against property in the form of valuable animals subject to Article 9 of the UCC.

Although the requirements for prenuptial and antenuptial agreements may vary from state to state, they typically include the following:

- Full names of the parties.
- Full names of each party's attorney.
- A detailed and current asset list, together with supporting documentation.
- Detailed and current liabilities list, together with supporting documentation.
- Full and complete disclosure of current income, including current cash income, with supporting evidence.
- Wedding date and the date the contract was signed (there may be a minimum statutory period).
- Use of accrual method.
- Prohibitions on spousal maintenance.
- Payments attributable to the duration of the marriage.
- Place for each party's lawyer to sign.
- Timely signing of agreements.

State laws differ with regard to the enforceability of prenuptial agreements, a type of agreement that courts used to view as contrary to public policy. The enforceability of any agreement should be researched. The agreement should be in writing pursuant to the statute of frauds and properly executed as the laws of the applicable state require.

Even if permitted in the state where the parties were married, if either party properly initiates a divorce in another state, the prenuptial agreement could be interpreted as contrary to public policy in the state with jurisdiction over the dispute, thereby impacting a pet custody claim. Other legal concepts that might impact the enforceability of the agreement include consideration, overreaching, unconscionable provisions, duress, void or voidable agreements, coercion, and whether the agreement is subject to the terms of the terms of the Uniform Premarital Agreements Act or its successor, the Uniform Premarital and Marital Agreements Act.[28]

28. *Uniform Premarital and Marital Agreements Act*, http://www.uniformlaws.org/shared/docs/premarital%20and%20marital%20agreements/2012_pmaa_final.pdf (last visited May 12, 2016).

For those who are old or ill, an enforceable prenuptial agreement may impact not only what happens in life but also what happens after death. Unless addressed in the prenuptial agreement, a decedent's pet may pass through the decedent's estate rather than remain in the home of the surviving spouse the animal has grown accustomed to and is happy in. If that outcome is not desired, this subject should be addressed in applicable agreements, including a pet trust.

UNIFORM COMMERCIAL CODE

Companion animals sold by a merchant may be deemed goods or products under the Uniform Commercial Code.[29] A fundamental principle of contract law is the requirement of a meeting of the minds on material terms of the agreement. When the seller is a merchant subject to the UCC, implied warranties such as fitness for a particular purpose or merchantability apply. The particular purpose could vary widely, including use for a particular sport, law enforcement, hunting, a therapeutic role, the show ring, or companionship. For example, if the animal subject to the UCC is delivered with a terminal medical condition, the contract could be voidable based upon the breach of an implied warranty of merchantability and fitness for a particular purpose.

Beyond the UCC's implied warranties, a contract may set forth an express warranty, such as that the animal does not have hip dysplasia. There may be additional laws in the applicable state pertaining to seller duties or obligations, including under consumer protection and lemon laws, which may be found within more general business laws. As states also vary on which UCC provisions have been adopted, be sure to review yours.

An interesting case on the subject of the applicability of the UCC was *O'Brien v. Wade*.[30] In this case, there was an implied warranty claim that the dog was suitable for hunting, as well as an express warranty claim. Express warranties do not exclude implied warranties.

Warranties can be made that do not appear in the written sales contract. They can arise in catalogs, brochures, advertisements, or from a seller's representations and assertions before, during, or after a sale. An integration clause in a contract, though available as a defense, is hardly iron clad. The validity of an express warranty does not depend on bad faith by the seller, as good faith is not a defense to a false assertion.

Under common law and the UCC, it is typical to see a specific performance action originating in replevin. Find out if the pending replevin action is based upon

29. *See* Sacco v. Tate, 175 Misc. 2d 901, 672 N.Y.2d 618 (App. Term. 1998); Cahill v. Blume, 8 Misc. 3d 1004(A), 801 N.Y.S.2d 776 (N.Y. City Civ. Ct. 2005); and Dempsey v. Rosenthal, 121 Misc. 2d 612, 468 N.Y.S.2d 441 (N.Y. City Civ. Ct. 1983).

30. 540 S.W.2d 603 (Mo. App. 1976).

a nonmerchant contract under the common law or under the UCC. If based upon common law, see if the claim is equitable and argue that the relief does not apply because of unclean hands if the facts warrant it.

The general rule of construction applies against the party that drafts a contract. Contracts containing a provision that this rule of construction will not apply may not be enforceable, particularly if the contract appears to be one of adhesion. A well-drafted contract that is clear, fair, and reasonable is more likely to be enforceable. Remember that there is an expectation that contracts will be entered into in good faith and represent a fair deal.

PET CUSTODY AND ACCESS CONTRACTS

Although contract terms are explored more thoroughly in the appendix, some of the basics are covered here. An example of the traditional but short approach would be, "The petitioner is awarded all right, title, and interest, as well as possession, to the dog commonly known as Scrapps." If you want to write this idea in a more modern way, you might say, "The petitioner is awarded the physical and legal custody of the dog, Scrapps." If you were to write a provision where one party was given title to the dog but the other party had access, visitation, or "pet time," the following language might be used:

> The petitioner is awarded the physical and legal custody of Scrapps, and the respondent is awarded pet time with Scrapps based upon the following schedule, subject to the conditions set forth after the schedule:
>
> 1) The respondent is granted pet time with Scrapps on the first Sunday of every month from 12:00 p.m. until 6:00 p.m.
> 2) The respondent is granted access to Scrapps every Wednesday from 6:00 p.m. until 8:00 p.m.
> 3) The respondent is granted vacation time with Scrapps each year from January 1st through January 7th and June 1st through June 7th.
>
> The respondent's pet time is conditioned upon the following:
>
> 1) The respondent is responsible for all transport of Scrapps between the parties.
> 2) The respondent will be timely in picking up and returning Scrapps.
> 3) The respondent will have limited and respectful communications with the petitioner.
> 4) If The respondent has a family emergency or a highly unusual work demand, or if there is severe weather, The respondent will promptly notify the petitioner by text message.
> 5) The respondent shall maintain homeowner's or renter's insurance with $100,000 liability coverage that applies to, and does not exclude, Scrapps's breed.

6) The respondent shall be vigilant in preventing Scrapps from getting loose or injuring another person or animal. In particular, the respondent will only allow Scrapps to run loose in a fenced-in yard or dog park while Scrapps is supervised by the respondent. This is a non-delegable duty.
7) Only the respondent will walk Scrapps, unless agreed to in writing by the petitioner, and when the respondent walks Scrapps, the dog will be on a leash no longer than six feet.
8) If Scrapps becomes involved in any type of dangerous dog proceeding while in the respondent's care, the respondent will pay for a lawyer to oppose or appeal this designation, and if applicable, pay for a lawyer to prepare a writ of certiorari, and the respondent's pet time will end unless the petitioner otherwise agrees in writing.

In addition to the above, the petitioner and the respondent will meet on an annual basis to discuss how Scrapps's best interests can be met and the schedule modified in the best interests for all concerned. If the parties cannot agree, the matter will be discussed in an alternative dispute resolution process agreeable to the parties. Unless the parties reach an agreement, the above terms shall not be modified by the court unless there is endangerment to Scrapps. If there is a claim that there is endangerment, the party alleging endangerment must prove by clear and convincing evidence that the endangerment exists.

If the parties seek joint ownership, joint custody, or co-ownership of Scrapps, some of the language utilized above could be used, along with the following:

- The petitioner and the respondent are awarded joint ownership and joint custody of the dog commonly known as Scrapps. Scrapps is a Schnauzer, and his microchip number is 12345.
- In exercising their co-ownership rights, the parties shall share Scrapps on a 5/2/2/5 schedule[31] as long as the parties reside within 60 miles of each other. If one of the parties moves more than 60 miles away from the other party, the parties will share Scrapps on a one month on, one month off schedule. Furthermore, the moving party will be fully responsible for transport of Scrapps to and from the other party's residence unless the parties otherwise agree in writing. Both parties also agree to use and pay for Best Pet Insurance, Plan B, and to equally share the cost of Scrapps's veterinary care and insurance and equally divide uninsured costs. Both parties will participate in making significant veterinary decisions and will be guided by seeking the best interests of Scrapps.

31. The above schedule reflects how many days apply.

ANIMAL TRANSPORT BY AIRLINE

No contract chapter pertaining to pets would be complete without reference to *Gluckman v. American Airlines, Inc.*[32] In this infamous 1994 decision, which shook animal owners to the core, a Golden Retriever named Floyd was put in a special crate and then placed in the airline baggage compartment, which lacked temperature control. When the dog died after suffering from heatstroke and brain damage, the airline took the contractual position that Floyd was "merely baggage." The court treated Floyd's death as a bailment action. If your client is considering using transport by airline to affect a visitation schedule, make sure your client is aware of implicit hazards and the best strategies to avoid them.

CONCLUSION

Because statutes and common laws do not yet consistently address where companion animals belong in American jurisprudence, an action that presents itself as a pet custody dispute may be more difficult than a lawyer expects. It is for this reason that a family lawyer serious about developing pet custody expertise must master the mechanics of contract law, including being conversant with the UCC. For lawyers bored by the repetitive aspects of many family court actions, pet law, in its pet custody dispute aspect, provides the opportunity to develop and utilize a very broad skill set. It is also foreseeable that your client will not appreciate how much effort it takes you to effectively represent them. It is advisable to inform your client early and often about presenting difficulties.

APPLICABLE CASE LAW

O'Brien v. Wade[33]

Year: *1976*
Category: *Contract Law*
Type of Action: *Breach of Contract, Warranty, Fraudulent Misrepresentation*
Animal: *Dog*
Pet Custody Concept: *Express and implied warranties apply to transactions subject to the UCC.*

In this 1976 court of appeals case, a man sought to purchase a registered dog that was obedience- and field-trained and otherwise suitable for duck hunting. The female Labrador sold to him, Zein, lacked hunting abilities. When Zein's buyer attempted to

32. 844 F. Supp. 151 (S.D.N.Y. 1994).
33. 540 S.W.2d 603 (Mo. App. 1976).

return her and get his money back, the sellers ignored him. The plaintiff sought compensable damages for the seller's failure to deliver Zein's registration papers and punitive damages based upon the seller's fraudulent representation.

After entry of judgment, the plaintiff appealed and was able to amend his petition to include a claim for breach of the implied warranty of fitness for the intended use of the dog as a retriever. At the subsequent trial, the jury found for the plaintiff and awarded him damages of $2,000. The defendant appealed what he called the "excessive" verdict.

Four and a half years passed from the time the plaintiff purchased Zein to the date of the appellate court decision; this case was subject to nine continuances. During this time, the plaintiff incurred boarding costs of $3,257.25 for Zein, a dog he did not want. The court said, "Dog lovers will applaud O'Brien's tenderhearted rejection of the possibility of destroying Zein upon learning that Wade would not agree to a rescission of the contract, but the law will not allow O'Brien credit for Zein's 4 1/2-year board bill." The court argued that one "cannot voluntarily keep and use worthless property with knowledge of its being worthless and thereby multiply damages or expenses chargeable to the vendor."

This decision included a discussion about warranty claims because one argument advanced by the defendant was that the circuit court erred by giving a jury instruction on both an implied warranty claim and breach of contract claim when "All of plaintiff's evidence pertained only to the breach of an express bilateral contract." The court rebuffed this line of reasoning, stating, "They are talking about express and implied warranties as to the same quality or characteristic, not as to different qualities or characteristics. An express warranty that pedigree papers will be furnished does not exclude an implied warranty that a dog is field trained for duck hunting." Furthermore, the court clarified that express or implied warranties should be construed as "consistent with each other and as cumulative." While reducing the damages amount awarded to the seller, the court of appeals affirmed the verdict on liability.

Practice Pointer: It is common for a disputant to argue that one type of claim means the exclusion of another. Be prepared for this and utilize this case if express and implied warranty claims are brought based upon different qualities or characteristics.

Connor v. Bogrett[34]

Year: *1979*
Category: *Contract Law*
Type of Action: *Breach of Contract, Warranty*
Animal: *Dog*
Pet Custody Concept: *In this jurisdiction, a dog is a good under the UCC.*

In this 1979 decision, a "dog aficionado" experienced in judging dogs in field trials became interested in a particular black Labrador Retriever. At first, the dog's owner offered to sell the dog for $14,000 but then reduced the sale price to $8,000 after

34. 596 P.2d 683 (Wyo. 1979).

the prospective buyer's veterinarian determined that the Labrador suffered from hip dysplasia.

According to the terms of the purchase agreement, the payments to the seller would be made in two installments. The first $6,000 would be paid on the date of sale and an additional $2,000 by another date certain. After taking possession of the dog but before paying the additional amount owed, the buyer trained the dog, entered the dog in field trials, and offered him for stud service.

When the dog's performance became impaired, the buyer had the dog "re-examined" by his veterinarian, who said the dog suffered from osteoarthritis due to his poor hips. Following a heated exchange, the buyer sought to rescind the sale and left the dog in the seller's yard. The seller counterclaimed that this behavior constituted an anticipatory breach of contract with regard to the outstanding payment of $2,000. He claimed that the buyer also owed him for the reasonable value of the services for maintenance, care, and training resulting from the buyer leaving the dog with him.

The buyer claimed that the seller expressly warranted that the Labrador could compete in field trials and that a summary judgment in favor of the seller was impermissible because there was a genuine issue of material fact regarding the dog's condition and abilities. Referring to the buyer, the court said, "It does appear that in at least one instance he shot the dog with a shotgun, which apparently is a recognized training technique for retrievers for field trial competition." The court further noted that later that year, the owner experienced difficulties with regard to "the willingness of the dog to perform in field trial competition."

The court determined that under the UCC, a buyer must pay at the contract rate when goods are accepted, and in this case, the dog had been accepted. The court looked to UCC remedies, including incidental damages, once goods are accepted. The Supreme Court of Wyoming agreed with the district court that "as a matter of law, the expressions of Bogrett relative to the potential of this retriever were only expressions of opinion or commendation." Accordingly, the buyer did not rely on the seller's statements.

Of interest was the court's discussion of whether there could be a warranty of future performance. Looking in part to Texas law, the Wyoming court said that because animals are "fragile creatures, susceptible to myriad maladies, detectable and undetectable," the warranty must be explicit for an express warranty of future performance of goods to pertain. The court observed language from a Mississippi court wherein "explicit" meant "something express or clearly stated and is more than merely implied."[35]

Practice Pointer: In a case where a warranty of future performance comes up, find out if the applicable state follows the Illinois doctrine, as exemplified in the landmark decision of *Whitmer v. Schneble*,[36] where animals are goods, or the New York doctrine, where animals are products under the UCC. The applicable doctrine may be outcome determinative.

---

35. Another issue was what constituted a final judgment for appeal purposes. The court determined that the filing of the stipulation to dismiss the second claim regarding compensation for services vested the court with appellate jurisdiction.

36. 29 Ill. App. 3d, 651, 331 N.E. 115 (1975).

BACHMAN V. ARTINGER[37]

Year: *1981*
Category: *Contract Law*
Type of Action: *Breach of Contract, Trespass, Assumpsit, Fraudulent Misrepresentation*
Animal: *Dog*
Pet Custody Concept: *Know the exceptions to the hearsay rule.*

The buyer of a miniature Schnauzer puppy claimed that the Schnauzer was unhealthy at the time of purchase, had a preexisting skin condition, and was not registrable with the American Kennel Club. She initiated an action against the seller based upon claims of breach of contract, fraudulent misrepresentation, trespass, and assumpsit. The buyer utilized a veterinarian expert witness to advance her claim. The trial court rejected the expert's medical opinion as not probative of the Schnauzer's health at the point of purchase.

The buyer claimed that the trial court erred by allowing hearsay; the seller was allowed to testify about an out-of-court statement regarding the puppy's bloodlines. Pointing out an exception to the hearsay rule, the court emphasized that "Testimony as to an out of court statement, written or oral, is not hearsay if offered to prove, not that the content of the statement was true, but that the statement was made." While the court observed that the seller had incorrect information about the dog's bloodlines, the buyer's claims of fraudulent representation required "clear and convincing evidence to have been made knowingly with the intent to deceive or in reckless ignorance of the truth or falsity of the matter." The claim of fraudulent misrepresentation failed because the seller did not have the requisite intent to deceive. She did not know about the animal's true sire until after the sale.

The court emphasized, "Every dog has its day," and concluded that despite the misinformation about the bloodlines, the Schnauzer was registrable with the American Kennel Club if the buyer sent in the correct forms. Judgment was affirmed in favor of the seller.

Practice Pointer: If an out-of-court statement is offered to prove that a statement was made, not the content of the statement itself, this may qualify as an exception to the hearsay rule. Knowing the hearsay rule and the exceptions thereto may make a difference in whether a case is won or lost.

37. 426 A.2d 702, 285 Pa. Super. 57 (Pa. Super. 1981).

BAZZINI V. GARRANT[38]

Year: *1982*
Category: *Contract Law*
Type of Action: *Breach of Warranty*
Animal: *Bird*
Pet Custody Concept: *To disclaim an implied warranty of merchantability under the UCC, a seller must mention it.*

The court began its opinion by describing this case as "a sad tale (or is it tail) of the noble, but late, toco toucan bird" and continued by saying, "Within two weeks after his physical, Bird suffered a seizure. (There was no evidence of foul play.)" The plaintiff temporarily nursed the bird back to health, but the bird died a week later.

The court carefully chose the words, "But this recovery enjoyed only the reign of a lame duck politician. Seven days later Bird was dead." Encouraged by its own humor, the court continued its opinion, "In life Bird was a bird—an animal of feelings, of flesh and blood and feathers. It is one of the sad aspects of the law that the heat and passion of life so often translate to cold, unfeeling words upon a page. This is such an instance for in death, notwithstanding his memory, Bird is a chattel."

The court did not make an effort to hide its sarcasm and mirth in this decision about a dead bird.[39] The following UCC provisions applied:

- UCC section 2-104(1), which applies to a merchant involved in the sale of goods,
- UCC section 2-314, which describes the implied warranty of merchantability, and
- UCC section 2-316(2) and UCC section 2-316(3), which detail how to modify a warranty.

The court specifically determined that UCC section 2-316(2) did not pertain because there was a requirement to mention the implied warranty of merchantability before excluding it. The court also determined that section 2-316(3) did not apply, as the examination of the bird occurred after the sale.

The purpose of pointing out and discussing the court's ridicule of the toucan, which is the most noticeable aspect of this decision, is because attorneys need to be prepared for these types of antics by other attorneys, court officials, and ADR providers when handling a case involving a companion animal. Clients should be prepared for the idea that their case may be the subject of hilarity, too.

In *Bazzini*, the defendant did not appear at the hearing to contradict the plaintiff's testimonial evidence, which was a notarized letter from her veterinarian and a receipt

38. 116 Misc. 2d 119, 455 N.Y.S.2d 77, 54 N.Y.2d 207 (N.Y. Dist. Ct. 1982).

39. Toucan birds are native to central or eastern South America, where they live in the wild. They are also commonly seen in captivity in zoos in the United States. It is unlikely that this court knew anything about the underbelly of capturing and shipping wild birds to the States, a practice that is both lucrative and results in high bird mortality rates. *Convention on International Trade in Endangered Species of Wild Fauna and Flora* (CITES), http://www.cites.org/ (last visited May 12, 2016).

of care for the bird. In deciding whether the facts offered proved that the defendant breached the implied warranty of merchantability, the judge proclaimed that he was not bound by the rules of evidence in small claims court. Thus, he said the veterinarian's letter could be considered. The veterinarian's letter indicated the bird probably suffered from a congenital defect. As the defendant failed to appear, the court justified an unfavorable inference against him and found, as a matter of fact, that "Bird was unmerchantable when sold."

More relaxed evidentiary standards may be used in small claims court. The judge followed his evidentiary commentary by saying, "That is, to be blunt and not cagey, Bird was not fit for the ordinary purposes for which toco toucans are used." Unable to help himself, the small claims court judge offered, "At least one purpose is to stay around as a live bird." The plaintiff was awarded $1,200.

Practice Pointer: Beware of jurists who are unknowledgeable about the plight of other animals and how they may take pleasure in making fun of them. True grit may need to be exercised to survive this type of crudeness.

Dempsey v. Rosenthal[40]

Year: *1983*
Category: *Contract Law*
Type of Action: *Breach of Warranty*
Animal: *Dog*
Pet Custody Concept: *The implied warranties of merchantability and fitness for a particular purpose apply to transactions under the UCC.*

The issue in this case was whether a consumer who purchased a Poodle for breeding and later discovered the dog had an undescended testicle should get a full refund based upon the dog being defective and nonmerchantable. According to the terms of the agreement between the pet store and the purchaser, if a veterinarian found the puppy was sick within two weeks, the dog could be returned. The dog was also subject to a return within 60 days based upon a health guarantee.

Five days after purchasing the dog, the purchaser took the dog to a veterinarian who examined him and told the purchaser that while in good physical health, the Poodle had a congenital defect. Later in court, two veterinarians testified as expert witnesses that the dog could be bred but would carry the genetic defect, as would the dog's progeny. The pet store's veterinarian examined the Poodle after the purchaser returned him to the pet store. Although finding "both testicles in the scrotum," the veterinarian observed that the right testicle was higher than the left.

The court first turned to the UCC and the implied warranty of merchantability and reviewed what would constitute minimal requirements with regard to sale of "goods." The first test was whether a good was of merchantable quality and would

40. 121 Misc. 2d 612, 468 N.Y.S.2d 441 (N.Y. City Civ. Ct. 1983).

"pass without objection in the trade under the contract description." The court stated, "This standard effectively sums up all of the various 'definitions' of merchantable quality since the principal function of the warranty of merchantability has been to give legal effect to a buyer's reasonable expectations based on trade understanding of the quality of goods normally supplied under such a contract."[41] If the implied warranty of merchantability was to be excluded or modified, this modification must be both in writing and conspicuous.

Given the hereditary nature of the dog's condition, the court determined that the Poodle was "not a merchantable dog" and then considered the subject of warranty of fitness for a particular purpose. The court summarized that the reasons underlying UCC sections 2-314 and 2-315 were (1) the seller must have reason to know the buyer's particular purpose, (2) the seller must have reason to know that the buyer is relying on the seller's skill or judgment to furnish appropriate goods, and (3) the buyer must rely on the seller's skill or judgment.

The court determined that merchants selling a pedigreed dog should "assume that the buyer intends to breed it." The court discussed how the dog's testicles had not descended at the time that the buyer rescinded the contract, although they descended later. While giving the buyer the opportunity to "examine the disputed goods" at the point of purchase, the court treated this opportunity differently than in the context of an unprofessional buyer, as in the instant case. The court concluded that the buyer revoked her acceptance and returned the Poodle lawfully under UCC section 2-608. Damages available under UCC section 2-711 required that the purchaser be reimbursed for the dog's purchase price of $541.25.

Practice Pointer: Although lawyers may know that warranties under the UCC could apply when a dog is purchased from a merchant, a lawyer may not be fully conversant with the definition of a merchant under the UCC. It is possible that warranties will apply not only when the seller is a professional breeder or business but also when the seller is a rescue. If representing a rescue, reread the UCC.

41. The court stated,

> The second through sixth tests of merchantability, set out in the U.C.C. are as follows: the goods must be at least such as: "(b) in the case of fungible goods, are of fair average quality within the description; and (c) are fit for the ordinary purposes for which such goods are used; and (d) run, within the variations permitted by the agreement, of even kind, quality and quantity within each unit and among all units involved; and (e) are adequately contained, packaged, and labeled as the agreement may require; and (f) conform to the promises or affirmations of fact made on the container or label, if any."

MIZAN ARABIANS V. PYRAMID SOCIETY[42]

Year: *1987*
Category: *Contract Law*
Type of Action: *Breach of Contract*
Animal: *Horse*
Pet Custody Concept: *When the prestige of a state is believed to be at stake, expect court deference to the state's interests.*

The plaintiff, a Minnesota partnership that breeds, shows, and sells Arabian horses, entered into an agreement with the defendant nonprofit to sell a horse at auction. According to their written contract, the horse could not be sold below the reserve bid of $65,000. If the reserve bid floor was not satisfied, the plaintiff would regain possession of the horse. The defendant received a $5,000 pre-sale consignment fee from the plaintiff. This fee was to be credited to a minimum of 12 percent commission on the reserve bid, or amount paid, whichever was higher.

Because of what the court determined was a misunderstanding between the parties, and neither bad faith nor fraudulent conduct, the horse was sold for $30,000 rather than for the $65,000 minimum sale price, known as the "reserve bid." Although the horse owners were in Minnesota and the auction was in Kentucky, the horse was moved to Arkansas, where the plaintiff filed suit in federal court against the prospective buyers and the defendant. In Arkansas, the plaintiff and the prospective purchasers agreed that they could have the horse for a total of $35,000. Following this sale, the district court granted the defendant's motion to transfer the case to the Eastern District of Kentucky, where a bench trial was held. The defendant appealed the court's determination of damages. This matter later came on before the federal court on the basis of diversity jurisdiction.

It was the defendant's position that because the horse once had a fair market value of $30,000, the plaintiff's damages recovery should have been zero. The court rejected this analysis by stating,

> The flaw in Pyramid's argument is that Mizan did not bargain for the "fair market value" of the horse. Rather, according to the terms of the agreement between the parties, Mizan justifiably expected one of two results: either (1) it would receive $65,000 or more for the sale of its horse, or (2) the horse would be returned. Neither expectation was fulfilled.

The court also considered the prestige of horse breeding and auctioning in Kentucky, together with the public policy aspect of the conflict, saying the business is "the Commonwealth's most prestigious and valued industry." The court held the auction to "strict scrutiny" given the "Commonwealth's interest in maintaining the integrity of its leading industry."

The court reaffirmed the lower court's award based upon the reserve bid, subject to certain offsets, including the amount paid for the horse and the 12 percent

42. 821 F.2d 357 (1987).

commission that applied, regardless of whether the horse was sold. The court emphasized that punitive damages are not an available remedy in a contract dispute. It was the court's position that denying the defendant its 12 percent commission was equivalent to requiring the defendant to pay punitive damages.

Practice Pointer: This case is useful for lawyers wanting to know the lingo in the horse business. The court was not shy about modifying the rule of law when it believed public policy issues were at stake. Here, public policy meant the good reputation of Kentucky's horse industry. It was because of this public policy aspect that the court applied a strict scrutiny standard. Public policy standards could also apply to disputes between parties when there is evidence of animal mistreatment or domestic abuse. Also, please note that unless a state law provides otherwise, punitive damages are not recoverable in a contract dispute.

ANDERSEN V. KOSS[43]

Year: *1988*
Category: *Contract Law*
Type of Action: *Replevin, Summary Judgment*
Animal: *Dog*
Pet Custody Concept: *The court should be cautious when considering summary judgment motions.*

This case involved an ownership dispute about a dog named San Island Sinclair. The plaintiff, a Skye Terrier breeder, shipped San Island Sinclair to the defendant, who paid the dog's transport costs and sent the plaintiff a check for $500. Instead of cashing the defendant's check upon receipt, the plaintiff sent the defendant a written contract to execute wherein the plaintiff would have a co-ownership interest in the dog. When the defendant refused to sign the contract, the plaintiff initiated a replevin action to regain possession of the dog. She alleged in her motion for summary judgment that as the purchase price of the dog was $500, the transaction was subject to the statute of frauds. When the lower court granted summary judgment to the plaintiff, the defendant appealed.

The court of appeals reversed the lower court's summary judgment decision for the defendant because the issues were not "determinable solely as a question of law." The court set forth the following guidelines for when a summary judgment would be appropriate:

- Grant when, after considering affidavits, depositions, admissions, exhibits, and pleadings, there are no material fact issues.
- Evidence is construed in favor of the nonmoving party.
- Do not grant when reasonable persons might draw different inferences from undisputed material facts.

43. 527 N.E.2d 1098, 173 Ill. App. 3d 872 (Ill. App. 1st Dist. 1988).

- The moving party's right should be free from doubt.

These standards are reflective of well-settled law. The court further reasoned that the parties' "conduct was sufficient to take the oral contract out of the statute of frauds" and offered a painstaking analysis as to the difference between accepting and contemplating unilateral action under the UCC. The court emphasized that the "receipt and acceptance either of goods or of the price constitutes an unambiguous overt admission by both parties that a contract actually exists."

An oral contract for the sale of goods that has been partially performed is enforceable by either party. As the court could not determine if the oral contract between the defendant and the plaintiff "was unenforceable as a matter of law," a summary judgment could not be granted. Although the application of equitable principles was not overtly stated in this opinion, the court's concern about due process and equity was transparent. The court stated that summary judgment dispositions constitute a "drastic means of disposing of litigation" and emphasized the importance that "the right of the moving party is free from doubt."

Practice Pointer: Pet custody disputes in dissolutions of marriage, as well as in a variety of civil disputes, often involve claims for replevin and summary judgment actions. Therefore, it is important to learn how they apply in the applicable state. A client might be able to gain the ear of the court by advancing a part performance argument, too. When the court of appeals decided that the issue could not be "determined solely as a question of law," imagine that the defendant offered the court a persuasive narrative. Regardless of how impersonal a judicial officer may seem, the court may know that a dog is not just personal property anymore, so always offer a compelling narrative.

Nuijens v. Novy[44]

Year: *1989*
Category: *Contract Law*
Type of Action: *Breach of Warranty*
Animal: *Dog*
Pet Custody Concept: *The UCC does not apply to all sellers.*

This case arose in a small claims court. Although the plaintiff purchased a very sick dog for $400, the seller was neither a merchant nor a pet dealer within the business law definitions that governed the sale of cats and dogs. Because the plaintiff did not buy the dog from a merchant, she could not claim a breach of express and implied warranties under the UCC. As the plaintiff failed to timely produce a licensed veterinarian certificate or return the dog within the five-day warranty period, she had no recourse.

It was conceded that the plaintiff had orally advised the seller that the dog had a urinary infection within the five-day guarantee. Aware of the low economic value of the animal, the court meticulously looked for a remedy that would be satisfactory to

44. 543 N.Y.S.2d 887, 144 Misc. 2d 453 (N.Y. Just. Ct. 1989).

the plaintiff, who opposed returning the dog to the seller. Finding none that would be acceptable to her, the plaintiff's action was dismissed.

Practice Pointer: The small claims court may try to help someone against a bad actor if there is any legal theory the court can hang its hat on. Pull out your old law books, and be light on your feet. Think outside of the box, and teach yourself to hop between substantive practice areas.

SCHNEIDER V. GREEN[45]

Year: *1990*
Category: *Contract Law*
Type of Action: *Breach of Contract, Breach of Contract Actionable in Tort*
Animal: *Dog*
Pet Custody Concept: *Courts may give more time and attention to cases where dogs have monetary, rather than relational, value and when there is a bad actor.*

This case is an excellent example of how courts are willing to give considerable time and attention to the upper class or to animals regarded as having economic rather than relational value. The plaintiff was the most distinguished Bearded Collie breeder in the United States and had "won more distinguished show prizes than those that the next ten breeders of Bearded Collies have collectively earned." The defendant, a newcomer to the show dog world, had the financial means to shoulder the extraordinary costs of bringing a dog to championship.

The plaintiff and defendant entered into an oral agreement regarding five Bearded Collies that were American Kennel Club (AKC) registered. According to the plaintiff, their agreement consisted of a breeding program where the plaintiff and defendant enjoyed co-ownership of the dogs that would live with the defendant. This would enable the dogs to "benefit from having an interested family of . . . [their] own." The defendant was responsible for the costs associated with the dogs' maintenance and dog shows. Although the defendant was not obligated to breed a dog or bring a dog to championship, the plaintiff retained various rights if bred, including the first and fourth picks of one litter or the second and third picks of the next.

When the parties had a falling out, the plaintiff claimed that they had a joint venture agreement with regard to the five Collies and because the defendant breached their agreement, there should be a dissolution of the joint venture, an accounting, and punitive damages. The plaintiff also sought declaratory relief as to the ownership and possession of the dogs and damages for defamatory statements made against him by the defendant. In contrast, the defendant claimed that she had sole title to three of the Collies and that they co-owned the other two. She also asserted that oral agreements were unenforceable based upon the statute of frauds.

In sorting out the claims, the court presumed the agreement that the plaintiff had with the defendant was similar to other oral agreements the plaintiff entered into,

45. 1990 WL 151142 (S.D.N.Y.).

wherein (1) AKC registration showed co-ownership, (2) the plaintiff had breeder approval rights, (3) the plaintiff had specified choice of litter rights, (4) the plaintiff had the right to approve which shows the dogs would participate in, (5) the resident co-owner would assume the costs of the dogs' maintenance, and (6) the resident co-owner could decide whether to breed or show the dogs.

Due to the oral nature of the alleged agreement, the court sifted through considerable testimony in order to determine which party was credible, or perhaps more credible, than the other. The plaintiff's testimony was consistent with an ownership agreement that suddenly surfaced close to the trial date. The court commented on "the obvious utility of this document" and said its late production cast "significant doubt on its authenticity." The defendant's version of the oral agreement was viewed as "inconsistent with her written and oral admissions, her testimony and the co-ownership arrangements of the other dogs purchased" during a trip to England. It seemed that the testimony of the defendant's star witness lacked credibility, too.

Certain evidence suggested that the plaintiff and defendant had co-ownership of particular dogs, while other evidence seemed consistent with individual ownership claims. The defendant registered one of the Collies in her own name with the AKC but registered the same dog as co-owned with the plaintiff in a "Dial-N-Entry."

A serious aspect of this dispute was the defendant's claim that a jointly owned dog might have the von Willebrand's factor disease. There were conflicting test results as to whether one of the Collies was a carrier. The plaintiff asserted a defamation claim, too, against the defendant. While the parties disagreed as to whether the offspring of the disputed dog could be registered, the AKC registered the offspring without the defendant's consent.

Among the claims and issues the court addressed were (1) the nature of the agreements between the parties, (2) whether the agreements between the parties were breached, and (3) the remedies available as compensation for the breach. Criteria used to determine if there was a joint venture included:

> 1) two or more parties entered into an agreement to carry on a specific enterprise or undertaking either for an expectation of profit or presence of adventure; 2) their agreement evidences their intent, either express or implied, to be joint venturers; 3) each contributes either property, financing, skill, knowledge, effort or other asset; 4) each has some degree of mutual control or management over the venture; 5) each has a property interest in the subject matter of the venture and 6) there exists a provision for the sharing of both profits and losses.

Part of what was intriguing about the court's criteria for a joint venture was a statement made by the court, relying on *Ramirez v. Goldberg*:[46]

> [A]bsence of a monetary contribution to the arrangement is not a barrier to the classification of the agreement as a joint venture as the individual who

46. 82 A.D.2d 850, 852, 439 N.Y.S.2d 959 (2d Dept. 1981).

offers services, for a share of the net profits from several transactions risks losing the value of those services, and therefor is subject to losses.[47]

Another issue was what impact the statute of frauds had on an oral agreement that "could not be performed within one year." The court somewhat artfully dodged the statute of frauds question without even discussing the subject of part performance by concluding that "the agreement conceivably could have been fully performed within one year." The court's finagling of the statute of frauds may be of interest to family lawyers whose pet custody practices include civil disputes.

As to the dissolution of the joint venture, the court looked at the requisite grounds for dissolution, including gross misconduct, lack of good faith, or "some cause which produces serious and permanent injury to the venture rendering it impractical to carry on business." The plaintiff claimed dissolution was warranted because his relationship with the defendant was "beyond repair." The court agreed that a dissolution was appropriate because it was no longer possible nor productive for the parties to have the joint venture.[48]

An interesting aspect of this 1990 opinion was the court's recognition that the normal process of granting an accounting for a dissolution of a joint venture, the liquidation and distribution of the assets, was not feasible due to the nature of the assets—the dogs. To find another solution, the court considered the decision in *Sherrier v. Richard*,[49] a case involving "valuable art objects not appropriate for liquidation," wherein the court utilized "equitable" powers with regard to distribution. Fashioning a remedy for the equitable distribution of the dogs was difficult. The court considered the terms of the joint venture and the purpose of contract law. A challenge for the court, notwithstanding the defendant's breach of the agreement, was that the award of contractual damages should be "limited to those losses within the contemplation of the defendant when the contract was made."

Ultimately, the defendant's breaches included (1) advertising a dog in a Westminster show catalogue without including the plaintiff's name, (2) failing to have the plaintiff participate in making show decisions, (3) failing to obtain the plaintiff's consent with regard to breeding decisions, (4) registering one dog at the AKC in the defendant's name only, and (5) failing to give the plaintiff puppies from one of the litters. Notwithstanding these contractual breaches, given the enormity of the defendant's economic contribution to the dogs, the court found that awarding her possession of a particular dog had the effect of providing her with a "partial recovery for her contribution."

Although the court was conservative in its initial analysis about how to resolve the contractual aspects of the parties' dispute, the court stated that an independent tort claim might arise even when the root of the claim was a contract breach, as

---

47. If this same reasoning was applied to family court, the reasoning implicit in the concept of a joint venture could apply when one of the parties contributes the money, such as purchase price and the cost of veterinary care, and the other party contributes services, such as the primary care and training of a pet.

48. If this subject was carried over to family court, the joint venture type of analysis could be applied to when courts should permit the parties to co-own an animal. Parties in a divorce action might be able to co-own a dog if they had an amicable and cooperative history and unable to co-own a dog in a situation where hostility between them was palpable.

49. 564 F. Supp. 448 (S.D.N.Y. 1983).

compared to independent contract and tort claims. Relying on *North Shore Bottling Co. v. C. Schmidt and Sons, Inc.*[50] and *Clark-Fitzpatrick, Inc. v. Long Island R. Col.*,[51] the court said, "A contracting party may be charged with a separate tort liability arising from a breach of duty distinct from, or in addition to the breach of contract." Furthermore, relying on *Albemarle Theatre Inc. v. BayBerry Realty Corp.*[52] and *Carmania Corp., N.V. v. Hambrecht Terrell Int'l.*,[53] the court added, "Where a contract creates a relationship of legal duty to another, independent of the contract obligation, and that relationship is breached by a 'trust betrayed [or] confidence abused,' those actions can make a 'breach of the contract actionable as a tort.'"

The court elegantly said,

> A breach of contract may be so intended and planned; so purposely fitted to time, and circumstances and conditions; so inwoven into a scheme of oppression and fraud; so made to set in motion innocent causes which otherwise would not operate, as to cease to be a mere breach of contract, and become, in its association with the attendant circumstances, a tortious and wrongful act of omission.

In the instant case, the court specifically found that the defendant's "conduct evinces a pattern of tortious behavior whereby Green breached the duty of finest loyalty and honesty imposed by law upon a joint venture, *Gramercy Equities Corp. v. Dumont*,[54] in order to promote her ambition to begin her own kennel, at the expense of the joint venture and plaintiff."

As the defendant severely damaged the plaintiff's reputation, the court ordered her to pay $15,000. On the subject of slander per se, when the defendant said at a prestigious kennel show that "Dick really didn't have a right to have sold those puppies because Henry had this disease and she wanted to be a reputable breeder," the court determined that the defendant's statement was "motivated by ill will, spite and reckless disregard for the truth." The court went even further and concluded that the defendant "was aware her statement was absolutely false." In addition to the monetary relief the court awarded the plaintiff for damages stemming from the tortious breach of contract and other claims, which altogether came to $37,000, the court granted the plaintiff another $5,000 for additional damages to punish the defendant for "willful or malicious conduct and to deter others from similar behavior."

Considerable attention in this opinion was given to evidence that the defendant was a bad actor. Even so, this decision only mildly addressed the best interests of the Collies that were the subject of the joint venture. Ultimately, the defendant received two of the five Collies for "humane" reasons.

Practice Pointer: First and foremost, the credibility of each party matters. Beyond that, in animal-related business ventures, courts can be swayed by the typical course of

50. 22 N.Y.2d at 179, 292 N.Y.S.2d at 92.
51. 70 N.Y.2d 382, 389, 521 N.Y.S.2d 653, 656–57 (1987).
52. 27 A.D.2d 172, 175–76, 277 N.Y.S.2d 505, 510 (1st Dept. 1967) (citing Rich v. New York Cent. & Hudson Riv. R.R. Co., 87 N.Y. 382 (1882)).
53. 705 F. Supp. 936 (S.D.N.Y. 1989).
54. 72 N.Y.2d 560, 534 N.Y.S.2d 908 (1988).

conduct in an industry where many deals are commenced with a handshake and unimpressed by statute of frauds assertions where there has been part performance. If your client is a bad actor, settle your case.

WERRONEN V. TAYLOR[55]

Year: *1992*
Category: *Contract Law*
Type of Action: *Enforcement of Partnership Agreement*
Animal: *Horse*
Pet Custody Concept: *Under partnership law, the term "co-owners" means the business, not the assets used in that business.*

A licensed horse trainer bought a thoroughbred racehorse for $5,500, and days later, the trainer received a payment from the plaintiff regarding the same horse for the same amount. Although the parties orally agreed that the trainer would train the horse and gain 50 percent of any purses or net profit upon the sale of the horse, the parties disagreed as to whether the plaintiff was to be the sole owner of the thoroughbred or whether the parties were co-owners.

The supreme court entered a judgment for the plaintiff. The defendant appealed to the supreme court's appellate division, alleging that the supreme court erred in refusing to include a jury instruction defining partnership law. When rendering its decision, the court emphasized that under partnership law, the term "co-owners" "refers to the business, not to the assets used in that business." Therefore, whether the parties formed a partnership was not relevant to the determination of who owned the horse. The court expressed confidence in the jury's assessment of witness credibility and verdict. Judgment for the plaintiff was affirmed.

Practice Pointer: In this case, be aware that the horse trainer may have lacked the quality of lawyer that the plaintiff had. This is a cautionary tale for the less affluent to be sure to enter into detailed written agreements with rich people.

55. 589 N.Y.S.2d 666, 187 A.D.2d 774 (N.Y. A.D. 3rd Dept. 1992).

Gluckman v. American Airlines, Inc.[56]

Year: *1994*
Category: *Contract Law, Tort Law*
Type of Action: *Bailment, Negligent and Intentional Infliction of Emotional Distress, Summary Judgment, Tort of Outrage, Loss of Companionship*
Animal: *Dog*
Pet Custody Concept: *Transport decisions can be deadly.*

This is an important case to remember when contemplating flying on an airplane with a pet in cargo or if the issue of shipping an animal arises. The plaintiff owned a two-and-a-half-year-old Golden Retriever named Floyd. When an airline denied Floyd transport in the passenger cabin of an airplane, Floyd's owner made arrangements with the agent for Floyd to be transported in the baggage compartment and bought a special crate for that purpose.

When Floyd was in the American Airlines baggage compartment, the temperature reached 140 degrees Fahrenheit due to an hour delay and the baggage compartment's lack of air conditioning. Floyd suffered heatstroke and brain damage. Following intensive care all night, Floyd was euthanized. The airline did not inform the plaintiff that there were fluctuating temperatures in the baggage compartment. In the eyes of American Airlines, the Golden Retriever was "merely baggage." The airline complained that the owner could have insured the Golden Retriever "for more than the standard, limited amount."

American Airlines' motion for dismissal of the plaintiff's claims for negligent and intentional infliction of emotional distress, loss of Floyd's companionship, and Floyd's pain and suffering were granted pursuant to the Federal Rules of Civil Procedure Rule 12(b)(6). The defendant's motion for summary judgment under Rule 56 of the Federal Rules of Procedure was denied, enabling the plaintiff to proceed with a bailment claim. The essence of this bailment claim was that the airline breached its obligation to deliver and return Floyd to the plaintiff in the "same healthy condition in which he was received."[57]

Practice Pointer: This powerful airline placed a family pet in cargo without any warning to the owner that there was no temperature control. Given the vagaries of airplane schedules, both plane delays and temperature changes were not only predictable, but. it was foreseeable that temperature changes could result in the death of a dog. Punitive or exemplary damages may be awarded when there is gross misconduct or negligence in a tort action, and where compensatory damages are an inadequate remedy.

---

56. 844 F. Supp. 151 (S.D.N.Y. 1994).

57. Pet owners should be aware that unless a pet is allowed to travel in the passenger cabin, letting the animal travel in the baggage compartment is risky. For this reason, private on-demand jets such as Jet Edge International now offer pet-friendly business models. Jennifer Kaplan, *Luxury Jets Pamper Pets with Pilaf, Room to Roam: Globetrotter*, Bloomberg Business, http://www.bloomberg.com/news/articles/2014-12-01/luxury-jets-pamper-pets-with-pilaf-room-to-roam-globetrotter (last visited May 12, 2016).

DIMARIO V. COPPOLA[58]

Year: *1998*
Category: *Contract Law*
Type of Action: *Summary Judgment*
Animal: *Horse*
Pet Custody Concept: *When it comes to oral agreements, the court can assert broad latitude in deducing contract terms in order to achieve a result the court likes and deems fair.*

At issue in this landmark case was whether an oral agreement between the plaintiff racehorse trainer and the owners of the horse named Runaway Groom[59] was enforceable and binding. In ascertaining whether an oral agreement was binding, the court considered whether there was (1) an express reservation, (2) the presence of partial performance, (3) the absence of material terms to be negotiated, and (4) the absence of complexity. Finding the existence of an oral contract, the court granted summary judgment to the defendants. The court found that the plaintiff was compensated according to the agreement and that when the subject matter of the dispute was governed by an oral contract, an unjust enrichment claim could not arise.

Framing its decision in a historical context, the court described the horse racing industry as "a long and rich tradition from which modern trade usage and custom is derived.[60] Contests of speed between horses are among the oldest diversions of humanity." Horse racing was developed by the ancient Greeks, who refined the sport of chariot racing. There was racing without chariots in the first Olympic games. Horse racing was also a "sport of kings" as well as a tradition of European nobles and aristocracy; the court described how the prevalence of "gentlemen's agreements" is part of that tradition.[61]

Based upon the standard and custom in the industry, a trainer is paid a per diem rate plus 10 percent of the horse's gross winnings during the trainer's employment and also receives certain breeding rights in the stallion. The defendants argued the

58. 10 F. Supp. 2d 213 (E.D.N.Y. 1998).

59. This horse won "The Travers Stakes" in Saratoga, "The Rafty" at Belmont Park, and the "The Prince of Wales" in Canada.

60. *The American Stud Book* dates back to 1873. The horse industry may restrict breeding methods, such as artificial insemination or embryo transfer, to maintain tradition and control. There are horse registries for purebreds. There are closed stud books, meaning that unless the animal has two registered parents, the horse cannot be registered; there are also partially closed stud books. APPALOOSA RELATED REGISTRIES, http://barnlot.tripod.com/registries.html (last visited May 12, 2016). The American Quarter Horse Association registers the offspring of numbered American Quarter Horses in its stud book. An Appendix American Quarter Horse could be a first-generation cross between a registered Thoroughbred and an American Quarter Horse. An Appendix Horse could also be a cross between a numbered American Quarter Horse and an Appendix American Quarter Horse. Horses in the Appendix registry can earn their way into the main stud book by meeting performance requirements. *Types of Awards*, AMERICAN QUARTER HORSE ASSOCIATION, http://aqha.com/Journal/Resources/Awards/Types-of-Awards.aspx (last visited May 12, 2016).

61. Nowhere in this exuberant discussion was there any hint of the dark side of the horse racing industry with regard to the horses that compete. Oresti Tsonopoulos & Jim Luttrell, *Horse Racing's Dark Side*, N.Y. TIMES, http://www.nytimes.com/video/sports/100000002924701/horse-racings-dark-side.html (last visited May 12, 2016).

trainer should receive "10% of the earnings derived from the syndication of the horse, namely 10% of the gross proceeds realized from the sale of forty equal shares of the horse."[62]

The court was dismissive of the defendants' contention that Article 2 of the UCC did not apply, as the sale of a racehorse was a sale of goods. The sale of fractional interests in a racehorse pursuant to a syndicate agreement was also a sale of goods under the UCC.[63] The court said that a syndicate share was "only one of the claimed elements of compensation." The court then offered a brief tutorial about the horse business, while describing how syndication works, saying,

> Each syndicate interest grants the holder a proportionate share in the profits and expenses of the stallion, and one breeding right per year, called a "season." A season, also referred to as a "cover" or "nomination," is the right to have a mare serviced by a named stallion during a particular [annual] breeding season.

The court added that "Just as a mare who is at the point in her estrous cycle when she is ready to breed is said to be 'in season,' the stallion who copulates with the mare 'covers' her back."

The court continued,

> [A]dditional seasons, or covers, are sold in a market commonly referred to as the bloodstock market. The stallion's seasons are sold to outside parties in two ways. First, on a guaranteed live foal basis if the offspring stands and nurses. Second, on a non-guaranteed basis, for the right to breed the horse with no guarantee of a live foal.

The court indicated in a number of ways that it utilized principles from the Restatement (Second) of Contracts. The court offered that choice of law rules did not apply in this diversity case subject to *Erie Railroad Co. v. Tompkins*.[64]

Impressed by an article that advocated flexibility with regard to contracts rather than the "former rigidly imposed requirements of certainty of terms,"[65] the court said that the "denigration of a formalistic approach to contract interpretation focuses on equitable and ethical considerations of fairness. It allows the recognition and enforcement of agreements that previously might have failed." It was interesting how the court gave itself considerable latitude to achieve "fairness." Simply put, the court summarized how it thought contract law should work in the context of the cultural tradition of horse racing and effectively said, "Let it be so.".

The defendants said the parties' oral agreement was unenforceable, as it failed to satisfy New York's statute of frauds. The court did not conceal its displeasure that this issue was raised for the "first time in their post-hearing memorandum." The court

---

62. In meticulous dicta, the court offered how syndication works and how the statute of limitations applies to a syndication agreement. A horse is syndicated "upon sale of one fractional interest."

63. John J. Kropp et al., *Horse Sense and the UCC: The Purchase of Racehorses,* 1 Marq. Sports L.J. 173–75 (1991).

64. 304 U.S. 64, 58 S. Ct. 817, 82 L. Ed. 1188 (1938).

65. Eyal Zamir, *The Inverted Hierarchy of Contract Interpretation*, 97 Colum. L. Rev. 1710, 1750 (1997).

cogently stated, "The statute of frauds was designed to prevent fraud in the proving of certain legal transactions particularly susceptible to deception, mistake and perjury" and that "There is no hint of fraud here. This was an employment agreement, largely completed. The only real issue is the meaning of the agreement."

Practice Pointer: This decision reminds attorneys involved in pet custody disputes that courts permit a certain amount of contractual latitude when they want to. In this case, latitude was given in an industry where gentlemen's agreements are class based and cultural, and reflective of a valued tradition.

Cahill v. Blume[66]

Year: *2005*
Category: *Contract Law*
Type of Action: *Breach of Warranty*
Animal: *Dog*
Pet Custody Concept: *When acquiring a companion animal from a pet store, it is foreseeable that the pet will have greater lifetime living expenses, as dogs purchased from pet stores are likely to be not only poorly bred but also sourced from a large confinement breeder.*[67]

A woman bought a puppy from a pet store subject to a one-year guarantee. When she learned that her pet had multiple congenital disorders, including hip dysplasia and ocular problems, she sued. Under the state's lemon law, her maximum recovery against the pet store was limited to the purchase price of the puppy. The UCC applied, as the puppy was considered a good under UCC section 2-105 and the pet store was considered a merchant under UCC section 2-104. Remedies available to the buyer under UCC section 2-714 included that she could accept the goods while recovering damages following notification based upon "any non-conformity of tender."

Even though the purchaser did not get the benefit of her bargain, the court said her claim was limited to the purchase price or premium paid for the dog because of the purchase price limit under the lemon law. UCC section 2-714(2) defined the measure of damages available for breach of warranty as the difference between the value of the goods when accepted and what the value would have been if the good was sold as warranted. The buyer was refunded the $760.37 purchase price of the dog.

66. 8 Misc. 3d 1004(A), 2005 WL 1422133 (N.Y. City Civ. Ct.).
67. A growing number of states prohibit pet store sales.

Practice Pointer: Buyer beware when purchasing an animal from a pet store.[68] There is a risk of buying a puppy from a large confinement breeder,[69] also known as a puppy mill, at both pet stores and on the Internet, and even from individuals pretending to be backyard breeders. When purchasing a dog this way, remedies are limited. It is foreseeable that poorly bred dogs will have health and pain-related problems that may in turn become behavioral problems.

Oats v. Whittaker[70]

Year: *2005*
Category: *Contract Law*
Type of Action: *Jurisdiction, Full Faith and Credit*
Animal: *Dog*
Pet Custody Concept: *Familiarize yourself with jurisdictional issues.*

The sellers, who specialized in protection dogs and called themselves Canine Industries, wanted to sell a number of dogs to a couple in Texas. When the dogs they sold, without a signed written agreement, did not work out, the sellers took the dogs back. The buyers requested their money back, but the sellers ignored this request. The buyers commenced a lawsuit in Texas alleging fraud, breach of contract, misrepresentation, and violations of the Consumer Protection Act. When the defendants failed to appear or answer within the time allowed, the Texas court granted a default judgment against the seller for $59,085 in actual damages, together with $213.80 in attorney's fees, $10,000 in exemplary damages, and $10,000 in additional damages.

The main issue addressed by the Commonwealth of Massachusetts Superior Court, when entertaining an action for the registration of a foreign judgment, was whether the Massachusetts court could enforce the Texas judgment under the Full Faith and Credit Clause, Article IV, Section I, of the U.S. Constitution and Title 28 of the U.S. Code. The court addressed whether it had personal jurisdiction over the

68. When the point of sale is a pet store, it is expected that the animals are sourced from large-scale confinement operations, even if the origin of the pet is hidden from a prospective buyer. The store may present the animal as a purebred from a well-known registry; this could be true, as many registries permit large confinement breeders to register. Large confinement operations place content on their websites regarding "satisfied customers." Reputable breeders oppose the sale of puppies or kittens in pet shops and carefully screen potential owners. California, Florida, Illinois, New Jersey, New Mexico, Texas, and Canada have already passed laws restricting pet store sales. *Ordinances*, Companion Animal Protection Society, http://www.caps-web.org/research-investigations/ordinances (last visited May 12, 2016).

69. Large confinement operations, also known as puppy mills and kitty mills, have earned poor reputations. If your client is unsure if his or her animal came from a large confinement breeder, here is some useful criteria for spotting online: the seller does not screen potential owners, puppies are less than eight weeks old when sold, the same images of puppies are advertised using various names and multiple sites, no refund or return policy is offered, more than 20 puppies are advertised as a group, images appear to be photoshopped or taken in artificial settings, and animals are offered as pets for a holiday, such as "Easter pets." *How Much Is That Doggie on My Browser? The Truth behind Online Puppy Sales*, International Fund for Animal Welfare, http://www.ifaw.org/sites/default/files/ifaw-report-how-much-is-that-doggie-on-my-browser.pdf (last visited May 12, 2016).

70. 18 Mass. L. Rptr. No. 29, 637 (MA 1/3/2005), 18 Mass. L. Rptr. No. 29, 637 (Mass. 2005).

defendants and found that because the sellers had minimal contacts with Texas, the grant of jurisdiction in Texas did not offend the traditional notions of fair play and substantial justice. Determining that the defendants failed to meet their burden of proof to show specific facts that would "raise the issue of lack of personal jurisdiction," the court found that the buyers had met their burden of proof as the moving party. Having properly acquired or exercised personal jurisdiction over the defendants, and demonstrating that no genuine issue of material facts existed, the plaintiffs were "entitled to judgment as matter of law."

Practice Pointer: It is risky for clients to avoid a limited appearance when litigation has commenced. When a client fails to do the right thing and appears to be a bad actor, expect damages to rise.

LIPNICK V. REISINGER[71]

Year: *2006*
Category: *Contract Law*
Type of Action: *Breach of Warranty*
Animal: *Dog*
Pet Custody Concept: *If your client has a teacup-sized animal, pay more attention to the potential of health problems.*

Lola, a "Teacup Yorkie," was sold to the appellee. At the time of sale, the appellee was informed of the small dog's special diet and was also told that it "was not uncommon for dogs of this size to have health problems." Pursuant to the terms of the sale agreement, Lola's buyer was required to take Lola to a veterinarian within 48 hours to verify her health. The seller's warranty specifically excluded the condition of hypoglycemia, which was the cause of Lola's death eleven days after purchase. This decision is somewhat challenging to read and understand, perhaps because the court said, "To facilitate our analysis, we have combined several of appellant's assignments of error."

In the court's discussion of the implied warranty of merchantability, instead of talking about the sale of a product as the court already had under "Assignment of Error I," the court discussed the "sale of any good" by a merchant. Lola had been inspected by a veterinarian within 48 hours, as required by the contract, but the veterinarian did not identify any health problems. Despite this finding, the higher court said the appellee could have produced evidence that the puppy had "health defects" when the puppy was sold to her, but the court said that as there were no defects at the time of sale, there was "no evidence to support the trial court's finding that the puppy was ill at the time it was sold to appellee."

The trial court crafted its own warranty for the seller based upon a code of ethics the court had read about in a magazine article that said breeders should keep puppies until they are twelve weeks old and concluded that the appellant breached her duty by selling the puppy at only eight weeks. Although the higher court stated, "We note that

71. 859 N.E.2d 600, 168 Ohio App. 3d 253, 2006 Ohio 3878 (Ohio App. 2006).

there is no basis in law for the trial court's creation of the above implied warranty," it was unclear from the opinion whether the higher court thought there should have been some additional obligation by the seller pertaining to the sale of teacup puppies known to have fragile health.

Finding that there was insufficient evidence to support any duty by the seller or flowing from an implied warranty of merchantability, the higher court poked fun at the trial court's implied ethical warranty while acknowledging that "other implied warranties may arise from course of dealing or usage of trade." It was the higher court's view that the municipal judge could have made evidentiary accommodations for the appellant in the small claims "layman's forum" and could have admitted the veterinary records about hypoglycemia without the need for a veterinarian to testify. Without much direction, the higher court remanded the case.

Practice Pointer: In small claims court, claimants may not know what they are doing and municipal judges who are not conversant in animal law may not know how to help them. When advising clients to go into small claims court alone, suggest that a lawyer help them draft their claims and at least walk them through the steps and evidence and tell them where the court has evidentiary discretion.

Appell v. Rodriguez[72]

Year: *2007*
Category: *Contract Law*
Type of Action: *Breach of Warranty*
Animal: *Dog*
Pet Custody Concept: *Small claims courts afford more substantive justice than other courts do.*

After the seller represented to the plaintiffs that a veterinarian had already examined the dog, the plaintiffs purchased a Great Dane puppy from a breeder. The contract at the time of sale stated that the puppy was in good health, "without defect or disease," but required that "any claims regarding the health of the dog be made within three business days of purchase." Two weeks after purchasing the puppy, the plaintiffs' veterinarian determined that the puppy had severe hip dysplasia. The plaintiffs filed a claim asking for the purchase price of the dog and the cost for the hip correction surgery. The trial court awarded the plaintiffs the $1,500 purchase price of the dog.

The New York court called the dog a "good" and the breeder a "merchant" under the UCC and emphasized that the standard of review for a small claims court judgment was whether there was "substantial justice" based upon "the rules and principles of substantive law." The higher court agreed with the trial court that the seller breached the UCC implied warranty of merchantability when he sold the plaintiffs

72. 2007 N.Y. Slip. Op. 50051(U) (N.Y. App. Term 1/8/2007), 2007 N.Y. Slip. Op. 50051 (N.Y. App. Term 2007).

a puppy with a congenital defect, notwithstanding the contractual three-business-day reporting deadline.

In explaining its decision, the higher court emphasized that "A small claims judgment may not be reversed absent a showing that there is no support in the record for the court's conclusions, or that the court's determination is otherwise so clearly erroneous as to deny substantial justice." Accordingly, the court affirmed the trial court's decision, granting the plaintiffs $1,500 in damages.

Practice Pointer: The concept of substantive justice, which is said to be based upon the rules and principles of substantive law, is commonly integrated with equitable principles in small claims court. When advising clients as to what might happen, tell them the court is more likely to place justice before the law than a court that applies the rule of law.

Maguire v. Mohrmann[73]

Year: *2007*
Category: *Contract Law*
Type of Action: *Consumer Fraud*
Animal: *Dog*
Pet Custody Concept: *When the court cares about wrongdoing, it will reject rigid legal interpretations that thwart justice.*

When the defendant, a private dog breeder, sold an English Springer Spaniel puppy to the plaintiff with a health certificate, she concealed the fact that the puppy had recently been treated for worms. When the plaintiff later called the defendant, she disclosed that the puppy had been ill but claimed that she had nursed him back to health. The plaintiff took the puppy to a veterinarian on day four following the Spaniel's purchase, and the puppy died on day five.

Evidence showed that while the plaintiff spoke to the defendant on the way to the plaintiff's veterinarian when the dog was critically ill, the defendant ignored the plaintiff's subsequent repetitive efforts to communicate with her by telephone, e-mail, and online messages. The trial court's decision was affirmed, notwithstanding shortcomings in meeting the regulatory requirements established by the Division of Consumer Affairs with regard to the Consumer Fraud Act. The plaintiff was awarded the purchase price of $1,000, together with veterinary costs of $399.52, with regard to her dead puppy.

Although not in strict compliance with her duties per the regulation requirements of the Division of Consumer Affairs, the plaintiff's efforts were found to be in "the spirit of this regulation" and constituted "substantial compliance." The trial court doubted that any examination had taken place by the defendant's veterinarian.

Recognizing that the defendant was a bad actor, the trial court cobbled together a decision reflecting contract, regulatory, and equitable principles. The appellate court expressed an idea, notwithstanding the plaintiff's tardiness in presenting a veterinary

73. 935 A.2d 1259, 397 N.J. Super. 103 (N.J. Super. 2007).

certification of unfitness in compliance with regulations, by stating, "We reject such a rigid interpretation of the regulatory procedures, which would undercut Maguire's consumer claim."

This was yet another New Jersey case where both the trial court and higher court were willing to invest judicial time to right a wrong in a dispute involving the greater principles of justice and fairness without utilizing a rigid interpretation of a rule of law. This is the kind of decision that may be of use to the family court.

Practice Pointer: Look at other decisions out of New Jersey and Vermont. These jurists seem to be advanced and care about fairness and justice. On the West Coast, look to decisions from the states of Oregon and Washington. Also look north to Alaska and south to Hawaii. In the Midwest, look to Illinois..

Scruggs v. Caba[74]

Year: *2007*
Category: *Contract Law*
Type of Action: *Breach of Contract*
Animal: *Dog*
Pet Custody Concept: *When people do not get along, the court will look for ways to avoid a co-ownership determination.*

The owner of a Poodle named Lucy initiated an action for her recovery and also sought damages resulting from the defendant's refusal to return the dog. One of two plaintiffs was a veterinarian and the registered owner of Lucy. This plaintiff had a close relationship with the defendant; they attended dog shows together and had contemplated co-ownership of Lucy. This plaintiff once allowed the defendant to keep Lucy for several months, but when the defendant offered to buy Lucy, this plaintiff declined.

The defendant argued that notwithstanding both plaintiffs' failure to sign her proposed agreement, she and the plaintiffs were co-owners of Lucy. She argued that the statute of frauds, which requires that a contract involving the sale of goods over $500 be in writing and signed by both parties, did not apply and asserted a special defense to the doctrine of equitable estoppel. The court said that "while there is a promissory estoppel exception to the statute of frauds, there is no equitable exception" and the "party seeking to avoid the bar must prove part performance of the contract."

The court required that the defendant introduce "acts offered as evidence of part performance when they do not compel the inference that there was some contract by which these acts were required of the plaintiffs and, therefore, explainable under no other theory. If the acts are reasonably explicable on some other ground . . . they are not sufficient to take the case out of the statute of frauds." The defendant, not able to produce evidence of acts proving part performance of her proffered agreement, instead sought compensation of $19,450 for grooming, showing, and feeding Lucy a

74. 2007 WL 866068 (Conn. Super.).

special diet. The defendant offered to waive reimbursement for these expenditures if awarded Lucy.

The plaintiffs demonstrated that others had watched Lucy without charge, and there was no agreement to compensate the defendant for Lucy's care. The court did not award damages to either party, classifying both damages claims as "speculative," and found that the plaintiffs were Lucy's lawful owners and were entitled to her immediate and continuing possession. Although Lucy lived with the defendant with the plaintiffs' permission for two months, and later for another four months, the defendant simply fell short in proving her position.

Practice Pointer: After informing your client that your efforts may prove unsuccessful, liberally raise equitable claims and exceptions, such as a promissory estoppel exception to the statute of frauds, if this will advance a client's position. Dig deep in the common law for ideas on how to proceed. Look for old legal maxims, and consider them as a treasure trove.

Budd v. Quinlan[75]

Year: *2008*
Category: *Contract Law*
Type of Action: *Breach of Warranty*
Animal: *Dog*
Pet Custody Concept: *Statutory remedies may not be exclusive.*

The plaintiff initiated a small claims action after purchasing a puppy from the defendant for $400. Finding that the puppy was sick, the plaintiff immediately spent $2,383 on veterinary expenses. Pursuant to the General Business Law, a purchaser can recover the price he or she paid for veterinary services up to the cost of the animal, or, when the seller is a merchant, the buyer may proceed on the alternative claim of breach of an implied warranty of merchantability under UCC section 2-314. The business law expressly states that the remedy set forth therein is not an exclusive remedy.

The supreme court increased the lower court's award of $400, which was the purchase price of the dog, to accomplish "substantial justice," taking into account the veterinary costs. The idea of substantial justice is associated with fair play and means that there has been justice to a sufficient degree, even if not necessarily in the form of the law, consistent with the Federal Rules of Civil Procedure Rule 8(f).

Practice Pointer: Carrying the idea of substantial justice over to family law and disputes regarding companion animals, the question arises as to whether substantial justice would mean consideration of human and animal best interests or perhaps a "justice for all" standard.

75. 19 Misc. 3d 66, 860 N.Y.S.2d 802, 2008 N.Y. Slip. Op. 28156 (N.Y. App. Term. 2008).

Hardenbergh v. Schulder[76]

Year: *2009*
Category: *Contract Law*
Type of Action: *Breach of Warranty*
Animal: *Dog*
Pet Custody Concept: *When the court is offended by one party's behavior, it may grant the other party more money than expected.*

The plaintiff purchased a puppy from the appellant merchant and subsequently sought medical treatment, alleging the puppy was in poor health at the time of sale. The court concluded that the defendant owed the plaintiff a sum equal to the cost of veterinary care that the plaintiff spent on the puppy. In this short but influential decision, the supreme court affirmed the decision of a civil court judge.

The court, finding that the sale of the dog represented the sale of a good under UCC section 2-105, and that the seller was a merchant under UCC section 2-104, allowed the plaintiff to seek damages based upon a claim for breach of the implied warranty of merchantability under UCC section 2-314. The court narrowly reviewed the civil court's action from a "substantial justice" standpoint.

Practice Pointer: If a seller is a merchant or a breeder, the court may include all or part of the cost of veterinary care, even if it appears that the remedy would otherwise be limited to purchase price.

Miuccio v. Puppy City, Inc.[77]

Year: *2009*
Category: *Contract Law*
Type of Action: *Breach of Statute Regarding Deceptive Acts*
Animal: *Dog*
Pet Custody Concept: *Let the court help you decide what your claim should be.*

The plaintiff bought a Shih Tzu/Maltese puppy that became lethargic and ill seven days after purchase. Even though the plaintiff failed to meet the statutory requirements for a breach of contract claim pursuant to applicable business laws, the court opened another door for her by stating, "Although the claimant cannot prevail on the breach of contract action, there are several problems with the contract from the defendant which give rise to a cause of action under General Business Law 349 which prohibits deceptive acts and practice in any business." More specifically, the court stated that "the differences between defendant's contract and the statutory requirements constitute a 'deceptive act or practice' in the conduct of defendant's business."

76. 2009 N.Y. Slip. Op. 52454(U) (N.Y. App. Term 12/1/2009), 2009 N.Y. Slip. Op. 52454 (N.Y. App. Term 2009).

77. 2009 N.Y. Slip. Op. 50404(U) (N.Y. Civ. Ct. 3/5/2009), 2009 N.Y. Slip. Op. 50404 (N.Y. Civ. Ct. 2009).

Although the court only awarded the plaintiff a nominal amount with regard to the defendant's deceptive acts, the court's help was reflective of what courts are doing elsewhere—helping worthy parties better frame their causes of action and legal theories so that justice may be served. In a pet ownership dispute involving a business, inform the court about seller deceptions.

Practice Pointer: Always share a compelling story with the court.

RIZZO V. PUPPY BOUTIQUE[78]

Year: *2010*
Category: *Contract Law*
Type of Action: *Breach of Warranty, Breach of Statute Regarding Deceptive Acts*
Animal: *Dog*
Pet Custody Concept: *Make sure your client is aware of how costly veterinary care can be.*

Two separate actions were initiated in New York City's small claims court. While one claimant was the mother and the other her daughter, the claims against the seller arose from a single transaction. Because the jurisdictional limit was $5,000, the court made its decision regarding the claim of only one of the claimants, Amanda Caruso.

The Puppy Boutique and Maria Santo sold a Yorkshire Terrier to Amanda Caruso for $1,630. Although the seller operated under the name "The Puppy Boutique," the Department of the State showed no business registered under that name. The Puppy Boutique lacked a license and a permit to operate its business. When selling the puppy, the defendants gave the buyer a waiver agreement to sign that conflicted with statutory requirements on the subject of veterinary care. At issue was whether the seller engaged in deceptive business practices contrary to the General Business Law.

Under the General Business Law, remedies were limited to (1) the return of the puppy for the puppy's purchase price, (2) the return of the puppy in exchange for another puppy, or (3) the reimbursement for veterinary costs not to exceed the puppy's purchase price. Even so, no similar limits pertained to relief available under the UCC. A claimant making a UCC claim can also recover incidental and consequential damages, which could encompass the veterinary expenses that the plaintiffs requested.

Pursuant to the General Business Law, an animal is unfit for purchase when, within 14 days of the sale, the animal becomes ill, shows a "congenital malformation" that impacts the animal's health, or has symptoms of a contagious or infectious disease. The court distinguished between congenital defects developed in utero from genetically "transmitted" hereditary defects. The General Business Law required the pet dealer to "issue a statement indicating that the dog has no known congenital or hereditary condition which would adversely affect the health of the dog at the time of sale or if the dog does have a congenital or hereditary condition a statement from a veterinarian that the dog is fit for sale." Treble damages could be sought for a violation of this provision.

78. 2010 N.Y. Slip. Op. 50926(U) (N.Y. Civ. Ct. 5/3/2010), 2010 N.Y. Slip. Op. 50926 (N.Y. Civ. Ct. 2010).

The buyer was allowed to bring a cause of action for a violation of an express warranty under UCC section 2-313 because the seller was considered a merchant and the puppy a good under the UCC. Although the buyer had paid $1,630 for the puppy, the veterinary bills had reached $6,000 by the time the puppy was euthanized. The buyer was awarded $4,989 for her incidental and consequential damages.

In concert with the UCC, this small claims court utilized the well-drafted General Business Law, with its consumer law features, to send a signal to merchants not to sell a sick puppy. The court issued a higher-than-expected award.

Practice Pointer: Notwithstanding the apprehension of a floodgate problem if custody disputes are allowed in the courthouse, America's small claims courts are demonstrating that they can effectively and efficiently accomplish substantive justice. If a seller is a merchant, the claim falls within the UCC and incidental and consequential damages, including for veterinary care, are available.

Gebbia v. Schulder[79]

Year: *2011*
Category: *Contract Law*
Type of Action: *Breach of Warranty*
Animal: *Dog*
Pet Custody Concept: *For conflicts at the point of sale, courts apply strict standards with regard to compliance with notice provisions.*

In this short decision, the court found that although an implied warranty of merchantability may have applied to the plaintiff's claim that she bought a genetically defective dog, because the plaintiff did not give the defendant notice of her claim within a reasonable time, the UCC remedy was not available. Accordingly, the plaintiff's breach of implied warranty of merchantability failed.

Practice Pointer: Inform clients about statutes of limitations and that courts are not sympathetic to claimants who slumber on their rights and are unlikely to make exceptions for them.

79. 2011 N.Y. Slip. Op. 51725 (N.Y. App. Term 2011).

MARTINELLI V. PETLAND, INC.[80]

Year: *2011*
Category: *Contract Law*
Type of Action: *Class Action*
Animal: *Dog*
Pet Custody Concept: *In the commercial context, the court set the bar high for a cause of action regarding misrepresentation of dogs sourced from large confinement breeders.*

The plaintiffs sought a federal class action certification under Rule 23 of the Federal Rules of Civil Procedure against Petland, Inc., a business that sold puppies at more than 100 locations. It was concealed from consumers that the animals they purchased were sourced from "a dog breeding operation in which the health of the dogs is disregarded in order to maintain a low overhead and maximize profits."[81] The defendant gave the purchasers health certificates and warranties.

In order to get their class certified, the plaintiffs were required to (1) show compliance with Rule 23(a) of the Federal Rules of Civil Procedure, (2) demonstrate that questions of law or fact were common to all class members, and (3) prove that the issues of the class predominated over issues pertaining to individuals, a standard known as a predominance requirement. The plaintiffs sought class certification to advance a claim for a violation of the Racketeer Influenced and Corrupt Organizations Act (RICO), under 18 U.S.C. § 1962, and pursuant to 18 U.S.C. §§ 1341 and 1343.

In order to proceed with a RICO claim, the plaintiffs were required to prove that the defendant had a scheme to defraud using the U.S. mails and wires, the defendant had the intent to defraud, and the defendant's fraudulent scheme proximately caused injuries to the plaintiffs.[82] The court scrutinized the third causation element because without enough reliance on the defendant's alleged fraudulent scheme, the court said the plaintiffs could not establish proximate cause.

The court, almost becoming an emblematic poster child for willful ignorance, scrutinized what would constitute first-party reliance with regard to the legal standard of causation. While willing to consider that specific oral representations to customers about how a puppy was sourced might have established reliance, the court seemed indifferent to what the plaintiffs described as the "pervasive, centrally orchestrated scheme to misrepresent the quality of puppies sold at its stores" through the company's website and brochures. The company asserted its "years of experience in raising quality family pets" and also claimed that the "finest available" puppies were healthy.

False representations were not enough to get the plaintiffs through the certification stage because of the possibility that pets were purchased from the defendant without relying on false representations. As the court put it, "If a class member did

80. R.I.C.O. Bus. Disp. Guide (CCH) 11738, 2009 WL 2424655 (D. Ariz. 2009); 274 F.R.D. 658, R.I.C.O. Bus. Disp. Guide (CCH) 12051, 79 Fed. R. Serv. 3d 587 (D. Ariz. 2011).

81. This is one definition of a puppy mill.

82. The plaintiffs also pursued claims based upon fraud and enrichment violations of the state consumer protection and state trade practices act.

not rely on the alleged fraudulent scheme, that class member cannot prove that the scheme caused his or her purchase and his or her injury."

Perhaps ironically, as the court was about to make a decision that would impact the mental and medical health of puppies sold throughout the country by big businesses to hide puppy mill sourcing, the court offered an emotional salvo about humans loving pets, saying, "A person might buy a puppy because he falls in love with it in the store window," and "a person who falls in love with a puppy in the store window might well purchase the puppy in the absence of any representation concerning its health."[83]

The court briefly considered whether causation was established based upon third-party reliance. The plaintiffs claimed that misrepresentations were made to Petland, Inc. franchisees that the corporation inspected and approved all breeders who supplied puppies, did not support puppy mills, and provided healthy animals. The court's rejection of this claim was based upon the idea that "they cannot be said to rely on that fraud and thereby satisfy the reliance requirement of causation" and that knowledge and culpability constituted an intervening cause that breaks the causal chain between misrepresentation and injury.

The court attributed the lack of reliance as an element of causation as the shortcoming that prevented class certification. Perhaps the court was disingenuous here and was more concerned about how to measure damages. The court's real concern could have been detected in its injury discussion and agreement with the defendant's argument that the proof of injury should be established on an individual basis and rejection of the plaintiffs' broad application of the "simple damage model."

How would the court evaluate individual past and future veterinary claims that could be in excess of the animal's purchase price? It seemed that the court's shortcoming was that it could not envision the connection between veterinary expenses and the scheme to defraud, even though presumably schooled in legal concepts such as credibility, foreseeability, and consequential damages.

The court envisioned a calculation for each class member, including factors such as "where the puppy was bred, whether the puppy satisfied the standards set forth in Petland's representations, where and how the puppy became ill, and what expenses are attributable to illnesses contracted at the breeder as opposed to elsewhere." The court added, "Such issues relate to more than damages; they relate to liability—whether class members were in fact injured by the alleged fraudulent scheme."

Practice Pointer: Let clients know that some court decisions will make right-thinking people mad.

83. By means of comparison, the court also thought the sales pitch to buy a bond was enough to utilize the pervasive fraudulent scheme standard in a securities fraud case but not in a case where there could be love at first sight. *In re* American Continental Corp., 140 F.R.D. 425 (D. Ariz. 1992).

Take Me Home Rescue v. Luri[84]

Year: *2012*
Category: *Contract Law*
Type of Action: *Breach of Contract*
Animal: *Dog*
Pet Custody Concept: *Rescue groups are insistent on enforcing spay and neuter adoption terms, and the court will back them up.*

The mission of Take Me Home Rescue, a nonprofit group based in Los Angeles, was to reduce pet overpopulation. When the rescue adopted a deaf Boxer dog named Lilly from the county, this placement was subject to the condition or contractual requirement that the rescue would not place Lilly in a permanent home before she was spayed.

The defendant, who saw Lilly on the rescue's website, where spay and neuter requirements as a prerequisite for adoption were emphasized, applied to adopt her. Because "Lilly could not be placed for adoption until she was spayed," the defendant was instead given a temporary foster opportunity to care for Lilly until her health improved, at which point she could be spayed and adopted. From the defendant's point of view, Lilly's foster status was a "mere formality."

Once the defendant had possession of Lilly, she changed Lilly's name to Felina and trained her as an agility dog. Upon learning that spaying Lilly might "interfere with Lilly's agility skills," the defendant decided not to spay Lilly and applied to the city of Los Angeles for an "intact license." When the rescue group learned of the defendant's behavior, they first considered whether they would make an exception but then decided they would not. When the rescue group requested a second time that Lilly be spayed and the defendant refused, they sent an e-mail demanding Lilly's return within 48 hours. When this request was not honored, the police were dispatched to the defendant's home, but no one responded.

There were additional communications from the rescue group to the defendant, including a letter advising her that she was in breach of the foster care agreement. The rescue expressed concern that given Lilly's history of mange, if she went into heat, this serious condition could resurface. Eventually, the defendant received a six-month "spay deferment" and then advocated that Lilly undergo a tubal ligation as an alternative to being spayed. Notwithstanding the grant of a spay deferment, the rescue sued the defendant, alleging breach of contract and conversion. The rescue sought declaratory relief as well as a preliminary and permanent injunction. The court was aware that when a sterilization certificate for Lilly was not timely provided by the rescue to the county, the county "threatened to suspend Take Me Home from its adoption program."

The defendant argued that she had been compliant with her foster care agreement, which contained no mandatory spay provision. She argued that the only remedy for a conversion claim was money damages. The defendant stated that the rescue did

84. 208 Cal. App. 4th 1342, 146 Cal. Rptr. 3d 461 (Cal. App. 2012).

not face irreparable damages because the county had only "threatened" to take action against the rescue. For the court's consideration, she offered an article, "Long-Term Health Risks and Benefits Associated with Spay/Neuter in Dogs,"[85] which included a review of scientific literature.

When the defendant failed to appear at the court hearing regarding the preliminary injunction, the court balanced the equities and determined that the rescue was more likely to suffer injury from the denial of the injunction than the defendant would suffer if the court granted a temporary injunction. After setting a bond for the defendant at $5,000, the court determined that if she had Lilly spayed by a veterinarian acceptable to the rescue, the defendant "could remain in possession of Lilly until the entire matter was adjudicated or parties resolved their differences."

The standard of review for a preliminary injunction involves two interrelated factors: (1) the likelihood that the plaintiff would prevail on the merits of the case at trial, and (2) the interim harm that the plaintiff was likely to sustain if the injunction was denied compared to the harm the defendant was likely to suffer if the preliminary injunction was granted. In assessing the second factor, the court needed to consider the inadequacy of other remedies, the degree of irreparable harm, and the necessity of preserving the status quo. Beyond that, if the party seeking the injunction made a sufficient showing of likelihood of success on the merits, the trial court could issue the injunction notwithstanding evidence that the balance of harms tipped in the other party's favor.

Between the parties' written foster care agreement and conversations regarding spaying Lilly, the court determined that they had a "partially integrated agreement that was supplemented by the collateral oral agreement that Lilly, as a foster dog, must either be spayed or returned to Take Me Home." Thus, the rescue had established that they had "a reasonable likelihood of success on the merits of its breach of contract claim." In discussing the subject of integration, the court indicated, "Where the parties execute a written agreement following negotiations, the agreement is at least partially integrated." Parol evidence could then be introduced to prove additional contract terms consistent with the express terms of the written agreement.

Next, the court addressed whether the parties intended for the foster care agreement to be the "exclusive embodiment of their agreement." This kind of intention could be established by a contractual integration clause. The foster care agreement had no material terms on the subject of a spay requirement. Even so, section 30503 of the state's Food and Agriculture Code required that a dog be spayed prior to adoption and the defendant agreed that she would have Lilly spayed. The court said, "The foster care agreement did not contain the entire agreement of the parties, and was only partially integrated." The court also noted that the code provision enabling a person to keep an intact agility dog did not apply to a rescue organization.

The last sentence of the court's discussion was instructive. "Luri is but one pet owner, and can either spay Lilly or adopt another dog; on the other hand, Take Me

85. Laura J. Sanborn, *Long-Term Health Risks and Benefits Associated with Spay/Neuter in Dogs*, Dogs Naturally, http://www.dogsnaturallymagazine.com/long-term-health-risks-benefits-spay-neuter-dogs/ (last visited May 12, 2016). When developing a pet custody practice, be conversant with this type of litigation, particularly if the contract negotiated for your client involves spay and neuter issues.

Home's entire existence depends on its ability to place pets that it obtains from shelters in adoptive homes." This consideration was a persuasive factor in the court's decision that the rescue was more likely to be injured if it did not grant the preliminary injunction, which it did.[86]

Practice Pointer: Agreements between rescue groups and fosters can be rocky. Great care should be taken to discuss expectations and there should be a meeting of the minds. This decision is a must read for lawyers representing rescue groups, clients who obtain their animals from rescue groups, and clients who have a combination of written and oral agreements with others. This case is a good reminder that contractual ownership and possessory rights may be conditioned upon compliance with the material terms of an agreement.

---

86. At least on the surface, there seemed to be limited consideration about the best interests of Lilly, except that there could be both positive and negative health effects from spaying her. Nothing is known about how important an activity like agility training might be to the self-esteem of a deaf dog with a history of potentially life-threatening mange. There was also no information provided about the ability of the defendant to promote Lilly's chastity, particularly if Lilly was involved in agility training with other dogs.

Chapter 6

Property Law and the Meaning of Things

"There are two means of refuge from the misery of life: music and cats."

—*Albert Schweitzer*

An interesting aspect of the development of property law as it pertains to animals is the absence or addition of emotional notes to these decisions. Some are devoid of empathy, some are insincere, and some are filled with emotional sentiment that serves as a springboard for new conceptualizations. They reveal that many believe that animals are property; others believe that animals are not property, while still there are others who believe that animals have mixed characteristics of property and not property.

Companion animals, as property, can be acquired in a variety of ways, including by purchase, gift, or inheritance; finding lost or abandoned property; trading property for property; or performing services for property. A seminal case regarding property rights in animals, discussed throughout this book, was *Sentell v. New Orleans Carrollton Railroad Co.*[1] In this decision, the court offered puzzling hierarchical property and quasi-property classifications. *Sentell* is where the concept of dogs as quasi-property emanated.

LOST AND FOUND ANIMALS

The plight of lost and found animals is a recurring theme in pet custody and ownership disputes. These cases fall primarily into two categories, one type involving

1. 166 U.S. 698, 17 S. Ct. 693, 41 L. Ed. 1169 (1897).

third parties asserting ownership rights[2] and the other type, the more traditional lost and found.[3] The latter concept used to be associated with missing agricultural animals gone "estray."

Title Passing through Operation of Law

When a companion animal is found and brought to an impound facility by operation of law, that entity has a duty to hold the animal for a specified time period as prescribed by ordinance or statute. The length of that hold time can vary; some are very short and unreasonable. Once the hold period is satisfied, a disposition can be made. If the original owner has not located his or her pet within the hold period, good title typically passes to a third party. Asserting the rights of the original owner in this context can be difficult and challenging.[4]

Title Not Passing through Operation of Law

In cases where title has not passed to a third party through operation of law, the dispute is typically between the original owner and the person asserting new ownership rights. Courts may use a balancing test to determine whether the loser or the finder should be awarded the pet. It may be outcome determinative, from an ownership perspective, how hard the owner looked for the pet and how diligently the finder looked for the pet's original owner. The court might be interested in the best interests of the animal, too.

Owners of Lost Animals

If the original owner, perhaps with a search team,[5] goes door to door looking for his or her lost animal; circulates posters with a current photograph of the animal; makes pleas on local radio stations; contacts animal control and all local rescue groups, humane societies, and animal control facilities; and posts on social media sites specializing in lost and found animals, these efforts will help the original owner's position if there is a later dispute. It will also help the original owner's position if the lost animal is microchipped, has a license, and is wearing a collar displaying that license and a tag with contact information.

---

2. A typical issue in this type of case is whether the animal was lost, improperly taken, or stolen.
3. Another way that companion animals come into the legal system is in the context of seizure. See the appendix for a sample animal seizure Memorandum of Law.
4. Unlicensed animals with no microchips are more likely to be euthanized than licensed animals given the reality of short hold period obligations by animal control.
5. A rescue group, including breed-specific groups, may be a great resource.

Owners of Found Animals

In contrast, if the finder of an animal posts the animal's name and photograph on Petfinder.com and similar national and local sites, calls the phone number on the animal's tag but finds it disconnected, locates a microchip through a scanner but finds it only reveals the name of a breeder who went out of business, and passes out leaflets about the animal in the vicinity where the animal was found, the finder will gain a credible position. Courts seem more likely to award the animal to the finder, and not the original owner, if the original owner's efforts to find the animal seem half-hearted and the finder was more diligent.

NOTTI LEGAL QUESTIONS

In the landmark decision of *Graham v. Notti*,[6] emanating from pleadings in a summary judgment action crafted by animal law trailblazer attorney Adam Karp, the appellate court talked about a lost Pomeranian named Harlee. The dog's "story raises questions about the nature of the property interest he represents and the political authority of animal protection agencies to sell or dispose of lost animals and, necessarily, the quality of title to those animals these agencies can convey."[7] The decision came down to jurisdiction—the pertinent question was whether Harlee was found in Spokane County or the city of Spokane. Jurisdiction alone was sufficient for the higher court to reverse the lower court's summary judgment in favor of Harlee's new owner and to remand the case for trial. Before doing so, the court laid out the following important questions that are worthy of your close attention:

- Did the new owner get valid legal title?
- Is an animal shelter under contract with a governmental entity limited to the same police powers that the governmental entity would have been able to exercise?
- Is a city's power to regulate limited by the city's general boundaries?
- How do a state's general laws impact a city's power to regulate?
- Does the UCC apply when there is no UCC transaction for purchase or entrustment?
- How do common law protections for bona fide purchasers impact the dispute?
- When a humane agency has voidable title to a pet, can that entity convey good title to a bona fide purchaser?
- Should the court's decision be impacted by whether the lost animal was unlicensed?

6. 196 P.3d 1070, 147 Wn. App. 629 (Wash. App. 2008).
7. *Id.*

- Should an animal shelter's possessory interest be superior to a citizen's ownership interest?
- If a state gives an entity an imperfect or qualified interest in a pet, does this impact the animal shelter's possessory interest?
- What common law arguments apply to the determination of whether a bona fide purchaser must relinquish ownership or possession of the animal?
- What equitable principles, including the doctrine of equitable estoppel, apply to a determination?
- Can the bona fide purchaser doctrine cure an ultra vives sale of property?

Problem Solving

All of these questions are useful to lawyers involved in ownership disputes regarding lost and found animals, and some of the questions on this list may help you develop your legal theory in other types of custody disputes as well. The answers depend on applicable statutes, common laws, and advocacy to modify, extend, and advance the existing law. Lawyers should know that if the proper entity has held the animal for the minimum hold period, typically title to the animal passes to that entity for dispositional purposes. This means an entity could transfer the animal to a research facility in states where pound seizures are permitted, or could euthanize the animal. Your client should be aware that time is of the essence.

KEY RESEARCH TERMS

Courts may be divided about whether they think lost animal provisions apply to commercial or agricultural animals versus companion animals, and courts are not naïve that their choice may be outcome determinative. Key words to include when researching this subject include estray, stray dog, or stray beast.

MICROCHIPS

The growing judicial expectation is that responsible animal owners will have their pets microchipped. The use of microchips will increase the likelihood that lost companion animals will be reunited with their owner because each chip has a unique number. A universal scanner that generates a radio signal can be used to read the number.[8]

8. A microchip is typically inserted into an animal's back, although it is possible that the chip will migrate over time. Not all scanners can actually read the microchip number because of manufacturer encryption practices designed to gain a competitor advantage.

CONCLUSION

Cases of particular importance in this chapter include *Sentell v. New Orleans Carrollton Railroad Co.*,[9] where the court classified dogs as quasi-property, unless dead or "subdued," thereby impacting police powers over dogs thereafter, and *Nahrstedt v. Lakeside Village Condominium Association, Inc.*,[10] where the court explored horizontal property rights and how they affect no-pets provisions. When looking for moving quotes about the benefits of pets to people of all ages, particularly the elderly and the young and those bedridden due to illness or injury, you will appreciate the poetic and persuasive dissent of Justice Arabian in *Nahrstedt*, a dissent that has in turn both influenced the progression of pet laws and caused the passage of a statute.

APPLICABLE CASE LAW

Sentell v. New Orleans Carrollton Railroad Co.[11]

Year: *1897*
Category: *Property Law*
Type of Action: *Constitutional Law*
Animal: *Dog*
Pet Custody Concept: *Dogs are only quasi-property.*

It is necessary to read this decision to fully appreciate how odd it is that courts keep citing it for its precedential value rather than overruling it. It is easier to understand this decision if you have awareness of the development of the English common law. According to a leading animal law professor, David Favre, animals were historically regarded as either useful or a representative of "ferae naturae," which meant they had a base nature.[12]

This 1897 U.S. Supreme Court decision was about the constitutionality of a state law that limited the value of a dog to the amount fixed on an assessment roll. In the lower court, it was held that the state law was "constitutional and valid as a police regulation to prevent the indiscriminate owning and breeding of worthless dogs." Determining that dog owners have only a conditional interest in this form of property, the supreme court upheld the Louisiana law and affirmed the judgment of the court of appeals. The court's rationale regarding police powers sounds like, and in fact is, out of the 19th century:

9. 166 U.S. 698, 17 S. Ct. 693, 41 L. Ed. 1169 (1897).
10. 33 Cal. Rptr. 2d 63, 8 Cal. 4th 361, 878 P.2d 1275 (Cal. 1994).
11. 166 U.S. 698, 17 S. Ct. 693, 41 L. Ed. 1169 (1897).
12. David Favre, *Living Property: A New Status for Animals within the Legal System*, Michigan State University Animal Legal & Historical Center, https://www.animallaw.info/article/living-property-new-status-animals-within-legal-system (last visited May 12, 2016).

> Property in dogs is of an imperfect or qualified nature, and that they stand, as it were, between animals ferae naturae, in which, until killed or subdued, there is no property, and domestic animals, in which the right of property is perfect and complete. They are not considered as being upon the same plane with horses, cattle, sheep, and other domesticated animals, but rather in the category of cats, monkeys, parrots, singing birds, and similar animals, kept for pleasure, curiosity, or caprice.

The court went on to say,

> They have no intrinsic value, by which we understand a value common to all dogs as such, and independent of the particular breed or individual. Unlike other domestic animals, they are useful neither as beasts of burden, for draught (except to a limited extent), nor for food. They are peculiar in the fact that they differ among themselves more widely than any other class of animals, and can hardly be said to have a characteristic common to the entire race.

In *Sentell*, a man took his valuable, pregnant, American Kennel Club (AKC) registered Newfoundland named Countess Lona for a walk. While "upon the streets, she stopped on the track of the railroad company, and, being otherwise engaged for the moment, failed to notice the approach of an electric car which was coming towards her at great speed; and being, moreover, heavy with young, and not possessed of her usual agility, she was caught by the car and instantly killed." Because the subject was not brought up on appeal, the court did not address the negligence of Countess Lona's owner in crossing the tracks with the pregnant Newfoundland.

The court distinguished between perfect property, which might include horses, cattle, and sheep, and property of an "imperfect and qualified nature." The court essentially established that cats, monkeys, parrots, and singing birds were third rate, meaning on a lower plane.

With regard to the animals not on the same plane, the court said, "All are more or less subject to attacks of hydrophobic madness." This court, in this often-quoted precedent, was aware of what was then widespread and deadly rabies. We now live in the 21st century, where rabies is well-managed.

Looking at the scope of police powers, the court said the state could use these powers to destroy personal property. These police powers extended to killing diseased cattle and destroying obscene books and gambling instruments. Although recognizing that due process rights were granted under the 14th Amendment, the court also said, "Although dogs are ordinarily harmless, they preserve some of their hereditary wolfish instincts." The court emphasized the need for a license, a tax, and identification of a dog by collar and tag.

The court, in utilizing the idea of a plane on which animals exist, did not place dogs above other domestic animals but rather below them.[13] It said that the animals "placed upon the assessment rolls" received the "same guarantees of law as other personal property." In summary, the court found that "it is only under these restrictions

13. Compare and contrast *Sentell* to the Wisconsin Supreme Court's admiration of dogs in *Rabideau v. City of Racine*, 627 N.W.2d 795, 797 (Wis. 2001).

that dogs are recognized as property."[14] Otherwise, it seemed that dogs would be free to roam with other wild animals.

Practice Pointer: If opposing counsel cites *Sentell* as a precedent, take the opportunity to remind the court about the place, and plane, of companion animals in the 19th century and the scientific basis for their disease-based vulnerability to "attacks of hydrophobic madness." Argue science when it helps you.

WILLIAMS V. TAM[15]

Year: *1900*
Category: *Property Law*
Type of Action: *Validity of Sale*
Animal: *Horse*
Pet Custody Concept: *Because a husband and wife may hold a racehorse as joint tenants, tenants in common, or community property, a person seeking to buy the horse should enter into an agreement with both.*

At issue in this somewhat muddy decision involving multiple transactions was the ownership of two racehorses named Midas and Sport McAllister. A married man, Williams, owned a horse with another man, Morris, and Morris sold his interest in Midas to a married woman, Mrs. Williams, the spouse of the above-referenced married man. There was some debate about whether the money used to buy this half-interest was from Mrs. Williams' separate property or from community property.

Another account of the same transaction was that when the married man, Williams, was owed money by his daughter, he refused to accept money from her. Mrs. Williams was able to secure a loan and used this money to buy a half-interest in Midas. The bill of sale from the seller in the half-interest in Midas was in the married woman's name. Midas's earnings were used to purchase the second horse, Sport McAllister.

The trial court determined that on April 9, 1897, the married man "conveyed his interest in said horses to the defendant." Although the wording was a bit unclear, the higher court also stated that "prior to such sale and conveyance defendant had notice of the said ownership of plaintiff in said horses."

When the purchaser of the horses argued that the trial court wrongly found that the married woman had a half-interest in the horses as separate property "by reason of their being purchased with this alleged gift," referring to the gift from father to daughter, the court reviewed the requirements for a valid inter vivos gift. To be valid, the gift must have taken place at once. The higher court recalled that if the gift would "take effect in the future it is no gift, only a promise to give." The court then said,

14. Another interesting aspect of this decision was when the court said, "While the higher breeds rank among the noblest representatives of the animal kingdom, and are justly esteemed for their intelligence, sagacity, fidelity, watchfulness, affection, and, above all, for their natural companionship with man, others are afflicted with such serious infirmities of temper as to be little better than a public nuisance."

15. 131 Cal. 64 (Cal. 1900).

"Here there was no revocation of the gift, and it was in fact received by the donee and appropriated to her own use."

The court explored whether the money used to purchase Midas was sourced from the separate property of the married woman or whether "she and her husband were copartners." If the latter, then the married man's "transfer to defendant was valid and transferred her interest." Next, the court reviewed what type of business the married woman was engaged in and determined that while this business involved training and running horses upon the racetrack, the business did not involve buying and selling horses for profit. The court said,

> A husband and wife may hold property as joint tenants, tenants in common, or as community property. There can be no implication arising from the use made of the horses, nor from the relationship of the parties, that Williams had any authority to sell his wife's interest in the horses, and no authority is shown to have been given him by the plaintiff for such purpose; nor was there any evidence of an agency, whether real or ostensible, for the sale of the plaintiff's interest in the horses.

The mere fact that the horses were in the possession and control of the married man did not affect his duty of "inquiry as to Dow Williams' authority to represent his wife in a transfer of the property." The court stated that the bill of sale for the horses made no reference to the married man having the authority to execute the bill of sale on the married woman's behalf. Based upon the above, the court said, "The motion for nonsuit was properly denied," which seemed similar to the concept that summary judgment for the married woman was granted. More so, the court expressly found "that prior to such sale and conveyance defendant had notice of the said ownership of plaintiff in said horses."

Apart from the court's particular attention to the right of a woman to have separate property rights and to not have those rights easily trounced on when her husband acted without her consent, it was interesting that there was the idea that "A husband and wife may hold property as joint tenants, tenants in common, or as community property" under the civil code.

This case reinforces the idea that when the animals in question are racehorses, anyone can have a half-interest, even though the transfer of these interests could be the subject of a later dispute.[16]

Practice Pointer: Enlighten the court that it is illogical to permit the co-ownership of animals valued for their earnings while denying co-ownership of animals valued for their relationship qualities, particularly when the parties have agreed that they can work together and have stipulated to use well-articulated mediation processes if future conflicts should arise.

16. When the dispute involves a companion animal with primarily relational value, courts sometimes hypocritically focus on the concept of finality of judgment.

Sandefur v. Jeansonne[17]

Year: *1942*
Category: *Property Law*
Type of Action: *Debtor Creditor*
Animal: *Mule*
Pet Custody Concept: *Animals may be used as collateral.*

Two brothers were very close and "partners in almost all of their dealings." They both deposited their business earnings in the bank account of "E. and T. Sandefur," which each could draw against. One of the brothers was married and had children, and the other was a bachelor. The bachelor purchased several mules in Baton Rouge that he used for logging purposes. He kept the mules on his brother's premises, where he lived until one year after his brother's death. The year of his brother's death, he gave a chattel mortgage to the bank regarding the mules he purchased.

When the bachelor moved to another location after his brother's death, he did not take the mules with him and they were used as working animals on the farm by his married brother's widow and his family. When the sheriff seized these mules subject to the chattel mortgage, his brother's widow claimed that the mules were hers and she sought an injunction to prevent their sale. She specifically sought prayer for a "rule nisi." When the rule nisi was issued, the defendants were ordered to show cause as to why an injunction could not be issued.

The gist of the court's decision seemed to be based on the statement, "While long possession is strong evidence of ownership, it is subject to explanation and will not stand up when in conflict with direct evidence of ownership in another." Not only did the higher court deny the widow's rule nisi, but also the court expressed regret that this matter was ever before them given the brothers' close relationship and history of business dealings.

Practice Pointer: Factors influence outcomes.

Romero v. County of Santa Clara[18]

Year: *1970*
Category: *Property Law*
Type of Action: *Employee Liability*
Animal: *Dog*
Pet Custody Concept: *Offer facts that support a valid claim.*

A city removed 48 dogs from their home and cited the dogs' owner with public nuisance. All 48 dogs were destroyed 60 days later. Believing that she had one year to initiate a lawsuit when it was only six months, the owner alleged that the wrong time period

17. 9 So. 2d 80 (1942).
18. 3 Cal. App. 3d 700, 83 Cal. Rptr. 758 (Cal. App. 1st Dist. 1970).

was given to her by an unidentified courthouse employee. The court characterized the plaintiff's contentions as "no more effective than baying at the moon" and emphasized that a person asserting estoppel "must aver and prove all of the required elements."

The court considered the plaintiff's amended complaint wherein she alleged that the defendants' actions were within the scope of their county employment and that, accordingly, liability attached. It seemed as if the court, in its 1970 decision, was unaware of the virtue of clarity of expression when it said, "The amended complaint does not aver that the myrmidons of the animal shelter or pound did something the laws or ordinances did not authorize them to do, at the end of 60 days, but we note Agricultural Code, sections 31107 and 31108."

The decision got worse with regard to what seemed to be unbridled contempt for the plaintiff, who notably had a Hispanic surname. The court said, "Appellant seeks to limit her attack on the augment of dismissal, to the order relative to the general demurrer. This is barking up the wrong tree." The court then stated that an order sustaining the demurrer was not appealable. Ultimately, the court of appeals affirmed the superior court's general demurrer and summary judgment decision in favor of the county.

Although 48 dogs were destroyed, there was no indication that any of the dogs were in poor health or not well cared for. Instead, the allegation was only that the owner was "keeping a public nuisance." It is unknown how much land the plaintiff had or whether she lived in an urban or agriculturally zoned area.

Although the owner received some due process, including a hearing involving the district attorney, it was unclear what authority the district attorney had to approve the dogs' destruction. Perhaps there was a local ordinance permitting the disposition of dogs at a shelter if not placed in a suitable home within 60 days, during which time the hold period ran. Hold periods are common in these kinds of situations. It was less clear why the plaintiff and her attorney thought a judge needed to sign an order as a predicate to the 48 dogs' destruction.

The higher court made fun of the plaintiff's moving affidavits, stating that they "have singular lacunae, for they do not present the facts which would illuminate the incident as a product of official action. When one wants to get a bear up a tree, he should use the whole pack and not a single dog." What the court was perhaps trying to communicate was that the plaintiff's affidavits were not on point for the legal issues at hand. After all, the court said, "These facts were sufficient to destroy the issue of estoppel" and then concluded that "the necessary elements for estoppel are not established as a matter of law." When estoppel was not established, the plaintiff's "failure to sue within the time specified was fatal to the causes of action." Given the court's earlier use of puns, perhaps using the word "fatal" was designed to further demean the plaintiff.

As a final and insincere salvo, the court offered, "We regret that appellant suffered the loss of her pets. But a nuisance is a right thing in the wrong place, like a pig in a parlor, or 50 dogs where the law says they should not be maintained under the conditions specified."

Practice Pointer: Step back and look at this 1970 decision in the next millennium. There is growing understanding of what due process is required before an owner may be deprived of property rights. This case stands out as indefensibly condescending, both regarding the unexplained killing of 48 dogs and because the decision has an arbitrary and capricious ring.

BROUSSEAU V. ROSENTHAL[19]

Year: *1980*
Category: *Property Law*
Type of Action: *Bailment*
Animal: *Dog*
Pet Custody Concept: *There are many ways to argue what a dog is worth.*

The plaintiff's dog died while boarded at a kennel, and the court carefully and thoroughly addressed the value of the dog to the woman who loved him. When the plaintiff left her healthy eight-year-old dog at a kennel, she entered into a bailment for the mutual benefit of herself and the kennel. Under these circumstances, a bailee is held to the standard of ordinary care.

When the plaintiff went back to the kennel a week later, she was informed that her dog had died four days earlier. Although the plaintiff consented to a necropsy, no report was forthcoming. The court found a "rebuttable presumption of negligence" against the bailee and awarded judgment to the plaintiff in the amount of $550, plus costs and disbursements.

In recognizing that the plaintiff had suffered "a grievous loss," the court considered many factors in determining the amount of damages she should receive. The court found that the dog did not have an ascertainable market value and the dog's age should not be used as a depreciation factor as "manifestly, a good dog's value increases rather than falls with age and training." Furthermore, the court declined to limit the plaintiff's recovery to a "merely nominal award."[20]

The court acknowledged that the woman received this mixed breed German Shepherd as a puppy upon the death of her husband. The dog was "her sole and constant companion" who provided her with protective value, and the court considered the loss of this dog's companionship value "as an element of the dog's actual value to this owner."

In thinking about this decision, consider the words of Martin Luther King, Jr., who said, "The arc of the moral universe is long, but it bends toward justice."[21] *Brousseau* leans in the right direction.

---

19. 443 N.Y.S.2d 285, 110 Misc. 2d 1054 (N.Y. City Civ. Ct. 1980).

20. In a footnote, the court indicated that although independent common law actions for damages for the loss of companionship related to the wrongful death of a dog were not permissible in New York, "the policies behind the loss of consortium cases impact upon the court's consideration in the instant case."

21. *Martin Luther King, Jr. Quotes*, GOOD READS, http://www.goodreads.com/quotes/111013-the-arc-of-the-moral-universe-is-long-but-it (last visited May 12, 2016).

Practice Pointer: This case represents a trend where the court took a dog's death seriously and struggled with how to value the loss of the dog. The court cited a well-written *New York Times* article on the subject of pet loss.[22] It is always a good idea to give the court copies of persuasive articles that relate to the subject before it.

Nahrstedt v. Lakeside Village Condominium Association, Inc.[23]

Year: *1994*
Category: *Property Law*
Type of Action: *Enforceability of Pet Use Restrictions*
Animal: *Cat*
Pet Custody Concept: *The transitional thinking described here about the hybrid nature of horizontal real property could be creatively applied to animal subjects.*

This seminal case is discussed in depth because where animals are permitted to live or prohibited from living is of central importance in a pet custody dispute. It is noteworthy that the California legislature later passed a law, perhaps for the reasons well articulated in the powerful *Nahrstedt* dissent, permitting the ownership of "at least one pet."[24] This decision impacted public policy and contains many arguments that can be borrowed and applied in a completely different pet law context. For example, horizontal property rights could be applied to advocate for a variety of ways that animals could be owned or shared outside of traditional ways.

Nahrstedt involved a pet restriction in a condominium complex that affected a homeowner's right to keep her cats. The homeowner believed the restriction was unreasonable as applied to her because her three cats lived indoors, were quiet, and did not constitute a nuisance. The California Court of Appeals supported the homeowner by determining that the restriction could only be enforced if the association could prove that these cats interfered with other homeowners' rights to "peaceful and quiet enjoyment of their property."

The California Supreme Court, by its decision, enforced the covenants, conditions, and restrictions embodied in the civil code and emphasized the presumption of the validity of the restriction. The court raised the floodgate problem of evaluating the reasonableness of a recorded use restriction on a case-by-case basis and applied the rule that a property use restriction in a common interest development was presumptively valid.

Justice Joyce Kennard, writing for the majority, presented an exhaustive overview of the general principles related to common interest types of homeownership, which included condominiums, cooperatives, and planned-unit developments. Justice Kennard explained that the "hybrid nature of property rights" reflected innovation. She traced the roots of these types of property rights to ancient Rome and medieval Germany,

22. A. Fischer, *When a Pet's Death Hurts Its Master*, N.Y. Times, May 8, 1980, at 3.
23. 33 Cal. Rptr. 2d 63, 8 Cal. 4th 361, 878 P.2d 1275 (Cal. 1994).
24. California Civil Code section 1360.50 prohibits "no pets" condominium deed restrictions.

and she applauded the concept of "horizontal property" or "strata" ownership, where "land can be divided into a series of strata or planes capable of severed ownership, making the ownership of things affixed to land separable from the ownership of the land itself."

The question she posed was why it took so long for this country to accept the idea of horizontal property ownership. Perhaps it was because the United States was sparsely populated and had undeveloped habitable land, and, while materials for building were affordable, there was "no great physical need for superimposing one dwelling upon another."[25] In writing about the development of horizontal property interests and the ability of those living in them to "limit the number of persons that can occupy each unit, and place limitations on—or prohibit altogether—the keeping of pets," Justice Kennard offered that "58 percent of highrise developments and 39 percent of town-house projects had some kind of pet restriction."

Quoting Professor Natelson,[26] Justice Kennard said that associations "can be a powerful force for good or for ill in their members' lives" and that anyone "who buys a unit in a common interest development with knowledge of its owners association's discretionary power accepts 'the risk that the power may be used in a way that benefits the commonality but harms the individual.'" Justice Kennard cited Florida's *Hidden Harbour Estates, Inc. v. Norman*[27] as follows:

> [I]nherent in the condominium concept is the principle that to promote the health, happiness, and peace of mind of the majority of the unit owners since they are living in such close proximity and using facilities in common, each unit owner must give up a certain degree of freedom of choice which he [or she] might otherwise enjoy in separate, privately owned property. Condominium unit owners comprise a little democratic sub-society of necessity, more restrictive as it pertains to use of condominium property than may be existent outside the condominium organization.[28]

The court had fleeting awareness that these common interest developments were "a more affordable alternative to ownership of a single family home" and that "as of 1988, more than 30 million Americans lived in housing governed by owners associations" and "32 million Americans are members of some 150,000 homeowners

---

25. In a similar vein, there is no need to classify all living creatures as personal property.

26. *Consent, Coercion, and "Reasonableness" in Private Law: The Special Case of the Property Owners Association*, 51 Ohio State L.J. 41, 47 (1990).

27. 309 So. 2d 180 (Fla. Dist. Ct. App. 1975).

28. Justice Kennard said, "Indeed, there was no statutory authority for the severing of real property ownership by planes or floors until 1804, when the French Civil Code (the Code Napoleon) acknowledged that 'the different stories of a house [could] belong to different proprietors,' and that in such cases 'the main walls and the roof [could be] at the charge of all the proprietors, each in proportion to the story belonging to him.' Not until nearly 160 years later did the notion of shared ownership of real property gain general acceptance in the United States." In a common law context, the court seemed to treat the Napoleonic Code, however loosely, as evidence of a precedent. It is noteworthy that in the court of appeal decision, *Nahrstedt* was permitted, as the supreme court later put it, to revive her "causes of action for invasion of privacy, invalidation of the assessments, and injunctive relief, as well as her action for emotional distress based on a theory of negligence."

associations and predicting that between 25 to 30 percent of Americans will live in community association housing by the year 2000."[29]

The court continued that in order for "new and innovative forms of ownership" to emerge, old ideas regarding ownership interests needed to be severed.[30] It explained that in many European civil codes and at English common law, "the owner of the soil possessed the exclusive right to control everything on, above, or beneath the land." This meant that fixtures attached to land "could not be severed from ownership of the land."

The court advanced the idea that the pet restrictions were in concert with constitutional principles and consistent with public policy considerations.[31] Even so, the

---

29. Consider Justice Kennard's projection that up to 30 percent of Americans would live in community association housing by the year 2000. Jumping ahead to the year 2013, according to the CATO Institute, "more than half of new housing is subject to association membership, including condominium buildings." Ilya Shapiro & Trevor Burrus, *Community Associations Have Property Rights Too*, CATO INSTITUTE, http://www.cato.org/blog/community-associations-have-property-rights-too (last visited May 12, 2016). The institute estimated that 60 million owners live in these types of associations. *Nahrstedt* is the kind of decision that bans, at least for the poor, who cannot afford single-family homes, pet ownership and all its known benefits, many of them articulated in the dissent. Following this logic in the family law context, if married or cohabiting couples move to less expensive housing subject to association restrictions following a separation, it is foreseeable that an unintended consequence of these breakups is that there is no affordable place for the family pets to go. Many senior citizens are forced to choose between owned housing and rental housing. The problem is that rental housing owners can decide if their tenants can bring their pets. Studies show that "moving was the most often cited of 71 reasons for relinquishing dogs and the third most common reason for relinquishing cats." John C. New, Jr. et al., *Moving: Characteristics of Dogs and Cats and Those Relinquishing Them to 12 U.S. Animal Shelters*, J. APPLIED ANIMAL WELFARE SCI. 2(2), 83, 84 (1999). According to the National White House Conference on Aging in 1981, "The forced separation of older persons from their companion animals upon entering housing projects for the elderly inflicts immeasurable emotional suffering and often leads to severe psychological trauma and consequent mental and physical deterioration, including the loss of the will to live. The comfort of a companion animal is a civil right not to be denied to responsible pet owners." FINAL REP. THE 1981 WHITE HOUSE CONF. ON AGING, VOL. 3, 127 (1981) (quoting Recommendation Number 244). Congress adopted a provision called "Pet Ownership in Assisted Rental Housing for the Elderly or Handicapped" (POEH) in 1983, which states that owners and managers of federally assisted rental housing for the elderly or handicapped cannot prohibit or prevent a tenant from owning common household pets. 12 U.S.C. §1701r-1(a) (2006). The definition of a common household pet is a "domesticated animal, such as a dog, cat, bird, rodent (including a rabbit), fish or turtle, that is traditionally kept in the home for pleasure rather than for commercial purposes." 24 C.F.R. Subtitle A § 5.306(1) (2012). Regulations state that the POEH is not applicable to health care facilities, including nursing homes or intermediate care facilities. 24 C.F.R. Subtitle A § 5.306(2) (2012). These facilities could have otherwise been included in the definition due to the facilities' use of mortgage insurance under the National Housing Act. *Id.* Nuisance pets can be removed under the POEH, which also "provides regulations creating guidelines for owners and managers with reasonable rules established by HUD." 12 U.S.C. § 1701r-1(b) & (c) (2006); HUD OCCUPANCY HANDBOOK 4350.3 REV-1, AT EXHIBIT 6-4 MANDATORY AND DISCRETIONARY PET RULES, *available at* http://portal.hud.gov/hudportal/documents/huddoc?id=DOC_35713.pdf (setting forth in table form the rules); 24 C.F.R. § 5.350(a) (2012). Pet rules may require pet owners to license their pets in accordance with state and local law under the discretionary standards. *Id.* § 5.318(f).

30. This case is a gift of reasoning that keeps on giving, as new and innovative forms of ownership with regard to companion animals could arise. If new thinking can occur with real property, the common law with animals could likewise evolve. When it comes to horizontal property, why are real property rights superior to other property rights associated with a public policy objective of a child's home environment promoting that child's school success? There is a growing body of evidence that children living with pets outperform children who do not.

31. This case can be taken apart and its logic used for a complete analysis for advocating other types of ownership for companion animals.

property owners' general expectations that the restrictions in place when they purchased their units would be enforced were not unlimited. The court emphasized how people "prefer a stable, planned environment."[32] Another important legal issue discussed was how the absence of "privity of contract between the party seeking to enforce the promise and the party resisting enforcement" affects the outcome.[33]

With regard to equitable servitude law pertaining to real property, the court emphasized that humans have a fiduciary duty to enforce the association restrictions as long as the use restriction was in good faith, its enforcement procedures were fair and applied uniformly, and the restriction was not arbitrary or capricious. The court then admitted how it was the beneficiary of "legal rules that are protective of recorded use restrictions," as bright lines on use restriction meant "fewer lawsuits challenging such restrictions" and that those challenges could be disposed of "expeditiously." This would be particularly true "if the rules courts use in evaluating such restrictions are clear, simple, and not subject to exceptions based on the peculiar circumstances or hardships of individual residents in condominiums and other shared ownership developments."[34]

The supreme court concluded that "the recorded pet restriction of the Lakeside Village condominium development prohibiting cats or dogs but allowing some other pets is not arbitrary, but is rationally related to health, sanitation and noise concerns legitimately held by residents of a high-density condominium project." The court said,

> Nahrstedt's complaint alleges no facts that could possibly support a finding that the burden of the restriction on the affected property is so disproportionate to its benefit that the restriction is unreasonable and should not be enforced. Also, the complaint's allegations center on Nahrstedt and her cats (that she keeps them inside her condominium unit and that they do not bother her neighbors), without any reference to the effect on the condominium development as a whole, thus rendering the allegations legally insufficient to overcome section 1354's presumption of the restriction's validity.

Next, the court provided a patriotic public policy rift wherein the court said, "All people are by nature free and independent and have inalienable rights. Among these are enjoying and defending life and liberty, acquiring, possessing, and protecting

32. Companion animals are not members of any fundamental protected class. Protected classes include sex, race, color, religion, ancestry, national origin, or disability. There is a growing body of evidence, in all facets of American life, that some animals are members of the modern family. When there is a question of enforcing a restriction, it could be discerned when the harm caused by the restriction is disproportionate to the benefit. If disproportionate, the restriction would not be enforced.

33. Family law practitioners should look at privity of contract issues in pet custody disputes. There could be contracts with breeders, rescue groups, fosters, licensees, creditors, and more.

34. This same logic could pertain to the enforceability of premarital, antenuptial, or partnership agreements, or marriage contracts, even if one person has long had sole possession of the animal and is advancing a claim for possessory rights. As applied to pets, in refusing to consider peculiar circumstances or hardships, the court becomes a beneficiary in terms of a lighter docket. Form sometimes prevails over substance.

property, and pursuing and obtaining safety, happiness, and privacy."[35] Interested in establishing societal privacy norms, the court said:

> The threshold question in deciding whether "established social norms safeguard a particular type of information or protect a personal decision from public or private intervention," we explained in *Hill*, must be determined from "the usual sources of positive law governing the right to privacy—common law development, constitutional development, statutory enactment, and the ballots arguments accompanying the Privacy Initiative."

From a pet ownership standpoint, the court little understood the public policy implications of its decision, although the court was modestly aware of disabled individuals living in rental housing and elderly persons living in publicly funded housing.[36]

The widely heralded dissent by Justice Armand Arabian began with an Albert Schweitzer quote, "There are two means of refuge from the misery of life: music and cats." Arguing that the pet restriction in *Nahrstedt* was arbitrary and unreasonable under the civil code, Justice Arabian said,

> Given the substantial benefits derived from pet ownership, the undue burden on the use of property imposed on condominium owners who can maintain pets within the confines of their units without creating a nuisance or disturbing the quiet enjoyment of others substantially outweighs whatever meager utility the restriction may serve in the abstract. It certainly does not promote "health, happiness [or] peace of mind" commensurate with its tariff on the quality of life for those who value the companionship of animals. Worse, it contributes to the fraying of our social fabric.

Arguing that the majority should have construed the plaintiff's pleadings according to a "substantive justice" standard, the dissent complained that the court instead held the plaintiff to an unreasonably high standard for specificity even though the plaintiff's pleadings should have been sufficient to establish that the pet restriction was unreasonable as a matter of law. He argued that "The burden on the affected property is so disproportionate to its benefit that the restriction is unreasonable and should not be enforced" and that the court should consider "the effect on the condominium development as a whole."

Justice Arabian reminded the majority of the "well-established and long-standing historical and cultural relationship between human beings and their pets and the value

---

35. The court framed constitutional privacy policies as existing in two classes, "(1) interests in precluding dissemination of confidential information (informational privacy); and (2) interests in making personal decisions or in conducting personal activities free of interference, observation, or intrusion (autonomy privacy)." The supreme court asserted that use restrictions for those who hold horizontal land rights rise to the level of a fundamental right.

36. The court said,

> Legislature has declared its intent that, in specified circumstances, these two classes of Californians be allowed to keep pets. Thus, section 54.1, which guarantees equal access to housing accommodations to individuals with disabilities, permits landlords to refuse to rent to tenants who have dogs, except when the prospective tenant is a disabled person needing the services of a guide, service, or signal dog. And, under Health and Safety Code section 19901, elderly residents in publicly funded housing are entitled to have up to two household pets.

they impart." Following the majority's lead for placing their arguments in a historical context, he said, "Archeologists in Israel found some of the earliest evidence of a domesticated animal when they unearthed the 12,000-year-old skeleton of a woman who was buried with her hand resting on the body of her dog" and "Cats were known to be household pets in Egypt 5,000 years ago and often mummified and entombed with their owners." A cat's loyalty to its master imprisoned at the Tower of London was "reputed to have located his master's cell and climbed down the chimney to join him during his imprisonment."

Conversant with the high regard for pets in the First Family, Justice Arabian said that people of all ages, particularly the elderly and young, and those bedridden due to injury or disease, "Experience a therapeutic, even spiritual, benefit from their presence." He went on to say that after the death of a family member or friend, animals offer comfort and for the lonely, companion animals can "offer a reason for living when life seems to have lost its meaning."

The dissent showed how Congress and state legislators had recognized the importance of animal companions as reflected in their express guarantee that "elderly and handicapped persons living in public assistance housing cannot be deprived of their pets." He emphasized that children and animals are "natural companions" and that "children learn responsibility and discipline from pet ownership while developing an important sense of kindness and protection for animals. Single adults may find certain pets can afford a feeling of security. Families benefit from the experience of sharing that having a pet encourages."

Justice Arabian characterized the homeowners' association board of directors as engaging in a form of "sophisticated bigotry," as the association failed to explain how its goals were compromised by the ownership of cats but not fish or birds. He described that this "inconsistency underscores its unreasonableness and discriminatory impact." Justice Arabian did not shy away from the language of emotion about cats when he stated, "Emotionally, they allow a connection full of sensation and delicacy of feeling."

Arguing that the plaintiff's pleadings were "sufficient to allege that the pet restriction is unreasonable as a matter of law," Justice Arabian argued that even if pet ownership was not a fundamental right, "it is an integral aspect of our daily existence, which cannot be lightly dismissed and should not suffer unwarranted intrusion into its circle of privacy."[37] He argued for balance between the growing rights of a condominium association and the freedom of the association. The dissent observed that "the majority's

37. Furthermore, Justice Arabian advocated that "Such inquiry should start with an evaluation of the interest that will suffer upon enforcement of the pet restriction. In determining the 'burden on the use of land,' due recognition must be given to the fact that this particular 'use' transcends the impersonal and mundane matters typically regulated by condominium CC & R's, such as whether someone can place a doormat in the hallway or hang a towel on the patio rail or have food in the pool area, and reaches the very quality of life of hundreds of owners and residents." If this logic of Justice Arabian's burden of proof argument could be applied to pet custody disputes, the difference between the impersonal and mundane could be compared to concepts such as health and happiness and reasons for living. The dissent also offered the idea of the "inversion of relative interests" and emphasized the "qualitative nature" of the pet restriction.

failure to consider the real burden imposed by the pet restriction unfortunately belittles and trivializes the interest at stake."[38]

Justice Arabian complained that the majority uncritically accepted "the proffered justification of preserving 'health and happiness'" and essentially considered "only one criterion to determine enforceability: was the restriction recorded in the original declaration?" He argued that a limited inquiry should have been permitted as a matter of law. The dissent traversed into territory less common for the bench—the language of emotion.[39]

In *Nahrstedt*, Justice Kennard said that a restriction must be "uniformly enforced" unless the individual could show that the restriction "otherwise imposes burdens on the affected land that are so disproportionate to the restriction's beneficial effects that the restriction should not be enforced." In contrast, the majority focused on a recorded declaration for a condominium complex that included covenants, conditions, and restrictions that were enforceable unless the declaration was unreasonable.[40]

Practice Pointer: The supreme court asked why it took so long for this country to accept the idea of horizontal property ownership. Today, this question can be reframed. Why is it taking so long for this country to amend the ideas of horizontal property ownership for pets in a divorce context? Co-ownership or joint custody of companion animals is allowed for valuable commercial dogs or cats. Contracts are drafted, signed, and enforced with regard to possessory interests, too.

While promoting "new and innovative forms of ownership" with regard to real property, one might wonder when courts will welcome innovation and ideas regarding pet ownership in a pet law custody context. For example, if the traditional concept of land ownership was vertical, including above and below the ground, but now can be horizontal, what prevents a divorcing couple from having joint ownership of a dog? Would the court prevent a divorcing couple from continuing to jointly own a condominium with negative equity, with the contractual obligation to sell the condominium at a future time post-decree? Why should courts permit co-ownership of companion animals raised by breeders focused on commercial interests but not reasonable individuals committed to their welfare and who love them?

A variety of arguments could be made by family lawyers about the evolution of forms of ownership, obligations, access, and standards concerning companion animals using the innovative issue of horizontal property by analogy. Animals classified as pets

38. The court observed that the majority opinion was "shorn of grace and guiding philosophy," and "devoid of the humanity that must temper the interpretation and application of all laws, for in a civilized society that is the source of their authority."

39. The subject of emotion is often linked to irrational behavior. Consider whether getting married for love or splitting up when the feeling of love departs are rational acts. The dissent in this case effectively integrated the language of emotion with persuasive rational arguments.

40. To the Supreme Court of California, the association's "no pets" policy meant no dogs or cats, "livestock, reptiles or poultry," but the restriction did not apply to birds or fish because the CC & R permitted these animals. Perhaps a societal irony is that the birds protected in *Nahrstedt* are specifically excluded from basic protection under the Federal Animal Welfare Act. This means if birds are subject to research experiments, there are no minimum requirements or anti-cruelty provisions for how they must be treated.

or companion animals might then be treated as special property.[41] Alaska now permits the consideration of animal welfare for companion animals by statute and many states include pets in orders for protection.[42]

In *Nahrstedt*, the court said that a "condominium use restriction appearing in originating documents which predate the purchase of individual units was entitled to greater judicial deference than restrictions promulgated after units have been individually acquired." By analogy, it would follow that a prenuptial agreement for a pet acquired might be more enforceable than a pet acquired pursuant to a binding contract entered into during a marriage.[43]

In the dissent, Justice Arabian asked if animals should be considered in the human circle of privacy and said that cats represented an aspect of freedom of association. These are novel arguments that good advocates can use. Lawyers can also utilize the types of arguments advanced by Justice Kennard for changing common law affecting common interest development to advocate for how laws related to companion animal ownership and access might advance. If representing a client when rational arguments alone are not conclusive, consider getting in the groove of the Arabian dissent. Learn from this master. One interesting aspect of this case was that happiness lies in certainty about use restrictions, and for the dissent, happiness can be gained from companionship with animals.

Ammon v. Welty[44]

Year: *1995*
Category: *Property Law*
Type of Action: *1983 Action*
Animal: *Dog*
Pet Custody Concept: *Make sure your clients are aware that if their pet becomes lost, time is of the essence.*

The owners of a dog named Hair Bear brought a federal civil rights complaint pursuant to 42 U.S.C. § 1983 and state tort law. Hair Bear's owners alleged that their dog was obtained deceitfully and, instead of being held for seven days as required by a Kentucky statute, was immediately shot and killed. The district court determined that the plaintiffs did not have a claim upon which relief could be granted and dismissed their complaint, which the plaintiffs appealed.

In an unpublished decision, the Sixth Circuit affirmed the district court's grant of the motion to dismiss. Although determining that the plaintiffs had a constitutionally

41. David Favre, *Living Property: A New Status for Animals within the Legal System*, 93 Marquette L. Rev. 1021 (2010).

42. Rebecca F. Wisch, *Domestic Violence and Pets: List of States that Include Pets in Protection Orders*, http://www.animallaw.info/articles/ovusdomesticviolencelaws.htm (last visited May 12, 2016).

43. *Uniform Premarital and Marital Agreements Act Approved*, Uniform Law Commission, http://www.uniformlaws.org/NewsDetail.aspx?title=Uniform%20Premarital%20and%20Marital%20Agreements%20Act%20Approved (last visited May 12, 2016).

44. 64 F.3d 662 (C.A. 6 Ky. 1995).

protected property interest in Hair Bear, and that the dog warden was not authorized to destroy him before seven days elapsed, the court utilized the logic that "Hair Bear's destruction by the dog warden was predictable and a predeprivation process unavailable," and "Kentucky provides a remedy for the alleged unlawful taking of plaintiffs' property." The federal court passed the buck to the state court and affirmed the federal district court's dismissal.

Practice Pointer: There is an old expression not to make a federal case out of it. When there is a remedy in state court, think before initiating a federal action unless the federal bench is better with animal claims than the state court is.

MORGAN V. KROUPA[45]

Year: *1997*
Category: *Property Law*
Type of Action: *Lost Property*
Animal: *Dog*
Pet Custody Concept: *Courts get to make the call on what law fits the best when there is more than one choice.*

The court granted possession of a mixed breed dog named Max to the plaintiff, who found Max after he became lost. Max's original owner made efforts to find him by notifying the nearby humane society, friends, and local businesses. The woman who found the dog notified the same humane society and made considerable efforts to find the dog's original owner by posting notices. She even had announcements made on a local radio station broadcast. When someone recognized the dog over a year later, not too far from the dog's former home, the original owner went to retrieve his dog. Although the finder refused to cooperate, Max jumped into the defendant's truck and the defendant drove away with the dog.

The trial court considered whether (1) to apply the lost property statute, (2) to make a best interests of the dog determination, or (3) to undertake an emotional attachment analysis. The court, with well-stated regrets, chose the lost property statute analysis. Determining that the plaintiff had substantially complied with her statutory obligations when she found the "lost property," the court awarded Max to her.

The court stated, "From its plain terms and judicial application over time it is evident that the statute—which dates from the late-eighteenth and early-nineteenth centuries—was designed for agricultural animals of substantial monetary value, not lost pets." The court continued that "stray beasts" meant animals such as cows, oxen, and horses, and then described other state laws that seemed out of date, including a statute that used the phrase "impound a beast." The court considered the wisdom of applying a statute meant for stray beasts to "mankind's companion throughout the ages."

Declaring that "a clear line cannot always be drawn between animals kept for economic reasons and those kept as pets," the court offered that some livestock owners

45. 702 A.2d 630, 167 Vt. 99 (Vt. 1997).

might be "emotionally attached to individual animals." The court observed how ideas about the value of animals are changing. To this court, the absence of statutory language clarifying how the lost property laws applied to domestic animals seemed important.

After stating that "pets generally do not fit neatly within traditional property law principles," the court recalled dicta in *Corso v. Crawford Dog & Cat Hospital., Inc.*,[46] where the court famously said that a "pet is not just a thing but occupies a special place somewhere in between a person and a piece of personal property." The court also explored applying an animal best-interest standard but lacked an idea as to how to do so efficiently. Looking for a way to resolve the lost dog case, the court was influenced by the public policy goal of encouraging finders to "take in and care for lost pets." The court also offered ideas for how those who lose pets could better search for them while stressing that the finders had obligations, too.

Practice Pointer: The court could think of three types of legal analyses to apply and chose the one it knew was meant for earlier centuries' lost agricultural animals but not lost dogs. This is a good case to review when considering what claims to advance and how the courts' ideas about laws, as applied to companion animals, are in transition.

Jersey City Management v. Garcia[47]

Year: *1999*
Category: *Property Law*
Type of Action: *Summary Judgment*
Animal: *Dog, Cat*
Pet Custody Concept: *No-pets provisions are not always enforceable.*

A tenant in a federally subsidized low-income housing project with a no-pets provision was subject to a summary disposition action. Notwithstanding this no-pets provision, the tenant had already lived in the project with her cat for eleven years and her dog for two. Before the tenant obtained the dog, she changed units within the housing project. The court addressed whether the no-pets provision was unreasonable.

In the original complaint, the landlord sought possession of the tenant's unit based upon the tenant's violation of the no-pets policy because she had a cat, without mentioning the dog, and then later amended the complaint to include the dog. After the tenant removed the dog from the housing project, she sought to vacate the judgment of removal. The court assisted her by construing her action as a motion for relief of judgment.

The superior court made a determination that the "defense of summary dispossess proceedings need not put tenants to the significant risk of lease forfeiture if their good faith defenses do not prevail."[48] The court said there was a good faith basis for

46. 97 Misc. 2d 530, 415 N.Y.S.2d 182, 183 (City Civ. Ct. 1979).
47. 729 A.2d 521, 321 N.J. Super. 543 (N.J. Super. 1999).
48. Jijon v. Custodio, 251 N.J. Super. 370, 598 A.2d 251 (Law Div. 1991).

the tenant's opinion that the relocation of the cat was "not violative of a reasonable application of the no-pet policy and, thus, for choosing to litigate that defense. Indeed, she was correct as to the cat." In addition, the court commented that upon the trial court's determination that she could not keep her dog, she removed the dog the same day, which had the effect of making the landlord's good cause grounds for eviction "curable." The court vacated the judgment of possession in favor of the landlord.

Practice Pointer: Always check to see if either party's residence is subject to a no-pets policy, and check zoning restrictions, too. Consider whether anything about a defendant's conduct is curable.

LAMARE V. NORTH COUNTRY ANIMAL LEAGUE[49]

Year: *1999*
Category: *Property Law*
Type of Action: *Lost and Found*
Animal: *Dog*
Pet Custody Concept: *Courts appreciate interesting and challenging advocacy.*

The plaintiffs' American Kennel Club registered German Shepherd puppy, Billy, "broke free" from her tether and became lost. The finder brought Billy to a kennel, who contacted animal control. As required by ordinance, animal control not only complied with all necessary postings but also held the puppy for nine days following impoundment. This hold period was greater than required by ordinance. Animal control then transferred care and control of Billy to an animal league. The league spayed Billy and adopted her out more than a month after she became lost.

In the meantime, the plaintiffs had learned that their dog was at the league, told the league that they had proof of ownership, offered to pay Billy's boarding costs, and filled out an adoption application to regain possession of Billy. The plaintiffs said they were informed by the league that their personal references needed to be contacted. They were not told that prior to submitting their application to adopt Billy, another person's application had already been approved. Although the plaintiffs' application references were never contacted, the plaintiffs were told that their application was denied because it was "not in the dog's best interests to be returned to them."

On appeal, the plaintiffs challenged the town's dog control ordinance as invalid because it was not authorized by state statute. They also asserted that their constitutional right to due process had been denied regarding the taking of Billy. In considering these claims, although the court said the plaintiffs had failed to name the town as a necessary party and should have brought in the attorney general, the court found that the judgment was not prejudicial to the absent party.

Although the court agreed with the plaintiffs that a municipality has only the power and functions granted to it, the municipality had controlling authority to transfer possession of the dog after the redemption period had passed. If the court utilized the

49. 170 Vt. 115 (1999).

plaintiffs' construction of the statute, the court complained, the town would need to "care for impounded domestic animals in perpetuity," and "we must construe statutes to avoid absurd results unintended by legislature." Accordingly, the ordinance reflected a "necessary and essential power under the enabling statute" that permits a town to regulate domestic pets running at large.

The court also distinguished claims under the town ordinance from the type initiated under the common law in *Morgan v. Kroupa*,[50] a case involving a dispute between private parties. The court's distinction was consistent with how courts treat cases involving third parties differently from cases involving the losers and finders of lost animals.

The next claim addressed by the court was whether the plaintiffs were denied due process when there was a disposition of property interests without the opportunity for them to be heard. The court said the *Mathews v. Eldridge*[51] factors were controlling. These factors are, "(1) the private interest affected by the state action; (2) the risk of erroneous deprivation of the affected private interest under the procedures used; and (3) the governmental interest involved, including fiscal and administrative burdens." With regard to the first *Mathews* factor, the court said that property interests in dogs are qualified as subject to police powers.[52] For example, a pet exposed to rabies could be confined, impounded, or killed, even though a dog is recognized as an inherently social creature whose "value derives from the animal's relationship with its human companions."

The court also cited *Morgan* for the proposition that an owner of a lost dog has a duty to "make reasonable efforts to locate an animal by contacting humane societies and other agencies and checking other public locations where notices may be posted." In the instant case, Billy was not wearing a license, and a common practice for someone with a lost puppy would have been to check with the local pound, humane society, and other public places. Given that the defendant was in full compliance with posting requirements, the court concluded that the plaintiffs were not deprived of due process rights. The court also distinguished due process rights when an animal is lost from due process rights when an animal is seized, as in *Porter v. DiBlasio*.[53] The court also weighed the qualified right to possession against the strong public interest of ensuring an animal was placed in a "suitable environment." The court pointed out that "courts elsewhere have uniformly upheld local ordinances authorizing the destruction or transfer of possessory rights in stray animals impounded for less than one week."

On the subject of the plaintiffs' motion to compel the disclosure of the new owner's identity, the court reiterated how discovery determinations were within the sole discretion of the trial court. Here, the trial court determined that the third party's identity was irrelevant. The court also said that there can be a compelling reason for nondisclosure, as addressed in *Johnston v. Atlanta Humane Society*,[54] because disclosure can lead to harassment or otherwise negatively affect pet adoptions.

---

50. 167 Vt. 99, 104, 702 A.2d 630, 633 (1997).

51. 424 U.S. 319, 335, 96 S. Ct. 893, 47 L. Ed. 2d 18 (1976).

52. The idea of "qualified" came from *Sentell v. New Orleans Carrollton RR. Co.*, 166 U.S. 698, 17 S. Ct. 693, 41 L. Ed. 1169 (1897).

53. 93 F.3d 301 (7th Cir. 1996).

54. 173 Ga. App. 416, 326 S.E.2d 585, 587 (1985).

Although the court found the league was "insensitive in its dealings with Plaintiffs," the court determined that the town had fully complied with the ordinance requirements consistent with the plaintiffs' due process rights. The court made a point of stating, "this is not to say that a future case seeking recovery for the emotional distress or other damages resulting from the negligent handling of an impounded animal—a claim not alleged here—would be unsuccessful."

Practice Pointer: First, always remember to let the court know if a bad actor is one of the disputants. Make sure to bring in all the necessary parties to an action and address how the factors described in *Mathews* apply in any case involving police powers. The court also stated that the subject of discovery regarding third parties was within the sole discretion of the court. Owners of lost dogs want this information if possible so that negotiations, including the offer of money, can be initiated. On the other hand, new owners may have valid concerns about trouble knocking on their door.

Prisco v. Forest Villas Condominium Apartments, Inc.[55]

Year: *2003*
Category: *Property Law*
Type of Action: *Summary Judgment*
Animal: *Dog*
Pet Custody Concept: *Courts are unpredictable when it comes to the subject of no-pets restrictions.*

The appellant overcame the court's grant of summary judgment in favor of a Florida condominium association when she raised the affirmative defense of selective enforcement of the terms of a no-pets restriction. In trial court, the appellant offered sworn affidavits of how cats were visible in windows and on balconies and one man even had a dog.

The trial court, finding that there had been no arbitrary or capricious enforcement of the condominium's bylaws, made a considerable effort to distinguish between cats and dogs, saying, "Cats are not the same as dogs, and the condominium allowing a cat on the premises does not equal to disallowing a dog 'because dogs clearly bark, cats do not, dogs need to be walked outside of their home, cats do not as they use litter boxes for the most part.'" The court even went as far as finding that "cats and dogs are not similarly alike."

The appeals court, perhaps not finding the trial court's analysis altogether compelling, focused on why another owner was permitted to have a dog. Although the condominium association had grandfathered in another tenant's dog after the bylaws had been passed, the trial court reasoned that this behavior did not constitute selective and arbitrary enforcement of the no-pets restriction.

55. 847 So. 2d 1012 (Fla. App. 2003).

The court of appeals analyzed the no-pets provision, which stated that except for fish and birds, "no pets whatsoever" were allowed. In order to apply this provision evenly, the court said, "The fact that cats are different than dogs makes no difference. What does matter is that neither a cat nor a dog is a fish or a bird, so both should be prohibited." Accordingly, the trial court's judgment was reversed and the case was remanded with the directive that the defendant could raise selective enforcement as an affirmative defense.

Practice Pointer: This case is reflective of the precarious future of companion animals when separating individuals are no longer able to afford living in single-family homes and instead are dependent upon the decisions of townhome associations that could adopt, or indiscriminately enforce, pet restrictions. A custody award should take into account whether a companion animal is allowed where the party is living.[56] Animals may end up suffering if they must live in a situation where their existence is forbidden.

Villa De Las Palmas Homeowners Association v. Terifaj[57]

Year: *2004*
Category: *Property Law*
Type of Action: *Pet Use Restrictions*
Animal: *Dog*
Pet Custody Concept: *Courts are unpredictable when it comes to no-pets rules.*

Relying on *Nahrstedt v. Lakeside Village Condominium Association*,[58] a case famous for denying a woman who had a "horizontal" real estate interest the right to keep her three cats, the California Court of Appeals addressed another horizontal type of dispute between a unit owner and a condominium association. The court determined that a "pet restriction contained in the amended declaration is enforceable" and constituted an "enforceable equitable servitude" under state law.

Although the legislature, following *Nahrstedt*, adopted a law requiring that "no governing documents shall prohibit the owner of a separate interest within a common interest development from keeping at least one pet within the common interest development, subject to reasonable rules and regulations of the association," the court observed that this new law did not have a retroactive application. The defendant had "actual knowledge of the no-pets rule prior to purchasing her unit." She not only violated this no-pets rule by having her dog in the unit but also had what the court may have viewed as the audacity to seek to change this rule. The association brought suit against her for injunctive relief, declaratory relief, and nuisance, while also seeking an award of attorney's fees.

When this action began, the condominium association, unsuccessful in its first effort for a preliminary injunction against the dog owner, subsequently adopted and

56. If moving, determine if no-pet policies or zoning restrictions apply.
57. 14 Cal. Rptr. 3d 67, 33 Cal. 4th 73, 90 P.3d 1223 (Cal. 2004).
58. 8 Cal. 4th 361, 33 Cal. Rptr. 2d 63, 878 P.2d 1275 (1994).

recorded an amended declaration and filed an amended complaint. Describing how amended declarations with equitable servitude were unenforceable if unreasonable, the higher court pointed to *Nahrstedt* for the proposition that a complete ban on pets was not unreasonable. The court also said that the presumption of reasonableness could be overcome if the restriction "(1) violates public policy; (2) bears no reasonable relationship to the protection, preservation, operation or purpose of the affected land; or (3) otherwise imposes burdens on the affected land that are so disproportionate to the restriction's beneficial effects that the restriction should not be enforced."

The court rejected the defendant's claim that "because the pet restriction was recorded after she purchased her property, she cannot be expected to have agreed to it and is therefore not bound by it." Finding her argument disingenuous, as she was aware of the ban, the court conceded that "reasonable people may share Terifaj's inverted viewpoint" but emphasized that the legislature did not. Referring to the *Nahrstedt* decision again, where the court distinguished between "originating CC & Rs [covenants, contracts, and restrictions] and subsequently promulgated use restrictions," the court said that *Nahrstedt* reasoning gave deference to a development's originating CC & Rs and protected the general expectations of condominium owners that "restrictions in place at the time they purchase their units will be enforceable."

The court of appeals held that the equitable servitude was enforceable and was not unreasonable. The unit holder was also required to pay the association's attorney's fees for the entire proceeding.

Practice Pointer: Be aware of judicial politics. Here, the court of appeals may have been more upset about post-*Nahrstedt* legislation than it was about enforcing a no-pets provision in the context of new legislation about to take effect. Courts usually search for legislative enactments to give them direction. This decision could have focused on the mere fact that both the lower and upper courts perceived the dog owner as sneaky and therefore a bad actor.

Pollard v. Southdale Gardens of Edina Condominium Association, Inc.[59]

Year: *2005*
Category: *Property Law*
Type of Action: *Real Property*
Animal: *Dog, Cat*
Pet Custody Concept: *The court may grant a renter, not just an owner, standing to challenge a no-pets provision.*

The appellants were residents of the Southdale Gardens condominiums and contractually subject to a no-pets clause, with an exception for day or overnight guests. Even so, it was common knowledge that the condominium association did not enforce the no-pets rule.

59. 698 N.W.2d 449 (Minn. App. 2005).

When three residents with pets were fined $10 per day for violating the no-pets rule, they sought a declaratory judgment that the rule was unenforceable, as the respondents (1) had waived their right to enforce the rule, (2) were equitably estopped from enforcing the rule, and (3) breached a duty to treat their residents equally by the use of selective enforcement of the rule. The respondents sought summary judgment in favor of the association and board of directors and prevailed in district court.

The higher court instead determined that a nonwaiver clause does not automatically prevent a waiver claim because a written contract could be modified by subsequent acts and party conduct. The respondents had failed to enforce the no-pets rule for 12 years and had also encouraged rule violations. There was a genuine issue of material fact as to whether the respondents "knowingly and intentionally waived their right to enforce the pet rule."

With regard to equitable estoppel, the higher court found that one cannot assert otherwise valid rights "where one has acted in such a way as to induce another party to detrimentally rely on those actions." The elements of equitable estoppel include "(1) that promises or inducements were made; (2) that they reasonably relied upon the promises; and (3) that they will be harmed if estoppel is not applied."

The court relied on *Dimond v. Manheim*,[60] where the court said,

> The authorities are . . . substantially all agreed upon the following general propositions. First, to create an estoppel, the conduct of the party need not consist of affirmative acts or words. It may consist of silence or a negative omission to act when it was his duty to speak or act. Second, it is not necessary that the facts must be actually known to a party estopped. It is enough if the circumstances are such that a knowledge of the truth is necessarily imputed to him. Third, it is not necessary that the conduct will be acted upon by the other party. It is enough that the conduct was done under such circumstances that he should have known it was both natural and probable that it would be so acted upon.

The court found that the respondents had failed to meet their burden of proof that a "nonwaiver clause precludes estoppel claims." Despite the respondents' argument that standing should only be allowed for condominium owners, the court granted standing to the residents, too, and did not reach the disparate treatment claim, as it had already determined that the no-pets clause burden of proof had not been met. The court said that the no-pets rule equally applied to residents and owners because both suffered the requisite "injury in fact." Based upon the above, the case was reversed and remanded.

Practice Pointer: Because someone's ability to keep a pet at his or her residence may affect who takes possession of an animal in a pet custody dispute, lawyers should be aware of how no-pets policies are evolving in the applicable jurisdiction.

60. 61 Minn. 178, 182, 63 N.W. 495, 497 (1895).

184 West 10th Street Corp. v. Marvits[61]

Year: *2007*
Category: *Property Law*
Type of Action: *No-Pets Provision*
Animal: *Cat*
Pet Custody Concept: *Advise your clients not to slumber on their rights.*

The enforceability of a no-pets clause in rental units has been litigated all over the country. In this case, the court determined that a no-pets provision did not apply to a woman with cats in a rent-controlled unit when a landlord failed to timely commence a holdover proceeding. The court determined that the landlord's action constituted a statutory waiver.

Practice Pointer: A no-pets clause in a rental or other agreement may affect what outcomes are possible in a pet custody dispute. Never assume anything about the result of litigation for a no-pets policy. Even when finding case law that seems to damage your case, do not forget to check the statutes. California implemented post-*Nahrstedt*[62] legislative pro-pet changes.

Feger v. Warwick Animal Shelter[63]

Year: *2008*
Category: *Property Law*
Type of Action: *Lost and Found*
Animal: *Cat*
Pet Custody Concept: *The courts, though generally protective of the identities of those involved in transactions with shelters, are capable of well-reasoned exceptions.*

The court provided a quick review of the long-standing traditions in New York of protecting animals, preventing animal cruelty, providing animals with a minimum standard of care, and even extending laws "to animals in areas which were once reserved only for people." The court stated that "the law now recognizes the creation of trusts for the care of designated domestic or pet animals upon the death or incapacitation of their owner. Companion animals may now be included as protected parties when orders of protection are issued in domestic disputes." The court also said, "These laws indicate that companion animals are treated differently from other forms of property."

The plaintiff's Persian cat, Kisses, was taken from her house. Ten days later, the plaintiff saw a picture of a cat named Lucy on an animal shelter's website that she alleged was her cat, Kisses. The shelter claimed that Lucy was a different cat than Kisses and that Lucy was brought to their shelter by an individual who had difficulties with

61. 59 A.D.3d 287, 874 N.Y.S.2d 403, 2009 N.Y. Slip. Op. 01327.
62. *See* Nahrstedt v. Lakeside Village Condominium Association, Inc., 33 Cal. Rptr. 2d 63, 8 Cal. 4th 361, 878 P.2d 1275 (Cal. 1994).
63. 59 A.D.3d 68, 2008 N.Y. Slip. Op. 10122, 870 N.Y.S.2d 124 (N.Y. App. Div. 2008).

a landlord regarding keeping the cat. The shelter informed the plaintiff that Lucy had already been adopted out. The plaintiff alleged that her cat was "brought to the shelter by an employee of the shelter, by an employee of a service provider of the shelter, or by an employee of a Warwick, New York law firm who received it from an employee at an affiliated law firm located near the plaintiff's home in New Jersey."

The plaintiff sought to find out the identity of the person who donated the cat to the animal shelter and the identity of the person who adopted the cat. The court granted the shelter a "protective order to prevent disclosure of the identities of the donor and adoptive owner of the cat" unless the donor was "an employee of the shelter, an employee of a service provider of the shelter, or an individual employed by the law firm." If the donor did not fall into these categories, then the disclosure of the identity of the donor would not be warranted.

The dissent argued that the "public interest encompasses not only the needs of the government, but also the societal interests in redressing private wrongs and arriving at a just result in private litigation," and then stated, "Where, as here, an unlawful taking is alleged, the interest directly implicated is that of the owner in obtaining the return of the missing animal. Since the interest of the public in arranging the adoption of strays is necessarily secondary, a discovery protection intended to benefit that interest at the expense of the pet's owner is, in my view, inappropriate." The majority and dissent agreed that there was no allegation of wrongdoing on the part of the adoptive owner. To the contrary, the adoptive owner was willing to cooperate with discovery.

Practice Pointer: When an animal is lost, the lawyer for the original owner should be resourceful about discovery requests. If it seems as though the animal has been re-homed based upon dishonest dealings, make the court fully aware of this concern. Some courts may permit limited discovery, particularly if there is good reason to believe that mischief is involved. Reasonable discovery-based disclosures could help the original owner secure the return of a cherished pet through negotiations as long as appropriate safeguards are in place.

Graham v. Notti[64]

Year: *2008*
Category: *Property Law*
Type of Action: *Lost and Found*
Animal: *Dog*
Pet Custody Concept: *How is valid title passed?*

This was a seminal pet custody case involving a dispute about a lost and found dog, a black Pomeranian dog originally named Harlee who was adopted by a third party. While still young, Harlee "inadvertently" got outside and "wandered away," and his owner's efforts to find him were unsuccessful. The original owners contacted a variety

64. 196 P.3d 1070, 147 Wn. App. 629 (Wash. App. 2008).

of services and shelters, including SpokAnimal C.A.R.E., and posted a lost dog notice on the SpokAnimal's webpage.

Harlee was found and taken in by a woman 12 days after he was lost. The woman promptly brought Harlee to SpokAnimal. They referred her to another entity called SCRAPS, which "impounded animals." Later, a staff member at SpokAnimal represented that Harlee's finder specifically said that she "found Harlee wandering on the Spokane city side of 44th Avenue, the street off of which Ms. Wilke lived. This street represented the border between Spokane County and the City of Spokane."

In the meantime, the same day Harlee was brought to the impound facility, a man saw Harlee at SpokAnimal and asked to adopt him. SpokAnimal waited the requisite 72 hours before adopting Harlee to the defendant. The adoption was completed about two weeks after Harlee went missing. Shortly thereafter, Harlee's original owner learned about the delivery of a black Pomeranian to SpokAnimal. She followed up and learned of Harlee's adoption.

Because SpokAnimal's website provided some information about Harlee's adopter, the original owner was able to contact him, express her attachment to the dog, and seek Harlee's return. When the adopter refused, she sent him a detailed letter pleading for the dog's return. The original owner sent another letter through counsel offering to pay the defendant money so she could get Harlee back. When the defendant refused, the plaintiff initiated a replevin action. The adopter responded by bringing a motion for summary judgment. The high court ultimately concluded that the adoption authority "of the agency, here SpokAnimal C.A.R.E, turns on whether Harlee was found in the City of Spokane or in Spokane County." The court reversed its earlier summary judgment determination in favor of Harlee's original owner and remanded the case for trial.

When Harlee's original owner sought replevin, she argued that the shelter could not pass valid title to Harlee because the shelter lacked valid title to pass because "the city's power to regulate is limited by its geographical boundaries and the state's general laws." Other arguments advanced were (1) SpokAnimal did not have voidable title to the dog under Washington's commercial code because the owner neither transferred the dog to the shelter for sale nor otherwise entrusted the dog to the shelter, (2) the dog's adopter was not a bona fide purchaser under Washington common law, and (3) the court should have applied Washington's lost property (finder) statute.[65]

The adopter argued that "an animal shelter need not pay value or otherwise obtain the voluntary relinquishment from the original owner in order to secure good or voidable title." The new owner further asserted that SpokAnimal had at least a voidable title to the dog because SpokAnimal did not exercise any authority outside the physical boundaries of Spokane city limits, and title can be transferred to a good faith purchaser despite the fact that the title was voidable. He argued that there was a compelling public interest for the state to recognize that a property interest in dogs "is imperfect or qualified rather than absolute;" he emphasized that finding shelter animals new homes promoted public policy interests.

The court determined that the claim initiated by the original owner was in the nature of a replevin or "claim and delivery" action and that to prevail, the plaintiff must

65. Washington state did not specifically exempt companion animals under this statute as other states do.

establish (1) the plaintiff was the owner of the property or was lawfully entitled to the possession of the property by virtue of a special property interest; (2) the defendant wrongfully detained the property; (3) the property had not been taken for a tax, assessment, or fine pursuant to a statute; (4) the property had not been seized under an execution or attachment against the property of the plaintiff; (5) if seized, the property was exempt from seizure by law; and (6) the approximate value of the property.

The higher court acknowledged the difficulty of applying "common law theories of personal property ownership, lost article statutes, or animal-specific legislation" to a lost dog ownership dispute. However, the court found that owners have property rights in their companion animals and that these rights "in dogs are subject to the legitimate exercise of state police power."

The defendant argued that dog owners only enjoy a "qualified property interest in their companion animals," as established by the U.S. Supreme Court in *Sentell v. New Orleans Carrollton Railroad Co.*[66] The court, not satisfied with this application of *Sentell*,[67] reiterated that a state's police powers may impinge on an individual's property interests. From there, the court leapt to the idea that as the state had delegated its police powers to SpokAnimal, it could transfer ownership of Harlee as part of that power. The court distinguished how title could be impacted by whether SpokAnimal transferred the dog as a private party or as a governmental entity. If it could be proven that the dog was not from the city, SpokAnimal could be treated as a private party.[68]

This case illustrates the benefit of digging deep and analyzing any legal theory that could impact the outcome of the case. By 2008, the Washington Court of Appeals was fully aware of the importance of one young Pomeranian to the individuals who wanted him and was also challenged by how the application of the existing rule of law was, at the end of the day, wanting.

With regard to who would get Harlee, the Appellate Court of Washington was silent. The authority of SpokAnimal C.A.R.E. "turns on whether Harlee was found in the City of Spokane or in Spokane County." The case was remanded for trial.

Practice Pointer: When engaged in advocacy for a client, look at the big picture through a microscope and look for any defects in the opponent's position. Title to a dog can be challenged. The concept of voidable title or a property interest in a dog can be imperfect or qualified rather than perfect based upon a 19th-century Supreme Court decision that, by any rational standard, is at variance with current conceptions regarding companion animals.

66. 166 U.S. 698, 17 S. Ct. 693, 41 L. Ed. 1169 (1897).

67. It is well worth the time to read *Sentell* before considering citing it as a precedent. At the time this decision was written, 1897, companion animals were regarded very differently than they are today.

68. The court considered Washington's lost property statute, also known as the "finder" statute. Essentially, the court found the obligations imposed under this statute, including a 60-day waiting period, were not "directly applicable to the animal context."

Northgate Cooperative v. Donaldson[69]

Year: *2008*
Category: *Property Law*
Type of Action: *Pet Use Restrictions*
Animal: *Dog*
Pet Custody Concept: *Learn when reasonable accommodation is required.*

The plaintiff, who had long suffered from anxiety and serious depression, was prescribed a variety of medications to alleviate her symptoms. As her condition deteriorated, she lost a secretarial position she had held for 22 years. The court found that if the plaintiff had the opportunity to care for a dog, this might have a positive benefit on her mental health, as caring for a dog would require her to be more active and have a routine, thereby mitigating her depression symptoms.

The plaintiff stated, "I am alone. I have friends and things like that, but it's like I am really alone, I just need something to hold and cuddle, to play with, to take with me when I go someplace, it's like a companion . . . it just makes me feel good, it makes me feel not depressed. It's kind of like depression, it comes in different waves, it's a different intensity, there are times I will sit in the corner and rock." The plaintiff had unsuccessfully attempted to have the co-op change its bylaws to allow dogs.[70] The plaintiff's doctor recommended that having a dog might not only alleviate the plaintiff's depression but also facilitate her social interaction and decrease her level of anxiety and isolation.

The co-op, unimpressed with the plaintiff's physician and his credentials, sought an opinion from a psychologist or similar medical provider that detailed why the plaintiff specifically needed a dog. Rather than complying with the co-op's request, the plaintiff filed a complaint. After considering the division's findings and the state's human rights law, the higher court determined that the plaintiff's request for a dog must be accommodated and that she would be awarded monetary damages for mental anguish and punitive damages.

Practice Pointer: Unlike the majority in *Nahrstedt v. Lakeside Village Condominium Association*,[71] where horizontal land use rights were more important than anything else, *Northgate* is a good example of how the court may consider another factor, human mental health, in the context of a no-pets policy, particularly in the case of someone who has long lived in a building. If told that a client cannot have the animal where he or she lives, do not accept this claim as the final word.

69. 54 A.D.3d 414, 863 N.Y.S.2d 469, 2008 N.Y. Slip. Op. 6646 (N.Y. App. Div. 2008).
70. The plaintiff had long lived in her apartment before it was converted to a co-op.
71. 8 Cal. 4th 361, 33 Cal. Rptr. 2d 63, 878 P.2d 1275 (1994).

PLACEY V. PLACEY[72]

Year: *2010*
Category: *Property Law*
Type of Action: *Domestic Abuse*
Animal: *Dog*
Pet Custody Concept: *The court may have the authority to determine the ownership of a pet in a domestic abuse proceeding.*

A 28-year-old woman suffering from mental illness lived with her parents. While living there, she adopted a dog named Preston from a humane society. In her adoption contract, she disclosed that she lived with her parents. Later, when the daughter became aggressive and violent and informed her parents exactly how she planned to kill them, the court granted her mother a protective order. Following the issuance of that order, the daughter brought motions for consideration requesting certain property, including the dog, Preston. The court had not reduced to writing what it had ordered from the bench.

The next summer, the daughter's fiancé forcibly took Preston away from his girlfriend's mother while she was walking Preston. The court thereafter rendered an order that the mother owned Preston and the daughter must return him to her. While the mother's contempt motion was still pending, the trial court certified a final judgment under the Rules of Civil Procedure, and the daughter appealed that judgment, arguing that the trial court lacked authority under the Protection from Abuse Act (PFAA) to permanently dispose of property. She also claimed that she was Preston's owner.

The court declared that even though the determination of ownership was not a "stated purpose of the PFAA," this did not mean the court lacked authority to make an ownership determination regarding this specific property, Preston. The court specifically said, "Because the Jefferson Family Court was acting in its capacity as a circuit court in its exercise of jurisdiction over the PFA action, that court would have had the same jurisdiction as a circuit court to consider, together with the PFA action, an action seeking to establish title to personal property, such as a detinue action."[73]

The higher court affirmed that the trial court had the authority to enter an order determining the ownership of Preston to "protect the mother from the daughter's continued, yet prohibited, contact." The court stated that as the daughter had brought motions for consideration, these pleadings were representative of her implied or expressed consent that the court could decide property issues, even when the court's authority had not been raised or sought in the pleadings.

It was a salient factor to the court that when the daughter executed the adoption contract, she did so with the representation that her parents would assist her with the "daily exercise, training, and care" of the dog. The court said, "We are not convinced that the contract of adoption necessarily decides the question of ownership." More so, the court said that the only state statute that defined "owner" for a companion animal was a statute concerning rabies. The rabies statute defined an owner as "any

72. 51 So. 3d 374 (Ala. Civ. App. 2010).
73. *See* § 30-5-3(b)(1) stating that a PFA action may be joined with any other civil action.

person having a right of property in a dog, cat, ferret, or other animal, or who keeps or harbors the animal, or who has it in his or her care, or acts as its custodian, or who permits the animal to remain on or about any premises occupied by him or her." The court continued that "it is instructive to note that ownership of an animal involves more than a mere right of property in an animal."

Although a documentary title and certificate of registration could create a prima facie presumption of title, the court said that when there were competing claims ownership was presumed to be in the person who possessed the animal. The court recognized that at times, other courts considered the best interests of an animal when making a property determination. In the instant case, the mother was Preston's primary caretaker. She paid all of Preston's veterinary bills, walked him daily, and bought him special and expensive food. Preston had lived for six years of his life in the family home with the mother. In contrast, the daughter was living in a hotel. The higher court positively commented on the fact that "the trial court considered the best interest of Preston in determining that the mother was Preston's true owner." The mother was awarded the dog.

Practice Pointer: You may be surprised about what the court does. In a domestic abuse proceeding, the court made an ownership determination regarding property. The court was probably interested in taking the best interests of the original owner's long-suffering mother and the dog into account, and detailed how there can be competing presumptions, such as title and possessory interest. Remember that bad actors often lose.

JKG v. SG[74]

Year: *2011*
Category: *Property Law*
Type of Action: *Possessory Rights*
Animal: *Dog*
Pet Custody Concept: *Courts may ignore the public policy aspects to a dispute.*

The plaintiff, the owner of a Dachshund/Border Terrier named Macho, gifted the dog to the defendant when the plaintiff needed emergency medical treatment. At the time of the gift, the defendant observed that the plaintiff stumbled, fell down, and appeared intoxicated, and that Plaintiff's apartment was filled with dog excrement.

Later, the plaintiff sought Macho's return, first by calling the police, next by trying to initiate mediation, and then by going to small claims court. As this particular small claims court only addressed money judgments, the plaintiff then tried the state supreme court and finally, as the court put it, "found the right venue." The court found that the plaintiff had a superior possessory right to Macho, and the dog was ordered to be returned to the plaintiff.

74. 2011 N.Y. Slip. Op. 21073, 31 Misc. 3d 639, 922 N.Y.S.2d 742 (N.Y. Civ. Ct. 2011).

Practice Pointer: This decision seems to be based upon only a very traditional property law analysis and seems out of step with modern views that dogs belong where at least their minimum welfare needs are met. Clients should be warned that an old-school type of decision is always possible. Although this case described a small claims court that only addressed money judgments, other courts bend the rules to achieve substantive justice.

O'Keefe v. Gist[75]

Year: *2012*
Category: *Constitutional Law, Property Law*
Type of Action: *1983 Action*
Animal: *Dog*
Pet Custody Concept: *Asserting due process rights is not easy.*

The plaintiff dog owner, who had regained possession of his dog, Boomer, brought an action against the defendants seeking relief under 42 U.S.C. § 1983.[76] The plaintiff alleged that his due process rights were violated when his dog was given to another without his consent and that he was denied pre-deprivation procedural due process. He also sought an order prohibiting the enforcement of the ordinance as it violated the Fourteenth Amendment of the U.S. Constitution.

The defendant police officer took possession of a stray dog that was microchipped but not wearing any tax or license tags. Although the officer looked for the dog's owner and conducted interviews, the officer failed to scan the dog for a microchip as he lacked a scanner. Rather than following established protocol and delivering the dog to animal control for disposal, the officer instead gave the dog to another.

The federal court took judicial notice that in a state action, the plaintiff had recovered possession of the dog after posting a $3,000 bond, and the plaintiff had also secured a judicial determination that he had full ownership of the dog following the return of the bond. Even so, the plaintiff was "deprived of his property from roughly July 2009 to December 2010." Although agreeing with the principle that an individual is generally entitled to notice and a pre-deprivation hearing, the court also described due process as a flexible concept and that post-deprivation procedures and common law judicial remedies could be adequate.

To prevail in a due process claim, the plaintiff needed to prove that post-deprivation remedies were insufficient. The court also scoffed at the plaintiff's claim that he was an owner, stating, "The defined term 'owner' is broad so that the city can hold individuals who have control over animals accountable for care and treatment of those animals. The definition is not operational and does not declare legal ownership interests in any animal." The court also said, "The dog further wore no tag and bore no other visible identification marks. A state actor cannot give notice to someone who is unknown."

75. 908 F. Supp. 2d 946 (2012).
76. A § 1983 action enables a private enforcement of a complaint.

Emphasizing that the officer did not know who the dog's owner was, the court further stated that "the constitution does not require municipal and state officials to do more that conduct a visual inspection of a stray cat or dog to attempt to determine ownership."[77] The court admitted that there were laws to scan stray animals for microchips, but perhaps with a chip on the court's own shoulder, the court declared that it was "unwilling to declare that the constitutional procedural minimum in this case requires every municipality to scan every stray cat and dog for microchips."

On the subject of declaratory judgment, as the plaintiff had the dog back, the court found that the plaintiff had failed to properly state a claim. The court also observed that the plaintiff's conversion claim was improperly pled.

Practice Pointer: The federal court seemed perplexed that after the plaintiff had his dog back, he had the audacity to go from state to federal court and make a federal case out of it. Lawyers should warn their clients that judicial reaction to any type of companion animal claim is unpredictable. Always remember, too, that the term "ownership" can be subject to a variety of interpretations.

PATTERSON V. CITY OF BELLMEAD[78]

Year: *2013*
Category: *Constitutional Law*
Type of Action: *Statutory Challenge*
Animal: *Dog, Cat*
Pet Custody Concept: *Disputes about companion animals, thus far, do not involve a fundamental right.*

The appellants owned many show dogs and cats and filed a lawsuit challenging a city ordinance that provided that any person who kept more than four dogs or cats on any one premise maintained a kennel and needed to pay an annual kennel fee of $300. Prior to this ordinance being passed, there was no fee. Instead of paying the fee for their "hobby farm," the appellants facially challenged the ordinance as unconstitutional and in violation of their Fourteenth Amendment equal protection and due process rights.

The court of appeals affirmed the trial court's summary judgment in favor of the city and denied the appellants' motion and request for discovery. The discovery sought by the appellants included the following:

> 1) Each and every governmental interest to which the City claims Section 3-40 is related. Also, the Pattersons requested that the City detail how it contends Section 3-40 meets, satisfies, relates, or has any connection to the particular

77. The court's arguments were a bit disingenuous for the simple reason that had the officer followed protocol and brought Boomer to animal control, it was likely that microchip scanners would have been readily available at these facilities, as the utilization of microchips for companion animals is an established process.

78. S.W.3d, 2013 WL 1188929 (Tex. App. 2013).

governmental interest. In doing so, the Pattersons also requested that the City state and describe upon what information, study, empirical data, or other evidence upon which these contentions are based. 2) The number and/or identity of the individual(s) and/or entity(ies) that the City has charged with a violation of Section 3-40 of the Municipal Code of the City of Bellmead from the time of the provisions' enactment until present.

Rejecting the appellants' discovery request, the court said, "Although the scope of discovery is broad, discovery requests must nevertheless show a 'reasonable expectation of obtaining information that will aid the dispute's resolution.'" Emphasizing that discovery must be "reasonably tailored" to relevant matters, the court said, "preemptive denial of discovery is proper if there exists no possible relevant, discoverable testimony, facts, or material which would support or lead to evidence that would support a claim or defense." The party opposing discovery has the burden of proving that the discovery requests failed to meet this requirement.[79]

In framing its decision, the court offered the explanation that "reasonable minds may differ as to whether Section 3-40 has a substantial relationship to public health, safety, morals, or general welfare; thus, the ordinance must stand as a valid exercise of the City's police power and the Pattersons' discovery requests are irrelevant to this matter." The court was dismissive of the appellants' claim that "Section 3-40 unfairly restricts dog and cat ownership but does not impose ownership limitations for other animals." In Texas, selective enforcement is permissible if it is not "intentional or purposeful."[80]

The court, not persuaded by the appellants' claim that the ordinance needed to have a rational relationship to a governmental function, instead said, "If reasonable minds may differ as to whether a particular ordinance has a substantial relationship to the public health, safety, morals, or general welfare, no clear abuse of discretion is shown and the ordinance must stand as a valid exercise of the City's police power." Emphasizing that there was a presumption of an ordinance's validity and that the person challenging the ordinance has the burden of proof, the court relied on the 1987 U.S. Supreme Court decision in *Nollan v. California Coastal Commission*[81] addressing the subject of property regulation. A city's action "will survive a substantive due process challenge if it could have rationally been decided that the measure might achieve the objective."

The city advocated that the state court should have utilized the same rational basis standard of review for a federal due process challenge. While not discussing the show dogs and cats impacted by this case, the court signaled the terrible powers of the government to destroy these animals. A representative who provided an affidavit for the appellants emphasized the negative public policy implications of the city's

---

79. The court justified its dismissal with the rationale that a plaintiff had failed to advance a claim for which relief could be granted. It seemed that the court would not permit the appellants' discovery because the constitutionality of the municipal code was "a pure question of law and does not permit the introduction of facts to support the Pattersons' assertions."

80. The court clarified that the equal protection guarantee is not a source of substantive rights or liberties. Instead, it is a right to be free from invidious discrimination through statutory classifications.

81. 483 U.S. 825, 107 S. Ct. 3141, 3147, 97 L. Ed. 2d 677 (1987).

ordinance. These pet-limit laws "lead to increased costs to the municipality, decreased animal adoptions, and increased animal deaths in municipal shelters."

Ultimately, the court found that the city's perspective about the ordinance differed from the appellants' viewpoint because "reasonable minds may differ as to whether a particular ordinance has a substantial relationship to the public health, safety, morals, or general welfare." Accordingly, the ordinance did not violate due process and represented a valid exercise of the city's police power.[82]

Practice Pointer: Over time, human relationships with pets may represent a legally recognized fundamental right. It is interesting to contemplate the court's conception of how "reasonable minds may differ."

STODDARD V. VANZANDT[83]

Year: *2013*
Category: *Property Law*
Type of Action: *Summary Judgment*
Animal: *Cat*
Pet Custody Concept: *Finders keepers, losers weepers.*

The plaintiffs sought return of their cat following a wrongful taking based upon the claim of "relief in the form replevin (return of the cat); wrongful possession; trespass and physical interference; and wrongful conversion." They also initiated a motion for summary judgment.

In this dispute about a cat named Freedom, the court detailed the standards applicable to the plaintiffs in the summary judgment action but plainly stated that animals were no longer personal property in the state of New York. Instead, animals—and more specifically cats—were in the category of companion animals. Companion animals were afforded special protections in New York, as reflected by the fact that they can be the beneficiaries of an estate, they can be the subject of an order for protection, and there are standards for their care.

Freedom's original owners had failed to microchip the cat, the cat had no collar or tags, and the cat "was wet and appeared to be abandoned." The finders of Freedom lived in the same complex as the original owners and inquired of the complex manager as to ownership. The finders took Freedom to the local humane society, where Freedom was posted as a found animal and held for five days, as required by statute.

82. The court addressed classifications that affect fundamental rights, saying that those classifications are subject to strict judicial scrutiny and should constitute the least restrictive means to achieving a compelling state interest. The court found that fundamental rights were not at issue because dog and cat ownership is not a fundamental right nor are dog and cat owners members of a suspect or quasi-suspect class that may be subjected to invidious discrimination claims. From there, the court applied the rational basis review standard to the appellants' equal protection claim and found it wanting.

83. 975 N.Y.S.2d 712, 2013 N.Y. Slip. Op. 51175(U), 40 Misc. 3d 1213(A) (2013).

When Freedom went missing, the original owners failed to check the humane society's webpage, although they claimed they had looked for the cat.

The court emphasized that in a summary judgment action, (1) the focus should be on issue identification, not issue determination; (2) the plaintiff must establish, by prima facie evidence, entitlement as a matter of law and must demonstrate by sufficient evidence the absence of material fact issues; (3) if the plaintiff could establish a judgment right as a matter of law, then the defendant had the burden of proving that there were "genuine issues" of material fact; and (4) evidence should be viewed in the light most favorable to the party opposing the motion for summary judgment.

The court, motivated by the public policy interest of finding placements for lost or abandoned cats, said companion animals were afforded the benefits of adoption "as an alternative to euthanization" and relied on *Feger v. Warwick Animal Shelter*,[84] wherein public policy favored encouraging pet adoption. The court acknowledged that the outcome of this case, though heartbreaking, was the "inevitable consequence of their [the plaintiffs'] inattention to their cat."

Practice Pointer: Always consider how to initiate and respond to public policy concerns.

Greater Houston German Shepherd Dog Rescue, Inc. v. Lydia Lira and Alfonso Lira[85]

Year: *2014*
Category: *Property Law*
Type of Action: *Lost and Found*
Animal: *Dog*
Pet Custody Concept: *Courts may resent the original owners of unsterilized dogs that become lost.*

This case received considerable attention in Texas. Brother and sister appellees Lydia and Alfonso Lira owned a German Shepherd that escaped through their open garage door. When the dog was not claimed within the city ordinance's limited hold period, the dog was transferred to a German Shepherd rescue group. When the appellees learned that their dog was at a rescue facility, they filed suit to recover possession of the dog utilizing several legal theories. The court of appeals determined that possession of the dog could not be recovered and took a strict constructionist approach with regard to what the higher court called "the exclusive procedures established by city ordinance for the redemption of an impounded dog." The court required that the dog be returned by the original owners to the rescue group.

84. 59 A.D.3d 68 (2d Dept. 2008).
85. No. 14-13-00240-CV, Trial Court Case No. 2013-03944 (2014).

It was pointed out that the loose dog did not have a license, rabies tag, identification tag, or microchip. The court seemed impressed by the expenses the city incurred as a result of the appellees' cumulative behaviors. The city had to photograph the dog, list the dog on a website for lost animals, and perform a medical evaluation, including a heartworm test. The medical evaluation revealed that the dog had not been sterilized and had a "weak positive" heartworm test result, which led to the dog being scheduled for euthanasia.

The appellees' behavior also caused the city, in addition to caring for the dog, to make the extra effort to have the rescue group treat the dog for heartworm and find the dog a home so that the scheduled euthanasia could be avoided. To recap, the appellees failed to pick up their dog from the city during the first three days of the dog's impoundment and during the time period that the dog was scheduled for euthanasia. On the fifth day of the dog's impoundment, the rescue group picked up the dog on the condition that the dog would be sterilized. The rescue group paid the costs for the dog to be evaluated, sterilized, and treated for heartworm, and they also had the dog microchipped.

In a footnote, the court described that the appellees had searched for the dog on the animal control website but did not find their German Shepherd, who was listed on the website under a different breed. The court cited *Strickland v. Medlen*[86] for the classification that dogs were personal property subject to ordinances related to police powers. With regard to city ordinances, the court said, "this procedure may not be circumvented by other means, such as by purchasing the dog."

It was difficult to tell if the court was influenced by the best interests of the dog or if the court was just angry at the expenses incurred by the city and the waste of everyone's time. The court merely mentioned in passing that there was evidence to support that if the original owners had attempted to reclaim their dog while the dog was still in possession of animal control, the owners "would not have complied with the redemption procedure," which involved sterilizing the dog, and the appellees were opposed to this. The court also said, "Although the dog tested positive for heartworms, the trial court also found that the Liras requested that no 'other medical procedures [be] done to him.'"

Practice Pointer: This case is representative of how *Strickland v. Medlen* affected the court's view about police powers in this lost dog case. Case law, rather than being vertical, is more horizontal, cutting across practice areas and state borders. There are significant cultural differences around the country on the subject of sterilization.

86. 397 S.W.3d 184, 185 (Tex. 2013).

HENNET V. ALLAN[87]

Year: *2014*
Category: *Property Law*
Type of Action: *Possessory Interest*
Animal: *Dog*
Pet Custody Concept: *Pets may be a special category of property.*

The court expanded the common law definition of personal property in this landmark decision, saying pets should be recognized as a "special category of property." A cohabiting couple who owned a black Labrador Retriever named Duke broke up, and the defendant signed a settlement statement so that the plaintiff could refinance the mortgage. At issue was whether the statement extended to Duke as personal property.

In examining this issue, the court emphasized that the modern trend to treat companion animals as more than just property was well articulated by Judge Cooper in *Travis v. Murray*.[88] In that decision, the court opted to use a "best for all concerned" standard. The court seemed to agree with Judge Cooper that the best-interest custody standard was unavailable when applied to pets. The court also looked at the evolving jurisprudence where companion animals were in a special category of property and were "afforded many protections under the law" and that in third-party liability tort claims, courts were "at a crossroads in determining whether a strict property analysis should still govern disputes between dog owners."

The court looked to the century-old decision in *Mullaly v. People*,[89] where dogs were brought into the protected category of personal property, saying, "artificial reasoning upon which these rules were based are wholly inapplicable to modern society." The court then added, "Today, we should take the next step in recognizing that pets are more than just 'personal property' when it comes to resolving a dispute between owners."

The court noted that the plaintiff issued two checks from an account to purchase Duke, but that same account held funds from the defendant's employment. Both parties' names appeared on the dog's title and registration. Given the strong relationship each party had with Duke, together with their "extensive involvement" in Duke's care, the case was remanded for review that would include the circumstances for how the dog was acquired and cared for, as well as what the arrangement was between the parties when they separated and the defendant moved out.

Practice Pointer: It is common in divorce decrees for each party to be awarded household goods, furnishings, and equipment, or even household goods, furnishings, equipment, and property. By not listing the companion animals individually, a lawyer runs the risk that this type of argument will arise. Generally speaking, if this claim does not arise within a year after the agreement, it is unlikely that any subsequent argument will impress a judge given the importance of timely action and possessory rights to the court.

---

87. 43 Misc. 3d 542 (2014).
88. 42 Misc. 3d 447, 977 N.Y.S.2d 621 (2013).
89. 86 N.Y. 365 (1881).

Chapter 7

Tort Law Affects Pet Law

"A man has honor if he holds himself to an ideal of conduct though it is inconvenient, unprofitable, or dangerous to do so."

—Walter Lippmann

According to the American Veterinary Medical Association, only 2.1 percent of pet owners view their animals as property, while 97.9 percent view them as family members or companions. Americans spend $28 billion annually on veterinary care. The evolving jurisprudence of tort law relating to companion animals is addressed in this chapter, together with what can be taken away from these tort cases and applied to family law in the pet law context.

OLD CONCEPTIONS OF ANIMALS

As companion animals become part of the modern family, some courts rigidly follow old common laws and precedents that reflect a different conception of companion animals. The 19th-century view is best captured in *Sentell v. New Orleans Carrollton Railroad Co.*[1] There, in the hierarchy of beings, dogs were quasi-property below horses, sheep, and other domesticated animals, and also below the category of animals kept for pleasure, curiosity, or caprice. The *Sentell* court only elevated a dog from quasi-property to lower tier property status if the dog was killed or subdued. There was no such restriction on horses.

1. 166 U.S. 698, 703 (1897).

HOW ANIMALS ARE VALUED

The question of damages awarded pursuant to a tort law claim could impact pet custody disputes when the rule of law is based more on principles of economic justice, something very rational that can be weighed and measured, rather than on principles that involve comprehending something more difficult, such as love, pain, emotion, and attachment.

If animals lack extrinsic or intrinsic value,[2] why should they be saved? Why should worthless animals be the subject of costly ownership disputes? This economic mentality might lead an owner to make a decision not to operate on a dog that cost very little but to operate on a dog that was expensive. This point of view also puts good veterinarians in poor positions when recommending a costly treatment in a situation where the value of a dog is thought about in purchase price economic terms. American culture is conflicted as to whether relational value or economic value is more important.

An example of what happens when pets are undervalued was exemplified by an action brought against a veterinarian in northern Minnesota. This veterinarian routinely overlooked the pain implications of surgery for cat declaws and other painful surgical procedures. Following a complaint against this veterinarian by the Minnesota Board of Veterinary Medicine, the board made a groundbreaking decision regarding the duty for a veterinarian to manage pain,[3] though "initially centered on allegations of an orthopedic procedure gone bad."[4]

TORT CLAIMS

When a tort action is initiated, the way the action is framed varies from state to state. For example, a claim may be brought based upon veterinary malpractice,[5] companionship loss, products liability, tortious interference with a contractual right, negligent or intentional infliction of emotional distress, a conversion claim,

---

2. Pets' prospects are worse if acquired inexpensively as gifts or impulse purchases. Dick Murray, *Unwanted Pets*, Urban Animal Management Conference Proceedings 1993, https://aiam.org.au/resources/file/conf-documents/1993/pub_pro93_dickmurray.pdf (last visited May 12, 2016); P. Arkow, *The Humane Society and the Human-Companion Animal Bond: Reflections on the Broken Bond*, 15 Vet. Clin. North. Am. Small An. Pract. 455 (1985).

3. *In the Matter of Carl W. Seemann,* Findings of Fact, Conclusions of Law and Final Decision and Order, https://mn.gov/boards/assets/SeemannC_2%202E7%202E08_tcm21-26761.pdf (last visited May 12, 2016).

4. Jennifer Fiala, *The Price of Pain: How a Veterinarian Facing License Revocation Exposes an Unwritten Mandate to Treat Animal Pain*, DVM 360, http://veterinarynews.dvm360.com/price-pain-0 (last visited May 12, 2016).

5. Christopher Green, *The Future of Veterinary Malpractice Liability in the Care of Companion Animals*, Michigan State University Animal Legal & Historical Center, https://www.animallaw.info/article/future-veterinary-malpractice-liability-care-companion-animals (last visited May 12, 2016).

or the new tort of outrage. In addition to the variations in claims, payers for damages also differ.

Economic Damages

Damages in tort law fall into three categories: economic, noneconomic, and punitive. With regard to economic damages, lawyers may request any kind of out-of-pocket expense or loss related to the companion animal. This may include purchase price, the cost of veterinary care and prescriptions, pet food and toy purchases, training and behavioral costs, expenditures for doggie daycare and grooming, loss of economic opportunity related to breeding, and the cost for a replacement animal. A lawyer might advocate that there is a relationship between how much money was spent on a companion animal and what the companion animal is worth to the owner.[6]

Do not be surprised if one court limits a claimant's economic loss to the fair market value or replacement value of the pet, while another court might add to this value what the court considers to be reasonable costs for veterinary services, while still others might be receptive to utilizing a broad spectrum of measures. The Texas court prefers that damages be based upon an animal's "true value," which leans on an agrarian usefulness analysis.[7]

Other courts embrace the idea that an animal may have a special economic value or intrinsic value,[8] especially when the fair market value or replacement value of the animal is difficult to ascertain. Relational or companionship value could be an aspect of economic loss, following the lead in the *Brousseau v. Rosenthal*[9] bailment decision. There, the court reasoned that "a good dog's value increases rather than falls with age and training." If, as you read on, you wonder if there is a clear line between the concepts of economic and noneconomic loss pertaining to companion animals, be comforted by the idea that there is not.

Noneconomic Damages

While it can be expected that courts will permit a claim for economic loss, it is less predictable when courts will allow a claim for a noneconomic loss. Unless the court refuses to entertain this type of claim altogether, the court focuses on the

---

6. When representing the owner of an injured or deceased animal, make a list of every commercial expenditure and then do a reality check as to how the courts in that jurisdiction might react to a broad economic claim.

7. *See* Strickland v. Medlen, 397 S.W.3d 184, 185 (Tex. 2013).

8. The term "intrinsic value" reflects an aspect of philosophical debates about morality and ethics. In philosophy, it has been argued that intrinsic value is a criterion for moral standing.

9. 443 N.Y.S.2d 285, 110 Misc. 2d 1054 (N.Y. City Civ. Ct. 1980).

human's suffering to the exclusion of the companion animal's suffering.[10] The court then determines whether the criteria for emotional distress has been satisfied, for example, by deciding whether the dog is a family member and whether the human who suffered the loss was within the zone of danger when the animal was harmed. How courts might address noneconomic loss is not static.

A landmark case on the subject of damages was *LaPorte v. Associated Independents, Inc.*,[11] a case where a garbage collector maliciously hurled a garbage can at a tethered and pedigreed Dachshund named Heidi; this action caused not only the dog's death but also the mental suffering of Heidi's owner.[12]

Courts seem to be in a catch-22 with regard to the concept of sentimental loss. For example, in 1987, the Illinois court in *Jankoski v. Preiser Animal Hospital, Ltd.*[13] observed that the state of Washington shunned consideration of the sentimental value of companion animals.

By contrast, loss of companionship was permitted as an aspect of sentimental value in the Pennsylvania decision of *Daughen v. Fox*,[14] a case where a dog died following an X-ray mix up by the veterinarian,[15] an error that was covered up. The court rejected the traditional formula for calculating damages because this method failed to take into account the reasonable and necessary costs for veterinary treatment. Finding that the typical personal property damages analysis approach was unjust, the trial court reasoned that the better method was to consider the intrinsic value of the animal because the value of an animal to the animal's owner may increase over time rather than decrease. Another sign of the changing times took place in Broward County, Florida. There, the court awarded a Rottweiler owner $20,000 based upon the dog's intrinsic value when a kennel failed to timely get the dog appropriate care for a respiratory condition.[16]

---

10. It will be interesting to see whether the concept of permitting noneconomic damages for only human suffering will change to both human and animal suffering through legislation or case law, particularly now that an animal can be a crime victim.

11. 163 So. 2d 267, 268 (Fla. 1964).

12. *See* Wilson v. City of Eagan, 297 N.W.2d 146 (Minn. 1980), Burgess v. Taylor, 44 S.W.3d 806 (Ky. App. 2001), and Propes v. Griffith, 25 S.W.3d 544 (Mo. App. W.D. 2000).

13. 510 N.E.2d 1084, 157 Ill. App. 3d 818 (Ill. App. 1st Dist. 1987).

14. 539 A.2d 858, 372 Pa. Super. 405 (Pa. Super. 1988).

15. Be aware of which causes of action are permitted involving veterinarians in your state because of the variance in statute of limitations deadlines. *See* Southall v. Gabel, 277 N.E.2d 230 (Ohio Ct. App. 1971), where the court concluded, "Until the Supreme Court speaks, veterinarians are not included in the definition of malpractice." *Id.* at 299. Determine whether a special malpractice period has been established by state statute. If the development of malpractice liability in the state is based upon common law rather than a statute, a personal injury or negligence statute of limitations could apply. There could even be an applicable statute of limitations for injury to personal property.

16. *What Is Your Pet's Intrinsic Value? A Judge in Broward County Says One Dog's Is $20,000*, Daily Vet Blog, http://m.petmd.com/blogs/fullyvetted/2009/may/what-your-pets-intrinsic-value-judge-broward-county-says-one-dogs-20000-6787# (last visited May 12, 2016).

Damages awards for noneconomic losses in medical malpractice cases may include amounts for pain and suffering, disfigurement, and loss of consortium. In veterinary malpractice cases,[17] compensation for noneconomic losses is rare.[18]

While courts have traditionally permitted awards of sentimental damages when a family heirloom is destroyed, the court may be averse to granting these types of damages for the loss of companion animal property.[19] Court rationales on this subject can be both difficult to follow and hypocritical. The court rejected consideration of the provision of sentimental damages in *Zager v. Dimilia*,[20] a case where an animal was injured when another dog broke loose from a tether.

Some judgments reflect the unique or special value of an animal to an owner. In a California case, a party was awarded $30,000 for the loss of his mixed breed dog, together with another $9,000 for veterinary bills.[21]

The court created "the unique approach" in *Campbell v. Animal Quarantine Station*,[22] a case that is almost emblematic of every pet owner's worst nightmare. Through the court's unique approach, the court enabled a pet owner to recover on a mental distress claim following the negligent destruction of animal property baked under the hot sun during transport.

It should also be noted that Tennessee has allowed some compensation for companionship loss.[23] This statute is subject to a ceiling and an exclusion. Now, all eyes are on how noneconomic damages claims will evolve.[24]

---

17. If you have a case involving veterinary malpractice, review the seminal article on this subject by Christopher Green, now the Executive Director of Harvard's Animal Law and Policy program. Christopher Green, *The Future of Veterinary Malpractice Liability in the Care of Companion Animals*, Michigan State University Animal Legal & Historical Center, https://www.animallaw.info/article/future-veterinary-malpractice-liability-care-companion-animals (last visited May 12, 2016).

18. *See* Oberschlake v. Veterinary Assocs. Animal Hosp., 785 N.E.2d 811 (Ohio Ct. App. 2003); Daughen v. Fox, D.V.M., 539 A.2d 858 (Pa. Super. Ct. 1988); and Corso v. Crawford Dog & Cat Hosp., Inc., 415 N.Y.S.2d 182 (Misc. 2d 1979) (the court found that a pet "occupies a special place somewhere in between a person and a piece of personal property").

19. *See* Arguello v. Behmke, 2006 WL 205097 (N.J. Super. Ch. 2006) (not reported in A.2d).

20. 524 N.Y.S.2d 968, 138 Misc. 2d 448 (N.Y. Vill. Ct. 1988).

21. Laura Parker, *When Pets Die at the Vet, Grieving Owners Call Lawyers*, USA Today, http://usatoday30.usatoday.com/news/nation/2005-03-14-pets-malpractice_x.htm (last visited May 12, 2016); *see* McDonald v. Ohio State Univ. Veterinary Hosp., 644 N.E.2d 750, 752 (Ohio Ct. Cl. 1994) (owner received $5,000 when his German Shepherd was paralyzed due to "exceptional circumstances"); and Petco Animal Supplies, Inc., v. Schuster, 144 S.W.3d 554, 563 (Tex. App. 2004) (owner not able to recover for "intrinsic value").

22. 632 P.2d 1066, 63 Haw. 557 (Haw. 1981).

23. T.C.A. § 44-17-403.

24. Lauren M. Sirois, *Recovering for the Loss of a Beloved Pet: Rethinking the Legal Classification of Companion Animals and the Requirements for Loss of Companionship Tort Damages*, 163 U. Penn. L. Rev. 1199 (2015), http://scholarship.law.upenn.edu/cgi/viewcontent.cgi?article=9478&context=penn_law_review (last visited May 12, 2016).

Punitive Damages

In addition to claims for economic and noneconomic damages, a lawyer might seek punitive damages, which seem to be granted in tort cases involving animals more often than one might expect. Perhaps the very courts who will not permit noneconomic damages are troubled when there is a wrong without a remedy. The behavior of the defendant, rather than emotional harm to the plaintiff, may be the test for punitive damages.[25]

TORT TRANSFORMATION

Tort law is out in front of other substantive areas when it comes to pushing past the boundaries of old conceptions about the value of a companion animal being limited to the animal's replacement cost.[26]

A good example of how existing common laws are being transformed or modified can be found in *Price v. Brown*.[27] When an English Bulldog died following a surgical procedure, the appellate court rejected a bailment claim, which is the type of claim typically brought against an automobile mechanic if the car ran when the car was brought in but was inoperable thereafter. The bailment action made no sense to the court in a claim involving a dog alive when brought to a veterinarian and then dead. The court thereby adopted the tort-based medical malpractice approach.

The dissenting judge in *Price v. Brown* still advocated the bailment approach.[28] Justice Castille said that it was well-suited for an action involving property, as it required that "the personalty shall be redelivered to the person who delivered it in the same or an agreed to altered form."[29]

To get a sense of the curious worldview of the courts and how the pendulum is swinging, examine *Corso v. Crawford Cat & Dog Hospital, Inc.*[30] There, the court specifically said, "This court now overrules prior precedent and holds that a pet is not just a thing but occupies a special place somewhere in between a person and a piece of personal property." This decision is emblematic of a court embracing morality by shaking off the shackles and precedents of the past.

---

25. Levine v. Knowles, 197 So. 2d 329, 331 (Fla. 3d Dist. App. 1967).
26. *See* Rabideau v. City of Racine, 627 N.W.2d 795, 797 (Wis. 2001).
27. 680 A.2d 1149 (Pa. 1996).
28. When reading bailment theories, reflect on the concept of Orwellian double speak.
29. *Price*, 680 A.2d at 1155 (Castille, J., dissenting). *See also* Williamson v. Prida, 89 Cal. Rptr. 2d 868 (Ct. App. 1999) (court found that medical malpractice standards apply to veterinary malpractice).
30. 415 N.Y.S.2d 182, 97 Misc. 2d 530 (N.Y. City Civ. Ct. 1979).

VETERINARY LIABILITY AND MEDICAL MALPRACTICE MODEL

Veterinary care in the United States has become a multi-billion-dollar industry.[31] Not only do pets receive annual examinations and vaccines, but they also get heartworm, flea, and tick treatments, and when the owners can afford it, major surgery to prolong their lives or chemotherapy to treat cancer. A growing number of dogs receive chiropractic care, and some with chronic conditions, such as hip dysplasia, receive acupuncture treatments. There are also many different medications available to help pets with anxiety, incontinence, and arthritis. Some dogs receive canine water therapy to help ease arthritis, increase joint flexibility, and decrease pain.[32]

Veterinarians and other providers often do not know with certainty who owns an animal, and they are faced with the dilemma of having to speculate.[33] As discussed throughout this book, ownership determinations are far from simple.[34] Courts are moving away from one-factor indicia of ownership to a multiple-factor analysis, and some take into account primary care and the history of possession. Accordingly, veterinarians are asked to provide veterinary services based on the representation of the human in possession of the animal, together with a name and signature on an intake form, although microchip evidence may support said ownership claim. They may be limited in what they can do to help an animal based upon a reputed owner's ability or inclination to pay for costly tests or treatments.[35] According to the current legal system, a veterinarian's actual client is the animal owner, not the animal.

Common law evolved in an agrarian society where actions against veterinarians varied and included claims for conversion, breach of bailment,[36] misrepresentation and fraud, strict products liability, and breach of contract. Case law about veterinary negligence, now usually pled as veterinary malpractice and not a breach of bailment claim, includes questions such as who is allowed in the family for liability purposes.[37] A threshold question, if a claim against a veterinarian is sought,

---

31. *Industry Statistics & Trends*, American Pet Products Association, http://www.americanpetproducts.org/press_industrytrends.asp (last visited May 12, 2016).

32. Alisa Advani, *Hydrotherapy: Dog Walk in Water*, The Bark, http://thebark.com/content/hydrotherapy-dog-walk-water (last visited May 12, 2016).

33. When Barbara J. Gislason spoke at an annual AAHA meeting, the subject of who owns the dog was of particular interest to prominent veterinarians.

34. Animal control laws tend to use a broad definition of ownership that extends to the keeper of an animal.

35. A new trend in association and professional organization benefits is to offer affordable health insurance for pets.

36. Katie J. L. Scott, *Bailment and Veterinary Malpractice: Doctrinal Exclusivity, or Not?* 55 Hastings L.J. 1009 (2004).

37. *See* Rabideau v. City of Racine, 627 N.W.2d 795, 797 (Wis. 2001).

is to determine whether the state where the action is brought holds veterinarians to a professional standard commensurate with the standards in medical malpractice.[38] Veterinary malpractice is a subject of intense interest for professors and scholars, as reflected in a variety of articles.[39]

The medical malpractice model begins with a predictable sequence of proofs: establish duty, breach of duty, proximate cause, and damages, and utilize a medical expert to establish the appropriate standard of care.[40] If liability is established, the verdict should represent equitable compensation for the injured party and further the societal goal, or economic efficiency, of preventing future injuries to others. Superficially, the models and tort objectives for veterinary and medical malpractice would be identical.[41] Exploring the detailed application of these models in each context and assessing the achievements of tort objectives may reveal them to be divergent.

In medical malpractice, as in the other human-focused tort law cases described herein, claims for compensatory damages focus on monetary losses, including lost wages, rehabilitation expenses, medical expenses, and other out-of-pocket losses resulting from an injury.[42] In sharp contrast, economic damages for loss or injury to companion animals are often limited to their fair market value or replacement cost, although the value of an animal to the owner may increase with age and a growing number of courts will allow reasonable compensation for out-of-pocket expenses and investments in the animal.[43]

According to Harvard's Christopher Green, the lack of consequences and accountability for wrongdoers is reflected in the very modest annual insurance costs for small animal veterinarians.[44] Because of the way damages related to liabilities for harm to companion animals are calculated, with an emphasis on economic value, veterinarian wrongdoers are little financially impacted by veterinary malpractice claims. Accordingly, veterinary insurance premiums are based primarily

---

38. *See* Downing v. Gully, D.V.M, P.C. 915 S.W.2d 181 (Tex. App. 1996) and Ladnier v. Norwood, D.V.M., 781 F.2d 490 (5th Cir. 1986).

39. Richard L. Cupp & Amber E. Dean, *Vets in the Doghouse: Are Pet Suits Economically Viable?* The Brief 42 (Spring 2002); Rebecca J. Huss, *Valuation in Veterinary Malpractice*, 35 Loy. U. Chi. L.J. 479 (2004).

40. Sarah L. Babcock, *A Veterinarian's Duty: Theories of Liability*, http://ocvets4pets.com/archive36/07_theories_liability.pdf (last visited May 12, 2016).

41. *See* McGee v. Smith, 107 S.W.3d 725 (Tex. App. 2003).

42. Raymund C. King, *Medical Malpractice and Tort Reform*, 6 Tortsource 1 (Spring 2004).

43. *See* Hohenstein v. Dodds, 10 N.W.2d 236 (Minn. 1943).

44. Christopher Green, *The Future of Veterinary Malpractice Liability in the Care of Companion Animals*, Michigan State University Animal Legal & Historical Center, https://www.animallaw.info/article/future-veterinary-malpractice-liability-care-companion-animals (last visited May 12, 2016). *See also* Steve Barghusen, *Noneconomic Damage Awards in Veterinary Malpractice: Using the Human Medical Experience as a Model to Predict the Effect of Noneconomic Damage Awards on the Practice of Companion Animal Veterinary Medicine*, Animal Law Lewis & Clark Law School, reprinted from Animal Law Volume 17, Issue 1, copyright 2010.

on general liability and defending complaints against veterinarians to a licensing authority.

Lack of meaningful civil damages and consequences in companion animal-related tort actions may have the undesirable effect of keeping incompetent, careless, and even cruel veterinarians licensed and in practice, and wrongdoers able to continue their bad behavior. It is ironic that some veterinarians, who devote their lives to advancing the importance of companion animals as family members, oppose noneconomic damages stemming from relational value, thereby subjecting animals to the logical and perhaps tragic consequences that tort law was designed to prevent.[45] It is understood that not only do all professionals, including veterinarians and lawyers alike, prefer not to pay malpractice premiums or practice defensive medicine or defensive law, but they also prefer to give their clients more affordable services that savings on insurance premiums could advance.

FUNDAMENTAL INTEREST TORT

Professor David Favre proposed a new tort called a fundamental interest tort at a Harvard Law School Conference called *The Evolving Legal Status of Chimpanzees*.[46] There, Favre stated,

> New and nameless torts are being recognized constantly, and the progress of the common law is marked by many cases of first impression in which the court has struck out boldly to create a new cause of action where none had been recognized before. The intentional infliction of mental suffering, the obstruction of the right to go where the plaintiff likes, the invasion of the right of privacy, the denial of the right to vote, the conveyance of land to defeat a title, the infliction of prenatal injuries, the alienation of the affections of a parent, and injury to a person's reputation by entering the person in a rigged television contest, to name only a few instances, could not be fitted into any accepted classifications when they first arose, but nevertheless have been held to be torts.[47]

45. *See* Strickland v. Medlen, 397 S.W.3d 184, 185 (Tex. 2013).

46. Professor David Favre teaches animal law at Michigan State University and is the editor of the Animal Legal & Historical Center website found at www.animallaw.info.

47. David S. Favre, *Judicial Recognition of the Interests of Animals—A New Tort*, 2005 Michigan State L. Rev. 333–67 (2005); MSU Legal Studies Research Paper No. 03-08. Professor David Favre argues that because animals are acknowledged by the legal system, it follows that they are within the legal community. Accepting their property status is not a barrier to recognizing and protecting their interests through the adoption of a new tort called the Intentional Interference with the Primary Interests of an Animal. *Primary Interests of a Chimp*, National Association for Biomedical Research, http://www.nabranimallaw.org/state/tort-law/primary-interests-of-a-chimp/ (last visited May 12, 2016). This tort would only pertain to a limited number of animal interests and would specifically exclude hunting, fishing, horses, zoos, aquariums, farms, and scientific research. The elements of the proposed cause of action Professor Favre described include (1) an interest is of fundamental biological, physiological, social, or nutritional importance to the animal; (2) the fundamental interest has been interfered with or harmed by the actions or inactions of the human; and (3) the weight and nature of the interest of the animal substantially outweighs the weight and nature of the interests of the human.

Professor Favre has also advocated that without questioning the property status of animals, animal interests may still be considered. The professor advocates that we understand that these interests matter, as we have passed endangered species and animal welfare laws, as well as the much-celebrated Chimpanzee Protection Act.[48]

OTHER CLAIMS AND CONCEPTIONS

As you wind your way through how courts regard the subject of companion animals in tort law, it is important to remind yourself about how key concepts differ across and between substantial practice areas. A subject of controversy among the states has been whether companion animals are more like products or goods in UCC contract disputes. The pro-products position was advanced in *Beyer v. Aquarium Supply Co.*,[49] where the court applied a strict liability standard in a tort action following the sale of sick hamsters. This product classification of animals is called the New York doctrine.

In contrast, the court in *Whitmer v. Schneble*[50] advanced an argument for a goods conceptualization of companion animals. Because dogs lack a fixed nature, the court proclaimed, "In short, all mankind, and this court as well, is aware that dogs bite and that bitches which have just whelped and are watching their pups will fulfill their natural maternal instinct and bite a stranger who approaches." This approach has come to be known as the Illinois doctrine, particularly as voiced by courts in other states debating whether to follow the New York or Illinois doctrine.

Latham v. Wal-Mart Stores, Inc.[51] synthesizes both of these doctrines and sprinkles in a *Restatement (Second) of Torts* analysis. The court ultimately rejected the New York product approach because of how the character of the property could be "changed and shaped" by the purchaser. More than that, the Missouri court recognized that a living creature has "mutability."

The logic of these goods and products classifications in tort and contract law is at odds with emerging ideas in other practice areas, including that companion animals belong in an interim category between property and personhood, or animals can be crime victims and trust beneficiaries. Envision a rant by Grammy-winning comedian Lewis Black ridiculing the two presenting UCC choices. Imagine

48. It is noteworthy that the federal Animal Welfare Act restricts scientific experimentation on some, but not all, animals; birds, rats, and mice receive no protection. *Rats, Mice and Birds Excluded from Animal Welfare Act*, American Psychological Association, http://www.apa.org/monitor/julaug02/rats.aspx (last visited May 12, 2016).

49. 94 Misc. 2d 336, 404 N.Y.S.2d 778 (N.Y. Sup. Ct. 1977).

50. 29 Ill. App. 3d 659, 331 N.E.2d 115 (1975).

51. 818 S.W.2d 673 (Mo. App. E.D. 1991).

that he dramatically shakes his head and gesticulates while saying, "One of the most important things, especially when you're leaving school, is to realize you're going to be dealing with a lot of idiots. And a lot of those idiots are in charge of things. . . ."[52]

It is noteworthy that when there is a "bad faith" or tortious breach of contract, lawyers are seeking to extend the tort remedies of compensatory and punitive damages to the commercial realm. It has been advocated that when contract remedies are grossly inadequate, courts are more likely to permit an alternative theory of recovery.

As a rule of thumb, contract damages are more in the realm of damages contemplated when the contract was formed and may include reasonably foreseeable damages at the time of contract formation; tort damages can result in consequential damages beyond commercial expectations in that compensation can be based upon the harm proximately caused. These ideas are derivative of the principle that all contracts imply a covenant, or implied duty, of good faith and fair dealing.

It is fascinating that notwithstanding the New York animals as products doctrine, New York is the state that birthed the landmark cases of *Corso v. Crawford Dog and Cat Hospital, Inc.*[53] and *Travis v. Murray*.[54] In *Crawford*, the court recognized that a "pet is not just a thing," and in *Travis*, the court preferred that when making pet custody determinations, the court utilize decision-making criteria that would result in the "best interests for all concerned."

TORT LAW IMPACTS FAMILY LAW

The emergence of noneconomic value for animals will impact family law and civil ownership disputes. If companionship loss, a type of noneconomic loss claim, is allowed as a tort claim, relational value may receive more attention in the family court context. If a tort of outrage because of animal cruelty is permitted in the tort system, ownership determinations in family law may be impacted by maltreatment behaviors. Tort reasoning impacts how courts perceive animal-related public policy.

The more a companion animal is differentiated from inanimate property in the tort system, the more the companion animal may progress as a subject worthy of

52. *Lewis Black Quotes*, Brainy Quote, http://www.brainyquote.com/quotes/authors/l/lewis_black.html (last visited Oct. 11, 2016).
53. 97 Misc. 2d 530 (Civ. Ct. Queens Cnty. 1979).
54. 2013 N.Y. Slip. Op. 23405 (N.Y. Sup. Ct. 2013).

the court's time and attention in family court.[55] Even so, we have passed the point of no return about how all animals, not just companion animals, may be treated. We are troubled by the idea of chickens or pregnant pigs not being able to turn around in their tiny cages or crates.

Cruelty to pigs is now the subject of comedy bits, as was famously represented on *The Daily Show with Jon Stewart*, where two comedians advanced their competing arguments about whether pregnant pigs should be able to turn around in their cages. The idea that the pigs should just stand still and face forward, as if pigs were inanimate objects, is a perspective buried in old precedents.

Courts used to give more time to disputants who co-owned famous show dogs, or pets owned by famous people, than those who own rescue dogs; some may be aware that adopting rescue companion animals is now considered to be politically correct. Even so, it is a priority for those who use animals in commercial ways to advocate for the continued use of inanimate property law conceptions. The progression of legal thought and changes in our culture regarding animal law affects all cases.

CONCLUSION

A new legal standard should be proposed, followed by creating workable model laws. It would be desirable for the Uniform Law Commission to take the lead in developing forward thinking pet law jurisprudence. The expansion of economic and noneconomic losses in animal and pet law cases should be appropriately crafted to promote tort equity and economic efficiency objectives. For the immediate future, it is unreasonable to exclude animal owners from compensation for their loss of sentimental property; animals, if still labeled property, should at least be considered to have noneconomic sentimental value in a similar way to wedding rings or family heirlooms. These are all subjects of importance that will be the subject of discussion, litigation, and legislation in this century.

The value of animals in the tort context impacts how all of pet law, including laws pertaining to pet custody disputes, will progress. The logic from a human perspective is that the more valuable companion animals are, the more they deserve the court's time and attention. Although in tort law, there is an idea that there is no wrong without a remedy, and that a remedy is typically more currency based, except when punitive damages apply, family courts could become more astute about relationships and bonds. It is as if we have two minds about how animals belong in the legal system; one version is that companion animals are members of our family, and the other is that they are not. Newer classifications of animals, such as in a special category of property, would be an appropriate beginning.

55. Remember that many courts have separate civil and family court calendars.

APPLICABLE CASE LAW

TAYLOR V. WELSH[56]

Year: *1907*
Category: *Property Law*
Type of Action: *Conversion*
Animal: *Cat*
Pet Custody Concept: *When a pet was wrongfully possessed and died, the owner was entitled to recover the difference between the cat's value at the time of possession and the cat's value when taken on the writ.*

The appellant acquired title to a white Persian show cat named Major in exchange for a picture. The cat had won prizes and honors at cat shows and was also regarded as "a money maker." Later, when the appellant was away and the cat was in the care of the appellant's mother, the appellee talked the appellant's mother into giving her possession of Major for $50.00. The appellee said this payment was on the condition that if the appellant did not ratify the sale, the appellant could get the cat back for $50.00.

Notwithstanding that she knew the appellant's mother was not the owner and lacked authority to even conditionally sell the cat, the appellee later accepted money from another woman to gain a half-interest in Major. The new half-owner had possession of the cat until the appellant's husband was able to take possession of the cat pursuant to a writ. According to the record, when taken on the writ, Major "was sick and nearly died."

Because the sale of Major was conditional, the appellee asserted that the appellant had the obligation to demand the cat before bringing suit, and the trial court agreed.[57] On appeal, it was determined that the appellant's mother, who was effectively a bailee, could not enter into any type of sale; the court determined that no title had passed to the appellee. Instead, "An unauthorized sale by a mere naked bailee is a wrongful conversion of the property, and the sale is void as to the owner." The court recalled the proposition that a buyer should take care to be sure that "the title was in his vendor. He having no title, the defendants acquired none." The court cited other authority that a bailee could not transfer good title, too.

Both the appellee and the new alleged co-owner knew, at the very least, that the transaction involving Major was only "conditional." The court also reviewed the right of the appellant to bring a replevin action and found a treatise, Coffey on Replevin, sec. 512, to be persuasive. The court also said that in a matter where a pound-master sold a horse without lawful authority, the purchaser contended that a proper demand was

56. 138 Ill. App. 190 (1907).

57. The higher court said, "The case was tried before the judge without a jury, and we can perceive no good reason for sending it back to the trial court for another trial, on probably the same evidence. The judgment will be reversed and judgment will be entered here in favor of the appellant and for $100 damages, appellant to recover her costs in this court and in the Superior Court of Cook county." The court's representation that there was "no good reason" to send this back to the trial court seemed reflective of considerable restraint regarding the court's disdain for this tribunal.

required before bringing suit. The court rejected this claim because when property was wrongfully in someone's possession, a demand was unnecessary.

At the time the writ was executed, Major was in the appellee co-owner's kitchen, dirty and vomiting, and he was unable to get up. He soon died at a veterinarian's office. In a post-mortem necropsy, it was determined that Major had a condition of dehydration and starvation resulting from an obstruction of his large intestines that caused blood poisoning.

The court determined that the appellant was entitled to recover the difference between the cat's value when the appellee took possession of him and the cat's value when taken on the writ. The court granted the owner $100 for damages but refused to cover the appellant's expenses of finding the cat. The court may have thought that the $100 damages were already quite extraordinary in 1907.

Practice Pointer: Bad actors often lose in pet ownership disputes. Have faith that bad decisions by poor trial courts will be overturned on appeal.

LaPorte v. Associated Independents, Inc.[58]

Year: *1964*
Category: *Tort Law*
Type of Action: *Malicious Tort*
Animal: *Dog*
Pet Custody Concept: *Courts look around for useful ideas relevant to a novel question.*

A garbage collector deliberately hurled a garbage can in the direction of a tethered, pedigreed two-year-old miniature Dachshund named Heidi. The perpetrator laughed while the tiny dog died. Following the death of her dog, Heidi's owner sought medical care and experienced emotional difficulties. At the subsequent trial, she was awarded $2,000 for compensatory damages and $1,000 for punitive damages. On appeal, the defendant challenged the trial judge's jury instruction and award of compensatory and punitive damages.

The court looked at precedent by examining *Kirksey v. Jernigan*,[59] where the trial court granted compensatory and punitive damages, including a mental suffering component, when the body of a deceased child was improperly embalmed and not returned to the child's parents. The higher court in *Kirksey* reversed the judgment because the "mental pain [was] unconnected with physical hurt" in a breach of contract action involving only simple negligence. Even so, the higher court permitted a claim of injury involving a wrongful act without malice. Malice was defined as "great indifference to the persons, property, or rights of others."

In the instant case, the court determined that the acts performed by the garbage collector represented malice and extreme indifference to the rights of Heidi's owner and distinguished it from *Kirksey*. The court then addressed whether damages should

58. 163 So. 2d 267, 1 A.L.R.3d 992 (Fla. 1964).
59. 45 So. 2d 188, 17 A.L.R.2d 766 (Fla. 1950).

have been limited to Heidi's market value or her "special or pecuniary value." While rejecting the idea of sentimental value for a dog, the court recognized that "the affection of a master for his dog is a very real thing and that the malicious destruction of the pet provides an element of damage for which the owner should recover, irrespective of the value of the animal because of its special training such as a Seeing Eye dog or sheep dog."

The court emphasized that "the anguish resulting from the mishandling of the body of a child cannot be equated to the grief from the loss of a dog but that does not imply that mental suffering from the loss of a pet dog, even one less an aristocrat than Heidi, is nothing at all." The court granted certiorari, quashed the judgment of the district court of appeals, and reinstated the judgment of the trial court for $2,000 compensatory and $1,000 punitive damages concerning the miniature Dachshund.

This landmark case represented an early decision in American jurisprudence where the court compensated a dog owner for the mental anguish suffered from witnessing her dog being maliciously killed. Cases involving noneconomic loss, mental anguish, and companionship loss are part of the greater pet law fabric where pets are important in human lives and impact their best interests.

Practice Pointer: Effectively communicate the relationship between a human and the companion animal in question.

Lincecum v. Smith[60]

Year: *1973*
Category: *Tort Law*
Type of Action: *Conversion*
Animal: *Dog*
Pet Custody Concept: *If someone claims to have found a valuable dog but fails to search for the original owner, the court will presume the worst.*

The court examined a claim involving the wrongful conversion of property by father and son defendants Udell and Darrell Smith. The plaintiff, the owner of a four-month-old Shih Tzu puppy and an adult Pekingese, left the animals alone in her unfenced front yard. When she could not find her puppy, she conducted a ground search and called her neighbors, local veterinarians, and the police. When she contacted local veterinarians again five days later, one veterinarian gave her the name of Udell Smith. Although Udell was a minister and he knew that his son, Darrell, had the puppy, he hid from the plaintiff that he knew where the Shih Tzu puppy was. In the interim, the puppy was euthanized.

Darrell claimed that he found a lost puppy in his father's front yard. Upon taking the puppy to a veterinarian, he learned that the puppy had a severe eye infection called keratitis and a corneal ulceration. After making a limited search for the puppy's owner, he told the veterinarian that he was taking the puppy to Baton Rouge and that

60. 287 So. 2d 625 (La. App. 3rd Cir. 1973).

if someone inquired about the puppy, that person should contact his parents. After going to Baton Rouge, Darrell took the puppy to another veterinarian, learned that the puppy was almost blind, that his prognosis was poor, and that treatment would be costly. Darrell had the veterinarian "put the dog to sleep." He admitted that his parents had failed to cooperate when contacted.

The plaintiff initiated a common law tort of conversion and sought to "recover the value of the puppy together with damages for embarrassment, humiliation, and mental anguish." For her conversion claim, the plaintiff was required to prove (1) a distinct act of dominion over another's property, (2) that the dominion was wrongfully asserted, and (3) that the dominion was inconsistent with the owner's rights. In Louisiana, "the destruction of goods by a positive and tortious act is a conversion" because "it is the effect of the act which constitutes the conversion." Accordingly, good faith and other equitable defenses were irrelevant.

For this claim, the court typically considers motive, intent, good faith, knowledge or ignorance, and care or negligence. Not convinced by Darrell's portrayal of himself as a good samaritan, the court found that he "did not do in our opinion what the law expected of him under the circumstances. It is evident from the record that any layman would have realized that this puppy of a Pekingese breed was not just a 'stray' dog." The court knew that Darrell was a local kennel club member, too. The court catalogued Darrell's minimal efforts in searching for the puppy's owner by pointing out that he "did not inquire about the dog from the neighbors, nor did he call the police, dog pound, or advertise in a newspaper." Furthermore, he exercised dominion and control over the puppy when he authorized the veterinarian to "put the dog to sleep."[61]

Ordinarily, the value of property is calculated based upon a dog's commercial value. The court found the dead puppy had less value than other puppies in the same litter because of his eye problems. Accordingly, the court determined that the puppy subject to the conversion had a value of $50. The court also awarded the plaintiff the sum of $100 for mental anguish and humiliation related to the conversion.

This is a case where the death of a four-month-old puppy, with a modest fair market value, drew the court's time and careful attention. It is also interesting that although courts around the country have denied emotional damages in other tort claims, the court readily awarded damages for mental anguish and humiliation in the plaintiff's conversion claim.

Practice Pointer: When a bad actor is involved, courts are receptive to the opportunity to find a reason to award damages.

---

61. Although there were originally two defendants in this case, the court held that Darrell's father, who originally declined to inform the plaintiff of the puppy's whereabouts, had not been involved in the conversion. Although the plaintiff's occupation was not discussed, the court described Darrell's father, Udell Smith, as a minister. The court considered whether the defendant minister's son was a "good samaritan." Reading between the lines, there was a sense that if the court had determined that Darrell had been a good samaritan, it would have made a different decision with regard to the award of $100 for the plaintiff's mental anguish and humiliation.

WHITMER V. SCHNEBLE[62]

Year: *1975*
Category: *Tort Law*
Type of Action: *Products Liability*
Animal: *Dog*
Pet Custody Concept: *Remember that the court may not reach some issues, such as the applicability of a statute of limitations, if others are outcome determinative.*

A Doberman Pinscher bitch with nine-day-old puppies bit a neighbor's child who got too close. When the owner was subsequently sued under an Illinois dog bite statute, the owner in turn brought a third-party complaint against the seller. The owner, who had the dog for two and a half years, alleged that the seller had breached an express warranty, failed to warn the purchaser of the dog's dangerous propensities, and claimed that the dog was an unreasonably "dangerous product" under strict liability laws. This claim was inconsistent with a bill of sale furnished by the sellers that said the dog was "medium aggressive" and the seller's literature, which described the breed as being an animal that could "love and fight with equal zeal" and was suitable for "true protection." The court was unimpressed by the claim of the dog's purchasers at the time of sale that the dog was described as a "docile dobe."

The court quoted extensively from the *Restatement (Second) of Torts*, section 290, and held that "this court will not infer a warranty that the dog will never bite from the language which was used. '[T]he law will not lend itself to the creation of an implied warranty which patently runs counter to the experience of mankind or known forces of nature. It will not read into any sale or bailment a condition or proviso which is unreasonable, impossible or absurd.'" The court said that it was "common knowledge" that dogs bite and that even a "gentle dog" who is nursing her puppies is likely to bite if "disturbed by strangers."

The court looked to 63 *Am. Jur. 2d Products Liability*, section 95 as the authority with regard to how a dog's personality changes over time. The court said that if a product is claimed to be viable, the product need not be manufactured, but "its nature must be fixed when it leaves the manufacturer's or seller's control."[63] The court quoted from the *Restatement (Second) of Torts*, section 402A, which said that the "purpose of imposing strict liability is to insure that the costs of injuries resulting from defective products are borne by those who market such products rather than by the injured persons, who are powerless to protect themselves."[64] The court never reached the issue of the statute of limitations, as the court determined that the seller was not liable to the buyer and that the buyer could not pursue a third-party action.

62. 29 Ill. App. 3d 659, 331 N.E.2d 115 (Ill. App. 1975).

63. The court presumed that in the two and a half years the owner had the dog, the owner shaped the character of the dog through the owner's own personality.

64. The products liability discussion in *Whitmer* sounds antiquated now that decades later, top scientists have reached consensus that animals have consciousness and a leading veterinarian group, the AAHA, has acknowledged pet sentience. Seth Davis, *AAHA Position Statement Classifies Animals as Sentient Beings*, NEWSTAT, http://www.aahanet.org/blog/NewStat/post/2012/10/17/521946/AAHA-position-statement-classifies-animals-as-sentient-beings.aspx (last visited May 12, 2016).

Practice Pointer: This decision, like so many older decisions, is somewhat disconcerting to read because the court, in rejecting the "product" approach, as reflected in the New York doctrine,[65] utilized a product analysis by comparing a pet dog to a shoe being slippery when wet. Even so, this decision is in many ways a more advanced analysis than others of its time in that the court is conversant with common animal behavior. "In short, all mankind, and this court as well, is aware that dogs bite and that bitches which have just whelped and are watching their pups will fulfill their natural maternal instinct and bite a stranger who approaches." A lawyer might also want to argue what is common knowledge.

Beyer v. Aquarium Supply Co.[66]

Year: *1977*
Category: *Tort Law*
Type of Action: *Products Liability*
Animal: *Hamster*
Pet Custody Concept: *Courts are capable of calling a companion animal a product because they are capable of suspending reason and logic to advance legal traditions.*

The plaintiff asserted a claim that the doctrine of strict products liability applied to injuries causally related to the sale of diseased hamsters. In this short 1977 decision, the court said, "The risk presented to human well being by a diseased animal is as great and probably greater than that created by a defective manufactured product and in many instances, for the average consumer, a disease in an animal can be as difficult to detect as a defect in a manufactured product."

Noting that the New York Court of Appeals had already determined that the doctrine of strict liability could be applied when the alleged defective product was from a spruce plank, the court determined that there was no requirement that the product, in this case the hamsters, be a "complex manufactured product." Accordingly, the plaintiff was allowed to proceed with this products liability claim.[67] The court strained to classify the hamsters as a product to allow for the application of the products liability doctrine to achieve the public policy objective of preventing breeders and distributors from selling sick animals to consumers. As is common in earlier court decisions, no concern was expressed for the sick hamsters, only for human well-being.

Practice Pointer: This case became known as the New York approach, as distinguishable from the goods method used in Illinois.[68] Because these are well-known

65. Know the difference between the Uniform Commercial Code New York products approach and the Illinois goods approach.
66. 94 Misc. 2d 336, 404 N.Y.S.2d 778 (N.Y. Sup. 1977).
67. Be aware of the potential for claims of upstream strict liability by pet producers or downstream strict liability for those who purchase or adopt these animals. Consider, from a products liability standpoint, how assisted reproductive technology practices related to companion animals may affect future claims, too.
68. *See* Whitmer v. Schneble, 29 Ill. App. 3d 659, 331 N.E.2d 115 (Ill. App. 2d Dist. 1975).

approaches about how animals are regarded in the legal system, it is probable that these and other remarkable conceptions about companion animals will emerge in pet custody and ownership disputes.

Baram v. Farugia S S[69]

Year: *1979*
Category: *Tort Law*
Type of Action: *Conversion*
Animal: *Horse*
Pet Custody Concept: *Be aware that one cause of action may be dependent on another.*

After a doctor bought a bay filly racehorse named Foxey Toni for $3,000, he hired a trainer, Dennis Fredella. Although the trainer had authority to enter Foxey Toni in races using Dr. Joseph Baram's name, he had no authority to forge his signature on the horse's Certificate of Foal Registration, thereby showing the trainer as the owner of the horse. Without Dr. Baram's knowledge or permission, these two raced Foxey Toni in Canada. The trainer then transferred both the horse's foal certificate and possession of Foxey Toni to his creditor, Farugia, who then brought in another co-owner.

The district court determined that "both Fredella and Farugia knew or should have known that the signature on the foal certificate had been forged and that Fredella had no authority to transfer Foxey Toni." Even so, when Dr. Baram accepted money from the trainer in the context of a criminal proceeding, he thereby lost his cause of action against the other wrongdoers based upon the court's strict application of the common law action of conversion. The court went to considerable lengths to explain how this modern common law originated from the concept of a forced sale in trover. In this type of action, damages equal the full value of the chattel at the time and place of conversion.[70]

The court found that Professor Prosser had captured the essence of a conversion claim in the *Restatement (Second) of Torts*, saying, "When the defendant satisfies the judgment in the action for conversion, title to the chattel passes to him, so that he is in effect required to buy it at a forced judicial sale. Conversion is therefore properly limited, and has been limited by the courts, to those serious, major, and important interferences with the right to control the chattel which justify requiring the defendant to pay its full value."

The court more than hinted that if the doctor had wanted to prove other types of damages, he should have initiated other causes of action. For example, if the doctor had initiated a common law action of trespass, he could have kept the horse and also received damages he sustained through the loss of possession. If he had brought an action in replevin, he could have regained possession of the horse, too.

---

69. 606 F.2d 42 (1979).
70. *See* Berry v. Heinel Motors, Inc., 162 Pa. Super. 52, 58, 56 A.2d 374, 377 (1948).

The higher court was not persuaded by the trial court's award of $3,000 against Farugia and Hackett for compensatory damages, as well as $5,000 against Farugia for punitive damages. Essentially, the court argued that when Dr. Baram accepted $3,000 for the value of the horse from Fredella, one of three defendants, his right to pursue the other defendants on separate actions of conversion extinguished his action against two other wrongdoers, saying, "a forced judicial sale had the effect of vesting title in Fredella retroactively from November 29, 1975, the date of the conversion."

The higher court was satisfied by its meticulous analysis when it said,

> We hold therefore that after receiving total satisfaction for the value of the chattel, Dr. Baram no longer possessed a common law cause of action in conversion for compensatory damages against Farugia and Hackett. The failure of his claim for compensatory damages also precludes his recovery of punitive damages, because under Pennsylvania law, "(t)he right to punitive damages is a mere incident to a cause of action . . . and not the subject of an action in itself . . ." (When the) plaintiff no longer has a cause of action of which his claim for punitive damages may be an element, that claim must fail."[71]

The judgment of the district court was reversed.

Practice Pointer: Sometimes, courts point out the failures of an inept lawyer. Be careful that lawyer is not you.

Corso v. Crawford Cat & Dog Hospital[72]

Year: *1979*
Category: *Tort Law*
Type of Action: *Emotional Distress*
Animal: *Dog*
Pet Custody Concept: *Courts may overrule prior precedents if they are convinced this is the right thing to do.*

In this famous decision from the civil court of the city of New York, the court examined the plaintiff's claims that the defendant wrongfully disposed of her dog's body. After euthanizing a 15-year-old Poodle, a pet hospital failed to deliver the Poodle's remains to a scheduled and well-planned funeral. Instead of the Poodle's remains, the body of a cat was delivered in the Poodle's casket. The owner of the Poodle brought a tort action, claiming that she had suffered mental distress and anguish and that she was entitled, from a damages perspective, to more than the fair market value of the dog.

In considering her claim, the court said something extraordinary: "This court now overrules prior precedent and holds that a pet is not just a thing but occupies a special place somewhere in between a person and a piece of personal property." The court added, "A pet is not an inanimate thing that just receives affection it also returns it."

71. *See* Hilbert v. Roth, 395 Pa. 270, 275, 149 A.2d 648, 652 (1959).
72. 415 N.Y.S.2d 182, 97 Misc. 2d 530 (N.Y. City Civ. Ct. 1979).

The court appreciated that the Poodle's owner had planned an elaborate funeral and a burial place with a headstone. Distinguishing a pet from an heirloom, the court found that the claim against the veterinary hospital was actionable and that $700 was reasonable compensation for the plaintiff's loss. Compared to other decisions from the 1970s, this case stands out because of the court's declaration that it had departed from prior precedent.

Practice Pointer: The court explicitly overruled existing precedent based upon the idea that pets represent more than just things in American culture. Now, companion animals are perceived to be sentient.

PELOQUIN V. CALCASIEU PARISH POLICE JURY[73]

Year: *1979*
Category: *Tort Law*
Type of Action: *Conversion*
Animal: *Cat*
Pet Custody Concept: *Courts are inclined to side with law enforcement.*

When an unknown cat caused repeated damage to a car, the defendants called their local animal control office and caused a trap to be set. A cat was seized two days later and was "put to sleep." The plaintiffs filed a suit against the complainants and animal control alleging that the defendants had converted and killed their pet cat, George. The defendants asserted at trial that the cat trapped and killed was not George, and the jury agreed.

The higher court's opinion began by saying, "This suit has been brought by Robert Peloquin, individually and on behalf of his two minor children, and by his wife, Ruth D. Peloquin." The court continued, referring to the date of the entrapment, that these were the same people who "testified their pet cat, George, disappeared that same night." Even so, the court ruled that "the Police Jury did act reasonable and proper under the circumstances of this case, and I find that they cannot be held liable to the Peloquin family for the death of a cat, which may or may not have been the cat named George." Finding that the plaintiffs failed to prove the identity of the dead cat by a preponderance of the evidence, the judgment of the trial court was affirmed.

This 1979 Louisiana case is emblematic of the evolving status of cats, with this case representing the old viewpoint. At one time in Louisiana, a trapped cat could easily be killed without any waiting period or notice to neighbors who might have owned the cat. Now that the state of Louisiana has been through Hurricane Katrina, one of the most horrific natural disasters in U.S. history, Louisiana is advanced in how to properly manage and help animals should a future disaster strike.

73. 378 So. 2d 560 (La. App. 3rd Cir. 1979).

Practice Pointer: If the applicable state has been subject to a national disaster, look for case law related to that crisis for helpful language regarding the value of companion animals to their owners.

CAMPBELL V. ANIMAL QUARANTINE STATION[74]

Year: *1981*
Category: *Tort Law*
Type of Action: *Emotional Distress*
Animal: *Dog*
Pet Custody Concept: *Courts can be creative and develop their own approach.*

The Supreme Court of Hawaii extended its "unique approach" to allow for the recovery of damages for mental distress suffered as a result of the negligent destruction of animal "property." When a family moved to Hawaii, their nine-year-old Boxer, Princess, was subject to quarantine. During this time period, the owners arranged for the Animal Quarantine Station to take Princess to a nearby hospital to receive treatment for a gum condition. During transport, Princess, left for more than an hour in a van, died of heat prostration.

When the plaintiffs sought damages for emotional distress, the court said, "We recognized that an individual's interest in freedom from negligent infliction of serious mental distress is entitled to independent legal protection." Observing that in *Rodrigues v. State,*[75] the court had "departed from the traditional standard and held that serious mental harm can be inflicted when a person endures negligently inflicted property damage," the court applied the same rationale to the death of Princess.

Announcing that it was "the first jurisdiction to allow recovery without showing a physically manifested harm," the court differentiated between a primary and secondary type of response, finding that although medical attention for the owners was an indicator of emotional distress, medical care was not a prerequisite for pursuing a claim. While acknowledging that a reasonable geographical restriction applied, the court found that the owners, whom the court regarded as victims, need not directly witness the harm in order to recover. The court also pointed out that there had been no floodgate problem following its decision in *Rodrigues.*

Campbell is an important case in pet law. The court's discussion about harm caused to Princess's owners was unapologetic and matter of fact. This case represents the court's appreciation of the human/animal bond and the harm caused when this relationship is lost.

Practice Pointer: Family court judges should be sensitive and compassionate about the grief resulting from the loss of pet companionship in the pet custody context. Courts are exploring more flexible standards for when damages are allowed.

74. 632 P.2d 1066, 63 Haw. 557 (Haw. 1981).
75. 52 Haw. 156, 472 P.2d 509 (1970).

Richardson v. Fairbanks North Star Borough[76]

Year: *1985*
Category: *Tort Law*
Type of Action: *Intentional Infliction of Emotional Distress*
Animal: *Dog*
Pet Custody Concept: *Courts open doors for present or future actions when presented with egregious facts.*

The appellants called the local dog pound when they were unable to find their missing dog, Wizzard. The pound had Wizzard and advised the appellants that Wizzard could be claimed between their business hours of 8:00 a.m. and 5:00 p.m. The appellants went to the pound immediately after work, arriving at 4:50 p.m., and could see Wizzard chained within the facility. The pound employee would not release him, saying that the pound was closed. The following day, the appellants left work early to retrieve Wizzard but found that he had been euthanized.

When this case came before the Supreme Court of Alaska in 1985, the court addressed damages for Wizzard's owners resulting from the municipality's negligence. The court considered whether the jury should have been able to consider Wizzard's value as a pet, economic damages, his owners' pain and suffering, and punitive damages. The dead dog's pain and suffering were not mentioned.[77]

After identifying Wizzard's legal status as an "item of personal property," the court said, "We recognize that the loss of a beloved pet can be especially distressing in egregious situations. Therefore, we are willing to recognize a cause of action for intentional infliction of emotional distress for the intentional or reckless killing of a pet animal in an appropriate case." The court rejected Wizzard's owners' emotional distress claim after deciding that the severity of the owners' distress did not cross the *Restatement (Second) of Torts*, section 46(1) (1965) threshold.

Punitive damages could not be awarded, according to the court, as punitive damages cannot be awarded against a municipality without underlying statutory authorization. The court determined that because this case involved the negligent exercise of police powers, an eminent domain taking had not occurred. In some circumstances, an eminent domain claim is made against a governmental body.

Even though Wizzard's owners did not prevail, the court dicta reflected changing ideas about how dogs should be valued. While the court rejected the concept of a "subjective estimation of Wizzard's value as a pet," the court recognized that other courts utilized different valuation approaches, particularly when a dog had a "mixed lineage" or when a pet was "maliciously killed." The court also signaled that it would award intentional emotional distress damages in an extreme case.

Practice Pointer: The value of a dog in the tort system is in flux, just as the value of a dog may be in flux in the family law context, too. If the court followed the array

76. 705 P.2d 454 (Alaska 1985).
77. With the passage of animal cruelty laws, the careless euthanasia of companion animals may now have greater consequences.

of valuation methods described in *Richardson*, it could deliberate between an objective fair market value method and a subjective method that might take into account the malicious treatment of the animal.

JANKOSKI V. PREISER ANIMAL HOSPITAL, LTD.[78]

Year: *1987*
Category: *Tort Law, Property Law, Equitable Principles*
Type of Action: *Companionship Loss*
Animal: *Dog*
Pet Custody Concept: *Courts can be rigid about how they provide access to the court.*

When their German Shepherd died due to the actions of a veterinarian, the plaintiffs initiated an independent cause of action based upon companionship loss and also sought to recover damages based upon this type of loss. Before dismissing the complaint upon the defendant's motion, the trial court afforded the plaintiffs the opportunity to proceed with a cause of action for property damage instead of loss of companionship.[79]

The court determined that regardless of how the plaintiffs characterized their loss, the Illinois wrongful death precedent was "distinguishable from the case at bar in one very important respect. The law involved human beings, not dogs. In the eyes of the law, a dog is an item of personal property." From there, the court reasoned that in some circumstances, "damages must be ascertained in some rational way from such elements as are attainable." It observed the recurring problem of what should be done when the personal property lacks market value and has what the court characterized as "sentimental value."

The court considered other jurisdictions' approaches. In Washington, the actual value to the owner did not include the "element of sentimental value."[80] In New York, loss of companionship was an "element to be used [for] measuring the actual value of the dog for purposes of calculating damages."[81] While concluding that some courts allow elements of sentimental value, these values, though not "merely nominal," were "severely circumscribed" according to the court. Even so, as the plaintiffs in this case had already disavowed the opportunity for a limited recovery for property damages, the court would not permit a new cause of action for companionship loss.

Jankoski is another decision representative of the courts being conflicted about where pets and companion animals belong in American jurisprudence and represents

78. 510 N.E.2d 1084, 157 Ill. App. 3d 818 (Ill. App. 1987).

79. Under prior Illinois law, the value of a dog was limited to commercial or market value. The Illinois Court of Appeals distinguished a "cause of action for loss of companionship" under the Wrongful Death Act from the line of Illinois cases that recognized "a cause of action for emotional distress." While acknowledging that it had previously recognized a new cause of action for the negligent infliction of emotional distress, the court said this only applied when the plaintiff was in the "zone of physical danger," where he or she was fearful for his or her own safety and suffered physical injury or illness that resulted from the emotional distress.

80. *See* Furlan v. Rayan Photo Works, Inc., 171 Misc. 839, 12 N.Y.S.2d 921 (N.Y. Mun. Ct. 1939).

81. *See* Brousseau v. Rosenthal, 110 Misc. 2d 1054, 443 N.Y.S.2d 285 (N.Y. Civ. Ct. 1980).

a disappointing search to find out if courts anywhere got it right. While the court was amenable to a new independent cause of action for humans in tort law, the court seemed out of its comfort zone regarding an independent action for loss of companionship. At the same time, the court revealed that it was fully aware that a nominal award to the parties was unfair.

Practice Pointer: Looking at the implications of the *Jankoski* decision for family court, perhaps the Illinois family court will one day recognize that as companion animals become family members, it is time that our laws grow to better reflect cultural values.

DAUGHEN V. FOX[82]

Year: *1988*
Category: *Tort Law*
Type of Action: *Emotional Distress*
Animal: *Dog*
Pet Custody Concept: *If at first you do not succeed, try, try again.*

An eight-year-old "mongrel dog called Cindy" died while in her veterinarian's care following an X-ray mix up. The appellants brought claims for trespass, the intentional infliction of severe emotional distress, and the loss of a unique chattel pet dog resulting in the owners' loss of companionship and comfort; they also asserted a "count in assumpsit,"[83] wherein the appellants claimed the hospital breached express and implied warranties through their negligent and reckless conduct. The trial court determined that Cindy's owners lacked a cause of action. Citing *Bartanus v. Lis*,[84] the appellants reminded the higher court that "the intentional infliction of emotional distress is an evolving tort and its scope has not yet been clearly defined."

The cascading series of errors impacting Cindy's life began when the veterinarian who performed the X-ray on Cindy advised the appellants that immediate surgery was necessary to remove an intestinal needle. When the needle was not found during surgery, additional X-rays revealed a bullet near Cindy's liver. By then, Cindy exhibited signs of lead poisoning and she, not strong enough to undergo another surgery, died a few days later. Although the appellee had "mixed up two x-rays of similar dogs," this fact was hidden from Cindy's owners.

The court discussed whether section 46 of the *Restatement (Second) of Torts* or the *Restatement (First) of Torts* section 868 (1939) controlled. The court described defects in section 46 of the *Restatement (Second) of Torts* and offered the entire footnote 5 from its decision in *Kazatsky v. King David Memorial Park*[85] as follows:

82. 539 A.2d 858, 372 Pa. Super. 405 (Pa. Super. 1988).
83. Assumpsit is a type of tort action rooted in contract and equity principles.
84. 332 Pa. Super. 61, 480 A.2d 1185 (1984).
85. 515 Pa. 183, 527 A.2d 988 (1987).

> It is interesting to note that this tort is not truly a judicial development simply "restated by the American Law Institute. Although it relies on prior cases, the Restatement in this area has generated the law more than it has restated it." . . . "Academics, rather than courts, were the prime movers in the development of the tort of intentional infliction of severe emotional distress by outrageous conduct: the modern tort was introduced in the pages of law reviews, and then refined and finally defined by the American Law Institute in its Restatements."

As the court struggled with what tort standard should apply, the court evaluated how to test outrageousness and framed the answer as a moral question. Should the court serve as society's conscience? The higher court found the instant case distinguishable from *Banasczek v. Kowalski*,[86] where the defendant intentionally shot two of the plaintiff's dogs. There, the court dismissed the preliminary objections of the defendant to the plaintiff's emotional distress claim in the nature of a demurrer, saying, "The more enlightened view is to allow recovery for emotional distress in the instance of malicious destruction of a pet."

Comparing the veterinarian's behavior in this case, which had the effect of causing Cindy to die, and then hiding the evidence, to the intentional shooting in *Banasczek*, the court determined that the threshold for outrageous conduct had not been met. Summary judgment in favor of the veterinarian was affirmed in this respect as the fundamental purpose of damages for an injury to property by tortious conduct of another was for compensation of the losses actually suffered. Not only did the court state that Cindy was personal property, the court also rejected the claim that this "mongrel dog" was a unique chattel. The court likened the appellants' claim for loss of companionship as akin to one for loss of consortium. As the appellants' mongrel was not a unique chattel, the owners' claims for loss of companionship and damages arising from sentimental attachment lacked merit. The higher court granted the appellants their right to proceed with the claim for breach of express and implied warranties.

Practice Pointer: This 1988 case was decided long before mixed breeds, rescues, or—as this court called them—"mongrel dogs" represented a badge of honor for their owners. By its tone, this case may represent the reason that future courts have become bold about overturning past precedents and granting special damages for dogs like Cindy, who previously enjoyed only "mongrel" status. Lawyers with custody disputes involving mixed breed dogs should be sensitive to the development of jurisprudence in this regard. While reading the progression of pet law cases, notice how courts shift to reflect some sensitivity to the plight of animals. Here, the property had a name, Cindy.

86. 10 Pa. D. & C. 3rd 94 (Luzerne Cnty. 1979).

ZAGER V. DIMILIA[87]

Year: *1988*
Category: *Tort Law*
Type of Action: *Negligence*
Animal: *Dog*
Pet Custody Concept: *A substantive justice approach might work well in pet custody disputes, too.*

Pet law case law is resplendent with quotes that justices like. In this case, the court began with a passage from Jack London's *The Call of the Wild* as follows:

> Old longings nomadic leap
> Chafing at custom's chain
> Again from its brumal sleep
> Wakens the ferine strain.

Contrary to leash laws in Pleasantville, a dog named McDuff broke his tether and injured another dog named Tucker. At issue was whether Tucker's damages should be determined based upon his fair market value or his actual value to Tucker's owner—called intrinsic value—or if some other standard should be utilized. In this small claims court decision, the judge applied the Uniform Justice Court Act to inexpensively affect substantive justice. This law enabled the court to use more relaxed rules of pleadings and practice, as well as evidentiary requirements.

In the first trial, McDuff's owner was found liable for the injury to Tucker and Tucker's fair market value was determined to be $10. Upon retrial on the damages issue, the plaintiff sought to recover out-of-pocket expenditures made related to Tucker, including payments for his adoption, sterilization, and recent veterinary services. The injured dog's owner also sought compensation for Tucker's intrinsic value and advanced the idea that the owner's long-term efforts to train the dog could be monetized. The court quickly disavowed granting any separate and distinct value for Tucker based upon "sentiment," citing relevant case law.[88] The court, having already heralded the dog species as man's best friend, grappled with how "it is impossible to reduce to monetary terms the bond between man and dog, a relationship which has been more eloquently memorialized in literature and depicted on the motion picture screen."

Looking for guidance on how to determine damages for a dog, the court rejected the agriculturally based precedent, as "this rule originated in cases involving working animals, valuable for their herding or hunting skills or show dogs, prized for their pedigree." Accordingly, the court found that utilizing a "traditional formula," with the factors including the age, health, and special traits or characteristics of value, did not pertain to the case before it. Under the "traditional formula," there was no "consideration

87. 524 N.Y.S.2d 968, 138 Misc. 2d 448 (N.Y. Vill. Ct. 1988).
88. *See* Smith v. Palace Transportation Co., 142 Misc. 93, 253 N.Y.S. 87 (Mun. Ct. 1931) and Stettner v. Graubard, 82 Misc. 2d 132, 368 N.Y.S.2d 132 (Town Ct. 1975).

of depreciation, presumably because a domestic animal's value increases, rather than declines as it becomes older and better trained."[89]

While valuing Tucker, the court was aware that Tucker was old and on his last legs, and that it was not unfair to take this into account from a damages perspective. The court readily embraced utilizing the "reasonable and necessary cost of reasonable veterinary treatment" for a damages calculation and offered an important rationale:

> In cases of injury to animals . . . the plaintiff ought to recover for expenses reasonably incurred in efforts to cure them in addition to the diminution in their value or their whole value when they are finally lost. The law would be inhuman in the tendency if it should prescribe a different rule, even where the animal eventually dies, since it would then offer an inducement to the owner to neglect its sufferings.

This was legal poetry at its best.

The court observed that in *Zager*, the acting village court found that "where there is no known market value, actual value to the owner or 'intrinsic' value is the criteria." The court noted that the "cost of repair should not exceed the market or 'intrinsic' value of the property" and "should not be applied in a case where neither market nor 'intrinsic' value is capable of calculation as a living creature is involved." It was groundbreaking when the court then used the words "living creature" in a personal property damages analysis.[90]

Ultimately, the court determined that the plaintiff had the burden of proof of establishing both the reasonableness and the cost of the treatment. Because the plaintiff did not fully meet the statutory requirement when presenting an "unitemized unpaid bill from the veterinary hospital," the court declined to give the plaintiff the full amount for veterinary services sought. Furthermore, the court determined that the plaintiff could not recover punitive damages, as the defendant's conduct must be "differentiated from that of his dog" and because a violation of a leash law was not "a sufficient predicate for punitive damages." The court awarded the plaintiff $300.

This case is interesting, from a psychological perspective, in that there is kind of a seesaw element to it as the stature or importance of a living creature seems to ebb, as in an inanimate object in need of repair, and flow, as in recognition that the property is alive, throughout this decision. It would be meaningful to future generations if we could simply admit the application of inanimate property language to living creatures is nonsensical, as to do otherwise is beneath the reasoning capability of rational human adults and children.

Practice Pointer: First, if you ever have a claim about an older dog, quote from this case the idea that a domestic animal's value increases with age. The fact that the court was sensitive to the potential of an owner neglecting an animal's suffering in order to achieve financial gain represents an early example of the court's appreciation of the importance of damages that advance the best interests of an animal from a public

89. This became a famous quote.
90. *See* 7C WARREN'S NEW YORK NEGLIGENCE, PERSONAL PROPERTY, § 2.02.

policy perspective. This is also a good example of how the court made an effort to advance the law even when the court was offered scant information about veterinary expenses.

Worrell v. Sachs[91]

Year: *1989*
Category: *Tort Law*
Type of Action: *Products Liability*
Animal: *Dog*
Pet Custody Concept: *Make public policy arguments.*

This case is one where the courts were conflicted about whether animals should be treated as property or goods for liability purposes. The plaintiff advanced a products liability claim for damages when a puppy carrying an unnamed parasite caused injury to a child. In this case of first impression, the court turned to the applicability of section 402A of the *Restatement (Second) of Torts*. This Restatement followed precedents from Illinois and the federal court that product liability laws should not pertain to transactions involving living creatures that are constantly interacting with their environment and are of a changing nature. By this, the court was advancing the concept that an animal is not a "product" but a "good."

The court crafted a burden of proof framework as to whether the injury caused was clearly attributable to the animal's preexisting condition, such as a disease, or perhaps the acquisition of the parasite was impacted by environmental circumstances and mutability principles. One way the court expressed this idea was by saying, "But it does not necessarily follow logically, that inability to prove a case because of mutability means that an animal is not a product at all." The court distinguished between proof of liability and status and said that different standards apply when products are "susceptible to a change in character over time."[92]

The Connecticut court then considered the public policy ramifications of permitting the sale of sick puppies without the availability of an appropriate remedy. Although the legislature already had limited recovery under its pet lemon law for the purchase price of the pet, notwithstanding this limitation, the court became bold. It determined that the legislature had limited recovery because it was already aware of the cause of action for products liability, which allowed the consumer to recover for injuries sustained by the defective product. Finally, the court rendered a decision so narrow that it pertained to the unique circumstances of this case. The sick puppy was a product, and damages flowed from the product liability laws.

---

91. 563 A.2d 1387, 41 Conn. Supp. 179 (Conn. Super. 1989).

92. This is reflective of the ongoing discussion about pets as products, following *Beyer v. Aquarium Supply Co.*, 94 Misc. 2d 336, 404 N.Y.S.2d 778 (N.Y. Sup. Ct. 1977), and what became known as the Illinois goods-based doctrine, where the language "mutable in nature" becomes a key concept.

Practice Pointer: This decision has a chameleon-like aspect, with an animal having a product status for some legal purposes but perhaps not others. Continue to pay attention to how animals are described and classified differently depending upon what type of civil claim pertains.

LATHAM V. WAL-MART STORES, INC.[93]

Year: *1991*
Category: *Tort Law*
Type of Action: *Products Liability*
Animal: *Bird*
Pet Custody Concept: *Keep a straight face while courts sort out the difference between inanimate products and living pets.*

A Wal-Mart employee specially ordered a parrot through his employer, Wal-Mart.[94] When the bird was found to have a communicable infection called psittacosis, an infection akin to pneumonia, the buyer initiated a strict products liability claim against his employer and others.[95] The Missouri court examined the following language from the *Restatement (Second) of Torts*, section 402A:

> One who sells any product in a defective condition unreasonably dangerous to the user or consumer or to his property is subject to liability for physical harm thereby caused to the ultimate user or consumer, or to his property, if (a) the seller is engaged in the business of selling such a product, and (b) it is expected to and does reach the user or consumer without substantial change in the condition in which it is sold. The rule stated in Subsection (1) applies although (a) the seller has exercised all possible care in the preparation and sale of his product, and (b) the user or consumer has not bought the product from or entered into any contractual relation with the seller.

The court then addressed whether a living animal could be a "product" under the Restatement and described the controversy in other states about the "products" versus "goods" approach. In particular, the court compared and contrasted the well-established New York doctrine, where hamsters were found to be products, with the Illinois doctrine, where dogs were classified as goods.

The Missouri court described *Whitmer v. Schneble*,[96] where the Illinois plaintiffs initiated a strict liability claim in a dog bite case based upon the assertion that the biting dog was an "unreasonably dangerous product." Although the *Whitmer* court recognized that the application of the Restatement was not limited to a manufacture, the

93. 818 S.W.2d 673 (Mo. App. E.D. 1991)

94. This was an unusual transaction, as Wal-Mart does not normally sell parrots. Although the defendant ordered the bird, the company had neither removed the bird from his container upon delivery nor handled the parrot "in any way."

95. Wal-Mart was a defendant in this action, along with a Wal-Mart manager and a business called General Petco Corporation. Through impleader, Gators of Miami also became a third-party defendant.

96. 29 Ill. App. 3d 659, 331 N.E.2d 115 (1975).

Illinois court decided that the Restatement required that the nature of the product "be fixed when it leaves the manufacturer's or seller's control."[97] In that case, the Illinois court concluded that notwithstanding worthy public policy objectives, the Restatement was inapplicable to "products whose character could be changed and shaped by the purchaser rather than the seller." Accordingly, animals were no longer products, as a matter of law, in Illinois.

The Missouri court then discussed the New York strict liability doctrine that arose in *Beyer v. Aquarium Supply Co.*[98] following the sale of diseased hamsters. The New York court had considered the equitable distribution of "the inevitable consequences of commercial enterprise" and also expressed its resolve "to promote the marketing of safe products." The New York court decided that because breeders, distributors, and vendors should be held accountable for placing a "diseased animal in the stream of commerce," the diseased hamsters fell within the definition of a product within the meaning of the Restatement.

The New York doctrine used the word "product" in a way that the Illinois court, citing *Anderson v. Farmers Hybrid Companies, Inc.*,[99] found defied logic. Living animals were, after all, in "constant interaction with the environment around them as part of their development." Accordingly, "living creatures have no fixed nature and cannot be products as a matter of law." Thus, comparing these two doctrines, the Illinois court arched its back and refused to classify a living animal as a product.

Practice Pointer: Look for emerging doctrines around the country and explain why the doctrine that benefits your client is superior to a competing doctrine. Throw in some Restatement analyses, and emphasize how much the pertinent practice area is evolving, too. Beyond that, do your part in making the laws better.

BUECKNER V. HAMEL[100]

Year: *1994*
Category: *Tort Law*
Type of Action: *Intentional Tort*
Animal: *Dog*
Pet Custody Concept: *Courts should seek to achieve a just result and, rather than be limited to one approach, should be able to utilize two.*

The court of appeals affirmed the lower court's award of damages to the appellees when their two dogs were deliberately shot and killed by a hunter. One dog was a Dalmatian and the other an Australian Shepherd. Both dogs were healthy, purebred females registered with the American Kennel Club; they were dogs that the owners

97. The court also emphasized the public policy rationale that "the costs of injuries resulting from defective products [should] be borne by those who market such products, rather than by the injured persons, who are powerless to protect themselves."
98. 94 Misc. 2d 336, 404 N.Y.S.2d 778 (N.Y. Sup. Ct. 1977).
99. 87 Ill. App. 3d 493, 42 Ill. Dec. 485, 408 N.E.2d 1194 (1980).
100. 886 S.W.2d 368 (Tex. App.–Hous. 1st Dist. 1994).

planned to breed. The dogs were chasing a deer when the hunter intentionally shot them. The court observed that the dogs were attacking neither a domestic nor a protected animal.

The trial court grappled with how to establish the loss of progeny or loss of stud fees in calculating damages. The court of appeals affirmed the actual damages award of $1,450, which included the value of prospective puppies, and also affirmed a punitive damages award of $2,500 in favor of the appellees. In addition to the damages award, this case is better remembered for the following concurring opinion by Justice Andell:

> I write, separately, however, to address what I consider to be a more substantial basis for affirming this award, namely, the intrinsic or special value of domestic animals as companions and beloved pets. The issue is whether bereaved pet owners must accept the market value of their pets as the measure of actual damages for their pets' wrongful killing, or if they have the option of accepting either the market value or the special value. I consider the general rule of market value to be inadequate for assessing damages for the loss of domestic pets. For the reasons in the following analysis, I would hold that the pet owners have the option of accepting either measure of damages. Hence, I would affirm, but on different grounds.

This concurring opinion represents a departure from other case law. The concept of special or intrinsic value is expanded from applying to mixed breed dogs, whose value on the market is not readily ascertainable, to purebred dogs.

Practice Pointer: The idea that the owner of a deceased dog could have the option of choosing which means of damages applies is intriguing. Think outside of the box.

McDonald v. Ohio State University Veterinary Hospital[101]

Year: *1994*
Category: *Tort Law*
Type of Action: *Damages Award*
Animal: *Dog*
Pet Custody Concept: *Let the court know about the marvelous bond between a person and an animal.*

Nemo was an exceptional dog that achieved the highest Schutzhund ranking and many awards. Although most of the activities that Nemo and his owner enjoyed were not profitable, the owner earned between $350 and $500 for each puppy Nemo sired.

The only issue before the court was the determination of damages. Nemo, an eight-year-old pedigreed German Shepherd, suffered irreversible paralysis following a negligently performed surgery. The dog was euthanized two years later notwithstanding

101. 644 N.E.2d 750, 67 Ohio Misc. 2d 40 (Ohio Ct. Cl. 1994).

his owner's repeated efforts to find a surgical procedure that would repair the damage to his spinal cord and reverse his paralysis.

At trial, the plaintiff's expert gave the opinion that Nemo's value was in the range of zero to $10,000. While the court recognized that market value was the typical standard used to determine a personal property loss, it was determined that this would merely be a guideline for a "dog of Nemo's caliber." The court described the plaintiff's relationship with Nemo as "similar to the bond between a highly skilled police dog and its handler." The court also emphasized that market value "is a standard not a shackle" and advocated that a more "elastic standard" be applied. While claiming not to be influenced by sentimentality, the court looked at the time and effort the plaintiff invested in the rigorous Schutzhund training and her two-year dedication to this "paralyzed animal." The court determined that Nemo's owner sustained damages in the amount of $5,000.

In looking at the court's decision and how the relationship between Nemo and his owner was discussed, the court conveyed the impression that it was humbled by the level of commitment Nemo's owner had to him. The court was also intrigued by the relationship between this human and canine. The award of money seemed to represent only a token of the court's respect.

Practice Pointer: Terminology in this case about "elasticity" or "standard not a shackle" may prove useful in advancing a legal argument.

DiGrazia v. Old[102]

Year: *1995*
Category: *Tort Law*
Type of Action: *Fraud*
Animal: *Horse*
Pet Custody Concept: *Fraudulent behaviors may estop other claims.*

Greatmate, a two-year-old thoroughbred filly horse, was being trained at a farm in Texas when she sustained a tendon injury. In subsequent care at a veterinary hospital, she died during an electrical storm. Although it was later learned through a necropsy that the horse probably died from septicemia, the horse's owners were led to believe that Greatmate died because of electrocution. Although Greatmate's owners sought the necropsy report, they were deceived with regard to the report's availability.

Later, when an action was commenced and the defendant used the two-year statute of limitations as a defense, the defendant achieved a favorable summary judgment. On appeal, Greatmate's owners asserted that the trial court should have denied summary judgment because fraudulent concealment behaviors prevented Greatmate's owners from discovering the cause of his death. The higher court framed its reversal by saying, "In a proper case, the invocation of fraudulent concealment estops a defendant from relying upon a statute of limitations as an affirmative defense to a cause of

102. 900 S.W.2d 499 (June 15, 1995).

action.[103] Fraud vitiates whatever it touches, and a party will not be permitted to avail himself of the protection of a limitations statute when by his own fraud he has prevented the other party from seeking redress within the period of limitations."

Greatmate's owners then had the burden of proving the following: (1) the existence of an underlying tort, (2) the defendant's knowledge of the tort, (3) the defendant's use of deception to conceal the tort, and (4) the plaintiffs' reasonable reliance upon the deception. When reviewing the evidence produced in the light most favorable to the non-movant, the higher court determined that the plaintiffs met their burden of proof.

The court distinguished between tolling the statute of limitations and the discovery rule, which is a judicially constructed test to determine when a cause of action accrues, as described in *Moreno v. Sterling Drug, Inc.*[104] This distinction is important because the key question becomes not when the statute of limitations begins to run but what has the effect of tolling or suspending the running of the limitation. Accordingly, knowledge of Greatmate's death was not equivalent to knowledge of tortious conduct.

Practice Pointer: Here, the assertion of a tort claim was dependent upon the owners' legal counsel knowing the difference between how to apply the statute of limitations and the discovery rule. Pay attention to legal technicalities.

HARLAN V. LOVETT[105]

Year: *1996*
Category: *Tort Law*
Type of Action: *Conversion*
Animal: *Horse*
Pet Custody Concept: *Know about lien law.*

The lessor entered into a month-to-month agreement with the lessee for the use of 83 acres of fenced land. The lessee neither met her financial obligations to the lessor nor returned his phone calls while the pasture lands subject to the lease became overgrazed. Although it is unclear how dire the situation for the horses became, it is known that the horses began grazing on adjacent property and a golf course.

The lessor decided to sell all the horses on the 83 rented acres. His rationale for doing so was that in addition to the lessee's abandonment of her horses, he could assert a pasturage lien, which is a type of lien akin to an innkeeper's lien. When he had a hauler sell the horses, the lessor subtracted the amount due him for rent from the proceeds the lessor received and he remitted the balance to the lessee. The lessee, and other plaintiffs, brought a conversion action against the lessor.

Although this case has a complicated procedural aspect, an important determination made by the court was that a pasturage lien did not apply to land that had been

103. *See* Borderlon v. Peck, 661 S.W.2d 907, 909 (Tex. 1983).
104. 787 S.W.2d 348, 351 (Tex. 1990).
105. 1996 WL 97590 (March 6, 1996).

leased. Although the plaintiffs were able to regain ownership of their horses, the jury awarded them significant compensation and punitive damages that were upheld on appeal.

Practice Pointer: The outcome of a court decision can be based upon whether a lien has statutory priority over other claims.

PRICE V. BROWN[106]

Year: *1996*
Category: *Tort Law*
Type of Action: *Veterinary Malpractice*
Animal: *Dog*
Pet Custody Concept: *New causes of action blur old distinctions between property and person.*

This was an important case nationally. The plaintiff brought her English Bulldog in for surgery on his prolapsed urethra. Following the surgery, the veterinarian promised that the dog would receive 24-hour monitoring, but this did not occur, and the dog died. The way the plaintiff stated her claim was that the veterinarian had made the bailment representation that her Bulldog would be returned to her in good health. When her dog died, the plaintiff initiated a cause of action against the veterinarian based upon a breach of bailment.

The court stated that a "cause of action for breach of a bailment agreement arises if the bailor can establish that personalty has been delivered to the bailee, a demand for return of the bailed goods has been made, and the bailee has failed to return the personalty." Even so, the court said, "Allegations which might give rise to a bailment are, without more, insufficient to state a cause of action against a veterinarian for death or damage to an animal entrusted to his or her care for veterinary treatment." In essence, the court was saying that it would not permit her bailment action.

The plaintiff lost her case, as she failed to meet the tort burden of proof for professional negligence. The plaintiff should have proven the following elements: "(1) the employment of the veterinarian or other basis for the duty; (2) the veterinarian's failure to exercise the appropriate standard of care; and (3) that the veterinarian's departure from that standard was the proximate cause of the animal's injury or death. A plaintiff must specifically allege that the veterinarian was negligent in the performance of his professional services." The majority elevated the standard necessary for recovery against the veterinarian to be consistent with human medical malpractice standards.

The chief justice of the Pennsylvania Supreme Court dissented, saying that the plaintiff had stated a cause of action upon which relief could have been granted based

106. 545 Pa. 216, 680 A.2d 1149 (Pa. 1996).

upon her breach of bailment theory.[107] The chief implied that the Bulldog's owner might have gotten recovery if she was allowed to proceed on the bailment theory, a claim that would have been easier to prove and more affordable. Another dissenting judge said, "I must disassociate myself from that portion of Mr. Justice Castille's dissenting opinion which characterizes the majority's decision as creating a new cause of action, that of veterinary malpractice."

Practice Pointer: It is always interesting to read a case where a new cause of action arises. Now animal law, in the limited context of veterinary professional services, proclaims a cause of action parallel to a cause of action for humans. It is as if we have two minds about how animals belong in the legal system: one version where animals are like humans and the other where they are not. Lawyers should remember this case for the proposition that animal law is a practice area full of surprising developments. The shift from bailment actions to malpractice actions is akin to the shift away from ownership disputes to the arise of custody disputes.

Faul v. Trahan[108]

Year: *1998*
Category: *Tort Law*
Type of Action: *Worker's Compensation*
Animal: *Horse*
Pet Custody Concept: *When a statute is challenged, constitutional review may apply to more than one "level."*

Before the plaintiff went to work at a farm, he had read the warning language in the state's Equine Immunity Statute. There was some dispute as to whether the plaintiff, who became injured, should have been riding horses owned by others who paid for a stall rental, or only horses that belonged to Franks Farms, the business that employed him. Employees were told not to ride horses other than those owned by the farm during working hours. It seemed that other employees knew that a horse named Passem All was a "flipper." Others thought that the horse "was crazy." The defendant was the trainer for Passem All. The trainer knew that the horse had a problem going into the starting gate and warned jockeys about this.

The question at issue was whether an employee of a racehorse training barn could only look to worker's compensation as an exclusive remedy for his injuries or whether he could seek damages based upon an intentional tort exception. It was alleged that the manager of the Opelousas location of Franks Farms knew that Passem All was dangerous and, accordingly, had a duty to warn potential riders. After weighing witness

107. Revisit *Smalich v. Westfall*, 440 Pa. 409 (1970), where the court outlined how to proceed on a breach of bailment theory, saying, "A bailment is a delivery of personalty for the accomplishment of some purpose upon a contract, express or implied, that after the purpose has been fulfilled, it shall be redelivered to the person who delivered it, otherwise dealt with according to his directions or kept until he reclaims it."

108. 718 So. 2d 1081 (Oct. 7, 1998).

credibility, given the conflicting testimony, the trial court determined that worker's compensation was the plaintiff's exclusive remedy and the higher court found no error in the trial court's determination.

Another claim was that the Equine Immunity Statute violated a constitutional guarantee of equal protection. Under this statute, equine was defined as "a horse, pony, mule, donkey, or hinny." The statute said,

> Except as provided in Subsection C of this Section, an equine activity sponsor, an equine professional, or any other person, which shall include a corporation or partnership, shall not be liable for an injury to or the death of a participant resulting from the inherent risks of equine activities and, except as provided in Subsection C of this Section, no participant or participant's representative shall make any claim against, maintain an action against, or recover from an equine activity sponsor, an equine professional, or any other person for injury, loss, damage, or death of the participant resulting from any of the inherent risks of equine activities.

The statute also sets forth terminology for the warning notice that appears on signs and in contracts.

On the subject of constitutionality, the court said, "Our jurisprudence mandates that all statutory enactments are presumed constitutional and every presumption of law and fact must be indulged in favor of legality."[109] The court emphasized how statutes are subject to constitutional review or scrutiny based upon three levels. Level one relates to race or religious beliefs. Level two relates to basis of birth, age, sex, culture, physical condition, or political ideas or affiliation. Level three is based upon laws that classify people on any basis other than those enumerated in the Louisiana Constitution. The court said that because the standard of review applicable here was level three, the plaintiff had to meet a stringent burden of proof and demonstrate that the law did not further an appropriate state interest. The court said,

> We conclude that La.R.S. 9:2795.1 encourages the ownership of horses by limiting an owner's liability except in certain enumerated circumstances including injuries caused by "willful or wanton disregard for the safety of the participant" and intentional injuries. . . . By removing a considerable risk of tort liability from the sponsor, La.R.S. 9:2795.1 encourages the participation of persons in supplying equine activities to the benefit of the industry as a whole. The court concludes that the statute is rationally related to the legitimate state interest of promoting equine related industry and did not violate the constitutional principal of equal protection.

Accordingly, the higher court affirmed the trial court's determination and denied the plaintiff's claim.

Practice Pointer: Rider beware.

---

109. *See* Moore v. RLCC Technologies, Inc., 95 2621 (La. 2/28/96); 668 So. 2d 1135; Polk v. Edwards, 626 So. 2d 1128 (La. 1993); and State ex rel. Kemp v. City of Baton Rouge, 215 La. 315, 40 So. 2d 477 (1949).

HYLAND V. BORRAS[110]

Year: *1998*
Category: *Tort Law, Equitable Principles*
Type of Action: *Damages*
Animal: *Dog*
Pet Custody Concept: *Methods for valuing dogs are in flux, and some courts prefer common sense to a mechanistic valuation method.*

The plaintiff brought an action for damages when the defendant's Bulldog attacked and badly injured her ten-year-old Shih Tzu. The plaintiff requested compensation of $2,500 for veterinary bills even though this demand exceeded the dog's fair market value of $500. As the defendant put it, the dog's "repair costs outweigh the replacement cost" regarding the property. The higher court said, "We agree that generally the measure of damages for the negligent destruction of personal property is the difference between its market value before and after the injury." The court then rejected the defendant's damages position as "overly mechanistic."

Relying on *New Jersey Power & Light Co. v. Mabee,*[111] where the intermediate court stated, "Our highest court recognized that the proper measure of damages 'rests in good sense rather than in a mechanical application of a single formula,'" the court utilized this analysis as the basis for a more flexible approach for allowing excessive damages in the instant case. Accordingly, the court recognized that "a household pet is not like other fungible or disposable property, intended solely to be used and replaced after it has outlived its usefulness." The court decided that the defendant was responsible for the necessary and reasonable expenses needed to restore the plaintiff's dog to the dog's condition before the attack.

Practice Pointer: Beyond the court's determination, consider how the rejection of the mechanistic application of a single formula, as conceptualized in *New Jersey Power & Light Co.*, could be applied to family law, with a little adjustment. The new doctrine could be that the companion animal be awarded based upon common sense rather than the mechanical application of a single criterion. By rejecting the single criterion approach, a family court judge could utilize multiple factors before arriving at a pet custody determination.

110. 719 A.2d 662, 316 N.J. Super. 22 (N.J. Super. 1998).
111. 41 N.J. 439, 197 A.2d 194 (1964).

Supchak v. Pruitt[112]

Year: *1998*
Category: *Tort Law*
Type of Action: *Negligence*
Animal: *Horse*
Pet Custody Concept: *The subject of who owns an animal may be hard to ascertain.*

When a horse owned by Boyce Pruitt living on Ruth Pruitt's 140-acre farm "collided" with a vehicle driven by the plaintiff, the plaintiff brought a lawsuit against Boyce Pruitt and Ruth Pruitt, as well as a business owned by Boyce Pruitt called Boyce Pruitt Livestock & Feed. It was alleged that "the fences around Ruth Pruitt's pasture were inadequate for the horse in question" even though the evidence before the trial court revealed that Ruth Pruitt "did not own, nor did she exercise custody or control over" this horse. Boyce Pruitt "admitted that he owned and had custody of the horse."

The court reiterated the duty of livestock owners to keep their animals from running at large and said, "our law defines an owner as 'any person, association, firm, or corporation, natural or artificial, owning, having custody of, or in charge of livestock.'" The higher court affirmed a summary judgment in favor of Ruth Pruitt and Boyce Pruitt Livestock & Feed, as they were not owners for the purposes of this action.

Practice Pointer: When bringing an action like this, it can be difficult to correctly identify the actual owner of the horse. Imagine if the above ownership definition was used in family law.

Rabideau v. City of Racine[113]

Year: *2001*
Category: *Tort Law*
Type of Action: *Noneconomic Damages*
Animal: *Dog*
Pet Custody Concept: *The dicta in this case is more powerful than the holding.*

This landmark case was poetic and soul searching, and is often quoted, as further described below. This case is respected even though the Supreme Court of Wisconsin failed to award noneconomic damages to Rabideau, the owner of a dead dog named Dakota. Rabideau and his off-duty police officer neighbor gave differing accounts of what happened before the off-duty police officer shot and killed Dakota. By the shooter's account, when Rabideau arrived at home, Dakota jumped out of his truck, entered the officer's yard, and attacked his dog, Jed. The shooter claimed that he, his wife, and his children were in danger and that he shot the dog three times in self-defense. Rabideau asserted that the dog was only on the curb, that the dogs were not fighting,

112. 503 S.E.2d 581 (Ga. Ct. App. 1998).
113. 627 N.W.2d 795, 797 (Wis. 2001).

and that no humans were threatened. Following Dakota's death, his owner collapsed and required medical treatment.

The majority said, in dicta, "Humans have an enormous capacity to form bonds with dogs, cats, birds and an infinite number of other beings that are non-human. Were we to recognize a claim for damages for the negligent loss of a dog, we can find little basis for rationally distinguishing other categories of animal companion."

Compared to the length and impact of the court's decision, little information was shared about why the supreme court found that "genuine issues of material fact exist as to whether Officer Thomas Jacobi was entitled as a matter of law to shoot and kill Dakota." Reversing the lower court's summary judgment determination in favor of the police officer, the Wisconsin Supreme Court focused on the "primary question" of whether Rabideau was entitled to emotional distress damages with regard to the death of a companion dog. While answering the primary question negatively, the court determined that Rabideau's claim, when "liberally construed, also encompassed a demand for damages for property loss."

The court stated, "We are uncomfortable with the law's cold characterization of a dog, such as Dakota, as mere 'property.'" The court continued that labeling a dog as property "fails to describe the value human beings place upon the companionship that they enjoy with a dog. A companion dog is not a fungible item, equivalent to other items of personal property. A companion dog is not a living room sofa or dining room furniture. This term inadequately and inaccurately describes the relationship between a human and a dog."[114]

After this historic declaration, the court detailed the domestication of the dog, going back to 6300 B.C., and also mentioned the discovery of a 12,000-year-old burial site where a human and a dog were buried together. The court stated that dogs perform useful services to their human companions and "provide humans with devoted friendship."[115]

Then, somewhat abashedly, the court applied the traditional legal doctrines with regard to Dakota's death. In reviewing Rabideau's negligent infliction of emotional distress claim, the court focused on whether Rabideau and his dog met the prerequisite of "close relative" as a basis for recovery. A close relative was defined as a spouse, sibling, parent/child, or grandparent/grandchild relationship. Because Dakota did not fit within this definition, Rabideau could not pursue his negligent infliction of emotional distress claim.

The court explored whether an emotional distress claim resulting from negligent damage to property was permissible and described the challenge of establishing a public policy framework that would allow recovery without unfairly burdening the tortfeasor. Although contemplating Rabideau's idea of "limiting liability to the human companion of a companion animal who is killed," the court found it difficult to define the class of individuals that would fit into the human companion category. The court

114. Consider the court's observation that relationships between humans and animals are "deeply embedded in the organization of our law and society." A persistent problem in pet law, and particularly the evolution of pet custody law, is that the organization of family life may be at odds with the organization of law.

115. A recent study in Japan showed that dogs are less likely to accept food from someone who has mistreated their owners.

acknowledged that Rabideau made "a substantial argument in good faith for an extension, modification or reversal of existing law."

In the end, the court stepped back from granting Rabideau relief because of the specter of the floodgate problem. While not categorizing companion animals as family members, the court permitted "friendship" and opened the door for an emotional distress claim for negligent damage to property.

In a concurring opinion, the chief justice of Wisconsin explored this subject somewhat differently when she drew heavily on an analysis from University of Chicago professor Martha C. Nussbaum, who effectively made a love and ethics distinction. Drawing from Nussbaum's scholarship, the chief justice said, "One's love of a pet should not be mistaken for concern about the ethical rights of animals" and further stated,

> Commonly, we conflate two sorts of people: animal lovers and people who are sensitive to the ethical rights of animals. This conflation is a great error. In human life, we can easily take its measure: men may be genuine lovers of women while treating them extremely badly. . . . Even people who treat well the particular women they love may not care at all about women's rights generally.

Practice Pointer: This case is reflective of how companion animals are on the continuum between property and person. Consider how the courts are construing claims with more flexibility and in this case, liberally construing the claim.

Burgess v. Taylor[116]

Year: *2001*
Category: *Tort Law*
Type of Action: *Tort of Outrage*
Animal: *Horse*
Pet Custody Concept: *Judges and juries in horse country, Kentucky, know what it means when horses and horse owners are inseparable and that bonds matter.*

This often-cited but sad case stands out as a powerful and influential decision in the fledgling jurisprudence of pet law, and it is rich in legal analysis. Judy Taylor owned two registered Appaloosa horses named Poco and P.J. for over 13 years. It was well known that Taylor "loved Poco and P.J. as if they were her children" and that the horses were "gentle and affectionate" and "inseparable."

Due to her declining health, Taylor needed a safe place for her horses to stay where she could continue to visit and interact with them. Lisa and Jeff Burgess offered to care for her horses in exchange for the enjoyment of them. In rural communities, these kinds of arrangements are known as "free-lease agreements."

116. 44 S.W.3d 806 (Ky. App. 2001).

Lisa Burgess represented to Taylor that "she loved and was knowledgeable about horses, that she had a nice pasture for them to live in together, that she liked helping people." Taylor entered into a free-lease agreement with Lisa and Jeff Burgess, and Taylor was invited to "come and visit the horses any time she wanted." The Burgesses took possession of the horses on August 31, and Lisa Burgess reassured Taylor that she had "led them around their new pasture and that the horses were doing fine."

By September 6, the Burgesses had secretly sold Taylor's horses to a slaughterhouse for $1,000. Coincidentally, the Burgesses told Taylor a series of lies about the horses' whereabouts and sent her off on senseless pursuits. As part of their intricate lies, the Burgesses enlisted a friend, Kenny Randolph, to misrepresent to Taylor that he had possession of the two horses at a "fictitious location in the Frenchtown, Indiana area." Randolph "refused to give her specific directions or the name of the 'gravel road' the pasture was supposedly on."

The jury, aware that Taylor had frantically searched for Poco and P.J. both before and after they were killed in late September, awarded Taylor $1,000 for the fair market value of the horses, $50,000 in compensatory damages, and $75,000 in punitive damages. The judgment of the trial court was affirmed on appeal. These awards were based upon the breach of the free-lease agreement, intentional infliction of emotional distress on Taylor, and a cause of action known as a "tort of outrage." The elements for this tort included that (1) the wrongdoer's conduct must be intentional or reckless, (2) the conduct must be outrageous and intolerable in that it offends against the generally accepted standards of decency and morality, (3) there must be a causal connection between the wrongdoer's conduct and the emotional distress, and (4) the emotional distress must be severe.

With regard to the first factor, the Burgesses, who had sold Poco and P.J. to Eugene Jackson, asked their friend Randolph "to lie for them so Taylor would not find out what they had done. There was significant evidence that the Burgesses were aware of Taylor's feelings for Poco and P.J.," which was why they attempted to cover up what had happened to prevent Taylor from rescuing the horses before they were slaughtered.

With regard to the second factor, the court cited the *Restatement (Second) of Torts* when it considered that the Burgesses' conduct "clearly rises to the level of being outrageous and intolerable in that it offends generally accepted standards of decency and morality, certainly a situation in which the recitation of the facts to an average member of the community would arouse his resentment against the actor, and lead him to exclaim, 'Outrageous!'" The court found that there was compelling evidence at trial regarding "Taylor's love for her horses and concern that they were in a good place."

Furthermore, the jury listened to evidence related to phone calls of "a distraught and frightened Taylor to Lisa Burgess and Kenny Randolph, begging to know where her horses were. The Burgesses knew that Poco and P.J. were heading to slaughter, and that Taylor was, in reality, pleading for their lives. Yet, in the face of Taylor's pleas for the horses she loved like children, the Burgesses continued to lie and refuse to tell her where they were. This Court cannot characterize this emotional torment inflicted by the Burgesses upon Taylor as anything other than 'heartless, flagrant, and outrageous.'"

With regard to the third factor, the court determined the causal connection between the Burgesses' actions and emotional distress and that there was sufficient evidence to consider that Poco and P.J. were slaughtered, even though the Burgesses argued there was not sufficient proof of this fact.

Regarding the fourth factor, the court determined that Taylor "suffered from many panic attacks, and has had major problems with high blood pressure for which she must receive medical care. She suffers from anxiety and depression, for which she takes medication, and has had many thoughts of suicide. She described overwhelming feelings of loss and failure. She testified she has trouble sleeping and has recurring nightmares in which she hears Poco's scream in her head. Taylor testified that she has sought help from her doctor and social workers but cannot get over what happened."

The court rejected the argument that the damages awarded should have been limited to the fair market value of the horses. The authority cited by the Burgesses to support their argument to limit damages to fair market value was *Cincinnati, New Orleans & Texas Pacific Railway Co v. Rankin*.[117] While *Cincinnati* involved a claim for emotional damages, there was no holding prohibiting a claim for the intentional infliction of emotional distress. In *Cincinnati*, the common carrier's liability regarding the transportation of livestock under a tariff contract was not relevant to this case involving pet horses.[118]

The court, too, addressed the Burgesses' criticism about the admission of hearsay statements at trial. The rules of evidence allowed prior statements of witnesses and admissions if (1) the declarant was not available as a witness, (2) the declarant was examined concerning the statement after the proper foundation was laid, and (3) the declarant's statement was inconsistent with the declarant's testimony at trial. The court observed that the problem with the forgetful witness in this case was not new to Kentucky courts and found that prior statements were properly admitted by the trial court.

Practice Pointer: With limited applicable case law in Kentucky, the court looked to other jurisdictions that had considered pet loss claims. In this horse country, the court recognized the human/animal bond and that people suffer when their pets are harmed or killed. Out of a contractual agreement involving a free lease, not only did a tort arise, but also a tort of outrage.

117. 153 Ky. 730, 156 S.W. 400 (1913).

118. The court also rejected the Burgesses' claims that the excessive award of damages for emotional distress did not pass the "first blush" rule, that jury instructions should have been given on the clear and convincing standard, and that "unclear and poorly defined punitive damages law" violated the Burgesses' due process rights.

Harabes v. The Barkery, Inc.[119]

Year: *2001*
Category: *Tort Law*
Type of Action: *Emotional Distress*
Animal: *Dog*
Pet Custody Concept: *In addition to reading the holdings, also review influential dicta and judicial signaling in pet law cases. Courts recognize their historical role.*

A pet grooming business sought summary judgment after the plaintiffs initiated claims for emotional distress and loss of companionship. The plaintiffs' dog, Gabby, died from medical complications after she was exposed to extreme heat for an extended period of time at a grooming business. It was conceded that the plaintiffs "were extremely close to their pet and that the death of their dog has been a traumatic experience."

The court remembered that in *Hyland v. Borras,*[120] the appellate division had permitted an award of damages for a pet that exceeded the replacement cost of the animal. In *Hyland*, the court did not address the subject of noneconomic damages when a pet was negligently injured or killed.

The New Jersey court cast a wide national net[121] on how to analyze companionship loss damages and considered Iowa's *Nichols v. Sukaro Kennels,*[122] saying, "We are mindful of the suffering an owner endures upon the death or injury of a beloved pet."[123] The court then reviewed the Texas decision of *Zeid v. Pearce,*[124] where the court said, "One may not recover damages for pain and suffering or mental anguish for the loss of a pet." The court also considered the more archaic decision in Minnesota's *Soucek v. Banham,*[125] where the court pragmatically proclaimed, "Compensatory damages for death of a dog, as an item of personal property, are limited to fair market value."

Finally deciding that damages would not be permitted when there was a negligent infliction of emotional distress claim, the court revealed that in the future, it would permit damages in an intentional infliction of emotional distress claim "if the conduct resulting in injury to or death of a pet is either intentional, willful, malicious, or reckless." The court cited Florida's famous *LaPorte v. Associated Independents, Inc.*[126]

The court made multiple references to Wisconsin's *Rabideau v. City of Racine,*[127] a case discussed throughout this book. Although in the instant case, the court here, too, was ultimately unwilling to make a pet or companion animal a family member, the court struggled with the difficulty of drawing a line but hoped one could be drawn to

---

119. 348 N.J. Super. 366, 791 A.2d 1142 (N.J. Super. Ch. 2001).
120. 316 N.J. Super. 22, 719 A.2d 662 (App. Div. 1998).
121. The higher court turned to decisions in Nebraska, Iowa, Alaska, Michigan, Texas, New York, Georgia, Minnesota, and Pennsylvania for guidance.
122. 555 N.W.2d 689, 691 (Iowa 1996).
123. Notwithstanding this pro-pet language, the court still denied the recovery of damages for this kind of emotional distress claim.
124. 953 S.W.2d 368, 369 (Tex. App. 1997).
125. 524 N.W.2d 478, 481 (Minn. Ct. App. 1995).
126. 163 So. 2d 267, 268 (Fla. 1964).
127. 627 N.W.2d 795, 797 (Wis. 2001).

identify "the class of animals for which a pet owner may recover."[128] The court granted the defendant's motion for summary judgment and dismissed the plaintiffs' claims for emotional distress and loss of companionship.[129]

Practice Pointer: The developing animal law jurisprudence is dynamic. Do not give up on courts reluctantly following old precedents.

JOHNSON V. DOUGLAS[130]

Year: *2001*
Category: *Tort Law*
Type of Action: *Emotional Distress*
Animal: *Dog*
Pet Custody Concept: *Remember that floodgate concerns are ever present for the courts.*

A "family dog" named Coco was killed by a speeding motorist on a residential road while on a walk with the plaintiff wife. At issue on appeal was whether Coco's owners' claims for emotional distress were permissible.

The court stated, "There is no doubt that some pet owners have become so attached to their family pets that the animals are considered members of the family. This is particularly true of owners of domesticated dogs who have been repeatedly referred to as 'Man's Best Friend' and a faithful companion." Notwithstanding this admission, the court compared the death of the family dog to the destruction of a family heirloom or a prized school ring. The court detailed how expanding emotional distress claims in a property loss context would result in a floodgate problem that would burden the court. The court discussed a particular aspect of an emotional distress claim, whether either plaintiff was in the zone of danger when Coco died. The court rebuffed the plaintiffs' claim that they were in the zone of danger, as the zone of danger pertained to "the observance of the death or serious injury of an immediate family member who is a person."[131]

Recalling a dissent by Judge Kaye in *Bovsun v. Sanperi*,[132] the court said, "While it may seem that there should be a remedy for every wrong, this is an ideal limited

128. One might ask if the "class of animals" question and line drawing issue are the same for tort law and family law purposes. In *Harabes*, the court considered the decision in *Nichols v. Sukaro*, 555 N.W.2d 689 (Iowa 1996), wherein the plaintiff's expert advocated "if a pet is thought of as a family member by its owners, its value is whatever the owner thinks it is." Thus far, the tort system for the loss or injury to an animal tilts toward a commercial scheme where justice is affected by the allocation of economic value, although that value is becoming less mechanical and more elastic.

129. This is the court that penned the famous case of *Houseman v. Dare*, 966 A.2d 24 (N.J. Super. Ct. App. Div. 2009), seven years later. What a difference a decade makes.

130. 723 N.Y.S.2d 627, 187 Misc. 2d 509 (N.Y. Sup. Ct. 2001).

131. For many lawyers reading this book, the common law has many peculiarities, and one of them pertains to a legal fiction called the zone of danger. This is essentially a line-drawing effort. Here, the line is drawn to exclude nonpersons. As a ship is a person, one might imagine that if a human "person" was close enough to a ship "person" that sunk, this aspect of a zone of danger claim would be satisfied.

132. 61 N.Y.2d 219 (1984).

perforce by the realities of this world. Every injury has ramifying consequences, like the rippling of the waters, without end. The problem for the law is to limit the legal consequences of wrongs to a controllable degree." The court dismissed the defendant's claim for private damages.

Practice Pointer: This court concedes, without despair, that there can be wrongs without remedies. This court applauds itself for being "realists." Never forget that there are jurists like this.

KOESTER V. VCA ANIMAL HOSPITAL[133]

Year: *2001*
Category: *Tort Law*
Type of Action: *Emotional Distress*
Animal: *Dog*
Pet Custody Concept: *Courts signal the need for legislative action.*

This decision involved the death of a dog seen by a veterinarian because of a salivary gland problem in the dog's neck. Following the dog's unexpected death, a necropsy report revealed that the dog had suffocated, as the dog's bandages were wrapped too tightly.[134] The plaintiff sought emotional distress damages arising from the veterinary defendants' negligence. The trial court dismissed the plaintiff's action for failing to plead "legally cognizable damages."[135] The court found no precedent that would "permit the recovery of damages for emotional injuries allegedly suffered as a consequence of property damage." For the plaintiff to establish a prima facie case for negligence, the plaintiff must prove the malpractice elements of duty, breach of duty, proximate cause, and damages.

The appellate court, recognizing that "pets have evolved in our modern society to a status that is not consistent with their characterization as 'chattel,'" hinted that the plaintiff's claim should have been framed as an independent cause of action and not as a basis for damages. The court expressed empathy for the plaintiff's position and looked to the legislature to create an appropriate remedy. Imploring the legislature to act is common in cases where the common law and statutes are out of step with the evolving status of pets as family members.[136]

As seen in *Koester*, the idea of lack of compensation for the loss of a companion animal is a recurring theme in tort law cases. There is a difference between loss of companionship in a tort law claim and loss of companionship in a family law dispute. In

133. 244 Mich. App. 173, 624 N.W.2d 209 (Mich. App. 2001).

134. The plaintiff initiated a negligence action and sought damages based upon claims of pain and suffering, extreme fright, shock, mortification, and loss of companionship. The plaintiff argued that the court should create an independent cause of action for pet owners that would allow them to recover for the loss of companionship when a pet is negligently injured by a veterinarian.

135. In addition to appearances by the plaintiff and the defendants, the appearance of Barbara H. Goldman from the State Bar of Michigan Animal Law Section was noted on the record. This is a prestigious and venerable animal law section and one of the earliest in the United States.

136. *See* Rabideau v. City of Racine, 627 N.W.2d 795, 797 (Wis. 2001).

one instance, the animal is dead, while in the other, the individual may simply lose his or her relationship with an animal that is alive. Despite the difference in how loss of companionship arises in tort law and family law, the common thread is that the relational value of an animal is not equivalent to the animal's economic value.

Practice Pointer: Point out well-reasoned cases where the courts, instead of hoping the legislature would eventually act, exercise leadership. Remember *Corso v. Crawford Dog and Cat Hospital, Inc.*[137]

Mitchell v. Heinrichs[138]

Year: *2001*
Category: *Tort Law*
Type of Action: *Emotional Distress*
Animal: *Dog*
Pet Custody Concept: *When courts say they are changing value conceptions, read the fine print.*

The plaintiff's two dogs were loose on a neighbor's property and reached a livestock pen where a goat had just given birth. The neighbor approached the plaintiff's dogs while carrying her shotgun and shot and killed one of the dogs. Later claiming that she felt personally threatened, she apologized and offered $250 to the owner of the dead dog. The plaintiff declined the offer and initiated a legal action with claims for conversion and intentional infliction of emotional distress. She also sought punitive damages.[139]

The supreme court affirmed the lower court's grant of summary judgment motion initiated by the defendant to stop the plaintiff's intentional infliction of emotional distress and punitive damages claims. While the lower court allowed the plaintiff to proceed with a conversion action, the same court ultimately dismissed the claim when the dead dog's owner conceded that her adult dog had no market value. The supreme court reversed the dismissal of the conversion claim and remanded; the supreme court also instructed the superior court to determine damages based upon principles outlined in an earlier decision.

In an earlier decision in Alaska, *Landers v. Municipality of Anchorage*,[140] the supreme court said, "the value to the owner, rather than the fair market value" was a standard applied where the "destroyed or lost property has no real market value or where the value of the property to the owner is greater than the market value." There, the owner lost chattel that had only a subjective emotional or sentimental value. Indicating that this approach was "consonant with the modern case law in other jurisdictions that have addressed the valuation of pet dogs," the court granted to the owner the right to seek compensation based upon the value of the dog to her. Applicable criteria the

137. 97 Misc. 2d 530 (Civ. Ct. Queens Cnty. 1979).
138. 27 P.3d 309 (Alaska 2001).
139. Be sure to check the applicable state for how to properly plead punitive damages. It can be a cumbersome process.
140. 915 P.2d 614 (Alaska 1996).

court mentioned included the replacement cost, the cost of immunizations, the cost of neutering, the cost of comparable training, and the value of breeding potential.[141]

Practice Pointer: This case is illustrative of how the value of a dog, from a valuation perspective, is continually evolving. In this turn-of-the-century decision, the valuation was still viewed through only an economic perspective.

BLAHA V. STUARD[142]

Year: *2002*
Category: *Tort Law*
Type of Action: *Products Liability*
Animal: *Dog*
Pet Custody Concept: *A dog is a living creature.*

A man bought a five-year-old Labrador and gave the dog to his father. The seller, who understood the Labrador was being purchased as a hunting dog, disclosed to the buyer before the sale was completed that the dog had once jumped on a child. The dog later bit both the buyer's father and his child. Although the child's guardian ad litem brought a personal injury lawsuit against the seller, the court began its analysis and decision by saying, "It is common knowledge that horses buck, cattle roam, cats stray and dogs bite."

Regarding the strict liability claim, in contrast to the New York approach established in *Beyer v. Aquarium Supply Co.*,[143] the court said, "Because the dog in this case is not a 'product,' according to the Restatement, no liability exists under a theory of strict liability."[144] The court reasoned that negligence and negligent infliction of emotional distress claims brought by the child's guardian ad litem might subject the child's father to liability, not the seller.

Pointing to minimal records offered into evidence, the court compared the facts of this case to *Gehrts v. Batteen*,[145] where the owner's dog "constantly barked, bared its teeth, and strained at its leash." The court went on to say that "this court has found nothing to support the contention that possessor's liability may be superimposed upon a seller." With regard to the buyer's claim of negligent infliction of emotional distress, the court determined that negligence arises under state or common law when there is a duty or the duty is breached, which results in proximate cause of the injury. The court found that there was no requisite breach of duty here. The court also explored whether there was a basis for a breach of an express or an implied warranty claim and concluded that there was no breach of any warranty because the seller disclosed to the buyer that the dog had previously jumped on a child and was protective of a porch area.

141. This case was unusual because breeding potential was mentioned.
142. 2002 S.D. 19, 640 N.W.2d 85 (S.D. 2002).
143. 94 Misc. 2d 336, 404 N.Y.S.2d 778 (N.Y. Sup. Ct. 1977).
144. RESTATEMENT (SECOND) OF TORTS.
145. 620 N.W.2d 775 (S.D. 2001).

Of particular interest to the court was whether the Labrador was a good or a product. The court observed that New York courts consider animals as products, whereas Illinois courts consider them to be goods. The South Dakota court was more persuaded by the Illinois classification, as living creatures "are by their nature in a constant process of internal development and growth and they are also participants in a constant interaction with the environment around them as part of their development. Thus, living creatures have no fixed nature and cannot be products as a matter of law." The court also emphasized that under the *Restatement (Second) of Torts*, animals could not be products. Classifying the Labrador as a good and not a product was outcome determinative.

Practice Pointer: Family lawyers should pay attention to the ever-present potential for a liability claim if a companion animal causes an injury, particularly if the parties are seeking co-ownership or access rights. Although this decision may seem unrelated to how courts might grapple with a pet custody dispute today, this case is useful in that the court explored public policy classification rationales.

Krasnecky v. Meffen[146]

Year: *2002*
Category: *Tort Law*
Type of Action: *Emotional Distress*
Animal: *Sheep*
Pet Custody Concept: *Some courts are interested in novel questions.*

The court asked the question of whether the plaintiffs' claim was "legally cognizable." An unusual aspect of this companion animal case was that the affected animals were sheep. The plaintiff owners considered their sheep to be family members; they spent six or seven hours a day with the sheep, who they considered their "babies." The owners patted, hugged, and brushed their sheep and went all out to celebrate each individual sheep's birthday. As little lambs, they were bottle fed and given house privileges. The owners did not sell the sheep's wool or milk.[147]

When seven of their sheep were killed in their backyard by a neighbor's dog, the plaintiffs claimed that they suffered from "significant emotional distress and related physical problems." Although the plaintiffs did not seek economic damages as a matter of principle because an award of market value for the loss of a family member was offensive to them, they did seek emotional distress damages and companionship loss damages.

146. 777 N.E.2d 1286, 56 Mass. App. Ct. 418 (Mass. App. 2002).

147. The court offered a footnote wherein a definition for a companion animal was provided from a veterinary ethics textbook. One aspect of this definition used by the court was that the relationship "brings a significant benefit to a central aspect of the lives of each, which is in some sense voluntary, and in which each party treats the other not just something entitled to respect and benefit in its own right, but also as an object of admiration, trust, devotion, or love."

In the jurisdiction where the plaintiffs lived, tort emotional distress damages were allowed "for emotional distress resulting from an injury to a third party." Even so, the pertinent case law interpreted third party to mean a "parent of or another person closely related to a third person directly injured by the tortfeasor's conduct." The court proclaimed that whether the companion animal would qualify as a third party was "a novel question."[148]

In contemplating the plaintiffs' emotional distress claim, the court pondered utilizing the zone of interest analysis but instead focused on the requirements of spatial and temporal proximity. The court framed its behavior by saying, "Plaintiffs' absence at the time of the killing of their sheep and the fact that they did not learn of the slaughter until the following day alone preclude any recovery for the emotional distress suffered by them."

The court also pointed out that it would not apply the wrongful death statute, as emotional distress claims were outside of the statute. As the court put it, "Contrary to the argument of the plaintiffs, and notwithstanding any perceived inadequacies in the wrongful death statute, it appears anomalous, absent legislation, to permit more extensive recovery for the death of an animal than for the death of a person."

Viewing a loss of consortium claim as preferable to the plaintiffs' loss of companionship claim, the court turned to the definition of "consortium" in *Black's Law Dictionary*. The dictionary definition included "companionship, cooperation, affection [and] aid." The court continued by explaining that the state's wrongful death statute sets limits or confines regarding the recovery of all damages to those instances in which a tortfeasor "causes the death of a person." The court also noted that because of the denial of an action for loss of filial consortium under the common law, the legislature needed to enact the statute permitting filial consortium. It is interesting that in 2002, a Massachusetts court went to such great lengths to justify its denial of the plaintiffs' claims.

The court was unpersuaded by the record that the dog owner had set in motion "in the usual course of events" a force that would damage the property of another and pointed out that the plaintiffs had failed to bring to the court's attention any case where "the negligent release of a dog has been held to support a trespass action." The court also distinguished the instant case from one where an injunction was brought to prevent authorized grazing. Based upon the above, the court determined that "the damages sought by the plaintiffs, in the circumstances, are unavailable to them, as matter of law, and that, at most, the only damages to which they are entitled are the nominal damages which they have been awarded."

Practice Pointer: The court was apologetic for the lack of meaningful remedy for the plaintiffs' suffering upon the death of their sheep. Even though the plaintiffs called their sheep "babies," the court was not judgmental about it. One of the interesting aspects of this case is the court's examination of the subject of time. In this case, the owners' awareness of their animals' deaths was not immediate, but instead, the next

148. Compare this Massachusetts court looking at the novel question of "third party" with the Oregon court's novel examination of whether an animal could be a crime victim in *State v. Nix*, 355 Or. 777, 334 P.3d 437 (2014), *vac'd*, 356 Ore. 768, 345 P.3d 416 (2015).

day. An unusual aspect of this decision was the court's comprehension of a human loving an animal and the animal loving in return.[149]

PETCO ANIMAL SUPPLIES, INC. V. SCHUSTER[150]

Year: *2004*
Category: *Tort Law*
Type of Action: *Gross Negligence*
Animal: *Dog*
Pet Custody Concept: *Courts are confounded about how to address our love relationship with companion animals. When in doubt, many rally around 19th-century precedents.*

A miniature Schnauzer puppy named Licorice was taken to Petco for grooming. When an employee took the dog outside for a routine bathroom break, Licorice slipped out of her restraint and ran away. Although the dog's owner searched for Licorice for four days, the court said that "tragically, the dog was found dead, having been run over by traffic." In a default judgment, the lower court awarded judgment against the defendant based upon contract, gross negligence, tort, and conversion property claims. The damages awarded were as follows:

Replacement Value	$500.00
Training	$892.00
Microchip	$52.40
Lost Wages	$857.68
Counseling	$160.00
Mental Anguish/Emotional Distress	$10,000.00
Intrinsic Value/Companionship Loss	$10,000.00
Exemplary Damages	$10,000.00
Attorney's Fees	$6,750.00

Instead of bringing a motion for a new trial, the defendant initiated a "restricted" appeal within the requisite time period. This type of appeal is limited to the "face" of the record. The appellate court can review legal and factual insufficiency claims. The defendant argued that (1) damages for mental anguish, counseling, loss of companionship, and lost wages were not permitted as a matter of law; (2) there was no evidence to support the award of exemplary damages; and (3) the attorney's fees were excessive. Petco also asserted that a double recovery based upon tort and contract theories was not permissible.

When facing a legal sufficiency challenge, the court will sustain a "no evidence point" when "(a) there is a complete absence of evidence of a vital fact; (b) the court is barred by rules of law or of evidence from giving weight to the only evidence offered

149. It is noteworthy that the plaintiffs' lawyer, Steven Wise, is a lawyer who distinguished himself by teaching the first animal law course at Harvard Law School at the turn of the 21st century. Wise is now advocating for chimpanzee personhood.
150. 144 S.W.3d 554 (Tex. App. 2004).

to prove a vital fact; (c) the evidence offered to prove a vital fact is no more than a mere scintilla; or (d) the evidence conclusively establishes the opposite of the vital fact." When the determination is by jury verdict, the court uses the sufficiency standard as meaning that the judgment is "so contrary to the overwhelming weight of the evidence as to be clearly wrong and manifestly unjust." Ultimately, the court found vital facts were unproven.

The court addressed whether all the plaintiff's damage claims were permissible. Citing *Heiligmann v. Rose*,[151] wherein damages principles related to the intentional death of a dog were established, the court reversed the damages awards to the plaintiff for mental anguish, counseling costs, the intrinsic value of loss of companionship, and lost wages. Emphasizing that *Heiligmann* "classifies dogs as personal property for damage purposes, not as persons, extensions of their owners, or any other legal entity whose loss would ordinarily give rise to personal injury damages," the court also emphasized that "Texas courts have continued to classify dogs as property for damage purposes."

The court also referenced *Arrington v. Arrington*,[152] a case where the court said, "A dog, for all its admirable and unique qualities, is not a human being and is not treated in the law as such."[153] By citing these two precedents, the Texas higher court reiterated its allegiance to "traditional classifications," including the *Heiligmann* "true rule of damages."[154] The supreme court stressed the importance of this 19th-century precedent, written in the same decade as the U.S. Supreme Court's decision in *Sentell v. New Orleans Carrollton Railroad Co.*[155] Both decisions were made when there were widespread, and deadly, rabies epidemics.[156] The court was steadfast that as in *Heiligmann*, true value could not be "attributed to companionship or other sentimental considerations."

In making its decision, the court revisited its earlier Texas decision in *City of Garland v. White*,[157] where mental anguish damages were awarded after a dog was fatally shot. The court recognized that this decision was a favorable precedent for the plaintiff's case and decided that *White* was not controlling because (1) there was an absence of an intentional act by Petco in causing Licorice's death, (2) the *White* court did not make a record of the defendant's position on mental anguish damages, and (3) the *Heiligmann* decision had not been cited.

Although the court found mental anguish damages were not available for a breach of contract claim, it found the record wanting in the instant case as to whether the

---

151. 81 Tex. 222, 16 S.W. 931 (1891).

152. 613 S.W.2d 565, 569 (Tex. Civ. App.–Fort Worth 1981, no writ).

153. In *Arrington*, the court refused to appoint a managing conservator for a pet dog but allowed visitation.

154. Even though a loss could be determined based upon market value, special value, or pecuniary value, the latter two were restricted in *Heiligmann* to be commensurate with the dog's usefulness and services. There is a national trend for appellate courts to better understand the place of animals in family life than supreme courts. As the appellate courts' members advance to the supreme courts, it is foreseeable that the supreme court will better understand that companion animals are not just property anymore.

155. 166 U.S. 698, 703 (1897).

156. This decision about an owner's ability to initiate a civil action regarding the killing of a dog was dependent upon the value the owner fixed by "himself" in the last assessment rolls, an idea similar to the idea of a prohibition against bringing an action unless a dog was properly licensed, and a high enough license fee paid.

157. 368 S.W.2d 12, 14–17 (Tex. Civ. App.–Eastland 1963, writ ref'd n.r.e.).

plaintiff was seeking damages "under her tort claims or breach of contract claim, or both." Finding that the plaintiff had not presented sufficient evidence regarding the reasonableness or necessity of the plaintiff's counseling expense, the court also rejected the plaintiff's claim that her "subjective feelings for Licorice" constituted proof of intrinsic value or loss of companionship. The court did not conceal that it was offended by the plaintiff's $280,000 companionship loss claim, either.

An amicus brief urged the court to "take account of the modern view of dogs as beloved friends and companions." The higher court complained that "one commentator cited in the brief went as far as to suggest Americans today view their pets as more akin to family members than mere property."[158]

While the court acknowledged that there were myriad "examples that Texans today view dogs as more companion, friend, or even something akin to family than as an economic tool or benefit,"[159] the ambivalence of the court was better captured by the statement, "As an intermediate appellate court, we are not free to mold Texas law as we see fit but must instead follow the precedents of the Texas Supreme Court unless and until the high court overrules them or the Texas Legislature supersedes them by statute." The court opposed molding the Texas law while strongly signaling its own viewpoint of how companion animals should be kept in their place.

The court rejected the plaintiff's effort to expand the concept of "intrinsic value" to include the subjective value of dog companionship.[160] Even so, the court added a "what if speculation" regarding an earlier supreme court decision, *Porras v. Craig*.[161] Though not applicable in this case, the court opened the door and said that intrinsic value may only be sought when property has neither market nor replacement value.[162] In the instant case, the court denied the plaintiff's claims for (1) lost wages, outside of the employment context; (2) property damages; and (3) exemplary damages. To be awarded exemplary damages as part of the plaintiff's tort claim, the plaintiff must have shown fraud or malice by Petco under agency law. Exemplary damages were not applicable in claims for breach of contract either.[163]

Based upon a breach of contract, the plaintiff was awarded damages for the dog's replacement value, training, microchip, attorney's fees, and court costs. While capable of characterizing the death of Licorice as tragic and admitting that "even Petco's counsel have publicly acknowledged 'the special bond between a pet and its owner,'" the court could not deviate in any way from the 19th-century true value rule. It was

158. From a historical perspective, it is noteworthy that this decision was made in 2004, the year before Hurricane Katrina made landfall in the gulf coast. Even from this court, one would not have expected this disdainful tone in a 2005 decision, especially when the state of Texas played such a large role, nationally, in saving companion animals.

159. The Texas court grappled with the developing pet law jurisprudence and tried to balance an avalanche of facts and statistics about the importance of pets or companion animals in the modern American family, as asserted in amicus briefs, against the perception of a floodgate problem.

160. The plaintiff cited cases where mental anguish damages were awarded arising "from the breach of duties incident to certain 'special relationships' including a 'very limited number of contracts dealing with intensely emotional noncommercial subjects.'" The court quipped that the dog grooming business did not qualify as an intensely emotional noncommercial subject.

161. 675 S.W.2d 503, 506 (Tex. 1984).

162. This type of valuation is particularly used with mixed breed animals.

163. Though not addressed in the case itself, the court pointed out in a footnote that mental anguish damages are not available when there has been a conversion.

unmoved by the idea that the Schnauzer puppy was the plaintiff's constant companion, "right by my leg," and that "If I went somewhere she could go, she went with me. . . . She was a companion to me and I miss her."[164]

Practice Pointer: Courts across the country differ in their ability to comprehend the affairs of the heart. Lack of what at times seems to be our collective understanding about emotion is somewhat intriguing given our cultural ideas about marrying for love and having soul mates, as well as our common values of adopting animals from rescue groups and contractually promising to give these animals forever homes. In terms of developing jurisprudence, we might ask how ideas such as vital facts might differ between a tort claim and a family law pet custody dispute. As companion animals continue to move into the interim category, vital facts may pertain to multiple decision making criteria.

Terral v. Louisiana Farm Bureau Casualty Insurance Co.[165]

Year: *2005*
Category: *Tort Law*
Type of Action: *Negligence*
Animal: *Dog*
Pet Custody Concept: *What is an owner? Let me count the ways.*

The plaintiff sustained injuries when a black dog ran in front of his motorcycle. When a lawsuit was filed against the defendant, Troyce Mangum, as the "alleged owner of the dog," both Mangum and his insurance company denied ownership. The plaintiff offered the following evidence to establish that the dog belonged to Mangum:

- A black dog similar to a Labrador had been seen.
- The dog spent a majority of time at Mangum's house.
- Mangum's neighbor considered the dog to be "living" at Mangum's residence.
- The neighbor had seen a resident at Mangum's home feeding and petting the dog.
- The dog at Mangum's residence was believed to be wearing a red collar.
- A black dog wearing a red collar was found dead in the road following the accident.
- A black dog had bothered others on Mangum's property.
- Neighbors had the impression that the dog belonged to Mangum.

---

164. No one could accuse this Texas Court of Appeals of overappreciating the importance of companion animals in American life.
165. 892 So. 2d 732 (La. 2005).

- A woman living at Mangum's house, following the accident, asked about the welfare of "her dogs."[166]

Mangum owned three registered dogs: a red Chow, a Chihuahua, and a Dachshund. Mangum said that although the black dog was not his, he did put food out on his front porch for his Chow and that the black dog ate the food on a regular basis. He further testified that he "never purchased anything for the black dog, never took it to the veterinarian, never walked it, never let it inside his trailer, and never told anyone that the dog was his." He pointed out that the three dogs he owned came into the trailer, went to the veterinarian, and rode in his vehicle.

The trial court determined that by feeding the black dog for a sufficient period of time, Mangum had "assumed ownership of it and, thus, responsibility for it." Under applicable state law, an owner of an animal is answerable for damages caused if the owner was negligent. Moreover, an owner of a dog is subject to strict liability for damages caused by the dog appropriate to the application of the doctrine of res ipsa loquitur.[167]

The court also looked at who was liable as an owner and said, "Despite the reference to 'owners' in La. C.C. art. 2321, the jurisprudence extends liability under the article to persons who harbor dogs through either actual or constructive possession and control of the animal."[168] The court further indicated that because a dog is "a corporeal moveable," the person in possession is presumed to have ownership.

Practice Pointer: There are many different ways that the term "ownership" can be understood. Ownership determinations are particularly broad when liability claims arise.

166. There was also evidence that a red Chow was loose at the time of the accident.

167. This is a legal principle based upon a Latin phrase meaning "the thing speaks for itself."

168. *See* Thompson v. Sicard, 385 So. 2d 334 (La. App. 1st Cir. 1980), *writ refused*, 386 So. 2d 355 (La. 1980); Tillman v. Cook, 3 So. 2d 230 (La. App. Orleans 1941); and McCoy v. Lucius, 36,894 (La. App. 2d Cir. 3/5/03), 839 So. 2d 1050, *writ denied*, 2003-1217 (La. 3/26/04), 871 So. 2d 344.

Womack v. Von Rardon[169]

Year: *2006*
Category: *Tort Law*
Type of Action: *Tort of Outrage*
Animal: *Cat*
Pet Custody Concept: *Assert traditional and novel claims.*

Three boys took a cat named Max off the porch of the house where he lived and brought him to a school where they poured gasoline on him and started a fire. The badly burned cat was then euthanized. Max's owner initiated claims for private nuisance, a tort of outrage, and a statutory waste claim against two of the boys and their parents.

In *Pickford v. Mason,*[170] the Washington court had already opened the door for the potential of emotional distress claims when a pet had been "maliciously injured." These emotional distress damages were permitted in the instant case for the burned cat when the court admitted that "[f]or the first time in Washington, we hold malicious injury to a pet can support a claim for, and be considered a factor in measuring a person's emotional distress damages."

The trial court denied nine of the plaintiff's 16 liability claims in a summary judgment decision. The claims at issue on appeal were a claim for private nuisance, the tort of outrage,[171] and a claim for statutory waste. With regard to the plaintiff's claim for private nuisance, the appellate court denied the claim and found that the loss did not relate to land or "property fixed to the land." The court further reiterated that "No appellate court has applied nuisance to the death of an animal" and "Cases in Washington involving an animal and nuisance are situations where the animal is a nuisance. At best, an Oregon court held an animal injuring or killing another animal is a nuisance."

With regard to the tort of outrage, the appellate court said the plaintiff must prove three elements: "(1) extreme and outrageous conduct, (2) intentional or reckless infliction of emotional distress, and (3) plaintiff's resulting actual severe emotional distress." Beyond these requirements, under *Kloepfel v. Bokor,*[172] the court said that intentional infliction of emotional distress claims must be predicated on behavior "so outrageous in character, and so extreme in degree, as to go beyond all possible bounds of decency, and to be regarded as atrocious, and utterly intolerable in a civilized community."

The court found that the plaintiff had not met the requisite burden of proof regarding the required intent on the necessary severity, while observing that the trial court had found liability based upon other theories. The plaintiff also offered a claim for statutory waste, a claim that, if granted, would have entitled the plaintiff to treble damages. The court denied this because the cat was free to roam, and therefore the cat was not attached to personal property on the land as the statutory waste statute

169. 135 P.3d 542 (Wash. 2006).
170. 124 Wash. App. 257, 262–63, 98 P.3d 1232 (2004).
171. The causes of action not dismissed by the trial court were for simple negligence (with the plaintiff as victim), gross negligence, trespass to chattels, conversion, statutory vicarious liability (for parents), negligent supervision (for parents), and negligent infliction of emotional distress.
172. 149 Wash. 2d 192, 195, 66 P.3d 630 (2003).

required. The court affirmed that the trial court did not err in considering Max's value and the plaintiff's emotional distress in the context of both malicious harm to Max and the harassment of the plaintiff's son.

Practice Pointer: If you are motivated to think outside of the box and want to understand the progression of pet law jurisprudence, read not only this decision but also the parties' trial court pleadings and memorandum of law. Each state has common laws that may provide unexpected opportunities.

Goodby v. Vetpharm, Inc.[173]

Year: *2009*
Category: *Tort Law*
Type of Action: *Wrongful Death*
Animal: *Cat*
Pet Custody Concept: *The court is unsure of where a pet belongs in a greater family system.*

Two cats suffering from hypertension were treated with a prescription of Amlodipine. When the prescription was refilled by the defendant veterinarians, the medication contained at least 20 times the drug dosage that appeared on the label. Following the onset of toxic responses, both cats died.

While acknowledging the nationally recognized precedents in the court's own home state of Vermont, *Morgan v. Kroupa*[174] and *Lamare v. North Country Animal League*,[175] the court said, "Pets have special characteristics as personal property." Emphasizing that the subject of their intangible value was not previously considered or addressed, the court entertained and then rejected the plaintiffs' emotional damages claims, stating that "emotional damages caused by their untimely loss merely does for the wrongful death of companion animals what the Wrongful Death Act does for the death of immediate relatives due to the fault of others."

The court seemed offended that the plaintiffs requested a judicial expansion of law to recover for the loss of a pet when that same law did not "allow for loss of a broad variety of critically loved human beings." The court complained that "Whether the familial quality of companionship between humans and their pets is relatively new or ancient, Plaintiffs seek a dramatic alteration to the law." Emphasizing that the extension of a wrongful death law should be by statutory enactment because expansion of the common law would require a compelling public policy reason, the court concluded, "Plaintiffs fail to demonstrate a compelling reason why, as a matter of public policy, the law should offer broader compensation for the loss of a pet than would be available for the loss of a friend, relative, work animal, heirloom, or memento—all of

173. 186 Vt. 63 (2009), 974 A.2d 1269, 2009 Vt. 52 (Vt. 2009).
174. 167 Vt. 99, 103, 702 A.2d 630, 633 (1997).
175. 170 Vt. 115, 122, 743 A.2d 598, 602 (1999).

which can be prized beyond measure, but for which this state's law does not recognize recovery for sentimental loss."

With regard to the plaintiffs' claim of negligent infliction of emotional distress, the court determined that the plaintiffs were not in the zone of danger[176] when the cats were administered the fatal dose of medication. This was because to be in the zone of danger, the plaintiff had to be within the zone "of an act negligently directed at him" by the defendant.

Practice Pointer: Avoid advocacy that rings the bell that companion animals would receive an advantage over humans.

SCHEELE V. DUSTIN[177]

Year: *2010*
Category: *Tort Law*
Type of Action: *Intentional Tort*
Animal: *Dog*
Pet Custody Concept: *It is not very difficult to read between the lines and see, just over the horizon, that this court will be ready to lead the country.*

The plaintiffs were traveling in Vermont when they stopped in a church parking lot to let out their family dog, Shadow, who crossed into an adjacent yard where a man was sitting on his porch, planning to shoot squirrels. When the man saw the nonthreatening Shadow, he shot him and caused his death by puncturing his aorta valve and causing the dog to hemorrhage.

Shadow's owners brought an action against the shooter seeking economic and noneconomic damages, as well as punitive damages. The parties agreed to stipulate to both findings and the amount of damages for various claims, with the exception of punitive damages. They left it to the courts to determine if there were claims upon which relief could be granted.

With regard to economic damages for the destruction of their property, the parties stipulated, without explanation, that one plaintiff had economic damages of $130 and the other plaintiff $25. On the subject of noneconomic damages for the destruction of property, emotional distress, and suffering, together with loss of companionship, the figures included "emotional-pain-and-suffering damages for each in the amount of $1,500; and damages for each in the amount of $1,500 for the destruction of the special relationship," which included "solace, affection, friendship and love."

The stipulation stated that the plaintiffs' distress included "the destruction of the special relationship that each had with Shadow." The plaintiffs' emotional distress claims arose from their having nightmares, sleeplessness, sadness, and stress, but not from

176. Although the words "zone of danger" have multiple meanings, one of them relates to being within the zone where the physical peril is presented and another is related to witnessing an injury to another. Another permutation of this idea is what is called the "impact rule," which requires that as a predicate to a claim, physical contact must occur.

177. 998 A.2d 697, 2010 Vt. 45 (Vt. 2010).

watching Shadow die. The plaintiffs believed that "the real worth of a pet is not merely financial and cannot be measured solely by the replacement value" and that noneconomic damages were appropriate when there had been malicious and intentional acts.

The trial court, relying on *Economou v. Carpenter*,[178] a case involving the conversion of another's property, reached the conclusion that Vermont law did not permit emotional distress claims for property loss, including the death of a pet dog. On appeal, the plaintiffs sought to extend the Vermont common law or the creation of a new common law cause of action for malicious injury to a pet dog. The plaintiffs also argued that the state's wrongful death law should not be interpreted to bar a loss of companionship claim with regard to a dog.

This matter came on before the Vermont Supreme Court following a determination by the superior court. Perhaps lacking gumption, the Vermont Supreme Court followed the "majority of jurisdictions," which "traditionally viewed animals, including pets, as a form of personal property, and this treatment continues up to the present." Despite traditional views about property, the supreme court conceded that the state had animal protection laws, and that property laws involving inanimate objects and pets differ, in part because the law imposed legal controls regarding pets.

The supreme court blamed its decision on the plaintiffs, observing that the plaintiffs had characterized Shadow as property in their brief when the court said, "Plaintiffs recognize as much in their brief, characterizing this cause of action as 'one for destruction of property.'"

The court justified its actions, and looked back to its own decisions, in sentimental language reminiscent of its own in *Morgan v. Kroupa*,[179] where the court said, "We have noted in the past that categorizing a beloved pet as mere property fails to recognize that an animal's 'worth is not primarily financial[;] . . . its value derives from the animal's relationship with its human companions.'" It is puzzling why courts use language such as "beloved pet" or "mourning pet owner," or concepts such as the "emotionless economic calculus of property law," when avoiding using their imagination and talent for how to advance the rule of law.

The court followed the Vermont precedent in *Goodby v. Vetpharm, Inc.*,[180] a negligence case where two cats died because of mislabeled medication, although the instant case involved the intentional tort of shooting Shadow. The court failed to distinguish between negligent and intentional acts from a noneconomic damages perspective and suggested that rather than the plaintiffs seeking noneconomic damages when a family dog was involved, a punitive damages claim might have been preferable. The court emphasized that in 1877, the Vermont court had permitted punitive damages for "a suit resulting from the intentional and reckless killing of a hunting dog."

The supreme court seemed fired up about what damages the court might have awarded if the plaintiffs had not waived their "initial prayer for punitive or exemplary damages by omitting the claim from the stipulation and not appealing this presumed waiver" and belittled the plaintiffs' "tactical decision." The court also suggested that it would afford more relief for the loss of a hunting dog than a family pet and described

178. 124 Vt. 451, 453–54, 207 A.2d 241, 243 (1965).
179. 167 Vt. 99, 103, 702 A.2d 630, 633 (1997).
180. 2009 Vt. 52, 7, 186 Vt. 63, 974 A.2d 1269 (Vt. 2009).

the slippery slope of permitting claims regarding the loss of friends, relatives, work animals, heirlooms, and mementos.

The Vermont court finally suggested a pro-pet allegiance in its holding when the court said, "In holding with the traditional view that the law recognizes animals as a type of property, we are not blind to the special place they hold in our lives. Indeed, pets occupy a legal realm somewhere between chattel and children."[181] This last sentence is worthy of repetition: "Indeed, pets occupy a legal realm somewhere between chattel and children."

Scheele is a good example of how courts will reach back a few centuries or across state lines to figure out where pets belong in American jurisprudence. The court limited the value of a family pet to economic value, even though the plaintiffs argued that Shadow's value was not "merely financial"[182] and said that punitive damages were not warranted.[183] The court seemed to try too hard to convince the reader that what the court had achieved was a just result notwithstanding strong misgivings. As other courts have done before, this court looked to the legislature to right wrongs.[184]

In dealing with companion animals, it seems that both humans and jurists swing between denying and embracing them. From a moral relativism standpoint, the court was aware that American culture will not accept the deliberate killing of a nonthreatening family pet. Thus, after conceding that "pets occupy a realm somewhere between chattel and children," what stopped the court from fashioning a loss of companionship common law claim for Shadow?[185]

The reader is reminded that other laws regarding wrongful death change with the times.[186] Where wrongful death claims for children were once prohibited, they are now lawful under statute. The inclusion of family pets in wrongful death or loss of companionship statutes and common laws can evolve, too.

Practice Pointer: Courts that award noneconomic damages and punitive damages in cases where animals have been cruelly treated may be more likely to advance the best interests of animals in a pet custody dispute. The focus of attention in a punitive damages determination is on the behavior of the defendant, not the subject of the harm. In a similar way, maltreatment of the family pet could be emphasized.

---

181. In the midst of a traditional decision, the court did something remarkable. The court is now conceptualizing animals as being in an interim category between property and person. Nationally, this is significant dicta.

182. How might this idea of "merely financial" or "not merely financial" be explored in a family law context? Begin with the concept of the "real worth" of a family pet. Once an animal has entered the family circle, financial value may be overshadowed by relational value. From a moral standpoint, putting a relational value on a divorce balance sheet seems indecorous, although some courts may prefer using a balance sheet entry to placate the other party. A more enlightened approach would be for the court to give considerable weight to best-interest conceptions.

183. Other courts have used outrageous facts to pave the way for a tort of outrage.

184. *See* Rabideau v. City of Racine, 243 Wis. 2d 486, 627 N.W.2d 795 (Wis. 2001).

185. One wonders if courts can be moral agents who know right from wrong.

186. John Fabian Witt, *From Loss of Services to Loss of Support: The Wrongful Death Statutes, the Origins of Modern Tort Law, and the Making of the Nineteenth-Century Family*, http://digitalcommons.law.yale.edu/fss_papers/397/ (last visited May 12, 2016).

DAMIANO V. LIND[187]

Year: *2011*
Category: *Tort Law*
Type of Action: *Negligence*
Animal: *Cat*
Pet Custody Concept: *Advance relevant facts as best you can.*

The Damianos' cat, Boo, was outside during the early morning hours. When Jill Damiano heard meowing coming from her neighbor's property, she thought her cat was trapped in her neighbor's garage. When she contacted her neighbor, Jon Lind, about her missing cat, he turned beet red, appeared sweaty and agitated, and stammered that he had not seen the cat, although Lind did disclose that he had set a trap near his deck.

The same morning that Boo disappeared, Lind provided a voluntary witness statement to the police that he had trapped a feral dark-colored cat in the early morning hours. According to the police officer, "Jon Lind admitted to me that he trapped the Damianos' cat, Boo, but did not know it was their cat until later that morning, after he allegedly released Boo and spoke to Mrs. Damiano."

Boo's owners extensively searched for him, to no avail. They later sought recovery against Lind based upon the emerging tort of outrage as well as claims of "bailment, negligence, malicious injury to a pet,[188] trespass to chattels, conversion, outrage, gross negligence, and fraud." Lind prevailed in a summary judgment action where the court found no evidence of an injury to their cat.

The Damianos asserted that Lind had a duty of care to reunite a lost trapped pet with the pet's owner, or at least had a duty not to harm, kill, or abandon an animal in violation of state laws pertaining to animal cruelty and pet taking. The court found a cause of action in negligence under statute or common law wanting.

The court said that conversion was "the act of willfully interfering with any chattel, without lawful justification, whereby any person entitled thereto is deprived of the possession of it," and wrongful intent is "not an element of conversion, and good faith is not a defense."[189] The court further stated that "neither good nor bad faith, neither care nor negligence, neither knowledge nor ignorance, are of the gist of the action [in conversion]." Trespass to chattels, less than a conversion, meant "the intentional interference with a party's personal property without justification that deprives the owner of possession or use. While a plaintiff must show that the interference was intentional, no intent to deprive the owner must be shown."

Based upon *Lincecum v. Smith*,[190] the court determined that the Damianos' conversion claim was not dependent upon a finder's law. Even so, to meet the evidentiary threshold established in *Lincecum*, the Damianos must prove "an intentional

187. 163 Wash. App. 1017, not reported in P.3d (2011).

188. Under *Womack v. Von Rardon*, 133 Wash. App. 254, 263, 135 P.3d 542 (2006), malicious injury could be a stand-alone cause of action.

189. In *Womack*, the plaintiff suffered emotional distress when her cat was set on fire. In the instant case, the court could not conclude that a malicious injury had occurred.

190. 287 So. 2d 625, 627 (La. Ct. App. 1973).

interference with a party's personal property without justification, depriving the owner of possession or use." As the Damianos properly raised a question of fact as to whether Lind willfully or intentionally interfered with their possession of Boo, the court held that they had raised a question of fact not appropriate for summary judgment. This meant that the plaintiffs could proceed with this claim.[191] The Damianos were also able to establish facts sufficient to raise material issues as to both their conversion and trespass to chattels claims.

With regard to the tort of outrage claim, the court reviewed the necessary elements. They are: "(1) extreme and outrageous conduct, (2) intentional or reckless infliction of emotional distress, and (3) actual result to the plaintiff of severe emotional distress."[192] The court concluded that the Damianos had failed to provide sufficient evidence to proceed with a tort of outrage claim.

The Damianos argued that Lind's failure to notify them that he had trapped a cat the morning that Boo had disappeared rose to the level of gross negligence rather than ordinary negligence. The Damianos asserted that Lind's behavior when Ms. Damiano inquired about her cat constituted fraud. The court of appeals said, "The Linds assert that Ms. Damiano had no right to rely on any purported statement made by Mr. Lind. Here, Ms. Damiano heard Boo's meows on the Linds' property and Boo had not returned home. Ms. Damiano had a right to rely on the statement made by Mr. Lind that he had not seen a cat. The court erred by dismissing the fraud claim."

Notwithstanding the earlier summary judgment determination by the court, the Damianos were able to proceed with the claims of trespass to chattels, conversion, and fraud, and remanded the case for trial. The Damianos' lawyer showed tenacity in a case where most lawyers might have felt they lacked the rudimentary evidence to proceed, such as the deceased body of Boo.

Practice Pointer: Assume that with the right facts and hard work, some courts will find a way to grant a party relief, advance the rule of law, or give the plaintiffs the chance to prove their case. In a similar way, strive in family court to get your case heard.

---

191. The court also ruled that although Lind claimed that he had set a trap for a public nuisance, mainly skunks, the court observed that a license was required to trap fur-bearing animals.

192. *See* Reid v. Pierce County, 136 Wash. 2d 195, 202, 961 P.2d 333 (1998).

Medura v. Town & Country Veterinary Associates, P.C.[193]

Year: *2012*
Category: *Tort Law*
Type of Action: *Negligence*
Animal: *Cat*
Pet Custody Concept: *Courts are beginning to realize that a pet's relational value exceeds the animal's economic value.*

The plaintiff brought an otherwise healthy nine-year-old cat into a veterinarian because the cat suffered from occasional lameness in one leg. Test results showed the cat had normal renal and liver functions. Although a variety of veterinary services were initially recommended, it was later determined that the surgeries, including tooth extractions, were unnecessary.

The veterinarian prescribed an antibiotic for the cat as well as an anti-inflammatory drug called Metacam. While not saying that the veterinarian failed to gain "informed consent" from the cat's owner,[194] the court said the owner was not told of symptoms or side effects caused by the drug. The cat slowly deteriorated in her owner's care over the next year and a half and ultimately died of acute renal failure.

After her cat's death, the owner proceeded with a summons and writ against the hospital and two veterinarians. She alleged negligent treatment, intentional misrepresentations about safe drug use, and negligent supervision. She sought damages attributable to emotional distress and restitution for her expenditures. The defendants made a motion to strike specific paragraphs in the plaintiff's prayer for relief.

The court considered other cases where similar issues had been raised. In *Myers v. City of Hartford*,[195] a Poodle was euthanized by animal control even though the owner had timely come forward to pick up the dog. The court, while not allowing recovery in that case, pointed out that the Poodle's owner was not a bystander when her dog perished.[196] The *Myers* court said, "Most significantly, claims for infliction of emotional distress are unavailable for the loss of a child or spouse, except when the bereaved is a bystander. Because our common law has not extended the right to sue for damages for the deprivation of such close human relationships when the plaintiff has not witnessed the fatal injury, it would be incongruous to extend it to emotional distress resulting to a person from the loss of a pet." The court in the instant case, too, considered whether the bereaved was a bystander and determined that she was not.

Despite determining that the cat's owner had "no familial connection" to her cat, the higher court seemed resolute in its recognition that the cat had relational value. While not going as far as establishing a "familial connection," the court said that "Myers

193. A.3d, 2012 WL 3871953 (Conn. Super.), 54 Conn. L. Rptr. 483.

194. Jennifer Fiala, *AVMA Redrafts Informed Consent: Rewrite Protects DVMs against Comparisons to Human Medicine, Officials Say*, DVM 360, http://veterinarynews.dvm360.com/dvm/Veterinary+news/AVMA-redrafts-informed-consent/ArticleStandard/Article/detail/479036 (last visited May 12, 2016).

195. 84 Conn. App. 395, 853 A.2d 621, *cert. denied*, 271 Conn. 927, 859 A.2d 582 (2004).

196. This is a zone of danger type of finding.

did not expressly foreclose a claim of severe emotional distress suffered by a bystanding owner who witnesses the fatal injury to a pet . . . the pet owner holds the status of a foreseeable victim of bystander emotional distress."

Rather than making a claim for negligent infliction of emotional distress, the plaintiff sought noneconomic damages in her prayer for relief. The court, while finding the two approaches comparable, thought the more important question was whether bystander liability could attach in a medical malpractice claim and, after reviewing the case law, determined that it could not.

The court, looking at a controlling precedent in *Maloney v. Conroy*,[197] said, "No matter how one reads *Maloney*, the same incongruity noted in *Myers*, that allowing recovery for loss of a pet but not a person, would be present here as well if the court ruled in the alternative." Accordingly, the court determined that allowing for a "plaintiff to recover damages for emotional distress due to the alleged malpractice of a veterinarian that resulted in the loss of a pet, but not allow recovery for a person to recover for emotional distress damages due to the alleged malpractice of the injured party's treating physician would defy common sense."

What was interesting about this discussion was that damages for the dead cat's owner were comfortably explored in the context of a comparable situation involving a human relative. There was no hint of the cat being an inanimate object, such as a sofa or a lamp, or even "mere" property. Thinking of *Hamlet*, it was evident that this court could differentiate "a hawk from a handsaw."[198]

Although the court did not allow the cat owner damages superior to what would apply to a human loss, the higher court embraced the plaintiff's restitution claim. A restitution claim allows a party to disgorge benefits that would be unjust for the other party to keep.[199]

This case told the story of an owner's dedication for one and a half years to her dying cat. It also makes one wonder whether the relational awareness the court demonstrated in *Medura* would be transferrable to family court. *Medura* represents the growing body of jurisprudence where an animal's relational value is understood.

Practice Pointer: This unpublished decision was extraordinary. Here are a few examples of the court's noteworthy vernacular:

- "nine-year-old cat"
- "cat's death"
- "the cat died"

---

197. 208 Conn. 392, 393, 545 A.2d 1059 (1988).

198. This is a Shakespearian phrase related to the ability to tell two things apart. *No Fear Shakespeare*, HAMLET, http://nfs.sparknotes.com/hamlet/page_116.html (last visited May 12, 2016).

199. The court distinguished between restitution based upon the common law principles of quantum meruit and unjust enrichment. Quantum meruit was described as an implied contract remedy typically related to the benefit of work and labor services received by the party unjustly enriched. In contrast to a quantum meruit claim, an unjust enrichment claim applies when there is no remedy available based upon a contract. Lack of remedy under contract is a precondition to either type of restitution claim. The court considered this type of factual determination to be within the province of the trier of fact.

- "the death of a pet"
- "the slow death of her cat over the course of a year and a half"
- "injury to such property as a pet"
- "labeling a pet as property fails to describe the emotional value human beings place on the companionship that they enjoy with such an animal"
- "although dogs are considered property, this term inadequately and inaccurately describes the relationship between an individual and his or her pet"
- "kill his pet dog"
- "the intrinsic value of the emotional attachment between a pet owner and his or her living, breathing animal"
- "witnesses the fatal injury to a pet"
- "the pet owner holds the status of a foreseeable victim of bystander emotional distress"
- "a human has no familial connection to a cat"
- "plaintiff had a close relationship with her pet"
- "her pet's passing is most unfortunate and tragic"

Tracey v. Solesky[200]

Year: *2012*
Category: *Tort Law*
Type of Action: *Negligence*
Animal: *Dog*
Pet Custody Concept: *Courts may apply nonscientific standards to breed identification.*

This was a very lengthy landmark decision that should be read in historic perspective. It centered on an important and contentiously debated label: Pit Bulls. Why is there such a fuss about Pit Bulls? They are often associated with news headlines when a child is maimed or killed. Few realize that many dogs identified as Pit Bulls are not in fact dogs of that breed; eyewitness misidentification is a common problem.[201]

This decision impacted not only Pit Bulls, but also other dogs the court deems or may deem are vicious. The court abandoned its one free bite doctrine for dogs, joining

200. A.3d, 2012 WL 1432263 (Md. 2012). Since this decision, the supreme court in *Tracey v. Solesky*, 427 Md. 627 (Md. 2012) determined that the decision applied to Pit Bulls, not Pit Bull mixes.

201. The chorus of pro-Pit Bull advocacy has discernable roots. Following Hurricane Katrina, many people lost what they believed were their Pit Bulls or Pit Bull mixes and went to extraordinary lengths to find them, and those who adopted Katrina dogs often became bonded to bully breeds, making them true believers about the positive traits of these dogs. Even Pit Bulls subject to the worst conditions imaginable at the Bad Newz Kennel operated by National Football League star Michael Vick have been rehabilitated in the hands of the kind people at Best Friends Animal Society. For all these reasons and more, a significant number of lawyers, veterinarians, and nonprofits in the United States are committed to due process and fairness for Pit Bulls and other bully breeds. The issues raised in *Tracey* are similar to other types of litigation involving profiling, which means judging a book by its cover.

an ever-growing host of states applying strict liability to any bite. This decision impacted prior case law on landlord liability and will influence leasehold no-pets policies.[202]

The court discussed the history in Maryland of "seven instances of severe maulings by Pit Bulls."[203] The focus of this discussion was on a dog named Clifford, who escaped from his pen. Once loose, he crossed the street, attacked a ten-year-old boy, and would not let him go. A witness who observed the incident killed Clifford. The court said Clifford "attacked at least two boys at different times on the same day" and emphasized the life-threatening injuries sustained by one of the boys, who needed multiple surgeries and long-term rehabilitation.

The plaintiff advanced a common law negligence theory against the landlord for the building where Clifford lived. The trial court granted judgment for the defendant landlord, stating that there was insufficient evidence to allow the common law negligence claim to be presented to the jury. The court of special appeals reversed the decision, as "the evidence had been sufficient to create a valid jury issue as to the extent of the landlord's knowledge as to Clifford's dangerousness in respect to the then common law standards in dog negligence cases."

The following questions were addressed on appeal:

1. Is the harboring of American Staffordshire Terriers (more commonly known as "Pit Bulls") by tenants an inherently dangerous activity for which landlords may be held strictly liable?
2. Does Maryland jurisprudence permit an inference of knowledge of prior vicious propensities of a domestic animal by a landlord based upon the existence of an exculpatory clause in a residential lease concerning bodily injury caused by the tenant's pets?[204]
3. Does Maryland jurisprudence permit an inference of knowledge of prior vicious propensities of a domestic animal by a landlord whose tenant harbors the animal in leased premises based upon the subjective conclusions as to the animal's temperament of neighbors who have limited observations of the animal's behavior which was never conveyed to the landlord?
4. May a landlord be held liable for injuries caused by a tenant's domestic animal due to the failure to require reasonable confinement of a domestic animal in the leased premises?

---

202. An important prior case on landlord liability was *Matthews v. Amberwood Associates Ltd. P'ships, Inc.*, 351 Md. 544 (1998). There, Pit Bulls were portrayed as having massive jaws that can crush a victim with 2,000 pounds of pressure per square inch. The court also observed how preventing future harm is quite important in the field of torts.

203. According to the court of appeals, in the 13 years prior to this case, there were seven severe Pit Bull "maulings" in Maryland, including the two boys in this case. The court reviewed the facts of all seven cases.

204. Be aware of contractual risk allocation. *See* Marie A. Moore, *Indemnification Provisions in Leases: What We Ask For and What Really Matters*, Probate & Property Magazine, http://www.americanbar.org/publications/probate_property_magazine_home/rppt_publications_magazine_2008_so_Moore.html (last visited May 15, 2017).

5. Should landlords that allow tenants to harbor dangerous or vicious animals in the leased premises be held liable in tort under any circumstances when the tenant fails to properly control its pet?
6. Should this Court's prior rulings in *Matthews v. Amberwood Associates Ltd. P'ship, Inc.*, 351 Md. 544 (1998) and *Shields v. Wagman*, 350 Md. 666 (1998) be overturned or significantly modified?

In its decision, the court of appeals said, "We answer appellant's first question in the affirmative and establish in this case, and prospectively, a strict liability standard in respect to the owning, harboring or control of Pit Bulls and cross-bred Pit Bulls in lieu of the traditional common law liability principles that were previously applicable to attacks by such dogs."[205] The court went on to state, "We are modifying the Maryland common law of liability as it relates to attacks by Pit Bull and cross-bred Pit Bull dogs against humans. With the standard we establish today (which is to be applied in this case on remand), when an owner or a landlord is proven to have knowledge of the presence of a Pit Bull or cross-bred Pit Bull (as both the owner and landlord did in this case) or should have had such knowledge, a prima facie case is established." There was also discussion of the court's ability to modify the common law "without the aid of a statute."

The court relied on *Mayor & City Council of Baltimore, et al. v. Clark*[206] for its "authority to change the common law." In that case, the court presented an overview for modifying common law rules as follows:

> The determination of the nature of the common law as it existed in England in 1776, and as it then prevailed in Maryland either practically or potentially, and the determination of what part of the common law is consistent with the spirit of Maryland's Constitution and her political institutions, are to be made by this Court. "Whether particular parts of the common law are applicable to our local circumstances and situation, and our general code of laws and jurisprudence, is a question that comes within the province of the Courts of Justice, and is to be decided by them. The common law, like our Acts of Assembly, are subject to control and modification of the Legislature, and may be abrogated, or changed as the General Assembly may think most conducive to the general welfare; so that no great inconvenience, if any, can result from the power deposited with the judiciary to decide what the common law is, and its applicability to the circumstances of the State, and what has become obsolete from non-user or other cause. *State v. Buchanan*, 5 H. & J. 317, 365–66 (1821)." Because of the inherent dynamism of the common law, we have consistently held that it is subject to judicial modification in the light of modern circumstances or increased knowledge.[207]

205. As stated in an earlier footnote, this decision was subsequently modified by the Maryland Supreme Court decision *Tracey v. Solesky*, 427 Md. 627 (Md. 2012), where the strict liability was limited to Pit Bulls, but not cross-bred Pit Bulls.

206. 404 Md. 13, 944 A.2d 1122 (2008).

207. Modern circumstances or increased knowledge would reflect, culturally, that companion animals are now in an interim category.

The court further emphasized the right of the judiciary to enter into a public policy debate where the legislature had failed to provide guidance on how the court should exercise its considerable discretion.[208] The court relied on *Polakoff v. Turner*[209] for the proposition that changes in the common law could be applied prospectively, as well as to the case triggering the change in the common law. The court described an article from *Annals of Surgery* titled "Mortality, Mauling, and Maiming by Vicious Dogs" wherein attacks by Pit Bulls were associated with higher morbidity rates, higher hospital charges, and more risk of death than attacks by other breeds. The court deduced that "strict regulation of pit bulls may substantially reduce the US mortality rates related to dog bites."

While the lower court relied on a statement attributed to the Centers for Disease Control (CDC) that "laws for regulating dangerous or vicious dogs should be promulgated and enforced vigorously," the higher court admitted that the CDC had not recommended breed-specific regulations.[210] Even so, further demonizing the Pit Bull, the court pointed to a disciplinary action in Florida resulting from two lawyers displaying the words "Pit Bull" in a television ad for their services.[211]

The court stated, "At least the following states have some form of strict liability statute in which the finding of dangerousness of the particular attacking dog is not necessary to establish the elements of negligence." These states were Arizona, Connecticut, Florida, Illinois, Iowa, Nebraska, New Jersey, Ohio, Oklahoma, and Wisconsin.[212]

Although it is assumed that the court was aware that through the utilization of DNA testing, which meant that Clifford's genetic origins could be identified, this court showed no interest in a science-based classification when it said,

> We hold that upon a plaintiff's sufficient proof that a dog involved in an attack is a Pit Bull or a Pit Bull mix, and that the owner, or other person(s) who has the right to control the Pit Bull's presence on the subject premises (including a landlord who has the right and/or opportunity to prohibit such dogs on leased premises as in this case) knows, or has reason to know, that the dog is a Pit Bull or cross-bred Pit Bull mix, that person is strictly liable for the damages caused to a plaintiff who is attacked by the dog on or from the owner's or lessor's premises. This holding is prospective and applies to this case and causes

---

208. Except for the state of Alaska, family courts have received no legislative guidance for how to make a custody decision about a companion animal.

209. 385 Md. 467, 484, 869 A.2d 837, 850 (2005).

210. The court also mentioned several criminal cases where Pit Bulls were used as dangerous weapons and emphasized the landmark decision by the Ohio Supreme Court ruling in *Toledo v. Tellings*, 114 Ohio St. 3d 278, 871 N.E.2d 1152 (2007), which upheld *Toledo*'s breed-specific regulations and reversed the judgment of the court of appeals that held that three laws were unconstitutional. The judgment of the *Toledo v. Tellings* court of appeals, 2006 WL 513946 (Ohio App. 6 Dist.) is worth reading, not only because it is a careful and well-crafted decision, but also because the court addresses expert witness testimony and how some statistics are not reliable and represent "bare statistics." The use of bare statistics impacts the misreporting about Pit Bull behavior.

211. There was no mention of the positive experiences by those who lost their Pit Bulls in Hurricane Katrina or those who saved them. The pro-Pit Bull position was merely described as constitutional issues "raised by Pit Bull advocates."

212. The court continued by saying that California, South Carolina, and the District of Columbia might be going in that direction, too. The court also stated that some local animal control laws are breed specific.

> of action accruing after the date of the filing of this opinion. Upon remand to the trial court, it shall apply in this case the modifications to the common law herein created.[213]

The other issues addressed in the appeal, though listed, are not included here. The dissent began by saying, "Today, the majority holds that a Pit Bull or any dog with a trace of Pit Bull ancestry (determined by what means the majority opinion leaves us entirely in the dark) shall be deemed hence forth vicious and inherently dangerous as a matter of law." The dissent alleged, "The majority transforms a clear factual question into a legal one in an effort to create liability," and then asserted that the majority "only compounds the problem created, driven by its apparent desire to reach a particular result in this case. Succumbing to the allure of bad facts leads inevitably to the development of bad law."

The dissent continued by saying, "Until today, the common law in Maryland was that the owner or keeper of a dog or other domestic animal would be held strictly liable for injuries caused by that animal, provided the plaintiff could show that the owner or keeper 'had knowledge of [the animal's] disposition to commit such injury,'" and added, "until today, a landlord would be held liable to a third party for an attack by a tenant's animal where the landlord had knowledge of the animal's presence on the leased premises and knowledge of its vicious propensities, and maintained control over the leased premises."

In contrast to the cases emphasized by the majority, the dissent highlighted the holding in *McDonald v. Burgess*,[214] where the court determined that "the mere fact that the dog in question belonged to a specific breed, which 'can and often does behave in a very vicious manner,' was insufficient to hold the owner legally responsible for his German Shepherd attacking another person." There was no showing that the German Shepherd was known to have a violent nature or that the Shepherd's owner "knew, or by the exercise of ordinary care should have known, of the dog's inclination or propensity to do the particular mischief that was the cause of the harm."

With regard to the modification of the common law, the dissent described the rule of stare decisis, which "promotes the evenhanded, predictable, and consistent development of legal principles, fosters reliance on judicial decisions, and contributes to the actual and perceived integrity of the judicial process." Accordingly, the dissent advocated for restraint in the modification of the common law.

Perhaps the dissent's more compelling argument was that "there is no good reason to modify the common law in this case." Criticizing the majority for relying on a report from the *Journal of the American Veterinary Medical Association* without disclosing that the American Veterinary Medical Association (AVMA) opposed strict liability for Pit Bulls, he pointed out that instead, the AVMA recommended "the consideration of factors completely unrelated to the breed or appearance of dogs, including their socialization, training, size, sex, and reproductive status."

---

213. Beware, dog owners, that although it is the Pit Bull today, the legislature or the court itself could deem another type of dog vicious tomorrow. Homeowner's policies are expanding breeds of dogs excluded from their policies, too.

214. 254 Md. 452, 458, 255 A.2d 299, 302 (1969).

The dissent further described how dog bite data can be misleading rather than provide an actual portrayal of dogs that bite. To understand dog behavior, he advocated that the better approach would be to examine "the owner's behavior, sterilization, socialization, supervision, breeding practices, educational outreach to potential dog owners, and screening of potential owners." Complaining that breed-specific rules were inferior, he said that behavior modification was "a better approach to controlling the problem of dog bites."

The dissent emphasized that at least 25 breeds of dogs were mistaken for Pit Bulls. The dissent briefly discussed the application of the Constitution's Due Process Clause, and the right of state legislation to exercise police power and highlighted the tenuous connection between a dog's appearance and a dog's actual breed, relying on the work of DNA expert Victoria L. Voith.[215]

Practice Pointer: Courts seem to be widening the net about just who could be liable for injuries caused by a Pit Bull, and no one knows which larger or bully breeds will be caught in the next net. If you have pet custody cases, be familiar with all the arguments advanced by the majority and dissent in this case, particularly when contemplating a joint custody or access plan for a Pit Bull or other type of dog that others might view as vicious. Recommend that your clients address liability responsibility and insurance obligations in whatever agreement is worked out.

Carefully review cases, such as the instant case, for arguments to utilize in a completely different context. In *Tracey*, the court cited *Matthews*, another tort case, for the proposition that the court had an important role not only with compensation but also with "the admonition of a wrongdoer." Ideas about wrongdoers could apply in family court no-fault divorces if the fault pertained to the maltreatment of a companion animal in an interim category. When thinking about the majority's description of its authority to modify obsolete common laws, it seems that advocacy about better decision-making criteria in cases involving a family pet would be a good place to start.

---

215. Victoria L. Voith, *Shelter Medicine: A Comparison of Visual and DNA Identification of Breeds of Dogs*, Proceedings of Annual AVMA Convention (July 11–14, 2009), http://www.nathanwinograd.com/linked/misbreed.pdf (finding that there is discrepancy between breed determination based upon physical attributes and scientific determinations) (last visited May 12, 2016).

STRICKLAND V. MEDLEN[216]

Year: *2013*
Category: *Tort Law*
Type of Action: *Sentimental Loss*
Animal: *Dog*
Pet Custody Concept: *Courts sometimes do not know whether they are coming or going and may be unable to distinguish animal-friendly perspectives from the other kind.*

Once in a while, a court decision registers as uniquely offensive. Such is this decision. What made this case particularly disturbing was the emotional salvos offered by the court about how "Texans love their dogs" in this "Lone Star State." The court's opinion started with this and other sentimental references about dogs, as if to hide the implications of this decision behind the facade of good will.

In the first paragraph of its opinion, the court began, "Even the gruffest among us tears up (every time) at the end of *Old Yeller*." If Justice Don Willett, who authored this opinion, was providing his personal perspective on what makes him cry, it seems fair game to ask why he is indifferent to the concept of noneconomic damages for the loss of companionship. He justified the award of damages when sentimental loss was involved for an inanimate object, such as a family heirloom, but drew the line at living property, writing his opinion as if to convince others that this was rational behavior.

In *Strickland*, animal control picked up a loose mixed breed dog named Avery. Although the owner timely went to claim the dog at the shelter, he lacked sufficient funds that day for Avery's release. The shelter hung a "hold for owner" tag on Avery's cage to "alert employees that the Medlens were coming for Avery." Notwithstanding this tag, "worker Carla Strickland mistakenly placed Avery on the euthanasia list, and he was put to sleep."

It is worthwhile to pause and examine the choice of words here, "mistakenly" and "put to sleep." Why was "mistakenly" used rather than "negligently?" When an employee ignores a hold tag that results in a pet's untimely death, why is the softer language "put to sleep" used? This is typical of language used with regard to animals that masks what is really being done—the court was signaling the denial of any recourse for Avery's owners. For example, the court did not specify whether Avery was put to sleep by carbon monoxide—a practice only very recently banned in Texas[217]—shot in the head, or euthanized by lethal injection.

The court used contradictory terminology regarding compassion for companion animals and indifference to their relational value when juxtaposed against the holding of this case. The confusing parade of phrases and words used by the court included the following:

- "cherished dog"
- "heartsick owner's heartfelt affection"

216. 397 S.W.3d 184, 185 (Tex. 2013).
217. Alana Rocha, *New Animal Law Is Welcome, But, at the Outset, Expensive*, N.Y. Times, http://www.nytimes.com/2013/05/31/us/new-texas-animal-euthanasia-law-is-welcome-but-expensive.html?_r=1& (last visited May 12, 2016).

- "bereaved dog owner"
- "relational attachment is unquestionable"
- "pets are property in the eyes of the law"
- "owner's subjective feelings"
- "a beloved companion animal is not a fungible, inanimate object like, say, a toaster"
- "the term 'property' is not a pejorative"
- "pet-death cases"
- "American pets now outnumber American children"
- "animal owners view their pets not as mere personal property but as full-fledged family members, and treat them as such"
- "70% of pet owners thought of their pets as family members"
- "50% of pet owners report being 'very likely' to put their own lives in danger to save their pets"
- "Americans spent roughly $53 billion on their pets"
- "the human-animal bond is indeed powerful"
- "Texas families share this pets-as-family view"

Although Justice Willett stated that he and other Texans view "pets-as-family," Willett himself seemed to prefer the "pets-as-property" classification, as evidenced by his ultimate failure to advance their place in our culture. After all, he had the opportunity to champion a new common law vision, but instead he upheld a 19th-century precedent called the "true rule."

The court said, "We must decide whether to adhere to our restrictive, 122-year-old precedent classifying pets as property for tort-law purposes, or to instead recognize a new common-law loss-of-companionship claim." The latter would allow recovery of "non-economic damages rooted solely in emotional attachment," a remedy the court stressed that the "common law has denied those who suffer the wrongful death of a spouse, parent, or child, and is available in Texas only by statute."[218] The court of course was aware that when a human dies, economic damages are often significant, and when a companion animal dies, they rarely are. The court put a shine on its denial of a remedy for a wrong by cloaking its position with traditional verbiage. The court said, "under established legal doctrine, recovery in pet-death cases is, barring legislative reclassification, limited to loss of value, not loss of relationship."

When this case was initiated, Avery's owners brought claims based upon his sentimental or intrinsic value because this mixed breed dog lacked market value. Upon rejecting this cause of action, the trial court encouraged Avery's owners to "state a claim for damages recognized at law." When they amended their complaint to seek

218. The court was disingenuous by its failure to disclose that most humans have meaningful economic value, whereas most family pets do not. Thus, unless the court looks at the totality of economic damages and noneconomic damages in both human and animal companions, the conclusion reached will be obfuscated in the same way as the well-known phrase about lies, damn lies, and statistics.

only damages for Avery's intrinsic value, the trial court dismissed their suit "with prejudice."

It is noteworthy that the Texas Court of Appeals reversed the trial court's decision, which enabled the respondents to proceed with a loss-of-companionship damages claim. The appeals court observed that "Texas law has changed greatly since 1891," when the *Heiligmann v. Rose*[219] decision was made, saying, "sentimental damages may now be recovered for . . . all types of personal property." Reinstating the respondents' claim, the court of appeals justified its holding by explaining that because of "the special position pets hold in their family, we see no reason why existing law should not be interpreted to allow recovery in the loss of a pet at least to the same extent as any other personal property."

Returning to the mixed message sent by Supreme Court Justice Willett about companion animals, he berated the court of appeals' decision and accused the court of pivoting on the plain meaning of the 19th-century *Heiligmann* decision. It seemed that Willett took issue with the lower court's pronouncement that dogs' devotion to their owners was an "iron truth" or that owners' reciprocal and deep attachment to their "beloved family pets" was also an "iron truth."

Although it was hard to decipher exactly where Justice Willett differed from the appellate court in his own view about human and dog relationships given his sensitivity to *Old Yeller*, it was pellucid that he did not view *Heiligmann* as supporting the appellate court's view that existing law should be extended to allow for the "recovery in the loss of a pet at least to the same extent as any other personal property." He opposed emotional injury damages being recoverable for the "negligent destruction of a dog."

Championing the *Heiligmann* "true rule" as still good law, Justice Willett said, "we classified dogs as personal property for damages purposes, not as something giving rise to personal-injury damages" and "we declared a 'true rule' for damages." This true rule had two elements: "(1) market value, if the dog has any, or (2) some special or pecuniary value to the owner, that may be ascertained by reference to the usefulness and services of the dog."[220] All one needs to do is read the true rule to realize that it harkens back to agricultural times before companion animals were prized for their relational value. The true rule seems so false by today's cultural standards that it might better be called the "deceitful rule."

The high court had a predilection for numbers. *Heiligmann* was a "122-year-old precedent," and *Brown v. Frontier Theatres, Inc.*[221] was a "decision a half-century ago." These precedential decisions were made before DNA was discovered and before there was growing consensus in the veterinary community about animal sentience.[222] Although Justice Willett was aware, and even informed us, that "Americans spent roughly $53 billion on their pets" and there are "377 million pets," he seemed unable

219. 81 Tex. 222, 16 S.W. 931 (1891).

220. The Texas "true rule" of 1891 makes one recall the *Sentell v. New Orleans Carrollton Railroad Co.* Supreme Court decision a few decades before, where the court reasoned that a dog was only quasi-property unless "dead or subdued."

221. 369 S.W.2d 299 (Tex. 1963).

222. Seth Davis, *AAHA Position Statement Classifies Animals as Sentient Beings*, NEWSTAT, http://www.aahanet.org/blog/NewStat/post/2012/10/17/521946/AAHA-position-statement-classifies-animals-as-sentient-beings.aspx (last visited May 12, 2016).

to conceive that the truth about the real value of companion animals to their owners was quite extraordinary, objectively speaking. Data he carefully included in his own opinion reveals this.

Perhaps factual display should have signaled to the Texas Supreme Court that companion animals are no longer only being valued for their work or use, or based upon their replacement value, but for what really matters to people—their companionship and relational value. This is why people spend over $15 billion on veterinary bills each year to keep their animals healthy. Categorizing the value of animals at market value or adopting the *Heiligmann* "use" value as the primary way to value animals seemed disingenuous. It is worth saying again that in contrast to Justice Willett's worldview, the Texas Court of Appeals said, with regard to *Heiligmann,* "Texas law has changed greatly since 1891" and "sentimental damages may now be recovered for . . . all types of personal property."

Ultimately, the Supreme Court of Texas decided that the use of the word "special" did not mean the special damages that the court of appeals described. Furthermore, the court clarified that its objective economic determination was unrelated to a dog's "ability to combat loneliness, ease depression, or provide security." It seemed that Justice Willett was again criticizing the lower court for its valuation criteria being "emotional and subjective," whereas his valuation criteria were "commercial and objective."

Justice Willett, unable to perceive the subjectivity of his own reasoning, projected that it was the Texas Court of Appeals that was emotional and subjective. If the supreme court wanted to be objective, it could revisit why $53 billion was spent on 377 million pets annually. The Texas Supreme Court's application of an outdated true rule for tort law did not address how animals help, to use Justice Willett's own terminology, "to combat loneliness, ease depression, or provide security."

Stating that family heirlooms were irreplaceable and "have their primary value in sentiment," Justice Willett emphasized the distinction between old heirloom property and non-heirloom property. If the property was non-heirloom, the court would exclude "any fanciful or sentimental considerations."[223] The court reaffirmed the default damages rule for "destroyed non-heirloom property lacking market or replacement value: 'the actual worth or value of the articles to the owner . . . excluding any fanciful or sentimental considerations.'" The reductionist expression, "fanciful or sentimental considerations" deserves to be classified as cringeworthy for those 50 percent of pet owners who Justice Willett described as very likely to risk their own lives to save their pets.

Justice Willett discussed *Porras v. Craig,*[224] a case relied on by the respondents. The question in *Porras* was how damages would be determined when, without the permission of a landowner, several large trees were cleared. The court comprehended that the owner may have lost the enjoyment of his trees even if the removal increased the land's market value. The Texas Supreme Court understood that it was proper to determine the ornamental and aesthetic value of the trees, as well as their utility and

223. If the court can distinguish between heirloom and non-heirloom property, the court should also be able to further refine living and nonliving property conceptions.

224. 675 S.W.2d 503 (Tex. 1984).

shade value, saying, "That assessment concerning real property is not rooted in an owner's subjective emotions, as here." It is as if the court believed concepts such as beauty and emotion could be separated by simple word choices.

If the court's quote was taken literally, it was okay to have a sentimental attachment to an heirloom, and be compensated for that, and to have an objective injury for the aesthetic and shade value of a tree. In contrast, it seems that having a subjective emotion about standing trees would be problematic in Texas jurisprudence. The court declined to "expand *Porras*'s notion of 'intrinsic value' to animal cases." The court even explained that "*Porras* itself excluded such subjective notions." Why was the court so shy about the true value of companion animals?

Next, Justice Willett turned to *City of Tyler v. Likes*,[225] another decision relied on by the respondents. He said, "The principal issue was whether mental-anguish damages are recoverable for the negligent destruction of personal property." Willett said that the sentimental value rule for property, the type found in *Tyler* where their home was flooded, did not pertain to an improper personal injury type of damages argument in the instant case. The court specifically said that it would not extend *Brown*'s family heirlooms rule to negligently destroyed pets.

What was surprising about how the supreme court viewed its own analysis was that in denying sentimental value, the court seemed to believe that this position was consistent with the court's high esteem for companion animals. Justice Willett explained how an "owner's attachment to a beloved pet is more" than fondness for a one-of-a-kind heirloom. He offered how the human and animal relationship was "emotional, formed over time and based on the pet's specific attributes, namely the rich companionship it provides."

Justice Willett said the court relied heavily on the *Restatement (Third) of the Law of Torts*[226] for the proposition that emotion-based liability should be prohibited because this type of claim should only be used for personal injury claims, not property damage claims.[227] Notwithstanding the supreme court's personal injury versus property example, the flexibility in legal tests is well revealed in the fact that courts nationwide permit veterinary malpractice claims based upon the medical patient model. Justice Willett has made a self-serving argument that is outcome determinative on the subject of noneconomic damages.

Justice Willett described how the true rule applied in Texas. "Where a dog's market value is unascertainable, the correct damages measure is the dog's 'special or pecuniary value' (that is, its actual value)—the economic value derived from its 'usefulness and services,' not value drawn from companionship or other non-commercial considerations." Applying this rule to the instant case, the loss of Avery was not compensable.

The supreme court, in a public policy discussion, contemplated and identified entities and associations that filed briefs who economically profit from the use of

225. 962 S.W.2d 489 (Tex. 1998).

226. Differences between the *Restatement (Third) of Torts* and the *Restatement (Second) of Torts*, pertaining to liability for pets and heirlooms, is well addressed in the following: John L. Diamond, *Rethinking Compensation for Mental Distress: A Critique of the Restatement (Third)* §§ 45–47, 16 Va. J. Soc. Pol'y & L. 141 (2008).

227. As the case law in this book will reflect, the progression of pet law cases will reflect that companion animals have entered an interim category between property and personhood.

companion animals, and had a substantial financial stake in the lucrative pet business, including breeder groups and veterinarians. In contrast, the court was dismissive of the opinion of nonprofits and law professors who also submitted amicus briefs.

Justice Willett speculated about the unintended consequences of veterinarians needing to practice defensive medicine and also opined the probability that veterinary costs would increase.[228] As a consequence, families with limited resources would "be more apt to euthanize a pet."[229]

Regarding police powers, Justice Willett said, "The Texas Municipal League and other government associations worry about police officers and animal-service employees being second-guessed for split-second decisions they must make in the field when they encounter loose and potentially dangerous animals." Without any reference to sovereign or governmental immunity on the subject of potential liability, the court speculated that insurance costs would rise, and perhaps insurance would not even be available.[230] The court said, "When recognizing a new cause of action and the accompanying expansion of duty, we must perform something akin to a cost-benefit analysis to assure that this expansion of liability is justified."[231]

One might ask what the Texas court would do in the family court context, with its conflagration of pro-pet and pro-property perspectives. The court could be jealous of extending rights for human family members to four-legged family members. The court said, "For all their noble and praiseworthy qualities, dogs are not human beings, and the Texas common-law tort system should not prioritize human-animal relationships over intimate human-human relationships, particularly familial ones. Analogous would be anomalous."

Although the highest court in Texas was appalled by the idea of treating a companion animal as a child in the tort system, would a justice such as Willett give the pet any best-interest consideration in family court? It is hard to tell, among all the rhetoric here, if Justice Willett was indifferent to the best interests of companion animals or if he actually cared about them. When Willet concluded, "No one disputes that a family dog—'in life the firmest friend'—is a treasured companion," one might ask whether this was meaningful dicta or empty rhetoric.

Practice Pointer: The ultimate irony in *Strickland* was that in some ways, the dicta was ideal for the advancement of the best interests of companion animals in family law. If the Supreme Court of Texas meant what it said about the significance of the

228. The societal benefit of limiting noneconomic damages in veterinary malpractice cases is well articulated in *Noneconomic Damage Awards in Veterinary Malpractice: Using the Human Medical Experience as a Model to Predict the Effect of Noneconomic Damage Awards on the Practice of Companion Animal Veterinary Medicine* by Steve Barghusen, Animal Law Lewis & Clark Law School, reprinted from Animal Law Volume 17, Issue 1, copyright 2010. While veterinarians will appreciate Dr. Barghusen's arguments, family law and animal law lawyers may think that these same problems present across disciplines.

229. There are many factors affecting the need for costly veterinary services. They include unhealthy conformation standards and the failure to maintain humane standards in large confinement operations.

230. Christopher Green, *The Future of Veterinary Malpractice Liability in the Care of Companion Animals*, Michigan State University Animal Legal & Historical Center, http://www.animallaw.info/article/future-veterinary-malpractice-liability-care-companion-animals (last visited May 12, 2016).

231. Under a Tennessee statute, there is a ceiling and exclusions for companion animal torts.

human and dog relationship, it can be hoped that Texas common law will be revisited so that human and animal best interests and even subjective emotional attachments can be considered by the court when making pet custody awards. Justice Willett said that the "relationship" attachment was unquestionable and that "Texas families share this pets-as-family view." Even if his embrace of companion animals was equivocal, let's hold him to it.

Chapter 8

Animal Cruelty, Crimes, and the Constitution

> **"The essence of humanity's dilemma is that we evolved genetically to accept one truth and discovered another."**
>
> —*E.O. Wilson*

In 1641, an early American settlement called the Massachusetts Bay Colony passed a law called "Body of Liberties." According to this law, "No man shall exercise any Tyranny or Cruelty towards any bruit Creature which are usually kept for man's use."[1] In 1862, in *State v. Avery*,[2] a man was criminally charged for whipping a horse and inflicting pain.

Despite early and continuing views that animal cruelty should be circumscribed, the national government failed to track animal abuse until 2014,[3] when the Federal Bureau of Investigation (FBI) entered a separate category in its database

1. *The Massachusetts Body of Liberties*, Bartleby.com, http://www.bartleby.com/43/8.html (last visited May 12, 2016).
2. 44 N.H. 392.
3. The U.S. Department of Justice, Office of Justice Programs, Bureau of Justice Statistics, tracks violent and property crimes but does not include animal abuse in these categories. *FAQ, What Type of Crime Does NCVS Measure?*, U.S. Dep't of Justice, Office of Justice Programs, Bureau of Justice Statistics, http://bjs.ojp.usdoj.gov/index.cfm?ty=qa&iid=473 (last visited May 12, 2016). The FBI also tracks certain crimes but not animal abuse. *Uniform Crime Reports, UCR General FAQs*, Fed. Bureau of Investigation, https://www2.fbi.gov/ucr/ucr_general.html (last visited May 12, 2016). There are a few databases available online that purport to track animal abuse. *Through Their Eyes, the National Animal Abuse Registry*, Bella Dog Magazine, http://www.belladogmagazine.com/humane-hearts/377-through-their-eyes-the-national-animal-abuse-registry (last visited May 12, 2016); *Database of Criminal Animal Cruelty Cases*, Pet-Abuse.com, http://www.pet-abuse.com/pages/cruelty_database.php (last visited May 12, 2016).

for animal cruelty; this was an aspect of the FBI's Uniform Crime Report National Incident Based Reporting System. Law enforcement now provides the FBI with incident reports on four categories: simple or gross neglect; intentional abuse and torture; organized abuse, including dogfighting and cockfighting; and animal sexual abuse.[4] The FBI has announced that animal cruelty may be charged as a Group A felony, along with homicide and arson.

HUMAN AND ANIMAL ABUSE LINK

Many people are aware of the link between animal abuse and human abuse.[5] Serial killers often have a history of animal abuse;[6] the three major predictors of serial killers are animal cruelty, bed-wetting, and fire starting. The National Center for Prosecution of Animal Abuse (NCPAA),[7] part of the National District Attorneys Association, was created "in partnership with the American Society for the Prevention of Cruelty to Animals (ASPCA) and Animal Legal Defense Fund (ALDF) to educate and train prosecutors and allied professionals on the effective handling of animal cruelty and neglect cases, including cases involving the co-occurrence of animal abuse and violence to people."[8] Their mission is to make people aware of animal cruelty and to "bring greater awareness to the often misunderstood nature of animal maltreatment and how it can interconnect with family violence and contribute to lethality issues for victims of interpersonal violence."[9] Animal abuse in the home is a predictor of human abuse.

Although at first glance, the work of the NCPAA may seem unrelated to the role of family lawyers in a pet custody dispute, this entity focuses on the same types of issues that arise in cases where there is domestic abuse. One way a warning is communicated to a family member is by threats of violence against an animal. If you are approached about representing a client in a case where domestic abuse has occurred, always remember to ask animal-related questions, too. If there has been recent harm to an animal, under state cruelty laws, and with the help of the

4. Sue Manning, *FBI Makes Animal Cruelty a Top-Tier Felony*, Detroit Free Press, http://www.freep.com/story/news/nation/2014/10/01/fbi-makes-animal-cruelty-top-tier-felony/16528367/ (last visited May 12, 2016).

5. Joan E. Schaffner, *Linking Domestic Violence, Child Abuse, and Animal Cruelty*, Michigan State University Animal Legal & Historical Center, https://www.animallaw.info/article/linking-domestic-violence-child-abuse-and-animal-cruelty (last visited May 12, 2016).

6. Lorna Benson, *Animal Cruelty May Be Sign of Deeper Human Problems*, Minnesota Public Radio News, http://minnesota.publicradio.org/display/web/2006/07/06/animalkillers (last visited May 12, 2016).

7. Before animals could be crime victims, businesses, nonprofits, and unions could.

8. *National Center for Prosecution of Animal Abuse*, National District Attorneys Association, http://www.ndaa.org/animal_abuse_home.html (last visited May 12, 2016).

9. *Id.*

NCPAA, a charge could be made and the conditions of release for the offender could ensure an animal's safety.

STATE ANIMAL-RELATED REGULATIONS AND STATUTES

There is a broad spectrum of laws and regulations at the state or local level pertaining to animal cruelty, animal safety public health, commerce, animal health, public safety, natural resources, captive wildlife, harmful exotics, endangered and threatened species, licensed breeders and dealers, pound seizures, trespass, emergency management, commercial interests, animal welfare, and animal cruelty.

Laws and regulations may also pertain to agro terrorism, animal enterprise terrorism, hunting and hunter harassment, animal fighting, abuse, cruelty, lost or estray animals, animals at large, service animals, harm to service animals,[10] overworking, owner obligations, exposure, sanitation, restricted or exotic species, transport, loading, traffic, guardianship, nuisance, veterinary reporting, liens, quarantines, seizures, destruction, humane killings, animals as prizes, and animals causing damage or injury.

ANIMAL SEX OFFENDERS

Another aspect of this subject is the number of registries with regard to sex offenders. While the state of Michigan once required that repeat animal offenders be listed under the state's Sex Offenders Registration Act, the Michigan Court of Appeals later determined that animals could not be victims of sex crimes under the state's law given the plain meaning of the word "victim."[11] This same "victim" problem came before the court six years later in *State v. Nix*,[12] a decision where the Supreme Court of Oregon found that animals were victims in a case involving cruelty to horses and goats.[13] Although the Oregon Supreme Court's decision in *Nix* was later vacated based upon a jurisdictional issue, the Oregon Court of Appeals reaffirmed this court's "animal as crime victim" approach in *State v. Hess*,[14] a case involving cat hoarding.

---

10. Bills are pending regarding making false claims about an animal being a service animal.
11. *See* People v. Haynes Michigan, 760 N.W.2d 283 (Mich. App. 2008).
12. 355 Or. 777, 334 P.3d 437 (2014), *vacated*, 356 Ore. 768, 345 P.3d 416 (2015).
13. In *Nix*, there was no allegation of sex with animals. *See* State v. Fessenden, 355 Or. 759 (Or. 2014) and State v. Hess, 359 P.3d 288 (Or. Ct. App. 2015).
14. 359 P.3d 288 (Or. Ct. App. 2015).

BESTIALITY

Bestiality is a form of animal cruelty. Laws on this subject are progressing swiftly. More than 40 states have laws that address sexual conduct between humans and animals.[15] The states that still lack these laws are Hawaii, Kentucky, Nevada, New Mexico, Ohio, Texas, Vermont, West Virginia, and Wyoming, as well as the District of Columbia.[16] For first-time offenders, sexual contact or penetration may result in a Class A misdemeanor; the same behavior could result in a Class B felony thereafter.[17]

The subject of bestiality interfaces with the subject of pet custody disputes, too. Although at one time, a strict property analysis might have been outcome determinative in an ownership dispute, there seems to be growing consensus that at the very least, animal cruelty should also be considered in the analysis. Even if a state has not made a crime out of sex with animals, hopefully civil courts will consider evidence on this subject when making a pet custody determination.

FELONY AND MISDEMEANOR ANIMAL CRUELTY LAWS

Animal cruelty and laws that pertain to animal protection have gained momentum in the United States. When South Dakota passed a felony law against animal cruelty in 2014, this meant that all 50 states had animal cruelty felony laws.[18] Egregious acts toward pets or companion animals increasingly subject perpetrators to felony prosecution and jail time.

There are two types of misdemeanor offenses; the first type involves an intentional act to harm an animal, including overdriving, overloading, torturing, cruelly beating, neglecting, unjustifiably injuring, maiming, mutilating, or killing an animal.[19] The second type is negligence based, including failure to act. For example, an individual state may establish minimums for food, water, shelter, and veterinary care.

15. In the state of California, animal sexual abuse is a misdemeanor and the definition of animal cruelty under Penal Code § 597 is "malicious and intentional maim, mutilation, torture, wounding or killing of a living animal." In the state of Alaska, sexual conduct involving animals is covered under the state's cruelty laws. Maria Turcios, *Bestiality Laws: Our Dirty Little Secret*, Hastings Women's Law Journal, http://hastingswomenslj.org/journal/2014/2/20/e3y5p9h4xformoldf658mebzcse7va (last visited May 12, 2016).

16. Rebecca F. Wisch, *Table of State Animal Sexual Assault Laws*, Michigan State University Animal Legal & Historical Center, https://www.animallaw.info/topic/table-state-animal-sexual-assault-laws (last visited May 12, 2016).

17. *Id.*

18. Chris Berry, *All 50 States Now Have Felony Animal Cruelty Provisions*, Animal Legal Defense Fund, http://aldf.org/blog/50-states-now-have-felony-animal-cruelty-provisions/ (last visited May 12, 2016).

19. *Animal Cruelty Laws State by State*, http://www.straypetadvocacy.org/PDF/AnimalCrueltyLaws.pdf (last visited May 12, 2016).

ANIMALS AS VICTIMS

As mentioned before, momentous decisions about animal cruelty include *State v. Nix*,[20] *State v. Fessenden*,[21] and *State v. Hess*.[22] *Nix*, which is still good law, as explained above, was a landmark decision. The Oregon court reasoned that although the word "victim" in a criminal statute typically pertains to a human person, the term may be interpreted differently in laws pertaining to animal welfare and cruelty. The logical interpretation of the word "victim" in animal welfare and cruelty statutes takes into account legislative history and legislative intent pertaining to animal protection.

PERSONHOOD

Just as *Nix* shows that the term "victim" is not restricted to mean human victims, the court in the companion decision of *Fessenden* also shifted the center of gravity about where animals belong on the continuum toward the concept of personhood.[23] There, an animal control officer was lawfully in a driveway when he saw an emaciated horse that he believed could easily fall, which would constitute a life-ending event. Using an emergency and exigent circumstances rationale, the court determined that the officer's warrantless search and seizure, as embodied by the officer's seizure of the horse, was permissible. In a carefully worded opinion, the court reminded the reader that animals are only property, while at the same time it promoted help for animal victims; victims are not just humans anymore.[24]

Following these two decisions, when it was necessary to vacate *Nix* because of a jurisdictional issue, as stated earlier in this chapter, the *Nix* decision was reaffirmed in the cat hoarding case of *State v. Hess*.[25] In *Hess*, the merger doctrine did not apply when sentencing the defendant, as each cat was a victim.[26]

ANIMAL MISTREATMENT

Although *Nix*, and its progeny, do not mention the words "best interests of the animal," the decision will be of great use to a practitioner looking for the types

20. 355 Or. 777, 334 P.3d 437 (2014), *vacated*, 356 Or. 768, 345 P.3d 416 (2015).
21. 355 Or. 759 (Or. 2014).
22. 359 P.3d 288 (Or. Ct. App. 2015).
23. Although *Nix* was reversed on procedural grounds, the holding was upheld in *State v. Hess*, 359 P.3d 288 (Or. Ct. App. 2015).
24. This is a worldwide breakthrough concept.
25. 359 P.3d 288 (Or. Ct. App. 2015).
26. Although the court meticulously avoided calling an animal a person, it would be fair to claim that in these recent Oregon decisions, animals are at least in an interim category between property and persons.

of elements that can be cobbled together to make a forceful best-interests legal argument. In a pet custody dispute, the court should not award a companion animal that has been the victim of any type of animal cruelty. In Minnesota, the court signaled in *Pratt v. Pratt*[27] that if a future case before the court involved "mistreatment" of a companion animal, the court could consider this behavior in rendering its decision.

PIT BULL CRUELTY

Animal cruelty may be directed at Pit Bulls, a dog breed that has received considerable attention in evolving pet law jurisprudence. When a malnourished Pit Bull was found in a garbage bag that had been thrown down a garbage chute,[28] the maintenance worker who found the dog took him to a humane shelter, where they found the dog's temperature was extremely low.[29] The shelter nicknamed the dog "Patrick" because he was found the day before St. Patrick's Day. Patrick's owner was charged with two counts of fourth-degree animal abuse and two disorderly person offenses.[30] In just three days, the hospital received more than $30,000 in charitable donations for Patrick's care.[31] A dispute about Patrick's ownership ensued. The court, utilizing a best-interest standard, awarded Patrick to the animal hospital that saved his life.

Another Pit Bull animal cruelty case that caught the public's attention and sympathy involved a dog named Louis Vuitton. Louis Vuitton's owner sprayed him with lighter fluid and set him on fire while beating him with a shovel. Sentenced to nine and a half years in prison when convicted at age 23, the owner presented the board with an early release petition.[32] The badly scarred dog and his new owner sat in the courtroom while the board voted three to zero to deny Louis Vuitton's previous owner early release.

National Football League (NFL) player Michael Vick, owner of Bad Newz Kennels, was involved in a "horrific dogfighting ring that killed Pit Bulls by

---

27. N.W.2d, 1988 WL 120251 (Minn. App.).

28. *Patrick the Pit Bull: New Jersey Woman Pleads Not Guilty to Charges Relating to Animal Cruelty*, L.A. Times, http://latimesblogs.latimes.com/unleashed/2011/05/patrick-the-pit-bull-new-jersey-woman-pleads-not-guilty-to-charges-relating-to-animal-cruelty.html (last visited May 12, 2016).

29. *Patrick, "Miracle" Pit Bull Who Survived Fall down Garbage Chute, Is on the Road to Recovery*, L.A. Times, http://latimesblogs.latimes.com/unleashed/2011/04/patrick-pit-bull-garbage-chute.html (last visited May 12, 2016).

30. *Id.*

31. *Patrick the Pit Bull: Judge Decides Abused Dog Should Stay at Animal Hospital for Now*, L.A. Times, http://latimesblogs.latimes.com/unleashed/2011/06/patrick-the-pit-bull-judge-decides-abused-dog-should-stay-at-animal-hospital-for-now.html (last visited May 12, 2016).

32. *Pit Bull Who Was Set on Fire And Beaten Attends His Abuser's Parole Hearing*, L.A. Times, http://latimesblogs.latimes.com/unleashed/2010/08/pit-bull-who-was-set-on-fire-and-beaten-attends-parole-hearing-for-his-abuser.html (last visited May 12, 2016).

electrocution, hanging and drowning."[33] *Sports Illustrated* described how dogs that were too young to fight were used for breeding or kept as bait dogs for the fighters to practice on and were kept chained to car axles in the woods.[34] Vick plead guilty to criminal charges related to interstate animal fighting and served 18 months in a federal prison.[35]

Some of the dogs Vick owned were subjected to humane euthanasia. For the remaining dogs, a federal judge issued a groundbreaking animal best-interests of the dogs order and appointed Rebecca Huss as a guardian and special master.[36] Huss placed a significant number of the surviving Pit Bulls with Best Friends Animal Society in Utah, an entity that rescued many Pit Bulls and Pit Bull mixes following Hurricane Katrina. Consistent with Huss's vision, the former Vick dogs were re-homed or rehabilitated, and one even ended up providing therapy dog services.[37]

There is a wide range of public opinion about what Vick did, the time he served, whether his star power in the NFL caused him to get special treatment, and whether redemption is possible.[38] Vick subsequently acquired a pet dog in 2012 and worked with Wayne Pacelle, the president of the Humane Society of the United States, as part of their "End Dogfighting" campaign. Vick testified in Congress in support of passing the Animal Fighting Spectator Prohibition Act.[39] In a speech to two high schools, Vick said, "I think I'm being used by God because all the laws have changed since my incident."[40]

33. *Tucker Carlson Says Michael Vick "Should Have Been Executed" for Dogfighting Crimes*, Washington Post, http://www.washingtonpost.com/wp-dyn/content/article/2010/12/29/AR2010122902775.html (last visited May 12, 2016).

34. Jim Gorant, *What Happened to Michael Vick's Dogs . . .*, Sports Illustrated, http://www.si.com/more-sports/2008/12/23/vick-dogs (last visited May 12, 2016).

35. *Vick, Michael—Associated Materials (2007, 2008)*, Michigan State University Animal Legal & Historical Center, https://www.animallaw.info/pleading/vick-michael-associated-materials-2007-2008 (last visited May 12, 2016).

36. Rebecca J. Huss, *Lessons Learned: Acting as Guardian/Special Master in the Bad Newz Kennels Case*, Valparaiso University, http://scholar.valpo.edu/cgi/viewcontent.cgi?article=1032&context=law_fac_pubs (last visited May 12, 2016).

37. Jim Gorant, The Lost Dogs: Michael Vick's Dogs and Their Tale of Rescue and Redemption (Gotham 2011).

38. Joyce Tischler, *An Open Letter to R.L. White, President of the Atlanta NAACP*, Animal Legal Defense Fund, http://aldf.org/article.php?id=156 (last visited May 12, 2016).

39. C.J. Ciaramella, *Humane Society Sics Michael Vick on Congress*, Daily Caller, http://dailycaller.com/2011/07/18/humane-society-sics-michael-vick-on-congress/ (last visited May 12, 2016).

40. *Michael Vick Tells High Schoolers "I Think I'm Being Used by God,"* L.A. Times, http://latimesblogs.latimes.com/unleashed/2010/11/michael-vick-dogfighting.html (last visited May 12, 2016).

HORSE CRUELTY

Horses are often subject to animal cruelty. These types of cases are challenging for prosecutors to win, in part because the appearance of a starving horse,[41] as reflected by the Henneke body conditioning scoring system,[42] may be impacted by other causes that require a fecal examination and blood testing. The Henneke body conditioning scoring method involves assigning a numerical value between one and nine to the horse's body condition based upon visual appearance of the horse's loin, ribs, tailhead, withers, neck, and shoulders.[43]

In one state's effort to keep horses fed and healthy, the Minnesota Horse Welfare Coalition (MNHWC) launched a cooperative called the Minnesota Hay Bank to bring caring citizens together to help responsible owners who had fallen on hard times. Noting that "[l]ocal elected officials, law enforcement, county prosecutors and judges have taken inconsistent and inadequate actions to hold individuals accountable for repeated practices of animal neglect and abuse,"[44] an article explored the possibility that the MNHWC could advocate for both legislative reform and more uniform law enforcement. The public was implored to be "keenly aware of the health of horses and find ways to work together to support struggling horse owners."[45]

ANIMAL HOARDERS

There has been a dramatic increase in the public's awareness of the plight of animals owned by hoarders. Photographs show that these hoarded animals are too thin and often have open sores, tumors, missing teeth, and eye diseases. It is estimated that 250,000 animals live in hoarding situations each year.[46]

According to the ALDF, "In terms of the number of animals affected and the degree and duration of their suffering, hoarding is the number one animal cruelty

41. In a horse boarding facility in East Bethel, Minnesota, seven horses were brought to the University of Minnesota Veterinary Center in 2011, as two of the horses were near death from malnutrition and most were 200 to 300 pounds below normal weight. Lowell Friday was not charged with a felony for his actions in Anoka County because the horses had not died or suffered great bodily harm under the pertinent statute. Friday was previously convicted in 2007 for misdemeanor maltreatment of animals. Paul Levy & Bill McAuliffe, *Seven More Starving Horses Seized*, Star Tribune, http://www.startribune.com/seven-more-starving-horses-seized/134159563/ (last visited May 12, 2016).

42. Craig H. Wood, *Body Condition Scoring for Your Horse*, University of Maine, https://extension.umaine.edu/publications/1010e/ (last visited May 12, 2016).

43. *Id.*

44. Stacy L. Bettison & Barbara Colombo, *We Must Take Care of Horses*, St. Cloud Times, http://minnesotahorsewelfare.org/wp-content/uploads/2013/02/We-must-take-care-of-horses-St-Cloud-Times-Op-Ed.pdf (last visited May 12, 2016).

45. *Id.*

46. *ALDF v. Woodley*, Animal Legal Defense Fund, http://aldf.org/press-room/press-releases/aldf-v-woodley/ (last visited May 12, 2016).

crisis facing companion animals in communities throughout the country."[47] The ALDF estimates that 72 percent of hoarders are women and that most hoarding involves cats and dogs. Hoarding behaviors include having an abnormally large number of animals, failing to provide proper nutrition, lacking insight about neglect, and displaying obsessive behaviors. Recidivism is pervasive.[48] From a pet custody aspect, courts need to be aware of these problems and consider that for the best interests of these animals, they must be relinquished.

FEDERAL LAWS

Federal laws that impact companion animals include the Animal Welfare Act, the Animal Enterprise Terrorism Act, and the Robert T. Stafford Disaster Relief and Emergency Assistance Act.[49] The U.S. Department of Agriculture has an Animal Disease Traceability Program; an Interstate Certificate of Veterinary Inspection or suitable alternative documentation is required for horses that cross state lines.[50] Horses in this program are identified by physical description, digital photographs, and an injectable non-ISO electronic method.[51]

HORSE PERMIT REQUIREMENTS

Lawyers should be aware of possible permit requirements for horses. For example, in the Southeast, there may be a requirement for an Equine Passport Permit, Equine Interstate Movement Permit, or Equine ID Card Program.[52] Utilizing the latter, the need to obtain a health certificate from a veterinarian every 30 days to travel out of state can be avoided. When trying to work out a schedule between two parties who live across state lines, this is the kind of knowledge about regulations and permit requirements that clients appreciate.[53]

---

47. *Animal Hoarding Facts*, Animal Legal Defense Fund, http://aldf.org/resources/when-you-witness-animal-cruelty/animal-hoarding-facts/ (last visited May 12, 2016).

48. *Id.*

49. *Robert T. Stafford Disaster Relief and Emergency Assistance Act (Public Law 93-288) as Amended*, FEMA, http://www.fema.gov/robert-t-stafford-disaster-relief-and-emergency-assistance-act-public-law-93-288-amended (last visited May 12, 2016).

50. *Animal Disease Traceability*, USDA Animal and Plant Health Inspection Service, http://www.aphis.usda.gov/traceability/ (last visited May 12, 2016).

51. Julie Fershtman, *The U.S. Department of Agriculture's New Animal Disease Traceability Program Will Impact Horses in Transit*, ABA Tort Trial & Insurance Practice Section Animal Law Committee Newsletter Winter/Spring 2013, at 17.

52. Dottie Burch, *Equine Interstate Passport Permit Programs Make Life Easier*, ABA Tort Trial & Insurance Practice Section Animal Law Committee Newsletter Winter/Spring 2013, at 7.

53. There is currently no federal ban on horse slaughter. It is a subject of controversy.

CRUSH VIDEOS

There has been strong congressional condemnation of sexual fetish videos; they include videos showing women crushing and killing small animals. Congress's first attempt to pass a federal law about this was struck down in *United States v. Stevens*;[54] the court used the rationale that the law was "too broadly written and violated First Amendment free-speech protections."[55] Justice Samuel Alito was the lone dissenter in *Stevens*, and in his dissent, he said, "The animals used in crush videos are living creatures that experience excruciating pain. Our society has long banned such cruelty."[56] He went on to say that the courts have "erred in second-guessing the legislative judgment about the importance of preventing cruelty to animals."[57] A more narrowly crafted version of this federal law, called the Animal Cruelty Violence Act of 2010, was passed by Congress and signed into law by President Barack Obama. A house sponsor said, "Animal torture videos are barbaric and have no place in a civilized society."[58]

U.S. CONSTITUTIONAL AMENDMENTS

First Amendment

Pet laws are impacted by the U.S. Constitution. The First Amendment of the U.S. Constitution states, "Congress shall make no law respecting an establishment of religion, or prohibiting the free exercise thereof; or abridging the freedom of speech, or of the press; or the right of the people peaceably to assemble, and to petition the government for a redress of grievances."[59]

Later in this chapter, you will learn that as of yet, the U.S. Supreme Court will not protect animals, at least when their welfare could impact First Amendment rights, or cause the court to reconsider who can be on what it calls "the list." It is interesting, from a First Amendment perspective, to imagine the same court issuing an opinion on a First Amendment constitutional challenge to the Animal Enterprise Terrorism Act (AETA).[60] At the end of this act, which criminalizes a variety of behaviors by animal advocates or their conspirators, Congress offers a "savings

---

54. 130 S. Ct. 1577 (2010).
55. *Id.*
56. Bill Mears, *Obama Signs Law Banning "Crush Videos" Depicting Animal Cruelty*, CNN, http://www.cnn.com/2010/POLITICS/12/10/animal.cruelty/ (last visited May 12, 2016).
57. *Id.*
58. *Senate Votes to Ban Distribution of "Crush Videos,"* L.A. Times, http://latimesblogs.latimes.com/unleashed/2010/11/senate-votes-to-ban-distribution-of-crush-videos.html (last visited May 12, 2016).
59. *First Amendment*, Cornell University Law School, http://www.law.cornell.edu/constitution/first_amendment (last visited May 12, 2016).
60. *See* Barbara J. Gislason, *Animal Enterprise Terrorism Act: Designing a Poison Pill for a Social Movement*, ABA Annual Meeting 2007.

clause." According to this savings clause, the AETA should not be construed to violate expressive conduct, including peaceful picketing or other peaceful demonstrations, protected by the First Amendment.[61] Even with this savings clause, examine the terrorism rhetoric used in this act and decide for yourself how the AETA is likely to chill free speech.[62] Imagine if this same statute were directed at a different social movement.

Fourth Amendment

The Fourth Amendment of the U.S. Constitution prohibits unreasonable searches and seizures and requires a predicate warrant based upon probable cause, meaning a good reason to believe a specific crime has been committed.[63] Probable cause is unnecessary when an exception to the warrant requirement applies. Exceptions include consent searches, motor vehicle searches, plain view, and exigent circumstances for those with legal authority.

Fourth Amendment issues arise in animal cruelty cases. If Fourth Amendment requirements are not satisfied, the "fruit of the poisonous tree," or the ill-gotten gains evidence, may be subject to the exclusionary rule, requiring that this evidence is inadmissible unless there are exceptions to the exclusionary rule. This type of exclusionary effort was made, unsuccessfully, in *Fitzgerald v. State of Maryland*,[64] where the defendant alleged that a canine sniff search in a hallway violated his constitutional rights. Fourth Amendment violations may come up in lawsuits under 42 U.S.C. § 1983, a law that enables citizens whose constitutional rights have been violated by government officials to sue.[65] Section 1983 actions are common in animal law.

Fifth Amendment

The Fifth Amendment of the U.S. Constitution protects citizens against the misuse of government authority, including the taking of property without just compensation.[66] This constitutional right is asserted when animals are seized in an animal cruelty investigation. Citizens also have the Fifth Amendment rights against self-incrimination and double jeopardy, which means being tried twice for the

61. There is concern by those involved in animal protection that the Animal Enterprise Terrorism Act has a chilling effect on animal activists' First Amendment rights.

62. Will Potter, *Analysis of the Animal Enterprise Terrorism Act (AETA)*, Green Is the New Red, http://www.greenisthenewred.com/blog/aeta-analysis-109th/ (last visited May 12, 2016).

63. *Fourth Amendment*, Cornell University Law School, http://www.law.cornell.edu/constitution/fourth_amendment (last visited May 12, 2016).

64. 384 Md. 484, 864 A.2d 1006 (Md. 2004).

65. The San Jose Charter of the Hells Angels Motorcycle Club v. City of San Jose, 402 F.3d 963 (9th Cir. 2005).

66. *Fifth Amendment*, Cornell University Law School, http://www.law.cornell.edu/wex/fifth_amendment (last visited May 12, 2016).

same crime. There can be confusion between the Fifth and Fourteenth Amendments when it comes to due process rights because, although the terminology is the same, only the Fourteenth Amendment pertains to the states. Fifth Amendment claims may arise as 42 U.S.C. § 1983 actions, too, as further discussed in this chapter.

Fourteenth Amendment

The U.S. Constitution's Fourteenth Amendment pertains to citizenship rights and equal protection of the laws regarding the actions of state and local officials but not private citizens.[67] It includes due process rights and makes these rights applicable to the states. Due process rights are of particular importance in dangerous dog cases. Due process is understood in two aspects: procedural due process, which centers on fairness, and substantive due process, a doctrine that requires the balancing of fundamental rights and liberties with governmental interests, including the interests of law enforcement, prosecutors, and the judiciary.[68] The Due Process Clause prohibits state and local government officials from depriving persons of life, liberty, or property without lawful authority.

Thus far, it seems that the term "life" only applies to human life, although animals can now be crime victims in the state of Oregon. The term "persons" does not apply to animals. Significant scholarly research has addressed this subject.[69] In the Uniform Law Commission Family Law Arbitration Act,[70] approved by the Uniform Law Commission on July 13, 2016, the definition of person is "an individual, estate, business or nonprofit entity, public corporation, government or governmental subdivision, agency, or instrumentality, or any other legal entity." It is foreseeable that in time, a special category of animal will be included on this list.[71]

The Fourteenth Amendment's Equal Protection Clause requires each state to provide equal protection under the law to all people within its jurisdiction. Equal

---

67. *Fourteenth Amendment*, Cornell University Law School, http://www.law.cornell.edu/constitution/amendmentxiv (last visited May 12, 2016).

68. *Due Process*, Cornell University Law School, http://www.law.cornell.edu/wex/due_process (last visited May 12, 2016).

69. Cass Sunstein & Martha Nussbaum, Animal Rights: Current Debates and New Directions (Oxford University Press 2005); Francis J. Beckwith, *Abortion, Bioethics, and Personhood: A Philosophical Reflection*, Southern Baptist Theological Seminary, http://www.sbts.edu/resources/journal-of-theology/sbjt-41-spring-2000/abortion-bioethics-and-personhood-a-philosophical-reflection/ (last visited May 12, 2016); Mary Midgley, *Fellow Champions Dolphins as "Non-Human Persons,"* Oxford Centre for Animal Ethics, January 10, 2010.

70. *Family Law Arbitration*, Uniform Law Commission, http://www.uniformlaws.org/Committee.aspx?title=Family%20Law%20Arbitration%20 (last visited May 12, 2016).

71. There is significant advocacy to promote personhood for chimpanzees.

protection arguments are made in animal law cases,[72] including concerning laws that emphasize a dog's breed.[73] Under the Fourteenth Amendment, law enforcement can seize an animal that has been cruelly treated when there is a public health aspect to the behavior toward the animal or a public health rationale, or with permission or consent.

ANIMAL CONTROL OFFICERS

As the work of animal control officers becomes more sophisticated, animal control officers seizing animals may utilize better protocols to establish that a crime involving a companion animal has been committed. These protocols include performing deoxyribonucleic acid testing, taking measurements, statements, and photographs, and confiscating other criminal evidence, such as weapons or animal fighting paraphernalia. Veterinarians may be utilized to describe physical injuries based upon an animal's weight, untreated medical conditions, or to diagnose a burn. Animal control officers may also draw on police powers to effect liens, forfeitures, and fines. It is good public policy that animals not live in situations where they have insufficient food, are tormented, or lack necessary veterinary care, or where there is indifference to their basic needs.[74]

ANIMAL FORFEITURES

According to experienced litigator Adam P. Karp, animal forfeiture cases are difficult.[75] These cases are not unlike drug forfeitures sought by law enforcement in civil and criminal actions, but there are distinguishable criteria. Karp stated:

> Unlike inanimate objects, seized animals require ongoing supervision, board, veterinary attention, and protection from the owner, all of which comes at a cost that more often than not exceeds the value of the seized animal. Perhaps unexpectedly, another current of jurisprudence that recognizes the familial-type bond between a person and animal companion, and the status of the animal as more than mere property, creates a doctrinal riptide that serves to protect the animal from the

72. William A. Reppy, Jr., *Broad Exemptions in Animal-Cruelty Statutes Unconstitutionally Deny Equal Protection of the Law*, http://scholarship.law.duke.edu/cgi/viewcontent.cgi?article=1414&context=lcp (last visited May 12, 2016).

73. *See* Tracey v. Solesky, A.3d, 2012 WL 1432263 (Md. 2012). While this decision originally applied to both Pit Bulls and Pit Bull mixes, the supreme court determined that its decision now only applies to Pit Bulls in *Tracey v. Solesky*, 427 Md. 627 (Md. 2012).

74. These problems may also arise in large confinement operations. The public is largely ignorant when animals sold online or in pet stores are sourced this way.

75. Adam P. Karp was the 2012 recipient of the Excellence in the Advancement of Animal Law Award from the ABA Tort Trial & Insurance Practice Section.

owner while at the same time protecting the owner from divestiture or termination of what amounts colloquially to a quasi-parental relationship.[76]

Criminal Forfeitures

A criminal forfeiture results from the criminal prosecution of a person. There could be a forfeiture of any property, real or personal, involved in a criminal offense, or any property traceable to this property.[77] A criminal forfeiture does not sever third-party rights, such as the rights of co-owners. Once third party interests are addressed, a court can issue a final order of forfeiture.

Civil Forfeitures

Civil forfeitures are different from criminal forfeitures. When there is a civil forfeiture, the focus is on the property rather than the owner being in violation of the law. The court may use the legal fiction of the "property's guilt."[78] The owner of a seized animal may face a civil forfeiture of his or her companion animal even if found not guilty in a criminal proceeding. Because there is no criminal proceeding, the individual involved in a civil forfeiture does not receive the constitutional protections that apply when there is a criminal forfeiture.[79] Property subject to civil forfeiture, in addition to contraband, proceeds from illegal activity, or tools used in a crime commission, may also include companion animals.

CONCLUSION

In summary, dating back to the Massachusetts Bay Colony, tyranny and cruelty toward "any bruit Creature"[80] was abhorred. Not only have states passed a broad spectrum of statutes to protect and advance animal welfare interests, and the federal government included animal abuse perpetrators in its FBI database, but also case law is moving animals along the continuum from merely property all the way to animals as crime victims. Companion animals in particular are entering the interim category between property and people. Lawyers are using the U.S. Constitution to promote animal interests.

---

76. Adam P. Karp, *Challenges to Pre- and Post-Conviction Forfeitures and to Post-Conviction Restitution under Animal Cruelty Statutes*, 70 A.L.R. 6th 329 (2011).

77. *Forfeiture*, Cornell University Law School Legal Information Institute, https://www.law.cornell.edu/wex/forfeiture (last visited May 12, 2016).

78. The law on this is comprehensively set forth in Asset Forfeiture Law in the United States by Stefan D. Cassella. *See also* Rebecca Huss, Ensuring Effective Tools For a Challenging Task: Amending the Civil Asset Forfeiture and Cost Reimbursement Language of the Animal Welfare Act's Animal Fighting Venture Provision.

79. *Id.* at 9. The Fourth Amendment exclusionary rules of res judicata and double jeopardy and the imposition of an excessive fine in violation of the Eighth Amendment may apply.

80. *The Massachusetts Body of Liberties*, Bartleby.com, http://www.bartleby.com/43/8.html (last visited May 12, 2016).

APPLICABLE CASE LAW

ANIMAL WELFARE INSTITUTE V. KREPS[81]

Year: *1977*
Category: *Constitutional Law*
Type of Action: *Standing*
Animal: *Seal*
Pet Custody Concept: *Consider raising a standing argument.*

The central issue in this case was whether the appellants had standing to sue the government when it waived the moratorium imposed by the Marine Mammal Protection Act so as to allow the importation of baby sealskin furs into the United States. The appellants identified themselves as organizations that bring "this action on behalf of themselves and their members, each of whom has a personal stake in the maintenance of a safe, healthful and productive environment and in the protection of marine mammals." The court determined that the appellants had standing. The basis for standing is well explained in *Animal Legal Defense Fund, Inc. v. Glickman*.[82]

Practice Pointer: In some cases, including one for a nonprofit against the government, a lawyer may need to make a standing argument.

FULLER V. VINES[83]

Year: *1994*
Category: *Property Law*
Type of Action: *1983 Action*
Animal: *Dog*
Pet Custody Concept: *Dogs matter.*

The court struggled with whether the plaintiff could pursue a 1983 civil rights claim when police officers not only shot and killed the plaintiff's dog but also "pointed a loaded gun at him when he objected to the killing of the dog." The court heard this matter following a grant of summary judgment in favor of the police officers by the lower court. In a de novo review of this determination, for summary judgment purposes, the higher court accepted the plaintiff's claims as true.

The plaintiff was outside with his dog, Champ, when police officers involved in investigative work passed by his yard. Champ merely stood up when the officers passed by, and despite the pleas of Champ's owner, an officer shot Champ twice. Following the shooting of Champ, the dog's owner was "wrestled to the ground by his friend out of fear of further confrontation" with the police. The evidence showed that the officer pointed his loaded gun at the plaintiff from a distance.

81. 561 F.2d 1002, 183 U.S. App. D.C. 109 (C.A.D.C. 1977).
82. 154 F.3d 426 (C.A.D.C. 1998).
83. 36 F.3d 65 (C.A. 9 (Cal.) 1994).

The plaintiff claimed that his procedural and substantive due process rights were violated. While the officers sought a summary judgment decision, the plaintiff brought a motion seeking to file an amended complaint alleging that "the officers unlawfully 'seized' the Fullers' property when they killed Champ and unlawfully 'seized' James Jr. when an officer pointed a gun at him, both in violation of the Fourth Amendment."

When the plaintiff's original complaint was found wanting, the lower court denied the motion to amend, as an amendment would not cure the complaint deficiencies. The plaintiff's Rule 60 motion for reconsideration was also denied because the original cause of action failed to plead a cause of action under the Fourth Amendment upon which relief could be granted; the amended motion was not curative, as a property seizure claim requires "meaningful interference with an individual's possessory interests in that property" under the Fourth Amendment.

In a major reversal, the higher court stated that the "destruction of property is 'meaningful interference' constituting a seizure under the Fourth Amendment" and continued that "[t]he officers' killing of their dog constituted a Fourth Amendment seizure" as "a dog is an 'effect' or 'property' which can be seized." Accordingly, the district court abused its discretion by determining that the plaintiff lacked a cognizable Fourth Amendment claim. Summary judgment on this issue was reversed.

In this 1994 decision, the court used the old language of calling a dog an "effect" in the same breath as "property." A little movement could be seen when the court recognized that not only had a "killing" occurred, but also the owner was so impacted by the injury to his dog that he, in effect, faced down an officer with a weapon ready to fire. The court was not indifferent to the emotional impact that killing a dog had on the dog's owner, though no concern was expressed for Champ, unless he was dignified by having his name acknowledged. This case is germane to the topic of pet custody because it represents the evolution of how pets are regarded in civil law.

Practice Pointer: The court determined that killing a dog was equivalent to property seizure contrary to a fundamental Fourth Amendment right. This case is a good example that sometimes, asserting a property right is beneficial. One of the challenges in further evolving animal law is how to advance pet law without losing the benefit of this type of decision.

Animal Legal Defense Fund, Inc. v. Glickman[84]

Year: *1998*
Category: *Constitutional Law*
Type of Action: *Standing*
Animal: *Primate*
Pet Custody Concept: *Assert an aesthetic injury.*

Although this is a landmark case involving animals, this discussion focuses on how the court addressed the subject of standing, which is an issue that may arise in disputes about who will be awarded a companion animal.

84. 154 F.3d 426 (C.A.D.C. 1998).

The subject of this case was whether a private citizen had standing to cause the government to enforce federal animal welfare laws that require animal dealers, research facilities, and exhibitors to enact and maintain minimum standards for the care of their animals, or, as some might phrase it, require compliance with minimal animal welfare standards. The Animal Welfare Act's (AWA) standards pertain to the humane handling, care, and transport of certain animals, including dogs, cats, and primates, but not birds or rodents.[85] The AWA,[86] with all its limitations,[87] reflects important animal welfare values. At least for dealers, research facilities, and exhibitors, the AWA requires the U.S. Department of Agriculture (USDA) to "adopt specific, minimum standards to protect primates' psychological well-being."

In the instant case, Marc Jurnove asserted that not only did the USDA fail to promulgate sufficient standards to govern the humane handling, care, treatment, and transport of primates, but also that because the USDA failed to meet its responsibilities, he suffered what he called an "aesthetic injury,"[88] which he argued gave him prudential standing[89] to sue.[90] Jurnove was granted prudential standing to challenge the secretary of agriculture as Jurnove had satisfied the Article III standing requirements under the U.S. Constitution, which are (1) he suffered injury in fact, (2) the injury was fairly traceable to the defendant's actions, and (3) a favorable judicial ruling will likely reduce the plaintiff's injury. In addition to the above, a plaintiff must meet prudential requirements to be granted standing.

Practice Pointer: This case is important because the court found that the plaintiff had standing well within the bounds of the law. It was the quality of this well-reasoned decision that made the plaintiff's standing appear obvious.

Brown v. Muhlenberg Township[91]

Year: *2001*
Category: *Tort Law*
Type of Action: *Fourth Amendment Violation*
Animal: *Dog*
Pet Custody Concept: *Courts abhor blatant cruelty.*

Immi was a three-year-old Rottweiler who was wearing "a bright pink, one inch wide collar with many tags" when her owners let her outside in their fenced yard. The latch

85. AWA, 7 U.C.C. § 2143 (a) (1994).

86. Enforced by the USDA. The USDA's Animal and Plant Health Inspection Service enforces USDA regulations.

87. The act does not address the use of animals for research purposes.

88. The concept of "aesthetic injury" typically arises in the context of public policy, where the public has an interest in avoiding an eyesore, perhaps caused by waste management or pests. This subject also arises in discussions regarding ecosystems and species health.

89. Prudential requirements relate to a plaintiff falling within the appropriate zone of interest.

90. The idea that primates cannot be protected unless the humans who see them in poor circumstances complain about their plight using the correct terminology of "aesthetic injury" is reminiscent of the awkward advocacy and reasoning in the pet law context. Thus, a lawyer might argue that the parties' child has a strong bond with the animal and not the other way around. In a similar way, a human's suffering, watching a beloved animal die, may be compensable, while the animal's suffering is incidental.

91. 269 F.3d 205 (3d Cir. 2001).

on the gate was not working, and Immi wandered into a parking lot near her residence, where Officer Eberly stopped his patrol car and tried to get the dog's attention. Eberly exited his car and drew his gun. One of Immi's owners saw what was happening from her house window and started shouting at the officer to stop, but after a slight hesitation, Eberly shot Immi five times, killing her.

In this civil rights decision, the Third Circuit reviewed several constitutional and state law claims brought by the appellants against a police officer for the officer's intentional shooting and killing of Immi. The court summed up the facts by saying, "We are thus faced with a situation in which a municipal law enforcement officer intentionally and repeatedly shot a pet without any provocation and with knowledge that it belonged to the family who lived in the adjacent house and was available to take custody." The court said that Immi's owner called out to the officer, saying, "That's my dog, don't shoot" before the officer shot. According to a witness, the dog had not acted aggressively.

The appellants alleged that Officer Eberly violated their Fourth Amendment right to be free from unreasonable government seizures of their property. The court agreed that pets are considered "personal property" and that therefore the appellants had a possessory interest in their dog. The court further explained what it means for citizens to be secure, including in their "effects." Relying on *United States v. Jacobsen*,[92] the court said, "Destroying property meaningfully interferes with an individual's possessory interest in that property."[93]

The court emphasized that the state's interest must be sufficiently compelling and that the seizure must not be "disproportionately intrusive." The court applied the test from *United States v. Place*[94] to "balance the nature and quality of the intrusion on the individual's Fourth Amendment interests against the importance of the governmental interests alleged to justify the intrusion." Utilizing the *Place* balancing test, where Immi was not an immediate threat and the owner was watching and trying to regain custody of the dog, the court concluded that the destruction of Immi was an unreasonable seizure. The court rejected Officer Eberly's qualified immunity defense, saying that if the facts alleged by the appellants were true, Officer Eberly's qualified immunity defense did not convince the court that a reasonable officer in Eberly's position would have concluded he could lawfully kill the dog. The dog had posed no imminent danger to the officer, and the owners were "known, available, and desirous of assuming custody."[95]

---

92. 466 U.S. 109, 124–25 (1984).

93. The court equated the killing of a dog with the seizing of a dog by an enforcement officer. In a footnote, the Third Circuit said that even though unlicensed, Immi was not abandoned as a matter of law, despite Officer Eberly's argument.

94. 462 U.S. 696, 701, 103 S. Ct. 2637, 77 L. Ed. 2d 110 (1983).

95. The Third Circuit further said,

> We predict that the Pennsylvania courts would permit a trier of fact to return a verdict for the plaintiff in an intentional infliction of emotional distress case where it is shown that a police officer's attention was called to the severe emotional distress of the pet's owner, he hesitated before shooting, and he then attempted to fire five bullets into the pet within the owner's view and without justification. In such cases, the malicious behavior is directed to the owner as well as to the pet, with the potential for serious emotional injury to the owner being readily apparent.

In order to prevail on a tort claim, the appellants would be required to demonstrate that (1) the officer's conduct was extreme and outrageous, (2) his conduct caused a person severe emotional distress, and (3) he acted with the intention of causing that person such distress or with knowledge that such distress was substantially certain to occur.[96] In this case, the court strongly indicated that an award for the intentional infliction of emotional distress was warranted.[97] The court limited the intentional infliction of emotional distress claim to only the owner present when Immi was shot but not Immi's other owner. As summary judgment in favor of Officer Eberly was reversed, the case was remanded for further proceedings consistent with the court's opinion.[98]

While the court denied summary judgment with regard to Officer Eberly, it found no causal link between a municipal policy and custom and Officer Eberly's shooting of Immi. Summary judgment was granted in favor of the police chief with regard to the appellants' inadequacy of supervision claim.

Practice Pointer: This decision is emblematic of the court recognizing that humans are bonded to their dogs. When outrageous conduct is directed at a family pet, the courthouse doors swing open. When raising a due process claim, distinguish between how the federal court views procedural defenses as compared to substantive due process defenses.

FITZGERALD V. STATE OF MARYLAND[99]

Year: *2004*
Category: *Constitutional Law*
Type of Action: *Unreasonable Search*
Animal: *Dog*
Pet Custody Concept: *In this case, the dog was elevated to a "government agent."*

The petitioner in this criminal case sought to suppress evidence based upon a search and seizure warrant that resulted in the taking of marijuana and contraband from his

96. The Third Circuit said,

> Officer Eberly argues in essence that the killing of a pet under any circumstances would not be recognized by the Pennsylvania courts as extreme or outrageous. We believe the Banaszek court was correct in rejecting a similar contention. Given the strength of community sentiment against at least extreme forms of animal abuse and the substantial emotional investment that pet owners frequently make in their pets, we would not expect the Supreme Court of Pennsylvania to rule out all liability predicated on the killing of a pet.

97. It is curious that the court promoted noneconomic damages in a criminal case.

98. There was a strong dissent emphasizing the testimony supporting the district court's finding and the "characteristics and nature of a Rottweiler that should be taken into consideration in assessing the reasonableness of Eberly's actions." In note six of the dissent, the court warned lawyers handling animal disputes to be cautious of the "quality required for substantive due process protection" when asserting a property interest. If the plaintiffs in *Brown* had properly raised a substantive due process claim, Officer Eberly may have been granted qualified immunity defense pursuant to the controlling decision in *DeBlasio v. Zoning Board of Adjustment*, 53 F.3d 592, 600 (3rd Cir. 1995).

99. 384 Md. 484, 864 A.2d 1006 (Md. 2004).

apartment. This case arose when an anonymous source alerted police to drug activities. The police entered the petitioner's apartment building with a "certified" drug detecting dog. Once in the hallway, the dog sniffed outside of four apartment doors, "alerting" the officers that narcotics were present behind the door to the petitioner's apartment. The officers obtained a warrant and arrested the petitioner, charging him with possession of marijuana with intent to distribute. The petitioner argued that the dog's sniff constituted an unlawful search and that without the "canine sniff," the police would have lacked probable cause for a warrant. The lower court denied the petitioner's motion to suppress the evidence.

The Supreme Court of Maryland, indicating this was an issue of first impression, addressed three issues: (1) Whether "a dog sniff constitutes a search under the Fourth Amendment of the United States Constitution or Article 26 of the Maryland Declaration of Right; (2) If so, was the sniff an unlawful search; and (3) If the dog sniff is unlawful and its results excised from Grim's affidavit, would the remaining information establish probable cause for a warrant?"

Citing the U.S. Supreme Court decision of *United States v. Place*,[100] the Maryland court noted that the use of a dog to sniff luggage at an airport was not a search under the Fourth Amendment. The court reasoned that this type of search was of a limited nature and had the effect of not subjecting the owner of the property "to the embarrassment and inconvenience entailed in less discriminate and more intrusive investigative methods."

The court addressed the petitioner's argument that the court should differentiate "sniffs from the exterior of the home from all other sniffs." The court explained why the facts of this case were distinguishable from other search and seizure cases because of where the government agent, in this case the dog, was located. The court said, "The dog, Alex in our case, occupied the same position as the government agent; he observed from the public space outside the residence. Were Alex to have entered the residence himself without a warrant, he would have conducted an unconstitutional search."

An interesting aspect of this decision was that the petitioner advanced the argument that the U.S. Supreme Court ruling in *Kyllo v. United States*[101] was relevant. In *Kyllo*, the police used a thermal imager, or sense-enhancing technology, capable of determining temperatures inside a residence. The U.S. Supreme Court had applied a restriction on sense-enhancing technology when the technology was not in "general public use." The court dismissed the petitioner's argument in the instant case when it said, "Even a perfunctory reading of *Kyllo* reveals that its standard does not apply to dog sniffs. *Kyllo* is an opinion about the need to limit 'advancing technology.'"

The court further added, "it is clear that *Kyllo* has no bearing on dog sniffs. First, a dog is not technology—he or she is a dog. A dog is known commonly as 'man's best friend.' Across America, people consider dogs as members of their family." The Maryland higher court went even further and clearly stated, "dogs are not 'advancing technology.' Even taking into account potential gains from evolution, breeding, and

100. 462 U.S. 696, 103 S. Ct. 2637, 77 L. Ed. 2d 110 (1983).
101. 533 U.S. 27, 121 S. Ct. 2038, 150 L. Ed. 2d 94 (2001).

improved nutrition, the limits to dogs' future ability to smell are not far from the current limits." A forceful dissent by Judge Greene followed.

Judge Greene stated, "When police intentionally use an investigative technique, in this case a dog, to detect the presence of drugs by directing the dog to a residence or person, that action constitutes a search." Furthermore, "The canine sniff at the door of Fitzgerald's apartment was not a detection of something in the hallway, but rather was a detection of something inside Fitzgerald's apartment—a private dwelling. In other words, it was not a search of the hallway—an area of limited expectation of privacy." The dissent also discussed situations where canines may falsely alert,[102] saying, "Mistakes can intrude significantly on one's legitimate expectations of privacy." The court continued, "One court has found that the reason dogs may alert falsely is because of the high percentage of cash that contains sufficient quantities of cocaine to trigger a response in a dog."[103]

Practice Pointer: It is amazing all the different ways that companion animals are conceptualized within the legal system. In this case, the dog was a government agent, a family member, and man's best friend. More specifically, while under the UCC, some animals may be classified as products. In this case, the dog was not technology.

---

102. *See* United States v. Six Hundred Thirty-Nine Thousand Five Hundred and Fifty-Eight Dollars ($639,558) in U.S. Currency, 955 F.2d 712, 714 n.2 (D.C. Cir. 1992) (pointing out that experts have concluded that anywhere from 70 to 99 percent of all currency in the United States is contaminated by detectable amounts of cocaine).

103. The dissent also argues that "there is no such half-way thing as a quasi-search of a residence requiring some lesser or intermediate justification. If the canine sniff is a search, the Fourth Amendment applies requiring a warrant based on probable cause. If it is not a search, the Fourth Amendment is inapplicable." In making its argument, the chief judge expressed considerable concern that these techniques would have a disproportionate impact on the poor, who more typically live in public access places.

MYERS V. CITY OF HARTFORD[104]

Year: *2004*
Category: *Property Law*
Type of Action: *Misapplication of Qualified Immunity*
Animal: *Dog*
Pet Custody Concept: *Good courts want to do the right thing.*

Responding to a neighbor complaint about roaming dogs, an animal control officer removed the plaintiff's dog from her premises and ordered that the dog be euthanized without following euthanasia protocol. Before acting, the officer should have: (1) contacted a veterinarian, (2) informed the owner of the search and seizure, and (3) advertised in a newspaper the fact that the municipality had possession of the dog.

On appeal, the plaintiff demonstrated that the trial court had misapplied the qualified governmental immunity doctrine. While conceding this, the court found that the plaintiff was not prejudiced because the same remedy was available in common law. The court reasoned, "Without the guidance of legislative history, we must look to the language of §§ 7-465 and 52-557n to determine a workable and logical interpretation of the interplay between these two statutes and the common law. We presume that the legislature intends sensible results from the statutes it enacts."

Under common law, a municipal employee is "liable for the misperformance of a ministerial act." Even so, because the common law did not recognize a claim for intentional or negligent infliction of emotional distress resulting from an injury to a pet, the plaintiff had failed to set forth a colorable common law claim and the municipality could not "be liable for indemnification when no liability can attach to its officers or employees." The trial court's directed verdict was affirmed.

In addition to the court's analysis of how the doctrine of sovereign immunity should be applied, this court, like so many others, hinted that it was consigned to the decision reached rather than proud of it. The court said, "Labeling a pet as property fails to describe the emotional value human beings place on the companionship that they enjoy with such an animal" and the term property "inadequately and inaccurately describes the relationship between an individual and his or her pet."

Practice Pointer: In this case, no claim for an unconstitutional taking of property was permitted. Do not give up on the court but exercise extreme caution when pursuing a case where a likely defense will be governmental immunity.

104. 84 Conn. App. 395, 853 A.2d 621 (Conn. App. 2004).

Bakay v. Yarnes[105]

Year: *2006*
Category: *Constitutional Law*
Type of Action: *1983 Action*
Animal: *Cat*
Pet Custody Concept: *Time is of the essence.*

The plaintiffs brought a 1983 action under 42 U.S.C. § 1983, alleging that in addition to violating state laws, the defendant violated the Fourth, Fifth, and Fourteenth Amendments of the U.S. Constitution. The plaintiffs also advanced a variety of tort, agency, property, and other claims.[106]

Following a neighbor's complaint to animal control, it was found that as many as 70 cats on the plaintiffs' property were being neglected. There was a substantial amount of urine and feces, together with the presence of an overwhelming smell. The officer received permission from the caretaker to perform an inspection around the perimeter of the house. Subsequently, law enforcement obtained a search warrant. When the officer seized 68 cats from the plaintiffs' Lost Mountain Cattery, the plaintiffs were informed that they had 15 days to petition the court for the cats' return; notwithstanding this statement, 40 cats were quickly "destroyed" without the plaintiffs' permission.

Although there was a history of disease at the plaintiffs' cattery, including highly contagious feline distemper, there was no evidence that any of the 40 euthanized cats had feline distemper. The plaintiffs asserted that the "primary motivation behind destroying the cats was the Humane Society's lack of space" and not the spreading of disease, and that the cats could have been successfully treated. The defendant argued that a veterinarian had recommended euthanasia, as the cats were "severely suffering and/or diseased."

The court considered the plaintiffs' procedural and substantive due process violation claims and found that due process, including both notice and the opportunity to be heard, "is required when a 'significant property interest' is involved." There is a difference between significant property interests and an interest in significant property. While the government is prohibited from a "taking" without due process, the court found that these due process laws do not apply when "exigent circumstances arise" and when it "serves the public interest to act immediately." The court described a

105. 431 F. Supp. 2d 1103 (W.D. Wash. 2006).

106. The plaintiffs alleged simple and gross negligence, violations of the plaintiffs' civil rights under the U.S. Constitution and the Washington Constitution, the doctrine of respondeat superior, conversion and trespass to chattels, breach of a bailment contract, the tort of outrage, statutory waste, breach of a fiduciary duty, and tortious interference with business expectancy.

"humanitarian purpose," or essentially a humanitarian purpose doctrine exception, to due process rights.[107]

The plaintiffs asserted a tort of outrage, a tort akin to an intentional infliction of emotional distress claim, where conduct is extreme or outrageous and causes distress, and emotional distress is suffered as a result of said conduct.[108] The court considered whether a tort of outrage was permissible when conduct is "so outrageous in character, and so extreme in degree, as to go beyond all possible bounds of decency, and to be regarded as atrocious, and utterly intolerable in a civilized community." Although the court determined that as a matter of law, the plaintiffs had not met the evidentiary hurdles to proceed with this claim, the court showed deference to considering this type of novel legal claim.

This case stands out because the federal court did not treat a case involving dead cats as frivolous or ridiculous, or question why the plaintiffs were making a federal claim out of the death of these cats. Instead, the court found this case deserving of a close analysis.

Practice Pointer: Perhaps the humanitarian doctrine exception described in *Bakay*, and offered in a due process context, could be applied to justify a best interests of the companion animal exception in a family law case, particularly when the animal has been the subject of abuse.

Northwest Animal Rights Network v. State of Washington[109]

Year: *2010*
Category: *Animal Cruelty*
Type of Action: *Legality of Statutory Exemption*
Animal: *Multiple*
Pet Custody Concept: *Courts may look to the legislature.*

This decision involved whether a statute could exempt certain animals from anticruelty laws. The plaintiffs framed their challenge under the Constitution and asserted that because of the non-delegation doctrine established in Article I, Section X of the U.S. Constitution, a state law violated both the Fifth and Fourteenth Amendments.

107. Another interesting aspect was the plaintiffs' claim that they "lost their Cat Fanciers' Association (CFA) license because of the publicity surrounding the seizure." *But see* Joan Miller, *Why Is CFA Opposed to Cat Licensing?*, Cat Fanciers' Association, Inc., http://www.ncraoa.com/articles/feline/WhyCFAOpposesCatLicensing.04.PDF (last visited May 12, 2016). Although a license is a revenue source for animal control agencies and humane societies, cat licensing was "rejected by the CFA because we recognize that this regulation is essentially a 'cat tax' unfairly targeted to segments of the public who are most visible—those individuals involved in caring for and helping to gain appreciation for cats—responsible cat owners, breeders/owners of pedigreed cats; unowned/feral cat caregivers."

108. The tort of outrageous conduct has emerged in toxic tort litigation. Jason R. Fulmer, *The Tort of Outrage: A Suggestion for a New Standard for Defining Outrageous Conduct in Arkansas*, 54 Ark. L. Rev. 47 (2001–02). For the seeds of the tort of outrage in animal law, *see* Burgess v. Taylor, 44 S.W.3d 806 (Ky. 2001).

109. 158 Wash. App. 237 (2010).

As laid out in *Northwest Greyhound Kennel Association, Inc. v. State*,[110] the court said a case is not justiciable when indispensable parties are not joined or when the case represents a political question that the judiciary should not resolve. In *Northwest Greyhound*, the political question related to whether professional gambling should be permitted. The court said, "We believe that defendant's challenge does not reach the issue whether the [Gambling Act] impedes equal protection of the law; rather it raises a political question and is not justiciable."

In the instant case, the court found that indispensable parties might have been beef ranchers, rodeo riders, 4-H members, veterinarians, recreational fishers, and university researchers. The court, as in *Northwest Greyhound*, examined what actions should be criminalized and found that this was a question for the legislature, not the judiciary. Citing *Rousso v. State*,[111] the court emphasized that if the judiciaries made public policy decisions, not only would this ignore the separation of powers, but it would also "stretch the practical limits of the judiciary."

Practice Pointer: It is always unpredictable whether courts will make decisions on moral issues or whether the court will decline and point to law-making bodies.

United States v. Stevens[112]

Year: *2010*
Category: *Constitutional Law*
Type of Action: *Free Speech*
Animal: *Cat, Dog*
Pet Custody Concept: *Courts cannot be counted on to prevent animal cruelty by classifying depictions of animal abuse as unprotected speech.*

Writing for the majority, Chief Justice Roberts permitted the making of crush videos involving helpless animals as an exercise of free speech, the kind of action one might associate with moral turpitude or the emerging concept of moral obscenity.[113] The federal law challenged was 18 U.S.C. § 48, and according to Chief Justice Roberts, this law was enacted "to criminalize the commercial creation, sale, or possession of certain depictions of animal cruelty." The court described crush videos as depicting "women slowly crushing animals to death 'with their bare feet or while wearing high heeled shoes,' sometimes while 'talking to the animals in a kind of dominatrix patter' over '[t]he cries and squeals of the animals, obviously in great pain.'"

Roberts continued, "The statute does not address underlying acts harmful to animals, but only portrayals of such conduct." He explained that the issue before the court was limited to "whether the prohibition in the statute is consistent with the freedom of speech guaranteed by the First Amendment." He defined animal cruelty as when "a living animal is intentionally maimed, mutilated, tortured, wounded, or killed, if

---

110. 8 Wash. App. 314, 318–19, 506 P.2d 878 (1973).
111. 170 Wash. 2d 70, __, 239 P.3d 1084 (2010).
112. 559 U.S. 460, 130 S. Ct. 1577, 176 L. Ed. 2d 435 (2010).
113. *Kerry: Syria Gas Attack a Moral Obscenity*, Aljazeera, http://www.aljazeera.com/news/middleeast/2013/08/2013826191025273764.html (last visited May 12, 2016).

that conduct violates federal or state law where the 'creation, sale, or possession takes place.'"[114] According to the chief justice, the pertinent law's "exceptions clause" meant the § 48(c)(1) prohibition did not apply to "any depiction 'that has serious religious, political, scientific, educational, journalistic, historical, or artistic value.'"

Then, Roberts turned to the issue, before the court, a § 48 challenge pertaining to dogfighting videos. One of the videos was titled "Pick-A-Winna." The chief justice said that § 48 was facially invalid under the First Amendment.[115] Emphasizing that the Third Circuit en banc[116] "declined to recognize a new category of unprotected speech for depictions of animal cruelty," the chief justice said that the Third Circuit was not persuaded that animal cruelty and child pornography depictions were analogous.[117] More specifically, Roberts said, "the Court of Appeals then held that §48 could not survive strict scrutiny as a content-based regulation of protected speech" because "the statute lacked a compelling government interest and was neither narrowly tailored to preventing animal cruelty nor the least restrictive means of doing so."

The chief justice reiterated that Congress is prohibited from passing laws that abridge the freedom of speech. Relying on *Ashcroft v. American Civil Liberties Union,*[118] Roberts said that the "government has no power to restrict expression because of its message, its ideas, its subject matter, or its content." Accordingly, § 48 was presumptively invalid, and the burden of proof to rebut that presumption must be overcome by the government. He opposed adding content-based speech restriction depicting animal cruelty to what he called "the list."[119] It seemed significant to the chief justice that even though the Massachusetts Bay Colony passed a law that "No man shall exercise any Tirranny or Crueltie towards any bruite Creature which are usuallie kept for man's use," the law was not "codified in the First Amendment."[120]

Roberts rejected the government's argument that "Whether a given category of speech enjoys First Amendment protection depends upon a categorical balancing of the value of the speech against its societal costs." His preferred standard is reflected as follows, "Within these categories of unprotected speech, 'the evil to be restricted so overwhelmingly outweighs the expressive interests, if any, at stake, that no process of case-by-case adjudication is required,' because 'the balance of competing interests is clearly struck.'" Rather than fashioning a doctrine or a principle that would further advance the "evil to be restricted" under § 48, Roberts dismissed the language of the law as "descriptive."

---

114. The statement "if that conduct violates federal or state law" is consistent with state law.

115. The district court found Stevens's actions were unprotected speech under the First Amendment, as are obscenity and child pornography. The constitutional application of the § 48 "exceptions clause" was sufficiently narrow.

116. Over a three-judge dissent.

117. It seemed that the court was unaware of the link between animal cruelty and human cruelty. Charles Siebert, *The Animal-Cruelty Syndrome*, N.Y. Times, http://www.nytimes.com/2010/06/13/magazine/13dogfighting-t.html?pagewanted=all (last visited May 12, 2016).

118. 535 U.S. 564 (S. Ct. 2002).

119. By "the list," Roberts presumably meant unprotected speech, such as incitement of illegal activity, the use of fighting words, and obscenity. It is also well understood there are categories of less protected speech, too, including commercial speech.

120. The U.S. Declaration of Independence was also not codified.

Roberts perhaps gave himself away when he cited *New York v. Ferber*,[121] a case where "the State of New York was found to have a compelling interest in protecting children from abuse, and that the value of using children in these works (as opposed to simulated conduct or adult actors) was de minimis." He then added, "We made clear that Ferber presented a special case: The market for child pornography was 'intrinsically related' to the underlying abuse, and was therefore 'an integral part of the production of such materials, an activity illegal throughout the Nation.'" He could embrace the restriction of evil aimed at innocent children but not innocent animals.[122] He said, "Maybe there are some categories of speech that have been historically unprotected, but have not yet been specifically identified or discussed as such in our case law. But if so, there is no evidence that 'depictions of animal cruelty' is among them." Roberts was unapologetic, if not defiant.

Next, Roberts addressed whether § 48 was facially invalid. Rejecting the typical approach to a facial attack, wherein "no set of circumstances exists under which [§ 48] would be valid," or that the "statute lacks any 'plainly legitimate sweep,'" the court instead preferred to use a different approach that was outcome determinative. The chief justice said, "a law may be invalidated as overbroad if 'a substantial number' of its applications are unconstitutional, judged in relation to the statute's plainly legitimate sweep."

What Roberts offered next was the specter of an overbroad application of § 48; he said this would create "a criminal prohibition of alarming breadth." He expressed concerns about the difficulty of applying the law in various jurisdictions. The examples that Roberts offered as evidence seemed to be descriptive, a quality he already admonished as lacking rigor in his criticism of the statute in question. Roberts's priorities were reflected in his criticism of the Endangered Species Act. He said, "Protections of endangered species restrict even the humane 'wound[ing] or kill[ing]' of 'living animal[s].'" Returning to § 48, he said that there was "a bewildering maze of regulations from at least 56 separate jurisdictions," and he added that these differences "extend well beyond hunting"; he then provided information about competing state powers involving livestock slaughter.[123]

Roberts foresaw that this law might negatively affect hunting videos, even though the government admitted that hunting videos have serious value and were distinguishable from films depicting or promoting dogfighting, which lack educational value. Roberts rejected the government's reliance on the *Miller v. California*[124] obscenity decision and was dubious about the government's claim that § 48 would only be used to prosecute cases involving "extreme cruelty." Claiming that § 48 was ambiguous, Roberts said, "We 'will not rewrite a . . . law to conform it to constitutional requirements.'" In

121. 458 U.S. 747, 102 S. Ct. 3348, 73 L. Ed. 2d 1113 (U.S. 1982).

122. Roberts seemed unable to make the connection that crush videos and dogfighting videos affect moral fiber. He also seemed unaware of the link between animal abuse behaviors and human abuse behaviors. *Understanding the Link between Animal Abuse and Family Violence*, American Humane Association, http://www.americanhumane.org/interaction/support-the-bond/fact-sheets/understanding-the-link.html (last visited May 12, 2016).

123. Although Roberts admitted that there was an exception clause to § 48 for lawful practices, he concluded that what would be required was an "unrealistically broad reading of the exceptions clause."

124. 413 U.S. 15, 93 S. Ct. 2607, 37 L. Ed. 2d 419 (U.S. 1973).

affirming the Third Circuit's decision, Roberts said, "However 'growing' and 'lucrative' the markets for crush videos and dogfighting depictions might be, they are dwarfed by the market for other depictions, such as hunting magazines and videos, that we have determined to be within the scope of §48." The court thereby affirmed the judgment of the U.S. Court of Appeals for the Third Circuit.

Justice Alito offered a passionate dissent. He explained that 18 U.S.C. § 48 "was enacted not to suppress speech, but to prevent horrific acts of animal cruelty—in particular, the creation and commercial exploitation of 'crush videos,' a form of depraved entertainment that has no social value." He also said, "Instead of applying the doctrine of overbreadth, I would vacate the decision below and instruct the Court of Appeals on remand to decide whether the videos that respondent sold are constitutionally protected."

He suggested that the records before the court failed to support "the Court's conclusion that §48 bans a substantial quantity of protected speech." Justice Alito pointed out that "A party seeking to challenge the constitutionality of a statute generally must show that the statute violates the party's own rights." He chastised the majority for violating a well-known tradition of the court that overbreadth should only be considered "as a last resort." He then discussed the subject of hunting as follows:

> I turn first to depictions of hunting. As the Court notes, photographs and videos of hunters shooting game are common. But hunting is legal in all 50 States, and §48 applies only to a depiction of conduct that is illegal in the jurisdiction in which the depiction is created, sold, or possessed. Therefore, in all 50 States, the creation, sale, or possession for sale of the vast majority of hunting depictions indisputably falls outside §48's reach.
>
> Straining to find overbreadth, the Court suggests that §48 prohibits the sale or possession in the District of Columbia of any depiction of hunting because the District—undoubtedly because of its urban character—does not permit hunting within its boundaries. The Court also suggests that, because some States prohibit a particular type of hunting (e.g., hunting with a crossbow or "canned" hunting) or the hunting of a particular animal (e.g., the "sharp-tailed grouse"), §48 makes it illegal for persons in such States to sell or possess for sale a depiction of hunting that was perfectly legal in the State in which the hunting took place.
>
> The Court's interpretation is seriously flawed. "When a federal court is dealing with a federal statute challenged as overbroad, it should, of course, construe the statute to avoid constitutional problems, if the statute is subject to such a limiting construction."

The dissent also found the majority view absurd in that the federal law impacted the methods of slaughter and dairy cow tail docking. Justice Alito said that "nothing in the record suggests that any one has ever created, sold, or possessed for sale a depiction of the slaughter of food animals or of the docking of the tails of dairy cows that would not easily qualify under the exception set out in §48(b)." He emphasized that the U.S. Supreme Court had "a duty to interpret §48 so as to avoid serious constitutional concerns, and §48 may reasonably be construed not to reach almost all, if not all, of the depictions that the Court finds constitutionally protected. Thus, §48 does not appear to have a large number of unconstitutional applications."

With regard to legislative intent, Justice Alito said the goal of Congress was to prevent the advancement of "the creation, sale, or possession of 'crush videos.'" He stated that crush videos exploit images of how a "kitten, secured to the ground, watches and shrieks in pain as a woman thrusts her high-heeled shoe into its body, slams her heel into the kitten's eye socket and mouth loudly fracturing its skull, and stomps repeatedly on the animal's head. The kitten hemorrhages blood, screams blindly in pain, and is ultimately left dead in a moist pile of blood-soaked hair and bone."

Justice Alito also emphasized that all 50 states and the District of Columbia have enacted statutes that prohibit animal cruelty. The law enforcement problem of identifying the "parties responsible for the torture" is not related to the issue of whether a certain kind of speech is prohibited. More so, he stressed the need for a federal law because "In the rare instances in which it was possible to identify and find the perpetrators, they 'often were able to successfully assert as a defense that the State could not prove its jurisdiction over the place where the act occurred or that the actions depicted took place within the time specified in the State statute of limitations.'"

Stressing the need for a federal law to stop criminal conduct and commercial exploitation, he appraised the importance of *New York v. Ferber*,[125] a Supreme Court decision where the Court made the link between child pornography and child molestation. He exclaimed that the majority could have made similar intellectual leaps when it came to the nexus of violent images and violence in *Stevens*. Relying on an amicus brief from the Humane Society, Alito said,

> The abused dogs used in fights endure physical torture and emotional manipulation throughout their lives to predispose them to violence; common tactics include feeding the animals hot peppers and gunpowder, prodding them with sticks, and electrocution. Dogs are conditioned never to give up a fight, even if they will be gravely hurt or killed. As a result, dogfights inflict horrific injuries on the participating animals, including lacerations, ripped ears, puncture wounds and broken bones. Losing dogs are routinely refused treatment, beaten further as "punishment" for the loss, and executed by drowning, hanging, or incineration.

From a public policy standpoint, Alito also said that the "harm caused by the underlying criminal acts greatly outweighs any trifling value that the depictions might be thought to possess." He concluded that the statute had a "substantial core of constitutionally permissible applications," and "respondent has not met his burden of demonstrating that any impermissible applications of the statute are 'substantial' in relation to its 'plainly legitimate sweep.'"

As Alito has demonstrated, while the court is eager to carve out an exception involving innocent human children exploited in the child pornography industry, and put a stop to it, the supreme court was unable to extend the same logic to the plight of innocent animals. This case may be useful to family lawyers as evidence of how the

125. 458 U.S. 747, 102 S. Ct. 3348, 73 L. Ed. 2d 1113 (U.S. 1982).

pendulum swings on issues such as where the public policy line is drawn on anticruelty issues. It was obvious that for Roberts, the hunting and agricultural implications of any law, no matter how indirect, were front and center, whereas for Alito, the idea of making a crush video killing a kitten with a high heel was beyond the pale. At the end of the day, this decision is really a morality tale involving Congress and the judicial system.

When thinking about the three branches of government, it is interesting that Congress reacted swiftly to this decision and even our often partisan Congress grasped the importance of thwarting animal cruelty and righting this wrong, a second time, whereas Roberts lacked sensitivity pertaining to the "evil to be restricted." Rather, he used his considerable legal talent to proclaim that in the 21st century, we lack the courage to prevent the exercise of "Tirranny or Crueltie towards any bruite Creature" traceable to one of our earliest colonies.

This case is interesting because it contrasts with a growing body of cases involving animals where the courts are apologetic that they could not do more and emphasize that it is really the lawmakers that must initiate policy change.[126] Thus, the Congress of the United States passed a law about animal cruelty, and the entire U.S. Supreme Court, except Justice Alito, held different values.

The challenge of animal law and pet law—and specifically pet custody disputes—will persevere even when the court acts in isolation from cruelty concerns or without comprehension of human/animal relationships, while at times claiming to do the opposite. On one day, it is possible to convince a court to look at the narrow and discreet issues in a particular case, such as "we separated a year ago and the dog has lived with me and I should be awarded the dog as the dog goes everywhere with me," while on another day, a judge may ridicule the same person for having the audacity to bring up the subject as if the court's stature would be impacted by deciding a case where an emotional investment had been made in a living "thing." Keep in mind that concerns about the future of companion animals, and who should have them, have not been the norm in America's jurisprudence. Thus, lawyers are actual players in what the new normal will look like.[127]

---

126. *See* Rabideau v. City of Racine, 243 Wis. 2d 486, 627 N.W.2d 795, 2001 WI 57.

127. Chief Justice Roberts's opinion in *Stevens* stands out in part because of what appeared to be his unapologetic insensitivity to the plight of animals. Even so, it is also well understood that he is a zealous proctor of the First Amendment. It is too early to rule him out as someone who would not write a more sympathetic decision pertaining to the plight of animals in a case involving state rights, the kind reflected in pet trust laws passed in 50 states. It is worthwhile to remember that the chief justice voted to uphold what is known as Obamacare. He also lives in a culture wherein there remains the possibility that a companion animal is, or could be, a family member. While on the subject of who belongs in a family, it is well understood that the dynamic of who can be in a family is reflected by the progression of artificial reproductive technology cases as well as decisions related to the general topics of gay rights and marriage equality. Emblematic language about how family institutions change with the times is reflected in *Obergefell v. Hodges*, 576 U.S. ___ (2015), where Justice Kennedy, writing for the majority, said, "The nature of injustice is that we may not always see it in our own times. The generations that wrote and ratified the Bill of Rights and the Fourteenth Amendment did not presume to know the extent of freedom in all of its dimensions, and so they entrusted to future generations a charter protecting the right of all persons to enjoy liberty as we learn its meaning. When new insight reveals discord between the Constitution's central protections and a received legal stricture, a claim to liberty must be addressed." While it is conceded that the *Obergefell* decision does not address the appropriate place of companion animals in our daily lives, or mention a relationship with an animal in the context of freedom or liberty, the momentous decisions of our day have effectively planted seeds that those advocating for a better future for companion animals may harvest.

Practice Pointer: Although Roberts was in the dissent in *United States v. Windsor,*[128] and wrote for the majority in *Stevens*, over time, he may come to shift his perspective as to which evils belong on "the list." As public opinion changes, so, too, will public opinions mirrored in the friends and families of Supreme Court justices. It is for this reason that those who read the *Stevens* decision should not despair. All social movements shall have their time, and "every dog shall have its day."[129]

Pasado's Safe Haven v. State[130]

Year: *2011*
Category: *Criminal Law*
Type of Action: *Constitutionality of a Statute*
Animal: *Livestock*
Pet Custody Concept: *An animal lawyer achieved standing for a client by bringing a taxpayer derivative action.*

Under a livestock slaughter act, it is permissible to kill livestock by one of two methods. The appellants, Pasado's Safe Haven, sought to eliminate one of those two methods and brought an action for declaratory judgment pursuant to the Uniform Declaratory Judgments Act. The action was commenced as a taxpayer derivative suit, which had the effect of giving the appellants standing.

Stating that the "remedy of partial statutory invalidation is not always available," the court focused its opinion on the subject of whether the appellants had a justiciable claim, which was defined as "(1) . . . an actual, present and existing dispute, or the mature seeds of one, as distinguished from a possible, dormant, hypothetical, speculative, or moot disagreement, (2) between parties having genuine and opposing interests, (3) which involves interests that must be direct and substantial, rather than potential, theoretical, abstract or academic, and (4) a judicial determination of which will be final and conclusive."

Concerned that a partial invalidation would affect a result not intended by the legislature, the court denied Pasado's requested relief.

Practice Pointer: It is noteworthy that standing was accomplished here through a taxpayer derivative suit.

128. 570 U.S. ___ (2013); 133 S. Ct. 2675; 186 L. Ed. 2d 808 (2013).
129. *Every Dog Has Its Day*, Free Dictionary, http://idioms.thefreedictionary.com/Every+dog+has+its+day (last visited May 12, 2016).
130. 162 Wash. App. 746 (2011).

People v. Tohom[131]

Year: *2013*
Category: *Criminal Law*
Type of Action: *Comfort Dog Courtroom Assistance*
Animal: *Dog*
Pet Custody Concept: *Dogs can fulfill the role of comforting children.*

The state sought to have a "therapy assistance animal" or "comfort dog" accompany a 15-year-old sexual assault victim on the witness stand. It was alleged that her father not only had frequent sexual intercourse with her but also that after impregnating her twice, he arranged for her to have abortions.

The People argued that Rose, a Golden Retriever therapy dog, would be of therapeutic benefit to the girl, as Rose previously helped the girl express her anxiety and verbalize her feelings, both in interviews and in therapy sessions. The child's therapist recommended that Rose should be present in the courtroom "to alleviate the apprehension, as well as the psychological and emotional trauma that such testimony might engender."

The issue of allowing a comfort dog to accompany a child onto a witness stand was one of first impression in New York. There was neither case law nor statutory authority on the subject. The People argued that the child qualified as a "special witness" under the criminal procedure law as well as under the executive law section 642-a. Under the latter law, it was allowed for a "person supportive of a 'special witness' to be 'present and accessible' during the testimony of the witness." The word "person" was of course problematic.[132]

While the defendant argued that Rose's presence would "clearly prejudice the jury against" him, the People countered that the jury could receive curative instructions. The jury instructions eventually given were as follows:

> Ladies and gentlemen, the next witness is J who is obviously sitting in the jury box. As you might recall, I previously spoke to you about the companion animal that's with her. As I indicated before and I reiterate to you now, during the testimony of J, she will be accompanied by a companion dog. The decision to allow this was one the court made and you may not speculate in any way as to why that decision was made. You must not draw any inference either favorably or negatively from either side because of the dog's presence. You

131. 2013 N.Y. Slip. Op. 5234 (N.Y. App. Div. 2013).

132. According to a licensed social worker from Child and Family Services, the child witness had long been the subject of sexual abuse and suffered from post-traumatic stress disorder. She had difficulty expressing her emotions, discussing her abuse, and sleeping. During regular therapy sessions, when Rose was in the child's presence, the child was "a lot more verbal." The social worker explained that "when Rose 'placed her head on J's lap, and J began to pet her, J was better able to talk about how she felt and how she would feel safer if Rose was present with her in the courtroom.'" The People were concerned that "having J testify in open court about the abuse would be tantamount to 'retraumatizing her and causing her to experience post-traumatic stress disorder symptoms and possibly increase those symptoms.'" Rose was trained "to sense stress and anxiety and act in such a way to help reduce that by raising herself up and offering herself to the person to be petted."

> must not permit sympathy for any party to enter into your considerations as you listen to this testimony, and this is especially so with an outside factor such as a companion dog permitted to be present in the courtroom. Each witness's testimony must be evaluated based upon the instructions I give you during my charge and on nothing more.

Although in its decision, the court addressed many fine points of criminal law, the most interesting was how the court interpreted the executive law. Instead of focusing on the word "person," the court discussed the intent behind the executive law when it said, "The purpose of the legislation was to address the emotional stress which a child victim might endure as a result of his or her necessary involvement with criminal proceedings."[133] Accordingly, the court found that executive law section 642-a applied.

The court recalled that in *People v. Gutkaiss*,[134] a child witness was afforded the comfort of holding a teddy bear while testifying at trial. In the instant case, the court observed that a live animal was involved, "as opposed to an inanimate object." The court emphasized its broad discretion "in fashioning an appropriate measure to address a testifying child witness's emotional or psychological stress, based upon the particular needs of that child." It was also noted that a comfort service dog named Ellie was permitted in the courtroom in *State v. Dye*[135] and the use of a therapy dog was permitted in *People v. Spence*.[136]

The court was not persuaded by the defendant's argument that the presence of a therapy dog adversely affected his constitutional right to confront the witness. The court said that the defendant's claim had "no basis," as the record clearly reflected that Rose sat unobtrusively with the witness, neither moving nor making any noises. During the trial, the prosecutor stated on the record that "the dog sat peacefully and quietly on the stand," and when defense counsel was asked by the court if this was a fair description of the dog's behavior, counsel agreed.

The court also noted that during the trial, defense counsel engaged in "extended and thorough" cross-examination of the witness and that the "record does not suggest to us that Rose impeded defense Counsel's right to cross examine the central witness."[137] The court utilized these sources to explain that even if it had conducted a "Frye" hearing, the defendant's argument was without merit because there was

---

133. In *State v. Nix*, 355 Or. 777, 334 P.3d 437 (2014), *vacated*, 356 Ore. 768, 345 P.3d 416 (2015), the court undertook a similar legislative intent analysis.

134. 206 A.D.2d 628, 614 N.Y.S.2d 599 (N.Y. A.D. 3 1994).

135. 283 P.3d 1130 (Wash. App. 2012).

136. 212 Cal. App. 4th 478, 151 Cal. Rptr. 3d 374 (Cal. App. 2012).

137. The court rejected the defendant's argument that the court should have held a "Frye" hearing to determine whether Rose should have been allowed during the victim's testimony.

significant research establishing that the presence of a dog can have a comforting emotional effect on humans.[138]

Of particular interest was the court's decision under the section titled "Use of Dogs for Emotional Therapy." In the court's opinion, there was a direct quote from a book by Andrew Leaser called *See Spot Mediate: Utilizing the Emotional and Psychological Benefits of "Dog Therapy" in Victim-Offender Mediation.*[139] "There is already a significant amount of research showing that the mere presence of a dog can have dramatic emotional and psychological benefits."

In the instant case, the supreme court affirmed the predatory sexual assault and child welfare endangerment conviction. The New York Supreme Court determined that a judge "conducting a public trial is empowered to control the proceedings in whatever manner may be consistent with the demands of decorum and due process." This case is indicative of how judges in New York may have extra sensitivity to the role of a therapy dog helping a child, whereas these same animals, cognitively advanced and empathetic, may only be products or goods under the Uniform Commercial Code.

Practice Pointer: This case demonstrated how dogs can be of benefit to children suffering from psychological trauma. In the same vein, it makes sense that the best interests of children whose parents are divorcing or splitting up should be considered in pet custody disputes.

State of Washington v. Peterson[140]

Year: *2013*
Category: *Criminal Law, Constitutional Law*
Type of Action: *Felony*
Animal: *Horse*
Pet Custody Concept: *Courts can interpret statutes in a reasonable way when they want to.*

The appellant started a horse breeding business that included breeding racehorses. Although leasing four acres of land from a man named Rock Borchardt, the appellant failed to feed or water the horses put there. Borchardt noticed a "bone dry" watering dish on a 100-degree day and testified that "the horses ate the grass down to the dirt."

---

138. The court quoted from Marianne Dellinger's *Using Dogs for Emotional Support of Testifying Victims of Crime*, 15 Animal L. 171 (2008) by saying, "Dogs have a natural ability to calm humans as well as a positive effect on our emotional and psychological states. They help us break down the barriers of fear, distrust, and anxiety so we can get to the truth and scientific studies have shown that dogs help people by reducing blood pressure, stress and anxiety, improving feelings of self-worth and decreasing loneliness." Next, the court quoted Michael Walsh's *Comfort Dogs Head to Help Victims of Boston Bombings*, NY Daily News, April 17, 2013, when it said, "There is also substantial anecdotal evidence that dogs have been found to have beneficial effects on the emotional and even physical well-being of hospital patients, residents of nursing homes, and those suffering from psychological trauma, including the victims of the recent shootings in Newtown, Connecticut, and the Boston Marathon bombings."

139. 20 Ohio St. J. on Disp. Resol. 943, 961 (2005).

140. 301 P.3d 1060 (Wash. App. 2013).

Borchardt told the appellant to "come take care of your horses or get them off my property."

The appellant rented additional acreage located on Trout Farm Road near Sultan. Janet Auckland, a nearby neighbor, testified that at first, the appellant kept "five or six horses" there and that "within a week, the tall grass on the property was gone, leaving nothing but dirt." Auckland said that there "wasn't anything for them to survive on." When she returned from a trip the next month, Auckland noticed many of the horses' ribs and bones were showing. Like Borchardt, Auckland observed lack of water for the horses.[141]

Both animal control and the sheriff's office obtained and executed a search warrant to seize the horses. The appellant was charged with cruelty in the first degree for six horses. The appellant challenged the first-degree animal cruelty statute, arguing that the statute terminology "unjustifiable physical pain" was constitutionally void for vagueness.[142] The court reviewed the black letter law as to how a statute need not meet impossible standards of specificity. The lack of definition of a statutory term did not make a term vague, especially if an individual with ordinary intellect could understand its meaning. The court was satisfied that the statutory language "unjustifiable physical pain" met an "objective standard of reasonableness."[143]

The court heard testimony from veterinarians on the subject of pain.[144] One veterinarian said that feeding a horse intermittently can cause pain because if a horse "is only fed once a day, its acid levels in the stomach will rise." The same veterinarian also explained how "overall demeanor, head carriage, and dull affect" were all evidence of horse suffering.

As animal cruelty in the first degree is not an intent crime, the state's proof of criminal negligence was enough.[145] The court affirmed that the statute on animal cruelty was not void for vagueness. Then, the court turned to the issue of whether starvation and dehydration were alternative means of committing the crime of animal cruelty in the first degree. The answer to the question depends on whether the words "alternative means" are definitional or descriptive of an element of the crime. The defense asserted the fine point that the horses were not suffering from dehydration.

The court held that "starvation, dehydration, and suffocation are different ways of committing the crime of animal cruelty in the first degree and are not merely

---

141. There was one exception to the poor care that this witness observed. In the midst of the starving horses, the appellant gave one stallion "alfalfa and water."

142. The burden of proof is on the appellant when there is a void for vagueness challenge.

143. The court defined pain as "a state of physical or mental lack of well-being or physical or mental uneasiness that ranges from mild discomfort or dull distress to acute often unbearable agony."

144. When the appellant acquired a horse with a foot condition called laminitis, a veterinarian said Tyme was "overall in good health, her laminitis is being well-managed, she walks quite comfortably, and she seems happy." Following complaints, the appellant again took Tyme to a veterinarian who found that Tyme had a "big sac, kind of a seroma," a wound that seemed to be draining, and a painful hoof condition called founder. The veterinarian recommended euthanasia, as Tyme had an extremely low body condition score. Another veterinarian who saw Tyme said that her ribs were "very discernible," that she was "nonambulatory," and that her demeanor was dull. Flies were observed crawling in and out of her draining wound. The second veterinarian also recommended euthanasia. At the time of Tyme's later necropsy, it was revealed that she had no subcutaneous fat.

145. When economic distress is an affirmative defense to animal cruelty in the second degree, it is not a defense to animal cruelty in the first degree.

descriptive or definitional but rather, separate and essential terms of the offense." Viewing the evidence most favorable to the state, the court concluded that the state had proved beyond a reasonable doubt that the appellant had "dehydrated the horses causing substantial and unjustifiable pain." Furthermore, the court said, "We hold that whether the horses suffered unjustifiable pain and suffering caused by dehydration is a matter of common knowledge and ordinary experience."[146]

Practice Pointer: Some courts may stretch the law when extreme cruelty to animals is involved.

State v. Fessenden[147]

Year: *2014*
Category: *Criminal Law*
Type of Action: *Felony*
Animal: *Horse*
Pet Custody Concept: *Under extreme circumstances, courts will advance animal protection.*

Following a citizen complaint, an officer lawfully parked in a driveway and observed a horse whose "backbone protruded, her withers stood up, her neck was thin, all of her ribs were visible, she had no visible fatty tissue in her shoulders, and she was 'swaying a little bit.'" Believing that the horse was in need of emergency aid and that exigent circumstances existed, the officer seized the horse and brought her to a veterinarian for care. The officer feared that if he waited for a warrant, the horse would fall and that would be the end of her. The officer also saw the horse strain to urinate, a behavior that to the officer signaled the risk of starvation-related kidney failure and the possibility that the horse's other internal organs would shut down. The officer believed the crime of first-degree animal neglect was in progress.

One of the co-owners of the starving horse was charged with first-degree animal neglect and first-degree animal abuse, and the other co-owner was charged with second-degree animal neglect. Their appeals were consolidated.[148] Both defendants maintained that the warrantless search violated their state and federal Fourth Amendment constitutional rights.

For the emergency aid exception to the warrant requirement, the court cited *State v. Baker.*[149] There, the court permitted entry to property without a warrant when the officers had an "objectively reasonable belief, based on articulable facts, that a

146. The court determined that the state was entitled to reimbursement for the costs incurred in caring for the seized horses, per statutory plain language that if convicted, "defendant is liable for the care of the horses."

147. 355 Or. 759 (Or. 2014). This was a companion case to *State v. Nix*, 355 Or. 777, 334 P.3d 437 (2014), *vacated*, 356 Or. 768, 345 P.3d 416 (2015).

148. It was not clear on appeal why the defendants faced separate charges, but as they co-owned the horse, it seemed probable that the defendant charged with the greater offense was the co-owner in possession of the horse.

149. 350 Or. 641, 649, 260 P.3d 476 (2011).

warrantless entry is necessary to either render immediate aid to persons, or to assist persons who have suffered, or who are imminently threatened with suffering, serious physical injury or harm." In *Fessenden*, the court of appeals determined that "animals were included in the class of 'persons' that officers may aid without a warrant." The court of appeals also found that there was a "societal interest in protecting nonhuman animals from unnecessary pain, injury, trauma, and cruel death."

The supreme court differentiated between the requirements for applying the emergency aid exception and the exigent circumstances exception. The emergency aid exception permits the "warrantless entry, search, or seizure, regardless of whether the officer has probable cause to believe that a crime has been or is being committed, as long as the officer reasonably believes it necessary to 'render immediate aid to persons who have suffered, or who are imminently threatened with suffering, serious physical injury or harm.'" In contrast, the exigent circumstances exception is further discussed below. Another aspect as to how these two exceptions may be distinguished pertains to the subject of scope. The emergency aid exception is specifically applicable to rendering aide to persons.

In rendering its decision, the court began by reviewing the arguments the defense advanced, stating, "Inanimate property *qua* property does not constitute a compelling societal interest equivalent to the interest in avoiding serious physical harm to persons." The defense also argued that "even if animals are considered 'sentient life' and not 'property,' society's interest in protecting animals from abuse and neglect is not sufficiently significant to invoke an exception" to the warrant requirement.

The defense cited Cass R. Sunstein for the proposition that the common law only protects animals to the extent that animals derived status as the property of their owners.[150] The court said, "Courts generally suggested that such cruelty was not unlawful unless it worked an injury to the owner, who was the essential rights holder; but on rare occasions, the courts concluded that cruelty could count as a common law misdemeanor." This was quite an interesting common law aside and could serve as an argument, by analogy, in a torts claim for expanding noneconomic damages.

The defense further contended that in passing animal cruelty laws, the same type of impact on owner analysis applied. Thus, animal cruelty laws did not represent concern about how animals were treated, but rather, the public policy objective was not to densensitize humans if this were allowed to happen. The defense challenged that even if societal interests afforded more protection to certain animals or when certain types of mistreatment occurred, the state still must overcome a clear and convincing threshold for a warrantless seizure. To do otherwise would be contrary to the ideal of a "clear, workable, and consistent" departure from the requirement of a warrant.

Although not reflective of legislative intent at the time these crimes were committed, the court observed that while this matter was before the courts, the state legislature had passed a law that "animals are sentient beings capable of experiencing pain, stress and fear."[151] The court recognized that although animals may be killed, their treatment is circumscribed by boundaries, including good animal husbandry and

150. Cass R. Sunstein, *Standing for Animals (with Notes on Animal Rights)*, 47 UCLA L. Rev. 1333, 1337 (2000).

151. ORS 167.305(1).

accepted veterinary practices. The court also explained that pets, including dogs and horses,[152] have a special place in human affection.

The court noted that "India's Central Zoo Authority recently banned the exhibition of dolphins after concluding that their status was closer to that of 'non-human persons.'" In addition, the court described current efforts in the United States pertaining to the establishment of legal personhood for chimpanzees. The supreme court said, "As we continue to learn more about the interrelated nature of all life, the day may come when humans perceive less separation between themselves and other living beings than the law now reflects. However, we do not need a mirror to the past or a telescope to the future to recognize that the legal status of animals has changed and is changing still."

In delivering its decision, the court focused on the exigent circumstances exception to the warrant requirement and reviewed cases where the exigent circumstances exception to the statute were not limited to cases where human life was threatened. Instead of requiring a threat to human life, these cases reflected that an investigating officer should act when a crime is in progress.

The court detailed that an officer believed that based upon the condition of the horse, the horse was at risk for serious imminent harm or death, particularly if the horse fell during the long time it takes to secure a warrant. The court said, "the officer had probable cause to believe that a crime was in progress." Accordingly, the exigent circumstances exception applied. The court stressed how the officer had acted based upon "specific, articulable facts" and that its decision was within "narrow confines." The court also noted that the Ninth Circuit's federal interpretation of exigent circumstances was similar to the state's. Next, the court determined that the "officer's warrantless seizure of the horse was lawful, and the trial court did not err in denying defendants' motions to suppress." The decisions of both the court of appeals and the circuit court were affirmed.

Courts around the country now have another case to cite as animal law jurisprudence moves surely forward. Here, as in the companion case of *State v. Nix*,[153] the court was willing, in the context of outrageous human behaviors directed at hoofed animals, to interpret the use of the word "person" to apply to animals even while maintaining that their animal status had not changed. The court was doing its best to protect animals and went as far as it rationally and logically could. This is the type of resourcefulness courts can utilize when there is an absence of just laws.

Practice Pointer: This case illustrates that certain animals are treated differently in certain circumstances than others. In the tradition of *Rabideau v. City of Racine*,[154] this case clearly shows that the court was "uncomfortable with the law's cold characterization of a dog as mere property." The court also seemed to reflect, as subtly

---

152. The court observed that development of animal welfare laws reflects this fact. The centuries-old ASPCA has long had a seal wherein an angel intervened to save a carriage horse from being beaten. The novel *Black Beauty* was credited with being influential in the passage of animal cruelty laws. *See* Rabideau v. City of Racine, 243 Wis. 2d 486, 491, 627 N.W.2d 795, 798 (2001).

153. 355 Or. 777, 334 P.3d 437 (2014), *vacated*, 356 Or. 768, 345 P.3d 416 (2015).

154. 243 Wis. 2d 486, 491, 627 N.W.2d 795, 798 (2001).

as possible, the sense that angels are on the side of animals. Rather than saying this directly, the court described the ASPCA seal with the angel intervening to stop animal cruelty. Lawyers can be just as subtle in using powerful images of good and evil.

State v. Nix[155]

Year: *2014*
Category: *Criminal Law*
Type of Action: *Sentencing*
Animal: *Horse, Goat*
Pet Custody Concept: *Animals are now in the interim category between property and persons.*

In this well-crafted and landmark opinion, the court undertook one of the most rigorous efforts in the history of animal law to discern legislative interest. Although the court later vacated its decision in *Nix* because it concluded that it did not have jurisdiction of the appeal, the Supreme Court of Oregon in *State v. Hess*[156] said, "we nonetheless are persuaded by the *Nix* court's reasoning on the merger question, and we adopt it. Hence, we conclude that the trial court did not err in entering convictions on all 45 of the animal-neglect counts."

The police, informed of animal abuse, entered the defendant's farm and found emaciated horses and goats that were either dying or already dead. The defendant was convicted of 20 counts of second-degree animal abuse, a verdict he did not agree with because, as animals are not persons, they cannot be victims. The trial court, agreeing with the defendant's position, merged the 20 verdicts involving 20 different animals and suspended imposition of a 90-day jail sentence, leaving three years of bench probation in place.

The court explored whether an animal could be a victim under Oregon statute and case law. Pursuant to statute 167.325(1), "A person commits the crime of animal neglect in the second degree if, except as otherwise authorized by law, the person intentionally, knowingly, recklessly or with criminal negligence fails to provide minimum care for an animal in such person's custody or control." The court then looked at language from more than ten statutes, extensive case law, various dictionary definitions, and Article I, Section 44(3) of the Oregon Constitution on whether animals can be victims., If they could, the defendant would then be punishable by as many offenses as there were victims under statute 161.067(2).

The court emphasized the following concepts:

- The interpretation of the word "victim" should be understood in the context of the "underlying substantive criminal law statute."
- Legislative history is one of several aids in statutory construction.

155. 355 Or. 777, 334 P.3d 437 (2014), *vacated*, 356 Or. 768, 345 P.3d 416 (2015). This holding was reaffirmed in *State v. Hess*, 359 P.3d 288 (Or. Ct. App. 2015).
156. 359 P.3d 288 (Or. Ct. App. 2015).

- Oregon statutes define minimum care as "care sufficient to preserve the health and well-being of an animal."
- Rather than being fixed, the meaning of "victim" is context specific.
- The applicable statute does not define the word "victim."
- Who the legislation wanted to protect should be determined.
- Dictionary definitions are useful.
- Constitutional provisions describing human victims as persons are useful.
- The ordinary meaning of the term "victim" can be expressly or implicitly understood within the criminal code.
- Most Oregon cases refer to a human victim for the purposes of the merger doctrine.
- The legislation has the power to designate, "either expressly or by an implication, a different meaning of victim than person."
- The public can be the victim of a criminal offense.
- The applicable statute is intended to protect animals by making their abuse a crime.
- Oregon statutes, beyond providing animals with water, shelter, and veterinary care, also articulate other welfare requirements.
- By passing a statute requiring minimum care, it is understood that the legislature has intended to protect the animals referenced in that statute.
- In its case law, the idea of victim has been broadened.
- It would be illogical to identify the perpetrator of a crime as the victim of that same crime.

The court concluded that "the victim under ORS 167.325 is not a person." From there, the court analyzed whether the victim of the animal abuse negligent crime should be "the animals themselves or the public at large." In weighing these alternatives, the court was persuaded that "even though animals usually are the property of persons, there is a broader public interest in their health, care, and well-being that requires vindication when they are neglected."

While the court observed that there were compelling reasons that the public might qualify as a victim, the court thought the better approach was to identify "both an actual harm and the particular subject who must suffer that harm in order for a violation of the statute to be complete." The court concluded that "it appears that the legislature's primary concern was to protect individual animals as sentient beings, rather than to vindicate a more generalized public interest in their welfare." The court also offered an extensive legislative history, including Oregon's revision of its animal cruelty laws in 1985, to support its interpretation.

Practice Pointer: Analyze the Constitution, every statute and case possible, and help the court take the next step in the ever-evolving animal law jurisprudence. In this case, the court found that an animal can be a crime victim.

State v. Hess[157]

Year: *2015*
Category: *Criminal Law*
Type of Action: *Appeal*
Animal: *Horse, Cat*
Pet Custody Concept: *Cats can be crime victims.*

Essentially reaffirming the holding in *State v. Nix*,[158] which was vacated based upon the court's conclusion that it lacked jurisdiction for the appeal, the court declined to apply the defendant's request to apply the merger statute, which meant that seven dead cats and thirty-eight live cats were individual crime victims. The trial court properly found that the defendant's expert testimony on her lack of capacity due to her obsessive-compulsive personality disorder was irrelevant. To the contrary, the court reiterated the minimal standard the state had for an omission to perform an act the individual was capable of performing and determined that the defendant had capacity.

Practice Pointer: Courts are not impressed by mental health excuses as a defense for the mistreatment of animals.

State v. Newcomb[159]

Year: *2016*
Category: *Criminal Law*
Type of Action: *Search*
Animal: *Dog*
Pet Custody Concept: *Animals are sentient and no longer "mere" property.*

One might not expect, in a misdemeanor case involving a beaten and starving dog, that the Oregon attorney general, Ellen F. Rosenblum, and Oregon's solicitor general, Anna M. Joyce, would both sign on to the state's brief, and also that briefs of amici curiae would be submitted by such a broad range of governmental entities and nonprofits, including the National District Attorneys Association, the Association of Prosecuting Attorneys, the Animal Legal Defense Fund, the Oregon Humane Society, and the Oregon Veterinary Medical Association. Yet, they all did.

In this landmark decision, the Oregon Supreme Court reversed the court of appeals and affirmed the circuit court decision of Judge Eric J. Bergstrom. This meant that in the course of the cruelty investigation of a dog named Juno, who was lawfully seized based upon probable cause of malnutrition, the veterinarian could draw blood

157. 359 P.3d 288 (Or. Ct. App. 2015).
158. 355 Or. 777, 334 P.3d 437 (2014), *vacated*, 356 Or. 768, 345 P.3d 416 (2015). This holding was reaffirmed in *State v. Hess*, 359 P.3d 288 (Or. Ct. App. 2015).
159. 359 Or. 756 (2016).

without a warrant to treat the animal because the veterinarian was not entering "a container" with information contrary to a constitutional search requirement. Instead, Juno was a living animal with physiological processes. The court realized that a dog is a dog inside and out.

The blood tests revealed that the dog's emaciated condition, as reflected on a score of 1.5 out of nine on a body condition score, was not attributable to parasites.

Practice Pointer: Keep an eye on the Oregon Supreme Court. It is at the forefront of redefining the place of animals in American history.

Chapter 9

Katrina, Katrina

"Think occasionally of the suffering of which you spare yourself the sight."

—*Albert Schweitzer*

In this chapter, we will take a close look at how ground operations worked following Hurricane Katrina, what legal questions arose, what role the American Bar Association played, and how carefully judicial officers struggled to make decisions in ensuing pet custody disputes. The legal decisions following Hurricane Katrina are emblematic of the shift in how companion animals are viewed in our legal system.

HURRICANE KATRINA SEQUENCE OF EVENTS

Before Hurricane Katrina made landfall, Governor Kathleen Blanco had already declared a state of emergency, forecasting that the Lake Pontchartrain levee near New Orleans could be toppled or breached. For the first time in the history of the city, Mayor Ray Nagin issued a mandatory evacuation order and the Federal Emergency Management Agency (FEMA) was authorized "to identify, mobilize and provide at its discretion, equipment and resources necessary to alleviate the impacts of the emergency."[1] The National Weather Service warned that in the event of a category four or five hurricane, most of the area would be uninhabitable for weeks, if not longer. Eighty thousand people were stranded in the city, beyond those trapped at the Superdome. There were also 50,000 stranded pets.

When the levee toppled and breached following the arrival of the category five hurricane, President George W. Bush, Department of Homeland Security Secretary

1. *Statement on Federal Emergency Assistance for Louisiana*, http://911review.org/Hurricane_Katrina/Federal-response-Hurricane-Katrina.html (last visited May 12, 2016).

Michael Chertoff, and FEMA Director Michael Brown were slow to comprehend what was unfolding or to offer adequate assistance. Even when Brown ordered 1,000 employees to be deployed to help affected citizens, there was poor communication between the White House and those in New Orleans. Looting escalated, and people began to die at the Superdome. The National Guard finally arrived in Louisiana, Mississippi, Alabama, and Florida.

Hurricane Katrina, perhaps more than any other event in American history, signified the inability of local, state, and federal governments to function during a crisis.[2] What happened was not forgotten and set the stage for professionalizing the command and control structures between local, state, and federal governments to work together. The concept of the role of a first responder became popularized.

Plight of Animals

With regard to the plight of animals and those who loved or tried to rescue them, news outlets showed them stranded on rooftops and trapped in dangerous waters. The public saw the faces of frightened, starving, and dying animals. Humans were risking their lives to protect their pets. The National Guard reported that an estimated "30 to 40 percent of the people who refuse to leave the affected areas are staying because they want to take care of their pets."[3]

Nonprofits such as the Humane Society of the United States (HSUS) and Best Friends Animal Society persevered against impossible odds. HSUS could barely maintain the perimeter of its own operation, where it lacked space, food, water, and support to take in countless numbers of rescued animals.[4] HSUS's rescue operation was in jeopardy from day to day because land use was at issue. Beyond understanding what law applied, there were widespread questions of who had the authority to issue an order, how a valid order would be disseminated, and how the order would be enforced.

Not only did Hurricane Katrina cause everyone to understand how we lacked an effective command and control center structure in a disaster context, but also we specifically recognized that companion animals had gained a new place in the American value system. Companion animals were, for a majority of pet owners along the Gulf Coast, more than just a piece of furniture. They were family.

---

2. Federal agencies were included.

3. Stanley Coren, *The Dogs of Hurricane Katrina*, Modern Dog Magazine, http://moderndogmagazine.com/articles/dogs-hurricane-katrina/151 (last visited May 12, 2016).

4. Wayne Pacelle, HSUS president, did not evacuate and leave the already rescued Katrina animals when a second hurricane was expected to hit HSUS's ground zero rescue location.

News Stories

According to HSUS, 60 percent of the pet-owning public regarded their pets as family members as the 2005 hurricane season approached.[5] *New York Newsday* reported that a man and his 16-year-old Dachshund Chihuahua mix survived for five days in a tree;[6] the rescuers saved the man but left his dog behind.

CNN showed an image of parents and their children on a roof with their family dog; the rescuers took the humans but left the family dog.[7] Anderson Cooper interviewed a blind woman who refused to evacuate for ten days without her service animal.[8] Because of Cooper, the woman was evacuated with her seeing eye dog. A little boy boarding a bus carrying a small white dog named Snowball began sobbing "uncontrollably" and then sank to his knees, vomiting, when Snowball was snatched from his arms by a police officer.[9] The little boy was forced to board the bus without Snowball.

While it was reported that some officers shot pets, others left food and water for stranded pets. Other animals were taken out of harm's way and turned over to rescue groups such as HSUS, which had a contract with FEMA, or Best Friends Animal Society, a group that had local land.

DIFFICULT QUESTIONS

During Hurricane Katrina, difficult questions about the rule of law included these:

- How can ownership be proven or determined?
- What hold period, if any, applies in a disaster context?
- Although most states have Good Samaritan laws pertaining to rescuing humans, do these laws apply to rescuing animals?[10]
- Can veterinarians act as Good Samaritans under the law when other members of the public cannot?
- When is it legal to break and enter into a home to save an animal?
- How would anyone know if permission for entry to a house had been granted by the animal's owner?

5. Wendy Burton, *Preparing Pets and Livestock for Hurricane Season*, University of Florida, http://bradford.ifas.ufl.edu/ag_prepare_pets_hurricane.shtml (last visited May 12, 2016).
6. Karen Dawn, *Shameful Policy Caused Many Pets' Deaths*, New York Newsday, http://www.dawnwatch.com/oped-september14-2005.htm (last visited May 12, 2016).
7. Karen Dawn, *Best Friends Need Shelter, Too*, Washington Post, http://www.washingtonpost.com/wp-dyn/content/article/2005/09/09/AR2005090901824.html (last visited May 12, 2016).
8. *Id.*
9. *Id.*
10. *Good Samaritan Law*, http://www.princeton.edu/~achaney/tmve/wiki100k/docs/Good_Samaritan_law.html (last visited May 12, 2016).

- Is it legal to break windows in homes to implement feed and leave efforts?
- Once a pet is saved, can the pet be taken out of state?
- If the original owners locate their pet, can they get their pet back? Are decisions impacted by class?
- Can lost and found registries be required to divulge information?
- How do the original owner's rights compare to the rights of those who newly bonded with the animal and paid for extraordinary veterinary care?[11]
- When can an animal be permanently re-homed?
- What if the new owners, pointing to evidence of scars, claim that the pet now in their care had been used for dog fighting or was otherwise neglected or cruelly treated?
- When, if ever, will the best interests of the animal be considered by the courts?

There were few readily available answers to these questions. The differences from state to state were significant, in part due to Louisiana's unique civil law system with roots in the Napoleonic Code, while the other 49 states' common law was largely derivative from English Common Law. It was difficult to sort out when to apply regular statutes and common laws and when to apply emergency laws and orders offered by various branches of government.[12]

In this chapter, there is commentary on the difficulty of answering some of the above questions. This commentary is presented to shed light on these difficult questions, and the discussion also reveals that in this century, we are only at the beginning of a long journey to sort out how we will decide the way companion animals will be treated in both emergency contexts and American jurisprudence.

SAVING KATRINA ANIMALS

Pit Bulls and Pit Bull mixes were common in the Gulf States impacted by Hurricane Katrina. When saved, many became known as "Katrina dogs."[13] Rescue groups, as well as what have been called "rogue" groups who saved and received animals, varied as to whether they had procedures in place to trace the origins of these animals before they were transferred within their home state or out of state. Groups differed as to whether their goal was for the animals to be later reunited with their original owners or for them to stay with a foster or new owner. It was challenging

---

11. It was common for Katrina animals to have heartworm problems.
12. Allen Anderson & Linda Anderson, Rescued: Saving Animals from Disaster (New World Library 2006).
13. Kim Borgen, Left Behind without a Choice: Hurricane Katrina Animal Rescue Documentary, 2009.

to determine what laws to apply to each individual situation when there were competing legal claims.

Hold Periods

Where should rescue groups, with limited financial means and significant communication problems, place found animals with great medical and emotional needs? Did it make sense to apply the three-to-seven-day hold period, pursuant to a local ordinance, when the owner was separated from an animal because of a mandatory evacuation order and animal transport was circumscribed? Did hold periods make sense in a disaster context when owners were unable to travel and animals might die? One viewpoint was that after a certain date, the rescued animals could be sent out of state and re-homed.[14]

There was also the matter of people looking for lost pets and whether the rescue groups should or could disclose that they were alive and had been re-homed. It was in this context of cultural upheaval and who belonged in a family that for the first time in American history, the American Red Cross placed a link on its website to PetFinder, a national animal database. This had the effect of some of the animals' original owners being able to find their lost companion animals.

Who Owns Katrina Animals

Post-Katrina conflicts occurred between original pet owners and those who had contractual relationships with rescue groups who spent extensive time and effort to rescue and rehabilitate suffering animals. Many who received Katrina animals viewed themselves as fosters, particularly if they were working under a contract with Best Friends Animal Society. Other rescues believed they had title to a rescued animal and, therefore, had the power to transfer title of the animal to another rescue or to new owners. It was common for volunteers who went to the Gulf Coast to come back with a Katrina animal.

Defining Crime

Another challenging aspect regarding the animals left behind in the wake of Katrina was what those trying to save them were legally permitted to do. If a search and rescue team saw a stray dog in a window, was it necessary that they find a sheriff or other law enforcement official to assist with breaking the window to rescue the dog? If not, were the rescuers involved in a trespass to chattels or were they committing crimes?

---

14. The difficulty posed by these questions related to hold periods caused the American Bar Association to pass a resolution on this subject, described later in this chapter.

Veterinary Services, Liability, and Workers' Compensation

From a veterinary malpractice perspective, what was the requisite standard of care for those providing veterinary services? Was the standard an emergency standard? Imagine the conditions of the animals coming into these makeshift care facilities. The challenges faced by individuals trying to help the animals included protocols for not hosing the dogs kept for fighting with water. The animals were dehydrated, starving, and frightened; some had heartworm and other medical and behavioral challenges attributable to these turbulent times.

Who was to decide which animals could be saved and which animals euthanized? Which veterinary ethics euthanasia standards applied? Could a decision to euthanize lead to an intentional infliction of emotional distress claim by the original owner? Could the animals be spayed or neutered and returned to the shelter so that they could not reproduce and suffer, or cause a health hazard? The subject of spaying and neutering was very contentious.

Could those working under the veterinarians claim negligent supervision during this impossibly busy time if they were bitten, and therefore sue their supervisor or a nonprofit? If helpers were bitten, could they file a workers' compensation claim? If so, would the claim be federal or state? Would the claim be filed in the state where they came from or the state they were helping in? There were also questions about who would qualify for workers' compensation if injured.[15]

Ground Operations

Much of the Gulf Coast was in a post-Katrina state of anarchy. Veterinarians needed pharmaceuticals and painkillers. Drug Enforcement Agency laws applied to the dissemination of controlled substances, and perimeters needed for the rescue and veterinary operations to protect pharmaceuticals and prevent saved animals from disappearing were dodgy and difficult, if not dangerous, to secure. Because there was no reliable infrastructure pertaining to the portability of veterinary licenses in an emergency context in 2005, volunteer veterinarians who came to the Gulf Coast risked censure and liability for practicing without a license, or for practicing outside of the scope of their practice area.

Lost and Found Animals

In the aftermath of Hurricane Katrina, rogue or unaffiliated volunteers sometimes rescued animals that had already been found and returned to their homes, causing

15. Liability claims and workers' compensation issues were addressed by the Uniform Law Commission, as later discussed in this chapter.

them to be lost again. The removal of animals from their home state, without adequate tracking procedures in place, escalated the challenges of family reunification. Some animals crossed state lines without veterinary care and health certificates, which created disease risks for both the animals and the public in the receiving states, including the spread of heartworm. There were unscrupulous volunteers who took trophy and valuable animals, justifying their takings by claiming that the original owners did not try hard enough to find their lost animals. Some volunteers advanced ownership arguments related to the animals' best interests.[16]

Lawyers tried to assist with all of the above issues.[17] To answer these questions, lawyers not only needed to research the individual state law but also needed to learn how those individual state laws would be impacted by emergency situations and orders from authorities. American Bar Association (ABA) lawyers worked on FAQs.

DEVELOPMENT OF ANIMAL LAW

During Hurricane Katrina's multiple landfalls, both animal law and emergency management law were in their infancy. The idea of teaching animal law according to traditional legal categories such as criminal law, tort law, and constitutional law had only recently been captured in animal law textbooks.[18] City and state animal law bar associations around the country were mostly in birthing stages and included people with animal rights identities and equine lawyers who were not sure they wanted to be associated with lawyers focused on animal protection.

Hurricane Katrina Case Law

Arguello v. Behmke[19] was a significant Hurricane Katrina decision where the original owner did everything possible to leave her dog at a shelter when she was required to evacuate. She made every effort to find her Great Dane, Chopper. Consistent with other court rulings that seem to be impacted by the behaviors of good actors and bad actors, the court characterized the original owner's placement of Chopper at an animal shelter as a bailment. The New Jersey court said that title to the chattel had not passed within the six-year statute of limitations in Louisiana.

16. When advancing an argument for an animal's best interests, it was often the case that the post-Katrina original owners had less financial means and resources than those in possession of the disputed animal.

17. Megan NcNabb, *Pets in the Eye of the Storm: Hurricane Katrina Floods the Courts with Pet Custody Disputes*, Michigan State University Animal Legal & Historical Center, http://www.animallaw.info/journals/jo_pdf/lralvol14_1_71.pdf (last visited May 12, 2016).

18. Bruce Wagman, Sonia Waisman, & Pamela Frasch, Animal Law: Cases and Materials (Carolina Academic Press 2009).

19. 2006 WL 205097 (N.J. Super. Ch. 2006) (not reported in A.2d).

Under Louisiana law, which draws from France's Napoleonic Code, ownership of a domestic animal cannot be achieved through occupancy.

The New Jersey court also stated that a pet has sentimental value and artificial value. On one hand, the court recognized how the original owner's search for Chopper was akin to a search for a lost child, where "no one would question the decision of the return," while in the next breath, the court referred to Chopper as chattel.

A Texas court went in the opposite direction in another post-Katrina case, *Augillard v. Madura*,[20] involving a black Cocker Spaniel called Jazz by one party and Hope by the other. Rather than making a bailment claim, as described above, the original owner asserted a property conversion claim and advanced an argument based upon DNA testing. Forensic evidence showed that between DNA attributed to Jazz and DNA attributed to Hope, there was an exact match on 17 DNA markers. Although Hope's owner asserted that the DNA evidence could have been tampered with, the court was dismissive of this allegation as a mere surmise or suspicion. Apart from how the court handled the forensic evidence, the court wrote about the pet custody conflict in Note 15 of its opinion, which said:

> We also note the obvious dissonance between the emotional investment at the heart of the human-pet relationship and the current legal system, which identifies this eleven-year-old cocker spaniel with chronic health problems as "property," subject to suit for conversion and identified in terms of her economic worth. Given the parties' considerable expenditure in this case, it goes without saying that Jazz's significance as a cherished member of Augillard's family—as well as her importance to her caretakers of almost three years, Tiffany Madura and Richard Toro—far exceeds her market value. Thus, while resolving this appeal in accordance with the applicable law governing ownership of chattel, we recognize that there are important non-economic interests at stake in this case. As one commentator has remarked,
>
>> People do not plan memorial services, or invest in serious medical treatment for their books or lawnmowers. They don't plan to pay more in insurance premiums than the purchase price or replacement cost of the property they seek to protect. Individuals do not leave money for their bicycles in their wills, or seek visitation arrangements for their televisions upon the termination of their marriages.

Because the lower court had denied Augillard's conversion claim based upon evidence that was factually insufficient, the trial court decision was reversed and the original owner prevailed on her conversion claim.

---

20. 257 S.W.3d 494 (Tex. App. 2008).

Pertinent Laws

Prior to Hurricane Katrina, the governing law in effect was the Robert T. Stafford Disaster Relief and Emergency Assistance Act (Stafford Act), passed in 1988 and amended in 2000.[21] It succeeded the Federal Civil Defense Act of 1950 and the Disaster Relief Act of 1974. Because the Stafford Act did not address public animal transport, many companion animals died following Hurricane Katrina. The Pets Evacuation and Transportation Standards (PETS) Act was introduced in the House on September 22, 2005 permitting pet transport.[22] On April 5, 2006, a more expansive companion bill was introduced in the Senate as S. 2548, which increased the scope to more phases of emergency management and addressed funding concerns.[23]

American Bar Association Resolution

The ABA and its 400,000 members passed a resolution in January 2006 supporting animal-related amendments to the Stafford Act.[24] The ABA advocated that statutory changes should include procedures for animal rescue, care, and management, and the applicable resources. The ABA described the need for a mechanism to determine authority among state and local governments and organizations during rescue and shelter activities.[25] Hurricane Katrina represented a pivotal point in the development of animal law not only because of the swift passage of the PETS Act by Congress but also because media coverage showed how much animals were loved and that their owners would risk their lives to save them.[26]

Animal Disaster Relief Network

Following Hurricane Katrina, the ABA Animal Disaster Relief Network (ADRN) was founded in order to educate lawyer and non-lawyer participants on how to address urgent matters, to create a resource directory, to educate newcomers about

---

21. *Robert T. Stafford Disaster Relief and Emergency Assistance Act, as Amended, and Related Authorities*, FEMA, http://www.fema.gov/pdf/about/stafford_act.pdf (last visited May 12, 2016).

22. The H.R. 3858 sponsor was Congressman Tom Lantos (D-CA). Co-sponsors were Christopher Shays (R-CT), Don Young (R-AK), James Oberstar (D-MN), and Barney Frank (D-MA).

23. *Bill Summary & Status 109th Congress (2005–2006) S.2548*, Library of Congress, http://thomas.loc.gov/cgi-bin/bdquery/z?d109:S2548: (last visited May 12, 2016). The bill was sponsored by Senator Ted Stevens (R-AK) and Senator Frank Lautenberg (D-NJ) and co-sponsored by Senator Lincoln Chafee (R-RI) and Senator Maria Cantwell (D-WA).

24. *Hurricane Katrina Related Legislation*, ABA, apps.americanbar.org/tips/tfdic/WORD/Katrina%20Memo.doc (last visited May 12, 2016).

25. The ABA Tort Trial and Insurance Practice Section Animal Law Committee and Chair-Elect Kristina Hancock led the effort that resulted in a resolution to support the PETS Act. The PETS Act was signed into law on May 22, 2006.

26. Prior to Hurricane Katrina, lawyer Melissa Rubin of the Humane Society of the United States (HSUS) made speeches throughout the United States encouraging audiences to be ready for a disaster. Rubin was destined to become a key HSUS player in the Gulf to help animals affected by Hurricane Katrina.

disaster relief basics, and to develop better laws.[27] The ADRN also built relationships between animal lawyers, veterinarians, and the U.S. Department of Agriculture. Another significant effort was an alliance between the ADRN and the Animal Legal Defense Fund, thanks to founder Joyce Tischler, to utilize both entities to further develop law-based FAQs related to disaster issues.[28]

Select Legal Panel on Emergency Management Regarding Animals

From the ADRN, the ABA Tort Trial and Insurance Practice Section (TIPS) Select Legal Panel on Emergency Management Regarding Animals emerged.[29] There were questions about whether animals fit into the legal category of surrendered, lost, or abandoned property and if replevin actions would be effective. The panel sought to create a useful law that would enable states to plan for legal issues related to animals in crisis should future disasters occur.[30] The panel created the "Model Act Governing Standards for the Care and Disposition of Disaster Animals" in March 2006.[31] Years later, following the support and input of an ABA special committee, this model act was embraced as an ABA resolution. The passage of this resolution influenced the passage of state laws.

Uniform Emergency Volunteer Health Practitioner's Act

When the Uniform Law Commission (ULC) was crafting a new law for the portability of medical licenses in a disaster context, veterinarians were at first excluded. Barbara J. Gislason asked Chairman Raymond Pepe for a rehearing, and with the cooperation of an equine veterinarian from the American Veterinary Medical Association, was able to convince the ULC to revise its uniform laws to apply to veterinary licenses. This uniform law, which Gislason helped revise, passed by the ULC and the ABA, was called the Uniform Emergency Volunteer Health Practitioners Act. [32] The ULC also addressed the subject of liability and workers' compensation claims.

---

27. Barbara J. Gislason founded the ADRN, which gained participants from more than 60 non-governmental organizations (NGOs), bar associations, federal and state governmental entities, and educational institutions.

28. *Frequently Asked Questions Arising from the Rescue of Animals Affected by a Regional Disaster*, Animal Legal Defense Fund, http://aldf.org/downloads/disaster_faq.pdf (last visited May 12, 2016).

29. The EMRA was founded by Barbara J. Gislason and was comprised of a broad spectrum of professionals, including from the American Veterinary Medical Association, the Centers for Disease Control, the National Alliance of State Animal and Agricultural Emergency Programs, NGOs, and others who had distinguished themselves post Hurricane Katrina or who had relevant subject matter expertise.

30. Professor David Favre, a former law school dean and expert in property law and animal law, was the principal drafter of the model act. Coauthors included Melissa Rubin and Barbara J. Gislason.

31. Passing the ABA resolution took five years and would not have been possible without significant input and political acumen of ABA TIPS leader James Carr.

32. *The Uniform Emergency Volunteer Health Practitioners Act*, Centers for Law & the Public's Health, http://www.publichealthlaw.net/ModelLaws/UEVHPA.php (last visited May 12, 2016).

AMERICAN RED CROSS

In the wake of Hurricane Katrina, human survivors knocked on American Red Cross (ARC) doors, pets in tow, only to be turned away into the dark night, as the ARC had a no-pets policy. In the aftermath of Hurricane Katrina, the ARC did an about-face. Since that time, the ARC has been committed to establishing co-location shelters for companion animals.[33] By the time Superstorm Sandy arrived in 2012, Jason Ross was able to keep his rescue Boxer, Coulton, and Siamese cat, Coco, with him at an ARC shelter.[34] The ARC and the Ocean County Animal Response Team (CART) realized that "people consider their pets an integral part of the family."[35] CART Supervisor Barbara Moser-Ward said, "People do not leave their pets. Pets are their family."[36]

FOOD DRIVES

The value of animals in religious and other institutions has also changed. Once, there were food drives for humans only, but now, many food drives include animals, and some are even specifically for animals. At one time, firefighters risked their lives to save humans only. Now, firefighters receive additional training on rescuing animals, and some carry special smaller masks designed to help pets recover from smoke inhalation.[37]

BLESSING ANIMALS

It is well known, particularly as Catholics now have a pope called Pope Francis, that the idea of blessing animals dates back at least to St. Francis of Assisi, who lived from 1181 to 1226. The idea of animals being included in American religious life seems to be growing and some bring companion animals to a house of worship for a blessing once a year.

---

33. *Red Cross, SMART Shelter Pets & Their Humans during Disaster*, American Red Cross, http://www.redcross.org/news/article/Red-Cross-SMART-work-together-to-shelter-pets-and–their-human-companions-during-disaster (last visited May 12, 2016).

34. *Pets Ride out Superstorm Sandy with Their Families*, American Red Cross, http://www.redcross.org/news/article/Pets-Ride-Out-Superstorm-Sandy-with-Their-Families (last visited May 12, 2016).

35. *Id.*

36. *Id.*

37. Lisa Flam, *Pet Oxygen Masks Can Save Animals' Lives in Fires*, Yahoo News, http://news.yahoo.com/pet-oxygen-masks-save-animals-lives-fires-194219196.html (last visited May 12, 2016).

CONCLUSION

A little more than a century has passed between the 1897 Supreme Court decision in *Sentell v. New Orleans Carrollton Railroad Co.*,[38] a decision where dogs were classified as only quasi-property, rather than a lower level of property, unless they were killed or subdued. One hundred eight years later, when Hurricane Katrina made landfall on the Gulf Coast, the American view about the value of dogs changed. Not only did humans regard dogs as family members, but also humans were willing to risk their lives to save them. For those who became lost, the public embraced and cared for precious Katrina animals. When animal survivors became the subject of pet custody disputes, the tone of the ensuing judicial decisions clearly revealed that the courts really did not view Katrina animals as chattel or property anymore.

APPLICABLE CASE LAW

Arguello v. Behmke[39]

Year: *2006*
Category: *Property Law, Contract Law*
Type of Action: *Bailment*
Animal: *Dog*
Pet Custody Concept: *Unless property is abandoned—which did not apply here, as the intake form the woman filled out was evidence of a bailment—the statute of limitations for passing title is six years.*

The court began this lengthy, unpublished decision by saying, "One of the well known equitable maxims is that equity will not knowingly become an instrument of injustice." The owner of a Great Dane dog named Chopper left him at an animal shelter with her two Beagles in the wake of Hurricane Katrina. She stated that she would pick them up seven days later. When she left the dogs, she signed an intake form that the court said created a bailment. The court defined a bailment agreement as when "personal property is delivered by one person into the possession of another person in trust for a specific purpose, under an agreement that the property will be returned to the owner, or accounted for, or kept for the owner to reclaim it, when the purpose is accomplished."

The owner was unable to retrieve Chopper within seven days. She spoke to a volunteer who orally granted her a two-week extension. Even so, the intake form at the shelter only indicated a one-week hold for the dog. It was because of this error that Chopper was moved from the Gulf Coast to New Jersey, where he was subsequently neutered and then adopted.

38. 166 U.S. 698, 17 S. Ct. 693, 41 L .Ed. 1169 (1897).
39. 2006 WL 205097 (N.J. Super. Ch. 2006) (not reported in A.2d).

After the shelter adopted Chopper out, the original owner went to the shelter to pick up her three dogs. After realizing that none of her dogs were at the shelter, the owner began a diligent search for them, and she recovered her Beagles from a humane society. She was unable to locate Chopper until she gained access to a database showing Chopper's new owner. The original owner sought possession of Chopper, but the new owner refused to release him, claiming that the original owner had misidentified the dog. The new owner asserted that the dog she had was a completely different dog named Pluto, not Chopper. The original owner initiated an action pursuant to an order to show cause and writ of replevin.

The court determined that (1) the dog was a "chattel" under the law, (2) the original owner did not intend to abandon or give up Chopper, (3) a bailment agreement had been reached between the original owner and the shelter, and (4) for title to pass to the possessor of chattel, the chattel must have been abandoned or the true owner must have demanded possession within the six-year statute of limitations. Accordingly, the court granted the order to show cause and writ for replevin in favor of the original owner.

Instead of hearing this case in the lower law division, the New Jersey court granted the Chancery Division "jurisdiction to enforce the restitution or delivery of a specific chattel which has a peculiar artificial value and for which, therefore, adequate compensation cannot be obtained at law."[40] The court took judicial notice that "few possessions, if any, have more sentimental and therefore peculiar artificial value than a pet, which also serves as a companion to its owner." In presenting his decision, New Jersey Superior Court Justice Williams quoted Henry David Thoreau. "It often happens that a man is more humanly related to a cat or dog than any human being."

Pursuant to New Jersey law, a replevin action was described as equitable in nature and could be brought by "a person seeking recovery of goods wrongly held by another." The *Arguello* court explained that it was "faced with a situation where both sides did nothing wrong." Although one might think the subsequent owner's failure to do something "wrong" was outcome determinative, the court was sympathetic to the original owner's situation as a Hurricane Katrina survivor. Not only did the court recognize her diligent efforts to retrieve her pets, but the court also observed that Chopper's new owner had bonded with him and had "performed a kind deed."

Another interesting aspect of this New Jersey decision was that the court analyzed the laws of New Jersey and Louisiana. Pursuant to Louisiana case law, specifically *Peloquin v. Calcasieu Parish Police Jury*,[41] someone who finds a lost, privately owned domestic animal in Louisiana does not acquire ownership by "occupancy." Even so, the New Jersey court also looked to its own case law and determined that the original owner had not abandoned Chopper because she did not intend to give up possession of her property, but rather, "quite the contrary." The court emphasized that "plaintiff took every reasonable step to attempt to track down her dog after Lamar-Dixon failed to

40. The use of the term "artificial value" for a companion animal is interesting, as the terminology almost goes back to the concept of "fictitious value" described in *Akers v. Sellers*, 114 Ind. App. 660, 54 N.E.2d 779 (Ind. App. 1944).

41. 367 So. 2d 1246 (La. App. 3d Cir. 1979).

deliver it to her when she arrived to pick it up and continued to this day by the filing of this lawsuit. Clearly, such acts defeat any assertion of abandonment."[42]

Of additional significance was that the new owner, rather than claiming to be a bona fide purchaser, relied on the "Memorandum of Understanding and Minimum Requirements for Satellite Sheltering of Katrina Animal Evacuees between People for Animals and the Humane Society of the United States." According to this document, if the animal was still "contained" by October 16, 2005, the contained animal would become the shelter's property. The court determined that the contract between these two entities was based upon a mutual mistake, as related to the possession of Chopper, which was a ground for rescission of the agreement. The court explicitly used "its equitable power to cancel the agreement" between the Humane Society of the United States and People for Animals.[43]

Although there were issues raised regarding Chopper's identification number and acknowledgment that his name was listed as Pluto upon adoption, the court, while not accusing the defendant of perpetuating a fraud upon the court, expressed doubt about her claim that the Great Dane did not respond to the name Chopper. The court's decision gained momentum as it progressed through the facts and advocated for the application of equitable principles. The Chancery court said, "even if it were to find all of the Contracts valid insofar as they allowed for the dog's transport and adoption, they would be invalidated by this court of equity. Even a contract fairly procured must not advance injustice or hardship." Accordingly, the decision should operate without "injustice or oppression to either plaintiff or defendant." This approach is consistent with the equitable maxim that "equity will not knowingly become an instrument of injustice."[44]

Going out of its way not to blame the nonprofit for the unfortunate developments in this case, and acknowledging that this disaster rescue group was working with limited resources and access to facilities, the court nevertheless proclaimed that the "equities demand this situation be considered beyond the strict confines of the law and exercise discretion guided by compassion. If this were a lost child, reunited with its parents who searched for it, no one would question the decision of the return." This

42. In this unpublished decision, the court reviewed every aspect of the bailment agreement that Chopper's original owner had with Lamar-Dixon, the HSUS rescue that had possession of Chopper before he was transferred to another rescue and then acquired by the defendant. With regard to the contractual terms of the bailment, the court observed that Chopper's original owner had written on Chopper's intake form "Call if shelter closes; dogs will be picked up." Because Lamar-Dixon did not cross out the plaintiff's handwritten additions, the court treated Lamar-Dixon's silence and inaction as an acceptance of these terms. Furthermore, the plaintiff gave Lamar-Dixon phone numbers where she could be reached, and a Lamar-Dixon volunteer later spoke to the plaintiff and promised to hold Chopper for two more weeks, which she reasonably relied on as an oral promise.

43. The court seemed offended by the defendant's argument that the plaintiff's search for Chopper lacked diligence when it said, "To expect plaintiff to conduct an online search for Chopper in an area of the country which to date has not fully been restored to its pre-storm condition with areas still lacking in electricity is a preposterous argument." The court paid considerable attention to the plaintiff's clean hands and that she deserved the court's equitable power when it said, "plaintiff's inability to recover Chopper prior to the October 15, 2005 deadline was due to Lamar-Dixon's mistake and through no fault of her own."

44. Unless codified, replevin actions are equitable in nature.

analogy was notable because just before the court used the child analogy, the court said that the Great Dane was a chattel.

Practice Pointer: Although this was an unpublished decision, the analysis and advancement of equitable principles were so strong that Lady Liberty could be perceived as riding a stallion; the court was determined not to permit any legal argument to prevent the reunification of a dog named Chopper with the original and diligent owner who loved him.

Augillard v. Madura[45]

Year: *2008*
Category: *Property Law, Contract Law*
Type of Action: *Conversion*
Animal: *Dog*
Pet Custody Concept: *Choose the right claim.*

In this post-Hurricane Katrina decision, the court was faced with choosing between the original owner of a black Cocker Spaniel,[46] who had raised the dog for eight and a half years, and the new owner, who had substantially invested in the sick dog's veterinary care. Although Augillard claimed to be the dog's original owner and claimed to recognize Jazz, the trial court rejected her claim for conversion of a dog called Hope. To prevail on a claim for conversion, she was required to establish, by a preponderance of the evidence, that (1) the plaintiff owned or had legal possession of the property or was entitled to possession; (2) the defendant unlawfully assumed and exercised dominion and control over the property to the exclusion of, or inconsistent with, the plaintiff's rights as an owner; (3) the plaintiff demanded the return of the property; and (4) the defendant refused to return the property. The trial court ruled that she had failed to meet her burden of proof.

Despite Hurricane Katrina, Augillard still had some of her dog's veterinary records and a brush containing her dog's DNA. She argued on appeal that the veterinary records showed that she had provided the dog with regular veterinary care, had given her heartworm medication, had treated her for a skin condition, and that the dog had been recently groomed. Augillard hired a DNA expert who testified that when fur from Jazz's brush was compared to fur from Hope,[47] there was a complete match on 17 DNA markers; it was asserted that this DNA evidence was conclusive. She also claimed the mitochondrial DNA from Jazz's sibling was consistent with Hope's and said

45. 257 S.W.3d 494 (Tex. App. 2008).

46. Jazz became lost when the National Guard would not let the owner's mother take the dog on a rescue boat. In the meantime, the original owner was working at the airport helping with the delivery of evacuation supplies. It was for this reason that Jazz was left at her mother's home with large quantities of food and water.

47. Augillard claimed that the DNA the expert used was from a brush that Augillard earlier used on Jazz. In contrast, Madura claimed that the DNA the expert used was from a brush that Augillard surreptitiously used on Hope during their brief meeting.

that this proved both dogs shared a maternal relative. Madura made no objection to the court receiving this DNA evidence. The only issue on appeal was whether Jazz and Hope were the same dog.

To the contrary, Madura and her veterinarian described the rescued dog as sick and overweight, and that Hope was suffering from hypothyroidism and large bladder stones.[48] The higher court criticized the trial court's finding that "the DNA evidence was not 'authenticated or identified thus indicating a high potential for tampering,'" and it emphasized that the "uncontradicted evidence at trial was that Augillard did not have an opportunity to obtain a DNA sample from Hope," as she was only permitted to briefly see the dog while in the presence of several other people.

Augillard had conclusively established every element of her conversion claim. The evidence was factually insufficient to support the trial court's judgment. The appellate court used the legal sufficiency of the evidence as the appropriate standard of review and said that neither a jury fact finder nor a trial court fact finder could disregard from a legally sufficient standpoint what the appellate court described as conclusions contrary to a vital fact. More specifically, the appellate court found that "When evidence contrary to a verdict is conclusive, it cannot be disregarded."

The court offered a history of Hurricane Katrina and the passage of the Pets Evacuation and Transportation Standards Act of 2006. Information was provided about the challenges resulting from 50,000 pets stranded in the New Orleans area, including 12,000 pets that were transported as far away as New Jersey, Arizona, and Pennsylvania. In this case, it should be emphasized that Madura's counsel had not challenged the DNA test results, only the source of the dog's hair.

The *Augillard* court, in ruling for the original owner, described its emerging worldview about companion animals in Note 15 of its decision as follows:

> We also note the obvious dissonance between the emotional investment at the heart of the human-pet relationship and the current legal system, which identifies this eleven-year-old cocker spaniel with chronic health problems as "property," subject to suit for conversion and identified in terms of her economic worth. Given the parties' considerable expenditure in this case, it goes without saying that Jazz's significance as a cherished member of Augillard's family—as well as her importance to her caretakers of almost three years, Tiffany Madura and Richard Toro—far exceeds her market value. Thus, while resolving this appeal in accordance with the applicable law governing ownership of chattel, we recognize that there are important non-economic interests at stake in this case. As one commentator has remarked,
>
>> People do not plan memorial services, or invest in serious medical treatment for their books or lawnmowers. They don't plan to pay more in insurance premiums than the purchase price or replacement cost of the property they seek to protect. Individuals do not leave money for their bicycles in their wills, or seek visitation arrangements for their televisions upon the termination of their marriages.

48. Notwithstanding Madura's claim, her own veterinarian had only recently detected these large stones.

Practice Pointer: The court proclaimed that more than economic interests were at stake and that there was an "obvious dissonance between the emotional investment at the heart of the human-pet relationship and the current legal system." The word "dissonance" is a good word to remember. The underlying analysis about value echoes the pronouncement about fictitious value in *Akers v. Sellers*.[49] Another important practice pointer to take away from this decision is if a client loses his or her dog, tell him or her to hold onto the pet's sweater and brush in case a DNA test is later needed. In time, it is also probable that DNA information will be more readily available to experts for companion animal identification purposes.

49. 114 Ind. App. 660, 54 N.E.2d 779 (Ind. App. 1944).

Chapter 10

Dangerous Dogs and Police Powers

"People must have renounced, it seems to me, all natural intelligence to dare to advance that animals are but animated machines. . . . It appears to me, besides, that [such people] can never have observed with attention the character of animals, not to have distinguished among them the different voices of need, of suffering, of joy, of pain, of love, of anger, and of all their affections. It would be very strange that they should express so well what they could not feel."

—*Voltaire*

This chapter will provide yet another perspective as to how pets are viewed in American jurisprudence. If you were beginning to think from earlier chapters that dog personhood was imminent, this chapter is a reminder that the state's constitutional police powers still emanate from *Sentell v. New Orleans Carrollton Railroad Co.*[1] In this bygone era, when the rabies epidemic was alarming, not only did dogs have a lowly status, but also this lowly status could be even less than property—only quasi-property.[2] Unless a dog was dead or "subdued," the dog did not gain any property status.

1. 166 U.S. 698, 17 S. Ct. 693, 41 L. Ed. 1169 (1897).

2. As is repeated often in this book, read the seminal case on animal law in the United States, the Supreme Court decision from 1897 in *Sentell v. New Orleans Carrollton Railroad Co.*, 166 U.S. 698, 17 S. Ct. 693, 41 L. Ed. 1169 (1897).

TRAVEL RISKS

From the perspective of pets traveling between households, this chapter is a reminder that these arrangements pose risks, as we are now living in litigious times. If a garage door or pasture gate is left open and the family pet gets loose, there may be unpleasant consequences. Learning about dangerous dog procedures is important because if the other party in your pet custody dispute is careless and irresponsible, in a post-decree context, the ramifications of this individual's negligence may mean that your client endures the heartache of a dangerous dog proceeding[3] or, worse yet, a resulting destruct order. Lawyers also need to know that where they live, certain breeds or breed look-a-likes may be the subject of urban legends.

IMPORTANT CASE LAW

Before getting into the nuts and bolts of a dangerous dog proceeding, there are a few cases in particular to be aware of. An important aspect of dangerous dog cases is whether the underlying statutes or ordinances pass constitutional muster. In *Garcia v. Village of Tijeras*,[4] the threshold for a state's legitimate exercise of police powers was minimal when residents were afraid of loose Pit Bulls.

Another problem you will likely be presented with is how state laws and local ordinances will be reconciled. A good example of how this occurs is reflected in *Hannan v. City of Minneapolis*.[5] There, the court looked at the conflicting state and local ordinances and applied four guiding principles: (1) the ordinance and the statute shall not contain express or implied terms that are irreconcilable, (2) the ordinance shall not permit what state law forbids, (3) the ordinance cannot forbid what the statute expressly permits, and (4) when no conflict exists between the ordinance and statute, the ordinance may contain additional or complementary terms to aid in furtherance of the statutory purpose.

After applying these principles, the *Hannan* court determined that the regulation of dangerous dogs by the applicable ordinance was not subject to the statutory preemptive doctrine because the ordinance was merely additional and complementary. More importantly, the court reminded the municipality that their regulations could not be breed specific.

---

3. When there is a dangerous dog proceeding, be forewarned that there may also be other civil and criminal litigation.
4. 108 N.M. 116, 767 P.2d 355 (N.M. App. 1988).
5. 623 N.W.2d 281 (Minn. App. 2001).

Until *Tracey v. Solesky*,[6] the most famous case in the United States involving Pit Bulls was *City of Toledo v. Tellings*,[7] a case where the opinions of the appellate court and supreme court were at odds[8] and the supreme court cited *Sentell* as a precedent.[9] Before getting into the details of *Tracey* and other decisions impacting Pit Bulls, we turn once more back to the *Sentell* decision. To get a sense of the 1897 worldview, here are selected excerpts from the landmark *Sentell* decision:

- "The facts, however, were not properly before the court, and the opinion was put upon the ground that the state law was constitutional and valid as a police regulation to prevent the indiscriminate owning and breeding of worthless dogs."
- "Property in dogs is of an imperfect or qualified nature, and that they stand, as it were, between animals ferae naturae, in which, until killed or subdued, there is no property, and domestic animals, in which the right of property is perfect and complete. They are not considered as being upon the same plane with horses, cattle, sheep, and other domesticated animals, but rather in the category of cats, monkeys, parrots, singing birds, and similar animals, kept for pleasure, curiosity, or caprice."
- "They have no intrinsic value, by which we understand a value common to all dogs as such, and independent of the particular breed or individual. Unlike other domestic animals, they are useful neither as beasts of burden, for draught (except to a limited extent), nor for food. They are peculiar in the fact that they differ among themselves more widely than any other class of animals, and can hardly be said to have a characteristic common to the entire race."
- "All are more or less subject to attacks of hydrophobic madness."[10]
- "While the higher breeds rank among the noblest representatives of the animal kingdom, and are justly esteemed for their intelligence, sagacity, fidelity, watchfulness, affection, and, above all, for their natural companionship with man, others are afflicted with such serious infirmities of temper as to be little better than a public nuisance."

---

6. 50 A.3d 1075 (Md. 2012). A.3d, 2012 WL 1432263 (Md. 2012).

7. 2006 Ohio 975 (Ohio 3/3/2006), 2006 Ohio 975 (Ohio 2006) (court of appeals decision), and 114 Ohio St. 3d 278, 871 N.E.2d 1152, 2007 Ohio 3724 (Ohio 2007) (supreme court decision).

8. In *Sawh v. City of Lino Lakes*, 800 N.W.2d 663 (Minn. App. 2011) (court of appeals decision) and 823 N.W.2d 627 (Minn. 2012) (supreme court decisions) and *Strickland v. Medlen*, 397 S.W.3d 184, 185 (Tex. 2013), the reasoning in the lower appellate court was noticeably more progressive, and reflective of the role of animals as valued family members, than the decisions by the supreme court.

9. 166 U.S. 698, 17 S. Ct. 693, 41 L. Ed. 1169 (1897). It is amazing that courts continue to cite *Sentell* with a straight face; it is from another era, before dogs advanced to companion animal status.

10. After reading this decision, think about the word "rabies." Then read it again.

Jumping to the 21st-century decision of *Tracey v. Solesky*[11] out of Maryland, the court determined that Pit Bulls were inherently dangerous and landlords, aware of their presence, would be strictly liable for damages caused.

In *County of Pasco v. Riehl*,[12] a case about the constitutionality of a dangerous dog statute, the court utilized the often cited U.S. Supreme Court decision in *Mathews v. Eldridge*[13] for the proposition that procedural due process requires that a person have the opportunity to be heard at a meaningful time and in a meaningful manner. A family dog named Sheba was labeled dangerous but there was no forum to advance the owner's procedural due process rights. Sheba bit a teenager during a game of pool after the boy had struck the dog several times with a pool stick. Her owner argued that Sheba had been provoked. The appellate court concluded that without an opportunity for a dangerous dog hearing, the statute was unconstitutional on its face, as due process was lacking.

A decision that reflects just how much discretion administrative agencies have over the future of a family pet, still only in property status, was well illustrated in *Pelzel v. St. Paul Office of License, Inspections and Environmental Protection*.[14] Upholding the dangerous dog designation of a Labrador Retriever, the court reminded us that appellate review is limited to (1) whether the agency who made the determination had jurisdiction; (2) whether the proceedings were fair and regular; (3) whether the decision was unreasonable, oppressive, arbitrary, fraudulent, or without evidentiary support; and (4) whether the decision was based upon an incorrect theory of the law. The court declared that it was modifying the common law. The most important aspect of this case for animal law practitioners is that because the court framed the agency as having only quasi-judicial powers, no de novo review was available. This decision is also useful because it reminds practitioners of the importance of finding out if the municipality has an open file policy when it comes to dangerous dog proceedings. If there is an open file policy, the advocate has more opportunity to prepare.

When looking at the emerging case law regarding dangerous dogs, it is interesting to observe how artful lawyers can be with their efforts to find proof of a legal theory. No one could accuse Washington lawyer Adam Karp of not being resourceful. In *Coballes v. Spokane County*,[15] a case involving a dangerous dog law, Karp prevailed when the court finally recognized what it characterized as a "statutory appeal in substance," as further discussed below. The lesson here is that even

11. A.3d, 2012 WL 1432263 (Md. 2012). Since this decision, the supreme court determined that the decision applied to Pit Bulls, not Pit Bull mixes, in *Tracey v. Solesky*, 427 Md. 627 (Md. 2012).
12. 620 So. 2d 229 (Fla. App. 2d Dist. 1993).
13. 424 U.S. 319, 335, 96 S. Ct. 893, 47 L. Ed. 2d 18 (1976).
14. No. A05-2534 (Minn. App. 9/12/2006) (Minn. App. 2006).
15. 274 P.3d 1102 (Wash. App. 2012).

for an experienced animal lawyer conversant with appellant rules, it is challenging to understand and apply them, as well as to imagine how new ideas can be pushed forward.

Coballes is somewhat entertaining, as the analysis takes lawyers back to law school days as Karp offered up six different approaches to justify appellate review: (1) statutory judicial review, (2) constitutional writ of certiorari, (3) statutory writ of review, (4) statutory right of appeal, (5) constitutional writ of review, and (6) an ex parte motion for writ of review, assignment of judge, and waiving bond. The court gave the plaintiff the right to appeal, having decided that he had come up with a statute appeal in substance; this determination gave the plaintiff a broader scope of review than would have been available under a writ.

To get a sense of the spectrum of opinions in dangerous dog cases on the subject of due process, it is worthwhile to read both the court of appeals decision and supreme court decision in *Sawh v. City of Lino Lakes*.[16] In the Minnesota court of appeals decision, the court worked through the three *Mathews v. Eldridge*[17] due process factors. In doing so, the appellate court recognized that the family pet is distinguishable from other types of property and that companion animals have a special place in their owners' lives. In applying the *Mathews* factors, the court also said that procedural due process requires the opportunity to be heard at a meaningful time and in a meaningful manner before a dangerous dog declaration is made.

In a unanimous opinion, the Minnesota Supreme Court in contrast dialed back the clock to *Sentell*,[18] but instead of calling a dog "quasi-property," per the *Sentell* dead nor subdued criteria, the Minnesota Supreme Court called the Labrador "tangible property." The court side-stepped the critical question impacting the city council's death row sentence on the subject of the "shall/may" dichotomy. The key idea of this dichotomy is that even when an ordinance uses the word "shall," the city council "may" still have discretion with regard to a dog's destruct order.

Instead of looking at the due process aspect of one of the decision makers' attempts to learn if the city council had discretion at a key life and death juncture, the Minnesota Supreme Court rolled over not only this question, but also the statutory defect that mischaracterized the subsequent offense as an act being performed by the animal's owner rather than the dog. As stated before, there are

16. 800 N.W.2d 663 (Minn. App. 2011) (court of appeals decision); 823 N.W.2d 627 (Minn. 2012) (supreme court decision). This case is significant in that a Golden Retriever was euthanized even though all three incidents could have involved human behaviors that provoked the dog. This supreme court's decision reflects almost a 19th-century point of view. A good rule of thumb as to which century's point of view about dogs is controlling in a state is to see if the court cites *Sentell*. In that decision, the U.S. the Supreme Court worried about all animals' vulnerability to "attacks of hydrophobic madness."

17. 424 U.S. 319, 335, 96 S. Ct. 893, 47 L. Ed. 2d 18 (1976).

18. 166 U.S. 698, 17 S. Ct. 693, 41 L. Ed. 1169 (1897).

dramatic differences between the tone and quality of the decisions between the court of appeals and the supreme court in *City of Toledo v. Tellings*[19] and *Strickland v. Medlen*.[20] From a normative and cultural perspective, some supreme court decisions seem to be not of the 21st century.

CONSTITUTIONAL DUE PROCESS PROTECTION

All dangerous dog proceedings have a common denominator—the dog's owner is entitled to constitutional due process protection. It may be difficult to predict what rules and procedures the hearing officer will use in advance, as the hearing officer[21] may not be a lawyer or may otherwise be unschooled in constitutional principles and how they apply, much less the common laws. If constitutional rights are violated, make a good record for appeal purposes. Many appeals are by writ.

In a dangerous dog proceeding, lawyers need to figure out what to emphasize, using evidence such as bite statistics and by advancing public policy objectives. Review dangerous dog cases that cite the U.S. Supreme Court case *Mathews v. Eldridge*.[22] Revisit the 1st, 4th, 5th, and 14th Constitutional Amendments, and bring a pocket-sized Constitution to the hearing. Do not hesitate to pull it out and look through it thoughtfully. Consider raising arguments on how these constitutional rights, particularly due process, might apply to a dangerous dog proceeding. Ask important *Mathews* due process questions, including these:

- Is any private interest affected by the official action?
- What is the risk of an erroneous deprivation of an interest through the procedures used?
- What is the probable value of additional or substitute procedural safeguards?
- How is the government impacted fiscally and administratively or by additions and substitutions?

Assert applicable constitutional due process rights by calling witnesses, presenting evidence, cross-examining witnesses, making arguments, establishing burden of proof, having a meaningful opportunity to be heard, having a de novo review, and filing a writ of certiorari. Oppose hearsay information in governmental reports, and offer rebuttable witnesses, if any. Make sure that a record is properly made at the administrative hearing.

19. 2006 Ohio 975 (Ohio 3/3/2006), 2006 Ohio 975 (Ohio 2006) (court of appeals decision) and 114 Ohio St. 3d 278, 871 N.E.2d 1152, 2007 Ohio 3724 (Ohio 2007) (supreme court decision).

20. 397 S.W.3d 184, 185 (Tex. 2013).

21. Hearings could also be before a government body, such as a city council.

22. 424 U.S. 319, 334, 96 S. Ct. 893, 47 L. Ed. 2d 18 (1976).

At the same time, be aware of how much power the decision maker has and how narrow and pro forma the scope of appellate review may be. Many of the same principles or ideas that apply to representing a client in a dangerous dog proceeding also apply to a pet custody dispute. The significant difference is that procedural due process rights in pet custody disputes are at its inception. Be imaginative in all claims made.

"SHALL/MAY" DICHOTOMY

Remember to ask basic questions. Is the ordinance or statute valid? Is it overly broad and ambiguous? If the law contains the word "shall," find out when and if the "shall/may" dichotomy applies. Is the word "shall" directory or mandatory? If mandatory, and law enforcement failed to comply with notice and other due process requirements, the case could be won if the government loses subject matter jurisdiction. Explore the option of having your client relocate, which may happen in a divorce anyway. Will the municipality agree to a lesser declaration in six months if the client spays or neuters the dog and works with a behaviorist? Use common sense to get the best disposition possible.

BREED-DISCRIMINATORY LEGISLATION

Lawyers handling dangerous dog matters will be more effective if they are aware of the legal implications associated with a variety of dog breeds. This includes breeds that have gained adverse notoriety as vicious or been the subject of breed-discriminatory legislation (BDL), also referred to as breed-specific legislation (BSL).[23] When a dog is labeled potentially dangerous or dangerous, the dog needs help right away because if there is another alleged wrongdoing, the probability of the animal's destruction based upon the police powers of local government increases, and possibly more so for dogs subject to BDL.[24]

There is another reason for a family lawyer to pay attention to BDL with regard to which party should be awarded a dog in a pet custody dispute. Because parties to an action may differ with regard to how responsible they are at managing the

---

23. *ABA Adopts Policy Based on Tort Trial & Insurance Practice Section Resolution Urging Adoption of Breed-Neutral Dog Laws and the Repeal of Breed Discriminatory (Pit Bull) Ordinances*, ABA Now, http://www.americanbar.org/news/abanews/aba-news-archives/2013/08/aba_adopts_policyba0.html (last visited May 12, 2016). *Breed-Specific Legislation (BSL) FAQ*, National Canine Research Council, http://nationalcanineresearchcouncil.com/dog-legislation/breed-specific-legislation-bsl-faq/ (last visited May 12, 2016). The Centers for Disease Control and the American Veterinary Medical Association have issued statements admitting that their own single-vector epidemiological studies are not accurate when it comes to identifying breeds most likely to bite or kill and therefore should not influence policy.

24. Joan E. Schaffner, The Lawyer's Guide to Dangerous Dog Issues (ABA Publishing 2009).

entrances and exits from a home, yard, or car, or how careful they are at making sure animal containment features such as a fence are secure, awarding the dog to the more vigilant owner might be in the dog's best interests, particularly if the dog has a notorious reputation.[25]

POTENTIALLY DANGEROUS DOG LABELS

Even a potentially dangerous dog declaration may have long-term consequences that are not readily apparent. For example, if a dog is declared potentially dangerous, the provocation defense may not be available if the dog is subject to another dangerous dog proceeding, even if the dog in question was provoked.

If the governmental entity suggests that the designation is only temporary and could be lifted in six months, find data to support the representation that the governmental agency routinely nullifies the designation.[26] Remember that if an animal owner does not immediately change his or her behavior to avoid future problems, which may include a change as simple as situational awareness or being educated about the meaning of the dog's body language, the dog's very life could be in jeopardy.

STRICT COMPLIANCE

Whether a dog is declared potentially dangerous or dangerous, the dog's life may depend on the owner's strict compliance with the determination of requirements by the appropriate authority, which might be an administrative hearing officer in one jurisdiction or a city council in the next, and even, possibly, a judge. Do not to rely on oral statements made by animal control if they are less rigorous than the terms of a declaration reflected in an order, unless the terms are modified in writing. When an animal is feared by the public or law enforcement and gets loose, not only could the animal cause harm, but the animal could also be harmed by someone carrying a weapon.[27]

---

25. The poor quality of information available about notorious dog breeds on social media is an aspect of our culture. One website claimed that "A study of dog bite data from 1982 to 2011 indicated that American Pit Bull Terriers, Rottweilers, crosses of these two breeds and Wolf Hybrids were responsible for most injuries and fatalities to humans." *The 9 Most Aggressive Dog Breeds*, Dog Temperament, http://www.dogtemperament.com/the-9-most-aggressive-dog-breeds/ (last visited May 12, 2016). This website ranks the nine most aggressive dogs without any explanation as to the criteria used for determining dangerousness.

26. Consider asking the clerk or filing a freedom of information request to learn how often dangerous dog or potentially dangerous dog designations are reduced.

27. Cynthia Bathurst et al., *The Problem of Dog-Related Incidents and Encounters*, COPS, www.dogwise.com/downloader.cfm?itemid=dogincidents&format=pdf (last visited May 12, 2016).

DECLARATION CONSEQUENCES

Consequences of a dangerous dog declaration could include the following:

- Reimbursement for veterinary or medical expenses of an injured person or animal,
- Fines,
- Administrative costs,
- Mandatory microchipping,
- Compliance with dog behaviorist recommendations,
- Fenced-in yard in compliance with very exacting specifications,
- Basket muzzle,
- Three-foot leash,
- Crating the dog when guests are present or having the dog in a "safe room," preferably a well-locked area,
- Escape-proof kennel subject to exact specifications,
- Medication for the dog,
- Follow-up meetings with an animal control-sanctioned evaluator,
- Sign posting, and
- Expensive liability insurance or surety bond.
- Adverse publicity in local publications.

DANGEROUS DOG PROCEEDING CONSULTATION

When someone is involved in a dangerous dog proceeding, he or she should schedule an appointment with an attorney immediately, even if the label the authorities seek to attach to the dog is only one of a "potentially" dangerous dog. Although this label sounds innocuous, the consequences for a dog receiving this label may prove deadly. The label could affect an owner's ability to advance a provocation defense if another incident occurs. If there is another incident, and the owner may be prohibited from asserting a provocation defense, a dangerous dog declaration may result in a client's costly requirement to pay a surety bond.

At the initial consultation, tell the potential client to bring all documents received from animal control, law enforcement, governmental entities, or anywhere else that has anything to do with the dog in question, including ownership or adoption records,[28] veterinary records, and photographs. To the extent

28. The owner may have no choice but to deal with animal control on subjects such as veterinary records for a rabies vaccine or on the subject of quarantine.

possible, tell clients to avoid communicating with anyone[29] about the case until there is an opportunity for a risk assessment. If the owner talks to an animal control officer before obtaining legal advice, there is a high chance that the individual will make an admission against interest and be unaware when a trap is sprung.

If asked to represent a dog owner in any dangerous dog proceeding, be careful to describe what you may do, but not whether your efforts will be effective given that there are so many variables in how a proceeding may be conducted and the law applied. Be precise with the scope of your representation in a legal fee agreement as in addition to a dangerous dog proceeding, an owner could be subject to a civil proceeding, including based upon a tort claim for an injury. An owner may also face a criminal misdemeanor charge, such as for allowing an animal at large.

When a dog is accused of doing something wrong, risks dramatically rise for both the dog and the dog's owner during the following six months. Unsolved problems can reoccur and other eyes are watching.[30]

Owners of dogs who "nip" or bite may blame innocent victims, thereby making their representation more challenging; owners often lack insight into how their own behavior contributed to the incident. The owners may lack a tall enough fence, believe they have their pet on voice command with words such as "come" or "stay," or lack a physical barrier between the dog and entries and exits.

Here are two examples of what dangerous dog cases may be like:

A Boxer is found caught in a hunting trap and is then moved between rescue and foster groups without the benefit of expensive veterinary attention for his injured limb. By the time the Boxer is adopted by an older couple in another state, the dog requires the amputation of his front leg, which could have been prevented if the dog had received timely veterinary care. Although the Boxer seems to have done well in a variety of settings before his leg was amputated, his anxiety increases following the loss of his limb. The couple notices the dog's mood shift and has an animal behaviorist over twice to help.

One fateful day, the doorbell rings when a delivery man delivers a package. Rather than fully opening the door, one of the retired owners signs for the package with the door slightly ajar and the dog pushes through the door and "nips" the delivery man. The next day, animal control shows up, the Boxer is declared a potentially dangerous dog, and one of the owners is charged with misdemeanor crimes for having a dog at large; a civil action also ensues.

Because the owners receive many confusing documents from the city, the person identified on the documents is called in order to clarify the form necessary to

29. A catch-22 in these proceedings is that the owner's behavior may impact if or when the government may return the seized dog.

30. It is common for there to be some type of surveillance by animal control once a declaration has been made.

meet the 14-day deadline to appeal the potentially dangerous dog determination. In the meantime, a form is made up by the couple's attorney and is submitted to the authorities in the hopes that it will satisfy the 14-day requirement under the ordinance.[31]

The city employee does not comprehend the importance of challenging the designation as a constitutional due process right. The couple asks the city employee for the appeal form, but the city employee tells them not to worry because if the dog does not have any further incidents within the next six months, and the couple seeks a rescission of the action, the city routinely grants it. Apparently, the couple is supposed to trust that this is how it will work even though one of the two owners had also been charged with a criminal misdemeanor and the victim may put pressure on the city not to change the declaration because of ensuing civil litigation.

The city attorney finally rescinds the potentially dangerous dog determination, and one month later, the couple attend a criminal court proceeding after calling the delivery man to learn about the severity of his bite, which is minimal. The prosecutor agrees to reduce the case to a petty misdemeanor when the couple agrees to pay a small fine. Family lawyers should avoid being offended when judges and prosecutors require some payment, even in cases where logic would dictate a dismissal was warranted.

In the second example, imagine an elderly woman living on the upper level of a house with her constant companion, a protective German Shepherd, a dog granted bed privileges. Consider this dog to be her protector. Assume others let the dog outside as needed and that only the elderly woman exits the outer door on the upper level of the split-level house; guests and other residents of the home only enter and exit the house through the lower level. One day, the elderly woman exits through the front door on the upper level and falls; her German Shepherd pushes the door open and bites a neighbor child coming to the elderly woman's aid. One year later, the same dog seriously harms the elderly woman's friend when she enters through the upper-level door carrying mail.

In this circumstance, how would we honestly look at what would be provocative to this German Shepherd? These scenarios reflect how fast a dog's future may be in jeopardy and also, why a dog needs an able and responsible owner.

INSURANCE POLICIES

An owner should put their homeowner's or renter's insurance carrier on notice about a potential liability claim following a dangerous dog declaration. Some

31. As a practice pointer, if a form cannot be found, lawyers should make up their own forms with appropriate headings so they can be filed by required deadlines.

insurance policies do not cover certain breeds of dogs, and a dangerous dog declaration may affect an owner's insurability and rates. If the insurance carrier excludes certain breeds, and the breed of the dog is ambiguous, the owner may need help in preparing an insurance claim.

IMPORTANT QUESTIONS

Expect the owner to be emotional in these types of proceedings. Learn in a fact-intensive, summary fashion what happened. Review photographs of the dog, including pet photos on smartphones. Some important questions to answer include these:

- What is a typical day like in the household? Does the dog go back and forth between households?
- Who is really the dog's owner? Work through conflicting indicia of ownership. Find out whose name is on microchip, veterinary, and licensing records.
- Could the dog have health problems that cause the dog to be easily provoked or irritable due to pain? Many people do not give their pets appropriate dental care, and poorly cared for teeth can be very painful, thereby affecting the dog's behavior.
- Has the dog threatened another or caused injury before? What would neighbors say?
- Could the case involve the mistaken identity of the offending dog?
- Has action been taken pursuant to a state statute, an ordinance, or both? If an ordinance, was it correctly passed?
- Were the statutory or ordinance notice deadlines met?
- Was there something unusual or troublesome about what the governmental entity did? If so, investigate whether this is a recurring problem.
- Were any statements made, either orally or in writing?
- Is the governmental entity bringing this action "by the book" per the local ordinance, if applicable?
- How well trained is the law enforcement person involved? Is the individual working for animal control, serves in a community serving function, or mostly doing police work?
- Is there a personal history between the owner and the accuser or anyone else of significance?
- Are there breed discrimination concerns?
- Do any decision makers, perhaps on a city council, have a conflict of interest?

RECORDS TO OBTAIN

Records and documents to obtain in dangerous dog cases, as well as in nuisance cases, such as barking dogs, include the following:

- Veterinary records establishing the animal's routine veterinary care;
- Aerial maps of the property where the incident occurred;
- Law enforcement daily planners, either hard copy or electronic;
- Government notices, including due process and hearing notices;
- Citations, forms, and correspondence; and
- Incident and other reports.

Make your record requests early and in writing.

EVIDENCE

The evidence collected by the government for initial as well as subsequent dangerous dog declarations can be more sophisticated than expected, especially if the owner lives in an area with well-trained animal control officers and there has been a prior incident. There could be use of electronic surveillance, video and sound recordings, and well-established protocols, including repeated neighborhood surveillance and detailed reports of observations. The dog catchers of the past may have become the professional animal control officers of today, and many are trained on laws and procedures and serve as first responders during a crisis.

STATUTES AND ORDINANCES

While gathering pertinent information and records, find out which law is referenced in the notice. Even if there is a state statute, it is possible that a local law or ordinance pertains to the declaration rather than a state law. When negotiating a deal, it might be better to have the declaration only under the local ordinance and not the state statute. A local declaration may provide more options if the worst happens and the animal needs to be re-homed. It is also a good practice to review all published and unpublished decisions about dangerous dogs in the pertinent state.

Even if dangerous dog proceedings seem simple, they can be time consuming and costly for clients because clerks and prosecutors may not be familiar with them. In some states, there are dangerous dog laws at the state level, but they can be pre-empted by stricter local laws. The local laws might incorporate portions of the state laws by reference, even if the terms are conflicting. Websites and phone numbers listed on government notices or forms received by clients may be nonexistent.

CLIENT FINANCIAL COMMITMENT

When a dog gets into trouble, expenses can quickly escalate for the dog owner. They could include quarantine expenses, attorneys' fees for three proceedings, a behavioral assessment, dog training, animal control fees, increased insurance rates, bond costs, and later, the costs of appeal. When a client hires a lawyer for a dangerous dog proceeding, he or she may expect a lawyer to win rather than apply that lawyer's best efforts. Lawyers should be cautious about accepting cases where the client wants any promise about what the lawyer can achieve given the amount of discretions a hearing officer has, and the limited scope of appellate review. A lawyer should also have a carefully worded and signed legal fee agreement where the difficulty inherent in this type of case is disclosed, and the client's commitment to paying legal fees clear.

LOWER EXPECTATIONS

If a lawyer, avoid promising clients what to expect or what result can be achieved. There is often lack of uniformity in how dangerous dog proceedings are handled from state to state and jurisdiction to jurisdiction, and between decision makers or elected governmental lawmakers, such as a city council.

Even if a lawyer has experience with dangerous dog proceedings and has achieved positive results in the past, this does not mean the owner's case will play out in the legal system in the same way. Keep in mind that the decision makers in these cases are selected and paid for by a governmental entity. Expect unseen pressures.

FILING PLEADINGS

If dealing with a judge in a courtroom context, it is wise to get applicable filings in as early as possible. Even so, these dangerous dog proceedings come on quickly and move so fast that it may be impossible to prepare and file your pleadings in a timely way, which the court will not appreciate. Let your client know ahead of time that late filings may result in judicial displeasure and may not be accepted, but as a practical matter, they are usually received and the preparation of documents helps the owner to be well prepared. When in doubt, argue constitutional principles on the record.

LAWYER STRATEGY

Another possible strategy, particularly given how informal these actions can be, is to enter the proceeding with lawyer-like documents. For example, consider having a seven-claim motion in hand about due process and other issues, together with an affidavit and memorandum of law on the subject of misidentification. It may be costly for the owner to pay for these pleadings.

At the hearing, provide these documents to the hearing officer and have the delivery reflected on the record, perhaps following up with a confirming letter after the hearing. On the other hand, if the hearing officer is known, be careful not to engage in what he or she might view as provocative behavior, given how much discretion the hearing officer has and the limitations concerning appellate standards of review. Consider utilizing a friendly approach rather than one where a hearing officer with discretionary powers takes offense. Be light on your feet and make the best judgment call you can.

HEARING OFFICERS

It bears repeating that lawyers should not tell their clients with any degree of confidence what will happen in a dangerous dog proceeding. It may be impossible to find out how much time will be allowed; what evidentiary rules, if any, will be applied; whether decision makers think they can accept hearsay evidence about the incident through an animal control officer's written report; whether there will be an opportunity to cross-examine a witness in person rather than by telephone; or whether there will be time available to call a rebuttal witness.

Generally speaking, most hearing officers are receptive to hearing testimony from a veterinarian or behavioral expert, although some may only accept a written report from an expert they approve of. Even so, if the hearing officer believes the person is an animal expert, it matters that the expert's view is not at odds with how the hearing officer views animal behaviors. For some decision makers, any bite to a human may be indefensible.

Keep in mind that if the hearing officer accepts a behavioral expert's report without testimony, the hearing officer may expect reciprocation by allowing the animal control officer to submit a report without any appearance by complainants or eyewitnesses. Because the opportunity to cross-examine adverse witnesses is important and lack of ability to perform this legal function may be outcome determinative, lawyers should keep clients in the loop in the decision-making process. It is advisable, even when these proceedings require preparation in a compressed time frame, to confirm that the owner understands the consequences of important decisions.

Unless appearing in front of an experienced administrative law judge or a knowledgeable individual who has handled many dangerous dog proceedings, be aware that the person in charge may not know whether any of the legal challenges raised are worthy of consideration. Evaluate whether to make an oral motion to reschedule the hearing in order to offer a pertinent legal memorandum. If there is a continuance, take the opportunity to negotiate a settlement.

Even if a lawyer has experience with dangerous dog proceedings in a particular jurisdiction, the simple substitution of a presiding hearing officer may result in a very different process, and there may be no advance notice of the substitution. While one officer may not permit an eyewitness to testify by telephone, another might. A different officer, paid for a three-hour proceeding, might offer an excellent deal in the first five minutes, and the client should be encouraged to consider it.

Sometimes, a good thing to tell a client is that the odds are against him or her, but perhaps by the time of the hearing, the odds can be changed with the credibility and effectiveness of either the accuser or the client's testimony being influential. Attorneys working with owners may be able to increase the odds of a favorable result. Expect the unexpected. Be light on your feet. If the owner is angry, the most important thing an attorney can do is to help him or her get that anger under control. Walk into the hearing with a good attitude. Imagine the hearing officer as just and wise.

ANIMAL CONTROL

Animal control is typically worried about being sued by the alleged victim or future victim if they fail to pursue a declaration and—by inaction—create another bite opportunity and adverse publicity. Even if animal control is not against the disposition you seek, they will typically offer no opinion on the record to the hearing officer, probably for liability reasons.

Keep ahead of governmental immunity laws. Animal control may be more receptive to pre-hearing negotiations if you can educate them on this subject. Hearing officers may not realize that they have immunity when performing a quasi-judicial function as long as that officer is acting within the scope of his or her authority.[32] Others are worried about adverse publicity in the news should another incident occur. It may surprise you that sometimes, animal control focuses on the severity of a bite, and sometimes, they want to classify what could just as easily have been a scratch from a nail on the dog's paw as a "nip."

32. Research every type of immunity law in your state.

MAKING A GOOD IMPRESSION

Help your client make a good impression at the hearing, including with regard to his or her physical appearance, attitude, facial expressions, body language, and tone of voice. The owner's written statements must be congruent with his or her other testimony.

WITNESSES

Probable witnesses include owners, caretakers, neighbors, eyewitnesses, veterinarians, and pet behaviorists. In addition to the owner, find out if there are others who made pertinent observations about the dog, as the owner may be biased or in denial. Analyze and discuss how to encourage and convince eyewitnesses, treating veterinarians, and character witnesses to cooperate.

EXPERTS

If the dog involved has any type of reputation for viciousness, make sure you have an expert who likes the breed of dog. Find out what dog breeds the expert owns or has owned. If you continue to practice in this area, learn which dog breeds are owned by animal control officers and hearing officers, too.

BODY LANGUAGE

There are many ways to interpret a dog's body language, facial expression, and vocalization. Aggressive dog behaviors were identified through wolf research when wolves' most aggressive and submissive behaviors were compared to the behaviors of different dog breeds. Aggressive behaviors included standing over the body of another dog and a dog standing erect, meaning the dog stood tall with an arched back and hackles standing up. Beware of dogs who are snarling, growling, or lunging; are stiff; have their tail tucked tightly under their body; have exposed teeth; have a direct gaze;[33] or are lip licking.[34] Quick movements can affect the likelihood of a dog to chase or bite.

Submissive dog behaviors include muzzle licks, very slowly turning the head away, and crouching. When a dog goes belly up, this is called a passive submit.[35] Injured or frightened dogs are more likely to bite, especially if their body is low

33. Cynthia Bathurst et al., *The Problem of Dog-Related Incidents and Encounters*, COPS, www.dogwise.com/downloader.cfm?itemid=dogincidents&format=pdf (last visited May 12, 2016).
34. *Id.*
35. *Id.*

to the ground or if they are hiding. Examples of a dog's positive body language include full-body wiggling; a relaxed face and relaxed fur; and a high tail, head, body, and ears.[36]

LEGAL ARGUMENTS

In some instances, it is a good idea to complain that the hearing officer does not have the right credentials, the municipal law's deadlines or service requirements were not met, the court cannot accept an animal control officer's report because it contains hearsay and impacts your client's right to cross-examination or violates evidentiary rules, or the state has not met its burden of proof. Given that legal requirements may not be well understood by the government officials implementing them, look for and emphasize deficiencies. For example, argue that the jurisdiction is wrong or that the law was enacted improperly. In other cases, being very courteous and polite might be more effective because your goal may be to negotiate deal terms, such as that the dog may be off leash in a private fenced-in yard with the fence subject to modest, rather than very expensive, modifications.

MISTAKEN IDENTITY

Defending a client in a dangerous dog proceeding is demanding, and the outcome is often influenced by the credibility and reliability of eyewitness identification,[37] particularly when multiple dogs are involved in a scuffle. Identifying the perpetrator can be difficult depending upon where an incident occurs, especially if in a dog park or in a neighborhood with an abundance of loose dogs.[38]

In one incident, a couple took their Sheltie to a dog park, and a Newfoundland[39] picked up the Sheltie and shook the dog like a ragdoll, causing the Sheltie to die from resulting injuries. The Sheltie's owners went to numerous dog parks trying to locate the Newfoundland and finally identified the probable Newfoundland and the dog's owner; the dead Sheltie's owners contacted animal control to initiate a dangerous dog proceeding.

---

36. *Id.*

37. Arye Rattner, *Convicted but Innocent: Wrongful Conviction and the Criminal Justice System*, LAW AND HUM. BEHAV., Vol 12(3), Sep 1988, 283-293.

38. Laurel Allen, *Dog Parks: Benefits and Liabilities*, UNIVERSITY OF PENNSYLVANIA SCHOLARLY COMMONS, http://repository.upenn.edu/cgi/viewcontent.cgi?article=1017&context=mes_capstones (last visited May 12, 2016).

39. Newfoundlands were once maligned, just as Pit Bulls are today, but they now have a reputation as gentle giants. Larry Cunningham, *The Case against Dog Breed Discrimination by Homeowners' Insurance Companies*, 11 CONN. INS. L.J. 1 (2004), *available at* http://www.animallaw.info/articles/arus11conninslj1.htm (last visited May 12, 2016).

At the hearing, the Newfoundland's owner testified that the injury was not caused by his dog and he asked the hearing officer to keep the record open. He later produced a receipt that proved he had an alibi for his whereabouts at the time of the incident. The owners of the dead Sheltie were chagrined that they did not have the ability to appeal the hearing officer's decision. Neither the Sheltie nor the dog's owner were parties to the action, which was initiated by law enforcement pursuant to the state's police powers.

It is possible that the Sheltie's owners did not find the correct Newfoundland who killed their dog or that the dog was with someone other than the dog's owner during the incident. The dog could have been a littermate, a relative, or a Newfoundland that looked nothing like the offending dog.[40]

On the other hand, if this particular Newfoundland did kill the Sheltie, did the Newfoundland, through free will, intend to kill the Sheltie? What if the Newfoundland had a toy dog he played with daily that was the same size as the Sheltie, and he shook the Sheltie by the neck the same way he shook his toy? What if the Newfoundland had a serious, painful dental problem that the owner ignored? What if the Newfoundland had been beaten earlier that day and was in a highly agitated state at the dog park? What if the Newfoundland had not been regularly fed?

When a dog is put on trial, a difficulty is that humans do not know to what extent the dog is an inherently vicious animal or what events and abuse by others impacted the dog's behavior.[41] For the couple wanting justice for the death of their Sheltie, it is worth asking if there should have been any mercy for the Newfoundland if the dog had been subjected to abuse.[42]

PROVOCATION

Family lawyers and lawyers for rescue groups should understand how dog ownership may affect their clients' liability risk. Although historically, dogs were entitled to one free bite, now people who own or keep dogs may be subject to strict liability unless there is sufficient proof of provocation. Provocation may reflect an anthropomorphic, human-based provocation standard or norm, such as self-defense, or a determination that there was a proportional reaction to an

40. Determining who killed the Sheltie might be possible today with DNA technology because a dog's DNA can be extracted from the bite wound and local law enforcement can obtain a warrant for a DNA test for the dog in question.

41. Knowing the difference between a reputable breeder and a large confinement operation with registered purebloods is important. To ascertain which kind of breeder your client had, it helps to learn about the time the animal was acquired.

42. Remember, a guardian and special master was appointed to save Michael Vick's fighting dogs. Should rescue groups be able to save abused animals subject to dangerous dog proceedings in circumstances where there is consensus that the dog's owner abused the animal?

attack. If a human on a leash would not be troubled by an unfamiliar screaming child running up and jumping on him or her, this might mean the dog should not be provoked either.

The concept of provocation for a dog's actions exemplifies the difficulty humans have with both embracing and rejecting anthropomorphic reasoning. It might be argued that pointing a gun at most dogs would not be provocative unless the dog had been around guns in the military or as a K-9 officer and understood what this meant. What about when a stranger approaches the dog's owner from behind? If a dog reacted to being called names, might it be the tone of the person's voice in combination with the actual words that affects the dog?

Scent might also be relevant to an animal's provocation. A dog could be provoked by the smell of a human cadaver, such as the deceased body of the dog's owner. A dog might come across other scents that have the effect of impacting a dog's behavior, such as the scent of a prior abuser's cologne. We do not know how hormones or pheromones are involved. Our understanding of what provokes dogs is wanting. The answer may be that the human preoccupation, thus far, has been to establish a standard for liability that does not account for species differences.

NATURE OR NURTURE

Pit Bulls have garnered attention in the nature or nurture debate, as they score well on an objective test instrument administered by the American Temperament Test Society (ATTS). As a breed, they have a score of 83.9 percent compared to the average score of 77 percent.[43] Even so, the ATTS now has a disclaimer saying, "The pass-fail rate is not a measure of a breed's aggression, but rather of each dog's ability to interact with humans, human situations, and the environment."[44]

---

43. Joshua-Paul Angell, *Pit Bulls Score Better on Temperament Tests Than the General Dog Population*, EXAMINER.COM, http://www.examiner.com/article/pit-bulls-score-better-on-temperament-tests-than-the-general-dog-population (last visited May 12, 2016).

44. *ATTS Breed Statistics*, AMERICAN TEMPERAMENT TEST SOCIETY, INC., http://atts.org/breed-statistics/ (last visited May 12, 2016). A mauling by a Pit Bull is regarded as evidence that the breed is bad, whereas serious injuries by a Golden Retriever might be viewed as an aberration. Beliefs about breed behavior may be based upon raw statistics rather than in relation to a particular breed's representation in the population. For example, if there were 100 Pit Bulls in a city and 10 Poodles, and there were five bites by the Pit Bulls and one bite by a Poodle, the raw statistic involving the Pit Bulls would be misleading. The raw statistic would suggest that the Pit Bull was five times more likely to bite than the Poodle. Clearly, this would be unfair given that in this scenario, the Pit Bull only had a 5 percent bite rate compared to the Poodle's 10 percent bite rate.

It is believed that dog behavior, in addition to genetics, is impacted by how the dog is initially socialized, ignored, or harmed by breeders and owners or sometimes successive owners.[45] Dogs that have had both a reputable breeder and a responsible owner have a good head start.[46]

DANGEROUS DOG PROCEEDINGS AND DIVORCE

Given the stress of a divorce process and the varieties in routine, it is possible for an incident that triggers a dangerous dog proceeding to occur during family law proceedings. When deciding whether or not to take on this type of case, be aware that dangerous dog proceedings are challenging, in part because administrative processes are often poorly established and clients may be in denial that an incident even took place. Others will resent paying for the cost of good representation or not understand a lawyer's candor is designed to diminish expectations.

If a dangerous dog proceeding occurs during a divorce action, immediately explore whether the dog should go to another home and how this move would impact the dangerous dog declaration. Notification may be required if the dog is moved, so be sure that your client changes the dog's address in compliance with applicable law and ordinances or a criminal charge could result.

Make sure your client knows exactly how many separate legal proceedings may be pending with regard to this one incident. It is common for clients not to recognize that a dangerous dog proceeding is different from a criminal proceeding against them personally and that they got the paperwork for both at the same time and may have missed a deadline. The dog owner may also be subject to a civil lawsuit. Again, ask your client to give you all of the documents he or she received because clients often misinterpret this information.

CLIENT TO-DO LIST

Clients who are at risk for a dangerous dog proceeding, perhaps because of a prior incident or the reputation of their dog's breed or based upon the perceivable fear-based reactions of others, should be given the following to-do list:

---

45. *Human-Canine Bond FAQ*, National Canine Research Council, http://nationalcanineresearchcouncil.com/responsible-pet-ownership/human-canine-bond-faq/ (last visited May 12, 2016).

46. *How to Form an AKC-Accredited Dog Club*, American Kennel Club, https://images.akc.org/pdf/rulebooks/RCFORM.pdf (last visited May 12, 2016); *Assured Breeder Scheme*, Kennel Club, http://www.thekennelclub.org.uk/assuredbreederscheme (last visited May 12, 2016); *What Is an Accredited Dog*, Canine Accreditation Program, http://canineaccreditation.org/ (last visited May 12, 2016).

- Know which animals are exempt from their homeowner's, renter's, and motor vehicle insurance. Be aware of insurance coverage in case the dog hurts someone or the dog is hurt.
- When taking road trips, keep in mind that laws, including BDLs, leash laws, and places where dogs are prohibited, may vary. Do not take the dog to places where BDLs are in effect. Also, choose your route with BDLs in mind.
- When bringing the dog on family vacations, make appropriate reservations in advance and get a confirmation number.
- Make sure any pet sitter is responsible about keeping the dog contained.
- If the dog has been aggressive or bitten before, or if the dog shows signs of aggressive behavior, proactive measures should be taken, including providing more exercise, taking the dog to a veterinarian to see if the dog has medical or dental problems or pain issues, giving the dog appropriate medication for anxiety, or getting help from an expert to assess the situation to help modify both human and dog behaviors.
- Have situational awareness of how other dogs could be confused with this dog, as it is easy for eyewitnesses to blame a similar-looking dog for the actions of another.

OWNING AN AT-RISK ANIMAL

Lawyers and other professionals should help clients evaluate the pros and cons of owning or keeping an at-risk animal, whether based upon legal proceedings or health problems. Consider the following:

- Do the owners know if the dog has bitten before, and if so, what was the severity level of the bite? Bites may be ranked from one to five, with five being the most severe.
- Would anyone claim that the dog has bitten or been aggressive before, even if the owner disagrees?
- Have the owners considered hiring an animal expert? Some experts treat themselves as neutrals and automatically communicate their reports to animal control, so choose an expert who will not share his or her result with anyone else without your permission.
- Are there any videos showing the dog interacting with others, including strangers?
- Have you met the dog on the dog's turf and given the owners feedback as to what you learned?

- Is the client willing to install appropriate physical barriers to prevent the opportunity for another incident? If not, help motivate the owner to make lifestyle changes or rehome the animal.
- Is the dog trained so that voice commands such as "stay," "leave it," and "no" are routinely used and understood? Keep in mind that voice commands should not be a substitute for physical barriers.
- Does the client have an invisible fence? Be wary of invisible fences, as dogs can go through them and they do not serve as a barrier if a person or another dog comes onto the property and through the invisible fence.
- Has the dog been socialized with people, particularly children, and other animals from a very young age, and has this socialization been ongoing? Dogs without extensive and varied, timely socialization are more at risk for dangerous behaviors.[47]
- Does the dog have a hereditary condition that causes pain that might impact the dog's behavior?[48] A dog's behavior can be impacted by poor hearing or eyesight, a painful tooth condition, and even the dog's medications.
- Is the dog going to be around small children? This might not be a good idea, as children lack judgment about what might provoke a dog. Impress upon your client not to leave the dog alone with any child, and make sure a child cannot undo locks. Install higher locks if necessary.
- Are there any warning signs that might signal a potential bite from the dog, including a growl or the dog attempting to back up? Clients should learn the dog's body language, including with regard to his or her tail, ears, mouth, or even by standing still, and the meaning of the dog's different vocalizations.
- Is your client following the requirements detailed in applicable insurance policies, and is he or she aware of which breeds are subject to exclusion from his or her homeowner's or renter's insurance policy? Clients

47. Christine Adkins & Ian Dunbar, *Puppy Socialization and Bite Inhibition: Bringing up Baby*, Modern Dog, http://moderndogmagazine.com/articles/puppy-socialization-and-bite-inhibition/271 (last visited May 12, 2016).

48. Benoit Denizet-Lewis, *Can the Bulldog Be Saved?*, N.Y. Times, http://www.nytimes.com/2011/11/27/magazine/can-the-bulldog-be-saved.html?ref=magazine (last visited May 12, 2016). This controversial article included a cover photo of a Bulldog, along with more than 20 closed captions describing Bulldog health problems including breathing difficulties, brain tumors, elbow dysplasia, and birthing difficulties. James Serpell, the Director of the Center for the Interaction of Animals and Society at the University of Pennsylvania, said that "our human tendency toward anthropomorphic selection is partly responsible for the modern bulldog's predicament." He also said that the Pug and the French Bulldog (brachycephalic breeds) have been bred to "play up the cute effect." Pugs, Pekingese, and Boston Terriers may suffer from the same syndrome as Bulldogs. This article advocates cross breeding to reduce extreme traits in well-loved breeds.

should obtain a current copy of their insurance policy and be aware of any new insurance amendments or endorsements.

- Is your client aware of behaviors that might provoke a dog? Entering a dog's home or yard or interfering with food, treats, or toys poses risks.

CONCLUSION

Although it is unlikely for people involved in a pet custody dispute to contemplate that their dog could someday be declared a dangerous dog, these things do happen. It is for this reason that superior lawyers handling pet custody disputes will be aware of future risks and advocate for a wise plan.

APPLICABLE CASE LAW

GARCIA V. VILLAGE OF TIJERAS[49]

Year: *1988*
Category: *Property Law, Constitutional Law*
Type of Action: *Ordinance Constitutionality*
Animal: *Dog*
Pet Custody Concept: *When thinking about challenging a statute or ordinance because of a client's concerns related to a pet custody case, the court will examine whether the law has a rational relationship to a legitimate legislative purpose.*

The constitutionality of an ordinance banning the ownership of American Pit Bull Terriers was challenged based upon constitutionally protected substantive and procedural due process rights and the constitutional prohibition against an impermissible taking without just compensation for private property. A determination was also sought that the ordinance be found void based upon vagueness. The ordinance was passed in a rural village with a large number of problem dogs and public outcry following the mauling of a nine-year-old girl.[50] The only criterion for delaying the destruction of the accused dog under the new ordinance was a proceeding to contest the dog's lineage.

The court reviewed whether the appellants had met their burden of proof that the enactment exceeded constitutional limitations beyond a reasonable doubt. The appellants claimed that the definition of an American Pit Bull Terrier between the American Kennel Club and the United Kennel Club lacked uniformity. The court found that the ordinance could not be challenged based upon vagueness when the

49. 108 N.M. 116, 767 P.2d 355 (N.M. App. 1988).

50. In this community, it was reported that perhaps 25 percent of the households had American Pit Bull Terriers who were believed to be responsible for injuring not only children but also other dogs, ducks, geese, and turkeys.

appellants' conduct was clearly subject to the ordinance per *Parker v. Levy*.[51] The court relied on testimony that Pit Bulls could be identified by phenotype. After commenting on Pit Bull biting style, the court was persuaded that these dogs were unpredictable, aggressive, strong, athletic, and vicious, and that they could be involved in what the court described as a "fighting frenzy."

On the subject of due process under the 5th and 14th Amendments, the appropriate test was whether the ordinance bore a rational relationship to a legitimate legislative purpose. As the "American Pit Bull Terriers presented a special threat to the safety of the residents of the Village," the court was satisfied by the rational relationship between the ordinance and a legitimate purpose. In justifying its substantive due process determination, the court offered an analysis that "Our ruling would be the same if eighteen out of the eighty households owned German Shepherd dogs, and German Shepherd dogs had been involved in a number of attacks on people and animals before being banned from the Village."

The court stated that the appellants' equal protection argument that the ordinance had no rational relationship to a legitimate purpose because it focused on only one breed rather than pure and mixed breeds was improperly constitutionally framed, as no fundamental right was involved and because a dog breed was not a suspect classification. Relying on *Garcia v. Albuquerque Public Schools Board of Education*[52] for the proposition that "If any state of facts can reasonably be conceived which will sustain the classification, the statute is valid,"[53] the court said the village could tailor its ordinance to deal with the specific attack dogs.

The appellants complained that the ordinance failed to expressly set forth provisions for a notice of hearing and right to appeal and pointed out that there were implicit prior notice problems for dogs traveling through the community. Even so, not having an express provision was not viewed by the court as a fatal flaw because the state laws were in concert with the procedural requirements of *Mathews v. Eldridge*,[54] and the ordinance could be interpreted to avoid constitutional conflict.

When the village properly exercised its police powers, the court said there was no due process violation of taking property.[55] The court rejected the appellants' preferred threshold for exercising police powers, which were "extreme, imperative or overruling necessity." Deprivation of private property simply had to meet the bare bones threshold of "justified as a legitimate exercise of the police power."[56] The district court

51. 417 U.S. 733, 94 S. Ct. 2547, 41 L. Ed. 2d 439 (1974).
52. 95 N.M. 391, 622 P.2d 699 (Ct. App. 1980).
53. *Id.*
54. 424 U.S. 319, 334, 96 S. Ct. 893, 47 L. Ed. 2d 18 (1976).
55. Relying on *Sentell v. New Orleans Carrollton Railroad Co.*, 166 U.S. 698, 17 S. Ct. 693, 41 L. Ed. 1169 (1897), where dogs only have the status of "quasi-property," the court said, "Even if it were assumed that dogs are property in the fullest sense of the word, they would still be subject to the police power of the State, and might be destroyed or otherwise dealt with, as in the judgment of the legislature is necessary for the protection of its citizens."
56. The court looked at two U.S. Supreme Court cases, *Webb's Fabulous Pharmacies, Inc. v. Beckwith*, 449 U.S. 155 (1980), and *Sentell v. New Orleans Carrollton Railroad Co.*, 166 U.S. 698, 17 S. Ct. 693, 41 L. Ed. 1169 (1897).

judgment regarding constitutionality of the ordinance was affirmed. There were two concurring but no dissenting opinions.

Practice Pointer: Between centuries and jurisdictions, dogs perceived as vicious or dangerous vary. More recently, owners have argued that the misidentification of their dogs could be revealed by genetic testing. Even so, if the parties involved in the dispute have different cultural beliefs, it must be addressed. As these dogs could be re-homed outside the village, the court was less troubled by the idea that a "taking" required compensation. This statement seemed disingenuous given the placement problems the court acknowledged for humane societies.[57]

American Dog Owners Ass'n, Inc. v. City of Minneapolis[58]

Year: *1990*
Category: *Constitutional Law*
Type of Action: *§ 1983 Action*
Animal: *Dog*
Pet Custody Concept: *Put § 1983 actions on your list of options if a problem arises about a dog between a governmental entity and your client.*

In 1990, the American Dog Owners Association (ADOA) challenged a Minneapolis ordinance pursuant to 42 U.S.C. § 1983.[59] The ordinance was facially attacked for lacking constitutionally mandated procedural due process. ADOA also claimed that the ordinance was unconstitutionally vague and overbroad.

While ultimately issuing a narrow ruling that the ordinance afforded procedural due process to dog owners under the 14th Amendment, and that lawyers who prevailed in this type of federal action were entitled to an award of attorney's fees, this decision focused on what constituted procedural due process. The court looked to the landmark decision in *Mathews v. Eldridge*,[60] where the majority stated that due process, "unlike some legal rules, is not a technical conception with a fixed content unrelated to time, place and circumstances." Furthermore, the court stated that due process "is flexible and calls for such procedural protections as the particular situation demands."[61]

Practice Pointer: Note that § 1983 actions are common in animal law. These ordinances impact where animals can live in a particular community. Always review *Mathews* when taking on a dangerous dog case.

57. The court declined to specifically address compensation for a "taking," giving the rationale that no dogs had been destroyed and the issue was not ripe.
58. 453 N.W.2d 69, 72 (Minn. App. 1990).
59. *42 USC § 1983—Civil Action for Deprivation of Rights*, Cornell University Law School, http://www.law.cornell.edu/uscode/text/42/1983 (last visited Aug. 15, 2014).
60. 424 U.S. 319, 334, 96 S. Ct. 893, 47 L. Ed. 2d 18 (1976).
61. *See* Morrissey v. Brewer, 408 U.S. 471, 481, 92 S. Ct. 2593, 2600, 33 L. Ed. 2d 484 (1972).

COUNTY OF PASCO V. RIEHL[62]

Year: *1993*
Category: *Constitutional Law, Government Law, Dangerous Dog*
Type of Action: *Constitutionality of Statute*
Animal: *Dog*
Pet Custody Concept: *Courts prefer following the due process requirement of* Mathews v. Eldridge[63] *and generally ignore how the 19th-century* Sentell v. New Orleans Carrollton Railroad Co.[64] *decision characterized dogs as quasi-property.*

The appellees owned a dog named Sheba who lacked a current rabies vaccination. Sheba bit a teenager named Eric while he was playing pool with several friends at the appellees' home. Eric was bitten after continually prodding Sheba with a pool stick and advancing toward Sheba with the pool stick in hand. Subsequently, Eric's mother filed a "dangerous dog affidavit." The appellees complained that although the dangerous dog statute allowed dog owners the right to defend against a dangerous dog classification, this right was compromised when no forum to advance this right was made available. The court considered whether a dangerous dog law was constitutional under the 5th and 14th Amendments of the U.S. Constitution. The county challenged the trial court's order enjoining enforcement of Chapter 767.12 of the Florida Statutes.

The appellees were neither interviewed about what happened nor received notice of a hearing prior to Sheba being classified as a dangerous dog. The appellees said that Sheba was incorrectly classified as a dangerous dog because the statute provided an exception that "a dog shall not be declared dangerous if the threat, injury, or damage was sustained by a person who . . . while lawfully on the property was tormenting, abusing, or assaulting the dog or its owner."

The hearing officer considered animal control's report, which included sworn affidavits. Following the 1976 U.S. Supreme Court decision *Mathews v. Eldridge*,[65] the Florida court observed that procedural due process meant that there needed to be an opportunity to be heard "at a meaningful time and in a meaningful manner." Even so, the requirements of procedural due process depended on "the character of the interest" as well as "the nature of the proceeding involved."

The court considered the *Mathews* factors, specifically (1) the private interest that would be affected by the official action, (2) the risk of deprivation of such interest through the procedures used, (3) the probable value, if any, of additional or substitute procedural safeguards, and (4) the government's interest, including the function involved and the fiscal and administrative burdens that the additional or substitute procedural requirements would entail. The court determined that a statute was unconstitutional on its face when there was "no opportunity for a hearing whatsoever." The court also enjoined the appellees from classifying Sheba as a dangerous dog.

62. 620 So. 2d 229 (Fla. App. 2d Dist. 1993).
63. 424 U.S. 319, 96 S. Ct. 893, 47 L. Ed. 2d 18 (1976).
64. 166 U.S. 698, 17 S. Ct. 693, 41 L. Ed. 1169 (1897).
65. 424 U.S. 319, 96 S. Ct. 893, 47 L. Ed. 2d 18 (1976).

Practice Pointer: Notwithstanding the importance of this decision, it is noteworthy that the court made a point of emphasizing that "domestic animals, commonly referred to as pets, are subjects of property or ownership." It was because of the pet private property status that the court determined that "the owner thereof cannot be deprived of the use thereof, except in accord with all of the elements of due process."

HANNAN V. CITY OF MINNEAPOLIS[66]

Year: *2001*
Category: *Dangerous Dog, Constitutional Law, Governmental Law*
Type of Action: *Conflict of Laws*
Animal: *Dog*
Pet Custody Concept: *Appealing a quasi-judicial decision may require the filing of a writ of certiorari.*

This was a case about whether destruction of a dog could occur when the state and local laws differed. When the relator failed to comply with his obligation to restrain and muzzle his dog, animal control officers took action and an administrative hearing was held. The relator challenged the power of animal control to order the destruction of an animal when the administrative agency permitted the use of written response over personal testimony.[67] The hearing officer ordered the dog's destruction. No information was offered about the dog.

Finding that the relator had properly sought review of a quasi-judicial agency decision by filing a writ of certiorari, the court considered whether the relator was granted due process in the agency proceeding and if the agency's decision was unreasonable and lacking evidentiary support.

With regard to the conflict doctrine between state law and local ordinances, four guiding principles were applied: (1) the ordinance and the statute shall not contain express or implied terms that are irreconcilable, (2) the ordinance shall not permit what state law forbids, (3) the ordinance cannot forbid what the statute expressly permits, and (4) when no conflict exists between the ordinance and statute, the ordinance may contain additional or complementary terms or aid in furtherance of the statutory purpose. The fourth principle applied to the instant case, and the state statute and local ordinance were allowed to coexist.

It was determined that the state statute neither implied nor expressed that the subject matter was solely a matter of state concern or that the state had fully and completely covered the subject matter. Based upon the above, the statutory preemption doctrine did not apply. The state law expressly allowed for local regulation and provided that the regulation was not breed specific. The court also declared that "the regulation and control of dangerous dogs is a wholly legitimate issue for municipal interest because it primarily affects the local populace."

---

66. 623 N.W.2d 281 (Minn. App. 2001).

67. The use of "enabling" due process procedures addressing dangerous dog designations was addressed in *In re Molly*, 712 N.W.2d 567 (Minn. App. 2006).

Practice Pointer: As this case reveals, the disposition of a dog can be a matter of life or death for the dog, especially if the dog is awarded to a reckless owner and dangerous dog proceedings are likely to ensue. The court, by making an ownership determination, in a family law proceeding may be doing more than making a disposition when it is foreseeable that the dog will get in trouble. Attorneys should know the Conflict of Laws Doctrine and its guiding principles.

City of Toledo v. Tellings[68]

Year: *2006*
Category: *Constitutional Law*
Type of Action: *Ordinance Constitutionality*
Animal: *Dog*
Pet Custody Concept: *When a court cites* Sentell v. New Orleans Carrollton Railroad Co.,[69] *a case where the Supreme Court described dogs as subject to "attacks of hydrophobic madness," watch out.*

Because of the national importance of this decision, for those interested in BSLs, also known as BDLs, this discussion will begin with the lower court's decision.[70]

The appellant owned three Pit Bull-type dogs that were both family pets and law abiding. When a health inspector checked for lead paint after observing the dogs in his home, the appellant was charged with violations of vicious dog laws and for failing to carry liability insurance. The appellant claimed that the municipal and state laws were unconstitutional, and a five-day hearing ensued with multiple dog and Pit Bull experts. The witnesses testifying on the appellant's behalf included experts on Pit Bull behavior, anatomy, temperament, and training. Other witnesses included canine geneticists, veterinarians, cruelty investigators, breeders, animal technicians, animal control consultants, and zoo directors.

The lower court articulated how Pit Bulls originated in England in the late 1800s and had been used for "bull baiting" and later to protect American settlers. The court said that American Staffordshire Terriers and American Pit Bull Terriers are types of Pit Bulls, and both are registered and "trained for confirmation and participation in other dog trial events, such as weight pulling and agility." The court addressed claims about Pit Bull musculature and concluded that the Pit Bull was not different from the Saint Bernard, Bull Mastiff, Rottweiler, Malamute, or other well-muscled dogs.

Together with pedigreed Pit Bulls, the appellate court noted that unpedigreed Pit Bulls can be family pets and also misused in criminal activities. Except for Pit Bulls trained to be aggressive, the lower court concluded that Pit Bulls were "highly obedient, eager-to-please, good family pets" and noted that a cruelty investigator witness

68. 2006 Ohio 975 (Ohio 3/3/2006), 2006 Ohio 975 (Ohio 2006) (court of appeals decision) and 114 Ohio St. 3d 278, 871 N.E.2d 1152, 2007 Ohio 3724 (Ohio 2007) (supreme court decision).

69. 166 U.S. 698, 17 S. Ct. 693, 41 L. Ed. 1169 (1897).

70. The lower and higher court decisions in this case should be required reading for any lawyer who wants to handle pet custody cases. These decisions are illustrative of the divergent views on animals and the challenges inherent in seeking a just result in the legal system.

had said he had never been bitten by a Pit Bull and did not find them "to be 'vicious' in comparison to other breeds."

The court also reviewed testimony regarding the urban legend that Pit Bulls have "locking jaws" and stated that dental records revealed no evidence to support this claim. Instead, the Pit Bull has characteristics similar to those of other dogs of the same size, though "some Pit Bulls have the innate ability to 'bite and hold.'" Some, but not all, Pit Bulls exhibit a quality called "gameness,"[71] which the court likened to "stick-to-it-iveness." The court observed that this breed's qualities make them good search and rescue dogs, military protective dogs, drug sniffing dogs, and therapy dogs.

The lower court was critical of the statistics presented against the Pit Bull, including in the fatality context. These were "bare statistics" that described incidents "without reference to the total number of dogs in each breed population." To the court, these types of statistics lacked relevance and meaning. The court seemed troubled by a dog warden's acknowledgment that "even if a dog was 50 percent Pit Bull, if it did not 'look like a Pit bull,' the owner would not be charged." It was the look of the dog that made the dog subject to the vicious dog laws, not the genetics.

Based upon the above, the Ohio Court of Appeals determined as a matter of law that the local and state vicious dog laws were unconstitutional and reversed the municipal court's determination. More specifically, the court of appeals offered that while some might believe that an owner should be able to refute a vicious declaration, "once a dog has been designated as a Pit Bull, even evidence that a dog has an unblemished bite history and good, non-aggressive, obedient behavior is still insufficient to prove that it is not a 'vicious' dog." The convictions against the appellant were vacated.

The Ohio Supreme Court reversed the judgment of the court of appeals and found that the government had validly exercised its state and city police powers. The court held that "the state and the city of Toledo possess the constitutional authority to exercise police powers that are rationally related to a legitimate interest in public health, safety, morals, or general welfare." The court further held that "the State of Ohio and the City of Toledo have a legitimate interest in protecting citizens from the dangers associated with Pit Bulls, and that R.C. 955.11(A)(4)(a)(iii) and 955.22 and Toledo Municipal Code 505.14 are rationally related to that interest and are constitutional."

The Ohio Supreme Court discussed how the "legislature is the primary judge of the needs of public welfare" and said that the court will not nullify a law unless the law represents "a clear violation of a state or federal constitutional provision." The court quoted from the Ohio Constitution by saying, "Private property shall ever be held inviolate, but subservient to the public welfare."[72] The ownership and control of dogs was described to be well within the legitimate exercise of police powers, as dogs are only private property to "a qualified extent." By "qualified extent," the court clarified that notwithstanding "special relationships" between humans and dogs, police powers could be used to destroy or "otherwise deal" with them.

71. The court identified "gameness" as a controversial topic and seemed to indicate that it was not clear whether this was attributable to nature versus nurture.

72. Ohio Constitution, Section 19, Article I.

Citing *Sentell v. New Orleans Carrollton Railroad Co.*,[73] the court emphasized how police powers were necessary to "protect the public against the nuisance posed by a vicious dog." While conceding that the ordinance could apply to dogs not inherently dangerous, the supreme court determined that the appellants had failed to meet their burden of proof and that the evidence supported the conclusion that "Pit Bulls pose a serious danger to the safety of citizens." The court also stated that the "state and the city have a legitimate interest in protecting citizens from the danger posed by this breed of domestic dogs." The supreme court extinguished the court of appeals' determination that the state and municipal laws were unconstitutional based upon the court's procedural due process, substantial due process, equal protection, and void for vagueness analysis.[74]

Practice Pointer: Note that the court relied on *State v. Anderson*[75] when it said, "In sum, we believe that the physical and behavioral traits of Pit Bulls together with the commonly available knowledge of dog breeds typically acquired by potential dog owners or otherwise possessed by veterinarians or breeders are sufficient to inform a dog owner as to whether he owns a dog commonly known as a Pit Bull dog." With regard to the place of dogs in American jurisprudence, link the case law back to the vintage *Sentell*, where dogs, rather than being private property, were only quasi-property unless dead or subdued. From a cultural perspective, young court of appeals judges may view animals as family members more often than older jurists serving on the supreme court do.

Pelzel v. St. Paul Office of License, Inspections and Environmental Protection[76]

Year: *2006*
Category: *Government Law*
Type of Action: *Appeal of Agency Determination*
Animal: *Dog*
Pet Custody Concept: *Appreciate just how minimal due process rights may be.*

In this Minnesota Court of Appeals case, a Labrador Retriever named Rory was designated a "potentially dangerous animal" after biting two children while running at large, and thereafter determined a "dangerous animal" when he was again running at large and bit another person. Both determinations were made by an agency utilizing the legislative code of the city of St. Paul.

Rory's owner appealed the agency's determination by a writ of certiorari to the court of appeals. In this unpublished decision, the court set out the procedure for

73. 166 U.S. 698, 17 S. Ct. 693, 41 L. Ed. 1169 (1897).

74. The court distinguished its interpretation of *State v. Cowan*, 103 Ohio St. 3d 144, 2004-Ohio-4777, 814 N.E.2d 846, from the court of appeals' interpretation. The current laws were deemed superior to the flawed, narrowly tailored laws that did not survive constitutional scrutiny. The court concluded that the laws represented valid exercises of police powers by what appeared to be merely evoking *State v. Thompkins*, 75 Ohio St. 3d 558, 560–561, 664 N.E.2d 926 (1996).

75. 57 Ohio St. 3d 168 (Ohio 1991).

76. No. A05-2534 (Minn. App. 9/12/2006) (Minn. App. 2006).

scope of review for an agency decision subject to the administrative law guidelines. Following *Hannan v. City of Minneapolis* precedent,[77] the appellate review was limited to (1) whether the agency who made the determination had jurisdiction; (2) whether the proceedings were fair and regular; (3) whether the decision was unreasonable, oppressive, arbitrary, fraudulent, or without evidentiary support; and (4) whether the decision was based upon an incorrect theory of the law.

While declaring its reluctance to interfere with the management of municipal affairs, the court framed agency quasi-judicial powers and found de novo review was not available based upon an administrative agency interpreting a legislative code to reach its determination. This limit was designed to protect the separation of governmental powers.

The court of appeals speculated on what actions it might take to safeguard constitutional guarantees. If the agency's findings were insufficient, the court might remand the case to the agency for additional findings or reverse the administrative agency's determination due to lack of substantive evidence. The court drew the line at "retrying the facts" or making "credibility determinations," saying that those actions were outside of its power.

One of the issues raised was to what extent a hearing officer could consider various records, including animal control records and police reports, without "further foundation." While not clarifying what "further foundation" meant, the court granted the administrative agency broad discretion to consider any records it wanted to.[78]

After listening to testimony from Rory's owner and an alleged victim, the agency considered correspondence, police reports, and animal control records detailing the investigation that animal control performed and declared Rory a dangerous dog. It seemed that the testimony of Rory's owner boosted the higher court's confidence in the agency's determination. The owner, while claiming that Rory was coming to her and that his feet were in her yard, stated, "I just know that my dog never left the yard." Deference was granted to the hearing officer as being in the position to observe the dog owner's credibility. While there was evidence of dangerousness, the lack of standards with regard to what records a hearing officer could consider without foundation was troubling.[79]

---

77. 623 N.W.2d 281, 284 (Minn. App. 2001).

78. The court explained that "The Saint Paul Legislative Code allows the hearing officer to consider '[t]he records of the office of license, inspections and environmental protection, including those of animal control, and any police reports relating to an attack or bite,'" relying on Saint Paul, Minnesota Legislative Code § 200.12(c)(1)c.

79. Although misidentification was not raised as an issue here, one can imagine a more sinister implication where the courts allow animal control reports in lieu of eyewitness testimony. An eyewitness, the source of information contained in an animal control report, might be unable to tell two yellow Labradors apart. The behavior of one dog could be attributed to another in a report that impacts the life expectancy of a family pet. In some situations, the accused dog could be subject to cruelty by neighbor children, adults, or passersby. It seems that when an animal is claimed to be running at large or causing an injury while in the animal's own yard, the consideration of reports only, without adequate foundation, is uniquely troubling because of behaviors that may have provoked the dog. Beyond that, for certain breeds of dogs, including the breeds subject to BDLs, courts must be sensitive to how human behaviors stemming from fear of a breed might be confused with the actions of an individual member of that breed.

Practice Pointer: For those who have not yet participated in an administrative hearing, it is difficult to learn in advance of a hearing how it will be conducted. For example, it can be hard to find out what procedures will be followed or if the hearing officer will be more concerned about the violation of an ordinance or statute. Here are some pertinent questions. Find out if the municipality has an open file policy in a dangerous dog proceeding. Will exhibits be shared at a reasonable time in advance of the hearing to allow the parties to determine what fact witnesses might be necessary? Will the hearing officer require a disclosure of the witnesses' names and contact information in advance of the hearing? Are continuances routinely granted when there are constitutional due process issues? Will a hearing officer delay a determination subject to an expert evaluation and opinion?

It would also be helpful to know what, if any, evidentiary rules the hearing officer intends to utilize and whether testimony will be permitted when someone is not physically present at the proceeding, such as if an eyewitness prefers to appear by telephone. It is important to know how much time is allocated for the proceeding, too, as this will impact whether you can call a rebuttal witness. In addition, the timeliness of action by animal control to make a declaration may be at issue. If six months pass before an owner is notified that a companion animal was at large, it becomes much more difficult for the owner to obtain evidence than if the complaint was timely made. In that situation, a due process objection could be made.

American Canine Foundation v. Sun[80]

Year: *2007*
Category: *Dangerous Dog*
Type of Action: *Constitutionality of an Ordinance*
Animal: *Dog*
Pet Custody Concept: *Freedom to contract and the Commerce Clause were subordinate to public safety concerns, as exemplified by the state exercising its police powers.*

The plaintiff challenged an ordinance requiring that dogs over the age of four months be spayed or neutered. The plaintiff claimed that this ordinance (1) preempted the federal Animal Welfare Act (AWA), (2) violated procedural and substantive due process rights, (3) violated equal protection rights, (4) represented an ex post facto law in violation of Article I, Sections 9 and 10 of the U.S. Constitution, (5) violated the Takings Clause of the Fifth Amendment, (6) adversely affected interstate commerce in violation of the Commerce Clause, (7) infringed the freedom of contract for those buying and selling dogs, (8) was unconstitutionally vague, and (9) violated the First Amendment right to freedom of association.

A U.S. District Court judge granted the defendants' motion to dismiss these claims. Before granting dismissal under Rule 12(b)(6), the court determined that the plaintiff had failed to establish one out of three elements required for standing, saying,

80. No. C-06-4713 MMC, March 21, 2007.

"neither the claim asserted nor the relief requested requires the participation of individual members in the lawsuit."

With regard to the AWA preemption, the court observed that the ordinance permitted unaltered dogs if their owner "obtained an unaltered dog license." The court was not persuaded that the AWA was intended to preclude the state and local regulation of animals. On the subject of procedural due process, the court criticized the plaintiff, as "the issue is not dangerous dogs, it is unsterilized dogs." In making this argument, the court referred to the 1897 decision of *Sentell v. New Orleans Carrollton Railroad Co.*,[81] which reflected an extreme view on animals as property, if not less than property.

The court also pointed out that even when a private interest was at issue, dogs were still property subject to the police powers of the state. Consequently, under *Wilkinson v. Austin*,[82] "any private interest in the ownership of unaltered dogs is subject to more limited procedural protections." The court also noted that because unsterilized dogs are more likely to stray, bite, or attack, the ordinance promoted public safety, which was a government interest. The court rejected the plaintiff's claim that the law was unconstitutionally vague or that it would cause "arbitrary, unreasonable and discriminatory law enforcement and serve no legitimate government purpose."

On the subject of equal protection, as the ordinance did not infringe a fundamental constitutional right or affect a suspect classification, and because plausible reasons existed for government involvement, the court found that there was a rational basis for the ordinance. The court was not persuaded by the ex post facto clause even though the ordinance could result in unanticipated costs to those who already had unaltered dogs. It was determined that no constitutional violation occurred because there was a grace period for an owner to apply for an unaltered license or to spay or neuter his or her dog before the penalty period would commence. The court paid more attention to the plaintiff's takings claim under the Fifth Amendment. Rejecting the plaintiff's claim that a taking was involved, the court said the ordinance only regulated use and pointed out that unaltered dog licenses were available for competition dogs.

Concerning the Commerce Clause, the court considered whether local regulations would "unjustifiably discriminate on their face against out-of-state entities" or "impose burdens on interstate trade." The court concluded that the ordinance was neutral, locally focused, and did not violate the Commerce Clause. The court further observed that "even if the ordinance could be said to impose some burden on interstate trade, any such incidental burden is not excessive in relation to the above-stated local benefits," referring to costs and losses associated with animal overpopulation.

Regarding freedom of contract, the court indicated that it was well-settled that contracts were subject to reasonable police power restrictions and again cited the 1897 decision of *Sentell*. The court viewed the public safety aspects of the ordinance as superior to how the ordinance might infringe on "the business of selling canines." In order for the plaintiff to cross the threshold and proceed on a constitutionally vague claim, the court, citing *Hotel & Motel Association of Oakland v. City of Oakland*,[83]

81. 166 U.S. 698, 703 (1897).
82. 545 U.S. 209, 224–25 (2005).
83. 344 F.3d 959, 972 (9th Cir. 2003).

said that a "party challenging the facial validity of an ordinance on vagueness grounds outside the domain of the First Amendment must demonstrate that the enactment is impermissibly vague in all of its applications." The court said the plaintiff did not even allege the ordinance was vague in all its applications.

Perhaps of greater concern to the plaintiff was the subject of arbitrary enforcement. Although not mentioned in the decision, it could be anticipated that breed discrimination was a consideration in the ordinance enforcement. The court dodged this concern and instead merely listed seven grounds upon which a dog license for an unaltered dog could be denied or revoked.

The plaintiff also claimed the ordinance violated the plaintiff's First Amendment right to freedom of association because of the "freedom from coerced association with groups holding views with which the nonmembers disagree." Contrary to the plaintiff's position, the court found that as long as the dog was registered with an approved registry and competed in at least one dog show or sporting competition, there was no requirement that the dog belong to a breed club.[84] The court concluded that "neither the benefits of an unaltered dog license nor compliance with the ordinance depends on club membership or club association."

Practice Pointer: Cast a broad net, and if that does not work, try, try again!

Downey v. Pierce County[85]

Year: *2011*
Category: *Constitution*
Type of Action: *Due Process Rights*
Animal: *Dog*
Pet Custody Concept: *If you want the court to be more thoughtful, emphasize* Mathews v. Eldridge[86] *principles.*

In 2011, the Court of Appeals of Washington state reversed, in part, a dismissal of all claims by the superior court in an action initiated by the appellant dog owner. The issues before the court, partly published and partly unpublished, included (1) whether the fee for the initial evidentiary review of a dangerous animal declaration, which took place before an auditor without subpoena authority and without creating a record, constituted a violation of the owner's procedural due process rights; (2) whether the subsequent fee for a de novo "appeal" hearing before a hearing examiner regarding the dangerous animal declaration was a similar due process violation; and (3) whether the dangerous animal declaration determination violated the appellant's due process rights, in part because of the lack of an evidentiary standard in the ordinance.

A seven-pound Pomeranian named Kayla, set loose by her owner to urinate, was grabbed by the stomach and carried away by another dog. Whether Kayla provoked

84. The court seemed unaware of its purebred emphasis.
85. 267 P.3d 445, 165 Wash. App. 152 (2011).
86. 424 U.S. 319, 334, 96 S. Ct. 893, 47 L. Ed. 2d 18 (1976).

the other dog and whether the other dog could be identified as a dog named Blizzard was unclear because the much later identification of Blizzard did not match earlier descriptions given to animal control and Kayla's owner had her back turned to Kayla when the incident took place. Blizzard's owner claimed that Blizzard was kenneled at the time of the incident. The hearing officer made findings, applied the preponderance of evidence standard, denied a motion for reconsideration, and upheld the dangerous animal declaration against Blizzard.

First, the court addressed the lower court's summary judgment dismissal of the appellant's derivative taxpayer claims regarding being charged for the proceeding. The court agreed with the appellant that the initial evidentiary hearing should have been without charge. The court emphasized that under *Mathews v. Eldridge*,[87] due process is a flexible concept whose exact contours would be determined by the particular situation. It required the consideration of the private interest, the risk of erroneous deprivation of that interest, and the governmental interest.

The court then articulated the private interests at stake, which included, "(1) pet owners' interests in keeping their pets, which is arguably more than a mere economic interest because pets are not fungible; (2) economic interests in not having to pay additional annual registration and inspection fees or acquire significant liability insurance in order to retain his or her property; and (3) potentially being subject to criminal liability for later violations of the County's dangerous animal restrictions."

The appellant was accordingly reimbursed $250 for an auditor fee, as well as the later fee for the hearing examiner, because the first review was insufficient to meet the *Mathews* standard for a public review and there was no record permitting appellate review by the hearing officer. Instead, the matter before the hearing officer was the first opportunity for the pet owner to have a hearing that avoided the *Mathews* erroneous deprivation problem.

Practice Pointer: Relying on *Mansour v. King County*,[88] the court agreed that the ordinance violated the appellant's due process rights, as it did not provide for adequate standards of proof. The court distinguished between utilizing a probable cause standard before issuing a dangerous animal declaration from an evidentiary standard that justified the "permanent deprivation of property." The court found that when a standard is not articulated, the preponderance of the evidence standard should apply.

---

87. *Id.*
88. 131 Wash. App. 255, 128 P.3d 1241 (2006).

Coballes v. Spokane County[89]

Year: *2012*
Category: *Civil Procedure*
Type of Action: *Scope of Review*
Animal: *Dog*
Pet Custody Concept: *The scope of review is narrower in a writ proceeding than on an appeal.*

Although the owner of a Rottweiler/Alaskan Malamute mix took precautions when a three-year-old girl was a guest in her house, the girl was bitten by the dog, hospitalized, and underwent surgery. The Board of Commissioners designated the Spokane County Regional Animal Protection Service (SCRAPS) to hold a dangerous dog proceeding, and SCRAPS affirmed the dangerous dog declaration. The appellant sought relief for this declaration by utilizing an artful array of actions, including a statutory judicial review, a constitutional writ of certiorari, a statutory writ of review, a statutory right of appeal, and a constitutional writ of review. The appellant also served an "Ex Parte Motion for Writ of Review, Assignment of Judge, and Waiving Bond."

In working its way through this complex array of claims, the court boiled down some controlling principles. When a statutory appeal is available, as it was in this case, a statutory or constitutional writ is not. The latter is only available when a remedy of appeal was not available, and this extraordinary remedy was only granted sparingly. More specifically, the court said the writ of certiorari was recognized by RCW 7.16.040 and a statutory writ of certiorari was the same as a statutory writ of review.

The court then offered that the scope of review was narrower in a writ proceeding than it was in an appeal. Pointing out that this limited scope of review could be fatal to the appellant's case, the court nevertheless construed the appellant's action as a "statutory appeal in substance." Next, the court considered the superior court's review on the merits and determined that the same appeal procedure applied as to appeals from district courts. The court also granted the appellant's request that if the court determined that she did not have an appeal of right to the superior court, she be granted leave to bring a motion for discretionary review and to proceed with any claim she had that satisfied RAP 2.3(d) criteria.

Practice Pointer: No matter what breed of dog a client has, make sure the client is careful when guests arrive, especially children. If the way to proceed in a dangerous dog action is less than clear, try everything; if you cannot find what you want in a statute, look for a good writ.

89. 274 P.3d 1102 (Wash. App. 2012).

Sawh v. City of Lino Lakes[90]

Year: *2012*
Category: *Dangerous Dog*
Type of Action: *Writ of Certiorari*
Animal: *Dog*
Pet Custody Concept: *Between substantive practice areas, courts may shift from one end of a continuum to another.*

Courts gain reputations, and in pet law, the Minnesota reputation in pet law was heralded following the unpublished decision in *Pratt v. Pratt.*[91] In that case, the court signaled that if a dog was mistreated in the future, this could be a factor in an ownership determination. The Minnesota courts were likewise ahead of the curve in *American Dog Owners Association, Inc. v. City of Minneapolis,*[92] where the court ruled against BSLs, later known as BDLs. It is for that reason that there were shock waves, both inside and outside of Minnesota, when this well-respected bench unanimously ruled that a yellow Labrador mix would be destroyed. Perhaps that decision is even more disturbing in that the supreme court displayed no awareness of how companion animals are treated differently than other property. This decision represents an old-time perspective; you can spot it as the court proudly cites *Sentell v. New Orleans Carrollton Railroad Co.*[93] as a precedent.

A yellow Labrador mix dog named Brody was involved in three different incidents. The first incident occurred when he was two years old; he ran through an invisible fence and jumped up on a passerby, either biting or scratching the man. The second incident occurred six months later when Brody was on a leash in his yard being groomed by his owner when an agitated neighbor walked by. The neighbor was making a 911 call about a nearby fire. Brody bit her once on the elbow and again on the hip. The neighbor complained that Brody, who was tethered in his own yard, "absolutely was not under the owner's control."[94] Brody's owner, referred to as the relator, admitted that she had "lost control" of Brody. The third incident occurred one month later when Brody was in his owner's home in the basement behind a closed door, lying in his kennel. When a delivery man erroneously went downstairs, Brody bit him, and the delivery man suffered a puncture wound on his hand.[95]

After the first incident, the relator received a written citation from the city declaring Brody as a "potentially dangerous dog." The citation gave the relator no information about how to exercise due process rights; she was not notified that she had a right to a hearing or the right to an appeal. After the second incident, Brody was classified as

90. 800 N.W.2d 663 (Minn. App. 2011) (court of appeals decision) and 823 N.W.2d 627 (Minn. 2012) (supreme court decision).

91. 1988 WL 120251 (Minn. App. Nov. 15, 1998).

92. 453 N.W.2d 69, 72 (Minn. App. 1990).

93. 166 U.S. 698, 17 S. Ct. 693, 41 L. Ed. 1169 (1897).

94. The injured woman later admitted that the "smoke and her nervousness" could have "aggravated the dog."

95. The delivery man injured in the third incident testified at the second hearing that "he hoped the dog would not have to be destroyed."

a dangerous dog. This determination was "predicated on the dog's earlier declaration as a potentially dangerous dog" according to the Minnesota Court of Appeals. When a dog is already branded a potentially dangerous dog, if another incident occurs, the dog's owner cannot offer a provocation defense.

At the time of the second incident, the relator was informed that challenging the first incident was "a separate process" and that she was required to follow up with another county on that matter. Although no information was provided on how she would exercise her due process rights in another county, the relator was provided with information for challenging the dangerous dog declaration for the second incident. The third incident occurred after the relator's first hearing had taken place in front of the city council but before the relator received written notice from the city council about the council's determination, whereby the owner's specific obligations as a result of Brody's dangerous dog declaration were particularized. At the first council meeting, the relator was told to secure a muzzle on Brody when he was outside of a "proper enclosure."

At the second hearing before the city council, which followed the third incident, it was learned that the delivery man had opened a closed door and entered the relator's basement, contrary to the relator's instructions.[96] The delivery man's bite was deemed as evidence of a subsequent dangerous dog offense contrary to the local ordinance. The dog languished in a pound for two years while this matter was in the courts. The statute pertains to the "owner of the animal" committing the subsequent offense, not the animal. This bears repeating.

Evidence offered by the relator at this death row-type hearing[97] included testimony from an animal behaviorist who said that Brody had "protective behavior" when defending "his territory," and that training Brody would benefit him. The council also received numerous letters detailing positive observations about Brody. Following these two consecutive city council determinations, the relator appealed Brody's "destruct" determination by writ of certiorari.[98] At issue on appeal was whether the relator was denied procedural due process and whether the city's decision "to designate Brody as 'dangerous' was arbitrary and capricious."

The analysis of the Minnesota Court of Appeals was substantially different than the reversal that followed by the Minnesota Supreme Court.[99] In the first instance, the court of appeals appreciated the special place companion animals have in their owners' lives and reasoned that higher due process standards should apply. This is a very important idea. The court of appeals emphasized that the relator's failure to timely

96. Although the legal system has long been comfortable using expressions such as *res ipsa loquitur* when a sponge is accidentally left inside a patient following surgery, it seems that both lawmakers and jurists have difficulty appreciating that dogs are protective of their territory.

97. As the Minnesota court has added medical malpractice to the standard to be applied in veterinary malpractice cases, it only seems fair to call this a death row-type of process, even though the court obfuscated its actions by using the word "destruction."

98. At the second city council meeting, when a question was asked about how to interpret the word "shall," the city was not informed about the fine points of the "shall/may" dichotomy with regard to whether a destruct order must be mandatory.

99. The cases are so different that if the educated reader was to guess in which decade each decision was written, the reader might have guessed that the supreme court's decision was from a different century than the court of appeals'.

raise a constitutional procedural due process claim when before the city council was not relevant because "constitutional issues are within the exclusive province of the judicial branch, and administrative agencies generally do not have jurisdiction to resolve constitutional issues."

As the city council action was quasi-judicial, the court of appeals relied on *Dietz v. Dodge County*[100] for the proposition that the reversal of a quasi-judicial body's decision was limited to "whether the order or determination in a particular case was arbitrary, oppressive, unreasonable, fraudulent, under an erroneous theory of law, or without any evidence to support it." As the U.S. Constitution Amendment XIV, Section 1 and the Minnesota Constitution Article I, Section 7 granted due process rights, the court of appeals said that the gravamen of a due process claim was that "the government has deprived a person of a constitutionally protected liberty or property interest." Citing *Brooks v. Commissioner of Public Safety*,[101] the court viewed procedural due process as "flexible" and that procedural protections vary as the particular situation warrants. The court then applied the three procedural due process factors set forth in *Mathews v. Eldridge*:[102]

> (1) the private interest . . . affected by the official action; (2) the risk of an erroneous deprivation of such interest through the procedures used, and the probable value, if any, of additional or substitute procedural safeguards; and (3) the government's interest, including the function involved and the fiscal and administrative burdens that the additional or substitute procedural requirement would entail.

In terms of balancing interests, the court of appeals said that although a "protected property interest was implicated," the city had a "high interest" in effective animal control. The first of the three *Mathews* factors was applied "in favor of the city." The court agreed with the relator that she should have been allowed to challenge the declaration of her dog as potentially dangerous in accordance with the second *Mathews* factor, which pertains to the risk of erroneous deprivation of property interest.

The court emphasized that the potentially dangerous dog declaration "can provide a basis on which the city later deems a dog 'dangerous'" because the local ordinance defined a "dangerous animal" as an animal that has done the following:

1. Caused bodily injury or disfigurement to any person on public or private property;
2. Engaged in any attack on any person under circumstances which would indicate danger to personal safety;
3. Exhibited unusually aggressive behavior, such as an attack on another animal;
4. Bitten one or more persons on two or more occasions; or
5. Been found to be potentially dangerous and/or the owner has personal knowledge of the same, [sic] the animal aggressively bites, attacks or endangers the safety of humans or domestic animals.

100. 487 N.W.2d 237, 239 (Minn. 1992).
101. 584 N.W.2d 15, 19 (Minn. App. 1998), *review denied* (Minn. Nov. 24, 1998).
102. 424 U.S. 319, 335, 96 S. Ct. 893, 903 (1976).

It followed that Brody's dangerous dog declaration at the first hearing before the city council was impacted by his potentially dangerous dog status because the relator was denied the "opportunity to be heard at a meaningful time and in a meaningful manner."[103] The court of appeals then turned to the third factor under *Mathews*, which reflects the government interest. Not persuaded by the claim of fiscal and administrative burdens regarding the third factor, the court said, "Because two of the three *Mathews* factors weigh in favor of relator, we conclude that his procedural due-process rights were violated." Reversing the city council decision, the court further determined that because this constitutional denial was dispositive of the matter, the court would not address the other issues raised on appeal.

The supreme court reframed the facts and applied the *Mathews* factors in a dramatically different way.[104] Now, the relator was not constitutionally entitled to challenge the first potentially dangerous dog declaration and ignored the impact of what could be an ill-advised potentially dangerous dog declaration on a dog's very life. Before applying the three factors in *Mathews*, the court utilized a "two-step analysis to determine whether the government has violated an individual's procedural due process rights." A protected property interest would not apply "when government action may lead to the deprivation of a property interest at some indeterminate point in the future based on certain unfulfilled conditions."

In rendering this procedural due process two-step analysis, the court cited *Board of Regents of State Colleges v. Roth*,[105] a case that discussed whether due process under the 14th Amendment of the Constitution required a hearing opportunity when a non-tenured teacher's contract was not renewed. The supreme court determined that the relator had no protected life, liberty, or property interest, although the supreme court offered no analysis as to how it made its determination of a "life" interest. Should the subject of property ever be treated differently in the legal system when the property is alive? What if the companion animal is on the continuum between property and person?

In then applying the *Mathews* factors, the court emphasized that an animal was "like any other item of tangible personal property."[106] On the first *Mathews* factor, the private interest affected by the official action, the court said the city prevailed. With regard to the second factor of erroneous deprivation, the court looked at the relator's argument about a meaningful opportunity to contest the potentially dangerous dog designation. The court indifferently said that "the City must find only that an animal control officer has previously declared an animal 'potentially dangerous' and provided

103. Based upon the review of the record of the city council meeting, the court also observed that the previous potentially dangerous dog declaration did not seem to be "up for debate" in any later proceeding.

104. 823 N.W.2d 627 (Minn. 2012) (supreme court decision).

105. 408 U.S. 564, 570–71 (1972).

106. For all the flaws of the Texas Supreme Court's decision in *Strickland v. Medlen*, 397 S.W.3d 184, 185 (Tex. 2013), where the court deemed noneconomic damages were not available for the owners of a dog negligently killed at an animal shelter, the Texas court at least understood that its decision impacted a pet as a family member. The Minnesota Supreme Court is far away from both the Texas and Vermont perspective, where in *Scheele v. Dustin*, 998 A.2d 697, 2010 VT 45 (Vt. 2010), the court said, "Pets occupy a legal realm somewhere between chattel and children."

written notice of that fact to the owner, not that the 'potentially dangerous' designation was correct."

The court reasoned that "the purpose of the 'potentially dangerous' designation is simply to put owners on notice of their animal's dangerous tendencies."[107] Under the second *Mathews* factor, the risk of an erroneous deprivation of such interest through the procedures used, and the probable value, if any, of additional or substitute procedural safeguards, "the City was not required to provide Sawh with an opportunity to challenge the correctness of that designation at a later hearing." With regard to the third *Mathews* factor, dealing with police powers, the court said that the city might want to avoid "the increased costs and administrative burdens that additional procedures would entail." Again, this was a court that embraced the 1897 U.S. Supreme Court decision of *Sentell*, where the court envisioned dogs as "subject to attacks of hydrophobic madness" and only advanced them from quasi-property to property if "dead or subdued." The Minnesota court may not have realized that this seminal case was based upon the world view of dogs as subject to rabies, in that dogs are subject to "attacks of hydrophobic madness."

The court found the two hearings provided to the relator were constitutionally sufficient even though the outcome of the second hearing was predicated on the lack of notice of procedural due process to the dog owner following the first. Ignoring the appeals court's analysis that the deprivation of a hearing at a meaningful time and place on the potentially dangerous dog designation violated the owner's due process rights, the supreme court must have disagreed with the court of appeals that the city council action was arbitrary or capricious. The supreme court offered scant details as to what happened at the city council meeting.

The supreme court said that "lack of provocation is only one of two means for proving that an animal is 'dangerous'" and "the other is to prove that an animal previously had been designated as 'potentially dangerous.'" The court continued, "Thus, whether D.I. provoked Brody during the October 15 incident is irrelevant because both parties appear to agree that the city relied on the prior 'potentially dangerous' designation, not the lack of provocation accompanying the incident, in declaring Brody 'dangerous.'"

With regard to the destruction order, the supreme court turned to the local code, which defined provocation as "purposely[108] excited, stimulated, agitated, or disturbed," and found no evidence that Brody was provoked.[109] To the contrary, the court pronounced that there was substantial evidence that Brody was not provoked. The supreme court further determined that the destruction of Brody was not a discretionary act because the local code mandated that an "animal control officer 'shall' order the animal destroyed in a proper and humane manner.

107. The court was disingenuous here in that any declaration at all, even a potential one, impacts a later proceeding, and even more so as the first declaration nullifies a provocation defense if there is a second incident, even when a dog is physically attacked.

108. If "purposely" means "with conscious intent," one would imagine that the fact of "conscious intent" is evidence of life. Should different due process standards apply when a life is at stake?

109. If a dog is not provoked by a stranger entering the dog's lair, one must wonder if the use of the term "provocation" is sensible.

The word 'shall' indicates a duty that is mandatory, not one that is optional or discretionary."

The court was so adamant that the city must destroy Brody that there was even a footnote explaining why Brody's destruction was mandatory. In footnote three of its decision, the court said, "Sawh argues that the use of the word 'shall' in the City Code is directory, rather than mandatory." The court then made a straight-faced argument that "the mandatory-directory dichotomy is irrelevant here because this case does not involve a question about the consequences of an entity's failure to comply with the duties imposed upon it."[110] It seemed that the court lacked the legal chops to discuss how the mandatory directory dichotomy could be deviated from when a companion animal's life was at stake. While the supreme court was very literal on the mandatory directory dichotomy, the court ignored the basics of statutory construction regarding Minnesota Statute section 503.16(4). In a footnote, the court dismissed the plain meaning of this statute when the court said,

> Sawh argues that section 503.16(4) requires the owner of an animal to commit the "subsequent offense," not the animal. While the Supreme Court correctly observes that the City Code refers to a violation by the animal's owner in defining a "subsequent offense," it is clear that the underlying acts constituting the "subsequent offense" must be committed by the animal, not the animal's owner.

Thus, the supreme court chose to supply words in order to reach the interpretation the court preferred while being resolute on the subject of ignoring the mandatory directory dichotomy.

As this case demonstrates, the pendulum dramatically swings across the country between embracing companion animals as part of the family or the family dog becoming an inanimate object or, as the Minnesota Supreme Court put it, "tangible property."

Though not discussed in *Sawh*, an argument could have been made that interests of deprivation could extend beyond the gray area between a liberty deprivation[111] and a property deprivation. This gray area was described in the treatise of William J. Keppel. "Since a threat to life rarely occurs in administrative law,"[112] there were two pertinent questions relevant to a due process clause in an adjudication hearing: (1) what kind of deprivation of one's liberty or property by a government agency requires process, and (2) what process or procedure is due a person before a final deprivation of that interest can occur? Keppel's due process explanation was offered within an administrative due process context, where, as Keppel pronounced, a threat to life "rarely occurs."

---

110. Hans Hagen Homes, Inc. v. City of Minnetrista, 728 N.W.2d 536, 541 (Minn. 2007).

111. For some, having a companion animal could be an aspect of liberty. Liberty is defined as "Freedom; exemption from extraneous control. The power of the will, in its moral freedom, to follow the dictates of its unrestricted choice, and to direct the external acts of the individual without restraint, coercion, or control from other persons." A liberty choice could be having the companionship of a pet. *What Is Liberty*, LAW DICTIONARY, http://thelawdictionary.org/liberty/ (last visited May 12, 2016).

112. WILLIAM J. KEPPEL, ADMINISTRATIVE PRACTICE AND PROCEDURE (Vol. 21, Minnesota Practice Series) (2d ed., Thomson West 2007).

The *Sawh* decision before the Minnesota Supreme Court showed the exception to this pronouncement as a Labrador mix named Brody was very much alive before his destruction at "some indeterminate point." This type of argument brings us full circle to an important question. Do only human lives matter, and if so, why do all 50 states have felony laws for animal cruelty, as well as pet trust laws? Keppel may be surprised to learn that threats to life occur in the administrative context in dangerous dog proceedings.

Practice Pointer: Surely, a case could be made that the deprivation of animal companionship affects not only a liberty interest but also an interest in preserving the "life" of special property. After all, humans are rational, and we know that the destruction of a living animal is different from the destruction of an inanimate object. It seems as if the deprivation standard should be applied differently if a life is involved, taking the nod from the Minnesota Court of Appeals that due process standards should be higher when certain types of rights are involved.

State of Ohio v. McColor[113]

Year: *2013*
Category: *Criminal Law*
Type of Action: *Sentence Appeal*
Animal: *Dog*
Pet Custody Concept: *Have your clients make the best impression possible.*

The appellant was cited for numerous violations after his uninsured Pit Bulls got loose and chased a child and her mother down the street. The dogs did not bite the victims, but the mother was injured after she fell down. The appellant was charged with four counts of violating the city ordinances and eight counts of violating the state dog statutes. The appellant took a plea agreement and was sentenced to two consecutive jail terms of 180 days, five years of probation supervision, fines, court costs, and restitution to the victims. In the sentencing process, the court offered the hyperbole that Pit Bulls "eat little children."[114]

When reading this unpublished decision, it was hard to tell if the court threw the book at the appellant because he had an extensive criminal history, because the mother and the daughter chased by the dogs were terrified, because of the appellant's lack of remorse in the courtroom, or perhaps all of the above. The reviewing court acknowledged that the trial court considered the appellant's criminal history, as detailed in the pre-sentence investigation report, which contained previous violations of the dog statutes.

An officer testified that he had several issues with the appellant in the past and had previously advised him that he needed to have a $100,000 insurance policy on each dog. During an extensive conversation with the appellant, the trial court said to

113. 2013 Ohio 1279 (Ohio App. 2013).
114. *See* Toledo v. Tellings, 114 Ohio St. 3d 278, 871 N.E.2d 1152, 2007 Ohio 3724 (Ohio 2007).

him, "I get the impression you are going to do what you want to do when you want to do it, how you want to do it." The court seemed to be particularly aggravated by the fact that the appellant tried to blame the testifying officer and dog warden for the problems with his dogs. The holding in this case was that the appellant's due processes were not violated in sentencing. The court then added, "The trial judge made a statement about Pit Bulls that may be described as hyperbole, but the statement was not facetious and was intended to highlight the danger posed by owners who do not control their vicious dogs."

Practice Pointer: Make sure your clients know that in legal proceedings involving dogs, the court's decision may be impacted by his or her viewpoint about breeds, whether expressed, as in the above case, or not expressed.

Chapter 11

Science and Technology

"Science is a way of thinking much more than it is a body of knowledge."

—Carl Sagan

Good lawyers will integrate ideas from both the social and hard sciences, as well as from both horizontal and vertical jurisprudence, to marshal the great arguments of our time.[1] In this chapter, we will discuss genetics, how conformation standards may impact animal health and behaviors, how assisted reproductive technology (ART) may impact contract law and pet custody disputes in the near future, and how patents and ideas from intellectual property law or concepts may be carried over and impact pet custody disputes.

GENETIC TESTING

"Big data" garnered from bioinformatics[2] may affect human and companion animal futures alike. Modern laboratories focusing on animal welfare are testing animals' deoxyribonucleic acid (DNA). The Veterinary Genetics Laboratory performs tests for various registries, on a contractual basis.[3] The Canine Health Information

1. The dissent in the California Supreme Court decision *Nahrstedt v. Lakeside Village Condominium Association, Inc.*, 33 Cal. Rptr. 2d 63, 8 Cal. 4th 361, 878 P.2d 1275 (Cal. 1994), represents how the law is emerging and is changing still, as the dissent influenced legislative changes.

2. This term references the collection and analysis of complex biological data.

3. *Contract Testing*, UC Davis Veterinary Medicine, https://www.vgl.ucdavis.edu/services/contract.php (last visited Oct. 14, 2016).

Center (CHIC)[4] and the Canine Genetic Diseases Network[5] represent two entities making significant contributions to the health of dogs. CHIC is "a centralized canine health database,"[6] and its mission is to provide "a source of health information for owners, breeders, and scientists that will assist in breeding healthy dogs."

As the CHIC database grows, it is expected that through genetic testing, useful information will become available and impact future generations of dogs. CHIC's database states that it "will be able to establish whether progeny will be clear, carriers, or affected."[7] CHIC argues that this is possible because their epidemiological studies enhance their knowledge of health issues affecting all breeds of dogs. Some breeders will not cooperate with the transparent DNA testing for health issues offered by CHIC due to concerns that the test results would negatively impact their breeding program. It will be challenging for CHIC to balance its ambitious mission with the commercial interests of its funders and preferences for conformation standards.[8]

CONFORMATION STANDARDS

Be familiar with the realities of the breeding business rather than believing in a false patina. The subject of conformation standards[9] has been controversial, particularly in instances referred to as "extreme breeding." In 2008, a well-publicized British Broadcasting Corporation (BBC) documentary by Jemima Harrison, called *Pedigree Dogs Exposed*, revealed high levels of disability, deformity, and diseases affecting pedigree dogs.[10] Problems identified included Spaniels whose brains were, effectively, too large for their skulls and Boxers suffering from epilepsy. Following the documentary, which received the BBC's "biggest-ever viewer response to a

---

4. *What Is CHIC*, Canine Health Information Center, http://www.caninehealthinfo.org/ (last visited May 12, 2016).

5. The Canine Genetic Diseases Network represents a collaboration of researchers that search for genetic mutations that cause disease and suffering. Canine Genetic Diseases Network, http://www.caninegeneticdiseases.net/ (last visited May 12, 2016).

6. CHIC is sponsored by the American Kennel Club/Canine Health Foundation and the Orthopedic Foundation for Animals.

7. *CHIC Benefits*, Canine Health Information Center, http://www.caninehealthinfo.org/chicinfo.html#benefits (last visited May 12, 2016).

8. CHIC does not address problems inherent in a particular breed's standards.

9. It is worthwhile for lawyers to understand how their clients acquired their companion animal. Did the prospective buyer go to the breeder or breeding facility and observe the animal carefully? Did the prospective buyer meet the sire and the dam and ask about the breeder's veterinarian? Did the breeding animals seem happy and in good health? When you assess how the companion animal in controversy was sourced, do not be overly impressed with health certificates and genetic testing results if the breed that is the subject of the dispute is known to have intractable and costly health problems.

10. *Pedigree Dogs Exposed*, Top Documentary Films, http://topdocumentaryfilms.com/pedigree-dogs-exposed/ (last visited Aug. 27, 2013).

single program," the BBC dropped Crufts, the oldest dog show in the world, after 40 years.[11]

Zoologist and animal behaviorist, Sir Patrick Bateson of the University of Cambridge (who was knighted in 2003), was invited as a neutral to issue a thought-provoking report.[12] He addressed the subjects of inbreeding, inherited diseases, and the practice of selecting for extreme morphology. Sir Bateson advocated that breeding practices should be changed in order to promote animal health and welfare.

As clients describe to you the animals they care about by breed or even hybrid or mixed breed, it will be easier to picture what unique challenges your client and companion animal may have. They may include that the animal has difficulty breathing, seeing, walking, jumping, or may be living with chronic pain. While a robust and healthy animal might be able to travel back and forth between households with two civil owners, animals with serious health problems may need the stability of a daily routine.

CLONING[13]

After 123 efforts, a dog named Snuppy was cloned in South Korea at Seoul National University in 2005. Snuppy was *Time*'s "Most Amazing Invention" in 2005.[14] The subject of cloned pets[15] is vexing and invites many ethical questions, as these experimental animals may suffer high mortality rates.[16] Genetically engineered and

---

11. Beverley Cuddy, *Controversy over BBC's Purebred Dog Breeding Documentary: BBC's* Pedigree Dogs Exposed *Strikes a Chord*, The Bark, http://thebark.com/content/controversy-over-bbcs-purebred-dog-breeding-documentary (last visited Oct. 12, 2016).

12. Patrick Bateson, *Independent Inquiry into Dog Breeding*, Cambridge University, https://www.ourdogs.co.uk/special/final-dog-inquiry-120110.pdf (last visited Oct. 12, 2016).

13. The cloning process utilizes a somatic cell nuclear transfer to replicate or copy the subject of interest. Cloned animals represent big business for the pharmaceutical industry, where farm animals may now become "pharmed" animals, or effectively, pharmaceutical manufacturers, in that they manufacture pharmaceuticals for commercial use in their own bodies.

14. Mark Honigsbaum, *Snuppy the Cloned Puppy Tops Poll of Amazing Inventions*, Guardian, http://www.theguardian.com/science/2005/nov/15/uknews (last visited May 12, 2016). After Dolly the sheep was cloned, subsequent cloning efforts were directed at cows, pigs, goats, horses, mice, rabbits, cats, and dogs. Reasons for cloning included food production, recreating a companion animal, saving endangered species, and utilizing clones in biomedical research. Although statistics vary, cloned animals are known to have significant mortality rates, deformities, and health problems. The surrogate for the cloned embryo could have different mitochondrial DNA or may suffer multiple miscarriages; the long-term medical effects of cloning are far from certain.

15. Beth Landman, *I Spent More Than $100,000 to Clone My Dog*, New York Post, http://nypost.com/2015/10/31/i-spent-more-than-100000-to-clone-my-dog/ (last visited Oct. 14, 2016).

16. *An HSUS Report: Welfare Issues with Genetic Engineering and Cloning of Farm Animals*, Humane Society of the United States, http://www.humanesociety.org/assets/pdfs/farm/hsus-welfare-issues-with-genetic-engineering-and-cloning-of-farm-animals.pdf (last visited Oct. 12, 2016).

cloned animals are subject to regulations under the Animal Welfare Act[17] because cloned animals are classified as breeding animals and the breeders must be licensed and comply with humane care regulations. Consider a contractual clause prohibiting the cloning of a companion animal; advance bioethics arguments in this regard.

BIOETHICS INVOLVING ANIMALS

Although there is lack of uniformity on just what the term "bioethics"[18] means, the areas of concern generally pertain to broad or narrow ethical questions that relate to biology, medicine, and technology practices. Subjects of interest, from a bioethics perspective, could include cloning and genetic engineering, which is a method used to affect inheritable traits. The notable institution concerned with bioethics involving animals is London's Nuffield Council of Bioethics.[19]

The guiding ethical principles for human research on animals are to reduce animal suffering by using what is commonly called "the 3Rs." The 3Rs are Replace, Reduce, and Refine.[20]

ART Common Law

Science, and the development of intellectual property laws, could affect the relief a party seeks in a pet custody dispute as well as the legality and enforceability of the terms in a family court settlement. A presenting question could be whether the parties to a dispute may clone a family pet.

ART issues will evolve to apply to companion animals. It is likely that there will be similarities and differences as to how ART issues affect humans and companion animals. Unless companion animals gain more status than they have now, ART rights may arise from contractual or ownership rights. Those rights might be divisible from a bundle of rights, as is discussed below in the copyrights section.

---

17. *USDA Responds Favorably to AAVS Petition: GE and Cloned Animals Gain AWA Protection*, No Pet Cloning, http://www.nopetcloning.org/aavspetition.shtml (last visited May 12, 2016). This topic is regulated by the U.S. Food and Drug Administration. *Animal Cloning*, U.S. Food & Drug Administration, http://www.fda.gov/AnimalVeterinary/SafetyHealth/AnimalCloning/default.htm (last visited Oct. 12, 2016).

18. According to the American Veterinary Medical Association (AVMA), all veterinarians should adhere to the Principles of Veterinary Medical Ethics. *Principles of Veterinary Medical Ethics of the AVMA*, AVMA, https://www.avma.org/KB/Policies/Pages/Principles-of-Veterinary-Medical-Ethics-of-the-AVMA.aspx (last visited Oct. 14, 2016).

19. *The Ethics of Research Involving Animals*, Nuffield Council on Bioethics, http://nuffieldbioethics.org/wp-content/uploads/The-ethics-of-research-involving-animals-full-report.pdf (last visited Sept. 23, 2016).

20. Georgetown University provides a useful list of resources on this subject ranging from the AWIC (Animal Welfare Information Center) Bulletin to the USDA Animal Welfare Information Center to IACUC .org (Institutional Animal Care and Use Committee). *Animal Research Ethics*, Bioethics Research Library at Georgetown University, https://bioethics.georgetown.edu/explore-bioethics/animal-research-ethics/ (last visited Sept. 23, 2016).

The right of ownership could be separate from breeding rights and ART rights. It is unknown how advocacy for the welfare of companion animals will shape the emerging jurisprudence. ART law cases pertaining to humans are briefly discussed below, as ART cases involving companion animals have not yet arisen.

In *Litowitz v. Litowitz*,[21] a divorcing couple had previously entered into an embryo disposition contract. If the parties could not agree on the use of the frozen embryo, they agreed to petition the court for instructions. Although the trial court and the court of appeals awarded the pre-embryo to the husband, the U.S. Supreme Court instead enforced the parties' cryopreservation agreement.[22] The Supreme Court indicated that the fertility clinic could follow its own procedures in dealing with unused embryos consistent with its opinion. The court thereby permitted the pre-embryo to be thawed and to expire at the end of five years.[23] The *Litowitz* court treated the dispute about a human frozen embryo as a property bailment. It is foreseeable that a similar bailment claims might be made about frozen embryos in a companion animal dispute.

In *Davis v. Davis*,[24] the court distinguished between an implanted fertilized human embryo and one that was not yet implanted. The divorcing husband was given the right not to have another child against his will through in-vitro fertilization (IVF). The court created a new category for pre-embryos. The court said, "pre-embryos are not, strictly speaking, either 'persons' or 'property,' but occupy an interim category[25] that entitles them to special respect because of their potential for human life."[26] It is noted that companion animals, too, may also be referred to as in an interim category (or words to that effect.)

The *Davis* court further explained that rather than a true property interest in the pre-embryos, the parents actually had "an interest in the nature of ownership, to the extent that they have decision-making authority concerning disposition of the pre-embryos, within the scope of policy set by law."[27]

It is unknown how advocacy for the welfare of companion animals will shape the emerging ART jurisprudence. It is possible that methods and principles used in intellectual property law will affect an owner's bundle of rights subject to legal or ethical restraints.

---

21. 146 Wash. 2d 514, 48 P.2d 261 (Wash. 2002).

22. *The Embryo Project Encyclopedia*, Arizona State University, http://embryo.asu.edu/index.php (last visited May 12, 2016).

23. Litowitz v. Litowitz *[Brief] (2002)*, The Embryo Project Encyclopedia, http://embryo.asu.edu/view/embryo:125164 (last visited May 12, 2016).

24. 842 S.W.2d 588, 597 (Tenn. 1992).

25. Companion animals, too, are emerging as belonging in an interim category.

26. *Recent Case Law on Division of Frozen Embryos in Divorce Proceedings*, Divorce Research Center, http://www.divorcesource.com/research/dl/children/03mar54.shtml (last visited May 12, 2016).

27. *Id.*

Near-Future Pet ART Issues

As technology continues to evolve and affect reproduction in humans and companion animals alike, there are many issues that could be contractually addressed in pet custody disputes of the future. ART practices could impact the progeny of a companion animal in the following ways: (1) low or very low birth weights; (2) cardiovascular, urogenital, muscular, and skeletal birth defects; (3) susceptibility to disease; (4) reduced reproduction capability; and (5) shorter life expectancy.

For your consideration, here is a list of contractual issues or concerns that may arise:

- Who will have possession of the pet?
- Who owns the cryopreserved eggs?
- Who has a right to consent to a particular ART procedure?
- Does anyone have the right to object on moral grounds if an issue arises with regard to cryopreservation?
- Can the property rights to the pet and the pet's offspring, natural or artificial, or even clone, be divisible?
- What if there is a risk to the female family pet resulting from the harvesting of eggs or health risks for the surrogate?
- Who would pay for the resulting veterinary bills or for loss of an injured animal?
- Could a companion animal be used as a surrogate?
- Where would a companion animal's biological materials be stored?
- What shelf life limitations should apply to a cryopreserved companion animal's eggs or sperm, also known as gametes?[28]
- Who would have control of the gametes?
- Who will gain custody and the responsibility for offspring?
- Who will have the right to make medical decisions?
- What rights will owners of the donors and surrogates have?
- Who can enforce the contractual rights?

Although at first blush, these issues might seem to only apply in the human realm, and for commercial animals, similar issues with regard to pets and companion animals may arise as pets become more embedded in family systems and as companion animals advance on the continuum to an interim category between property and person. Breeder contracts may involve ART issues, too.

Other questions that may arise include what action should be taken concerning genetic test results, who decides whether there will be multiple gestations,

28. With emerging technologies, the shelf life of gametes increases if there is less water involved and fewer ice crystals that could cause gamete damage.

who decides what the time between gestations will be, who decides how gametes will be disposed of, and who decides when a gamete is abandoned?

Future companion animal issues may be impacted by a family that selects future pets from a broker of custom-made embryos for IVF, or from a breeder who opposes utilizing an embryo procedure, such as twinning. Twinning is a procedure that stimulates the fertilized egg to divide and create an identical embryo as a cryopreserved backup plan. There are many choices to make, and all of them have ethical dimensions, the type a bioethicist might address.

FAMILY VALUES

The Supreme Court of New Jersey[29] proclaimed that family values can be embodied in "biological families, step-families, blended families, single parent families, foster families, families created by modern reproductive technology, and in families made up of unmarried persons."[30] In New Jersey, in a concurring opinion, the court proclaimed that it was capable of "dealing with the realities, not simply the legalities, of relationships, and have adjusted the rights and duties of parties in relation to that reality."[31] Give these issues pause for consideration as to how this changing family conception may impact companion animals.

DEFINING PATENTS

It may surprise you that in the future, companion animals and their offspring may be affected by breeding related patent rights. Already, we have described concerns about animal clones and what was called the invention of a cloned dog named Snuppy. The United States Patent & Trademark Office (USPTO) defines a patent as "a property right granted by the Government of the United States of America to an inventor 'to exclude others from making, using, offering for sale, or selling the invention throughout the United States or importing the invention into the United States' for a limited time in exchange for public disclosure of the invention when the patent is granted."[32] A patent "may be applied for only in the name(s) of the

---

29. V.C. v. M.J.B., 748 A.2d 539, 566-57 (N.J. 2000) (Long, J., concurring).

30. Charles P. Kindregan, Jr. & Maureen McBrien, Assisted Reproductive Technology: A Lawyer's Guide to Emerging Law and Science 7 (ABA Publishing 2006).

31. *Id.*

32. United States Patent and Trademark Office, http://www.uspto.gov/main//faq/stopfaq.htm (last visited May 12, 2016).

actual inventor(s)." The USPTO's website also details what cannot be patented, and this list includes laws of nature and physical phenomena.[33]

What Is Patentable?

Although the USPTO does not utilize moral lines with regard to a determination of patentability, a line was drawn in a patent application test case[34] related to a process that combines human embryo cells with cells from embryos of another primate, which would result in a chimera.[35] This patent application was denied because human genes were involved; both constitutional and moral principles were central to this particular patent decision-making process. The patent office drew the line because it understood that with the issuance of this type of patent, the constitutional right to privacy, including a human's right to decide whether to procreate, would be jeopardized, and the 13th Amendment prohibition on slavery would be violated.

Another moral line was drawn by the USPTO with regard to an invention that would enable the patent user to keep the disembodied head of a primate alive.[36] Notwithstanding the above, the USPTO permitted the patentability of the Harvard "oncomouse,"[37] where through genetic modification, a chimera or transgenic mouse carried a gene that increased the mouse's susceptibility for cancer.[38] Macaque monkeys have been legally subjected to genetic modification so that they carry a genetic trait called MeCP2 duplication syndrome that affects humans. This

33. When a patent is granted in the United States, the patent, which operates much like a monopoly, is in effect for 20 years for a utility patent and 14 years for a design patent. When considering the duration of a patent, it is reasonable to take into account that for pharmaceutical companies, the drug development process can take many years, patented pharmaceutical inventions might not work, and developed drugs must pass clinical testing before commercialization is possible.

34. Stuart A. Newman, *My Attempt to Patent a Human-Animal Chimera*, L'Observatoire de la genetique, http://www.omics-ethics.org/observatoire/zoom/zoom_06/z_no27_06/za_no27_06_01.html (last visited May 12, 2016).

35. A chimera is an animal with genes or physical traits from more than one species. The idea of a chimera was exemplified by the flying monkeys in the *Wizard of Oz*. An angel is also a variation of a chimera conception.

36. *Device for Perfusing an Animal Head*, Google Patents, http://www.google.com/patents?id=DxktAAAAEBAJ&printsec=abstract&zoom=4#v=onepage&q&f=false (last visited May 12, 2016).

37. *Bioethics and Patent Law: The Case of the Oncomouse*, World Intellectual Property Organization, http://www.wipo.int/wipo_magazine/en/2006/03/article_0006.html (last visited May 12, 2016).

38. In Europe, Article 53(a) excludes patents for invention contrary to the "ordre public," a public policy doctrine made up of social, moral, and economic values that tie a society together. The European Patent Office (EPO) used the utilitarian balancing test on the oncomouse, and the oncomouse patent was permitted. Despite that, the EPO set a boundary and denied the patent application filed by the Upjohn pharmaceutical company on another type of transgenic mouse that would lose hair through genetic modification in order to be tested for cosmetics.

syndrome is inheritable by the macaque offspring and is believed to cause autism-like symptoms.[39]

Animal Patents

The USPTO has granted 660 animal patents ranging from cats, dogs, and rabbits to chimpanzees and other primates, as well as mice, but rescinded other patents after patent re-examination.[40] One rescinded patent pertained to rabbits modeling a dry eye condition. Another was rescinded when the methods used to contaminate Beagles' lungs with a fungal infection caused their death.[41] The purpose of the Beagle experiments was to study disease-related secondary lung infections.

Patent Case Law

In the seminal 1980 Supreme Court decision of *Diamond v. Chakrabarty*,[42] the Court proclaimed that "anything under the sun that is made by man" is patentable. A microorganism that was genetically engineered to clean up oil spills thus became patent protected.

It is hard to know just how far jurisprudence will go in the United States in permitting non-human animal biological materials, as well as human biological materials, to become patented intellectual property. In a landmark decision, *Mayo Collaborative Services v. Prometheus Laboratories*,[43] the U.S. Supreme Court invalidated two medical diagnostics patents held by Prometheus Laboratories, a biotech company owned by Nestle.[44]

In *Association for Molecular Pathology v. Myriad Genetics, Inc. et al.*,[45] the U.S. Supreme Court addressed whether human genes associated with breast cancer were patentable. The holding was that naturally occurring DNA sequences, even if isolated from the body, are not patentable, but artificially created DNA is patent eligible.

---

39. Ian Sample, *Genetically Modified Monkeys Created to Help Scientists Study Autism*, The Guardian, https://www.theguardian.com/science/2016/jan/25/genetically-modified-monkeys-created-to-help-scientists-study-autism (last visited May 12, 2016).

40. *Animal Patents*, American Anti-Vivisection Society, http://aavs.org/our-work/campaigns/animal-patents/ (last visited May 12, 2016).

41. *AR-News: AAVS ACTION: Revoke Beagle Patent*, http://lists.envirolink.org/pipermail/ar-news/Week-of-Mon-20040315/021942.html (last visited May 12, 2016).

42. 447 U.S. 303, 100 S. Ct. 2204, 65 L. Ed. 2d 144, 206 U.S.P.Q. 193 (1980).

43. 566 U.S. ___, 132 S. Ct. 1289 (2012).

44. Ethan A. Huff, *Supreme Court Rules Biotech Prometheus Laboratories Can't Patent "Laws of Nature,"* NaturalNews.com, http://www.naturalnews.com/035368_patents_laws_of_nature_Supreme_Court.html (last visited May 12, 2016).

45. 569 U.S. ___, 133 S. Ct. 2107 (2013). Association for Molecular Pathology et al. v. Myriad Genetics, Inc., et al., *Certiorari to the United States Court of Appeals for the Federal Circuit*, Supreme Court of the United States, http://www.supremecourt.gov/opinions/12pdf/12-398_1b7d.pdf (last visited May 12, 2016).

Cases such as *Prometheus* and *Myriad* represent that instead of the court permitting the patentability of any life form under the sun, an idea espoused from *Chakrabarty*, the Supreme Court is now swinging toward a jurisprudence expressing limited awareness of the moral and public policy implications of granting patents. It remains to be seen how courts will factor in moral implications for non-human animals in future cases. Perhaps companion animals embraced as family members, or non-human animals such as great apes, dolphins, ravens, and even cephalopods such as octopuses, all known to have exceptional cognitive abilities, may receive something akin to the most favored animal status with regard to moral line drawing.

Tech Transfer

If someone wants to use an invention (which now includes a cloned dog named Snuppy) that is patent protected, that person may seek to enter into a tech transfer agreement or licensing agreement. There has been controversy about how this works in the patent system in recent years due to the emergence of patent trolls. In legend, trolls usually stopped people from passing bridges unless the troll was satisfied with an offering. In the patent system, some companies buy patent rights as an investment and are then in a position to extract money from a business that needs a patent license, sometimes through demanding acceptance of onerous terms. This is all big business.

If a family lawyer is handling pet custody disputes involving ART issues, at least a cursory tracking of the evolving patent law would be desirable. Know the basics of a tech transfer agreement, a "process by which a technology expertise, know-how or facility developed by one individual, enterprise or organization is transferred to another individual, enterprise or organization. Effective technology transfer results in the commercialization of a new product or process."[46] Imagine if the clone of a family pet became the subject of a tech transfer agreement. There is a great need for lawyers who care about companion animals to help develop humane laws as this subject continues to evolve.

COPYRIGHTS

The purpose of this copyright discussion is quite limited and does not have anything to do with copyrighting animals. Instead, the subject of copyrights serves as a template for how horizontal "property" rights have been addressed in one substantive area of the law, which may have application to another. Our key focus

46. *Overview of Contractual Agreements for the Transfer of Technology*, http://www.wipo.int/sme/en/documents/pdf/technology_transfer.pdf (last visited May 12, 2016).

will be on the idea of a bundle of rights. Copyrights are permitted under the U.S. Constitution, Article I, Section 8, as follows: "The Congress shall have Power . . . To promote the Progress of Science and useful Arts, by securing for limited Times to Authors and Inventors the exclusive Right to their respective Writings and Discoveries."[47]

The key copyright idea is that the holder of the copyright has, or could assign or license, the following rights: (1) to reproduce the copyrighted work in copies or phonorecords; (2) to prepare derivative works based upon the copyrighted work; (3) to distribute copies or phonorecords of the copyrighted work to the public by sale or other transfer of ownership, or by rental, lease, or lending; (4) in the case of literary, musical, dramatic, and choreographic works, pantomimes, and motion pictures and other audiovisual works, to perform the copyrighted work publicly; (5) in the case of literary, musical, dramatic, and choreographic works, pantomimes, and pictorial, graphic, or sculptural works, including the individual images of a motion picture or other audiovisual work, to display the copyrighted work publicly; and (6) in the case of sound recordings, to perform the copyrighted work publicly by means of a digital audio transmission.[48]

Copyright is a form of protection offered under Title 17 of the U.S. Code,[49] as well as internationally under the Berne Convention. Within the copyright bundle of rights (which can be separated and subject to the terms of a license), there are rights concerning reproductive distribution, the creation of derivative works, and the right of public performance. There are exceptions to protection under Section 107 of the 1976 Copyright Act based upon "fair use."[50] In some instances, even when one party owns the copyright, that party can be forced to grant a compulsory license. In copyright law, one person could own an original painting while a completely different person could be licensed the painting's reproduction and derivative rights. An example of a derivative right would be the right to modify or add to a copyrighted work.

As described earlier in this chapter, this model for divisible rights could be applied to companion animals, particularly when it comes to the subject of ART, as well as possessory rights, such as access. Not only may dogs be co-owned, but also the breeder could retain or restrict breeding rights. One of several owners might have the pick of the litter, and so forth. Patent holders may further influence the need for contractual provisions.

---

47. *The Constitutional Provision Respecting Copyright*, Copyright Law of the United States of America, http://www.copyright.gov/title17/92preface.html (last visited May 12, 2016).

48. *17 U.S. Code § 106—Exclusive Rights in Copyrighted Works*, Cornell University Law School, https://www.law.cornell.edu/uscode/text/17/106 (last visited Sept. 23, 2016).

49. *Copyright Basics*, United States Copyright Office, http://www.copyright.gov/circs/circ01.pdf (last visited May 12, 2016).

50. *Id.*

Due to rapid changes in reproductive technology, as couples separate, disputes may not only be about the pet but also about the bundle of rights the companion animal genetically represents, ranging from standard breeding rights all the way to cloning, or the prohibition of cloning given the suffering of many of the failed offspring or harm to the surrogate. Depending upon how ART law and intellectual property law evolve, both could become part of pet law American jurisprudence in unexpected ways.

CONCLUSION

In our culture, everything is affected by science and technology. It is for this reason that even in pet custody disputes, being aware of what legal issues may arise not only puts you ahead of the rest but also gives you an opportunity to help shape the law's evolution.

Chapter 12

Potpourri of the Predicates of Change

"The fact that man knows right from wrong proves his intellectual superiority to the other creatures; but the fact that he can do wrong proves his moral inferiority to any creatures that cannot."

—*Mark Twain*

In the first chapter, it was stated that companion animals, rather than being consistently viewed as property, may instead be viewed as having legal status based upon a continuum between property and person, now called "the continuum." It was also suggested that the reason for this shift was that companion animals typically have a greater relational value than commercial value. In this chapter, we will explore some of the antecedents of this cultural shift.

CHARLES DARWIN

At the end of the 19th century, Charles Darwin offered his theory of evolution. He emphasized three principles: (1) serviceable habits, wherein emotional expression could be hereditary; (2) antithesis, an expression in opposition to a useful one; and (3) actions of the nervous system of the body. Darwin promoted the idea of the adaptive use of emotions and identified the universal emotions of anger, happiness, sadness, disgust, fear, and surprise, emphasizing that the difference between species is actually a difference in degree, not kind. This idea is now called evolutionary continuity.[1]

FREUD AND JUNG

Following the turn of the same century, Sigmund Freud advocated that humans have a conscious and unconscious mind; an id, ego, and superego; life and death instincts; and defense mechanisms.[2] He also famously said, "In the small matters trust the mind, in the large ones the heart." Carl Jung, Freud's Viennese contemporary, developed personality archetypes[3] that became the basis of the Myers-Briggs Type Indicator personality test popular among lawyers today. Jung also advanced the idea of a collective unconscious and had considerable influence on dream interpretation and symbolization.[4]

B. F. SKINNER

In stark contrast to Freud and Jung and their work on the inner workings of the mind, B. F. Skinner investigated an idea called operant conditioning.[5] Skinner advocated that human and animal behaviors could be shaped by positive and negative reinforcement.

NEUROSCIENCE

The United States has embraced and funded the Brain Research through Advancing Innovative Neurotechnologies (BRAIN).[6] This research is predicated on the belief that our brain is the source of thoughts, emotions, perceptions, actions, and memories.

Through neuroscience, we are gaining a comprehensive understanding about what our brains are like in action, including how brain circuits utilize neurons and how brain systems are distributed and affect behavior. One of the goals of the

---

1. Charles Darwin, The Expression of the Emotions in Man and Animals (John Murray 1872).

2. Kendra Cherry, *Sigmund Freud - Life, Work and Theories*, About Health, http://psychology.about.com/od/sigmundfreud/p/sigmund_freud.htm (last visited May 12, 2016).

3. Kendra Cherry, *What Are the Jungian Archetypes*, About Health, http://psychology.about.com/od/personalitydevelopment/tp/archetypes.htm (last visited May 12, 2016).

4. Humans have observed that animals appear to dream when asleep. Thus far, it is unknown what animals dream about.

5. B. F. Skinner performed animal testing in a chamber or box that became known as the Skinner box. Saul McLeod, *Skinner-Operant Conditioning*, Simply Psychology, http://www.simplypsychology.org/operant-conditioning.html (last visited May 12, 2016).

6. *Brain Research through Advancing Innovative Neurotechnologies (BRAIN) Working Group Report to the Advisory Committee to the Director, NIH*, National Institutes of Health, https://www.braininitiative.nih.gov/pdf/BRAIN2025_508C.pdf (last visited Oct. 4, 2016).

BRAIN initiative is to utilize rigorous theory and statistical models to produce a new conceptual foundation for understanding the biological basis of mental processes. A correlate to this idea is to discover how dynamic patterns of neural activity become cognition, emotion, perception, and action.

Functional magnetic resonance imaging is a method that enables scientists to observe brain activity and learn about neural circuitry by detecting changes in blood flow.[7] Neuroscientists have revealed that both humans and dogs have neurons that light up when they hear the voices of their own species in a brain region that is sensitive to emotional expressions.[8] This groundbreaking work suggests that both humans and dogs use "acoustic parameters" to interpret the feelings in a sound.[9]

ANIMAL EMOTIONS

We understand that animals have emotions because people we trust, including Jane Goodall, told us they do. Jane Goodall witnessed chimpanzees appearing dazed after their infants died and mothers carrying the dead bodies of their young. Sea lions, geese, bears, and moose react strongly to the death of a loved one.[10] Dr. Marc Bekoff, an evolutionary biologist and ecologist, has emphasized the sheer number of articles that have been published on this subject, including, "Joy in Rats," "Grief in Elephants," and "Empathy in Mice."[11] Bekoff suggests that the important question is not *whether* animals have emotions but *why* they evolved. Reminding us that all mammals share neuroanatomical structures associated with emotions, including the amygdala and neurochemical pathways in the limbic system, Bekoff suggested that the burden of proof be placed on the shoulders of those who assert that other mammals lack emotional expression.[12]

---

7. *What Is fMRI?, Imaging Brain Activity*, UC San Diego School of Medicine, http://fmri.ucsd.edu/Research/whatisfmri.html (last visited Oct. 4, 2016).

8. Gregory S. Berns et al., *Scent of the Familiar: An fMRI Study of Canine Brain Responses to Familiar and Unfamiliar Human and Dog Odors*, ScienceDirect, http://www.sciencedirect.com/science/article/pii/S0376635714000473 (last visited May 12, 2016).

9. Michaeleen Doucleff, *How Dogs Read Our Moods: Emotion Detector Found in Fido's Brain*, NPR Health, http://www.npr.org/blogs/health/2014/02/21/280640267/how-dogs-read-our-moods-emotion-detector-found-in-fidos-brain (last visited May 12, 2016).

10. Jessika Toothman, *Do Animals Have Emotions?* Animal Planet, http://animals.howstuffworks.com/animal-facts/animals-have-emotions.htm (last visited May 12, 2016).

11. Marc Bekoff, *Do Animals Have Emotions? Of Course They Do*, The Bark, http://www.thebark.com/content/do-animals-have-emotions (last visited May 12, 2016).

12. *Id.*

SENTIENCE

While it was long believed that animals lacked consciousness[13] and were irrational, modern science is only beginning to suggest the opposite. The American Animal Hospital Association, the second-largest veterinary organization in the United States, recently recognized that animals have sentience, or effectively, feelings.[14] This determination was viewed as groundbreaking.

Rational thought and logic, prized in legal frameworks, are not divisible from emotions; instead, the rational mind and emotions work together.[15] Emotions are integral to reason and logic, as reflected by evidence that emotions promote the brain's ability to create somatic markers, thereby helping the individual keep multiple facts in the mind for analytical purposes. Emotions also enable us to use storytelling, a method of communicating that has emotional resonance, as a vehicle for effective communications. Jaak Panksepp identified the four core emotions as fear, anger/rage, panic/separation anxiety, and seeking.[16]

ANIMALS AS DEFENDANTS

From the 13th to the 20th centuries, domesticated and wild animals were defendants in legal actions where they were granted full judicial formalities, including access to a lawyer. According to historical records, sentences for guilty animal defendants included being buried alive, hanged, or mutilated. In one case, a murderous pig was hanged, but her six piglets were spared.[17] A judge, bailiff, and hangman might all be present in both secular and ecclesiastical trials.[18]

It is interesting to speculate about why these trials were held and how the guilt or innocence of animals was determined. Finding an animal guilty of violent acts might suggest that the animal was able to think, feel, and act intentionally. If humans in previous centuries believed that non-human animals had free will, formed intentions, or should be held accountable for their actions, these ideas would be in sharp contrast to those advanced by René Descartes,[19] a 17th-century

---

13. *The Cambridge Declaration on Consciousness*, Francis Crick Memorial Conference, http://fcmconference.org/img/CambridgeDeclarationOnConsciousness.pdf (last visited Oct. 11, 2016).

14. Seth Davis, *AAHA Position Statement Classifies Animals as Sentient Beings*, NEWStat, http://www.aahanet.org/blog/NewStat/post/2012/10/17/521946/AAHA-position-statement-classifies-animals-as-sentient-beings.aspx (last visited May 12, 2016).

15. Antonio Damasio, Descartes' Error: Emotion, Reason, and the Human Brain (Penguin Books 2005).

16. Temple Grandin & Catherine Johnson, Animals Make Us Human: Creating the Best Life for Animals 1 (Houghton Mifflin Harcourt 2009).

17. Peter Dinzelbacher, *Animal Trials: A Multidisciplinary Approach*, 32 J. Interdisciplinary Hist. 405–21 (2002).

18. E. P. Evans, The Criminal Prosecution and Capital Punishment of Animals (The Lawbook Exchange, Ltd. 2009).

19. He is famous for his theory, now called Cartesian dualism, whereby the human mind and body are viewed as separate.

philosopher. He advocated that animals were more like machines. From a Cartesian viewpoint, it would be irrational to punish animals.

There is now scientific evidence leading to an entirely different theory of the world because of neuroscience and genetics. We could speculate that our legal precedents today would be quite different if someone with Descartes's intellect could both have understood modern neuroscience and have articulated the continuum of cognitive abilities and emotional qualities across species.

Did the animal defendants of yesteryear have something in common with the dangerous dog defendants of today? What is interesting about our use of the provocation standard for dogs in both dangerous dog and civil proceedings is that the burden to prove provocation typically falls to the defendant. An animal behaviorist might agree that provocation is impacted by the dog's temperament and the circumstances of an event. This is called a motivational analysis. Another way to approach the same subject is to wonder what an intentional act by a dog would look like. If animals think and feel, why do so many humans want to pretend they are like inanimate objects?

PERSONHOOD

What is the meaning of "person"? Would an IBM computer named Watson, who many agree can not only think but outthink some humans, qualify? A human is a type of person, as is a ship and a corporation. In the Uniform Law Commission Family Law Arbitration Act,[20] "person" is defined as "an individual, estate, business or nonprofit entity, public corporation, government or governmental subdivision, agency, or instrumentality, or any other legal entity."

Labeling a ship as a person and not an animal seems illogical. A principal argument used to advance animal law has centered on the fact that laws are applied differently to persons and property, otherwise known as things.[21] Although persons are not equivalent to humans, cultural expressions add to confusion about misidentification of species when personhood advocacy is encouraged for nonhuman animals, most notably in recent years for chimpanzees. None believe that all persons, including ships and the family cat, should have the right to vote.

---

20. *Family Law Arbitration*, Uniform Law Commission, http://www.uniformlaws.org/Committee.aspx?title=Family%20Law%20Arbitration%20 (last visited May 12, 2016).

21. Temple Grandin, *Animals Are Not Things: A View on Animal Welfare Based on Neurological Complexity*, http://www.grandin.com/welfare/animals.are.not.things.html (last visited May 12, 2016).

HUMAN PROPERTY

While some resent animals moving away from the type of property conceptions articulated in the often-quoted and strangely worded U.S. Supreme Court decision in *Sentell v. New Orleans Carrollton Railroad Co.*,[22] it appears that while animals are moving in the direction of personhood, an aspect of what was uniquely human is moving in the direction of property. This concept is perhaps best articulated in a popular book where a cell was extracted from a woman with cervical cancer, without her permission, and a cell line grown from it that became known to scientists all over the world as HeLa.[23]

Perhaps the most famous case in the country addressing whether human body parts may be treated as property is *Moore v. Regents of the University of California*.[24] Moore brought an action against the university based upon the legal claims of lack of informed consent, breach of fiduciary duty, and conversion with regard to his doctor's use of his cancer cells to develop a cell line that was commercialized. The court ruled that Moore had discarded his cells and he therefore lacked property rights and a commercial interest in his "discarded" cells.[25] Humans are becoming more like property in the legal system at the same time that animals are becoming more like persons.

There have also been efforts for decades to expand personhood rights to non-human animals. Current efforts to advance personhood rights for chimpanzees are being brought forward by the Nonhuman Rights Project. The initial plaintiffs were chimpanzees living in New York, a state believed to have common laws more likely to support writ of habeas corpus-based lawsuits.[26] The distinction between persons and things matters in this regard because only a person can assert rights and objections. Although it is understandable that those involved in animal enterprises fear that their profitability may be impacted if an animal gains personhood status, in part because animal use could be impacted, the inability to use the term "person" means less opportunity to advance more humane standards for companion animals, too.

22. 166 U.S. 698, 17 S. Ct. 693, 41 L. Ed. 1169 (1897).

23. Rebecca Skloot, The Immortal Life of Henrietta Lacks (Broadway Books 2011).

24. 51 Cal. 3d 120, 271 Cal. Rptr. 146, 793 P.2d 479 (1990).

25. Justice Arabian, famous for his dissenting opinion concerning the subject of a no-pets policy in *Nahrstedt v. Lakeside Village Condominium Association, Inc.*, 33 Cal. Rptr. 2d 63, 8 Cal. 4th 361, 878 P.2d 1275 (Cal. 1994), indicated in a concurring opinion that the deep philosophical, moral, and religious aspects of this decision were beyond the reach of the court.

26. Chris Hegedus & D. A. Pennebaker, *Animals Are Persons, Too*, N.Y. Times, http://www.nytimes.com/2014/04/23/opinion/animals-are-persons-too.html?_r=0 (last visited May 12, 2016).

CARSON, SINGER, AND REGAN

In the mid-20th century, Peter Singer popularized the utilitarian principles earlier advanced by economist Jeremy Bentham about achieving the greatest good concerning animal interests and advanced the concept of equal consideration.[27] Philosopher Thomas Regan said that animals are "subjects of a life" because they have beliefs, desires, memories, and a sense of their own future.[28]

The utilitarian principles advanced by Singer and the moral rights ideas advanced by Regan followed Rachel Carson's inspiring observation of a "silent spring." Carson's book showed the specter of a world without wild animals.[29] Carson informed the world about the toxic properties of chemicals such as DDT, widely used on farms, farms that no longer saw elegant creatures cross their vistas. Carson contemplated the very death of spring.

Carson, Singer, Regan, and others set the stage for the emergence of newer ideas that would lead to a 21st-century version of animal law and a jurisprudence that would reach beyond the property and contractual priorities embodied in commercially based animal laws. The deep history of animal law reflects a blending of established laws with regard to agricultural animals and horses and emerging laws reflecting animal welfare and animal protection ideals.

TEMPLE GRANDIN

Temple Grandin is a transformative figure in animal welfare and protection; she has led a life so amazing that an award-winning movie was made about her, a movie simply called *Temple Grandin*. It begs the mind to comprehend how a woman with autism stares down and changes big agriculture by getting those in the industry to open their eyes, while earning a Ph.D. in animal science. It is Grandin who warns against the use of abstract language and tells audiences of veterinarians, lawyers, and food producers that it is not enough to stop animal neglect and cruelty. Based upon her observations and research, she offers what enrichment and positive experiences would look like, in very practical terms, species by species. She warns against anthropomorphism in this regard. She motivates those who hear her to want to change.

---

27. Peter Singer, Animal Liberation (Pimlico 1975).
28. Thomas Regan, The Case for Animal Rights (University of California Press 1983).
29. Rachel Carson, Silent Spring (Houghton Mifflin 1962).

GUARDIANS

Historically, a guardian has a fiduciary obligation and a duty of loyalty. A criminal case that garnered national attention on the subject of dog fighting was brought against prominent National Football League star and legend Michael Vick, who utilized dogs cruelly in dog fighting. In his case, a federal court issued an order wherein Professor Rebecca Huss was appointed as both a guardian and special master for his severely injured Pit Bulls.[30] She, effectively, was to promote these dogs' best interests.

The term "guardian" may be related to duties regarding the temporary possession of an animal, or it could mean that a guardian is subject to enforceable rights and obligations. More recent ideas about terminology are reflected in the use of the terms "guardian" and "companion animals"[31] for pets. Laws were passed in Boulder, Colorado; Berkeley and West Hollywood, California; St. Louis, Missouri; Woodstock, New York; and the state of Rhode Island[32] that promote the idea that humans have certain obligations toward their companion animals, and if these obligations are not met, the local government may impose a remedy.

In 2012, Rhode Island passed the first law of its kind in the world that required animals to have an appointed advocate in abuse or neglect cases.[33] Rhode Island also became the first state in the country to amend its animal cruelty laws to include the concept of guardians.[34] Rather than using the term "owners," the legislation permitted the terms "owner" and "guardian" to be used interchangeably.

The concept of guardianship, when applied to companion animals, means that animal guardians are held to a higher standard than a mere owner and that this higher duty, if not fulfilled, could result in the animal being removed from the guardian.[35]

It is curious that there is so much organized opposition to a change in language that seems, thus far, to reflect aspirations of how companion animals should

---

30. Rebecca J. Huss, *Lessons Learned: Acting as Guardian/Special Master in the Bad Newz Kennels Case*, Valparaiso University, http://scholar.valpo.edu/cgi/viewcontent.cgi?article=1032&context=law_fac_pubs (last visited May 12, 2016).

31. *See, e.g.*, R.I. Gen. Laws § 4-13-1.2(6), (10) and § 4-19-2(28) (2006); Boulder, Colo., Code § 6-1-2 (1985); Berkeley, Cal., Code § 10.04.010 (2001); S.F., Cal., Code art. I § 41(m) (2003).

32. *See* R.I. Gen Laws § 4-1-1(a)(4) (2006); *Ownership v. Guardianship*, National Association for Biomedical Research, http://www.nabranimallaw.org/state/ownership-v-guardianship/ (last visited May 12, 2016).

33. *Rhode Island to Give Animals Legal Representation in Cruelty & Neglect Cases*, Animal People, http://newspaper.animalpeopleforum.org/2016/02/21/rhode-island-to-give-animals-legal-representation-in-cruelty-neglect-cases/ (last visited May 12, 2016).

34. Gary Block, *Guardianship Revisited: Rhode Island Law Passes 10-Year Mark*, Humane Society Veterinary Medical Association, http://www.hsvma.org/guardianship_rilaw (last visited May 12, 2016).

35. Joan Schaffner & Julie Fershtman, Litigating Animal Law Disputes: A Complete Guide for Lawyers 84 (ABA 2009).

be treated in society.[36] Advocates for expanding the use of guardianship terminology seek more responsible pet ownership, while opposition to the use of this term seems to be based upon the idea that this vernacular change could result in the imposition of greater duties with regard to companion animals in society. For example, there might be a duty to give a companion animal reasonable access to veterinary care. Even if the use of the words "guardian" or "companion animal" by governmental units has nominal legal effect, the American Veterinary Medical Association also opposes this terminology.[37]

COUNCIL OF STATE GOVERNMENTS

The Council of State Governments passed the "Resolution on Animal Guardianship and Liability Legislation." This resolution asserts that the proper balance between responsible animal care and the rights of pet owners and livestock producers is already in the existing legal framework.[38] The resolution formally opposes two types of legislative change: legislation that reclassifies pet, livestock, or animal owners as guardians or that otherwise alters the legal status of the animals; and legislation permitting the recovery of noneconomic damages for the loss or injury of a pet, livestock, or other animal. Reasons advanced for the resolution include that owners' freedom of choice in caring for their animals would be limited, third parties would be permitted to petition for a pet's custody, a legal challenge would be permitted regarding treatment choices an owner makes with regard to a veterinarian, and it would generally threaten the legal balance between the rights of pet owners and the well-being of animals.[39]

Animal laws, in any form, are controversial for many reasons, including that human livelihood and profit may involve animal use; animal laws reflect who is a predator and who is prey. Our human ancestors were often the prey, and of course, humans are still predators, as reflected not only by the food we eat but also by how we fight over territory.

Attitudes about animal use may relate back to the ideas of scarcity and competition. If an animal gets something, such as the use of the forest, quality food, or

---

36. Susan J. Hankin, *Not a Living Room Sofa: Changing the Legal Status of Companion Animals*, 4 Rutgers J. L. & Pub. Pol'y 2 (Winter 2007).

37. *AVMA Position Statements, AVMA Opposes "Pet Guardianship" in the Ownership vs. Guardianship Debate*, Washington State University, http://campusvet.wsu.edu/news/avmapositions.htm (last visited May 12, 2016).

38. Based in Lexington, Kentucky, the CSG's mission is to champion excellence in state governments to advance the common good. *The Council of State Governments*, http://csg.org/ (last visited May 12, 2015).

39. *Id.*

court time, do humans get less? Animals may be regarded as both human competitors and innocents. Animals are loved, they are hated, and they are feared.

ANIMAL LAWYER LABELS

The impact of elevating animals in any way, including in family court, can be trivialized or exaggerated. The labels directed at animal lawyers, no matter how conservative or midstream the individual lawyer, could include animal rights, animal rights activist, animal activist, and terrorist. While some of the lawyers receiving these labels may have self-identified with the animal rights activist label or consider themselves to be part of the animal rights movement, others do not. The labeling process seems to have the effect of intellectual anesthesia, wherein the human brain cannot discern the variety of views held by those who advocate for animal welfare or the advancement of animal laws. It is for this reason that animal advocacy by those already highly respected within the legal profession is so important.

THE 21ST CENTURY

By the end of the 20th century, ideas about how to advance and promote animal law became more sophisticated. As the millennium changed, law school textbooks were organized into substantive headings according to traditional legal categories such as criminal law, tort law, constitutional law, contract law, and family law, and overriding questions were asked, such as what is an animal?[40] Major federal statutes and treaties had already been passed, including the Animal Welfare Act,[41] the Endangered Species Act,[42] and the Convention on International Trade in Endangered Species of Wild Fauna and Flora.[43]

In the late 20th and early 21st centuries, lawyers were able to start committees and sections in their state and city bar associations, and they attracted long-respected legal talent. Animal law programs were offered at many of the best law schools in the United States, beginning with Harvard Law School and expanding to Duke University School of Law, Northwestern University School of Law, Stanford Law School, and many more, thereby influencing acceptance of animal law as a worthy subject nationwide. Now, over 160 law schools offer animal law courses

---

40. Bruce Wagman, Sonia Waisman, & Pamela Frasch, Animal Law: Cases and Materials (Carolina Academic Press 2009).

41. Bernard E. Rollin, *The Moral Status of Invasive Animal Research*, The Hastings Center, http://animalresearch.thehastingscenter.org/report/the-moral-status-of-invasive-animal-research/ (last visited May 12, 2016).

42. *Endangered Species Act Overview*, U.S. Fish & Wildlife Service, http://www.fws.gov/endangered/laws-policies/ (last visited May 12, 2016).

43. *About CITES*, Convention on International Trade in Endangered Species of Wild Fauna and Flora, http://www.cites.org/ (last visited May 12, 2016).

in the United States, and course offerings are expanding in Australia, India, Spain, Switzerland, Canada, and China.[44]

THE ROLE OF THE AMERICAN BAR ASSOCIATION

Acceptance of the Animal Law Committee (ALC)[45] in the American Bar Association (ABA) Tort Trial & Insurance Practice Section (TIPS) also influenced the acceptability of animal law as a mainstream national phenomenon.[46] In TIPS, concerns about animal law have expanded beyond long-standing concerns about animals' property status and lack of standing. Tort issues have been on the front burner in TIPS because there are wrongs without remedies when animals are negligently or intentionally harmed or injured.[47] The ALC has initiated numerous Resolutions that were approved by the ABA House of Delegates, thereby becoming policy of this professional association, including the following:

- Legislative Recommendations to Prohibit the Possession, Sale, Breeding, Import, or Transfer of Dangerous Wild Animals (105) (2015)
- Legislative Recommendations to Ensure Due Process in Canine Ownership (100) (2012)
- Guidelines for Service Animal Policies to Comply with the ADA (303) (2012)
- Guidelines Regarding Animal Seizures (108B) (2011)
- Model Act Governing the Care and Disposition of Disaster Animals (103A) (2010)[48]
- PETS Evacuation and Transportation Standards Act (H.R. 3858) (2006)[49]

44. *Animal Law Courses*, Animal Legal Defense Fund, http://aldf.org/animal-law-courses/ (last visited May 12, 2016).

45. Bliss Foster, *Speaking Up for Animals: Lawyers Organize a Network for Better Management and Protection of Companion Animals in Disaster Situations*, Bark Magazine, http://www.americanbar.org/content/dam/aba/marketing/tips/magazine_animal_law_bark_magazine.authcheckdam.pdf (last visited May 12, 2016).

46. Animal law was successfully launched in the American Bar Association (ABA) by Barbara J. Gislason in 2004. In 2008, Kathy Hessler, a professor at Lewis & Clark with a long history with the Animal Legal Defense Fund (ALDF), founded the Animal Law Section of the American Association of Law Schools.

47. In 2007, the TIPS ALC presented a groundbreaking national program at Duke University School of Law called *Animals & Bioengineering: A Consideration of Law, Ethics and Science*. The program stood out because of the broad range of opinions expressed by top legal and science experts ranging from scientists involved in the early cloning efforts of Dolly the sheep to Professors David Favre, William Reppy, and Steven Wise. This program, due to the efforts of Jill Mariani, had broad co-sponsorship with other ABA sections, including the Section of Science and Technology and the Special Committee on Bioethics and the Law.

48. *Animal Law Committee*, ABA Tort Trial & Insurance Practice Section, http://apps.americanbar.org/dch/committee.cfm?com=IL201050 (last visited May 12, 2016).

49. *Public Law 109-308—Oct. 6, 2006*, http://www.gpo.gov/fdsys/pkg/PLAW-109publ308/pdf/PLAW-109publ308.pdf (last visited May 12, 2016).

In the recent history of animal law, lawyers who traditionally participated in agricultural and equine practices were influenced by lawyers primarily motivated by animal welfare or animal rights concerns. Now, most are less comfortable with companion animals only being things, akin to inanimate objects. As the human species evolves, the rule of law can be reshaped to fit the current times and to embrace four-legged family members.

Beyond TIPS, other Sections of the ABA are expanding their base on animal subjects. They include the Section of Family Law, where this book was born, as well as the Section of Dispute Resolution, the Section of Individual Rights and Responsibilities, and the Section of International Law.

CONCLUSION

Although subjects of great importance have only been addressed in cursory form in this chapter, it is worthwhile to realize how our ideas today have been shaped by other visionaries. What were yesterday's facts may be tomorrow's curious beliefs.

Chapter 13

Law Office Basics, Anatomy of a Case, and Expert Testimony

"There is special providence in the fall of a sparrow."

—*William Shakespeare*

If you are a lawyer or other professional contemplating offering services of any kind related to pet law, begin with the premise that the case will likely be more difficult than you imagine and that a prospective or current client may undervalue your efforts and not want to pay for them. As this book demonstrates, not only is the law pertaining to pets far from settled, but personal attitudes and beliefs about companion animals will impact what happens in both expected and unexpected ways. Beyond that, no one may ever know how discretionary decisions, when applicable, are made.

It could be said that if you are a lawyer with a good reputation, your client will expect you to win, notwithstanding bad facts or the lack of predictability as to how the law is applied or decisions are made. Thus, you may be expected to read a jurist's mind as to whether they are old school or not, even if this is a case of first impression. Clients may also think that property law applications are set in stone and in their favor, while case law around the country suggests that no result can be guaranteed as the times are changing.

Do your best to reduce your clients' expectations, whatever your talent, as there are too many variables to forecast an outcome. Even the best animal law litigators in the country, many of whom try to push the envelope, have lost more cases than they have won. Even so, as you can see with the chronology of cases in different substantive areas, the jurisprudence continues to evolve and progress as the courts, who are part of a culture, contemplate change and sometimes, proclaim old precedents must be set aside.

The point is that no lawyer in this country has the magic touch to achieve any outcome; a good lawyer can help increase the odds of a good outcome. A presenting challenge is for lawyers and their clients to be on the same page regarding costly charges in a legal environment where anything can happen. Lawyers involved in these cases must, in effect, practice law defensively.

FINDING POTENTIAL CLIENTS

To find potential clients, attend events involving animals, visit social media sites that address animal issues, and give speeches on companion animal law. One way to develop your practice is to build solid relationships with people who know when a lawyer or mediator is needed. People able to make referrals to pet lawyers and mediators include doggie day-care providers, dog walkers, horse trainers, behaviorists, veterinarians, animal control officers, people working at humane events, and people involved in animal rescue, as well as people who enjoy the same types of activities and groups that you do.

Beyond basic marketing, it is wise to do a good job on the work you have. Satisfied clients are the best source of business, and over the years, your good relationships will result in a continuing stream of business opportunities.

INITIAL CONSULTATION

During the initial consultation, if the case is described as a pet custody or companion animal dispute, ask about the person's past significant relationships with animals. Get information about how the animals were acquired and what breeds they are. Instead of describing an animal as a cat, dog, or rabbit, a client may say he or she has a rescue animal, a mutt, a designer mix or cross breed, or a particular breed, such as a Schnauzer or Siamese. Most clients will be impressed if their lawyer is knowledgeable about their specific animal, and lawyers who are well informed about animals are perceived as better able to serve and advocate for their clients in companion animal disputes.

It is also important to be aware of pertinent statistics, such as the results of an American Animal Hospital Association pet owner survey. According to this research, 93 percent of people said they would risk their life for their pet, 86 percent include their pet in holiday celebrations, 67 percent take their pets with them on vacation, and 63 percent celebrate their pet's birthday.[1] Selectively share information with your clients that reflects your expertise.

EVALUATING POTENTIAL CLIENTS

When meeting with clients, explore why they are in your office, what goals they have, and what services they are willing to pay for. Evaluate if what they want seems reasonable and realistic. While they talk, pay attention to their body language. Look at their face. Notice if their arms are crossed, whether they are talking very fast or loud, and whether they are doing their best to rely on paper for information rather than their own perspective and recollection of key facts.

Does the client perceive himself or herself as powerful or weak? What is the motivation behind their stated position? Are they truly concerned for the animal or only concerned about their own emotional attachment? Are they in a power dispute with the other side? Is infidelity a factor? Are there chemical dependency issues, including someone transporting the animal while under the influence? Assess whether the person is an effective communicator, and if not, discuss how to help them improve this skill set.

LACK OF PREDICTABILITY IN THE LEGAL SYSTEM

As described in the introduction to this chapter, during the first meeting, explain the lack of predictability in the legal system when it comes to pet and companion animal legal issues. Inform them that judicial officers' viewpoints vary significantly as to whether they regard a pet or companion animal dispute as being worthy of their time and attention. Point out that courts may open their doors for ownership disputes involving very expensive animals, or disputes concerning hunting animals, but if the value of the animal is not of a commercial or traditional kind, the client should expect a broad spectrum of judicial interest and attention.

Clients must understand that some jurists, if willing to consider a pet custody dispute at all, might only lean toward a traditional property or contract analysis. Some courts are indifferent to the plight of companion animals and treat them as similar to a lamp or sofa and may threaten to order the parties to sell or auction "all the property" if the parties cannot agree on a disposition.

1. *The Pet Services Industry Today*, Zoom Room, https://www.zoomroomonline.com/the-pet-services-industry-today/ (last visited May 12, 2016).

It is because of the unknown proclivities of jurists that attorneys often lead by giving the court their most convincing traditional arguments, including ownership, title, and economic arguments, before adding in relational and best-interest criteria and maltreatment arguments. Help your clients appreciate the importance of artfully wrapping the most compelling best-interest factors into a story that bends toward the ideals of justice. Good stories matter. Even so, it is always desirable to warn clients that if the judge is intent upon making a decision based upon a traditional analysis, which the court may state represents well settled law, the court may criticize the attorney reflecting the type of decision making criteria used by Judge Chu in her order, contained in these appendices.

LEARNING ABOUT THE CASE

When first meeting with potential clients, do not solely rely on the forms they fill out and the documentation they bring in because important information can often be gleaned only from a careful interview. The interviewer should ask questions that a client's answers lead to, using a curious mind. Watch for hesitations. Some sample questions might include:

- Who wanted to get the animal?
- What is the animal's name?
- What is the animal's age and date of birth?
- How was the animal obtained (purchased, adopted, gifted, found, or other)?
- What source of funds was used to purchase the animal (individual or joint credit card, individual or joint checking account, or cash)?
- What is the name and contact information of the animal's veterinarian?
- What payments have been made to the veterinarian by either party? Are there records that support this?
- Has the animal had any significant veterinary expenses, and if so, for what diagnosis? Who paid for these expenses? Who took the animal to the hospital?
- What will microchip information show?
- Does the animal have veterinary insurance? Whose idea was that?
- Has the animal had significant behavioral and training expenses, and if so, for what reason? Who paid for these expenses?
- Has the animal had a history of any other significant expenses, and if so, for what? Who paid for these expenses?
- What evidence do you have to back up your claims?

- What type of food, supplements, and medications are given to the animal? Why? Who paid for these expenses?
- Have you ever been involved in a court dispute? If so, was the case resolved in the courtroom or through a mediation process?
- If applicable, what did you like or dislike about the mediation process?
- Has there been any allegation of substance abuse regarding either party involved?
- In the current dispute, what accusations have the parties made about each other?
- Has either party been subject to a domestic abuse or temporary restraining order, or has either party been convicted of any criminal offense?
- What is each party's relationship with the animal? (Press the client for many specific examples.)
- Who cares for the animal on a regular basis, including during the week and on weekends?
- Are there children, adults, or other animals who have a significant relationship with the animal? If so, please describe.
- Has a child abused the animal?
- Does anyone work from home? Does anyone bring the animal to work?
- Why do you think you should be awarded the animal?
- What are the most significant factors that you think will help you?
- What are the most significant factors that you think will hurt you?
- Did you bring any records or evidence with you that have not already been covered?
- What questions do you want to ask me?

Listen for a while before you continue and make sure the client feels heard. In addition to obtaining very basic information about the case, it is important to understand the client's point of view and values. Ask questions to learn about the person's background and history with humans and other animals.

Understanding Points of View

If retained, further understanding each party's point of view in a dispute is important. Ask clients for details about the opposing party's life. Pay attention to major milestones. If a business interest or a third-party interest is involved, ask questions about this. If applicable, learn how the parties' relationship began and ended. Get a feel for personalities and values. Is the client emphasizing monetary and property values or best-interest and relational values? Ask clients to speculate about the worst allegations the opposing party might make about them and what compliments they might give, too.

Role-Playing

Ask your clients if they are comfortable role-playing. If they say yes, make sure they know what role-playing is as otherwise, they may think you are criticizing them. If they are interested in role-playing, literally have them leave the office and come back in, offer them a different chair, and address them as someone else by name; help them stay in character. You should play another character, too.[2] Pay attention to whether allegations during this point-of-view role-playing reveal information not previously described with regard to domestic abuse, chemical dependency, criminal history, power and control, or medical and mental health challenges. Was there an earlier peaceful, friendly, and even loving relationship with the adverse party?

FEARS

If the dispute is based upon your client's fears that the animal will be mistreated, will suffer if the opposing party is awarded the animal, or will get loose, find out if these fears are well founded. Think about specific ways to address the problem. For example, is there evidence you could secure for an order for protection where the court can award the animal to your client? If one party travels often, could the other party have the right of first refusal to care for the animal? If one party feeds the animal too many table scraps and the animal has diabetes, could the parties agree that if weight and blood sugar levels are not maintained, title to the animal will be promptly transferred?

PROBLEM SOLVING

When listening to a client express fears and emotions, begin your problem-solving efforts right away, perhaps writing down key words. Determine if a satisfactory negotiation could occur without the need for a mediation process, or if the mediation process is necessary. Even if you think alternative dispute resolution would be futile, explain mediation and other alternative dispute resolution options to your client and the range of results that might be expected. Your client may be more willing to participate if the mediation professional has skills on animal issues

2. If playing another character, make sure your clients understand that what you will be saying "in character" is not your viewpoint.

and is comfortable discussing human and animal best-interest factors. If you are convinced there will be no good faith cooperation, learn how soon an action can be commenced.

CLIENTS TO AVOID

Avoid clients who essentially want you to operate in a shadow role, as they may ultimately be angry when they receive your bill, because as they see it, they did all the work. If the individual does not value legal services, they can be pro se. If you accept this type of client, proceed with caution and make sure to establish clear boundaries.

Troublesome clients often have relationship problems with everyone and may indicate that they are willing to cheat to gain the upper hand. Consider the likelihood that their anger and manipulative ways may be later turned against you. Know when to say no.

CLIENT FINANCIAL COMMITMENT

Find out if the client is willing to litigate the issue and how far he or she wants to take the case. For example, a client may be willing to pay $5,000 for the dispute but nothing beyond that. It can be difficult to tell which clients are fully committed to the future of their companion animal and which ones simply have a preference if they can afford it. The subject of money should be brought up in a way that does not promise them anything; you will not know whether they will get what they believe is their money's worth. Go through the likely process and types of decisions that may come up along the way. If the dispute seems rooted in anger between the parties, consider how to effectively address that anger without having the animal represent the symbolic victory for either party. Suggest possible outcomes and find out if the client's interests are really centered on the animal.

PREPARING QUALITY PLEADINGS

If mediation or another type of alternative dispute resolution does not occur, lawyers may want to prepare and file multiple tightly constructed affidavits with evidentiary attachments that overlap on key points. Not only may these affidavits prove useful in court, but also the preparation will help you and your client better understand the strengths and weaknesses of the action. Quality pleadings can make a difference if the court is delayed in making a decision following oral arguments or if the judge can no longer remember the details of what happened in the courtroom during the decision-making time period permitted. Artful and well-crafted affidavits may help the decision maker resolve the case in your client's favor. All correspondence, pleadings, and settlement proposals should be of an excellent quality. Always maintain a good standard, as your reputation depends upon it.

IDENTIFYING POTENTIAL EXPERTS

For family lawyers new to animal law issues, identifying potential experts for cases is not as easy as one might expect. People who have demonstrated capabilities with animals may have know-how but lack typical expert qualifications that please the court. Historically, veterinarians were used as expert witnesses in animal cases, but more recently, applied animal behaviorists are being sought.[3] A broad spectrum of people with animal expertise may qualify to give expert opinions depending on the courts. Although lawyers may expect veterinarians to be experts, unless they have had an applicable companion animal residency,[4] they might actually know less than those who work in the field training animals or addressing behavioral problems.

CONCLUSION

Last, but not least, be pleasant and sympathetic to everyone who comes through your door. Your clients will appreciate kindness.

3. *Certified Applied Animal Behaviorists*, http://certifiedanimalbehaviorist.com/ (last visited May 12, 2016).

4. There are two types of board certifications available for veterinarians offered through the Animal Veterinary Medical Association to demonstrate that the veterinarian has either expertise regarding a certain type of veterinary medical care and expertise relevant to which animals can be treated in his or her practice setting. *AVMA American Board of Veterinary Specialties*, American Veterinary Medical Association, https://www.avma.org/professionaldevelopment/education/specialties/pages/default.aspx (last visited May 12, 2016).

Conclusion

> **"Whether I shall turn out to be the hero of my own life, or whether that station will be held by anybody else, these pages must show."**
>
> —*David Copperfield*

THE HEROIC JOURNEY

A true hero's journey involves taking a great risk. A hero may emerge through the recognition that the popular beliefs are not equivalent to truth. A hero is the person who stands up in front of a moving tank or the student who enters a segregated school. On a hero's journey, the individual risks falling into the abyss and struggles with how to navigate through complex problems without simple answers.

As difficult as the heroic journey is, the context of the quest may be to acquire knowledge or achieve a goal. In animal welfare, the valiant include Jane Goodall, Bernard Rollin, and Temple Grandin because they have shifted the foundation of popular beliefs. Jane informed us that chimpanzees are individuals who deserve names, not numbers. She also helped us understand their social systems. Bernard, both resolute and tenacious, took on the research industry. He was able to change what was acceptable in research practices through his singular role in the passage of the federal Animal Welfare Act. Recruited by Bernard at Colorado State University, Temple changed agricultural practices through her ability to articulate to ranchers and corporate executives alike that it was time to stop talking abstractly about pain and suffering. It was time to stop it. Her words were uniquely impactful because she, as an autistic person, related to and could explain the animal perspective like none before her.

Rule of Law

The rule of law has been glorified as it protects us against tyranny and chaos. Many seek to export this high ideal. Before holding ourselves out as a moral beacon, it is worthwhile to undertake some soul searching. The rule of law today can be a mechanistic and simplistic application of economic principles used to achieve monetary goals and certainty, devoid of consideration of the social and moral context in which legal disputes arise.

Justification for how we normatively behave may reflect our allegiance to reason, logic, linear analysis, and rational decision-making processes without adequate consideration of greater principles. When guiding and higher order precepts are interjected, some perceive them as derogating the legal system.

Legal institutions have been built to justify how things are done and name their output as justice. Over time, we have relied on case law from other centuries, reverently utilizing terms such as precedent or stare decisis, locution that seems to embody the symbolic image of a star. We do not deserve a gold star when we sacrifice the innocent by ignoring the rightfulness or wrongfulness of our actions, then hide behind the shield of willful ignorance thereby distancing ourselves from the affairs of the heart. Helen Keller famously observed that "The only thing worse than being blind is having sight but no vision." In the same figurative sense, one may have a heart but be unable to follow it.

Lawyers trained to solve problems based upon a belief system focused on commercial value may be uncomfortable with the complex and emotional characteristics that family law cases have long presented, let alone those arising with companion animals. Some lawyers only deal with legal problems on the surface and act almost as if their clients are not real; their work is somewhat rote. Other lawyers are unaware that what they imagine to be their own rational decision-making processes have an indivisible physiological-emotional component. But, lawyers ultimately know that their clients are in pain. Because of the way the legal system is designed, some of them will not get justice—the kind of justice that we want to believe in, the kind of justice that exclaims, "When there is a wrong, there is a remedy" or "justice for all." Lawyers are often burdened with the idea that in some fundamental way, the justice system will let them down. Morale needs to be re-infused into our legal system. We can quell our fears and aspire to new standards of excellence.

Science

Through genetic modification or pharmaceutical neuro enhancements, humans are arguably becoming transhuman, meaning part human and part not. Not only is augmented reality (AR) upon us, but human body parts can become a cell line, such as HeLa, and classified as property, too. We also know that there are more microbe cells within our own bodies than human cells.

At the same time that we are changing ourselves, and are perhaps startled to learn which aspect of ourselves is human, we now have sufficient scientific tools and evidence to discern that other animals think and have feelings. Aware that other animals experience joy and pain, we are passing laws making animal abuse a crime. Courts are recognizing that animals subject to abuse can be crime victims, regardless of whether a statute uses "person" verbiage. Lawmakers are promoting animal welfare through local, state, federal, and international laws.

Children and Best-Interests Decisions

When it comes to children, there is now resolve *not* to treat them as chattels or property, as was done throughout human history. Instead, through the rule of law, decisions about children are viewed through best-interest factors, which embody concepts such as emotional bonds and history of devotion and capacity to provide primary care. The rule-based decision-making process requires that children be raised consistent with societal norms. Child endangerment is prohibited.

Companion Animals in the Family

Century after century, ideas about who can be in a family evolve. Historic barriers to family membership could be based on bride prices, economic class, royal bloodlines, race, ethnicity, citizenship, religion, sexual practices or identity, genetic contributions by three parents, and species, as well as based upon other legal and cultural rules and laws. Sociologically speaking, families have been expected to promote other members' physical, emotional, and social well-being, which would include leading a life that is fulfilled. The definition of who is in a family is a subjective concept and is of great importance to society.

We are now beyond the question of what happens if the companion animal enters our family system; it has already happened. We value our companion animals enough that we devote a significant portion of our earnings to support them and provide them with quality care. Someone cared enough to buy and read this long book.

Knowing what we know about companion animals being integral to family life, we can recognize, too, that our laws and common laws concerning them are outdated. When we question old ways, answers will arise. We are the promise and messengers of tomorrow and bring an enduring purpose.

The parts of ourselves that are capable of morality and mercy may be denied, be observed, or they can grow. It is regrettable when humans, working in a legal context, compartmentalize their feelings for the very pets that add richness, dimension, and companionship to all aspects of even their own family systems. Some have hypocritically hobbled a legal system that could develop cost-effective methods wherein the best interests of animals could be positively considered. The honorable among us can use our minds, creativity, and power to declare that companion animals are more than personal property. They are our family members.

Role of Courts and ADR Alternatives

More and more, it seems as if poorly funded courts are losing their ability or resolve to address valid moral and social concerns and thereby impact the status quo in what they call, in effect, their administration of justice. This trend may cause the role of courts to become less essential, less respected, and more marginalized. Contemporaneously, with an exodus from the courts in progress, there have been efforts to refashion justice in mediation and in other ADR processes. When considering how this is done, some ADR systems may have the same mechanistic shortcomings as the courts.

In the private sector, facilitative and transformative mediators have more ability to explore problem solving in a more comprehensive context when they have been given permission to reconstruct what justice looks like in ways not afforded courts or evaluative mediators. The question is open as to whether mediators and other dispute resolution professionals can go outside of their established human-centric comfort zones when helping to resolve conflicts involving companion animals. If stipulations or private agreements are reached, it will remain to be seen if good efforts to achieve private justice will be thwarted by the finality of judgment rule or other rules of law.

Pet Custody and Ownership Disputes

There are many ways lawyers can engage in the practice area of pet custody and ownership disputes involving companion animals who uniquely serve as the objects, if not subjects, of human affection. In the context of family law, the court has wide discretion to consider moral and social values, relational and equitable principles, and the best interests of the human and animal in making an award. This is true in part because, when companion animals' fates are determined, unless a law requires particularized findings, the exercise of discretion may be oblique.

Life, liberty, and the pursuit of happiness[1] were prized, presumably for chosen humans only, in yesteryear; we now know that a person can be anything we want a person to be. Ultimately, a legal system that lacks a heart, a soul, and a conscience becomes small in the eyes of the citizenry. In the past, great jurists were praised for being able to envision and construct new pathways for justice that had not existed

1. This concept was central to the U.S. Declaration of Independence. Under the 5th and 14th Amendments of the U.S. Constitution, a government may not deprive any person of "life, liberty, or property" without due process.

before. Giving pets and companion animals a special place and status in our justice system improves our resolve to positively get the measure of who we are.

FINAL THOUGHTS

Although the law concerning pet custody disputes is far from settled, this first comprehensive book on the subject encourages resourcefulness by offering you a broad array of ideas and arguments. By examining thorny and tangled structures and upholding enduring principles, you can resolve to understand the full dimensions of a dispute, to conceptualize just solutions, and to reimagine the rule of law.

You have learned already about how to effectively manage a pet custody dispute. You have grown to appreciate how these struggles arise in a social, cultural, and historical context and at the crossroads of many practice areas, including family law and animal law, with their presenting difficulties. The unfolding of laws pertaining to pet custody disputes involves these questions: Where does the classification of a companion animal lie on the continuum between property and person? Should we call this the interim category? Will the animal have fictional, economic, special, relational, or intrinsic value, or all of the above? What are the indicia of animal ownership? What duties do, or should, owners have? To what extent do ownership, custody, and guardianship conceptualizations imply a duty? How should decision-making criteria and methods be reframed? What due process standards should apply? Should due process standards be thin or robust? How can neutral biases be identified and addressed? What are the pros and cons of each alternative dispute resolution process? Will the courts enforce private agreements, and if so, under what circumstances will they retain jurisdiction? When should animal interests and welfare be advanced? Are we willing to stop animal cruelty?

There may be no other area of law that more fully reveals a dual conception of the place of an animal in the world than pet law cases do. Once an animal is classified as a companion animal, growing case law reflects that treating this animal as "merely" property is no longer in concert with our social and cultural values; at the very least, companion animals are distinguishable as special compared to other tangible property. We are aware that significant financial resources are expended to promote these animals' health and lifestyle and, for a growing number, to preserve their ashes at the end.

Although legal analysis has deductive logical reasoning aspects, as the significant case law analysis herein portrays, within the footings of this book the effort was made to reveal the diversity of human points of view about "the other" in the animal kingdom. Since our laws are for humans, and animals are not our children, we struggle with where our moral compass should point and whether to put a face on the presenting problem.

If you make the decision to use this book as a journey, you will be transformed by it because you will be able to utilize the ideas of many to feel the moral axis shift, across the centuries, about how we think about animals. When jurists avoid moral conceptions in their decision-making processes, they never enter the visionary territory revealed in poetry. From time to time, emotionally intelligent jurists recognize that humans love their pets and their pets love them back. Some jurists, such as Justice Arabian, change the world by revealing their hearts and their brains.

Social and cultural shifts are upon us about animal subjects and methods of resolving conflicts. Particularly in the realm of pet custody disputes, it is foreseeable that justice will be redistributed from the public sector to the private through alternative dispute resolution (ADR) processes where human-centered ADR approaches will contrast with, or merge with, pet-centered ones. Beyond the challenges regarding experts, biases, and neutrality in the ADR method, appreciate that not all jurists will welcome private pet custody agreements wherein the court has continuing jurisdiction to enforce joint ownership or pet time arrangements, much less want to deal with the subject of change of ownership upon credible evidence of animal mistreatment or abuse.

You are aware, too, that courts may be more willing, perhaps pretentiously, to retain jurisdiction over ownership and possession arrangements concerning animals prized for their commercial and economic value more than for their relational value. Practitioners must be aware that courts, too, can jealously suggest that when court time or attention is given to companion animals, the ubiquitous human children are implicitly deprived. For some, it is as if you dare say it. Silence regarding their plight may be deafening.

The reasoning goes something like this: if a dog is given a bone, a child will suffer. It is ironic that there is enthusiasm to refer to companion animals on one hand as akin to inanimate objects, and on the other, as beloved in a similar way as children. Somehow, the problem is set up as an either/or, when in reality, better processes can be designed to assist in achieving outcomes that promote animal welfare, if not the best interests for all concerned standard advanced in *Travis v. Murray*.[2]

Instead of being shackled by the old order, which relies on monetary and mechanistic Cartesian ideas, improving how companion animals should be treated in our legal system enhances, rather than diminishes, human greatness. Maybe, in the end, it is as simple as who you love. If you are a lover of animals, or a lover of a world that is better where the moral axis tips in favor of kindness, then measures to make their lives better will be embraced. For those who value animals only in

2. 42 Misc. 3d 447, 977 N.Y.S.2d 621 (2013).

economic terms, a central theme of this book will not be understood. The rule of law, at its best, represents high legal ideals and benefits from the practice of examining the moral and ethical principles, a practice that we say constitutes our conscience.

We have taken a deep dive into the subject of who companion animals are and who we are. Companion animals are not just property anymore, and for those who say otherwise, your time may come. Fascinated not only by their minds, but also by their love for us, we have brought them into our homes and families. We have risked our lives to save them.

Because we value companion animals, we can utilize our legal system to not only protect them, but also to fairly and cost-effectively consider and advance their best interests. As you have learned, to be effective in pet custody dispute processes, avoid rigidity about terminology regarding where pets belong on the continuum between property and person. Instead, consider how a wide variety of subject matter animal law cases, when knit together, will help you advance the just outcome you seek. School your client about the difficulty of challenging the established order. Be prepared to play the long game.

Animal law, and hence pet custody disputes, still retains troublesome roots in a 19th-century precedent, *Sentell v. New Orleans Carrollton Railroad Co.*[3] This U.S. Supreme Court decision was penned in a time when hydrophobic disease, also known as rabies, was prevalent. Why else would this court describe all animals as "more or less subject to attacks of hydrophobic madness"? With regard to dogs, the *Sentell* Court expounded that they could only advance from the status of quasi-property to a lower plane of property if they were dead or subdued. Of all members of the animal kingdom, then, the dog was the lowliest. At the same time that some courts still heed 19th-century precedents, aspects of humans are being reduced to property conceptions as well demonstrated in *Moore v. Regents of the University of California*[4] and the book *The Immortal Life of Henrietta Lacks*.[5]

We may come full circle in our 21st-century case law about dangerous dogs. We swing about in how we conceptualize dogs. They may have thoughts, feelings, and intentions, the type of ability that enables them to serve in the military or on a police force. These qualities impact how they respond to stimuli and provocations. On the other hand, at their essence, it is said that they are *ferae naturae*, meaning wild by nature. Is this because we perceive the wild beast inside of us? Ask yourself the difficult questions.

3. 166 U.S. 698, 17 S. Ct. 693, 41 L. Ed. 1169 (1897).
4. 51 Cal. 3d 120, 271 Cal. Rptr. 146, 793 P.2d 479 (1990).
5. Rebecca Skloot, The Immortal Life of Henrietta Lacks (Broadway Books 2011).

Animal law cases influence each other in what could be conceptualized as a series of vertical and horizontal intersections. The vertical lines in this model might be the established practice area of family law, while the horizontal lines reflect ideas such as how value is determined across many subject areas. Monetary value of companion animals, for example, remains dominant in tort law while relationship value is gaining momentum in family law. Through the concept learning opportunity this book provides, you now see how tort law, criminal law, constitutional law, and contract law have and will impact the growing body of pet law and custody law jurisprudence.

We can communicate our deepening knowledge to other lawyers, jurists, lawmakers, law enforcement officers, ADR professionals, and clients. We will envision what our rule of law will be, inspire others, and invest in the future one case at a time. Benefiting from the useful tools in the form of checklists, questions, agreements, and pleading critiques, together with extensive case analysis and practice pointers in this book, all may contribute their own ideas to grow this pet custody practice area, a practice area that will be revisited in the second edition of this book. To that end, you are invited to share your ideas and accomplishments with this author at barbara@gislasonlaw.com.

In closing, the author expresses her gratitude to you for your perseverance in reading what she hopes is a groundbreaking work. For her, this book represents a five-year labor of love. She also appreciates the American Bar Association Section of Family Law for giving her this opportunity to contribute toward the inspired design and realization of a more advanced justice system.

Also, it is time for the big reveal about the identity of the elephant in the room. It is you. Now that you know your form, you may change any aspect of yourself. All is possible.

Epilogue

Life with Dogs

"The tree which moves some to tears of joy is in the eyes of others only a green thing that stands in the way. Some see nature all ridicule and deformity . . . and some scarce see nature at all. But to the eyes of the man of imagination, nature is imagination itself."

—*William Blake*

SIGFUS

Shortly after purchasing a home with a large fenced backyard, I walked into a humane society, saw a puppy in a box, picked him up, adopted him, and left. It was love at first sight. Days later, this small Husky/Golden mix puppy, given the name Sigfus, disappeared from my backyard. A runner at a nearby lake found Sigfus and, through an act of kindness, returned him to me. It was amazing how fast I attached to this animal. Our relationship continued to grow. He was family.

Years later, the Minnesota State Bar Association's first Animal Law Committee members gathered at my home for a party. Sigfus, then 13, was in all of the photos. A week later, and quite suddenly, he was in the process of dying. I took the day off to be by his side. His breathing changed. It was hard for him to go down the stairs and outside to the quilt where the veterinarian was waiting for him. His life passed through my hands.

BJORNA

The next night, Bjorna, my nine-month-old yellow Labrador, seemed to be watching all kinds of activity, none of which I could see. On an off chance, I asked her, "Where's Sigfus?" Instead of looking around the room, Bjorna planted her eyes on the place just next to me as if she was looking at him. The next night I was reading in the same place and asked Bjorna, "Where's Sigfus?" She again looked at the same spot next to me.

VALDOR

When Sigfus passed, I had no plans to get another dog. Even so, at the end of the week, in the early afternoon, I had a premonition that I should go to a particular humane society. There were a couple of reasons that this persistent thought puzzled me. First, I did not want another dog, and second, if going to a humane society, I would not have gone to the small one, which was out of my way, but rather the big one on my way home where I found Sigfus.

Yet the thought remained, and when I had a bit of time before my next appointment, I decided to go. But after I got in my car at about 3:00 p.m. and turned left onto the major road, I blew a tire. By 6:00 that night, I had completed additional appointments and, with a spare tire in place, was ready to go home. Instead, I found myself driving to the small humane society.

I walked in, saw a thin male yellow Labrador mix, and said to him, "What are you doing here?" As it turned out, he had been transferred to the small humane society around the time I had tried to drive out there earlier in the afternoon. If I had gotten there when I first tried, I would have missed him by minutes. Valdor had been receiving medical treatment at the big humane society, and they transferred him to the small humane society at about 3:00 p.m. that day.

Valdor was about a year old, near the same age as my female Labrador, Bjorna. When he was rescued 30 days earlier, he was near starvation; another dog he had been traveling with on the street had been hit by a car. Bjorna and Valdor immediately took to each other and would often be seen paw to paw. In fact, when Bjorna was recovering from major surgery, for days, Valdor surrounded her bandaged body with his.

NIKOLAS AND JATGEIRR

Later, after Bjorna passed, I acquired two English Cocker Spaniels named Nikolas and Jatgeirr who rejuvenated Valdor's spirits and became a happy force in my life.

They are loving and energetic lap dogs who watch television and not only bark at live animals on the screen but also animal cartoons.

CONNECTING WITH ANIMALS

Humans typically experience other creatures and their triumphs and struggles in an abbreviated life cycle compared to their own. We watch as animals struggle with fear, loneliness, anger, and pain. They can model for us how to extract grace from life, how to live in the moment, and how to stay true to the end. We can connect with these animals as more than just observers, moving past calling them "it," "things," "objects," or "commodities." It is not trivial to explore their place in our lives and our families or seek to extend our time with them through the pursuit of pet custody or access. They are worthy of our best efforts.

Appendix 1

Pet Custody Questionnaire

This is an all-purpose intake questionnaire that is easily adaptable depending upon your intended use. It offers ideas of information to collect for lawyers, mediators, rescue groups, and experts. Courts could also utilize aspects of this questionnaire to make determinations for special handling.

QUESTIONNAIRE

1. What is the animal's common name and, if applicable, registry name?
2. What are the identifying characteristics of the animal, including breed, height, weight, color, markings, whether ears or tail are docked, and type of coat? Attach a recent photograph.
3. What is the animal's microchip company and number, if applicable?
4. Are there other humans or animals present in the applicable household? Please identify.
5. Does the animal travel well? If not, describe the animal's travel problems and state whether they can be addressed through the help of professionals.
6. Is the animal showing signs of emotional difficulty at this time? If so, describe the symptoms (lethargic, nonresponsive, change in appetite, defecating, barking, crying).
7. What are the likely causes of any presenting issues?
8. Describe the animal's general emotional behaviors with specificity (human friendly, dog aggressive, fearful, anxious, confident, happy).
9. Describe the quality of interaction between the animal and each member of any applicable household (children, parents, each party, roommates, other third parties, other animals).

10. Describe how each individual in a household, or someone who is often there, acts toward the animal (tone of voice, threats, physical attention, petting, grooming, walking, training, showing, exercising).
11. Other than the parties, does the animal have a special relationship with another human or animal? If so, please describe in detail.
12. Has the animal been harmed, yelled at, or teased? Has someone threatened to harm or injure the animal? If so, describe in detail.
13. Does the animal seem to be afraid of a particular human or another animal? If so, describe in detail.
14. Do you have concerns about the animal injuring a human or another animal? Describe any prior incidents, including those involving animal control or other law enforcement.
15. Do you have concerns about the animal being injured? Why?
16. Has anyone ever complained about your animal or any other animals in your household? If so, describe in detail.
17. Does anyone in the household have an issue with chemical dependency, substance abuse, anger management, or behavioral problems that might result in the mistreatment or neglect of the animal? If so, describe in detail and attach relevant documents, including court and medical records.
18. Has anyone in the household been involved in any special activities with the animal (athletic or competitive, training, behavioral)? If so, describe in detail and provide the contact information for others who have witnessed these activities. Attach photos.
19. Has the animal been used for hunting? If so, describe in detail.
20. Who takes care of the animal in the morning, afternoon, and evening (walking, exercise, environmental stimulation, meals, water, removing waste, basic training, advanced training)? If applicable, describe care changes in the past year.
21. Has anyone provided extraordinary care to the animal (taking the animal to the veterinarian for a chronic condition or disease, providing medication, giving vaccines, preparing or providing special meals to address dietary problems, arranging social interactions with other animals, participating in training or behavioral classes)? If so, please describe.
22. What is the animal's typical day like in the household?
23. How is the animal maintained when not in the care of a human (barn, kennel, crate, run of the house, tethered)? Describe fencing or invisible fencing and any issues with fencing, doors, or gates.
24. What are the most likely ways the animal could become loose or at large (digging, climbing, quality of restraint, escaping through an open door)? Who has made efforts in the past to keep the animal confined?

25. Is the animal typically at a daycare facility or barn? Describe the quality of the care and identify everyone who provides this care. Provide contact information.
26. Are there any anticipated changes in human or animal family members in the household in the next year? If so, describe.
27. At the time of acquisition, was there an intention that one individual would own the animal or was there an intention for joint ownership? Explain in detail.
28. How was the animal purchased (check, credit card, cash), and who paid? Attach purchase and payment records and photographs at the time of acquisition.
29. Was the animal purchased from a reputable and responsible breeder or from a backyard breeder? If so, how was this breeder identified and who, if anyone, visited the breeder's residence or breeding facility?
30. Was the animal purchased from a pet store, from a large confinement breeder, and/or on the Internet? Provide all the details of purchase, including the representations made by the breeder, animal broker, or individual through written, electronic, or oral means. Attach relevant records and contracts.
31. Was the animal adopted? Describe the details of this acquisition (the search for the animal, home visits, breeder visits, foster visits, rescue group visits, names and signatures on the application form, conditions and restrictions by breeders or nonprofit sellers). Attach copies of the application and any signed agreements.
32. Is there an argument that the funds used to purchase the animal came from more than one party, such as from a joint checking account or credit card or cash payment? If the funds or credit card came from one party, was there any reimbursement for advancing these funds or credit to the other? Attach any supporting evidence, even evidence of a cash withdrawal or a social media posting near the time of purchase.
33. If the animal was a gift, who was the donor? Explain the reason the gift was made (the original owner was disabled, moving, offspring of pet, found, birthday or engagement gift). Attach any evidence proving there was a conscious desire to make a gift, known as donative intent.
34. Was the animal found? If so, describe in detail each and every effort made to find the original owner. Include the names of animal control, humane and rescue entities contacted, social media sites visited, ads run in newspapers, circulation of flyers, and hard copy postings. Attach any evidence of the finder's efforts.

35. Was the animal ever lost? If so, describe each and every effort made to find the lost animal, and attach evidence.
36. Whose name appears on the animal's records at the time of acquisition and later on (microchip records, animal licenses, veterinary records, emergency care facility records)? Attach these records.
37. Which party made expenditures on behalf of the animal? If both parties contributed, who paid which bills and how? How were other expenses shared between the parties? Attach or describe any evidence that supports your claim, including relevant checks, credit card records, store receipts, debt equalization records, and veterinary, grooming, training, day care, and dog walking bills.
38. Has one of the parties spent more money on the animal? What was the source of said money? Explain in detail. Create a balance sheet showing respective expenditures by each party on an annual basis.
39. Has one of the parties objected to the payment of certain expenses, such as recommended veterinary care, for the animal? If so, explain the objection and the availability of funds at the time that were not utilized.
40. Is there any indication based on the breed of the animal or the animal's health history that there will be extraordinary veterinary expenses in the future? If so, what is the estimate for said expenses? Attach any evidence that supports your projection, including data about typical veterinary problems of a particular breed.
41. What behavioral, veterinary, dental, farrier, grooming, and other care does the animal receive on an annual basis? Attach evidence establishing animal expenses.
42. What are the estimated monthly costs for maintaining the animal, including food, shelter, medications, daycare, training, and veterinary care? Attach supportive records.
43. Do you have adequate veterinary insurance, homeowner's or renter's insurance, and automobile insurance pertaining to the animal? Attach each policy.
44. What are the exclusions for animals on the homeowner's or renter's policy? (Note that some companies exclude ten or more breeds from their insurance coverage unless there is a rider at an additional fee.) If an animal has already been identified as vicious or declared dangerous, state which party can afford the insurance coverage or applicable bond.
45. Is a veterinary insurance policy in effect for the animal? If so, can it be transferred, without change in coverage, from one party to another? Does the animal have any significant or costly preexisting conditions? If so, please explain.

46. What are the animal's current insured and uninsured veterinary and dental costs, including for medication? If treatment has been delayed, explain the reason for the delay and attach relevant veterinary records.
47. Is there anything about how the animal was acquired—such as the animal was found and you did not search for the original owner, you are violating the terms of a rescue group or foster or breeder contract, or you are violating the terms of an artificial reproductive technology agreement or infringing intellectual property rights—that would cause you to believe that ownership of the animal might be disputed by a third party? If so, please describe and provide relevant information, including contracts, agreements, and written communications.
48. Is there any reason that the parties to a dispute would not be able to have a pet sharing agreement (they live too far apart, the animal is afraid while traveling, there is a "no-pets" policy or zoning ordinance, one party is unreliable, the parties constantly argue, or there is a history of domestic abuse or stalking)?
49. If a third party could assert ownership or other rights, what is your expectation as to whether that party would participate in mediation or alternative dispute resolution to reach a settlement? Explain why.
50. Are the applicable parties likely to follow whatever determination the court makes? If not, why?
51. If a shared possession agreement were reached, would the applicable parties be able to agree on major veterinary treatment, including euthanasia, as well as cost sharing? If not, indicate how you would prefer these decisions be made.
52. Do you suspect that someone has an ulterior motive for a pet custody dispute, such as making threats, as payback for a grievance (such as a sexual behavior), or to gain an unfair bargaining position? If so, describe.
53. If both parties sign an agreement, would they treat this as their bond, even if the court would not sign an order allowing joint custody or parenting time and the agreement was unenforceable? Explain why you believe this.
54. Which is more important to you, that you are happy or that any companion animal relevant to this dispute is happy?
55. Would either party risk his or her own life to save the life of the animal? If so, explain.
56. What values do you believe the other party has? How are your values the same or different when it comes to companion animals?
57. Would you be willing to bring in an expert—such as a veterinarian, behaviorist, or animal trainer—to help resolve the dispute? If so, explain what qualifications would be the most credible to you

(veterinarian, behaviorist credentials, or experience in the field). Give your recommendations.

58. Is it more important to you that property or contractual rights be enforced or that the best interests of all the humans and animals involved be considered?
59. If you were unable to keep the animal or afford the animal's expenses, would you prefer the animal be awarded to the other party or someone else? If someone else, explain who and why.
60. What is your position on selling the animal? If applicable, describe in detail how you would like this sale to occur.
61. Would you be willing to go into an alternative dispute resolution process—such as mediation, collaborative law, or arbitration—to explore how to resolve the dispute? If so, describe what you would like this process to be like. Would you prefer that a lawyer prepare you for this opportunity or accompany you?
62. Which of the following criteria is important to you: (1) contract rights, (2) property rights, (3) possessory rights, (4) equitable rights, (5) best interest of humans, (6) best interest of animals, (7) best interest for all concerned, or (8) all of the above? Which criteria or factors do you think should be given the most weight in resolving the dispute? How about the least weight?
63. Would you be willing to work with an alternative dispute resolution professional or grant jurisdiction to the court to consider the following: (1) the animal's bond with each party, (2) the animal's bond with each child, if applicable, (3) the animal's bond with each adult who lives in a household, (4) the animal's bond or conflict with any other animal, (5) the animal's bond with any third party, (6) the animal's veterinary and mental health needs, (7) the animal's protection, (8) the animal's other needs, (9) the animal's standard of living, or (10) financial resources and ability to meet these needs?
64. Describe your ideal mediator or arbitrator. Give your recommendations.
65. Is it important for you to explore how to achieve the best outcome possible for the animal, based upon best interest of the animal criteria, without litigation?
66. What do you feel would be the fairest process possible?

Appendix 2

Values Clarification Exercise

Part of the objective of this book is to help the reader become more conversant with biases and points of view about the animal kingdom as a tool to better understand the perspectives of other attorneys, adverse parties, experts, judicial officers, and alternative dispute resolution professionals. A useful beginning point is to inventory your own views as follows:

1. Would others describe you as a leader or a follower?
2. Are you more likely to follow laws based upon a belief that they represent a higher order or because of the consequences if you do not?
3. Are you more likely to comply with the terms of a contract that you sign because your word is your bond or because you would be worried about a lawsuit if you did not comply?
4. Would you characterize yourself as being in the mainstream or being out of the box?
5. Do you view humans as primates or not primates?
6. Which do you think better describes animal rights: equal to human rights or minimum welfare standards?
7. Do you think of animal rights in an abstract way, such as a universal principle, or in a specific way, such as a particular wrong that you are aware of?
8. Would you be more likely to eat an animal-based protein or a non-animal-based protein?
9. Do you believe vegans are fanatical or morally superior?
10. Do you think a successful researcher would learn more about an animal's behaviors in a highly controlled laboratory experiment or through long-term field observation?

11. Would you rather spend time outdoors in a completely natural environment or in a beautifully planned and developed garden?
12. Would it be better if animals promptly responded to commands or if they were mostly self-directed?
13. Do you believe humans operate on instinct more than non-human animals do or operate on instinct less than non-human animals do?
14. Do you believe that emotions are a part of your rational thinking process or that emotions are irrational?
15. Do you think close emotional bonds between humans and companion animals reflect affection that would be better directed at another human or that there are valuable interspecies bonds?
16. Would you be more influenced to change your actions based upon what you learn through science or based upon what you learn through experience?
17. Which trait do you think is more important for a non-human animal to have, sentience or intelligence?
18. Who do you believe provides better care of companion animals, women or men?
19. Would you be more afraid if a companion animal that you cared for tried to bite you or tried to leave you?
20. Do you think that humans who buy an animal from a reputable breeder are superior to humans who adopt a rescue animal or are inferior to humans who adopt a rescue animal?
21. Do you think it is better to select a purebred animal based upon a registry or based upon an on-site visit?
22. Would you prefer that feral cats be killed so that they do not harm other wildlife or be spayed and neutered so that their population declines?
23. Should a utilitarian concept, making a choice that promotes the greatest good, be applied to all animals or to humans only?
24. Should a sustainability model apply to the survival of all animals or to humans only?
25. Do you think a love bond between a human and another animal is better exemplified by the time spent with the animal or by who the animal goes to when called?
26. If you had a companion animal, would you prefer that the animal sleep in your bedroom or outdoors?
27. Do you consider yourself to be an animal person or not an animal person?
28. If you were left alone on a deserted island, would you prefer the company of another human or a companion animal?

29. Are your views about non-human animals affected more by your family of origin or your education?
30. Are your views about companion animals affected more by science or religion?
31. When you have experienced loneliness or depression, have you ever had a companion animal offer you what you perceived to be help?
32. If you own an animal that dies, would you prefer to bring the animal in for cremation or let someone take the animal's body away?
33. If you were facing a natural disaster, would you be more inclined to leave home without your animal or risk your life save your animal?
34. In a disaster, can you understand why some humans would not evacuate without taking their companion animal?
35. In nature, do you typically have the sense that the wildlife around you can make decisions using their cognitive abilities or that the wildlife behaves based mainly upon instinct?
36. Would you prefer that humans who own companion animals have a duty to reasonably care for them or no duty at all?
37. Do you think that most humans are emotionally bonded to their companion animals?
38. Do you believe that a companion animal can suffer from depression?
39. Do you think most companion animals are bonded to the humans that care for them or mainly respond to positive reinforcement?
40. Do you think addressing emotional bonds between humans and companion animals in an ownership dispute is worthy of legal consideration or a burden on the legal system?
41. Do you think humans involved in experiments on companion animals are justified or morally inferior?
42. With regard to animal experiments, which do you care more about, the type of animal being experimented on or the worthiness of the experimental research?
43. In the legal system, do you think pet custody laws should focus more on the best interests of the human or the companion animal?
44. When a scientific research study concludes that humans are superior to other animals, do you find the study to be credible or not credible?
45. When a scientific research study concludes that a non-human animal is superior to a human in some way, do you find the study to be credible or not credible?
46. Would you be more likely to discipline a companion animal for eliminating in the house or threatening another?

47. Do you believe that behavior modification techniques used on animals are beneficial or harmful?
48. When training an animal, which technique do you think is more effective, positive reinforcement or negative consequences?
49. If there are universal moral principles, do they apply to all animals or only to humans?
50. In your peer group, would you be more admired for eating meat or living a lifestyle with a low carbon footprint?
51. When you think of a microorganism, do you typically think of germs or a necessary part of the ecosystem?
52. When you think of the world, do you perceive it as hierarchical, with humans first, or as one complex, interrelated system?
53. Would you describe yourself more as kind to non-human animals or indifferent to non-human animals?
54. If souls exist, do you think it is more likely that all animals have them or that only humans have them?
55. If animal souls exist, do you think they are hierarchical or not hierarchical?
56. Should the value of companion animals in the legal system be based more upon their economic value or relational value?
57. Is poor animal care an indication more of human cruelty or poor mental health?
58. Do you think that companion animals should be regarded the same as other domestic animals or different from other domestic animals?
59. When humans get a companion animal, do they have a moral obligation to take care of the animal for the rest of the animal's life or only as long as it is convenient?
60. If you had a dog that barked too much and bothered your neighbors, would you be more likely to find a professional to address emotional or veterinary needs or buy a no-bark collar?
61. In a family system, do you believe a companion animal would be more bonded to the human with whom the pet sleeps or the human who feeds the animal?
62. How would someone better demonstrate that he or she cares for an animal, by discipline or by physical affection?
63. If an animal best interest standard is utilized in a decision-making process, should the focus be more on the quality of care or the absence of maltreatment?
64. If another animal's language was understood, would you expect this to change your idea about how you should behave or would it have little impact on your behavior?

65. Who gains more when a human is kind to a non-human animal, the human or the non-human animal?
66. When making a pet custody decision, should the court pay more attention to the animal's cognitive ability or emotional needs?
67. If non-human animals were capable of expressing love, do you think this would best be exemplified by the animals grooming the subject of their love or protecting the subject of their love?
68. If an animal was closely bonded to an owner, would you expect the animal to grieve the owner's loss or be incapable of grief?
69. If a human provoked an animal, would you expect the animal to intentionally retaliate or to react based solely upon instinct?
70. What behaviors are more likely to provoke an attack by a companion animal, going into the animal's territory or taking the animal's food?
71. With regard to other primates, would you respect someone more who promoted experimentation or protested experimentation?
72. If your companion animal were threatened by a stranger, would you risk physical harm to save your pet or make your own safety your first priority?
73. If an animal were being tormented on private property, would it matter more if the animal were a wild animal or a farm animal?
74. Whom do you regard as more important, companion animals or all animals?
75. Should the minimum standards for animal care be food and shelter or food, shelter, veterinary care, and exercise?
76. If there were laws setting minimum standards for the care of companion animals, would it be more important that the animal have an enriched living environment or that the animal have sufficient opportunities to play and exercise?
77. If a human fails to meet the minimum standards of care for a companion animal, should another human be able to take ownership and possession or should the other human mind his or her own business?
78. Should minimum standards for the care of a non-human animal be higher for a companion animal or be the same for all animals?
79. When looking at a sunrise or sunset, do you feel at one with the universe or do you quickly move on to the next thing?
80. If you had affection for a particular animal, would this influence you to avoid eating the same kind of animal or would it have nothing to do with your food preferences?
81. When someone protests animal research, do you assume that the person is an animal rights extremist or a principled individual?

82. If a group's goal were to improve animal welfare, would the group be more effective if they engaged in nonviolent protests or disclosed personal data about alleged wrongdoers on social media?
83. Do you think the rapid extinction of non-human animal species is more attributable to humans or nature?
84. Would you be more likely to select the company of someone who talks about humans or nature?
85. Would you rather watch an action film or a film that analyzes relationships?
86. What better describes civilized behavior, humans conquering the natural world or humans living in harmony with the natural world?
87. If someone came onto your property and intentionally injured your companion animal, would you be more likely to seek revenge or recover your out-of-pocket veterinary costs?
88. Do you think that a person's desire to eat animal protein is impacted more by blood type or family of origin?
89. Do you think it is better to judge others or understand others?
90. Do you think non-human animals are capable of altruism or incapable of altruism?
91. Which idea is more important to you, risking your own life to save your pets or your pets risking their lives to save you?
92. Do you consider a wild animal in a zoo with enrichment activities to be comparable to the same animal in a natural habitat or significantly different from a wild animal in a natural habitat?
93. Do you think non-human animals are capable of evil intentions or jealousy?
94. Do you think the subject of genocide through the killing of an entire human race is a new idea or an old idea?
95. If you traveled through the galaxy and met a sentient being on another planet, would you classify that being as a non-human animal?
96. Do you think the major decisions you make in your life are more influenced by determinism or free will?
97. Do you interpret companion animals that will not leave their deceased owner's body as grief or as a lack of behavioral substitute pattern?
98. Do you refer to a pet as a male or female or as "it"?
99. If a researcher involved in cloning cows referred to healthy calves as "babies" and other calves as "experimental animals," would you find the researcher's use of language to be hypocritical or acceptable?

100. Do you think all humans have a primal instinct for the hunt or only some humans have a primal instinct for the hunt?
101. Do you think domesticated cats primarily hunt for food or are primarily engaged in a seeking activity?
102. Do you think vegan cat owners should never feed animal protein to cats or consistently feed animal protein to cats?
103. If human civilization fails in the next 100 years, would you expect the cause to be forces of nature or human shortcomings?
104. Do you feel more accountable to moral law or the rule of law?
105. Do you think the best genes for companion animals are reflected in purebreds or mixed breeds?
106. Do you think great apes under age five and human beings under age five have similar cognitive abilities or vastly different cognitive abilities?
107. Do you think companion animals rely mostly on sight or smell?
108. Do you trust your sense of sight or sound more?
109. Do you think an octopus or a dolphin is more intelligent?
110. Do you think it is more important for a breeder to test a breeding pair for genetic disorders or to raise animals in a family home?
111. Do you think breeding standards would be better if animals were crossbred to improve breed vigor or if animals were purebred?
112. Do you believe that humans have dominion over non-human animals?
113. If you answered yes to the question above, does dominion give humans the right to an unlimited use of the animal kingdom or does dominion give humans stewardship responsibilities for the rest of the animal kingdom?
114. Would you prefer to be remembered as courageous or successful?

Upon completing this values clarification exercise, determine if you have learned more about yourself or gained insight into the cognitive biases and points of view of others. Imagine how decision makers or alternative dispute resolution professionals might differ from you or your client in their responses. Assess which responses would be useful to you in determining if that individual would consciously or unconsciously lean in the direction of strict and rigid adherence to a property type of analysis in a pet custody dispute, and which responses would signify flexibility in utilizing a broader spectrum of outcome determinative factors.

Consider developing your own instrument to help reveal underlying viewpoints or biases. An inherent challenge is to learn about psychometrics and discern what values and biases could be explored to acquire the necessary data to inform more advanced public policy positions. It would be interesting to learn if any particular responses correlate to what might be typed as sympathy to the plight of animals or indifference to them.

Thus far, little is known about what viewpoints about companion animals, wild animals, or farm animals might correlate with viewpoints about what a fair and just result might mean in a pet custody dispute context. The near future will bring ample opportunity to utilize test instruments and big data to advance knowledge on this subject.

Appendix 3

Lost and Found Dog Pleadings

A couple that owned a Terrier was out of state when their dog went missing. The wife was out of the country mourning lost relatives, and her husband was receiving medical care.

The couple had left their Terrier, who had a microchip, in the care of a responsible family member. Even so, the Terrier, who was allowed outside to relieve himself without his collar on, disappeared in 20-degree-below-zero weather; the caretaker was unable to find him.

Once notified that her dog was missing, the wife immediately returned to Minnesota and, together with friends and family, continued to search for her dog. Humane societies were called, and information about the dog, including the dog's photograph, was posted on three national registries.

Because English was the wife's second language, she did not realize that the microchip she had implanted in the dog was not automatically registered by her veterinarian with her address. While searching for his missing dog, the husband checked with the microchip company and learned that an inquiry had been made by a veterinary hospital; the couple followed the trail and learned that their dog had been adopted out three days before. The rescue group refused to provide the couple with any information about the adopter.

What followed was an exchange of letters between the wife and the rescue group. The wife's letters were compassionate and eloquent and explained in compelling detail the unique place this dog had in her family. She told the rescue group how her husband was in recovery from a disease process and how an important aspect of his recovery was his daily walk in the park with the dog. She explained how she picked the dog up from doggie daycare on her way home from work each day to spend time with him before she picked up her daughter. There was no doubt about the depth of her love or the couple's commitment to this dog.

The letters from the rescue group had a steely tone. They wrote the wife short letters with a shaming quality asserting that the dog would be dead if not for them. The rescue group demanded that she leave them alone. In this case, the rescue group acted in the capacity of animal control and the statutory hold period had expired.

Once a rescue group makes an adoption, it is a challenge to recover possession of the animal. The general rule is that if an animal has been properly held by animal control for the statutory hold period, animal control can pass good title to a rescue group that can in turn pass good title to another. Even so, there are times that good lawyering can be effective for the original owner in this predicament. For example, it can be argued that courts may exercise discretion on whether to order the disclosure of the entity or individual in possession of the dog. If a disclosure is mandated, the original owner would then have an opportunity to negotiate financial terms, if not access terms, with the new owner.

In the case of the missing Terrier, the rescue group hired an attorney who filed an answer with a general denial to the plaintiffs' pre-litigation discovery motion. Once in the courtroom, it was clear that the judge had read the motion and the original owners' affidavit. Attached to the affidavit were a Summons and Complaint that the plaintiffs were contemplating serving if a further legal action was necessary. The judge was intensely interested in getting the Terrier back to his original owners and immediately ordered the rescue group to disclose the name of the adopter. A week later, following negotiations, the Terrier was home.

The pleadings that follow may be challenging to understand unless you realize (1) they were written many years ago,[1] (2) they were strategically designed to motivate the judge to order the disclosure of the identity of the person in possession of the dog, (3) they were designed to motivate the rescue group to cooperate, (4) the summons and complaint attached to the affidavit do not represent pleadings sufficient for a summary judgment, and (5) information has been changed on the pleadings to conceal the names of the parties, the county of the action, and other pertinent details.. The summons and complaint were attachments to the affidavit but were not the action itself because in Minnesota, a discovery deposition may be permitted under Rule 27 of the Rules of Civil Procedure before an action is brought. It is repeated that the motion and affidavit appear before the summons and complaint in this appendix because they were only illustrative of the action that the original owners would commence. This is why the motion heading is at variance with the headings in the summons and complaint.

1. If written today, these pleadings would have emphasized that there is a growing trend toward considering multiple factors in an ownership dispute, not simply the transfer of ownership following the hold period. The pleadings would also not refer to an interest in a dog as being the same as property rights and chattel rights. More modern pleadings would emphasize that this is how the subject used to be viewed, but in the context of emerging jurisprudence, a companion animal may be regarded as being in an interim category between property and persons, and to some, as a family member.

STATE OF MINNESOTA
COUNTY OF ANOKA

DISTRICT COURT
TENTH JUDICIAL DISTRICT
CIVIL COURT DIVISION
Court File No. 12345

In Re the Matter of:
Craig Swanson and Julie Swanson,

Plaintiff,

and

Animal Finder, Inc., and
Minnesota Animal Retrieval, and
John and Jane Doe,

Defendants.

NOTICE OF MOTION AND MOTION[2]

You will please take notice that upon the attached Affidavit and upon all of the files, records, and proceedings herein and the Court being duly advised in the premises, Plaintiffs, by their attorney, Barbara J. Gislason, will move the above-named Court at the Anoka County Courthouse, in the County of Anoka, State of Minnesota, on the 1st day of March, 2009, at 1:30 p.m. for an Order as follows:

1. Issuing an Order compelling Defendant Animal Finder, Inc. to disclose the current contact information, name, phone number, and address of John and Jane Doe, who have possession of Topper.
2. Determining that withholding information about John and Jane Doe is not permitted pursuant to the Minnesota Rules of Civil Procedure.
3. Permitting other just and equitable relief.

Said Motion will be based upon this Notice and the appended Affidavit of Craig Swanson and Julie Swanson, filed herewith, and upon all the pleadings, files, and records herein in the office of the Clerk of District Court, Anoka County, Minnesota.

2. These pleadings have been modified and do not reveal the actual party names.

All responsive pleadings shall be served and mailed to or filed with the Court Administrator no later than five (5) days prior to the scheduled hearing. The Court may, at its discretion, disregard any responsive pleadings served or filed with the Court Administrator less than five (5) days prior to such hearing in ruling on the Motion or matter in question.

Dated: ______________________________ ______________________________

Barbara J. Gislason
Atty ID No. 124011
Attorney for Plaintiffs
Law Office of Barbara J. Gislason
7362 University Avenue NE
Suite 120
Fridley, MN 55432
Telephone: (763) 5729297

STATE OF MINNESOTA	DISTRICT COURT
COUNTY OF ANOKA	TENTH JUDICIAL DISTRICT
	CIVIL COURT DIVISION
In Re the Matter of:	Court File No. 12345

Craig Swanson and Julie Swanson,

Plaintiff,

AFFIDAVIT OF PLAINTIFFS

and

John and Jane Doe

Defendants.

Craig Swanson and Julie Swanson, being duly sworn upon oath, depose and say:

1. We are the owners of Topper, a five-year-old Terrier, who is like our family member. Many more details are set forth in Plaintiffs' Summons and Complaint, which are on file with this Court and incorporated by reference.
2. We seek the contact information for Defendants John and Jane Doe, who have possession of our dog.
3. Defendants are indebted to Plaintiffs in the amount of $10,000.00 by reasons of the following facts: $10,000.00 for the wrongful detention of Plaintiffs' property.
4. Plaintiffs are lawfully entitled to the immediate possession of that certain personal property which is described as follows: A five-year-old male Terrier that answers to the name of Topper and who has a microchip with the number 123456. Family photographs further demonstrate his identity.
5. We believe a good faith approximation of the current value of the property being claimed is $10,000.00 because of his intrinsic value to our family.
6. Defendants, being in default as set forth above, are wrongfully detaining said property from Plaintiffs.
7. Appendix A, entitled Summons and Complaint, is attached hereto and incorporated by reference.

8. We also believe that in the attached Complaint, we have demonstrated the probability of success on the merits if a replevin action is commenced and that we will be entitled to recover possession of our property.

FURTHER YOUR AFFIANTS SAYETH NOT, except that this Affidavit is made in good faith and for the purposes set forth.

____

Craig Swanson, Plaintiff

Subscribed and sworn to before me
this ________ day of ________________, 2009

____

Notary Public

____

Julie Swanson, Plaintiff

Subscribed and sworn to before me
this ________ day of ________________, 2009

____

Notary Public

STATE OF MINNESOTA	DISTRICT COURT
COUNTY OF ANOKA	TENTH JUDICIAL DISTRICT
	CIVIL COURT DIVISION
In Re the Matter of:	Court File No. 12345

Craig Swanson and Julie Swanson,

Plaintiff,

SUMMONS

and

John and Jane Doe

Defendants.

THE STATE OF MINNESOTA TO THE ABOVE-NAMED DEFENDANTS:

You, and each of you, are hereby summoned and required to serve upon attorney for Plaintiffs, an Answer to the Complaint which is herewith served upon you, and to serve a copy of your Answer to said Complaint on the subscribers at their office, 7362 University Avenue NE, Suite 120, in the City of Fridley, State of Minnesota, within twenty (20) days after service of this Summons upon you, exclusive of the day of service. If you fail to do so, Judgment by Default will be taken against you and each of you for the relief demanded in the Complaint.

ALTERNATIVE DISPUTE RESOLUTION

Please take notice pursuant to Minn. Stat. §543.22 that the Alternative Dispute Resolution process may be available and apply to this proceeding to facilitate possible resolution of the claims set forth herein, through arbitration, mediation, neutral fact finding, settlement conferences, and other procedures more fully described in Rule 114 of the Minnesota General Rules of Practice for the District Courts.

Dated: ______________________________

____

Barbara J. Gislason
Atty ID No. 124011
Attorney for Plaintiffs
Law Office of Barbara J. Gislason
7362 University Avenue NE
Suite 120
Fridley, MN 55432
Telephone: (763) 5729297

STATE OF MINNESOTA
COUNTY OF ANOKA

DISTRICT COURT
TENTH JUDICIAL DISTRICT
CIVIL COURT DIVISION
Court File No. 12345

In Re the Matter of:
Craig Swanson and Julie Swanson,

Plaintiff,

COMPLAINT

and

Animal Finder, Inc., and
Minnesota Animal Retrieval, and
John and Jane Doe,

Defendants.

As and for their Complaint against Defendants, Plaintiffs state and allege as follows:

I.

Plaintiffs Craig Swanson and Julie Swanson (hereinafter "Craig" and "Julie") are residents of the City of Coon Rapids, County of Anoka, State of Minnesota.

II.

Defendant Animal Finder, Inc. is a corporation located at 555 Lost Animal Way, Minneapolis, Minnesota (hereinafter "Corporation").

III.

Defendant Minnesota Animal Retrieval is located at 10 South Street, Wayzata, Minnesota (hereinafter "Animal Control").

IV.

Defendants John and Jane Doe are residents of the State of Minnesota at an address to be determined.

V.

Craig and Julie are the licensed owners of a five-year-old male Terrier named Topper Swanson (hereinafter "Topper"). They reside at 123 West Drive, Coon Rapids, Minnesota.

VI.

The interest the parties have in their dog is the same as the property rights and chattel rights people have in other domestic animals such as cats, horses, and poultry.

VII.

Ownership of domestic animals can be differentiated from the ownership of wild animals, which can be acquired through possession.

VIII.

Plaintiffs continued to own Topper even when he was not under their immediate control.

IX.

Julie Swanson was born in Korea and moved to the United States in 1999 to study the English language. While in Minnesota, she formed a close relationship with her host father, William Johnson of Minneapolis, Minnesota, and was introduced to her future husband, Craig Swanson, by a friend. Julie married Craig on November 21, 2003.

X.

Topper was born on September 29, 2004 and was purchased by Julie and Craig at a pet store in Minneapolis, Minnesota, on or about December 1, 2004. Topper continuously lived with Julie and Craig since he was a puppy, and more recently, with their daughter, Sally Swanson, age two. Topper received excellent care from Julie and Craig. Julie stopped home every day to spend time with him, to pet and play with him, and to give him some brief exercise before picking up her daughter at daycare. Topper rode along in the car to get Sally; Sally was delighted by Topper's company.

XI.

After acquiring Topper in December 2004, Craig and Julie fed him Pets Plus dog food at $24.00 per bag and purchased many items for him, including chew toys, collars, leashes, and soft bedding, as well as routine veterinary care and heartworm treatment. Topper was microchipped and neutered.

XII.

The parties regarded Topper as a precious family member and conscientiously took him on daily walks since he was born, walking him about 25 miles per week. When Craig came home during the course of the evening, he gave Topper more vigorous exercise, taking him to a park for one to two hours, even in cold weather, when Topper would wear a sweater. The parks Craig and Topper frequented most were Sandy Park, South Street Park, and Woodrow Park, although they also walked along the creek and along the Mississippi River. This was great exercise for both Craig, who was in recovery from a disease, and Topper, who was an unusually healthy and muscular dog.

XIII.

Topper, in addition to bed privileges with Julie and Craig at night in their king-sized bed, had two beds of his own, one on the kitchen floor and one on the couch. He also had a blanket. He frequently sat on Julie's lap and she affectionately called him "Teddy Bear." Topper also had a close relationship with Delilah, a Golden Retriever that he played with three or four times a week for a few hours. Delilah belongs to Craig's sister, Melody Swanson.

XIV.

Topper is bilingual and understands both English and Korean. Julie and Craig have taught Topper many behaviors, including how to sit, shake, lay down, play dead, jump (through hoops and over legs), speak, dance, sit up, crawl, kiss, roll over, stay, and come. He also knows hand signals.

XV.

For Topper's protection, Julie paid to have Dr. Alan Johnson, a veterinarian, implant a Home Again microchip in Topper on May 9, 2005 at the We Love Pets Animal Hospital, and she had Topper neutered at the same time. However, at the time Topper was microchipped, Julie was challenged with her English as a second language and failed to understand that her veterinarian would not complete the microchip registration process.

XVI.

Even so, the microchip number implanted in Topper can be traced to Julie and Craig. Topper's registration with Home Again was finally completed on the Home Again website on December 4, 2009.

XVII.

Craig was recovering from a disease and went for continuing treatment in Texas from approximately February 18, 2009 through March 2, 2009. During this treatment, he was to have no contact with the outside world as he was enduring intensive detoxification from the therapy he had undergone. He did not learn that Topper was missing until near the end of his treatment.

XVIII.

Julie lost her Minnesota host father, her best friend, and her grandmother in December 2008 and went to Korea from February 11, 2009 through February 22, 2009 to express sympathy to her loved ones' survivors and to grieve the loss of her loved ones in surroundings where two of them had lived. She also brought her daughter Sally with her to comfort her father, who had lost his wife.

XIX.

When Craig left Minnesota on February 18, 2009, seven days after his wife and daughter went to Korea, he left Topper in the care of his sister, Melody Swanson, and her husband, Leonard Peterson, who reside in Minneapolis, Minnesota. They live adjacent to a large wooded area. This is where Delilah lives, the dog Topper often played with.

XX.

Topper was only going to be with Craig's sister for three days while both parties were gone. Julie's American cell phone did not work in Korea.

XXI.

The evening of February 19, 2009 was unusually cold, and Melody took Topper and her dog, Delilah, into her backyard to relieve themselves. It was then that Topper got away from Melody and became lost. Melody took immediate action to locate Topper, carefully searching in her neighborhood and adjacent neighborhoods. She contacted the local Humane Society and Animal Control the next day and along with her husband, circulated 150 lost pet notices that she created. She also left a voicemail for Julie, then in Korea, notifying her of Topper's disappearance.

XXII.

On February 19, 2009, Topper was found by an Animal Control Officer near Elko, Minnesota, and was transported to Defendant Animal Control.

XXIII.

Pursuant to Minn. Stat. §347.14, subd. 2, an officer with possession of a dog has the obligation to notify the owner, including ascertaining the owner "with reasonable effort."

XXIV.

Although Defendant Animal Control lawfully had temporary possession of Topper, their rights were not superior to the rights of the lawful owners who, together with their friends and family, made substantive and continuing efforts to find him through humane organizations, animal control, numerous searches, distribution of notices, and the posting of notices.

XXV.

Julie returned from Korea on February 22, 2009, three days after Topper was lost, and despite significant jet lag after a 12-hour flight, she immediately went to Animal Control, but Topper was not there. She also attempted to visit the local Humane Society, but it was closed. Julie also searched in the vicinity where Topper disappeared.

XXVI.

On February 23, 2009, Julie's friends helped her call several animal control locations and the police to inquire about Topper, sent emails, left a voicemail message at an animal rescue about him, and also posted a lost pet notice on the Minneapolis area Craig's List and two national databases, Petfinder.com and Fidofinder.com.

XXVII.

On February 23, 2009, Julie traveled to both the Animal Control and Humane Society to look for Topper. She also continued to search for him in the vicinity where he was lost. That same day, another friend, Deb, called the Minneapolis Animal Control looking for Topper. Deb also posted lost pet notices on the Minneapolis area Craig's List, even though this posting was duplicative of an earlier posting.

XXVIII.

Within the next week, Julie, together with friends and family, continued to search for Topper and posted 160 color notices that Julie made at home using PowerPoint. The notices said, "Lost Terrier," and showed that Topper had been missing since February 19, 2009. The notices included three photographs of Topper.

XXIX.

While Julie, together with her friends and family, searched for Topper, he was in the possession of Defendant Animal Control from February 19, 2009 through February 28, 2009.

XXX.

Although a scan was used by Defendant Animal Control to see if Topper had a microchip, the microchip he had was not found.

XXXI.

The only posting Defendant Animal Control did regarding its possession of Topper appeared on its website.

XXXII.

Defendant Animal Control had no ownership or possession rights in Topper. Because Defendant Animal Control never acquired title to Topper, the physical transfer of Topper to Defendant Corporation did not constitute transfer of a valid title.

XXXIII.

While Defendant Animal Control had temporary possession of Topper, Defendant Animal Control failed to provide reasonable notice that they had found a lost dog. Although Defendant Animal Control had posted information about lost dogs before on the national database Petfinder.com, Defendant Animal Control never posted finding Topper on Petfinder.com nor checked Petfinder.com for Topper's lost dog notice.

XXXIV.

Pursuant to Minn. Stat. §347.14, subd. 2, Defendant Animal Control should have posted written notice in at least three public places regarding its possession of

Topper. The only notice Defendant Animal Control posted was on its own website. Posting information about Topper on its website did not constitute a reasonable posting and violated Plaintiffs' constitutional due process rights. Said behavior by Defendant Animal Control also violated 42 U.S.C. 1983.

XXXV.

At the time Topper was delivered from Defendant Animal Control to Defendant Corporation, information about Topper had been available for one week on three national websites. The lost dog date on these websites corresponded with Topper's pickup date by Defendant Animal Control. The internet postings described Topper and stated that he was a five-year-old male Terrier.

XXXVI.

On February 28, 2009, Defendant Corporation, a non-profit corporation, assumed possession of Topper.

XXXVII.

Defendant Corporation had no title to Topper, was in illegal possession of him, and was subject to this Court's injunctive powers of Replevin. Plaintiffs continued to have ownership and possession rights in Topper.

XXXVIII.

While Defendant Animal Control and Defendant Corporation may assert there was an effective transfer of ownership, and that they have an opportunity to prove their claim in court, their disagreement with Plaintiffs was not sufficient to assert privilege or confidentiality concerning Defendants John and Jane Doe.

XXXIX.

Since the transfer of possession of Topper from Defendant Animal Control to Defendant Corporation to Defendants John and Jane Doe, Plaintiffs retained the exclusive ownership of Topper. No ownership rights transferred from Plaintiffs to any Defendant at any time.

XL.

On February 29, 2009, Defendant Corporation posted the availability of Topper for adoption on its website.

XLI.

On February 29, 2009, Defendant Corporation posted the availability of Topper for adoption on the Petfinder.com website.

XLII.

Prior to posting Topper's availability for adoption on the internet, Defendant Corporation failed to check three major registries that clearly described a five-year-old male Terrier who disappeared on February 19, 2009, including Petfinder.com, where Topper had been listed since February 23, 2009. As stated above, Defendant Corporation was well-aware of Petfinder.com as it had posted information about Topper there on February 29, 2009.

XLIII.

Defendant Corporation was aware, at all times relevant to this proceeding, that it is a common practice for people with lost animals to post information about them on national websites. Defendant Corporation itself has an internet website that, among other information, provides an updated count on how many dogs it has placed.

XLIV.

From February 28, 2009, when Defendant Corporation took possession of Topper, until March 2, 2009, when they delivered possession of Topper to Defendants John and Jane Doe, they failed to look for Topper's rightful owners on any of these three national sites: Craig's List, Petfinder.com, and Fidofinder.com.

XLV.

Defendants John and Jane Doe had no title and they were in illegal possession of Topper. They are subject to the court granting to Plaintiffs the exclusive power of replevin.

XLVI.

Defendant Corporation's website contains no disclosure that it made any reasonable inquiries for the rightful owners of pets in its possession prior to listing them for adoption on its website.

XLVII.

On March 4, 2009, Plaintiff Craig Swanson, back from rehabilitation treatment, spoke to his dog's veterinarian, Dr. Alan Johnson, at the We Love Pets Animal

Hospital, and learned that the microchip that was implanted in Topper was microchip number 123456. If Defendant Corporation had contacted Dr. Alan Johnson to inquire about which dog the microchip number belonged to, the veterinarian would have been able to give Craig the name of Defendant Corporation on March 4, 2009 when Craig called Dr. Johnson.

XLVIII.

After securing Topper's microchip number, Plaintiff Craig Swanson called the microchip manufacturer, Home Again, to check on Topper's registration information. It was then that he learned that a Certified Veterinary Technician named Christopher, who worked at Northland Animal Hospital, had scanned Topper's microchip. The Home Again agent gave Craig the phone number of the Northland Animal Hospital.

XLIX.

Craig then contacted Christopher and obtained the name of an individual and the number of the organization that had brought Topper to that hospital. Although Craig understood that Christopher would ask someone from this rescue group number to call him, when a call was not forthcoming, Craig called this number directly, only to learn it was a cat line, not a dog line.

L.

Craig then called the dog line and spoke to a woman who identified herself as Allison. Craig provided to Allison the details about Topper, including his microchip number. Allison informed Craig that Topper had been adopted out on March 2, 2009 and she said she would provide Craig's phone number to the people who adopted Topper. No one ever called Craig, so he went on the internet and was able to ascertain that the phone number he was calling belonged to Defendant Corporation. Feeling that Allison would not contact the adoptees, Craig and Julie decided to write an email describing their situation in more detail. They hoped to present their case without being cut off.

LI.

On March 5, 2009, Matthew Robinson, an employee of Defendant Corporation, sent Julie an email saying that Topper had been adopted on March 2, 2009 to a "good forever home." Matthew further stated, "I am sorry for your loss, but unless the new legal owners decide they can't keep him, which I doubt will ever happen, he will stay with them for the rest of his life."

LII.

Furthermore, Defendant Corporation was well-aware of the website Petfinder.com as Matthew disclosed to Craig's sister, Melody, on March 5, 2009 that Defendant Corporation posted that Topper was available for adoption on Petfinder.com on February 28, 2009.

LIII.

Matthew also claimed that Defendant Corporation had rescued Topper from "death row," but made no offer to find out if the new owners, who had only had Topper for five days, would return Topper. Matthew falsely communicated to Julie and Craig that Topper was on death row because he knew that Defendant Animal Control did not in fact euthanize dogs.

LIV.

On March 6, 2009, Julie wrote to the President of Defendant Corporation on behalf of her family indicating that she was writing to her because "you are our last hope, help me get my dog back."

LV.

On March 8, 2009, Julie and Craig received an email response from Matthew clarifying that John and Jane Doe would not return Topper to them, and he provided an attachment of a city ordinance that addressed hold periods and animal destruction. Said ordinance did not describe the statutory duty of Defendant Animal Control to reasonably post information about found animals nor described Plaintiffs' constitutional due process rights.

LVI.

Pursuant to *Smith v. St. Paul City,* 82 N.W. 577 (Minn. 1900), a municipal ordinance authorizing a police officer to destroy a dog not wearing a collar does not authorize a third party to kill the animal or relieve a third party from damages from lawful destruction. The logic of this case can be extended to possession but it is not equivalent to a third party having authority to transfer title of a dog.

LVII.

Defendant Animal Control may claim that Plaintiffs lost their legal right to Topper pursuant to the city running at large ordinance. Although said ordinance gives the "county dog catcher" the right to hold, and later, destroy, a dog, said ordinance does not give the "county dog catcher" the authority to pass title to a dog.

LVIII.

The city ordinance also requires that if the owner is known, the owner must be notified of the abandonment.

LIX.

Any claim by Defendants that Topper was abandoned must be proved by unequivocal claims and decisive evidence.

LX.

Critical to the determination of an abandonment claim is evidence of actual intent to relinquish or part with the rights or rights claimed to be abandoned.

LXI.

"Abandoned property is property to which the owner has relinquished all rights, title, claim, and possession, with intention of not reclaiming it..." *Black's Law Dictionary 13 (rev. 4th ed 1968).*

LXII.

There has been no clear and convincing evidence that Plaintiffs intended to relinquish all right, title, or claim to Topper.

LXIII.

Determining the obligation to reasonably conclude the identification of an owner has changed with advancement in technology, including the emergence of well-known national registries such as Petfinder.com that gained notoriety following Hurricane Katrina. It is now easier to find the owners of lost dogs by simply checking national registries.

LXIV.

Plaintiffs' dog was listed on Petfinder.com, Fidofinder.com, and Craig's List as of February 23, 2009, long before Defendant Animal Control transferred him to Defendant Corporation or Defendant Corporation attempted to transfer title and possession of Topper to Defendants John and Jane Doe.

LXV.

Contained within the burden of Plaintiffs' property interests in Topper are present and future possession and ownership rights, as well as claims for rents and profits. Their interests may be possessive in whatever fashion or degree and under whatever conditions the fee simple owner desires.

LXVI.

Plaintiffs' monetary claim will increase if Topper is not returned, forcing Plaintiffs to incur additional attorney's fees and costs for delay.

COUNT ONE: REPLEVIN

LXVII.

Based upon the above, Plaintiffs seek the return of their personal property through an action in Replevin.

LXVIII.

Plaintiffs re-allege paragraphs I through LXVI above.

COUNT TWO: UNJUST ENRICHMENT

LXIX.

Plaintiffs seek the return of their dog based upon the fact that they have expended time and resources in training their dog and provided him with food and care, and that Defendants' possession of said animal constitutes unjust enrichment.

LXX.

Plaintiffs re-allege paragraphs I through LXVI above.

COUNT THREE: NEGLIGENT INFLICTION OF EMOTIONAL DISTRESS

LXXI.

Plaintiffs have a very close emotional bond to their property, chattel, and family dog, named Topper.

LXXII.

Plaintiffs re-allege paragraphs I through LXVI above.

Wherefore, Plaintiffs demand Judgment against Defendants as follows:

1. Ordering and directing such relief as may be appropriate pursuant to Minnesota Statutes Annotated Sec. 325D.45, including, but not limited to, damages, costs, disbursements, and interest.
2. Granting judgment in favor of Plaintiffs for all other claims in an amount in excess of Twenty-Five Thousand Dollars and No/100 ($25,000.00), together with reasonable costs and disbursements.
3. For such other relief the Court deems just and equitable under the circumstances.

Dated: ______________________________ ______________________________

Barbara J. Gislason
Atty ID No. 124011
Attorney for Plaintiffs
Law Office of Barbara J. Gislason
7362 University Avenue NE
Suite 120
Fridley, MN 55432
Telephone: (763) 5729297

Appendix 4

Animal Seizure Memorandum of Law

For decades, those familiar with animal cruelty and abuse proceedings were aware that while defendants were afforded their constitutional due process rights, the needs of their seized companion animals were often unmet and costly. Seized animals, spared from euthanasia, languished in limbo while their treating veterinarians were uncertain of what quality of services to provide.[1]

In recent years, lawyers in several states, concerned about the plight of these animals, crafted and developed very traditional legal arguments to help re-home them. Retired Pepper Hamilton attorney, J. Gregg Miller, was one lawyer who rolled up his sleeves. He was kind to provide a current and redacted exemplar of his work below.

MEMORANDUM OF LAW IN SUPPORT OF THE PETITION OF THE PENNSYLVANIA SOCIETY FOR THE PREVENTION OF CRUELTY TO ANIMALS ("PSPCA") TO ESTABLISH THE PSPCA'S OWNERSHIP OF CERTAIN ANIMALS THAT HAVE BEEN SUBJECTED TO ANIMAL CRUELTY AND HAVE BEEN ABANDONED

The Petitioner herein, The Pennsylvania Society for the Prevention of Cruelty to Animals ("PSPCA"), by and through its attorneys, J. Gregg Miller, Esquire, Jessica A. Rickabaugh, Esquire, and Kristopher Berr, Esquire, hereby files the within Memorandum of Law in Support of the Petition of The Pennsylvania Society for

1. In 2016, when the Oregon courts began recognizing animals as crime victims, this recognition was effectively breaking news in law schools across the country.

the Prevention of Cruelty to Animals ("PSPCA") to Establish the PSPCA's Ownership of Certain Animals that have been Subjected to Animal Cruelty and have been Abandoned.

STATEMENT OF FACTS

Petitioner, The Pennsylvania Society for the Prevention of Cruelty to Animals ("PSPCA"), is a Pennsylvania non-profit corporation whose headquarters are located at 350 East Erie Avenue, Philadelphia, Pennsylvania 19134.

The PSPCA is organized, in part, to receive and investigate criminal complaints of animal cruelty, abuse, neglect or abandonment, and to prosecute suspects under the Animal Cruelty Law, 18 Pa. C.S.A. §5511.

The Humane Society Police Officers ("HSPOs") maintained by the PSPCA are empowered to enforce the Animal Cruelty Law, 18 Pa. C.S.A. §5511, by virtue of statutory authority conferred upon said Society's officers upon the satisfaction of various criteria, 22 Pa. C.S. §§ 3704, 3705 and 18 Pa. C.S.A. §5511(i):

> POWER TO INITIATE CRIMINAL PROCEEDINGS. An agent of any society or association for the prevention of cruelty to animals, incorporated under the laws of the Commonwealth, shall have the same powers to initiate criminal proceedings provided for police officers by the Pennsylvania Rules of Criminal Procedure.

The HSPOs are also authorized by the Dog Law, 3 P.S. §459-102, to perform "Dog Control," which includes "apprehending, holding and disposing of stray or unwanted dogs." All nine (9) of the animals that are the subject of this Petition are dogs.

The HSPO involved in the investigation that is described in this Petition was authorized and commissioned within Philadelphia and was sworn in by the Court of Common Pleas of Philadelphia County.

The primary mission of the PSPCA with respect to animals in their possession is to safely house, feed, care for, treat, provide elective veterinary care (such as sterilization) and to adopt out to loving families such animals. The PSPCA also has the power to euthanize animals under certain circumstances, but the greatly preferred alternative is to adopt out the animals to loving families. To adopt out the animals, the PSPCA needs clear title and ownership of the animals that are the subject of this Petition, and termination of any right, title and interest that the respondent may have had in these animals.

During the past year, the PSPCA's Humane Society Police Officer investigated a complaint of animal cruelty, neglect and abandonment that was alleged by a third party against the respondent(s).

In this case, nine (9) animals were recovered by the HSPO from premises owned or inhabited by the respondent(s) pursuant to authority contained in

§5511(l), which authorizes a Humane Society Police Officer to obtain a search warrant and to seize an animal that is subject to animal cruelty, including abandonment, and to take it to the PSPCA for care and treatment. In this case, a search warrant was obtained before the animals were taken.

As set forth in the affidavit of Humane Society Police Officer Jason Martinez that is attached as Exhibit A to the Petition, each of the animals that are the subject of this Petition was subjected to animal cruelty and was abandoned in violation of Pennsylvania law. 18 Pa. C.S.A. §5511(c) and 3 P.S. §459-601(c).

The PSPCA has provided veterinary care, food and shelter for the animals that were alive. Such care is expensive. The PSPCA should not be expected to continue to care for the animals for the rest of their lives, when adoption is a better alternative for both the animal and the PSPCA. The PSPCA wishes to put the animals up for adoption to a good home. However, in order to adopt out the animals, the PSPCA must have ownership of the animals in order to convey good title to an adoptive family, free and clear of any later claim of ownership by the respondent. It is for this reason that the within Petition has been filed with the Court.

ARGUMENT

In this case, the animals were subjected to animal cruelty at the hands of one or both of the respondent(s), which is a crime under 18 Pa. C.S.A. 5511(c). However, as indicated in the attached affidavit, the defendant has fled, thereby avoiding conviction for its crimes and forfeiture of the animals by statute, 18 Pa. C.S.A. 5511(m).

At this time, the PSPCA is entitled to ownership of the animals because (i) the animals have been abandoned, (ii) the PSPCA has spent, and continues to spend on a daily basis, time, effort and money in the housing, care, feeding and maintenance of the animals for which it has a statutory lien, and (iii) the respondent has been accorded ample due process of law with respect to any rights it may have had in the animals.

THE ANIMALS HAVE BEEN ABANDONED, AND THE PSPCA MAY TAKE TITLE TO THEM

In the above case, the animals were abandoned by their owner. In Pennsylvania, “abandonment” is a crime under both the Animal Cruelty Law, 18 Pa. C.S.A. §5511(c) and under the Pennsylvania Dog Law, 3 P.S. §429-601(c). Under Pennsylvania law, a dog is personal property. Dog Law, 3 P.S. §429-601(a). Specifically, the Dog Law §459-601 provides, in pertinent part, as follows:

> (a) DOGS TO BE PERSONAL PROPERTY.—All dogs are hereby declared to be personal property and subjects of theft.

(c) ABANDONMENT OF ANIMALS BY OWNER.—

(1) It shall be unlawful for any person to abandon or attempt to abandon any dog within the Commonwealth. Anyone convicted of abandoning or attempting to abandon any dog within the Commonwealth shall pay a fine of not less than $300.00 and not more than $1,000.00, plus costs.

Under well-established principles of Pennsylvania law, if property is abandoned, then a third party (in this case the PSPCA) may claim ownership of such property. Under Pennsylvania law, cats are also personal property, Neefe v. Neefe, 16 Just. 16 (1900); The Cat and the Law, 12 Temple L.Q. 89 (1937). Wild animals are not subject to ownership until reduced to actual possession, custody or control, at which time such animals become personal property. 1 Pennsylvania Law Encyclopedia—Second Edition, "Property" §1. Reptiles and fish sold by pet stores, such as snakes, alligators, turtles and goldfish, are considered personal property. Therefore, the animals that are included in this Petition are personal property subject to abandonment under Pennsylvania law.

Under Pennsylvania law, property may be abandoned if there is "an actual and voluntary relinquishment of possession and ownership," in which case "the property ceases to be the property of any person and becomes the subject of appropriation by the first taker." 39 Pennsylvania Law Encyclopedia—Second Edition, "Property" § 31. In Fidelity-Philadelphia Trust Co. v. Lehigh Valley Coal Co., 294 Pa. 47, 143 A. 474 (1928), the Pennsylvania Supreme Court held that a decedent had abandoned and relinquished all title and interest in a culm bank when he deposited the culm on land owned by another person, the culm was valueless, and for an extended period of time the decedent exercised no dominion over the culm and failed to prohibit others from taking from the culm bank. In Calhoon v. Neely, 201 Pa. 97, 50 A. 967 (1902), the Pennsylvania Supreme Court held that a lessee had abandoned an oil and gas lease which had a 15-year term when, after drilling a test well and finding no oil, the lessee removed its equipment and abandoned the site for 9 years. Then, a third-party drilled successfully, and the initial lessee returned, becoming "active at the sight of oil flowing from wells drilled by others." The Court held that the initial lessee had abandoned the lease, stating:

> Abandonment is a question of fact to be determined by the acts and intentions of the parties. An unexplained cessation of operations for the period involved in this case gives rise to a fair presumption of abandonment and, standing alone and admitted, would justify the court in declaring an abandonment as a matter of law.

More recently, the Pennsylvania Superior Court has held that a man abandoned a shotgun to the chief of police when he asked the chief to destroy or otherwise dispose of the gun, Commonwealth v. Wetmore, 301 Pa. Super. 370; 447 A.2d 1012 (Pa. Super. 1982). The U.S. Bankruptcy Court for the Eastern District of

Pennsylvania has held that a coal company abandoned a quantity of silt that contained some coal after it deposited the silt on property owned by a third-party, did not segregate or mark the silt deposit, and did not claim an interest in the silt for an extended period of time, In re: G.M.P. Land Company, 33 B.R. 729 (Bankr. E. D. Pa. 1983).

In the instant case, the respondent has abandoned its animals by fleeing the premises, leaving the animals behind, and failing to claim them or otherwise respond to notices from a Humane Society Police Officer of the Pennsylvania SPCA. Under these circumstances, the Pennsylvania SPCA is entitled not only to seize the animals but also to become their owner.

In addition to the foregoing general principles of Pennsylvania law regarding abandonment, the Dog Law provides at 3 P.S. §459-102 the following definitions:

> "ABANDON." To forsake entirely or neglect or refuse to provide or perform the legal obligations for the care and support of an animal by its owner or its agent.
>
> "ABANDONMENT." Relinquishment of all rights and claims to an animal by its owner.

When taken together, these definitions indicate that, in circumstances where an animal owner will "neglect or refuse to provide or perform the legal obligations for the care and support of" its animal, then the animal will be deemed "abandoned;" and the consequence of such "abandonment" will be the "relinquishment of all rights and claims to" the animal by its owner. Thus, pursuant to the Dog Law and Neefe v. Neefe, the respondent in this case has "abandoned" his animals by failing to provide the legal obligations of care and support that he owed to such animals. As a consequence of such "abandonment," he has relinquished all rights and claims to such animals pursuant to the Pennsylvania Dog Law, 3 P.S. §459-102 and Neefe v. Neefe. Therefore, the PSPCA may properly assume ownership of the animals, may take over the obligations of care and support, and may dispose of them as it decides best, preferring adoption over euthanasia.

THE ANIMALS ARE SUBJECT TO A LIEN FOR THE COSTS AND EXPENSES OF THE PSPCA WHICH ARE PAYABLE BY THE RESPONDENT; AND IT IS INEQUITABLE TO BURDEN THE PSPCA WITH ONGOING COSTS AND EXPENSES WHEN THE MORE FAVORED ALTERNATIVE OF ADOPTION IS AVAILABLE.

The costs and expenses that the PSPCA has incurred with respect to each of the animals gives the PSPCA both an equitable right to the animals and a legal claim to the animals. The Animal Cruelty Law provides that the PSPCA has a lien on the animals in the amount of the costs and expenses that the PSPCA has incurred in housing, caring for and feeding the animals in each case where, as here, a search warrant is obtained before the animal is seized and removed to the PSPCA for care and shelter, 18 Pa. C.S.A. 5511(l):

> SEARCH WARRANTS.—Where a violation of this section is alleged, any issuing authority may, in compliance with the applicable provisions of the Pennsylvania Rules of Criminal Procedure, issue to any police officer or any agent of any society or association for the prevention of cruelty to animals duly incorporated under the laws of this Commonwealth a search warrant authorizing the search of any building or any enclosure in which any violation of this section is occurring or has occurred, and authorizing the seizure of evidence of the violation including, but not limited to the animals which were the subject of the violation. Where an animal thus seized is found to be neglected or starving, the police officer or agent is authorized to provide such care as is reasonably necessary, and where an animal thus seized is found to be disabled, injured or diseased beyond reasonable hope of recovery, the police officer or agent is authorized to provide for the humane destruction of the animal. The cost of the keeping, care and destruction of the animal shall be paid by the owner thereof and claims for the costs shall constitute a lien upon the animal. (Emphasis added.)

In view of the extended time periods during which the PSPCA has cared for the animals that are the subject of this Petition, the costs and expenses exceed the market value of the animals. Therefore, the animals are unlikely to be reclaimed by the respondent. If respondent did try to reclaim the animals, it would be unable to do so unless it first paid the PSPCA the dollar value of the costs and expenses that have been incurred by the PSPCA and which constitute a lien on each of the animals 18 Pa. C.S.A. 5511(l). The PSPCA submits that it is inequitable to burden the PSPCA with ongoing costs to care for the animals when they could be adopted by responsible families.

THE RESPONDENT HAS BEEN ACCORDED DUE PROCESS OF LAW.

The Pennsylvania SPCA's operating procedures require its Humane Society Police Officers to search for missing animal owners as follows:

(i) check U.S. Post Office for forwarding address;

(ii) check with neighbors and relatives, if any, for current location or forwarding address;

(iii) check jail records if neighbors or relatives indicate that the missing owner is in jail.

The Humane Society Police Officer checked with neighbors and sent a certified letter to attempt to locate the missing owner who is the respondent in this matter.

The U.S. Constitution's Due Process Clause requires that a person whose property is being taken be provided with notice and opportunity to respond. Cleveland Board of Education v. Loudermill, 470 US 532 (1984). Also, the Pennsylvania Supreme Court has held that the basic elements of procedural due process are adequate notice, the opportunity to be heard, and the chance to defend oneself before a fair and impartial tribunal. Commonwealth of Pennsylvania vs. Wright, 599 Pa. 270, 293, 961 A.2d 119, 132 (2008); Commonwealth of Pennsylvania vs. Clayton, 546 Pa. 342, 351, 684 A.2d 1060, 1064 (1996); Parker vs. Kensington Hospital, 483 Pa. 106, 130, 394 A.2d 932, 945 (1978). This legal principle applies in connection with the taking and disposition of animals. Commonwealth v. Gonzalez, 403 Pa. Super. 157, 588 A.2d 528 (1991); but see, Commonwealth v. Barnes, 427 Pa. Super. 326, 629 A.2d 123 (1993).

The respondent has been accorded ample notice and an opportunity to claim its animal(s). The respondent has failed to do so. Now, the within Petition is being served on the respondent at its last known address from which the animals in question were removed by the PSPCA. Service of the Petition provides the respondent with a final notice and opportunity to be heard in Court. Under all the circumstances of the case, the respondent has been accorded ample due process of law.

CONCLUSION

Based on the foregoing authority, this Court should establish ownership in the PSPCA of the animals that are the subject of this Petition, so that the PSPCA may fulfill its mission by putting the animals up for adoption by a caring family.

The Pennsylvania Society for the Prevention of Cruelty to Animals respectfully requests an order of this Court establishing its ownership in the animals that are the subject of the within Petition.

Appendix 5

Companion Animal Custody and Ownership Family Law Statute Amendment: Model Language

When making a decision about the award of custody and ownership of a companion animal, the court shall consider the best interests of the companion animal. The court may also consider and determine the weight of the following factors: the best interests of all concerned, property claims, contractual claims, possessory claims, and claims based upon the operation of law.

If the parties have reached an agreement about an award of joint custody and ownership or a time-sharing arrangement, the court may enter an order based upon this agreement as long as the parties have demonstrated that the arrangement would be in the best interests of the companion animal and the parties have shown an ability to cooperate and have agreed to a sufficiently detailed and reasonable conflict resolution plan.

This plan shall address welfare standards, veterinary and dental insurance and uninsured expenses, the maintaining of appropriate liability, homeowner's, and renter's insurance, and how expense and cost-sharing decisions would be made. The agreement shall address how conflicts about the mistreatment of the companion animal, or problems that might arise if the companion animal became loose or displayed emotional problems, behavioral problems, or dangerous propensities, would be resolved.

Nothing in this statute shall be construed to apply to a service animal.

Appendix 6

Pet Custody Statutory Provisions[1]

The purpose of appendix 6, compared to appendix 5, is to consider what language might be included in a longer form pet custody statute. Think of this appendix as examples of provisions that could be utilized rather than a statute itself.

Challenges to bringing a long form model statute to the next level include the following:

1. What factors should be considered?
2. Which presumptions of ownership, if any, should be rebuttable?
3. What standard of proof should apply?
4. How would third-party interests be addressed?
5. Under what circumstances should any presumption of ownership be nullified based upon public policy reasons?
6. Should equitable principles apply?

WORK IN PROGRESS

Definitions.

"Owner" is the person who holds legal title to a companion animal as property. An owner would include a person who (1) lawfully purchased a companion animal, (2) adopted a companion animal from a title holding entity, (3) received a

1. The court in Alaska is now required to take "into consideration the well-being of the animal." Karen Brulliard, *In A First, Alaska Divorce Courts Will Now Treat Pets More Like Children*, The Washington Post, https://www.google.com/amp/s/www.washingtonpost.com/amphtml/news/animalia/wp/2017/01/24/in-a-first-alaska-divorce-courts-will-now-treat-pets-more-like-children/ (last visited May 12, 2017).

companion animal as a gift, (4) otherwise received title through the operation of law, or (5) was awarded good title in a legal proceeding.

"Presumption of Ownership" means that if the parties entered into a prenuptial agreement, marital agreement, co-habitation agreement, partnership agreement, or other written agreement regarding the ownership of an animal, the rights granted in said agreement would be presumptive.

"Primary Caregiver" is the person who provides day-to-day care of the companion animal's basic needs.

"Extraordinary Care" is the care provided to an animal due to an injury, disease, or significant need.

"Guardian" is a person who has assumed, by operation of law, certain elevated owner responsibilities as defined by a statute or ordinance.

"Domestic Animal" is an animal that has been domesticated and would include, but not be limited to, dogs, cats, horses, rabbits, ferrets, birds, small mammals, small reptiles, pigs, cows, chickens, and fish.

"Companion Animal" is a domesticated animal whose physical, emotional, behavioral, and social needs can be achieved as a companion in a home or who has a close daily relationship with a human wherein they keep each other company. Criteria for identifying a companion animal include the following:

- Purchased or acquired to be a family pet
- Provides companionship
- Has a name
- Provides no significant source of income
- Receives appropriate food, water, shelter, and veterinary care
- Is bonded to a family member
- Is held out as a pet or companion animal
- Lives indoors
- Owner describes himself or herself as "mom" or "dad"
- Image appears in family photographs, including on social media
- Image is reflected on a computer or cell phone screen saver
- Name is included in family listings
- Acts like a pet
- Brings pleasure
- Provides protection
- Has a guardian
- Is treated kindly and affectionately

Criteria for animals that might not be considered companion animals include the following:

- Not regularly fed
- Not domesticated
- Not named
- Not bonded to a family member
- Sleeps outside
- Not properly cared for
- Used for sports, entertainment, or performance
- Used for research purposes
- Primary purpose is breeding
- Is a service animal
- Performs work
- Is not permitted under federal or state laws

"Commercial Value" is fair market value.

"Relational Value" is the value of an animal to a human based on emotional bonds, attachment, or love.

"Governmental Title Holding Entity" is an entity that has received good title to a companion animal after satisfying requisite hold periods, or following a legal forfeiture or other operation of law.[2]

"Animal Abuse" or "Cruelty" is an action by an individual that causes a domestic animal to suffer because of negligent, reckless, and intentional acts, including (1) the failure to provide for basic needs, including adequate food, water, veterinary care, exercise, and shelter; and (2) engaging in behaviors that endanger the animal's physical or emotional well-being, including yelling, kicking, punching, throwing, or causing physical injury, unreasonable fear, or death.

"Legal Proceeding" is the initiation of an action or procedure in a court of law for the purposes of acquiring a benefit, interest, right, or enforceable remedy.

"Sole Custodian" is a human awarded sole custody and ownership of a companion animal.

"Joint Custodian" is a human awarded joint custody, joint ownership, or co-ownership of a companion animal.

"Financial Contribution" is a reasonable contribution to the cost of the companion animal's necessary licenses, grooming, training, veterinary and dental insurance, and uninsured veterinary and dental expenses, including medication. The cost of food, shelter, daycare, barn, trainers, behaviorists, and other care by third parties consistent with an established standard of living may also serve as the basis for financial contribution.

2. A typical title holding entity is animal control.

"Custodial Responsibility" means the duty to provide for the companion animal's welfare and includes the provisions of food, water, shelter, veterinary care, exercise, protection of the companion animal from harm, and compliance with state laws and ordinances.

"Access or Visitation" is the schedule or plan for the non-custodian to have time with the companion animal. The same idea can be expressed using the terminology "Pet Time."

"Access or Visitation Responsibilities" means the duty of the person granted access or visitation to provide food, water, shelter, veterinary care, exercise, protection of the companion animal from harm, prevention of the companion animal from causing harm, and compliance with state laws and ordinances.

"Third Party" is a party who has a contractual right or interest in a companion animal that is the subject of a pet custody dispute.

"Rights to Possession" are based upon any contractual or court-ordered custody or access schedule.

"Third-Party Rights" are the rights to enforce contractual rights.

"Human Best Interests" are the disposition that would most benefit one or more humans.

"Human Best Interest Factors" would include, but not be limited to, companionship, human/animal bond, lowered blood pressure, prolonged life expectancy, promotion of academic performance, decreased depression, alleviation of anxiety, impact on disease processes, reduction of arthritic inflammation, exercise opportunities, a sense of well-being, and happiness.

"Animal Bond" is an emotional bond between a companion animal and another.

"Animal Best Interests" are the disposition that would most benefit the companion animal involved.

"Animal Best Interest Factors" would include, but not be limited to, companionship, standard of living, quality of care, animal/human bond, animal/animal bond, survival, and absence of maltreatment, abuse, or cruelty.

"Special Activities" means the inclusion of the companion animal in special activities, including, but not limited to, competitions, agility training, therapy work, and hunting.

"Alternative Dispute Resolution (ADR)" refers to methods of resolving disputes outside of the courtroom.

"Alternative Dispute Resolution (ADR) Methods" include mediation, early neutral evaluation, negotiation, arbitration, and collaborative processes.

"Exception to Finality of Judgment" means the court has jurisdiction to modify custody or access if animal mistreatment, abuse, or cruelty has occurred or if there has been a material breach of contract.

"Duty to Participate in Alternative Dispute Resolution (ADR) Processes" means that if the joint custodian or sole custodian and individual with access or visitation rights have a conflict, they have a duty to engage in an ADR process in good faith before seeking recourse in the court. Duty to participate in ADR does not apply if domestic abuse, animal mistreatment, abuse, or cruelty is alleged and is being addressed in an appropriate legal forum.

"Decision-Making Criteria" means all the factors the court may consider in making a determination regarding pet custody, ownership, and guardianship, as well as visitation or access.

WORK IN PROGRESS

Determination—General.

When making a determination about pet custody and ownership, the court must consider the best interests of the companion animal. The court may also utilize the following factors as decision-making criteria with regard to the subjects of sole custody, joint custody, and access:

Property and Contract Criteria

- Ownership claims
- Possessory claims
- Third-party rights and interests
- Circumstances of acquisition
- Expenditure history
- Legal presumptions

Applicable History

- Duration of the relationship
- Quality of the relationship
- Provision of primary care
- Provision of extraordinary care
- Animal's standard of living
- Animal's involvement in and enthusiasm for special activities
- Bond between companion animal and others
- Conflicts with others
- Services provided by the companion animal to others
- Administrative and legal proceedings
- Ability of the companion animal to travel
- Determination if joint custody or access advocated

- Injuries sustained by or inflicted upon the companion animal
- History of animal mistreatment, abuse, or cruelty

<u>Demonstrated Commitment to Companion Animal</u>

- Willingness to continue or improve the companion animal's standard of living
- Commitment to keep the companion animal from getting loose
- Commitment to address behavioral, veterinary, and dental needs
- Willingness to cooperate with an access or visitation schedule and standards of care
- Ability to cooperate on major health care and dental decisions
- Ability to meet financial obligations for the quality care of the companion animal
- Willingness to be held accountable for financial contributions
- Recognition of liability risks posed and commitment to maintain appropriate liability insurance

<u>ADR Processes</u>

- Likelihood of commitment to use ADR processes
- Quality of ideas for dispute resolution
- Reasonableness of a proposed schedule
- Commitment to geographic area
- Past use of ADR processes

WORK IN PROGRESS

Continuing Jurisdiction.

The court retains jurisdiction to make further orders, as it deems just and proper, concerning:

- The sole custody or ownership of a companion animal
- The joint custody or ownership of a companion animal
- Access to a companion animal

WORK IN PROGRESS

Notice Requirements.

The court may want to utilize the following notice requirements:

- The right to know about a dangerous dog proceeding
- Updates on the companion animal's veterinary care
- The right to know if the animal is in an accident or has a serious medical or dental condition or injury
- Death of the companion animal

Appendix 7

Joint Custody and Joint Ownership Agreement

This agreement is between Tatum Thompson, who resides at Springfield, Maine (hereinafter referred to as "Tatum"), and Logan Longview, who resides at Manchester, Maine (hereinafter referred to as "Logan"). This agreement pertains to a male Husky dog named Peyton (hereinafter referred to as "Peyton").

WHEREAS, Tatum purchased Peyton on May 1, 2015, for the sum of $2,000.00; and

WHEREAS, Peyton is not subject to any lien, security interest, or encumbrance; and

WHEREAS, Logan moved in with Tatum and Peyton on June 1, 2015; and

WHEREAS, Tatum and Logan each paid one-half of the lease and utility payments where they lived from June 1, 2015, through one month before the execution of this agreement; and

WHEREAS, on August 1, 2015, Logan assumed the primary care of Peyton due to Tatum's out-of-town business demands; and

WHEREAS, Tatum has primarily paid for Peyton's food, toys, and training; and

WHEREAS, Logan has primarily paid for Peyton's veterinary insurance and uninsured veterinary expenses, including prescription medications; and

WHEREAS, Tatum and Logan desire that Peyton undergo a veterinary examination twice a year; and

WHEREAS, Tatum and Logan desire that Peyton's teeth are brushed every morning and Peyton's coat is brushed every evening; and

WHEREAS, Peyton is current on his rabies vaccine and takes heartworm medication and other medications recommended by Peyton's veterinarian and has also been neutered; and

WHEREAS, Tatum and Logan desire that appropriate medications continue to be purchased for and given to Peyton; and

WHEREAS, Peyton has a microchip; and

WHEREAS, Tatum and Logan realize that it is likely that Peyton will have substantial veterinary costs in the future given the propensity of Peyton's breed to develop hip problems and cancer; and

WHEREAS, Peyton's veterinary records have accurately listed both Tatum and Logan as Peyton's co-owners since August 15, 2015; and

WHEREAS, Peyton's annual license had been in Logan's name, and paid by Logan, since 2015; and

WHEREAS, Peyton has enjoyed daily morning and evening walks of at least one mile per day and Tatum and Logan desire that this level of exercise continue; and

WHEREAS, Peyton has been socialized, in part, by going with Tatum and Logan to a dog park at least twice a week and both desire that these types of socialization efforts continue; and

WHEREAS, Peyton has slept with Tatum's Siamese cat since Peyton was a puppy; and

WHEREAS, Peyton has spent considerable time with Logan's four-year-old daughter, who is disabled, and both Tatum and Logan agree that Peyton helps reduce this girl's anxiety; and

WHEREAS, Tatum and Logan's neighbors have called animal control twice when Peyton became loose during social gatherings at their home; and

WHEREAS, Tatum and Logan are aware that because Peyton is a large and muscular dog, if Peyton becomes loose again, it is foreseeable that there will be a reportable incident; and

WHEREAS, Tatum and Logan each recognize the importance of developing and implementing a safety plan with an agreed-upon expert at each of their new homes so that Peyton may enjoy a high quality of life; and

WHEREAS, Tatum and Logan recognize the importance of providing Peyton with ongoing behavioral training and of each having liability insurance that covers Peyton's breed in case an incident should occur; and

WHEREAS, Tatum and Logan agree that Peyton should be kenneled or otherwise put in a safe and secure place when a stranger of any age enters or leaves either Tatum's or Logan's current or future household premises. This practice should also apply when doors are opened for any type of delivery or visitor; and

WHEREAS, Tatum and Logan agree that they are, and believe they will continue to be, on amicable terms; and

WHEREAS, neither Tatum nor Logan anticipate any changes to their future residences or the addition of human or non-human members of their households within the foreseeable future; and

WHEREAS, both Tatum and Logan recognize that unless there is maltreatment or an imminent threat of danger to Peyton, Alternative Dispute Resolution (ADR) processes shall be utilized to resolve any future conflicts; and

WHEREAS, both parties agree that should a future conflict emerge, the guiding principle for the resolution of the conflict shall be in Peyton's best interests; and

WHEREAS, Tatum and Logan each agree that if Peyton gets loose again, this occurrence will be relevant to the subject of Peyton's best interests.

BASED UPON THE ABOVE, Tatum and Logan agree as follows:

1. Tatum and Logan shall have joint custody of Peyton and share all right, title, and interest in Peyton as co-owners.
2. Peyton's primary residence shall be with Logan.
3. Tatum will have possession of Peyton every weekend, for a two-week annual vacation, and at other times mutually agreed to by the parties.
4. Tatum and Logan's rights under this agreement are nontransferable, unless by written Addendum.
5. Tatum shall buy all of Peyton's premium dog food and provide the appropriate quantity of food to Logan for when Peyton is at Logan's residence.
6. Logan shall maintain and pay for Peyton's veterinary insurance currently in effect.
7. Tatum and Logan shall each pay one-half of Peyton's reasonable uninsured medical and dental expenses.
8. Tatum and Logan agree to keep each other informed of any pending professional appointments for Peyton, including, but not limited to, veterinarian, chiropractor, acupuncturist, trainer, or behaviorist appointments.
9. Tatum and Logan shall each maintain homeowner's liability insurance that covers Peyton in the minimum amount of $300,000.00.
10. Logan shall bring Peyton to the veterinarian for a comprehensive examination at least twice a year.
11. Tatum and Logan shall maintain Peyton at a reasonable weight consistent with veterinary recommendations.
12. Each party shall make a good faith effort to communicate with each other on subjects concerning Peyton's welfare, including, but not limited to, veterinary and mental health concerns, physical condition, and dangers. Each party shall develop a safety plan for Peyton and utilize expert services to design this plan.

13. Tatum and Logan shall each pay one-half the cost associated with behavioral training and, if applicable, therapy dog training for Peyton.
14. Dr. Casey Hanson shall continue to be Peyton's veterinarian, and Blue Jewel shall continue to be Peyton's urgent or emergency care facility unless the parties otherwise agree or if these providers are too far away when exigent circumstances arise. Tatum and Logan shall follow the reasonable recommendations of Peyton's medical and dental providers.
15. Logan shall license Peyton annually.
16. If Tatum or Logan want to introduce new members to their households, they shall schedule a meeting with Peyton's behaviorist first and before the move occurs to maximize the success of the new family unit.
17. Tatum and Logan shall cooperate to provide Peyton with ongoing training.
18. Tatum and Logan agree to keep each other informed as to each other's contact information, including their current address, phone number, and email address.
19. Peyton shall wear a collar that has a tag or plate that identifies Peyton's name and both owners' phone numbers and includes Peyton's license.
20. If Peyton is missing, lost, or stolen, Tatum and Logan will cooperate with regard to search and recovery efforts, including, but not limited to, ground search, notification of the authorities, social media and paper postings, advertisements, and utilization of rescue groups.
21. Tatum and Logan recognize the possibility of an emergency or disaster. They agree that if a dire circumstance arises, the following people may provide care for Peyton: Nancy and Leroy Swanson in Fargo, North Dakota; Eric Larson in Des Moines, Iowa; and Shasta Goldman in Milwaukee, Wisconsin. They also agree to amend this agreement to further detail an emergency plan.
22. Tatum and Logan shall equally share transport responsibilities for Peyton. Unless otherwise specified in writing, transport obligations shall shift between the parties on a weekly basis. If either party moves more than 30 miles from his or her current residence, that party will assume resulting additional transport responsibilities unless otherwise agreed.
23. Tatum and Logan shall use their best efforts to give love, affection, and humane and responsible care to Peyton.
24. Tatum and Logan shall provide Peyton with a safe environment, and the parties shall annually exchange in writing their goals on how a safe environment can be achieved.
25. Tatum and Logan shall be courteous and polite to each other in the presence of Peyton.

26. Peyton shall not be left alone on a leash, and Peyton shall only be left alone in a fenced-in yard for a length of time appropriate for the outside climate or for Peyton's temperament. With respect to the "fenced-in yard," the fence should be at least five feet high and the entrances and exits to the yard well secured.
27. Neither Tatum nor Logan, nor anyone added to either party's household, shall neglect or abuse Peyton.
28. Peyton shall be walked on a leash frequently, unless regularly exercised at a dog park. If at a dog park, Peyton's activities shall be closely supervised.
29. Peyton's microchip provider shall immediately be furnished with updated contact information for both parties.
30. Neglect, abuse, or maltreatment of Peyton shall constitute a material breach of this agreement.
31. The above duties with regard to the welfare of Peyton are in effect throughout Peyton's lifetime.
32. In the event of Peyton's death, Peyton is to be taken to the veterinarian for a necropsy, unless the parties otherwise agree. This expense would be divided equally.
33. Tatum and Logan agree to euthanize Peyton if recommended by Peyton's veterinarian and Peyton is in pain and is unlikely to further enjoy living.
34. Unless the parties otherwise agree in writing, if one of the parties to this agreement dies, the other party shall be awarded sole ownership and sole custody of Peyton and this agreement shall be binding on each party's heirs and assigns.
35. If either party materially breaches this agreement, the breaching party shall give possession of Peyton, if requested, to the other party until ADR processes are completed.
36. Tatum and Logan shall reasonably discuss revisions to their schedule based on change of residence, change of work hours or place of employment, and unforeseen family demands.
37. If the parties reach an impasse, the parties shall participate in an ADR process, beginning with mediation, unless time is of the essence.
38. The parties agree, if necessary, to utilize Dellwood Smith, or as an alternative, Patsy English, as their mediator unless the parties otherwise agree.
39. If the parties' dispute is not resolved in mediation, the parties agree to utilize Jody Abel for binding arbitration, or as an alternative, Ling Xu, unless the parties otherwise agree.

40. If this joint custody and ownership agreement is unsustainable or harmful to Peyton, Tatum and Logan shall delegate and grant to the arbitrator the authority to transfer the ownership of Peyton from joint ownership to sole ownership and to change custody from joint custody to sole custody without any right of access by the other party.
41. The terms of this agreement shall be utilized in any ADR process.
42. Each party shall pay one-half of ADR costs in a timely manner.
43. The court shall retain subject matter jurisdiction to ensure the parties participate in ADR processes, to enforce an arbitration award, and to render a decision if Peyton is endangered. The court may also award attorney's fees and court costs against the party who failed to participate in ADR processes or comply with the terms of the arbitration award.
44. Tatum releases Logan from any and all liability, costs, or damages caused by Peyton while Peyton is in Tatum's care and holds Logan harmless from paying same.
45. Logan releases Tatum from any and all liability, costs, or damages caused by Peyton while Peyton is in Logan's care and holds Tatum harmless from paying same.
46. This agreement shall be governed by and construed in accordance with Minnesota law.
47. Even if one provision of this agreement is unenforceable, all other terms shall remain in full force and effect.
48. Failure to enforce any of the terms and conditions of this agreement shall not be deemed a waiver of any rights or remedies that a party may have and shall not be deemed a waiver of any subsequent breach or default of any of the terms and conditions of this agreement.
49. Tatum and Logan reiterate that Peyton's best interests are of the greatest importance.

Dated: ______________________	______________________ Tatum Thompson
Dated: ______________________	______________________ Signature of Tatum Thompson
Dated: ______________________	______________________ Logan Longview
Dated: ______________________	______________________ Signature of Logan Longview

Appendix 8

Characteristic Rescue Adoption Contract

While two parties may believe that an ownership dispute is only between them, a third party, such as a rescue group, might assert an interest in the companion animal, too. A good rule of thumb is that if the contract terms suggest that the rescue still has continuing ownership rights, the rescue might, and they could have liability exposure, too. Also, beware that for title of an animal to pass, the statutory hold period must be satisfied by the correct legal entity.

Below is an illustrative example of a rescue contract.[1] The rescue may view the transfer of ownership by the adopter to another party, such as a spouse, a significant other, or a relative, to be a material breach, and they may take action to have the subject animal returned.[2]

1. When drafting a rescue contract, be mindful of the applicability of the Uniform Commercial Code and carefully research the question of liability in your state. Legal issues, including health requirements, can arise when companion animals are moved from state to state.

2. Animal control is typically the correct legal entity.

ADOPTION CONTRACT

Rescue Information

____________________ is a non-profit organization[3] incorporated under the laws of the State of ____________.

Address: ____

Phone: ____

Email: ____________________ hereinafter "Rescue"

Adopter Information

Name: ____

Address: ____

Phone: ____________________

Email: ____________________ hereinafter "Adopter"

Companion Animal Information

Name: ____________________ hereinafter "Animal"

Rescue ID: ____________________

Gender: ____________________

DOB or Approximate Age: ____________________

Right Body Markings: ____

Left Body Markings: ____

Coloring: ____________________

Microchip Number: ____________________

Registration Number: ____________________

A current photograph of the Animal is attached hereto.

WHEREAS, the parties to this agreement prefer to use language that reflects respect for animals; and

WHEREAS, the parties agree that the nature of this agreement is an adoption and that the seller is the Rescue and the purchaser is the Adopter; and[4]

WHEREAS, the parties intend that together with a transfer of custody from the Rescue to the Adopter, there shall also be a transfer of all right, title, interest, and ownership subject to specified material conditions; and

WHEREAS, the Rescue represents that it has the authority to transfer title to this Animal under applicable state law and that minimum hold periods have been satisfied.

---

3. Almost anyone can say they are a rescue group, so check the rescue out and learn who is on the Board of Directors and if state records support the rescue's non-profit claim.

4. Although these types of transactions are most likely sales subject to the Uniform Commercial Code, many rescues use donation-type language.

WHEREAS, the Rescue acknowledges that this agreement is subject to warranties and implied warranties of merchantability and fitness for a particular purpose under the Uniform Commercial Code,[5] unless said warranties are expressly and individually waived below; and

WHEREAS, the Adopter, in consideration for the placement of an animal by the Rescue, agrees to be bound by the terms of this agreement as set forth below.

I agree that this adoption is subject to the following terms and conditions:

1. I adopt the Animal "as is."
2. I acknowledge that the Rescue has disclosed that the Animal may have the following:
   a. Health Problems/Issues: ________________________________.
   b. The Rescue has disclosed the following information to me about the animal's history:[6] ________________________________.
   c. Behavior Problems/Issues observed at the Rescue include, but are not limited to, the following:

      ____.
3. I have received the following records concerning the Animal as an attachment to this agreement: ________________________________.
4. I understand that the Rescue has reasonably provided me with the above information and documentation and I acknowledge that the Rescue is not responsible for, and I hereby release the Rescue from, any errors or omissions in the information and documentation provided to me about the Animal.[7]
5. I agree to promptly contact the Rescue if my home address, telephone number, or email address change and to provide the Rescue with my updated contact information.
6. The welfare of the Animal is my responsibility, and I agree to give the Animal quality care, which shall include, but not be limited to, the following:
   a. I agree to provide the Animal with proper, healthy, and nutritious food and fresh water.
   b. I agree to provide the Animal with adequate companionship and exercise.

---

5. As a practical matter, most rescues are unaware that their actions may be subject to the Uniform Commercial Code.

6. Disclosure is important, as it puts the new owner on notice of the animal's dangerous propensities, if any, known to the rescue. If the rescue fails to disclose this information to the adopter, and the animal injures another, there may be recourse against the rescue. Disclosure about health problems is also important.

7. Waivers and releases from claims vary in their effectiveness.

c. I agree to provide the Animal with all necessary and appropriate medical/veterinary care and behavioral care so that the Animal will enjoy good physical and mental health.
d. I agree to provide the Animal with a regular heartworm prevention regimen, annual checkups, and appropriate vaccinations.

7. I understand that I am exclusively responsible for the Animal's veterinary expenses, and I shall hold the Rescue harmless from paying them.
8. I agree that the Animal may have a congenital defect, disease, or other problems due to environmental factors, such as inadequate socialization, mistreatment, or animal abuse.
9. I agree to spay or neuter the Animal, if not already done, no later than the age of three months or as otherwise agreed between the Adopter and the Rescue in writing.[8]
10. I am adopting the Animal as a companion animal for myself, and I will treat the Animal with affection and kindness.
11. I am not adopting the Animal for another person.
12. The Animal shall not be used for breeding, medical, or experimental purposes.
13. I will not subject the Animal to neglect, abuse, or cruelty or allow others to do so.
14. The Animal shall not be trained for aggression.
15. I acknowledge that it may take weeks for the Animal to adjust to the Animal's new surroundings, and for us to adjust to each other, develop trust, and establish a routine.
16. If I can no longer keep the Animal or provide the Animal with good care or the Animal is in jeopardy, I shall notify the Rescue and return the Animal to a designated representative of the Rescue within a reasonable time after the decision to return the Animal has been communicated to the Rescue.[9]
17. I will not surrender the Animal to a dog pound-type facility, humane society, or animal shelter where the Animal could be destroyed.
18. I will not give, transfer, or otherwise release the Animal to another without the express prior written consent of the Rescue.

---

8. Many rescues consider failure to comply with this provision a material breach of the contract. Some rescues prefer earlier or later spaying or neutering. This provision may be controversial because some animals have late-developing sexual characteristics. For most rescues, harm to an animal caused by early neutering or spaying is secondary to their mission to eliminate euthanasia of unwanted animals.

9. Should the adopter later be in a pet custody dispute, perhaps with a new spouse or partner, this is an important provision to review.

19. If I believe the Animal should be euthanized to alleviate suffering, I will notify the Rescue of my decision and seek the Rescue's input.[10]
20. I will notify the Rescue upon the death of the Animal.[11]
21. I will comply with all local, state, and federal ordinances and laws.
22. I will obtain all licenses necessary for the Animal.
23. I will keep the Animal clearly identified at all times when outside my home with a collar containing tags with my contact information and the Rescue's contact information.
24. I will microchip the Animal within 30 days and if already microchipped, I will cooperate with the Rescue to have the microchip provider show my name in its records.
25. I will not use a shock collar of any type on the Animal.
26. I will keep the Animal only as an inside house pet.
27. When outside, I will keep the Animal on a leash or in a safe and secure fenced yard.
28. I will not allow the Animal to otherwise run free, except in appropriate places such as dog parks where the Animal is properly supervised.
29. I agree not to leave the Animal outside unsupervised in inclement weather.
30. If the Animal is deaf, I will provide a safe and secure fenced yard.
31. If I place the Animal on a leash, tie, or cable, I will limit the time period to 30 minutes.
32. I SPECIFICALLY UNDERSTAND AND AGREE THAT THE ANIMAL IS NEVER TO BE TRANSFERRED OR COSMETICALLY ALTERED (INCLUDING EAR CROPPING AND TAIL DOCKING) WITHOUT THE RESCUE'S WRITTEN CONSENT AND TO DO SO WILL BE CONSIDERED A MATERIAL BREACH OF THIS AGREEMENT AND THE RESCUE WILL HAVE THE RIGHT TO IMMEDIATELY RESCIND THIS AGREEMENT AND TAKE POSSESSION OF THE ANIMAL WITHOUT THE NECESSITY FOR ANY PRIVATE PROCEEDINGS OR NOTICES. BY INITIALING THIS PARAGRAPH, I CONSENT TO AND AGREE TO ABIDE BY AND BE BOUND BY THIS POLICY. [_______][12] Your initials must appear here.
33. I will contact the Rescue immediately if the Animal becomes loose or is otherwise lost or stolen and I will make every effort to locate the Animal,

---

10. If this does not occur, a rescue may treat this as a material breach of the contract and the rescue may seek the return of other animals in the adopter's care.

11. A big issue for rescues is euthanasia without their input or permission.

12. This provision invites the question of whether this is the only material provision in the contract. Look to see if there is saving language that this provision does not represent the only material term from a breach of contract perspective.

including placing flyers, notifying local law enforcement officials, regularly checking with local animal control, animal shelters, pounds, and humane shelters, and I will fully cooperate with the Rescue in searching for the Animal.

34. The Rescue may contact me for further verification of compliance of the terms of this agreement, and I agree to cooperate by providing whatever information and documentation is reasonably requested.
35. I will reasonably permit the Rescue to access my home and yard as well as access to the Animal if there is an allegation of a material breach of this agreement, including, but not limited to failure to spay or neuter, animal neglect, or animal cruelty.
36. I hereby acknowledge that I am not relying on any representations or express or implied warranties made by the Rescue about the Animal.[13]
37. I admit that the Rescue has made no express or implied representation or warranty regarding the Animal's fitness for a particular purpose.
38. I understand that the Animal may be neither of merchantable quality nor suitable as a companion animal.[14]
39. I agree to the assumption of the risk and to indemnify, defend, and hold the Rescue harmless from any and all costs, expenses, claims, losses, damages, liabilities, and attorney's fees whatsoever arising out of any actions or occurrences involving the Animal while under my care, custody, and ownership, including, but not limited to injuries, death to humans or other animals, or damage to property.
40. I understand and acknowledge that this adoption is conditioned upon my compliance with the terms of this agreement, which are intended to promote the welfare of the Animal and prevent animal neglect and cruelty.
41. If I have provided the Rescue with false information in order to obtain the Animal, the Rescue shall have the sole discretion to rescind this agreement and send a representative from the Rescue to take possession of the Animal.
42. I stipulate and agree that if an action is brought against me for replevin and/or specific performance by the Rescue if I fail to fulfill my obligations pursuant to this agreement, I will be liable for the Rescue's attorney's fees and court costs. Said obligation may well exceed the monetary value of the animal.

---

13. This type of warranty language may be utilized in a variety of animal-related contracts. It may not be sufficient. Waiver of warranty language should be particular as to each implied or express warranty.

14. This is not the same as a waiver.

43. I agree that this agreement is to be construed under the laws of the state of the Rescue, and any litigation, arbitration, or other legal matters or proceedings regarding this agreement or the Animal adopted hereunder are to be in the jurisdiction of County of __________, State of __________ and that the laws of said state shall apply.
44. I acknowledge and agree that the failure of the Rescue to insist upon strict performance of any of the terms and conditions of this agreement shall not be deemed a waiver of any rights or remedies that the Rescue may have and shall not be deemed a waiver of any subsequent breach or default of any of the terms and conditions of this agreement.
45. If I refuse to relinquish or surrender the Animal following my breach, I understand that the Rescue may initiate legal proceedings to enforce this agreement and recover the Animal.
46. I understand that the Rescue is a 501(c)(3) charity and that my payment of $__________, as well as the payment of a state sales tax for the Animal, is NON-REFUNDABLE.[15]
47. I understand that the invalidity, unenforceability, or failure by a party to enforce a clause or parts of this agreement will not affect the validity or enforceability of any other provisions herein.
48. I represent that I have never been convicted of a crime, other than traffic related, and am not and have never been the subject of an Order for Protection. I further represent that neither I, nor anyone in my household, has been the subject of any animal abuse allegation.
49. I agree that the Rescue will be entitled to possession of the Animal, without bond, if litigation against me is commenced by the Rescue because of my material breach of this agreement.
50. I agree that the transport of the Animal shall be inside a vehicle and not in an area exposed to the elements.
51. I will not leave the Animal in a motor vehicle if the temperature outside poses a danger.
52. I understand that this agreement shall be binding upon the Adopter, the Rescue, and their successors or beneficiaries.
53. I acknowledge that oral representations by the Rescue, if any, as well as any other communications in any form, shall merge into this written agreement.

---

15. Clients may ask their lawyer if they will get a tax credit when adopting a dog from a 501(c)(3) rescue. Consider that the rescue may not have satisfied all its qualifying nonprofit requirements. Many exist on a very modest budget.

54. I have fully read and understand this agreement and have received a copy.
55. I AGREE THAT IN THE EVENT THAT THIS CONTRACT, INCLUDING ALL OF ITS COVENANTS AND CONDITIONS, IS BREACHED BY ME, THE RESCUE HAS THE RIGHT TO RESCIND THIS CONTRACT AND DEMAND THE RETURN OF THE ANIMAL.
56. I agree that an officer of the Rescue may sign this agreement electronically.

This Agreement is made on the ________ day of ____________, 20____ by and between ______________________, the Rescue, and ______________________________, the Adopter.

Dated: ______________________________ ______________________________
Adopter's Signature

Dated: ______________________________ ______________________________
Adopter's Printed Name

Dated: ______________________________ ______________________________
Rescue Representative's Signature

Dated: ______________________________ ______________________________
Rescue Representative's Printed Name

Appendix 9

Breeder Agreement for Pet-Quality Dog

It is important for lawyers representing clients to be familiar with breeder contracts and to anticipate legal problems that may arise because of them. It is also important to know whether the breeder is reputable and knows each dog individually, or if the breeder is a large confinement breeder whose interest in a dog is mostly financial. Below is a sample breeder agreement.

AGREEMENT[1]

This Agreement is between ____________, who resides at ________________ (hereinafter referred to as "Seller"), and _________________, who resides at _________________________ (hereinafter referred to as "Buyer"), concerning a dog born on ______________, (hereinafter referred to as "Dog.") The Dog is further described as follows: ________________________ and a photograph is attached hereto.

Payment Terms

1) The Seller hereby sells the Dog to the Buyer as a pet/companion for the total sum of $________, including the deposit of $________ paid on ________. The total sum paid is hereinafter referred to as "Purchase Price."

Warranties

2) The Seller warrants that the Dog is fit for the particular purpose of being a companion animal.
3) The Seller warrants that the Dog is of merchantable quality.
4) The Seller does not warrant the Dog for obedience training, agility training, therapy training, show ring performances, or breeding purposes.

Seller's Representations

5) Pertinent information regarding the Dog's lineage is as follows:

SIRE:		DAM:	
AKC #:		AKC #:	
CHIC #:		CHIC #:	
OFA—Hips:		OFA—Hips:	
OFA—Elbows:		OFA—Elbows:	
Patellas:		Patellas:	
Eyes:		Eyes:	
BAER:		BAER:	
Cardiac:		Cardiac:	
Legg-Calve-Perthes:		Legg-Calve-Perthes:	

1. This is a sample agreement for a breeder who is particularly concerned that the buyer take good care of the dog and that the dog not be bred. Be sure to check any laws that pertain to breeders in the applicable state.

6) The Seller has made an effort to reduce the risk that the Dog would have certain congenital defects, as reflected in the information about the Sire and Dam provided above.
7) The Dog is a result of the Seller's breeding program that strives to improve the health and wellness of the breed of this Dog.
8) The Dog is a pet-quality dog and not a show dog.
9) The Dog is of sound health and temperament at the time of delivery.
10) The Seller has all right, title, and interest in the Dog, and is the Dog's sole legal owner.
11) The Dog is not subject to any lien, security interest, or encumbrance.
12) The Seller does not co-own the Dog with any other person or entity.[2]
13) A licensed veterinarian has examined the Dog, and the Dog's veterinary records and/or health certificate are attached hereto.
14) If the Dog suffers from a bacterial or viral infection at the time of the Dog's first veterinary examination while in the Buyer's possession, and the Buyer prefers to keep the Dog, the Buyer shall pay limited and reasonable veterinary charges to treat the bacterial or viral infection. Upon providing the Seller with the applicable test and veterinary records, the Seller will reimburse the Buyer for veterinary costs not to exceed One Thousand Dollars and No Cents ($1,000.00). This offer by the Seller is null and void if the Buyer does not take the Dog in for a comprehensive examination by a licensed veterinarian within three (3) business days following the Buyer's possession of the Dog and provide proof thereof.
15) If the Dog suffers from a bacterial or viral infection at the time of the Dog's first veterinary examination while in the Buyer's possession, and proof thereof is provided, and the Buyer prefers to return the Dog to the Seller, the Buyer shall receive a full refund. This offer by the Seller is null and void if the Buyer does not take the Dog in for a comprehensive examination by a licensed veterinarian within three (3) business days following the Buyer's possession of the Dog and provide proof thereof.
16) The Dog has received parvo inoculations, has been de-wormed, and has received other vaccinations appropriate for the Dog's age.
17) The Seller will cooperate with the Buyer so that the Dog may have a limited AKC registration.
18) The Seller will cooperate with answering the Buyer's reasonable questions about the Dog and the Dog's breed.

---

2. This type of provision can be tricky depending on how many people co-own one or both dogs that constitute the breeding pair.

19) The Seller recommends that the Buyer provide the Dog with puppy and adult training and obedience classes and other structured training methods so that the placement of the Dog in the Buyer's home will be successful.
20) In the event that the Seller's veterinarian writes a credible written report that the Dog has one of the following congenital defects: _______________, and said defect is identified by a licensed veterinarian on or before the time the Dog reaches one (1) year of age, the Seller shall pay the Buyer no more than the Purchase Price of the Dog upon the transfer of possession, together with all right, title, and interest, as well as limited AKC registration, of the Dog back to the Seller, unless the Seller and the Buyer otherwise agree in writing.
21) If the Dog is diagnosed by a licensed veterinarian with luxating patellas or a dysplastic condition by the time the Dog reaches the age of one (1), and the Buyer seeks to keep the Dog, and if a veterinarian selected by the Buyer has the reasonable opportunity to examine the dog and reaches the same diagnosis, the Seller will reimburse the Buyer one-fourth (1/4) of the Purchase Price of the Dog. If the Buyer prefers to transfer possession, together with all right, title, and interest, as well as limited AKC registration, of the Dog back to the Seller, the Seller will refund the entire Purchase Price of the Dog to the Buyer, unless the Seller and the Buyer otherwise agree in writing.
22) If a licensed veterinarian diagnoses the Dog with grade three or higher luxating patellas on or before the time the Dog reaches the age of one (1), and both the Seller and the Buyer's veterinarians reasonably recommend surgery, the Seller shall promptly reimburse the Buyer for one-half (1/2) of any uninsured out-of-pocket costs the Buyer pays for the surgery, if and only if the Buyer has obtained veterinary insurance, as further described herein. The Buyer's lifetime contribution to the Dog's patella-related uninsured expenses, and other expenses described above, shall not exceed the Purchase Price of the Dog.
23) If the Dog dies and both the Buyer's and Seller's veterinarians reasonably determine the death of the Dog was caused by a genetic disorder, the Seller shall provide the Buyer with another pet-quality dog of the same breed within two (2) years.
24) The Seller shall notify the Buyer if the Seller has a change of address.
25) If the Dog dies, if the Seller requests a necropsy, the Seller will pay for it.

Buyer's Representations and Obligations

26) The Buyer acknowledges that if a false material representation is made by the Buyer in the Buyer's Application to purchase the Dog, which is attached hereto, said material representation shall constitute a breach of contract. Material misrepresentations would include, but not be limited to, number

of human occupants living at the Buyer's residence, number and type of nonhuman animals in the Buyer's residence, the lifestyle the Dog would be provided, and history of humane care of companion animals by the Buyer.

27) The Buyer shall bring the Dog to the Buyer's veterinarian for a comprehensive examination within three (3) business days of sale and shall immediately provide the Seller with copies of these veterinary records. The Buyer acknowledges that this is a material term of this agreement.
28) The Buyer acknowledges that the Seller has already provided the Buyer with a recommended vaccination protocol to be used for the Dog. The Buyer agrees to immediately share these guidelines with the Buyer's licensed veterinarian and to have the veterinarian follow the vaccination recommendations. The Buyer acknowledges that failure to follow this vaccination protocol may result in adverse reactions to vaccinations.
29) The Buyer shall not allow the Leptospirosis or Coronavirus vaccines to be administered to the Dog, unless agreed to in writing between the Seller and the Buyer.
30) The Buyer agrees to maintain the Dog at a reasonable weight and to exercise the Dog daily.
31) The Buyer shall pay for all veterinary costs, medical costs, behavioral costs, and other costs and fees related to the Dog, subject to reimbursements by the Seller to the Buyer only as expressly set forth herein.
32) The Buyer shall diligently take precautions to prevent the Dog from reproducing.
33) If the Dog is female, the Buyer shall have the Dog spayed by the time the Dog reaches six (6) months of age, but not before the Dog has reached five (5) months of age. The Buyer recognizes that this requirement is designed to promote the Dog's health and to prevent the Dog from having any litters.
34) If the Dog is male, the Buyer shall have the Dog neutered by the time the Dog reaches one (1) year of age, but not before the Dog has reached eleven (11) months of age. The Buyer recognizes that this requirement is designed to promote the Dog's health and to prevent the Dog from having any litters.
35) The Buyer represents that the Dog will be examined by a licensed veterinarian at least two (2) times per year for checkups and that the Buyer will follow the reasonable recommendations of the Buyer's licensed veterinarian for the Dog's ongoing care, which will include, but not be limited to, an annual fecal exam, an annual dental exam, and continued heartworm prevention.
36) By this Agreement, the Buyer authorizes the Seller to have access to and receive copies of the licensed veterinary records regarding the Dog throughout the Dog's lifetime.

37) The Buyer shall license the Dog annually and pay said fee.
38) The Buyer is not acting as an agent for any other person or business in the purchase of the Dog, such as a large confinement breeding operation.
39) The Buyer may not transfer right, title, interest, or possession of the Dog to another without the Seller's written permission.
40) The Buyer represents that disclosures about the Buyer's residence and human and animal occupants are reflected in photographs attached hereto and incorporated by reference.
41) The Buyer does not anticipate any changes to the Buyer's residence or human or animal members of the Buyer's household within the foreseeable future other than as set forth in the Buyer's Application.
42) The Buyer represents that neither the Buyer nor anyone else living at the Buyer's residence has ever been accused of, or convicted of, domestic abuse or a violent crime.
43) The Buyer represents that neither the Buyer nor anyone else living at the Buyer's residence has ever been accused of animal cruelty or neglect.
44) The Buyer is familiar with the characteristics of the Dog's breed.
45) The Buyer shall give love, affection, and humane and responsible care to the Dog.
46) The Buyer shall utilize his or her best efforts to provide the Dog with a safe environment.
47) The Buyer shall exercise the Dog daily.
48) The Buyer shall feed the Dog nutritious food and shall not overfeed the Dog.
49) The Buyer represents that the Dog shall reside with the Buyer in the Buyer's residence.
50) The Buyer shall immediately microchip the Dog, or, if a microchip is already in place, the Buyer will cooperate with the Seller to update the records with the applicable microchip manufacturer to list the Buyer and the Seller as individuals to contact in case the Dog becomes lost.
51) The Buyer shall obtain and maintain reasonable veterinary insurance for the Dog within twenty-four (24) hours following the Dog's initial veterinary examination and have a deductible on said insurance of no more than One Thousand Dollars and No Cents ($1,000.00) per annum unless the Seller and the Buyer otherwise agree in writing to other insurance provisions.
52) If the Buyer moves or the Buyer's telephone number or email address changes, the Buyer shall promptly provide the Seller with updated contact information for both the Buyer and the Dog's veterinarian.
53) The Buyer represents that the Dog will not be left alone on a leash and that the Dog will only be left alone in a fenced yard for the length of time appropriate for the outside climate and the Dog's temperament.

54) The Buyer shall not neglect or abuse the Dog.
55) The Buyer agrees that if the Buyer or someone in the Buyer's household neglects or abuses the Dog, this behavior represents a material breach of this agreement.
56) The Buyer represents that the Buyer's obligations are in effect throughout the Dog's lifetime, unless otherwise agreed to in writing between the Seller and the Buyer.
57) The Buyer will inform the Seller annually about the veterinary care and training the Dog receives and shall reasonably communicate with the Seller about the Dog's well-being.
58) The Buyer hereby agrees that if at any time during the Dog's lifetime, the Buyer will not or cannot continue to own or take proper care of the Dog, the Buyer shall contact the Seller and make arrangements to deliver the Dog back to the Seller, as well as pay said cost. The Buyer will also transfer possession and all right, title, and interest, as well as limited AKC registration, of the Dog to the Seller, unless the parties otherwise agree in writing.
59) The Buyer shall promptly notify the Seller upon the Dog's death.
60) The Buyer agrees that following the Dog's death, if requested by the Seller, the Buyer will cooperate in the Dog having a necropsy.
61) The Buyer admits and recognizes that the reputation of the Seller's kennel is the result of many years of work and professional experience, and inappropriate breeding of the Dog from the Seller's kennel damages the reputation and value of the Seller's kennel name and other litters.

Remedies

62) If the Buyer decides not to keep the Dog for any reason, the Buyer shall return the Dog to the Seller within three (3) days of purchase, and transfer possession and all right, title, and interest, as well as limited AKC registration, of the Dog to the Seller. Upon fulfillment of these obligations, the Seller shall promptly refund the Dog's Purchase Price to the Buyer.
63) If the Buyer decides not to keep the Dog following the above-described first (1st) comprehensive veterinary examination, the Buyer may return the Dog to the Seller within three (3) days following the examination, and transfer possession and all right, title, and interest, as well as limited AKC registration, of the Dog to the Seller. Upon fulfillment of these obligations, the Seller shall promptly refund the Dog's Purchase Price to the Buyer.
64) If the Buyer materially breaches this agreement and fails to return the Dog to the Seller upon written demand or fails to otherwise cooperate so that the Seller regains possession and all right, title, and interest, as well as transfer

the limited AKC registration of the Dog to the Seller, the Buyer shall pay the Seller's reasonable attorney's fees and court costs to enforce these terms.

65) If the Buyer materially breaches this agreement and fails to cooperate to update the Dog's AKC registration so that the registration is in the Seller's name, upon written demand, the Buyer shall pay for the Seller's reasonable attorney's fees and court costs to enforce this obligation.

66) The Buyer shall direct the Buyer's personal representative, guardian, or attorney not to transfer the Dog to any person upon the Buyer's incapacity or death without the Seller's written consent.

67) The Buyer shall notify the Seller if the Buyer is unable to meet the Seller's obligations described herein, and the Buyer shall not abandon the Dog to the streets, a shelter, or sell or give the Dog away.

68) If the Dog is sold or given away without the Seller's written consent, the Seller may take legal action against the Buyer and the Buyer shall be responsible for the Seller's reasonable attorney's fees and court costs to regain all right, title, interest, and possession of the Dog.

69) The Buyer's representations and obligations stated hereinafter shall apply to the Buyer's estate, if applicable.

70) If the Dog is returned to the Seller under any terms of this agreement, the Buyer shall personally transport and deliver the Dog to the Seller's address and pay the cost thereof, unless the Seller and the Buyer otherwise agree in writing.

71) The Buyer shall not euthanize the Dog without first offering to transfer all right, title, interest, and possession, as well as limited AKC registration, back to the Seller, unless otherwise agreed to in writing. This provision shall not apply if the Dog is in an accident, is not expected to survive, or if a delay would be cruel.

Liquidated Damages

72) The Seller has endeavored for many years to protect the above-described breed from irresponsible owners and cruel and abusive treatment. To the contrary, the Seller breeds dogs to enjoy a high quality of life in a forever home. If the Buyer surrenders or transfers the Dog to another party without the Seller's written permission, the Seller may elect whether to seek repossession of the Dog through a replevin action or to have the Buyer pay the Seller liquidated damages of Ten Thousand Dollars and No Cents ($10,000.00).

73) The Buyer recognizes that intentional or negligent breeding of the Dog is detrimental to the breed and to the Seller's kennel name. Furthermore, this is contrary to the Seller's commitment to a breeding program designed to promote the health of the breed and prevent genetic defects. Acknowledging the intrinsic value of the Seller's kennel name and the difficulty of precise damage

calculations for breach of the contract, the Buyer agrees to pay the Seller Ten Thousand Dollars and No Cents ($10,000.00) per litter born as a result of any such breeding, unless waived by the Seller in writing.

Indemnity and Release

74) The Buyer releases the Seller from any and all liability, costs, or damages caused by the Dog after placement with the Seller, including, but not limited to, damage to or destruction of property, and injury or death to any human or animal.

75) If any action or failure to act on the part of the Buyer shall result in any claim, suit, loss, damage, injury, death, or liability against the Seller, the Buyer agrees to defend, indemnify, and hold the Seller harmless and to pay all of the Seller's costs and expenses, including reasonable attorney's fees and court costs and any amount paid in settlement, and any award or judgment with respect thereto.

General Terms & Conditions

76) This agreement shall be governed by and construed in accordance with the laws of the state of ________..

77) If any provision of this agreement is unenforceable, all other terms shall remain in full force and effect.

78) This agreement represents the entire agreement between the Buyer and the Seller. Any prior agreements, promises, representations, or warranties, either expressed or implied, are nullified, unless expressly set forth in this agreement or a fully executed addendum thereto. This nullification extends to any representations made on websites and on social media.

79) The Seller shall have the right to enforce provisions of this agreement in a court of law.

80) The Seller has the right to determine the AKC registered name of the Dog prior to or after the sale or receipt of deposit. This AKC name will include any name and the kennel name of the Seller's choice.

81) If the Seller regains possession of the Dog for any reason, the Buyer will cooperate to update all AKC registration records so that the Seller is reflected as the Dog's sole owner.

82) Should the Buyer violate any of the material terms of this agreement, the Seller shall have the right to repossess the Dog and regain all right, title, and interest to the Dog.

______________	______________	______________
Date	Name of Seller	Signature of Seller
______________	______________	______________
Date	Name of Buyer	Signature of Buyer

POSSESSION OF THE DOG

1) I acknowledge that the Dog has been delivered to me and is in my possession and appears to be in good health. I have also received the Dog's Health Certificate and/or veterinary records, copies of which are attached hereto.
2) I signify that the Dog appears to be in general good health and I have examined the Dog to my satisfaction and I see no visible signs of illness. Even so, I will bring the Dog to a veterinarian for a comprehensive examination within the next three (3) days.
3) I have read and understand the terms of this agreement and will abide by them. The date below signifies the date of possession.

______________________	______________________	______________________
Date	Name of Buyer	Signature of Buyer

Appendix 10

Pet Custody Discovery

There are many ways to draft discovery documents with regard to custody and ownership disputes regarding companion animals. Some examples that may prove useful are provided below. These discovery documents used and the responses given were from one of the author's cases wherein the parties' sharing of a dog proved unsuccessful. Names and factual information have been altered from the original to provide anonymity.

STATE OF MINNESOTA	DISTRICT COURT
COUNTY OF PINK	SIXTH JUDICIAL DISTRICT
	CASE TYPE: OTHER CIVIL
Melissa Cox,	Court File No. 12345
Plaintiff,	
	DEFENDANT'S INTERROGATORIES TO PLAINTIFF
vs.	
Jennifer Hadley,	
Defendant.	

TO: PLAINTIFF MELISSA COX, 123 COURT STREET, MINNEAPOLIS, MINNESOTA 55414.

PLEASE TAKE NOTICE that Defendant demands, pursuant to the Minnesota Rules of Civil Procedure, full and complete Answers to the following Interrogatories, under oath, within thirty (30) days of the date of service hereof.

In answering these Interrogatories, furnish such information as is available to you, however obtained, including hearsay information known by, or in the possession of your agents, including your attorney. If any Interrogatory cannot be answered in full after exercising due diligence to secure the information, answer to the extent possible, specifying your inability to answer the remainder, stating whatever information and knowledge you have concerning the unanswered portion, and detailing what you did in attempting to secure that unknown information. These Interrogatories are deemed to be continuing so as to require supplemental answers if additional information is obtained between the time the Answers are served and the time of trial.

DEFINITIONS AND INSTRUCTIONS

1. The Interrogatory or sub-part thereof being answered shall be restated immediately preceding the Answer to such Interrogatory or sub-part thereof.

2. All knowledge and/or information which is in the possession, custody, or control of you or your attorney, investigators, employees, agents or such other representatives or persons acting on your behalf shall be divulged.

3. In the event an objection is made with respect to any Interrogatory on the grounds that it calls for the divulgence of privileged communications between attorney and client, state the following:

   a. The date on which the communication took place;
   b. The parties to the communication;
   c. The manner in which the communication took place, i.e., personal conversation, telephone conversation, or written communication;
   d. The identity of any persons who were present when the communication took place or who overheard or read the communication as the case may be; and
   e. The identity of all persons to whom the communication has been divulged.

4. In the event an objection is made with respect to any Interrogatory or sub-part thereof on the grounds that it calls for the divulgence of information allegedly protected by the limited "work-product" doctrine, state all facts on which you rely to support the validity of such objection.

5. In the event that the Answer to an Interrogatory or sub-part thereof is "not applicable," or any similar phrase or answer, describe in detail why the Interrogatory or sub-part thereof is not applicable.

6. In the event that the Answer to any Interrogatory or sub-part thereof is "unknown" or any similar phrase or answer, describe in detail all efforts made to obtain information that would pertain to the Interrogatory or sub-part thereof.

7. "You" and "your" when used herein shall refer to the party or parties to whom these Interrogatories are directed, and all persons acting on your behalf, including, but not limited to, attorneys and their associates, investigators, employees, agents, and other representatives.

8. "Person" shall mean any natural person and/or any entity, including, without limiting the foregoing, all proprietorships, corporations, partnerships, joint ventures, groups, associations or organizations, or other legal or business entity.

9. "Document" or "Documents" shall mean all written, printed, typed, drawn, reported, recorded, graphic, or photographic matter and sound reproduction of tapes, records, or other devices, of every nature, within the scope of Rules 26 and 34 of the Minnesota Rules of Civil Procedure, however produced or reproduced, now or at any time, in your possession, custody, or control, and any drafts, copies, or reproductions of the foregoing items and copies or reproductions of the foregoing upon which notations in writing have been made

which do not appear on the originals. The term "Document" or "Documents" also includes all electronically stored information (E.S.I.).

10. "Expert" shall mean any person whom you claim or may claim possesses a special skill or knowledge derived from his or her experience and who is qualified or whom you claim or will claim is qualified to have an opinion or to state a conclusion concerning any matter at issue in this litigation or who you claim or may claim is capable of aiding the jury in determining the facts.

11. The terms "Identify" or "Identity," "Identification," "Describe" or "Description:"

a. When used in reference to an individual shall mean to state his or her full name, present or last known residence, business or official affiliation, and business address;

b. When used in reference to a firm, partnership, incorporated or unincorporated association or other legal or commercial entity, shall mean to state the entity's full name and trade name, if any, the state in which it is incorporated or otherwise registered by law or organized, the address and telephone number of its principal place of business, and the names and titles of those officers, directors, managing agents or other employees who have knowledge of the matters involved in the Interrogatory and its nature; and

c. When used in reference to a document shall mean its date of preparation, author, addressee(s) or other intended recipient, subject matter, type of document (e.g., letter, memorandum, inventory lists, notes, telegram, contract, charts, etc.), its title, hearing, or other designation, a summary of its content or other means of identifying it, and its present location or custodian, or, if any such document or file was, but is no longer in your possession or subject to your control, the disposition that was made of it.

d. When used in reference to a conversation, conference, meeting, or communication shall mean that you shall state the following:

(1) The date and time thereof;

(2) The location at which it occurred;

(3) The identity of all persons participating or attending;

(4) The identity of all documents recording or summarizing or otherwise arising from the conversation, conference, or meeting; and

(5) The method of communication utilized, e.g., telephone, in-person communication, or other means; or if the method of communication was by telephone, specify the caller and the person called.

e. When used in reference to a factual situation, include the persons and documents plus specification of places, dates, exact words used in conversation (or substance of conversation if exact words are not remembered) acts, events, occurrences, etc. State with particularity all facts known which bear upon or are related to the matter which is the subject of the inquiry.

f. When used in reference to the source of information upon which an Answer to an Interrogatory is based, shall mean to identify the person, communication, or documents from whom or which information constituting all or part of the basis of the Answer has been derived.

12. "Events" as used herein means describe with particularity what took place or happened (e.g., all occurrences, acts, or admissions to acts) and when, giving conversations and identification of persons or documents, if appropriate.

INSTRUCTIONS CONCERNING ELECTRONICALLY STORED INFORMATION

If any of the information requested in the following Interrogatories is stored in a computer or any other means of electronic data compilation or storage, provide hard, i.e., printed copies.

ADMONITION

Pursuant to the provisions of the Minnesota Rules of Civil Procedure, the foregoing Interrogatories shall be deemed to be continuing in nature and if information is discovered or comes to your attention after these Interrogatories are answered which would change or supplement the Answers given, demand is hereby made that said information shall be furnished immediately.

INTERROGATORIES

1. Identify each person completing these Interrogatories, including the individual's address, place of employment, and title.

2. Identify all persons who have any knowledge or information about any of the allegations, claims, facts, or other matters asserted in the Complaint, Answer, and either party's discovery responses.

3. For each person identified in response to Interrogatories No. 1 and No. 2, state the following:

a. Describe in detail the knowledge or information possessed by each person identified, and identify the bases or sources from which the knowledge or information has been derived;

b. The identity of all persons to whom the individual has communicated any of the knowledge or information possessed, together with the time, date, place, and circumstances of the communication, and identification of any documents that memorialize the communication.

c. State the full name, present address, occupation, age, present employer, and said present employer's address of each veterinarian, veterinary assistant or technician, or other veterinary personnel who treated, cared for, examined, or otherwise attended to the companion animal during the animal's lifetime. With regard to every such individual, please state:

1) Each date upon which said individual attended to the companion animal;

2) The nature of the treatment or care rendered to the companion animal on each date;

3) The qualifications and area of specialty of each individual;

4) The present address of each individual;

5) The person who paid for said expense; and

6) The source of funds for said expenditure.

4. Identify all persons whom you expect to call as expert witnesses at trial in this matter, and for each such person, state the following:

a. Describe the subject matter of the expert's testimony;

b. State the area of expertise and basis for the claim of expertise; and

c. State a summary of the facts and opinions to which the expert is expected to testify and a summary of the grounds for each such opinion, including the specific factual data upon which the opinion will be based.

5. Identify each person whom you believe has or may have any knowledge or information concerning any facts relating to the claims, defenses, and/or subject matter of this litigation, and, for each such person, describe all such knowledge, information, and facts and set forth the basis of each such person's knowledge or information.

6. Identify each person who may be called by you as a witness at the trial herein and for each such person, describe all information and facts as to which such person is expected to testify.

7. Describe all facts that in any way support, refute, or otherwise relate to any of the claims, defenses, and/or subject matter of the above-entitled action.

8. Identify all documents or conversations that in any way support, refute, or otherwise relate to any of the claims, defenses, and/or subject matter of the above-entitled action.

9. Identify each document or conversation supporting, refuting, or otherwise relating to any allegation in any pleading, and, for each such fact, identify each person who you believe has or may have knowledge or information relating to the fact, and for each such person, describe in detail all such knowledge, information, and facts, and set forth the basis of each such person's knowledge and information.

10. Identify every person who provided information used in answering these Interrogatories and specify each Interrogatory for which each such person provided information.

Dated: ______________________________ ______________________________

Barbara J. Gislason
Atty ID No. 124011
Attorney for Defendant
Law Office of Barbara J. Gislason
7362 University Avenue NE
Suite 120
Fridley, MN 55432
Telephone: (763) 5729297

STATE OF MINNESOTA
COUNTY OF PINK

DISTRICT COURT
SIXTH JUDICIAL DISTRICT
CASE TYPE: OTHER CIVIL
Court File No. 12345

Melissa Cox,

Plaintiff,

vs.

DEFENDANT'S REQUEST FOR PRODUCTION OF DOCUMENTS TO PLAINTIFF

Jennifer Hadley,

Defendant.

TO: PLAINTIFF MELISSA COX, 123 COURT STREET, MINNEAPOLIS, MINNESOTA 55414.

YOU ARE HEREBY REQUESTED, pursuant to Rules 26 and 34 of the Minnesota Rules of Civil Procedure, that within thirty (30) days of the date of service upon you of this Request for Production of Documents, you, and each of you, produce copies of all requested documents in the possession, custody, or control of the above-named Plaintiff and that they be made available to the undersigned at the office of the undersigned located at 7362 University Avenue NE, Suite 120, Fridley, MN 55432, or, alternatively, that legible copies of the same be provided to the undersigned.

DEFINITIONS AND INSTRUCTIONS

1. "You" and "your" when used herein shall refer to the party or parties to whom these Requests are directed, and all persons acting on your behalf, including, but not limited to, attorneys and their associates, investigators, employees, agents, and other representatives.

2. "Person" shall mean any natural person and/or any entity, including, without limiting the foregoing, all proprietorships, corporations, partnerships, joint ventures, groups, associations, organizations, or other legal or business entities.

3. "Document" or "documents" shall mean all written, printed, typed, drawn, reported, recorded, graphic or photographic matter and sound reproduction of tapes, records, or other devices, of every nature, within the scope of Rules 26 and 34 of the Minnesota Rules of Civil Procedure, however produced

or reproduced, now or at any time, in your possession, custody, or control, and any drafts, copies, or reproductions of the foregoing items and copies or reproductions of the foregoing upon which notations in writing have been made which do not appear on the originals. The term "document" or "documents" also includes all electronically stored information (E.S.I.). This includes all documents that may come under your custody or control between the time your Responses are served and the date of trial.

4. The terms "identify" or "identity," "identification," "describe," or "description" shall mean:

a. When used in reference to an individual shall mean to state his or her full name, present or last known residence, business or official affiliation, and business address;
b. When used in reference to a firm, partnership, incorporated or unincorporated association or other legal or commercial entity shall mean to state the entity's full name and trade name, if any, the state in which it is incorporated or otherwise registered by law or organized, the address and telephone number of its principal place of business, and the names and titles of those officers, directors, managing agents, or other employees who have knowledge of the matters involved in the Request and its nature;
c. When used in reference to a document shall mean its date of preparation, author, addressee(s) or other intended recipient, subject matter, type of document (e.g. letter, memorandum, inventory list, note, telegram, contract, chart, etc.), its title, hearing, or other designation, a summary of its content, or other means of identifying it, and its present location or custodian, or, if any such document or file was, but is no longer in your possession or subject to your control, the disposition that was made of it;
d. When used in reference to a conversation, conference, meeting, or communication shall mean that you shall state the following:
   (1) The date and time thereof;
   (2) The location at which it occurred;
   (3) The identity of all persons participating or attending;
   (4) The identity of all documents recording or summarizing or otherwise arising from the conversation, conference, or meeting; and
   (5) The method of communication utilized (e.g. telephone, in-person communication, or other means), or if the method of communication was by telephone, specify the caller and the person called.

e. When used in reference to a factual situation, include the persons and documents plus specification of places, dates, exact words used in conversation (or substance of conversation if exact words are not remembered), acts, events, occurrences, etc. State with particularity all facts known that bear upon or are related to the matter that is the subject of the inquiry.

f. When used in reference to the source of information upon which a Response to a Request is based, shall mean to identify the person, communication, or documents from whom or which information constituting all or part of the basis of the Response has been derived.

You are hereby requested, pursuant to Rules 26 and 34 of the Minnesota Rules of Civil Procedure, to produce and permit Barbara J. Gislason, attorney for the Defendant, to inspect and copy the following designated documents:

DOCUMENTS REQUESTED

1. All documents read, reviewed, used, relied upon, or consulted in preparing your Responses to this Request for Production of Documents.

2. All documents identified, referred to, or relied upon in your Responses to this Request for Production of Documents.

3. All documents supporting any of the allegations, facts, denials, defenses, or other matters in any pleadings in this case.

4. All documents that refute or tend to refute allegations made by the other party.

5. All documents regarding or pertaining to any laws, rules, regulations, procedures, policies, or standards that support, or tend to support, any of the facts, denials, defenses, or other matters asserted in your pleadings or discovery responses.

6. All "statements" concerning the subject matter of the lawsuit within the meaning of Rule 26.02 of the Minnesota Rules of Civil Procedure.

7. All documents that you claim to be admissions against interest made by the other party relating to your claims or the other party's defenses.

8. Your curriculum vitae and resume.

9. All documents of veterinary or other medical treatment of the companion animal.

10. All documents that support your claim that you made expenditures to purchase and care for the companion animal, including, but not limited to:

a. Breeding
b. Veterinary and dental services
c. Food
d. Toys
e. Grooming
f. Training
g. Behaviorist
h. Boarding
i. Transportation
j. Dog walking or daycare
k. Any other payments

11. Any and all contracts, written agreements, or any document, letter, or record related to any agreements between the parties regarding the companion animal.

12. Any evidence, including, but not limited to, photographs, images, audio recordings, or social media communications, that contradicts the other party's pleadings, claims, or defenses.

13. All documents related to your homeowner's or renter's insurance coverage, automobile insurance, or pet insurance coverage that applies to the companion animal.

14. Any and all contracts, written agreements, co-ownership agreements, or any document, letter, or record related to any agreements between the parties or any third party, including, but not limited to, a breeder or rescue.

15. Any and all records that support your claim, if any, that the parties routinely exchanged physical custody or possession of the companion animal pursuant to a written or oral contract.

16. All records directly or indirectly related to your payments for veterinary or other medical treatment or examination of the companion animal by anyone.

17. All records that document any expenditures not previously disclosed that you have made on behalf of the companion animal.

18. Any and all documents and records of any kind, including, but not limited to, litter applications, registrations, and other AKC documents related to the companion animal.

19. All records pertaining to the licensure of the companion animal.

20. Copies of all police reports or animal control records or other complaints related to the companion animal.

21. Copies of any insurance claims made with regard to the losses sustained or caused by the companion animal or anyone injured by a companion animal in your custody, care, or control.

22. All other documents as defined within the above definitions which have not been specifically requested in the foregoing demands, but which are in your possession and relate to the subject matter of this litigation.

23. All photographs and videos you have, including electronic, that include the companion animal.

24. All documents which you may use as evidence at a trial or hearing in this matter.

25. Signed veterinary and dental releases for this office to obtain copies of all records and information from all professionals who have provided services to the companion animal or other animals that have been under your care, custody, or control within the past three (3) years.

26. Your complete personal and business federal and state income tax returns, with all attached schedules, beginning one (1) year before the companion animal was born or acquired, whichever was later, to the present.

27. Any and all documents that you currently have in your possession or which you could obtain through reasonable effort pertaining to the companion animal in which you claim any interest, including purchase agreement, adoption agreement, security agreement, certificate of title, certificate of breeder, and written appraisal. Include receipts, cancelled checks, charge account statements, and electronic records evidencing any and all expenses associated with, related to, or for the benefit of the companion animal.

28. All documents that reflect email, text message, social media, or any other kinds of communications between you and the other party that directly or indirectly refers to the companion animal.

29. All of your cell phone records from one (1) year before the commencement of this action to the present.

Dated: ______________________________ ______________________________

Barbara J. Gislason
Atty ID No. 124011
Attorney for Defendant
Law Office of Barbara J. Gislason
7362 University Avenue NE
Suite 120
Fridley, MN 55432
Telephone: (763) 5729297

STATE OF MINNESOTA	DISTRICT COURT
COUNTY OF PINK	SIXTH JUDICIAL DISTRICT
	CASE TYPE: OTHER CIVIL
Melissa Cox,	Court File No. 12345
Plaintiff,	
vs.	**DEFENDANT'S REQUEST FOR PRODUCTION OF STATEMENTS TO PLAINTIFF**
Jennifer Hadley,	
Defendant.	

TO: PLAINTIFF MELISSA COX, 123 COURT STREET, MINNEAPOLIS, MINNESOTA 55414.

Pursuant to Rules 26 and 34 of the Rules of Civil Procedure for the Minnesota District Courts, you are hereby requested to produce for inspection or copying by counsel for Plaintiff, within forty-five (45) days of the date of this request, the following statements:

1. All statements in your possession, custody, or control that in any way concern this lawsuit or its subject matter.

If you maintain that any such statement need not be produced in response to this request, provide information sufficient to identify and describe that statement for purposes of a ruling by the Court under Rule 26.02(3), including the following:

1. The identity of the person who gave the statement;
2. The identity of the person who took the statement;
3. The means of taking the statement;
4. The date of the statement; and
5. The general nature of the subject matter of the statement.

For the purpose of this request, a statement is (1) a written statement signed or otherwise adopted or approved by the person making it, or (2) a stenographic, mechanical, electrical, or other recording, or a transcription thereof, which is a substantially verbatim recital of any oral statement by the person making it and contemporaneously recorded.

You may produce a photocopy in lieu of the original of any statement which has been reduced to writing. As to any statements which have not been reduced to writing, you may identify the location and custodian of each such statement and the times and conditions upon which it will be made available for inspection and/or transcription.

This is an ongoing Request for Production of Statements now in existence or hereafter taken or obtained at any time prior to the final entry of Judgment in the above-captioned matter.

Dated: ______________________ ______________________

Barbara J. Gislason
Atty ID No. 124011
Attorney for Defendant
Law Office of Barbara J. Gislason
7362 University Avenue NE
Suite 120
Fridley, MN 55432
Telephone: (763) 5729297

STATE OF MINNESOTA	DISTRICT COURT
COUNTY OF PINK	SIXTH JUDICIAL DISTRICT
	CASE TYPE: OTHER CIVIL
	Court File No. 12345

Melissa Cox,

Plaintiff,

vs.

DEFENDANT'S ANSWERS TO PLAINTIFF'S INTERROGATORIES

Jennifer Hadley,

Defendant.

TO: PLAINTIFF MELISSA COX, 123 COURT STREET, MINNEAPOLIS, MINNESOTA 55414.

Pursuant to Rule 33 of the Minnesota Rules of Civil Procedure, Defendant Jennifer Hadley submits the following Objections and Answers to Plaintiff's Interrogatories and states as follows:

All Answers are made without in any way waiving or intending to waive, but on the contrary, intending to preserve and preserving:

1. All questions as to competency, relevancy, materiality, privilege, and admissibility of evidence for any purpose in any subsequent proceedings or the trial of this or any other action.

2. The right to object to the use of these Answers, or the subject matter thereof, in any subsequent proceedings or the trial of this or any other action on any ground.

3. The right to object on any ground at any time or to demand for further response to these or any other Interrogatories or other discovery proceedings involving or relating to the subject matter of the Answers herein.

4. The right to supplement and/or amend these Answers based upon the recollection of persons presently unavailable or the discovery of additional documents or information.

GENERAL OBJECTIONS AND COMMENTS

1. Defendant objects to the instructions set forth in Plaintiff's Interrogatories to Defendant to the extent that same set forth requirements which are

outside of the scope of the Minnesota Rules of Civil Procedure. Without waiving the foregoing objection, Defendant will Answer the Interrogatories in accordance with the Minnesota Rules of Civil Procedure and the Rules of Practice for Civil Actions.

2. Defendant objects to each Interrogatory to the extent that the information requested by such Interrogatory is protected by the attorney/client privilege, the work product doctrine, or other available privileges under the Minnesota Rules of Civil Procedure, Minnesota Rules of Evidence, trade secrets, and other applicable law.

3. Defendant objects to each Interrogatory to the extent that the information requested therein is not required to be provided by the provisions of Rule 26 of the Minnesota Rules of Civil Procedure.

4. Defendant objects to each Interrogatory to the extent that it attempts to impose duties on Defendant that are not provided for by the Minnesota Rules of Civil Procedure or other applicable law.

5. Because of the cumulative nature of the information sought by these Interrogatories, much of the information supplied by Defendant in any Interrogatory is also responsive to other Interrogatories. In many instances, an Answer to an Interrogatory may refer to Answers given in prior Interrogatories. However, Defendant may not have made all of the applicable cross references. Consequently, the Answers to these Interrogatories are to be read as a whole.

6. Much of the information requested by these Interrogatories is contained in various documents within the possession of the Defendant and/or Plaintiff. Defendant hereby incorporates all of the information contained in the documents which Defendant has produced or will produce, as well as the information contained in the documents which are in the possession of Plaintiff.

7. Many of these Interrogatories request that Defendant specify "each" or "every" relating to certain matters, facts, or documents. It is doubtful that any person or entity could provide "each" or "every" piece of information or identify every person arguably having knowledge of facts or that is related to certain claims or aspects of a case. Defendant has made a diligent inquiry and has supplied the information to provide reasonably complete and accurate Answers to these Interrogatories under the circumstances. Further, she hereby offers Plaintiff access to relevant records or documents in her possession in the event that the same contain, or are believed to contain, additional information which may relate to this litigation.

8. Defendant reserves the right to revise, correct, add to, supplement, and clarify any of her Answers.

9. The dog at issue in this case will be referred to as the "companion animal."

Without waiving any of the above-stated objections, Defendant, as and for her Answers to Plaintiff's Interrogatories, responds as follows:

INTERROGATORY NO. 1

Identify each person whom you believe has or may have any knowledge or information concerning any facts relating to the claims, defenses, and/or subject matter of this litigation, and, for each such person, describe all such knowledge, information, and facts and set forth the basis of each such person's knowledge or information.

ANSWER TO INTERROGATORY NO. 1

Objected to as overly broad and ambiguous. Without waiving her objection, Defendant states that the companion animal was Defendant's constant companion at her work at Denver School and as a softball coach and to Answer this Interrogatory would require the disclosure of all the administrators, faculty, athletics spectators, students, students' relatives, parents, other employees, and independent contractors that Defendant had contact with while at Denver School, and people who have seen Defendant walk the companion animal all over the United States, including in Minnesota, Arizona, and New York. Without waiving this objection, Defendant discloses the following:[1]

- Defendant's mother, Debbie Frankfurt, saw the companion animal in Defendant's company at the parties' home in Minnesota; at Defendant's sister's home in Minnetonka, Minnesota; at Defendant's mother's home in Texas; and in New York. She has observed the excellent care Defendant gives the companion animal. Defendant's mother made a harness for the companion animal that Defendant uses. While in Defendant's company, she saw Defendant feed the companion animal twice a day, plus a snack at night, exercise her, pet her, and saw the companion animal sleep by Defendant's side. She has noticed that when traveling, the companion animal is always close by Defendant's side.
- Defendant's friend, Sara Jorgensen, saw the companion animal at her house for a play date between the companion animal and Sammy, Sara's Cocker Spaniel. She also saw the companion animal in New York twice,

1. In this action, before providing Plaintiff with her client's discovery responses, Defendant's attorney also warned of her intention to seek relief from a judgment under Rule 60. Once Plaintiff received Defendant's discovery responses, Plaintiff promptly dismissed her action.

once in 2008 and once in 2010. She has observed the excellent care Defendant gives the companion animal. She saw Defendant feed the companion animal twice a day, plus a snack at night, exercise her, pet her, and knows that the companion animal went into the same room where Defendant slept. She has noticed that when traveling, the companion animal is always close by Defendant's side.

- Defendant's sister, Alexis Stein, watched the companion animal when the parties took trips out of town. When Defendant visited Alexis and her kids, Defendant brought the companion animal on weekdays and on weekends. Alexis also saw the companion animal at the parties' home and has observed the excellent care Defendant gives the companion animal. She saw Defendant feed the companion animal twice a day, plus a snack at night, exercise her, pet her, and saw the companion animal sleep by Defendant's side when Defendant stayed at her home. Alexis also often saw Defendant and the companion animal at Denver School, where Alexis' kids attended, and often went to softball games where the companion animal was with Defendant. Alexis sometimes helped Defendant with score keeping at these games.
- Defendant's niece, Madeline Stein, saw the companion animal with Defendant at the parties' house and at her house. Because Defendant tutored Madeline once a week for one year, Madeline was at the parties' home a lot and saw the companion animal with Defendant.
- Defendant's nephew, Christopher Stein, saw Defendant and the companion animal all the time as he attended Denver School, was in Defendant's class in 2006 and 2007, and sat in Defendant's office during his free period at school with the companion animal (many kids did that). He also saw the companion animal at his mother Alexis Stein's home and the parties' home. He has also seen the companion animal in the summer in New York for the past three years.
- Defendant's nephew, Bradley Stein, saw Defendant and the companion animal all the time as he attended Denver School. He also saw the companion animal at his mother Alexis Stein's home and the parties' home. He also saw the companion animal in the summer in New York for the past three years.
- Defendant's partner since 2007, Jessica Fink, sees the companion animal with Defendant all the time. She delivered the companion animal to Plaintiff in Minnesota in August 2009 when Plaintiff insisted that Defendant miss a family reunion to fulfill Plaintiff's preferred access schedule. She has observed Defendant taking the companion animal to the veterinarian,

making her homemade food of rice, chicken, and sweet potatoes, and watched her nurse the companion animal back to health when she was ill. She has seen Defendant work with the companion animal and a dog trainer for basic manners. She accompanies Defendant on some of the companion animal's daily walks. She has observed the companion animal having bed privileges and Defendant grooming her, brushing her coat every day, and taking her to a groomer every three weeks, as evidenced by how the companion animal looks when Defendant returns her. She has watched Defendant's care getting the companion animal into and out of a travel carrier and how when she packs for the dog, she includes toys the companion animal enjoys. For a while, she observed that Defendant even transported the companion animal's bed back and forth to Minnesota as she helped Defendant handle these items at the airport. She is also aware of how difficult Plaintiff is in working out travel schedules and her refusal to cooperate to pick up the companion animal upon Defendant's arrival in Minnesota or share expenses.

- Defendant's friend, Lindsay King, often saw Defendant in 2004 through 2007 to have lunch with Defendant and also went to the parties' house often. Defendant would bring the companion animal to Lindsay's house. Lindsay's dogs, a Yorkshire terrier and a Labrador, had play dates with the companion animal once a month at her home. She moved to Tennessee for a position at a clinic. She saw the companion animal go everywhere with Defendant for years.
- Janet Grant coached softball and Defendant coached the Denver team. They played each other every summer and the companion animal was there. Janet also saw the companion animal in Arizona at Defendant's house and was able to observe how well the companion animal was doing. She has seen the companion animal in all kinds of places and situations, including at the parties' home and later, Defendant's apartment.
- Mark Brick, a Denver teacher and past dean, saw the companion animal at school, usually in Defendant's office. He saw her at softball games while Defendant coached.
- Defendant's sister, Allison Leonard, saw the companion animal at the parties' home after she returned to Minnesota.
- Defendant's aunt, Donna Wendt, and her partner, Patricia Brandt, saw the companion animal in New York for six summers. They have seen Defendant walk the companion animal and observed that she behaves by Defendant's side.
- Defendant's brother, Trevor Hadley, moved to Minnesota in 2008 after Defendant moved out of state. Defendant stayed overnight at her brother's

when she transported the companion animal to Minnesota rather than just getting on another airplane the same day and flying home. He also observed all the dog supplies Defendant brought back and forth with her on the airplane and how she would put the companion animal in a dog carrier for travel when picking up or retrieving the companion animal.

- Laurie Peters, an old friend of Defendant's, has seen the companion animal and Defendant in Arizona and in New York. She has seen Defendant walk the companion animal many times and how well they interact.
- Emily Andrews, Denver School Counselor, saw the companion animal in Defendant's office year after year. She saw the companion animal interacting with the students in the classroom while Defendant taught.
- Garrett Foster saw Defendant with the companion animal in the classroom and at department meetings in Defendant's office. He saw the companion animal on average four days a week and was one of the first teachers to see Defendant when Defendant returned from New Hampshire with the companion animal as a small puppy. He saw the small kennel for the companion animal in Defendant's office and her water bowl and toys. The companion animal was always behaved, calm, never barked, and obeyed simple voice commands from Defendant. The companion animal was off leash in the building and everyone saw the companion animal walking close to Defendant down the school halls. If Defendant asked, "Where's the classroom?" the companion animal would run down the hall to her office.
- Michelle Frank, one of Defendant's closest friends and former dean of Denver School, saw the companion animal at school and the parties' home. She saw the companion animal arrive at Denver School in the mornings and saw the companion animal at Defendant's apartment after the parties separated. She also saw the companion animal with Defendant on the softball field.
- Richard Klepp was the head of the Math Department at Denver School and he saw the companion animal in the office, classroom, and department when he was in the building, probably three to four days a week.
- Kristy Knowles taught across the hall from Defendant's classroom and saw the companion animal three to four times a week in the classroom, department meetings, and office. She saw the companion animal in her kennel in Defendant's office and under the desk hanging out with the children.
- Linda Frank, a French Teacher at Denver School, saw the companion animal in the classroom and went on walks with the companion animal around the school and the lake. She also saw her in New York in the summer of 2010 and at her own house a few times.

- Carla Hunter, a Denver School teacher who taught with Defendant, saw the companion animal four or five times a week in the classroom and walking down the halls.
- Nicole French shared a classroom with Defendant. She saw the companion animal four to five times a week. Sometimes she would watch the softball team or class and see the companion animal with Defendant.
- Sophie Hanson, a student who often visited the companion animal in Defendant's office at Denver School, saw the companion animal once or twice a week. She would play with the companion animal, often hugging and kissing her.
- Missy Porter, a science student on the softball team (although she was not on Defendant's team), saw the companion animal on the field and she went to Defendant's office often to talk to Defendant and play with the companion animal.
- Lisa Sorenson, a student on Defendant's softball team, saw the companion animal on the field two to three times a week and also on vacation.
- Rebecca Marsh, a science student on Defendant's softball team, saw the companion animal in the school and on the Lacrosse field.
- Cooper Walsh, a student on Defendant's softball team, saw the companion animal in the school and on the softball field.
- Holly Thompson taught at Denver School and was on Defendant's softball team and she saw the companion animal in the school and on the softball field.
- Maggie Stein, a student and softball player, often saw the companion animal.
- Anne Hart, a student and softball player, saw the companion animal at the parties' home and around Defendant at the school.
- Martin Anderson, a student, went to the Denver School office a lot and saw the companion animal with Defendant.
- Christine Field, a student and on Defendant's softball team, saw the companion animal both in the school and on the field.
- Molly Campbell, a science student and on the softball team, saw the companion animal both in the school and on the field.

INTERROGATORY NO. 2

Identify each person you may call as a witness at the trial herein and for each such person, describe all information and facts as to which each such person is expected to testify.

ANSWER TO INTERROGATORY NO. 2

Defendant reserves the right to call the parties and all witnesses identified in Answer to Interrogatory No. 1, which is incorporated by reference, as well as those listed in her other discovery responses. All witnesses will describe the observations they have made concerning the companion animal and the parties over the years. Other names may be supplemented as discovery continues.

INTERROGATORY NO. 3

Describe all facts that in any way support, refute, or otherwise relate to any of the claims, defenses, and/or subject matter of the above-entitled action.

ANSWER TO INTERROGATORY NO. 3

Defendant's Answer and Counter Claim and Answers to Plaintiff's Interrogatories and Responses to Plaintiff's Request for Production of Documents are incorporated by reference. Plaintiff has possession of Defendant's relevant records. Discovery is continuing.

INTERROGATORY NO. 4

Identify all documents or conversations that in any way support, refute, or otherwise relate to any of the claims, defenses, and/or subject matter of the above-entitled action.

ANSWER TO INTERROGATORY NO. 4

Objected to as overly broad and ambiguous. Without waiving her objection, see Defendant's Responses to Plaintiff's Request for Production of Documents, which are incorporated by reference. Discovery is continuing. Defendant regularly paid for the companion animal's expenses while the parties lived together, took the companion animal to school with her each day, and paid for dog walkers, dog groomers, and doggie daycares when she could not. This is all evidence that the companion animal was Defendant's dog. The parties have had countless conversations about how or why Plaintiff might sue Defendant.

INTERROGATORY NO. 5

Identify each person you may call as an expert witness at the trial herein and for each such person state the following:

a. The subject matter on which the expert is expected to testify.
b. The substance of the facts and opinions to which the expert is expected to testify.

ANSWER TO INTERROGATORY NO. 5

No expert witness has yet been identified. Defendant will notify Plaintiff if an expert is retained.

INTERROGATORY NO. 6

Identify each person that you are aware has given an oral, written, or recorded statement to anyone concerning facts which in any way pertain to any of the claims, defenses, or subject matter of this litigation, specifying and identifying the date and place each statement was taken, the person(s) presently in possession of each statement, the person(s) taking the statement, and the content of the statement. For the purposes of this Interrogatory, the word "statement" means any statement within the meaning of Minn. R. Civ. P. 26.

ANSWER TO INTERROGATORY NO. 6

Defendant has taken no statements.

INTERROGATORY NO. 7

If you allege that you are not liable to Plaintiff as set forth in the Complaint, then describe with particularity each reason you believe you are not liable to Plaintiff, identify each document or conversation supporting, refuting, or otherwise relating to such allegation, and, for each such fact, identify each person who you believe has or may have knowledge or information relating to the fact, and for each such person, describe in detail all such knowledge, information, and facts, and set forth the basis of each such person's knowledge and information.

ANSWER TO INTERROGATORY NO. 7

Objected to as overly broad and ambiguous. Without waiving her objection, Defendant states that the parties lived together and often discussed the companion animal. Furthermore, this Interrogatory seeks legal opinion subject to attorney/client privilege and is therefore impermissible. See Answer to Interrogatory No. 1, which contains detailed information about many people who have knowledge of the relationship between Defendant and the companion animal.

INTERROGATORY NO. 8

For each of the Affirmative Defenses set forth in your Answer to the Complaint, please state separately and in detail:

a. Describe all facts that in any way support, refute, or otherwise relate to such Affirmative Defense;

b. Identify all documents or conversations that in any way support or otherwise relate to such Affirmative Defense; and
c. Identify each person whom you believe has or may have any knowledge or information concerning any facts relating to such Affirmative Defense, and, for each such person, describe all such knowledge, information, and facts and set forth the basis of each such person's knowledge or information.

ANSWER TO INTERROGATORY NO. 8

Defendant objects to this Interrogatory as overly broad and ambiguous. Without waiving her objection, Defendant refers Plaintiff to her Answer and Counter Claim, her Responses to Plaintiff's Request for Production of Documents, and her other detailed Answers to Interrogatories.

INTERROGATORY NO. 9

Identify every person who provided information used in Answering these Interrogatories and specify each Interrogatory for which each such person provided information.

ANSWER TO INTERROGATORY NO. 9

Objected to as subject to attorney/client privilege. Without waiving her objection, Defendant incorporates by reference Defendant's document production.

Dated: ______________________ ______________________

Barbara J. Gislason
Atty ID No. 124011
Attorney for Defendant
Law Office of Barbara J. Gislason
7362 University Avenue NE
Suite 120
Fridley, MN 55432
Telephone: (763) 5729297

STATE OF MINNESOTA	DISTRICT COURT
COUNTY OF PINK	SIXTH JUDICIAL DISTRICT
	CASE TYPE: OTHER CIVIL

Melissa Cox,

Court File No. 12345

Plaintiff,

vs.

DEFENDANT'S RESPONSES TO PLAINTIFF'S REQUEST FOR PRODUCTION OF DOCUMENTS

Jennifer Hadley,

Defendant.

TO: PLAINTIFF MELISSA COX, 123 COURT STREET, MINNEAPOLIS, MINNESOTA 55414.

Pursuant to Rules 26 and 33 of the Rules of Civil Procedure, Defendant submits the following Objections and Responses to Plaintiff's Request for Production of Documents:

GENERAL OBJECTIONS AND COMMENTS

1. Defendant objects to each Request to the extent that the information requested by such Request is protected by the attorney/client privilege, the work product doctrine, or other available privileges under the Minnesota Rules of Civil Procedure, Minnesota Rules of Evidence, and other applicable law.

2. Defendant objects to each Request to the extent that the information requested therein is not required to be provided by the provisions of Rule 26 of the Minnesota Rules of Civil Procedure.

3. Defendant objects to each Request to the extent that it attempts to impose duties on Respondent that are not provided for by the Minnesota Rules of Civil Procedure or other applicable law.

4. Because of the cumulative nature of the information sought by these Requests, much of the information supplied by Defendant in any Response is also responsive to other Requests. In many instances, a Response to a Request may refer to Responses given in prior Requests. However, Defendant may not

have made all of the applicable cross-references. Consequently, the Responses to these Requests for Production of Documents are to be read as a whole.

5. Some of the Requests ask that Defendant produce "any" or "all" documents relating to certain matters, facts, or documents. It is doubtful that any person or entity could provide "any" or "all" documents arguably that relate to certain Requests. Defendant has made a diligent inquiry and has supplied all documents which are reasonably responsive in order to provide complete and accurate Responses to Plaintiff's Request for Production of Documents under the circumstances.

6. Defendant objects to each Request to the extent that it requests documents to which Plaintiff has equal access, or which are in Plaintiff's possession. All such documents to which Plaintiff has equal access or which are in the possession of Plaintiff are incorporated in Defendant's Response and Defendant deems same to be "produced."

7. Defendant reserves the right to revise, correct, add to, supplement, and clarify any of her Responses.

8. The Responses given by Defendant are subject to these general objections, as well as the objections, if any, made to each specific Request.

9. Defendant gives these Responses without conceding that Minnesota or this Court have jurisdiction to decide this case.

10. Council for Defendant invites discussion with counsel for Plaintiff with respect to the Request for Production of Documents and the Responses and objections thereto, with the expectation that discussions between counsel may eliminate or modify objections, reduce burdens on Defendant, or otherwise result in the mutually satisfactory resolution of objections contained herein.

Without waiving any of the above-stated objections, Defendant, as and for her Responses to Plaintiff's Request for Production of Documents, states as follows:

REQUEST NO. 1:

Provide all photographs, slides, films, moving pictures, videotapes, or other types of photographic representations in your possession relating to the subject matter of this litigation.

RESPONSE TO REQUEST NO. 1:

Objected to as overly broad and ambiguous. Attached hereto are photographs pertaining to the companion animal.

REQUEST NO. 2:

Provide curriculum vitaes or resumes for each individual that you may call as an expert witness at the trial of this case.

RESPONSE TO REQUEST NO. 2:

No expert witness has been retained. Defendant reserves the right to retain an expert.

REQUEST NO. 3:

Provide any and all work papers, notes, and documents in the file of any expert witness who may testify, or of any expert witness who has written a report which is or will be relied upon in whole or in part by a testifying expert.

RESPONSE TO REQUEST NO. 3:

No expert witness has been retained. Defendant reserves the right to retain an expert.

REQUEST NO. 4:

Provide each document identified in any Answer to Plaintiff's Interrogatories to Defendant.

RESPONSE TO REQUEST NO. 4:

See Defendant's other Responses, which are incorporated by reference.

REQUEST NO. 5:

Provide all correspondence between the parties or other persons related to the subject matter of this litigation.

RESPONSE TO REQUEST NO. 5:

Relevant correspondence is in Plaintiff's possession or subject to attorney/client privilege.

REQUEST NO. 6:

Provide any and all contracts or agreements drafted regarding the subject matter of this litigation.

RESPONSE TO REQUEST NO. 6:

Plaintiff has possession of these documents, if any. Other records are objected to as they are subject to attorney/client privilege. Without waiving her objection, Defendant produces the companion animal's purchase agreement.

REQUEST NO. 7:

Provide all other documents, as defined below, which have not been specifically requested in the foregoing demands, but which are in your possession and relate to the subject matter of this litigation.

RESPONSE TO REQUEST NO. 7:

Defendant has yearly calendar records available at her attorney's office for viewing. Defendant's relevant Visa records and cancelled check records are attached, as well as ledgers reflecting dog walking, veterinarian expenses, food/accessories, boarding, airfare, and grooming expenses paid by Defendant, as well as ledgers showing airfare, car rental, parking, hotel, and veterinarian expenses paid by Defendant, together with receipts and veterinary records. Records that are more extensive will also be available for review at her attorney's office as Defendant has ordered additional credit card records from her bank and they have confirmed with Defendant that they have been located and will be mailed soon. In addition, attached hereto is a summary of Defendant's expenditures for the benefit of the companion animal to date, with the exception of food and grooming after the parties' separation, and the records pending from her bank. Other records are in Plaintiff's possession. Defendant reserves her right to supplement this Response.

Dated: ______________________________ ______________________________

Barbara J. Gislason
Atty ID No. 124011
Attorney for Defendant
Law Office of Barbara J. Gislason
7362 University Avenue NE
Suite 120
Fridley, MN 55432
Telephone: (763) 5729297

STATE OF MINNESOTA | DISTRICT COURT
COUNTY OF PINK | SIXTH JUDICIAL DISTRICT
CASE TYPE: OTHER CIVIL
Court File No. 12345

Melissa Cox,

Plaintiff,

vs.

DEFENDANT'S RESPONSES TO PLAINTIFF'S REQUEST FOR PRODUCTION OF STATEMENTS

Jennifer Hadley,

Defendant.

TO: PLAINTIFF MELISSA COX, 123 COURT STREET, MINNEAPOLIS, MINNESOTA 55414.

Defendant, as and for her responses to Plaintiff's Request for Statements, states as follows:

REQUEST NO. 1:

All statements in your possession, custody, or control which in any way concern this lawsuit or its subject matter. If you maintain that any such statement need not be produced in response to this request, provide information sufficient to identify and describe that statement for purposes of a ruling by the Court under Rule 26.02(3), including the following:

1. The identity of the person who gave the statement;
2. The identity of the person who took the statement;
3. The means of taking the statement;
4. The date of the statement; and
5. The general nature of the subject matter of the statement.

For the purpose of this request, a statement is (1) a written statement signed or otherwise adopted or approved by the person making it, or (2) a stenographic, mechanical, electrical, or other recording, or a transcription thereof, which is a substantially verbatim recital of any oral statement by the person making it and contemporaneously recorded.

RESPONSE TO REQUEST NO. 1:

Defendant has no statements in her possession, custody, or control related to this lawsuit or its subject matter.

Dated: ______________________________ ______________________________

Barbara J. Gislason
Atty ID No. 124011
Attorney for Defendant
Law Office of Barbara J. Gislason
7362 University Avenue NE
Suite 120
Fridley, MN 55432
Telephone: (763) 5729297

Appendix 11

Order Denying Replevin

Looking at a replevin action from several different angles can be helpful. Below is an example of a well-crafted and groundbreaking public Order Denying Replevin from a judge in Hennepin County, Minnesota. The order is reflective of how courts can utilize both traditional ideas about animal ownership and newer ideas about the best interests of both humans and animals. It is probable that Judge Chu's order will be typical of orders to come. Here are some of the highlights from the court's findings of fact:

- The parties intended to jointly adopt the rescue dog.
- The plaintiff paid a very small purchase price.
- The defendant spent a significant amount on veterinary expenses.
- The defendant had possession of the dog for the past two years.
- The defendant lives in a desirable location near a dog park.
- The plaintiff has a large yard.
- The plaintiff is unwilling to share possession of the dog.
- The plaintiff is subject to a harassment order involving the defendant.
- The plaintiff initiated a replevin action following an unfavorable result in a separate civil proceeding.

Based upon these factors, the court considered the plaintiff's initial expenditures for the dog of $26.63 and that he later paid veterinary bills totaling $226.06. In comparison, the defendant paid more than $2,733.04 for veterinary fees. In exercising her discretion, Judge Chu's decision was impacted by the following:

- Traditional jurisprudence is that animals are personal property.
- Animal protection laws address the subjects of torture, neglect, cages, abandonment, transport, seasonal health requirements, and prohibition

on poisoning, dog fighting, and regulation of housing based upon climate regulations that distinguish nonliving animals from nonliving chattel. Laws permit felony prosecutions.
- Cases that inspired or impressed Judge Chu included *Rabideau v. City of Racine*,[1] *Bueckner v. Hamel*,[2] *State of Ohio v. Anderson*,[3] and *Fitzgerald v. State*.[4]

Judge Chu offered her analysis on the subjects of animal domestication, philosophy, and science. More specifically, she stated the following:

- Dogs became domesticated in 6300 BC.
- Deceased humans have been buried with their dogs for 12,000 years.
- Dogs provide work, including in law enforcement and friendship.
- Cartesian views, referring to philosopher René Descartes, are out of date.
- Societal views about companion animals have changed.
- Animals are sentient and emotive beings.
- Animals provide companionship to the humans with whom they live.
- Taking into account a dog's best interest is consistent with turning tides.
- Human participants have worthy interests, too.

Judge Chu also described the ownership dispute with the dog to be a "custody" issue and explained that legislature recognizes dogs as living beings that deserve basic legal protections. With regard to the human participants, Judge Chu considered their emotional connections to the dog, as well as their financial investment in the enjoyment of a relationship with the dog.

The four factors the court utilized as decision-making criteria were (1) which party selected the dog for adoption and paid the initial adoption fee, (2) the extent to which each party provided care and love for the dog, (3) the extent to which each party provided financial support for the dog, and (4) which result is in the dog's best interest. Utilizing all of these factors, Judge Chu awarded the dog to the defendant even though it was the plaintiff who paid the dog's nominal purchase price.

1. 627 N.W.2d 795, 797 (Wis. 2001).
2. 886 S.W.2d 368, 377 (Tex. App. 1994).
3. 566 N.E. 1224, 1225–26 (Ohio 1991).
4. 864 A.2d 1006, 1015 (Md. 2004).

STATE OF MINNESOTA | DISTRICT COURT
COUNTY OF HENNEPIN | FOURTH JUDICIAL DISTRICT

Case Type: Conciliation Appeal

Phillip Nelson, | Judge Regina M. Chu

Plaintiff,

ORDER DENYING REPLEVIN

vs. | File No. 27 CV 08-4388

Roxanne Radeck,

Defendant.

The above-entitled matter came duly on for a court trial before the Honorable Regina M. Chu, Judge of District Court, on April 23, 2009, upon Defendant's Removal of a Case from Conciliation Court to District Court. Christopher Keyser, Esq., appeared for and on behalf of Plaintiff. Defendant appeared *pro se*. Plaintiff Phillip Nelson testified on his own behalf. Defendant Roxanne Radeck testified on her own behalf. Exhibits were offered and received.

Based on the testimony and exhibits admitted at trial, and all the files, records, and proceedings herein, the Court makes the following:

FINDINGS OF FACT:

1. In April 2001, Defendant moved into Plaintiff's residence located in Rockford, Minnesota. The two were involved in a romantic relationship.

2. In approximately April 2003, the parties jointly decided to adopt a dog. They made several visits to the Lakes Area Humane Society in Alexander, Minnesota, in hopes of finding a dog.

3. Defendant and Plaintiff mutually agreed to adopt a golden retriever/yellow lab mix. They jointly decided to name the dog "Sammy." The adoption form associated with this adoption listed the "Adoptee/Owner" as Plaintiff. The form only allowed one individual to be named as the adoptee.

4. The parties were not able to take Sammy home on the same day in which they decided to adopt him. Instead, Plaintiff had to return to the Humane Society on April 11, 2003, to physically take Sammy home. Defendant did not

participate in picking up Sammy because she was working at the time of the scheduled pick up. Plaintiff paid $25.00 for Sammy, plus $1.63 in tax.

5. The parties and Sammy lived together in a residence owned by Plaintiff until August 3, 2007, when Plaintiff and Defendant ended their romantic relationship. The break-up of the parties' relationship involved substantial conflict.

6. In an effort to reduce tensions, Plaintiff left his residence while Defendant moved her stuff out of the house. Among the belongings removed from the residence by Defendant was Sammy.

7. Between April 11, 2003 and August 3, 2007 (when Defendant moved out), Defendant made the following payments associated with Sammy: (a) a $61.40 vet bill dated April 29, 2003; (b) a $57.31 vet bill dated June 23, 2003; (c) a $121.50 vet bill dated August 22, 2003; (d) a $79.01 vet bill dated April 27, 2004; (e) a $50.50 vet bill dated July 2, 2004; (f) a $44.46 vet bill dated October 16, 2004; (g) a $60.50 vet bill dated April 25, 2005; (h) a $116.35 vet bill dated August 9, 2006; and (i) a $143.00 vet bill dated May 14, 2007. Besides the $26.63 adoption fee, Plaintiff has made the following payments associated with Sammy: (a) a $ 41.59 vet bill dated August 26, 2004; and (b) a $157.84 vet bill dated August 16, 2004.

8. In May 2008, Defendant paid for a surgical procedure to repair an injury to one of Sammy's hind legs. This procedure cost over $2,000.

9. Sammy has resided with Defendant since August 2007. Defendant lives in a house in South Minneapolis. There are a number of parks near her residence, including a dog park in which Sammy is able to roam free of a leash. Defendant takes Sammy to the dog park almost every day.

10. Plaintiff currently resides in a residence with a large yard that would enable Sammy to roam free. Plaintiff testified that he considers Sammy to be his dog, and that a dog "has one master." Since August 2007, Plaintiff has not seen Sammy.

11. Although both parties have genuine affection for Sammy, the Court finds that Defendant has an extremely close and lovely relationship with the dog. Defendant's demeanor while testifying demonstrated a sincere concern for Sammy's well being.

12. On September 18, 2007, Defendant got a harassment restraining order against Plaintiff. On October 8, 2007, Plaintiff violated the restraining order.

13. On October 11, 2007, Plaintiff filed a conciliation court claim seeking possession of Sammy and the return of certain computer speakers. The conciliation court found in favor of Plaintiff on January 23, 2008.

14. On February 20, 2008, Defendant removed the case to District Court.

CONCLUSIONS OF LAW

1. Historically, the law has regarded a dog as a mere item of personal property that could be used or abused as its owner saw fit. *See, e.g., Corn v. Sheppard*, 229 N.W. 869, 492 (Minn. 1930); *Chapman v. Decrow* 45 A. 295, 298 (Me. 1899); *Vaughn v. Nelson*, 62 S.E. 708, 709 (Ga. Ct. App. 1908) (noting that dogs are property and "may be levied on and sold"); Amie J. Dryden, *The Inadequacies of Animal Cruelty Statutes and the Property-Based View of Animals*, 38 Idaho L. Rev. 177, 181 (2001). Under the traditional view, courts analyzed claims regarding the ownership of a dog in the same manner as it evaluated disputes concerning any other item of personal property. Barbara Newell, *Animal Custody Disputes: A Growing Crack in the 'Legal Thinghood' of Non-Human Animals*, 6 Animal L. 179, 179 (2000).

2. In recent years, the law has begun to reject the historical view of a dog in strictly property terms. For example, a number of Minnesota statutory provisions prohibit the abuse or neglect of dogs and other animals. *See* Minn. Stat. § 343.21 subd. 1 (prohibiting a person from torturing, neglecting, unreasonably caging without "exercise and change of air," or abandoning any animal); Minn. Stat. § 343.24 subd. 1 (regulating the manner in which animals are transported to prohibit cruel or inhumane conditions); Minn. Stat. § 343.26 (prohibiting a person from keeping an animal in an unsheltered place between November 1 and May 1 if the animal has had its hair removed by clipping or shearing within the past 60 days); Minn. Stat. § 343.27 (prohibiting the unjustifiable poisoning of any animal); Minn. Stat. § 343.31 (providing that anyone who promotes dog-fighting is guilty of a felony); Minn. Stat. § 343.36 (prohibiting contests "in which a pig, greased, oiled or otherwise, is released and wherein the object is to capture the pig"); Minn. Stat. § 343.40 (regulating the use of dog houses to ensure that dogs have adequate protection from the elements). Legislation of this sort recognizes a distinction between companion animals and other pieces of non-living chattel, which enjoy no protection from abuse or neglect. *See Rabideau v. City of Racine*, 627 N.W.2d 795, 797 (Wis. 2001).

3. Recent case law has eloquently spoken of the changing societal views of companion animals. In *Bueckner v. Hamel*, 886 S.W.2d 368, 377 (Tex. App. 1994), the Court of Appeals of Texas said:

> The law must be informed by evolving knowledge and attitudes. Otherwise, it risks becoming irrelevant as a means of resolving conflicts. Society has long since moved beyond the untenable Cartesian view that animals are unfeeling automatons and, hence, mere property. The law should reflect society's recognition that animals are sentient and emotive beings that are capable of providing companionship to the humans with whom they live.

4. These changing attitudes reflect the fact that a dog is not a mere item of personal property. Unlike a car or other item of chattel, dogs are living beings that have emotions and are uniquely responsive to human interaction. *See State of Ohio v. Anderson*, 566 N.E. 1224, 1225-26 (Ohio 1991). They are commonly referred to as "man's best friend." *Fitzgerald v. State*, 864 A.2d 1006, 1015 (Md. 2004).

5. The Wisconsin Supreme Court recently discussed the longstanding bond between dog and human. The Court noted:

> Dogs have been a part of human domestic life since 6300 B.C. Archaeologists have uncovered a 12,000-year-old burial site in which a human being and a dog lay buried together. 'The arm of the person was arranged on the dog's shoulders, as if to emphasize the bonds that existed between these two individuals during life. Dogs are so much a part of human experience that we need not cite to authority when we note that dogs work in law enforcement, assist the blind and disabled, perform traditional jobs such as herding animals and providing security, and, of course, dogs continue to provide humans with devoted friendship.

Rabideau v. City of Racine, 627 N.W.2d 795, 798 (Wis. 2001) (internal citations omitted).

6. When evaluating the present dispute concerning the custody[5] of Sammy, it is appropriate to consider the best interest of the dog. A custody determination that did not take into account Sammy's best interest would be contrary to the trend towards recognizing dogs as living beings deserving of basic legal protections. This does not imply that Sammy's best interest is the sole consideration. The human participants in this claim have certain interests as well, both in terms of their emotion connection to Sammy as well as their financial investment in the enjoyment of a relationship with Sammy.

7. To resolve this dispute, the Court will consider the following factors: (1) which party selected Sammy for adoption and paid the initial adoption fee; (2) the extent to which each party provided care and love for Sammy; (3) the extent to which each party provided financial support for Sammy; and (4) which result is in Sammy's best interest.

8. The parties jointly selected Sammy for adoption. Plaintiff physically paid the adoption fee, although this fee was only $25.00. Because both parties participated in selecting Sammy and the adoption fee was minimal, this factor does not weigh in favor of either party.

---

5. Courts traditionally viewed this sort of case as one involving "ownership" of a dog rather than "custody" of the dog. Given the changing attitudes towards companion animals, the Court feels the term "custody" is more appropriate in this case.

9. Defendant provided the bulk of care for Sammy. Defendant testified that she was Sammy's primary caregiver, and the Court finds this testimony credible. This factor therefore weighs in favor of Defendant.

10. Defendant has incurred the bulk of expenses associated with caring for Sammy. This factor consequently weighs strongly in favor of Defendant.

11. Defendant has genuine affection for Sammy and is the best position to ensure Sammy's well being. She is familiar with Sammy's habits and health concerns, and she is able to provide Sammy with daily exercise in a dog park located near her home. Sammy and Defendant have formed a solid and loving bond, and any disruption to this relationship would be stressful to Sammy. Therefore, Sammy's best interests are served by remaining with Defendant.

12. Taken as a whole, the relevant factors weigh in favor of Defendant retaining possession of Sammy. For that reason, Plaintiff's demand for replevin is denied.

IT IS HEREBY ORDERED:

1. Plaintiff's demand for replevin of a golden retriever/yellow lab mix named "Sammy" is **DENIED**.
2. All other demands for replevin made by Plaintiff are **DENIED**.
3. This matter is **DISMISSED WITH PREJUDICE**.

LET JUDGMENT BE ENTERED ACCORDINGLY

Dated: April 27, 2009 **BY THE COURT:**

____

Regina M. Chu
Judge of District Court

Appendix 12

Replevin Pleadings and Analysis

The purpose of this appendix is to help you learn how to look for holes, or half-truths, in the adverse party's claims before you learn anything about your own client's claims. In this appendix, you will see a summons, complaint in replevin, plaintiff's notice of motion and motion for summary judgment, and plaintiff's memorandum of law in support of summary judgment, all written by a well-known family lawyer, together with the plaintiff's reply to defendant's counterclaim. These pleadings represent very traditional and conservative replevin and summary judgment property arguments.

The response/answer in this appendix was drafted by a pro se defendant. The defendant's pleadings, followed by the pleadings by the attorney she ended up hiring, are also provided with commentary. The defendant's attorney reasoned that the state should not consider traditional ownership criteria when there was an animal safety issue and advanced equitable arguments. She further argued that awarding the dog to the defendant would be in both the defendant's and the dog's best interests. More specifically, the defense maintained the following:

- Because the documents the plaintiff relied upon did not clearly establish ownership, the subject of ownership was a material fact.
- The court should have treated the pro se party's failure to specifically deny the plaintiff's ownership of the dog in a pleading as a clerical mistake.
- The pro se defendant using the words "I will not admit" in her response to the plaintiff's request for admissions was equivalent to a denial.
- The plaintiff's failure to annually license the dog was evidence of lack of ownership.

- Under *Pratt v. Pratt*,[1] the court could consider evidence of the mistreatment of a dog in a divorce context.

The names and information in the following pleadings filed with the court have been altered to provide anonymity. As stated above, the comments are intended to show the family lawyer ways to analyze and criticize an opposing party's work product and to begin the process of conceptualizing possible counterarguments without the benefit of any other pertinent information about the case. It might be useful to attempt to deconstruct each party's pleadings yourself before you look at the footnotes.

1. 1988 WL 120251 (Minn. App. Nov. 15, 1998).

STATE OF MINNESOTA DISTRICT COURT
COUNTY OF SMITH FIRST JUDICIAL DISTRICT
CIVIL COURT DIVISION

In Re the Matter of: Court File No. 123

Andy Anderson,

Plaintiff,

SUMMONS

and

Nicole Davis

Defendant.

THIS SUMMONS IS DIRECTED TO: NICOLE DAVIS, DEFENDANT ABOVE-NAMED, 222 FIRST AVENUE, WILCO, MINNESOTA 55304.

1. **YOU ARE BEING SUED.** Plaintiff has started a lawsuit against you. Plaintiff's Complaint against you is attached to this Summons. Do not throw these papers away. They are official papers that affect your rights. You must respond to this lawsuit even though it may not yet be filed with the Court and there may be no Court file number on this Summons.

2. **YOU MUST REPLY WITHIN 20 DAYS TO PROTECT YOUR RIGHTS.** You must give or mail to the person who signed this Summons a written response called an Answer within 20 days of the date on which you received this Summons. You must send a copy of your Answer to the person who signed this Summons located at: Johnson Law Office, 100 Seventh Street, Minneapolis, MN 55408.

3. **YOU MUST RESPOND TO EACH CLAIM.** The Answer is your written response to Plaintiff's Complaint. In your Answer, you must state whether you agree or disagree with each paragraph of the Complaint. If you believe Plaintiff should not be given everything asked for in the Complaint, you must say so in your Answer.

4. **YOU WILL LOSE YOUR CASE IF YOU DO NOT SEND A WRITTEN RESPONSE TO THE COMPLAINT TO THE PERSON WHO SIGNED THIS SUMMONS.** If you do not answer within 20 days, you will lose this case. You will not get to tell your side of the story, and the Court may decide against you and award Plaintiff everything asked for in the Complaint. If you do not want to contest the claims stated in the Complaint, you do not need to respond. A default judgment can then be entered against you for the relief requested in the Complaint.

5. **LEGAL ASSISTANCE.** You may wish to get legal help from a lawyer. If you do not have a lawyer, the Court Administrator may have information about places where you can get legal assistance. Even if you cannot get legal help, you must still provide a written Answer to protect your rights or you may lose this case.

6. **ALTERNATIVE DISPUTE RESOLUTION.** The parties may agree to or be Ordered to participate in an Alternative Dispute Resolution process under Rule 114 of the Minnesota General Rules of Practice. You must still send your written response to the Complaint even if you expect to use alternative means of resolving this dispute.

Date: ____________________ ______________________________

Jacob Johnson
Johnson Law Office
100 South Seventh Street
Minneapolis, MN 55408

STATE OF MINNESOTA
COUNTY OF SMITH

DISTRICT COURT
FIRST JUDICIAL DISTRICT
CIVIL COURT DIVISION
Court File No. 123

In Re the Matter of:
Andy Anderson,

Plaintiff,

COMPLAINT IN REPLEVIN

and

Nicole Davis

Defendant.

Plaintiff, Andy Anderson, for his Complaint against Defendant, Nicole Davis, states and alleges as follows:

PARTIES

1. Plaintiff Andy Anderson, a Minnesota resident, resides in Smith County, Minnesota.

2. Defendant Nicole Davis, a Minnesota resident, resides in Smith County, Minnesota.

JURISDICTION

3. The Court has jurisdiction over the subject matter and parties to the above-captioned case; the County of Smith is the proper venue for the above-captioned case pursuant to Minn. Stat. §542.06.

4. This action is brought pursuant to Ch. 565 of the Minnesota Statutes.[2]

2. Actions to recover the possession shall be tried in the county in which the property is situated.

FACTUAL BACKGROUND

5. Plaintiff is the sole owner of a Shiba Inu dog named Millie (hereinafter "Millie"). Millie was born on November 15, 2007 in Alexandria, Douglas County, Minnesota.[3]

6. On or around January 21, 2008, Plaintiff traveled to Alexandria, Minnesota, to pick up Millie. Plaintiff purchased Millie for $500.00 from the Best Mates Animal Society of Alexandria, Minnesota. All monies used for the purchase of Millie were that of Plaintiff. Alex Gustafson, the breeder of Millie, will attest to Plaintiff's legal ownership of Millie. Alex Gustafson, the breeder of Millie, has completed an American Kennel Club Litter Record, a true and correct copy of which is attached hereto as Exhibit A.[4]

7. Thereafter, Millie resided with Plaintiff at his one-bedroom apartment located at 111 Smith Street in Wilco, Minnesota.

8. Plaintiff chose the name for Millie without any help from others.[5] Millie was named after his mother.

9. In April 2010, Millie landed awkwardly on her left front leg and broke it. Plaintiff took Millie to an emergency veterinary clinic located in Minneapolis, Minnesota. The veterinarians worked quickly to take x-rays and set the broken bone. The next day, Plaintiff took Millie to #1 Animal Hospital. The attending veterinarian took additional x-rays and recommended surgery by an orthopedic surgeon.[6]

10. The Friday of that same week in April 2010, Millie had surgery. Pins and screws were required and remain in place to date. Millie had a successful recovery. Plaintiff paid all costs of the surgery, which exceeded $4,000.00. Since Millie was Plaintiff's separate property, it was Plaintiff's responsibility alone to pay all healthcare costs for Millie's health and well-being.[7]

---

3. It is typical for pleadings involving animals, even in equine disputes, to identify an animal by name. This is in stark contrast to cases involving children, where their names are avoided.

4. Because of the lack of specificity as to the source of funds, it is likely there is no record. Be careful about making a claim that the breeder would attest to ownership. Proof of American Kennel Club registration, though of evidentiary importance, is not the same as proof of the source of funds for the dog's purchase.

5. He seems to be stating his intention to get the dog for himself, though not very well. If he intended to obtain Millie for his exclusive use, he should say so.

6. The plaintiff's attorney was wise to be proactive in describing this injury rather than waiting for the defense to bring it up. Even so, the plaintiff's explanation of how the dog awkwardly landed is not compelling. His explanation for his effort to get the dog veterinary care is somewhat curious and noticeably more detailed than the injury explanation.

7. This seems like a lot of money for someone to pay to help a dog that was deliberately injured. Was the dog inadvertently hurt when the plaintiff was in a rage or under the influence? Is his claim that there was simply an accident true? How he is viewed may be impacted by whether he has ever been subject to orders for protection or harassment restraining orders or has a criminal record reflecting violent propensities, or if there are veterinary records involving the same animal, a different animal, owned by the defendant where the injury was described as an accident.

11. Millie continued to live with Plaintiff at 111 Smith Street in Wilco, Minnesota, for the next five months and had minimal contact with Defendant.[8]

12. On or around July 1, 2010, Plaintiff moved in with Defendant at her townhome having the common address of 222 First Avenue, Wilco, Minnesota.[9]

13. Defendant would rarely take the time to walk Millie, aid in training and obedience, or let Millie out early in the mornings or after work in order to permit Millie to relieve herself.[10]

14. Despite living and sharing a co-residence with Defendant, Plaintiff was responsible for paying Millie's healthcare, special weight management dog food, grooming every six weeks at Dog Groomers Palace, and other related expenses, including the cost to have Millie spayed (costs of approximately $500.00). Plaintiff also paid to have an identification microchip embedded into Millie and other registration costs. Millie is registered in Plaintiff's name.[11]

15. Countless neighbors situated in Wilco, Minnesota, and mutual friends of Plaintiff and Defendant would attest that it was Plaintiff who would walk and care for Millie. More importantly, these close mutual friends would also confirm that Millie was Plaintiff's dog.[12]

16. Defendant's only significant financial contribution to Millie is a current health insurance policy that Defendant purchased for Plaintiff and Millie as a Christmas gift.[13]

17. Unbeknownst to Plaintiff, over the course of the past few years, Defendant has made misrepresentations to third parties regarding her legal rights to Millie's ownership. More specifically, Defendant made an attempt to license Millie in her name alone, and has changed the owner's name on various accounts with third

8. Is there contradictory evidence, such as photographs, social media postings, cell phone records, or banking and credit card records that might constitute evidence of deception? For example, has the plaintiff been making gasoline purchases or running errands in the locale where the defendant lives, or do cell phone tower records suggest where he was actually living?

9. Look for a written agreement and all records, both before and after the plaintiff claims he moved in, to see if there was any discernable difference in his expenditures. If not, why not?

10. Was the defendant not able to walk Millie due to health problems? Was she concerned about walking her because Millie was dog aggressive? Find out what the neighbors have to say about Millie's care and exercise. Look for records that would confirm claims about work hours.

11. Are there any records to back up these claims? When was Millie microchipped? Was it after the action commenced? How was money handled when the parties were not together? Did they have joint bank or credit card accounts?

12. Get witness contact information and statements and learn about witness neutrality. Develop your own witness list.

13. Health insurance policies can be expensive for dogs and are typically paid on a month-to-month basis. Get the date and amount of this expense and all related records. Find out whose name or names the defendant put on the insurance application she submitted.

parties, including #1 Animal Hospital. All of Defendant's actions were done without the knowledge or consent of Plaintiff.[14]

COUNT I

Replevin/Claim and Delivery of Millie

18. Plaintiff restates and realleges the foregoing paragraphs as though fully stated herein.

19. Millie's physical description is described as follows: wedge-shaped head with small ears, dark eyes, and a coat of orange, white, and cream colors. A true and correct photograph of the same is attached hereto as Exhibit B.[15]

20. At all times material hereto, Plaintiff was the sole owner of one Shiba Inu dog named Millie and having the physical description as set forth above. As such, Plaintiff is entitled to immediate possession of the property.[16]

21. On or around August 23, 2011, Plaintiff was locked out of his co-residence and Defendant wrongfully detained Millie.[17]

22. Defendant's detention and taking of Millie is wrongful and unlawful.[18]

23. Plaintiff made demand to Defendant for the safe return of Millie.[19]

24. Defendant has intentionally refused, neglected, or failed to return Millie to Plaintiff.[20]

25. Therefore, Plaintiff seeks an Order from this Court directing Defendant to return and deliver possession of Millie to Plaintiff.[21]

---

14. This is an unusual claim. Check to see if the defendant's name appeared as an owner on the veterinary records at the same time she got the pet insurance. The defendant's application for veterinary insurance could help or hurt the defendant's case. Did the plaintiff give Millie to the defendant, or did he hold Millie out to be their dog? Find out why the defendant got the license. Perhaps the defendant did so because the plaintiff did not get around to it and she saw the form sitting on the kitchen table. The plaintiff's allegation that the defendant "changed the owner's name on various accounts with third parties" deserves close attention.

15. It is a good idea to attach a photograph.

16. This is a classic property allegation.

17. It would be interesting to learn if the plaintiff called anyone, including the police, to complain about this wrongful detainment, or if the plaintiff posted anything on social media sites about this incident. Learn about the posting habits of both parties and whether postings about the dog were typical. If they were, the absence of postings would be important, too. An inquiry should be made as to why the plaintiff failed to hire a locksmith to get into his joint residence and what communications he had with the defendant or the landlord to attempt to gain reentry. What reasons did the plaintiff have to avoid police involvement?

18. This is a classic legal argument that might be successful if legal title is the only decision-making criteria that the court utilizes when making an ownership determination.

19. It is important to know more about the timeline and method concerning the plaintiff's alleged demands.

20. This is a reasonable allegation. Is there evidence to support that she refused continuing demands?

21. This is concise and straightforward.

COUNT II

Injunctive Relief

26. Plaintiff restates and realleges the foregoing paragraphs as though fully stated herein.[22]

27. To the best of Plaintiff's knowledge, Defendant currently possesses Millie.[23]

28. Defendant's detention of Millie is wrongful and unlawful.[24]

29. Plaintiff is entitled to immediate possession of Millie.[25]

30. Unless restrained by an Order from this Court, Defendant will continue to act against Plaintiff's property in furtherance of her own interest and to the detriment of Plaintiff.[26] Plaintiff has no adequate remedy at law against Defendant, except for return of the property and an injunction, permanent or temporary, pursuant to applicable law.[27]

31. The injunctive relief requested by Plaintiff will not damage or deprive Defendant of any legal rights because Plaintiff is likely to prevail on the merits regarding Defendant's misrepresentations to third parties, common law and statutory violations, and Plaintiff should ultimately prevail in retaining Millie as his sole property.[28]

32. Greater injury will be inflicted upon Plaintiff should this Court refuse to grant Plaintiff's request for injunctive relief.[29]

33. Based on the foregoing, Plaintiff is entitled to an Order enjoining Defendant from claiming any right, title, or interest in Millie, including the rights to visitation and injunctive relief to protect Plaintiff's property interests.[30]

---

22. This is a standard provision.

23. Venue, which means the location where the case is heard, may depend upon several factors, including where the property "is situated." One reason replevin actions are prompt is to prevent the property from being "situated" somewhere else.

24. This is s standard provision.

25. This is a standard provision.

26. What does "acting against Plaintiff's property" at face value mean? Even if the plaintiff is using the language of case law correctly, the language itself suggests that by taking an action "against" the plaintiff's property, the defendant harmed Millie the dog. The plaintiff does not seem to be asserting any best interests of the dog standard.

27. This is pretty boilerplate and explains why monetary damages are insufficient.

28. This is somewhat confusing. It would be better if each subject were treated individually.

29. This is pretty boilerplate.

30. This is pretty boilerplate, except the prohibition on visitation has come up for the first time here and sounds out of left field, and the wording is clumsy.

DEMAND FOR RELIEF[31]

WHEREFORE, Plaintiff requests relief as follows:

1. For a judgment in favor of Plaintiff and against Defendant awarding the immediate return and possession of the property described therein, Millie.[32]

2. For an injunction prohibiting Defendant from claiming any right, title, or interest in Plaintiff's dog, Millie. Such injunction shall also prohibit Defendant from any visitation[33] rights with Millie.[34]

3. For reasonable attorney's fees incurred in bringing this action, together with Plaintiff's costs and disbursements.[35]

4. For a judgment sounding in equity to properly and justly implement the orders and judgments of the Court.[36]

5. For such other relief as the Court concludes is appropriate.[37]

Date: ____________________ ________________________________

Jacob Johnson
Johnson Law Office
100 South Seventh Street
Minneapolis, MN 55408

---

31. This is boilerplate.
32. It might have been better to describe Millie in a more compelling way than just as property.
33. It would have been better to add the word "possession," too.
34. This is a boilerplate provision except on the subject of visitation rights. Let your client know that sometimes the courts will permit this type of arrangement when an action is pending.
35. This is a boilerplate provision. While most lawyers demand attorney's fees, it is well known that the courts are often reticent to award them.
36. The plaintiff has not advanced a strong claim for an order based upon equitable principles. For a great example on equitable arguments, read *Marvin v. Marvin*, 176 Cal. Rptr. 555, 122 Cal. App. 3d 871 (Cal. App. 2d Dist. 1981).
37. This is a boilerplate provision.

STATE OF MINNESOTA
COUNTY OF SMITH

DISTRICT COURT
FIRST JUDICIAL DISTRICT
CIVIL COURT DIVISION
Court File No. 123

In Re the Matter of:
Andy Anderson,

Plaintiff,

and

Nicole Davis

Defendant.

PLAINTIFF'S NOTICE OF MOTION AND MOTION FOR SUMMARY JUDGMENT

TO: NICOLE DAVIS, DEFENDANT ABOVE-NAMED, 222 FIRST AVENUE, WILCO, MINNESOTA 55304.

NOTICE OF MOTION

PLEASE TAKE NOTICE that on January 25, 2012, at 9:00 a.m. or as soon thereafter as counsel can be heard, Plaintiff, Andy Anderson, through undersigned counsel, will bring the following Motion for Summary Judgment against Defendant, Nicole Davis, before the Honorable John Anderson, Judge of Smith County District Court, at the Smith County Courthouse, 55 State Street, Minneapolis, Minnesota.

MOTION

Plaintiff moves the Court, pursuant to Rule 56 of the Minnesota Rules of Civil Procedure, for an Order for Summary Judgment on the grounds that there are no material facts in dispute and that Plaintiff is entitled to summary judgment as a matter of law. This motion is based upon all the pleadings, files, affidavits, memoranda, arguments of counsel, records, and proceedings herein.[38]

Date: ____________________

____
Jacob Johnson
Johnson Law Office
100 South Seventh Street
Minneapolis, MN 55408

38. This notice of motion and motion is boilerplate. The plaintiff forgot to address the subject of attorney's fees. This is where you might notice that the plaintiff also failed to include an affidavit with her motion. Even if the claims in a complaint and affidavit overlap, the court typically requires both under the rules.

STATE OF MINNESOTA
COUNTY OF SMITH

DISTRICT COURT
FIRST JUDICIAL DISTRICT
CIVIL COURT DIVISION
Court File No. 123

In Re the Matter of:
Andy Anderson,

Plaintiff,

and

Nicole Davis

Defendant.

PLAINTIFF'S MEMORANDUM OF LAW IN SUPPORT OF SUMMARY JUDGMENT

INTRODUCTION

Plaintiff Andy Anderson submits this Memorandum of Law in support of his Motion for Summary Judgment as to all of his claims against Defendant Nicole Davis.

This case concerns the legal ownership of a Shiba Inu dog named Millie. Plaintiff was forced to commence this lawsuit in replevin to recover lawful possession of his own dog, Millie. Plaintiff is the sole owner of Millie and purchased Millie from a breeder named Alex Gustafson in Alexandria, Minnesota, prior to sharing a co-residence with Defendant.[39]

On August 23, 2011, Plaintiff was intentionally locked out of his co-residence and Defendant refused to permit his entry. All of Plaintiff's belongings (except those items and effects not returned as of yet) were bagged in garbage bags and piled in the parties' garage. Defendant refused to allow Plaintiff's entry into his co-residence without police presence and will not discuss any matters relating to Plaintiff's dog, Millie.[40]

Defendant mistakenly claims that Plaintiff abandoned Millie and that she now is a co-owner.[41] Defendant has failed to present any evidence[42] demonstrating that

39. This paragraph is persuasive.

40. This paragraph is persuasive, at least at first. If the plaintiff's name appeared on the lease, it would be unlikely the police would interfere with his right of entry. Perhaps the plaintiff laid low for a while so the defendant would not bring an order for protection against him.

41. Over time, abandonment would result in the defendant's sole ownership.

42. The plaintiff already admitted that the defendant paid for Millie's veterinary insurance.

she is in fact a co-owner of Millie and likewise cannot establish superior title.[43] Regardless of any equitable arguments that Defendant may assert at the summary judgment motion hearing or during continued litigation, Defendant's continued efforts to license Millie in her name alone, while ostensibly making certain representations to employees at #1 Animal Hospital to change the account holder's name on file with Millie's veterinarian to hers, does not extinguish Plaintiff's lawful ownership.[44] Ultimately, Defendant's wrongful detention of Millie acts to intentionally hinder, delay, and defraud Plaintiff's right to immediate possession.[45]

There being no question that Plaintiff is the owner of Millie, Plaintiff is entitled to summary judgment along with all costs and attorney's fees incurred in bringing this action.[46]

ISSUES

I. Should Plaintiff be granted summary judgment because his ownership of Millie is clearly established by a Bill of Sale issued by breeder Alex Gustafson, coupled with Plaintiff's American Kennel Club litter record and registration?[47]

II. Should summary judgment be granted in favor of Plaintiff because Defendant has not presented any evidence to create a genuine issue of material fact and has failed and/or refused to cooperate in discovery by answering admissions?[48]

43. Look for evidence that a gift between fiancés resulted in co-ownership.

44. This point is made well. If the plaintiff can establish that the defendant was sneaky and dishonest, and she is a bad actor, this will help his case. Even so, if the plaintiff abandoned Millie, it would be appropriate for the defendant to update her records.

45. This helps his case. Cases can be won and lost because of social media posts, the kind that say, "Here we are with our dog, Millie" or "Here is a picture of our family" or "Here is Millie sleeping by her mom, as always" or even a posted photograph of the defendant taking Millie for a walk during a blizzard.

46. Well, there is a question. Perhaps the plaintiff meant a meritorious question.

47. It would be worth finding out if the breeder in question was a friend of the plaintiff or the plaintiff's family. Although the plaintiff made a point of saying in his affidavit that he physically went and picked up Millie, it is not clear whether the defendant actually found the breeder and had presale communications with the breeder. Find out if there was a contemporaneous withdrawal of cash from the defendant's, rather than the plaintiff's, bank account. Perhaps the defendant gave him cash for her share of the dog's purchase and neglected to tell you thinking she could not prove it. Your client may be unaware that testimony can be direct evidence.

48. This is stated well.

STATEMENT OF DOCUMENTS COMPRISING THE RECORD[49]

Affidavit of Jacob Johnson with true and correct copies of the following Exhibits:

Exhibit 1: American Kennel Club Litter Record;

Exhibit 2: Bill of Sale and Affidavit of Alex Gustafson;

Exhibit 3: American Kennel Club Registration;

Exhibit 4: Letter with enclosures from attorney Steven Brown to Defendant Nicole Davis dated September 19, 2011;

Exhibit 5: 2008 Dog License Application dated June 28, 2008;

Exhibit 6: Home Again Microchip Registration and Full Service Subscription Renewal Payment Receipt;

Exhibit 7: Letter from Jacob Johnson to Defendant Nicole Davis dated September 1, 2011;

Exhibit 8: Plaintiff's Complaint in Replevin (without Exhibits A and B);

Exhibit 9: Defendant's Answer;

Exhibit 10: Plaintiff's Interrogatories to Defendant (Set I);

Exhibit 11: Plaintiff's Request for Production of Documents to Defendant (Set I);

Exhibit 12: Plaintiff's Request for Admissions to Defendant (Set I);

Exhibit 13: Defendant's Answers and Responses to Plaintiff's Interrogatories, Request for Production of Documents, and Request for Admissions;

Exhibit 14: *Behnke v. Green Behnke*, A03-1039, 2004 WL 376984 (Minn. Ct. App. Mar. 2, 2004); and

Exhibit 15: Affidavit of Plaintiff.[50]

---

49. There are many ways to establish who owns or jointly owns an animal. Purchase records are only one of them, although traditional documentary evidence at the point of purchase can have a persuasive impact on the court. An American Kennel Club registry, at least in past years, carried an implication that the animal has economic value. Some courts are able to understand economic value better than relational value. More recently, because puppies sourced from large confinement breeders can now be registered, once-famous registries have lost some of their patina.

50. This list is satisfactory, with the exception that the plaintiff's counsel failed to prepare an affidavit for the plaintiff, as indicated at the top and bottom of this list. Also, in paragraph 15 of the plaintiff's complaint, he described "countless" neighbors and mutual friends that would "confirm" his ownership of Millie. The absence of statements or affidavits to this effect is conspicuous. The plaintiff's affidavit is also lacking.

SUMMARY JUDGMENT STANDARD

Rule 56.03 of the Minnesota Rules of Civil Procedure provides that judgment shall be entered forthwith if the pleadings, depositions, Answers to Interrogatories and Admissions on file, together with the Affidavits, if any, show that there is no genuine issue as to any material fact and that either party is entitled to judgment as a matter of law. Minn. R. Civ. P. 56.03; *Marose v. Hennameyer*, 347 N.W.2d 509, 510-11 (Minn. Ct. App. 1984). In deciding a Motion for Summary Judgment, the Court does not resolve issues of fact; rather it determines whether a genuine issue of material fact exists. *Nord v. Herreid*, 305 N.W.2d 337, 339 (Minn. Ct. App. 1981).[51]

Rule 56.05 of the Minnesota Rules of Civil Procedure states that a party opposing summary judgment "may not rest upon the mere averments or denials of the adverse party's pleadings but must present specific facts showing that there is a genuine issue for trial" (emphasis added). The non-moving party cannot rely on conjecture and speculation to meet its burden of showing a genuine issue of material fact. *Lubbers v. Anderson*, 539 N.W.2d 398, 402 (Minn. 1995). Rather, the non-moving party must present sufficient evidence to permit reasonable persons to draw different conclusions. *Gradjelick v. Hance*, 646 N.W.2d 225, 231 (Minn. 2002); citing *DLH, Inc. v. Russ*, 566 N.W.2d 60 (Minn. 1997). To preclude summary judgment, the non-moving party must offer more than mere averment and conclusory allegations. *Metge v. Cent. Neighborhood Improvement Ass'n*, 649 N.W.2d 488, 495 (Minn. Ct. App. 2002), review dismissed (Minn. Oct. 15, 2002) (emphasis added).[52]

To defeat a motion for summary judgment, the evidence offered in opposition must be admissible at trial. *Murphy v. Country House, Inc.*, 240 N.W.2d 507, 511 (Minn. 1976). "Speculation, general assertions, and promises to produce evidence at trial are not sufficient to create a genuine issue of material fact for trial." *Nicollet Restoration, Inc. v. City of St. Paul*, 533 N.W.2d 845, 848 (Minn. 1995). "A material fact is one of such nature as will affect the result or outcome of the case

---

51. Because a pro se individual answered discovery, it can be expected that the court will give defects less weight, particularly if once she retains counsel, the discovery responses are properly amended and they reveal a material factual dispute. This claim suggests the defendant's discovery responses were not sufficiently detailed and should be amended, and a motion should be brought to permit this if the plaintiff objects. Check to see if any of the cases the plaintiff cited relate to pet custody or ownership disputes.

52. Look for exceptions to this rule in any case around the country involving a companion animal along the lines of Judge Regina Chu's replevin order. Look at the concerns the appellate court emphasized in *Houseman v. Dare*, 966 A.2d 24 (N.J. Super. Ct. App. Div. 2009). Research how equitable doctrines interface with summary judgment principles. A valuable aspect of equity is that it has the ability to create new rights through conscience-based actions. If you do not like where a decision is heading, consider how to reconstitute and reimagine the equitable arguments of yesteryear. Stephen N. Subrin, *How Equity Conquered Common Law: The Federal Rules of Civil Procedure in Historical Perspective*, 135 U. Pa. L. Rev. 909 (1987), http://scholarship.law.upenn.edu/cgi/viewcontent.cgi?article=3957&context=penn_law_review (last visited Apr. 29, 2017).

depending on its resolution." *Zappa v. Fahey*, 245 N.W.2d 258, 259-260 (Minn. 1976). **If a non-moving party fails to meet the burden of producing facts that could create a genuine issue, summary judgment is proper.** *Thiele v. Stich*, 425 N.W.2d 580, 583 (Minn. 1988) (emphasis added).[53]

III. Should Plaintiff be granted summary judgment because his ownership of Millie is clearly established by a Bill of Sale issued by breeder Alex Gustafson, coupled with Plaintiff's American Kennel Club litter record and registration?[54]

RELEVANT FACTS[55]

Millie, who is the subject of this litigation, was born on November 14, 2007 in Alexandria, Minnesota. On January 21, 2008, Plaintiff traveled to Alexandria, Douglas County, Minnesota, to receive Millie, the dog he picked out a few weeks earlier from breeder Alex Gustafson. The dog was named Millie after Plaintiff's mother. *(See Exhibit 15)*. Plaintiff paid cash in the amount of Five Hundred and no/100 Dollars ($500.00) for Millie's purchase price. All monies used for Millie's purchase were that of Plaintiff. *(Id. at paragraph 5)*. Breeder Alex Gustafson has confirmed that Plaintiff is the sole owner of Millie. *(See Exhibit 2)*.

After receiving transfer papers for Millie on January 21, 2008, Plaintiff also received a document most commonly referred to as an American Kennel Club ("AKC") Litter Record. *(See Exhibit 1)*. This document includes an AKC puppy number, the name of the puppy, and new owner information. Listed under the *"new owner"* section found on this document is the name of Plaintiff *(See Id.)* (emphasis added). According to breeder Alex Gustafson, this litter record is a legal form.[56]

After receiving Millie from breeder Alex Gustafson, Millie lived with Plaintiff at his one-bedroom apartment located at 111 Smith Street, Wilco, Minnesota.[57] To comply with the "pet policy" at his apartment complex, Plaintiff was required

---

53. Neighbor and friend witnesses might be able to address equitable issues and contradict assertions made by the plaintiff. Even the postal carrier or UPS or FedEx delivery person might be a good witness. Also, be sure to learn whether the defendant was a domestic abuse victim.

54. Although the plaintiff could have evidence that he was the original owner of Millie, there may be other evidence, even based upon the equitable doctrine of promissory estoppel, that he gave Millie to the defendant. Consider public policy and unconscionability arguments. The most suspicious fact in the complaint is about Millie's accident. If the plaintiff substantially hurt Millie, others might have observed something very wrong in his mistreatment of her.

55. This is an effective way to present relevant facts.

56. This argument is a bit upper class. Even so, some judges will be more interested in giving their time to cases involving pedigreed dogs with economic value rather than animals with less well-recognized lineage. With an AKC registration, some courts would give the plaintiff a rebuttable presumption in his favor.

57. It could be that the plaintiff and Millie rarely slept there. Where is the evidence that he did more than retain an address?

to complete their standard Pet Policy Agreement and pay an additional damage deposit in the amount of $300.00. *(See Exhibit 15).*[58] As Millie lived alone with Plaintiff during her early life, it was Plaintiff who not only was Millie's legal owner, but also her master. *(Id. at paragraph 11).*[59] Plaintiff also enrolled and attended a dog obedience training school with Millie. *(Id.)*[60]

To further evidence his ownership, Plaintiff prepared and submitted a 2008 Dog License Application with the City of Wilco *(See Exhibit 5)*. A dog license is required by Minnesota law, more specifically, Section 347.09 of the Minnesota Statutes. The applicable statutory section provides "The owner of any dog (the word 'owner,' when used in sections 347.08 to 347.21, in relation to property in, or possession of, dogs shall include every person who owns, harbors, or keeps a dog)." As such, Plaintiff listed his name alone as "owner" on the license application to comply with the law.[61] The name of Defendant is not found anywhere on Millie's license application.[62] Additionally, Plaintiff had a microchip implanted in Millie bearing microchip number 12345 (the "Microchip Registration") to ensure Millie's safety and well-being should she ever be lost or stolen. *(See Exhibit 6).*[63] This Microchip Registration, together with the AKC Litter Record and Registration, displays the high level of joy and pride Plaintiff enjoys in owning Millie. *(See Exhibit 15).*[64]

After selling each of their real properties, Plaintiff and Defendant moved in with each other on July 1, 2008 at 222 First Avenue, Wilco, Minnesota. The parties shared the property as a co-residence.[65] Along with Plaintiff came Millie, who began living with Plaintiff and Defendant until Plaintiff was intentionally locked out on August 23, 2011.[66] Since then, Millie has been wrongfully detained by Defendant

58. This is a very good argument.

59. This "master" term seems both a bit obsequious and from another time and place.

60. It seems suspicious that the obedience training school was mentioned but not the name of the school. Find out if the defendant attended any of these classes or if the plaintiff dropped out.

61. It is good for the plaintiff to show that he complied with his legal licensing obligations. The court will like this.

62. Given the plaintiff's penchant for excessive detail, the plaintiff should be able to prove that he licensed Millie every year.

63. Find out if the defendant's address was on this microchip registration during a time when the plaintiff claimed to have been living alone.

64. The plaintiff made a best interest of the human argument, though not well. Instead of disingenuously writing about a "high level of joy and pride," the plaintiff's attorney, in the underlying affidavit that the motion should be based on, could have done better by writing something such as, "I usually got home from work around 4:30 p.m. As soon as I walked in the door, Millie would jump right into my arms and cover me with kisses. Quickly, I would get her leashed and we would go for a short walk, usually about one-fourth of a mile. After that, Millie and I would sit on the couch where I would brush her and she would then put her head in my lap while I watched a movie." It is better if the court gets the picture rather than getting the adjective of "joy." A basic writing tip is "show me, don't tell me."

65. The plaintiff was all about his ownership of Millie, but sparse on the details of the parties being co-residents of the townhouse, which was presumptively a rental. Learn more about this.

66. How could she have done this if it was a co-residence, like he was claiming? The plaintiff's portrayal of these facts sounds farfetched.

despite Plaintiff's demands for Millie's safe return.[67] Defendant has not complied with Plaintiff's requests and now is claiming ownership of the same. Counsel for Plaintiff has made written demand for the immediate delivery of Millie prior to the commencement of this action. *(See Exhibit 7).*[68]

In the present case, ownership of Millie is evidenced by a Bill of Sale, the AKC Litter Record, and AKC Registration. Defendant, by not denying paragraph 5 of Plaintiff's Complaint, has confirmed that "Plaintiff is the sole owner of a dog named Millie." *(See Exhibits 8, 9).* The Court should take Defendant's admission as further evidence to support Plaintiff's motion that is before this Court.[69]

Specifically, Defendant, in her Answers to Plaintiff's Interrogatories to Defendant (Set I), made it clear that the dog is owned by Plaintiff as his separate personal property:

(See specifically Exhibit 10, Plaintiff's Interrogatories to Defendant (Set I) and Exhibit 13, Defendant's Answers and Responses to Plaintiff's Interrogatories, Request for Production of Documents, and Request for Admissions (Set I).[70]

> Interrogatory No. 5: If you claim legal ownership of Millie, please identify all documents and/or records that support your claim of legal ownership, which may include, but is not limited to, a Registration Certificate or Litter Record from the American Kennel Club.
>
> Answer to "Plaintiff's Interrogatories to Defendant (Set I)"
>
> Interrogatories: 3-9
>
> All requested information is presently in the possession of aforementioned Plaintiff.

Defendant has similarly confirmed through discovery that she did not purchase Millie or contribute any money towards Millie's purchase price.

---

67. Again, learn specifically how long he waited before making this demand and how he made it. Find out if the letter the plaintiff listed above is his sole evidence. Most people would promptly show up with the police and their AKC registry records and demand that their girlfriend hand their dog over. This makes you wonder if the plaintiff owed his co-resident money.

68. The specific information listed by the plaintiff's counsel making a written demand suggests that the plaintiff was slow to ask for his dog back a second time.

69. Purchase is not the only economic factor courts look at to establish ownership anymore, especially in situations where a dog's veterinary expenses can well exceed the dog's purchase price. Courts may look at the best interest of the dog factors, including mistreatment or relational value. Find out if the veterinary expenses were covered by the pet insurance the defendant bought for Millie. Find out everything about the veterinary bills of each and every animal the plaintiff ever owned, and look for other evidence of suspicious animal injuries. Go to the courthouse and see if the plaintiff is a defendant in any civil or criminal actions. Learn if any of the plaintiff's prior girlfriends had suspicious injuries, if not an order for protection. Ask the defendant about what medical attention she had lately. Look closely at the law on abandonment, and consider making equitable arguments such as quantum meruit, promissory estoppel, and equitable trust.

70. The plaintiff made a strong, traditional claim.

Interrogatory No. 6: Please identify any and all documents, if any, which substantiate or support your claim that you were the person who purchased (or made a contribution of money thereof) Millie from breeder Alex Gustafson.

Answer to "Plaintiff's Interrogatories to Defendant (Set I)"

Interrogatories: 3-9

All requested information is presently in the possession of aforementioned Plaintiff.

The documentation requested in Plaintiff's Request for Production of Documents also, in a large part, were ignored by Defendant as no documents were provided in response. *(See Exhibits 11, 13).*

To date, Defendant has not produced any documents evidencing that she is the legal owner of Millie or that she has acquired superior title in the same by detaining Millie from Plaintiff since August 23, 2011. *(See Exhibit 15).*[71]

Following the breakup, Plaintiff contacted Millie's veterinarian at #1 Animal Hospital. *(See Exhibit 15).* A #1 Animal Hospital employee told Plaintiff that he was no longer listed as Millie's "owner" on the account. *(See Id.)*[72] Counsel for Plaintiff contacted #1 Animal Hospital and the matter was referred to its legal counsel.[73] Upon receiving a copy of Millie's Bill of Sale, Plaintiff's account with #1 Animal Hospital was properly restored and #1 Animal Hospital's mistake was corrected. *(See Exhibit 15).*[74] Attorney Steven Brown then sent a letter to Defendant giving her notice that Plaintiff, as owner of Millie, was entitled to Millie's records. *(See Exhibit 4).* This incident, along with many others, should demonstrate the emotional and financial strain Plaintiff continues to endure because of Defendant's wrongful detention of Millie. *(See Exhibit 15).*[75]

71. In a situation where there has been abandonment, this would not be required. Consider that the defendant may be able to prove that the plaintiff failed to contact her for a lengthy period.

72. It is a better practice to secure the name of the person being referenced. Given the dog's suspicious injury history, try to learn if there was concern at the veterinary office that the plaintiff displayed threatening behaviors.

73. The fact that a lawyer unfamiliar with animal law told the veterinarian to change the records to the plaintiff's name does not prove that they were in the plaintiff's name in the first place. It could prove that the veterinarian's lawyer was risk averse in the context of pending litigation between the parties. It seems more probable, as the defendant long carried veterinary insurance on Millie, that Millie's veterinary records showed both parties' names.

74. Again, this may be a misrepresentation. Get more information.

75. This may only show that both parties were asserting their ownership rights.

ANALYSIS

The right of property generally includes the right to freely possess, use, enjoy, and dispose of the things[76] which are subject to ownership. *Congdon v. Congdon*, 200 N.W. 76, 82-83 (Minn. 1924). The Common Law has always given an owner of property an extensive power of imposing [his/her] will with respect to [his/her] property—a power known as the power of dominion. *(Id. at 83)*. The definitions of the word 'property' in the law dictionaries insist on a right to possess, use, and enjoy a determinate thing. The definition from Black's Law Dictionary provides the following: "Any external thing over which the rights of possession, use, and enjoyment are exercised." *See Black's Law Dictionary 1335 (9th Ed. 2009)*. "In its widest sense, property includes all a person's legal rights, of whatever description." *See Id. at 1336; John Salmond, Jurisprudence 423-24 (Glanville L. Williams ed., 10th ed. 1947).*[77]

Replevin is a Common Law action in which a party alleging to be entitled to immediate possession of personal property seeks to obtain possession of the property from another. "The real test as to whether a replevin action can be maintained turns upon the question whether Plaintiff is, at the time of the institution of the suit, entitled to the immediate possession of the property claimed." *Warren v. Driscoll*, 227 N.W. 199 (Minn. 1929). "When it is said that to maintain replevin Plaintiff's possession must have been lawful, it means merely that it must have been lawful as against the person who deprived [him/her] of it; and possession is good title against all the world except those having a better title." *Anderson v. Gouldberg*, 53 N.W. 636 (Minn. 1982). **"One who takes property from the possession of another can only rebut this presumption by showing a superior title in [himself/herself] . . . "** *Id.* (emphasis added).

The Minnesota Supreme Court explained that an action for replevin may only be used for the recovery of personal property in *Washburn v. Cutter*, 17 Minn. 335 (Minn. 1872). In this case, Plaintiffs sued for the wrongful taking and detention of certain logs by Defendant. The Court held that such entry and removal of the timber by Defendant, who was a trespasser, entitled Plaintiff to recover the logs in replevin. The Court also concluded that property severed from realty becomes personalty and may be recovered in a replevin action.[78]

---

76. The property rights described herein are at odds with legislative enactments throughout the country that promote animal welfare and penalize animal cruelty. Also, the old idea that companion animals are mere property, akin to inanimate objects, is out of step with the progression of national case law about companion animal ownership but still consistent with dangerous dog statutory interpretations.

77. This is a traditional legal analysis that looks as if it came directly out of a popular Minnesota treatise. Again, this is where a lawyer should come in with how ideas about animals as only property are changing with regard to estate planning or the kinds of changing legal standards and concerns raised in Judge Chu's replevin order. The courts, as stated in *Pratt v. Pratt*, 1988 WL 120251 (Minn. App. Nov. 15, 1998), are willing to consider the mistreatment of an animal in reaching a decision.

78. The plaintiff argued well-settled law based upon inanimate property. This would have been more persuasive if he had examples of the court proceeding with a replevin action in the last 50 years where a pet was involved.

Like in *Washburn*, Plaintiff was forced to commence this action because of Defendant's wrongful taking and detention of his personal property. As demonstrated by various exhibits, the facts indicate that Millie was purchased by Plaintiff prior to moving into the 222 First Avenue, Wilco, Minnesota, property[79] where he cohabited with Defendant. In plain terms, Plaintiff brought Millie, as his separate property, into his three-year relationship with Defendant.[80] However, after the breakup, Defendant has asserted that she has somehow acquired an ownership and possessory interest in Millie.[81] In fact, Defendant has unlawfully retained Millie without Plaintiff's consent. Plaintiff has made various demands for the immediate return of Millie and never told Defendant that he would be relinquishing ownership.[82] Additionally, Plaintiff did not make any clear and definite promises, oral or written agreements, and/or other assurances to Defendant that Millie would be hers.[83]

It is already established Defendant failed to deny paragraph 5 of Plaintiff's Complaint.[84] As a result, this paragraph is admitted and the Court should rule in Plaintiff's favor. Even if Defendant can make equitable arguments to support her claim that she is a co-owner of Millie following her breakup with Plaintiff, it has already been established that the initial sale of Millie was made by and between breeder Alex Gustafson and Plaintiff.[85] Again, Defendant has failed to produce a scintilla of evidence showing that she holds any right, title, or interest in Millie. Possession by Plaintiff was lawful when he first acquired Millie.[86] In order to rebut this presumption, Defendant must demonstrate that she holds superior title. Defendant can neither rebut this presumption now nor can she at trial. Therefore, this Court should enter summary judgment in favor of Plaintiff and against Defendant as a matter of law.

II. Should summary judgment be granted in favor of Plaintiff because Defendant has not presented any evidence to create a genuine issue of material fact and has failed and/or refused to cooperate in discovery by answering admissions?

---

79. Not a great word pick here.

80. The plaintiff seems to be saying his relationship began with the defendant when he moved in with her. This sounds disingenuous.

81. This contradicts the plaintiff's earlier allegation.

82. Again, dates of these various "demands" were not detailed.

83. This is a fact question.

84. Using a judicially created doctrine, it could be argued that the defendant substantially denied paragraph five.

85. Purchase could be a rebuttal presumption of ownership or represent one of a variety of factors the court can consider in determining ownership.

86. This sounds good.

RELEVANT FACTS[87]

Plaintiff, in his Request for Admissions to Defendant (Set I), also asked the following:

(See specifically Exhibit 12, Plaintiff's Request for Admissions to Defendant (Set I) and Exhibit 13, Defendant's Answers and Responses to Plaintiff's Interrogatories, Request for Production of Documents, and Request for Admissions, (Set I).

Request No. 1: Admit that Plaintiff purchased Millie from breeder Alex Gustafson.

Request No. 2: Admit that Millie, who is the subject of this litigation, is registered in Plaintiff's name alone.

Request No. 3: Admit that you, Defendant, received a letter dated September 19, 2011 from Steven Brown, attorney for #1 Animal Hospital, which states in pertinent part that "Plaintiff has provided the Animal Hospital with written evidence that he is the owner of a Shiba Inu named Millie."

Request No. 4: Admit that you, Defendant, have wrongfully retained Millie without the consent of Plaintiff, Millie's registered owner.

Request No. 5: Admit that Plaintiff is listed as owner of Millie in the American Kennel Club Litter Record, a true and correct copy of which was incorporated by reference into Plaintiff's Complaint as Exhibit A.

As answer to "Plaintiff's Request for Admissions to Defendant (Set I)"

Pursuant to admissions:

1-5 I will not admit.

Defendant's responses, however, fail to set forth in detail the reasons why Defendant cannot truthfully admit or deny the matter as required by the Minnesota Rules of Civil Procedure.[88] Here, the facts show that Defendant has failed to not only provide responses to Plaintiff's Admissions, but all of Plaintiff's discovery requests. A party's stubborn refusal to cooperate in discovery in good faith does not create a question of fact.

---

87. At some point, there is a feeling that by repeating the same points over and over again, the plaintiff was trying to create the illusion that he had more evidence than he in fact had. An experienced judge would notice this.

88. The plaintiff's attorney might want to exercise more caution. When a pro se individual vaguely denies a request for admissions, the pro se defendant's failure to detail the reasons for a denial may be the basis for a discovery-related motion with an award of attorney's fees requested rather than as the basis for a dispositive motion. The question may arise as to whether the pro se defendant's response to the request for admissions should be interpreted based upon the four corners of all the pleadings she filed, including her answer, or handled from perhaps a substantive fairness perspective. Although a lawyer would know enough to incorporate other pleadings by reference, a pro se defendant would not. Regardless of whether discovery is timely, the defense attorney should file amended discovery responses and also ask the court to exercise discretion, after service is achieved, to extend leniency. It is probably a better idea to include this type of statement when there is some level of complexity to the facts. However, what the plaintiff's attorney did here may work. If the judge assigned to this case had a heavy docket and perceived this case as inconsequential because the dispute was only about a pet, a subject beneath the dignity of the court, the court could seize upon this strict constructionist opportunity to decide the case in favor of the plaintiff.

ANALYSIS

Further, when addressing a Motion for Summary Judgment, the sole function of the Court is to determine whether there is a fact question to be tried.

> Rule 36.01 of the Minnesota Rules of Civil Procedure provides, in pertinent part, that [a] party may serve upon any other party a written request for the admission, for the purposes of the pending action only, of the truth of any matters within the scope of Rule 26.02 set forth in the request that relate to statements, opinions of fact, or the application of law to fact . . . [t]he matter is admitted unless within 30 days after the service of the request . . . the party to whom the request is directed serves upon the party requesting the admission a written answer or objection addressed to the matter, signed by the party or by the party's attorney . . .
>
> If objection is made, the reasons therefore shall be stated . . . An answering party may not give lack of information or knowledge as a reason for failure to admit or deny unless the party states that a reasonable inquiry has been made and that the information known or readily obtainable by the party is insufficient to enable the party to admit or deny. Minn. R. Civ. P. 36.02.[89]

Thus, a party upon whom Admissions are served must respond within 30 days or the matters contained in the request are deemed "conclusively established." Minn. R. Civ. P. 36.02. As the Court is well-aware, any denial should fairly meet the substance of the request, especially if such request is reasonably calculated to lead to admissible evidence.[90]

Based on the evidence presented to the Court, the record clearly indicates that Plaintiff is the sole legal owner of Millie. As previously noted, Plaintiff sent written Requests for Admissions to establish that he is the rightful owner of Millie and that he continues to suffer hardship as a result of Defendant's wrongful actions. All of the requests served on Defendant concern matters within her knowledge and involve the subject matter of this litigation. In any event, the requested admissions go directly to the merits of this case. A court may deem the requests admitted and enter summary judgment based on a party's failure or refusal to answer admissions. *Behnke v. Green-Behnke,* 2004 WL 376984 * 7, *see also Western Horizontal Drilling, Inc. v. Jonnet Energy Corp.*, 11 F.3d 65, 70 (5th Cir. 1994) (holding that deemed admissions may serve as the basis for summary judgment). *(See Exhibit 14).*

"A party opposing a motion for summary judgment must come forward with affirmative evidence sufficient to create a genuine issue of material fact and may not rely upon mere averments in the pleadings or unsupported allegations."

---

89. It is always good practice to remind the court of the exact language in a pertinent statute.

90. It would have been better for the plaintiff to have added a case on this point. The counterargument is probably that courts have discretion, particularly when a pro se individual provides a good faith effort in answering the complaint.

Musicland Group v. Ceridian Corp., 508 N.W.2d 524, 530-31 (Minn. Ct. App. 1993).[91] Here, Defendant's practical refusal to cooperate in discovery does not by itself create any issues of material fact. It is therefore within the Court's discretion to grant summary judgment in favor of Plaintiff because Defendant failed to respond to Plaintiff's Request for Admissions.[92]

As a result of Defendant's failure or refusal to respond to Plaintiff's Request for Admissions, even if the Court does not rule in favor of Plaintiff on alternative grounds, the requests should be deemed admitted, and as there are subsequently no material facts in dispute, the Court should enter summary judgment in favor of Plaintiff.

CONCLUSION

For the above reasons, Plaintiff respectfully requests that this Court grant his Motion for Summary Judgment.

Before looking at the pleadings by the defense, it is worth noting that many jurists lack experience in family law, animal law, or both. In these pleadings, the plaintiff offered the court enough in terms of facts, evidence, and the law[93] for the court to grant the plaintiff the relief sought if the court was both conservative and traditional with regard to the application of the law, was indifferent to animal welfare concerns, and forgot that replevin actions are rooted in equitable principles.

If a client brings his or her case to you to defend this action, you cannot minimize the risk that a grant of summary judgment could occur. It is better to approach what you do as making an effort to change the probabilities. The defense cannot expect to get a progressive judge. The defense may be able to prove that the plaintiff was deliberately deceiving the court and cause the court not to grant the relief sought because of a material fact question or based upon common law equitable considerations. It is also possible that a judge would deny the plaintiff's action based upon a well-articulated summary of recent companion animal case law.

As we proceed to analyze the defendant's pleadings, you will see that in the pro se defendant's response/answer, she simply copied the plaintiff's complaint and typed in the word "Denied" under several paragraphs of the plaintiff's complaint. Only the paragraphs where she included a response have been included here.

91. When companion animals are involved, consider whether traditional replevin and summary judgment standards should apply.

92. This was actually a misrepresentation to the court. The defendant did respond to the plaintiff's request for admissions but did not fully meet the requirement under the pertinent rules.

93. Notwithstanding this claim, the plaintiff failed to file a mandatory affidavit in the instant case.

DEFENDANT'S RESPONSE/ANSWER

DENIED

8. Plaintiff picked the name for Millie without any help from others. Millie was named after his mother.

DENIED

9. In April 2008, Millie landed awkwardly on her left front leg and broke it. Plaintiff took Millie to an emergency veterinary clinic located in Minneapolis, Minnesota. The veterinarians worked quickly to take x-rays and set the broken bone. The next day, Plaintiff took Millie to #1 Animal Hospital. The attending veterinarian took additional x-rays and recommended surgery with an orthopedic surgeon.

DENIED

10. The Friday of that same week in April 2008, Millie had surgery. Pins and screws were required and remain in place to date. Millie had a successful recovery. Plaintiff paid all costs of surgery, which exceeded $4,000.00. Since Millie was Plaintiff's separate property, it was Plaintiff's responsibility alone to pay all healthcare costs for Millie's health and well-being.

DENIED

11. Millie continued to live with Plaintiff at 111 Smith Street in Wilco, Minnesota, for the next five months and had minimal contact with Defendant.

DENIED

12. On or around July 2008, Plaintiff moved in with Defendant at her townhome having the common address of 222 First Avenue, Wilco, Minnesota.

CORRECTION OF DATE: JUNE 28, 2008

13. Defendant would rarely take the time to walk Millie, aid in training and obedience, or let Millie out early in the mornings or after work in order to permit Millie to relieve herself.

DENIED

14. Despite living and sharing a co-residence with Defendant, Plaintiff was responsible for paying Millie's healthcare, special weight management dog food, grooming every six weeks at Dog Groomers Palace, and other related expenses,

including the cost to have Millie spayed (costs of approximately $500.00). Plaintiff also paid to have an identification microchip embedded into Millie and other registration costs. Millie is registered in Plaintiff's name.

DENIED

15. Countless neighbors situated in Wilco, Minnesota, and mutual friends of Plaintiff and Defendant would attest that it was Plaintiff who would walk and care for Millie. More importantly, these close mutual friends would also confirm that Millie was Plaintiff's dog.

DENIED

16. Defendant's only significant financial contribution to Millie is a current health insurance policy that Defendant purchased for Plaintiff and Millie as a Christmas gift.

DENIED

17. Unbeknownst to Plaintiff, over the course of the past few years, Defendant has made misrepresentations to third parties regarding her legal rights to Millie's ownership. More specifically, Defendant made an attempt to license Millie in her name alone, and has changed the owner's name of various accounts with third parties, including #1 Animal Hospital. All of Defendant's actions were done without the knowledge or consent of Plaintiff.

DENIED

21. On or around August 23, 2011, Plaintiff was locked out of his co-residence and Defendant wrongfully detained Millie.

ANSWER: Plaintiff was asked to leave my residence due to the discovery of multiple extracurricular intimate relationships—and his acknowledgment of same—with multiple female partners in Minnesota and outside Minnesota, placing my health in serious jeopardy, due to this secret activity and multiple indiscretions over an extended period of time—during our relationship while continuing to refer to me as his "fiancé," even most recently in the presence (meeting) of an attorney.[94]

94. The defendant raised the possibility that her reason for keeping or pursuing Millie was payback for the plaintiff's indiscretions. Her answer would have been better if she had emphasized her primary care of Millie and weaved in her indignation about the plaintiff's extracurricular activities with a more precise depiction of the extent of the plaintiff's absences. While a pro se individual may be able to get away with the type of fault argument that the defendant made here, a judge would not appreciate this type of argument being advanced by an attorney. Even so, because this dispute arose in a cohabitation rather than a dissolution of marriage context, the court may have been willing to listen to limited fault-based evidence, particularly as the plaintiff is seeking the historically equitable remedy of replevin and while the defendant may have had a legal basis for claiming abandonment.

24. Defendant has intentionally refused, neglected, or failed to return Millie to Plaintiff.

DENIED

25. Therefore, Plaintiff seeks an Order from this Court directing Defendant to return and deliver possession of Millie to Plaintiff.

29. Plaintiff is entitled to immediate possession of Millie.

ANSWER: Plaintiff, for weeks at a time, and repeatedly, has abandoned Millie, while engaging in out of state and in town affairs with multiple female partners, claiming to be working over extended periods of time, while deceiving Defendant. Additionally, this extra relationship activity has put Defendant in physical and health jeopardy as a result.[95]

30. Unless restrained by an Order from this Court, Defendant will continue to act against Plaintiff's property in furtherance of her own interest and to the detriment of Plaintiff. Plaintiff has no adequate remedy at law against Defendant, except for return of the property and an injunction, permanent or temporary, pursuant to applicable law.

ANSWER: Plaintiff owes Defendant more than Ten Thousand Dollars ($10,000.00 plus) due to his refusal to share in the mutually agreed upon household expenses, bounced checks never made good, etc.[96]

REQUEST FOR RELIEF[97]

WHEREFORE, Defendant requests relief as follows:

1. For a judgment in favor of Defendant and against Plaintiff awarding the immediate possession of the property described therein, Millie.

2. For an injunction prohibiting Plaintiff from claiming any right, title, or interest in Defendant's dog, Millie. Such injunction shall also prohibit Plaintiff from any visitation rights with Millie.

3. For reasonable attorney's fees incurred in bringing this action, together with Defendant's costs and disbursements.

4. For a judgment sounding in equity to properly and justly implement the orders and judgments of the Court.

---

95. It is impressive that a pro se individual came up with an abandonment claim. She should have developed the abandonment facts more. She also had other possible claims, such as for promissory estoppel, consideration of maltreatment of Millie, co-ownership, or gift, that she did not raise here.

96. It seems this idea could be expanded to indicate that, in effect, they both paid for the living expenses.

97. In addition to amateur but somewhat effective denials and answers, the pro se defendant did prepare a decent request for relief.

5. For the return of the $10,000.00 owed to Defendant by Plaintiff for his refusal to adhere to our agreement to share household costs for the time he spent in our "co-residence," and for the "bounced checks" never made good to me.[98]

6. For such other relief as the Court concludes is appropriate.

Before continuing, it is worth stating that the pro se defendant did enough in her answer/response to cause a reasonable judge to evaluate whether the plaintiff, if lacking candor in his recital of facts to the court in some important respects, was not eligible for the equitable relief that a replevin order represents.

Note that for the next pleading, the defendant hired an attorney at the eleventh hour. Although comments are provided about how the defendant could have further developed the legal issues in this case or redone the answer and supplemented her responses to request for admissions, this is a pretty good brief for an inexperienced attorney writing against the clock. Even so, when you read the court order, you will find that the defense counsel missed something important.

98. As the defendant did not make a counterclaim, this prayer for relief is not appropriate. Even so, it may help her cause.

STATE OF MINNESOTA
COUNTY OF SMITH

DISTRICT COURT
FIRST JUDICIAL DISTRICT
CIVIL COURT DIVISION
Court File No. 123

In Re the Matter of:
Andy Anderson,

Plaintiff,

and

Nicole Davis

Defendant.

DEFENDANT'S MEMORANDUM OF LAW IN OPPOSITION TO PLAINTIFF'S MOTION FOR SUMMARY JUDGMENT

Defendant, by and through her undersigned counsel, now submits this Memorandum of Law in opposition to Plaintiff's Motion for Summary Judgment. Plaintiff argues that there is no genuine issue of material fact and that he is entitled to judgment as a matter of law for that reason. As discussed below, Plaintiff's Motion should be denied because there is a genuine issue of material fact and because Defendant is the proper owner of the dog, Millie.[99]

BACKGROUND

This case arises out of the end of the parties' romantic relationship. Plaintiff has commenced a lawsuit for replevin of Millie and now has a Motion for Summary Judgment pending before this Court. Plaintiff asserts that Millie is his sole property and that he has borne sole responsibility for Millie throughout her life. In reality, Defendant has been the primary caretaker and provider for Millie and is better suited to remain Millie's owner.[100]

STATEMENT OF THE RECORD

Pursuant to Minn. R. Gen. Prac. 115.03 (d)(2), the record on which this Memorandum relies, is the pleadings and the entire file in this case, as well as:

99. The idea of "proper owner" is legally appealing and carries a bit of equitable gravitas.
100. This is a pretty good and concise statement except that concerns about Millie's "accident" should have been emphasized more.

1. Affidavit of Defendant with Exhibits[101]

    a. Exhibits 1 and 2: Picture of Defendant in Alexandria with Millie's litter
    b. Exhibit 3: Plaintiff's 2008 dog license application
    c. Exhibit 4: Receipt for 2011 dog license purchased by Defendant
    d. Exhibit 5: Email correspondence from VPI
    e. Exhibit 6: AKC litter record
    f. Exhibit 7: Copies of Millie's vet records
    g. Exhibit 8: Veterinary bills paid by Defendant
    h. Exhibit 9: Spreadsheet showing Defendant's expenditures for Millie
    i. Exhibit 10: Spreadsheet showing Plaintiff's debts to Defendant
    j. Exhibit 11: Defendant's bank statements and Plaintiff's returned check
    k. Exhibit 13: Copies of emails regarding attempts of Defendant and others to get Plaintiff into treatment
    l. Exhibit 15: A list of dates that Plaintiff abandoned Millie
    m. Exhibit 16: Emails between Defendant and Plaintiff's assistant
    n. Exhibit 17: Copies of Plaintiff's employment probation notices
    o. Exhibit 18: Pictures of damage to Defendant's house caused by Plaintiff
    p. Exhibit 19: Picture of Plaintiff's black eye
    q. Exhibit 20: Picture of damage to Defendant's garage door caused by Plaintiff
    r. Exhibit 21: Pictures of Millie and Bella

2. Affidavit of Rebecca Roberts with a copy of *Pratt v. Pratt*, 1988 WL 120251 (Minn. App. Nov. 15, 1998).

FACTS

In December of 2008, Defendant traveled with Plaintiff to Alexandria, Minnesota, to inspect a litter of two puppies. (*See Affidavit of Defendant*). According to the American Kennel Club Litter Record, a dog named Millie was purchased by Plaintiff, who listed his address as 123 Birch Street. Plaintiff never resided at the Birch Street property. Defendant solely owned and occupied the Birch Street residence. (*Id*).[102]

101. The defendant's affidavit is not included in this appendix.
102. *Id.* is what is used when referring to a case, not a pleading.

Millie and Plaintiff moved in with Defendant in June of 2008. Once Plaintiff and Millie moved in, Defendant became Millie's primary caretaker.[103] Defendant gets up with Millie three times each night,[104] takes Millie for walks,[105] and sees to it that Millie is fed[106] and receives the care of a veterinarian when necessary.[107] Since 2008, Defendant has spent $2,391.59 on Millie. (*See Affidavit of Defendant*).[108]

Plaintiff purchased a one-year license for the dog in 2008. (*See Affidavit of Defendant*). Plaintiff never renewed Millie's license and Defendant purchased a license for Millie on August 28, 2011 after the City of Wilco alerted her to the problem. (*Id.*).[109]

Defendant and Plaintiff planned to be married before their relationship ended.[110] In anticipation of the planned marriage,[111] and with Plaintiff's full knowledge and consent, Plaintiff and Defendant listed "Andy and Nicole Anderson" as Millie's owners on Millie's account at #1 Animal Hospital as well as several other veterinary facilities.[112] (*Id.* at paragraph 10 and Exhibit 7).

Plaintiff has struggled with addictions and substance abuse[113] and has a tendency towards violence. Plaintiff ripped the face off of a drawer in Defendant's home and damaged Defendant's garage door by kicking it.[114] (*See Affidavit of Defendant*). Defendant believes that Millie's broken leg was actually caused by Plaintiff,

103. This should have more detail.

104. Is there something wrong with Millie because of her accident? Does Millie cower? Is Millie anxious?

105. Who observed this?

106. What does this mean? Does she buy her food and feed Millie consistently, or only feed her if the plaintiff forgets or is away?

107. Meaningful details should be provided, particularly if Millie is apt to need more than annual veterinary care following her accident. It might also be relevant if Millie had been seen for a condition, such as anxiety.

108. Proving that the defendant paid large amounts of veterinary fees is significant and consistent with her claim that she has an ownership interest in Millie.

109. Be specific as to how the defendant was alerted to the problem. Was she at a dog park and asked for Millie's license by animal control? Did a notice come in the mail?

110. Did he give her a ring? Was their engagement announced on social media?

111. A planned marriage, alone, does not make the defendant a co-owner.

112. Why is Millie going to more than one veterinary facility? What medical problems does she have?

113. Provide details. The defendant probably knows whether the plaintiff had drunken driving convictions or was in treatment or attended sobriety meetings. The defendant might also know how many milligrams of OxyContin the plaintiff took a day and where he obtained it. Given that courts know misuse of pain pills is a major concern in the United States today, provide the court with as many details as possible about the severity of the plaintiff's use.

114. Look for police reports to verify and add dates or years and seasons.

perhaps while he was under the influence of alcohol or illegal drugs.[115] (*Id.* at paragraph 20). Additionally, Plaintiff once insisted that Millie's stomach be pumped because he was afraid that Millie had eaten an OxyContin. (*Id.* at 19).[116]

Plaintiff regularly left the home that he shared with Millie and Defendant for days or weeks at a time[117] without telling Defendant where he was going, or even that he was leaving. On these numerous occasions, Defendant continued to care for Millie as she had been since 2010.[118] (*Id.* at paragraph 29).

ARGUMENT

Summary Judgment Standard

Summary judgment is appropriate only when "the pleadings, depositions, Answers to Interrogatories, and admissions on file, together with the Affidavits, if any, show that there is no genuine issue as to any material fact and that either party is entitled to a judgment as a matter of law."[119] Minn. R. Civ. P. 56.03. The Court must view evidence in the light most favorable to the non-moving party, and the movant must clearly sustain its burden of proving that there is no genuine issue of material fact and that it is entitled to judgment as a matter of law. *Vacura v. Haar's Equipment, Inc.*, 364 N.W.2d 387, 391 (Minn. 1985). A party opposing summary judgment "cannot rely upon mere general statements of fact but rather must demonstrate at the time the motion is made that specific facts are in existence which create a genuine issue for trial." *Hunt v. IBM Mid Am. Employees Fed. Credit Union*, 384 N.W.2d 853, 855 (Minn. 1986). Summary judgment is not appropriate when reasonable persons might draw different inferences from the evidence presented.[120] *DLH, Inc. v. Russ*, 566 N.W.2d 60, 69 (Minn. 1997).

---

115. The defendant simply did not go far enough and given the traditional arguments advanced by the plaintiff about property claims, the quality and completeness of this portion of the pleadings is likely to be outcome determinative. For example, the defendant might have said, "While the plaintiff was generally tolerant of Millie when sober, he was a mean drunk toward both Millie and me and he was typically drunk on weekends. His alcohol of choice was whiskey and he also took whatever he could inexpensively 'score' from his childhood friends, a few of which have served time. When drunk, he would throw heavy objects and punch holes in doors and walls from time to time. I also noticed that especially when he was drunk, Millie sometimes cringed around him or cowered when he lifted his hand."

116. This makes the plaintiff sound responsible. It is not clear whose OxyContin Millie swallowed and why Millie would have access to this drug. If the defendant was asserting that the plaintiff's behavior was impacted by his addiction to pain medication, she should have said so.

117. The more the defendant can establish that the plaintiff was frequently away and left Millie in her care, the better.

118. The defendant made an animal best interest argument by suggesting that the plaintiff was unreliable.

119. This is a decent leading argument.

120. This is an appropriate boilerplate legal summary.

Contrary to Plaintiff's assertion, there is a genuine issue of material fact in this case, and this Court should deny Plaintiff's Motion.[121] Plaintiff alleges that there is no genuine issue of material fact as to Millie's ownership and that Defendant has not cooperated in discovery, thus Plaintiff seeks to have this Court deem his Requests for Admission and certain allegations in his Complaint admitted. Plaintiff's ownership is not clear and Defendant has clearly denied Plaintiff's Requests for Admission.

I. PLAINTIFF'S MOTION SHOULD BE DENIED BECAUSE THERE IS GENUINE ISSUE OF MATERIAL FACT AS TO MILLIE'S OWNERSHIP.

Plaintiff argues that "ownership of Millie is evidenced by a Bill of Sale, the AKC Litter Record, and the AKC registration." (*See Plaintiff's Memorandum of Law in Support of Summary Judgment*). Plaintiff further argues that Defendant has not denied paragraph 5 of Plaintiff's Complaint and that the allegations therein should be deemed admitted. Plaintiff's Motion should fail because the documents referenced by Plaintiff do not provide clear evidence of Plaintiff's ownership[122] and because taken as a whole, Defendant's Answer should be fairly read to deny the allegations in paragraph 5 of the Complaint.[123]

A. The Documents Relied Upon By Plaintiff Do Not Clearly Establish Plaintiff's Ownership.

Plaintiff relies on a Bill of Sale, the AKC Litter Record, and the AKC registration as evidence of his ownership of Millie. These documents do not establish Plaintiff's ownership.

The first document, a purported Bill of Sale, is only a letter from the breeder advancing Plaintiff's argument at his request. (*Exhibit 2*). The statement from the breeder is undated, but was notarized on September 16, 2011, after Plaintiff's September 1, 2011 demand for Millie (*Exhibit 7*).[124] A true "Bill of Sale" would be dated from the time that Millie was purchased. The statement from the breeder should not be construed as dispositive of the ownership of Millie.

---

121. It would have been better to talk about issues of material fact being plural rather than singular.

122. The defendant asserted a clear evidence standard. Does the defendant mean by a preponderance of the evidence or based upon a clear and convincing evidentiary standard?

123. Taken as a whole, this was a good argument, but it would have been better if he had presented a case to support this interpretation.

124. Great job.

The second document relied upon by Plaintiff is the AKC litter record. (*Exhibit 1*). Plaintiff asserts that the AKC litter record is a "legal form" based upon the representation of the breeder, but provides no other support for that assertion. The document lists Millie's "New Owner" as Plaintiff, and lists his address as 123 Birch Street. Plaintiff never resided at the Birch Street property. Defendant solely owned and occupied the Birch Street residence. That the address is one where Defendant lived, but Plaintiff never did, shows that there is a genuine issue of material fact as to who owns Millie.[125]

Finally, Plaintiff points to a document that he calls an "AKC Registration." (*Exhibit 3*). The document is submitted without any supporting information, and even a cursory review of the document leaves wide open the question of what it shows, if anything. On its face, the document appears to be only a coupon for a free office visit for the newly registered dog. The coupon should not be construed as evidence of ownership.[126]

Because the letter from the breeder is not a "Bill of Sale," because the AKC litter record lists Defendant's address where Plaintiff never lived, and because the "AKC Registration" is only a coupon for a free veterinary checkup, there is a genuine issue of material fact, and Plaintiff's Motion should be denied.

B. Plaintiff's Motion Should Be Denied Because Taken as a Whole, Defendant's Answer Should Be Fairly Construed to Deny Paragraph 5 of Plaintiff's Complaint.

Plaintiff argues that "Defendant, by not denying paragraph 5 of Plaintiff's Complaint, has confirmed that 'Plaintiff is the sole owner of Millie.'" *(Plaintiff's Memorandum of Law in Support of Summary Judgment)*. Plaintiff's argument is without merit.

Defendant prepared her Answer without the assistance of counsel. As a pro se party, this Court should construe Defendant's pleadings liberally to do substantial justice.[127] Defendant denied nearly every allegation in Plaintiff's Complaint.[128] Her lack of any response to paragraph 5 was merely a clerical mistake.[129] (*See Affidavit of Defendant*). Looking at Defendant's Answer as a whole, this Court should

125. The argument about the American Kennel Club registration was very confusing, but it suggested an issue as to material fact.

126. The defendant effectively threaded the needle with example after example of the plaintiff's lack of candor with the court.

127. This is a good argument. It would have been even better if the defendant had quoted someone, such as Learned Hand, or added relevant companion animal case citations.

128. This is a bit misleading; The defendant did not address every paragraph.

129. This is a bit dodgy. If there was a case supporting the idea that a poor-quality pleading by a pro se individual should be treated under the rules as a clerical error, the defendant should have so informed the court..

reasonably conclude that Defendant intended to, and does deny the allegation contained in paragraph 5 of the Complaint.

Such a reading of Defendant's Answer is consistent with the standard that this Court must use in ruling on the instant Motion. This Court must view evidence in the light most favorable to the non-moving party. *Vacura v. Haar's Equipment, Inc.*, 364 N.W.2d 387, 391 (Minn. 1985). Taking all the evidence presented in the light most favorable to Defendant, this Court should construe her Answer as denying the allegation contained in paragraph 5 of the Complaint.[130]

C. Plaintiff's Conduct Creates a Genuine Issue of Material Fact as to the Ownership of Millie.

Plaintiff's claim of sole ownership of Millie is further undermined by the facts in this case. Defendant helped to pick out Millie and has even provided a picture of the event.[131] (*See Affidavit of Defendant*). Defendant's address, where Plaintiff never resided, was provided as the address of Millie's new owner on the AKC litter form,[132] and since Millie moved into Defendant's home in 2008, Defendant has gotten up with Millie three times each night, taken Millie for walks, and seen to it that Millie is fed and receives the care of a veterinarian when necessary.[133] Since 2011, Defendant has spent $2,391.59 on Millie. (*See Affidavit of Defendant*). Millie's records with #1 Animal Hospital were listed under "Andy and Nicole Davis" because the parties contemplated marriage and with Plaintiff's knowledge and consent, and in July of 2011, Plaintiff verbally indicated that Defendant could "have Millie."[134] (*See Affidavit of Defendant*).[135] These facts all indicate that Defendant, and not Plaintiff, is the true owner of Millie.

Plaintiff's lack of ownership in Millie is further evidenced by the fact that he failed to license the dog after 2009. Minn. Stat. §347.09 requires that:

---

130. The defendant could have reminded the court that Millie's best interests were at stake and said something such as, "Furthermore, from a public policy standpoint, there is evidence that Plaintiff has a history of substance abuse, Plaintiff has damaged Defendant's property, Millie had a suspicious accident while under Plaintiff's care and control, and Plaintiff has simply left Millie for weeks at a time without making any inquiries about her welfare." It is important to find out which judge is assigned to your case before deciding what argument to make. Consider if your intended audience is really the court of appeals.

131. Good job!

132. The defendant should have added, "and is a fact consistent with Defendant's claim that the parties co-own Millie."

133. This sounds improbable. The defendant's lawyer should have either explained what was wrong with Millie that caused her to get up three times at night or cautioned her to amend her underlying affidavit.

134. Given the plaintiff's lifestyle, a stronger claim for gift, co-ownership, or promissory estoppel could have been asserted. It is a weakness that the defendant did not offer affidavits by neighbors aware that the plaintiff was often gone and how the defendant took good care of Millie.

135. Although the defendant's affidavit was properly filed, it was not included in this appendix.

> In every county in which sections 347.08 to 347.21 shall become operative every dog more than six months of age must have a license. The owner of any dog (the word "owner," when used in sections 347.08 to 347.21, in relation to property in, or possession of, dogs shall include every person who owns, harbors, or keeps a dog) shall, on or before February 1 each year, obtain a license for the dog, and shall pay for such license the fee prescribed by the county commissioners, which shall not be less than 50 cents nor more than $1 for a male dog and not less than $1 nor more than $2 for a female dog; such payments to be made to the town, or city clerk or deputy. The application for such license shall be in such written form as prescribed by the county auditor, and shall state the name, sex, breed, age, color and marking of the dog for which the license is sought.[136]

Likewise, the City of Wilco has an ordinance which reads, "No person shall own, keep or harbor any dog over the age of 16 weeks without first obtaining a dog license from the city." Wilco City Code (Minn.) § 8-626.[137]

Plaintiff purchased a license for Millie in 2008 and not thereafter. Defendant purchased a license for Millie on August 28, 2011 only after the City of Wilco alerted her that Plaintiff had not purchased a license in three years. That Plaintiff did not meet the legal obligation of a dog owner to purchase a license under both Minn. Stat. §347.09 and Wilco City Code (Minn.) § 8-626, shows that Plaintiff is not Millie's owner and that there is a genuine issue of material fact for trial. Accordingly, this Court should deny Plaintiff's Motion.[138]

Because the facts of this case and the conduct of the parties show that Defendant is the true and proper owner of Millie, there is a genuine issue of material fact, and this Court should deny Plaintiff's Motion.

II. THIS COURT SHOULD NOT DEEM PLAINTIFF'S REQUESTS FOR ADMISSION TO BE ADMITTED.

Plaintiff argues that Defendant has refused to cooperate in discovery and the Court should deem Plaintiff's Requests for Admission to be admitted.

Minn. R. Civ. P. 36.01 provides that an Answer to a Request for Admission "shall specifically deny the matter or set forth in detail the reasons why the answering party cannot truthfully admit or deny the matter." Defendant's Answer should be fairly read to deny each of Plaintiff's Requests for Admission. "I will not admit" is a

136. The defendant could have gone further and stated that past this point, the couple, now engaged, co-owned Millie based upon the type of equitable principles explored in *Marvin v Marvin*, 176 Cal. Rptr. 555, 122 Cal. App. 3d 871 (Cal. App. 2d Dist. 1981). Also, be aware of making a choice between asserting ownership and co-ownership rights.

137. It is always a good idea to include pertinent laws.

138. Sometimes, it is okay to throw in the kitchen sink because it is never really known what will be persuasive to a judge.

clear denial and not a refusal to admit or deny. Responding to discovery requests is a technical matter not well understood by non-attorneys, and Defendant's Answers should be construed liberally.[139]

Minn. R. Civ. P. 36.01 goes on to provide that "The party who has requested the admissions may move to determine the sufficiency of the answers or objections." Plaintiff has made no such Motion here, nor has Plaintiff requested any further clarification or response to his discovery. Plaintiff's request that the Court deem his Requests for Admission to be admitted is not properly before this Court and the Court should not deem the Requests to be admitted.

Because Defendant denied each and every of Plaintiff's Requests for Admission and because Plaintiff has not brought a proper Motion before this Court, Plaintiff's Requests for Admission should not be deemed admitted.[140]

III. DEFENDANT IS THE PROPER OWNER OF MILLIE BECAUSE MILLIE HAS BEEN AND WILL BE MISTREATED BY PLAINTIFF.

At its very root, this case is about the breakup of a relationship.[141] Because Millie has been mistreated at the hand of Plaintiff, and likely will be again, Plaintiff should not be granted ownership of Millie.[142]

In *Pratt v. Pratt*, 1988 WL 120251 (Minn. App. Nov. 15, 1998), the court held that in the context of divorce, a court cannot apply the child custody standards of Minn. Stat. §518.17, but the trial court can award a dog based in part on evidence of mistreatment of the dog. *Pratt*, 1988 WL 120251 at *1. While this case is not divorce per se, it is analogous to the dissolution in *Pratt*.[143]

Plaintiff has struggled with addictions and substance abuse and has a tendency towards violence. Plaintiff ripped the face off of a drawer in Defendant's home and damaged Defendant's garage door by kicking it. (*See Affidavit of Defendant*). In April of 2008, Millie suffered a serious broken leg. Defendant believes that

139. This is a really good argument. It would have been even better if the defendant had cited a case describing under what circumstances that answer would be liberally construed.

140. This point was well made.

141. Actually, at the very root, this case was about whether Millie was co-owned from the beginning, and if not, if she was co-owned later, and if not, if the defendant became the owner later because of a gift, abandonment, or even the acquisition of a possessory right. If Millie was co-owned, the court could utilize the factors offered by Judge Regina Chu earlier in this appendix in its decision-making process. Argue that the individual purchase of an animal by one party was not dispositive of all the ownership issues.

142. In these situations, attorneys should check the Bureau of Criminal Apprehension as well as any registry pertaining to animal abusers, including the National Animal Abuse Registry Database Administration System, a site used to screen potential pet adopters, and a newly evolving registry akin to New Hampshire's Task Force for the Humane Treatment of Animals.

143. Good job.

Millie's broken leg was actually caused by Plaintiff, perhaps while he was under the influence of alcohol or illegal drugs or both. (*Id*). Additionally, Plaintiff once insisted that Millie's stomach be pumped because he was afraid that Millie had eaten an OxyContin. (*Id*).

Because Millie has been mistreated at the hand of Plaintiff and likely will be again, Plaintiff's Motion should be denied and this Court should recognize Defendant as the true and proper owner of Millie.

CONCLUSION

For the foregoing reasons, Defendant respectfully requests that this Court deny Plaintiff's Motion in full and award Defendant attorney's fees and costs associated with this Motion.

STATE OF MINNESOTA	DISTRICT COURT
COUNTY OF SMITH	FIRST JUDICIAL DISTRICT
	CIVIL COURT DIVISION
In Re the Matter of:	Court File No. 123
Andy Anderson,	
Plaintiff,	
	PLAINTIFF'S REPLY TO DEFENDANT'S COUNTERCLAIM
and	
Nicole Davis	
Defendant.	

Plaintiff, Andy Anderson, for his Reply to Defendant's Counterclaim, states as follows:

GENERAL DENIAL[144]

1. Unless otherwise admitted, qualified, or otherwise explained, Plaintiff denies each and every allegation of Defendant's Answer and Counterclaim.

REPLY TO COUNTERCLAIM

2. In response to the allegations set forth in paragraph 12 of Defendant's Answer and Counterclaim, Plaintiff admits only that he moved in with Defendant on or around July 1, 2008.

AFFIRMATIVE DEFENSES

3. Pending discovery to preserve all affirmative defenses, Plaintiff incorporates all affirmative defenses set forth in Rule 8.03 of the Minnesota Rules of Civil Procedure. Plaintiff also reserves the right to assert or supplement any additional defenses it may have in this case.[145]

---

144. The court does not expect anything elaborate with this kind of reply. It was good for the plaintiff to get one in. This reply does the job. Even so, the plaintiff's failure to deny many of the defendant's assertions seemed to create the impression that the plaintiff was not forthright.

145. This is lawyer-like.

4. Affirmatively alleges that Defendant's Answer and Counterclaim fails to state a claim upon which relief may be granted against Plaintiff.[146]

5. Affirmatively alleges that if Defendant has sustained any damages, it is the result of her own fault, conduct, and responsibility, or the fault, responsibility, or liability of parties over whom Plaintiff has no control.[147]

6. Affirmatively alleges that Defendant's claims may be barred, in whole or in part, by the doctrine of waiver, laches, consent and/or estoppel.[148]

7. Affirmatively alleges that the granting of Defendant's demand would result in unjust enrichment, as Defendant would retain money it is not entitled to.

8. Affirmatively alleges that Plaintiff's claims may be barred, in whole or in part, by the doctrine of unclean hands.[149]

WHEREFORE, Plaintiff requests relief as follows:

1. That Defendant takes nothing from its pretended Counterclaim and that Plaintiff be awarded the relief as described in his Complaint.

---

146. This is always a good claim to make.

147. This is a poor example of throwing in the kitchen sink. This language appears to have been cut and pasted from a dog bite pleading.

148. Remember to include equitable defenses. There may be a promissory estoppel argument to make against the defendant. Notice that in all of the plaintiff's pleadings, the tone is very legalistic, if not righteous, about the plaintiff's claim that he owns Millie. The plaintiff did little to establish that he loves and is attached to Millie, or that keeping Millie with him would be in his or Millie's best interests. Because this was a summary judgment action, where it was important that there was no material fact dispute, the plaintiff may have decided not to develop the record on this for strategic reasons. Even so, the plaintiff's attorney may have been too cautious.

149. If the court wanted to feel good about a quick decision on a summary judgment motion, it would have been a good idea for the plaintiff to undermine the credibility of the defendant. For example, if the defendant got fired from her job for stealing during the parties' relationship, this is the kind of fact that might muddy the equitable waters. Here, the plaintiff's unclean hands argument seemed to be that the defendant first provided Millie's veterinary clinic with her name as Millie's owner in a situation where she paid for the dog's veterinary insurance, but later took steps to remove his name without his permission or authority. Whenever manipulation of records goes against the other party, assert this and get the full name of your source.

STATE OF MINNESOTA
COUNTY OF SMITH

DISTRICT COURT
FIRST JUDICIAL DISTRICT
CIVIL COURT DIVISION
Court File No. 123

In Re the Matter of:

Andy Anderson,

Plaintiff,

and

Nicole Davis

Defendant.

ORDER DENYING PLAINTIFF'S MOTION FOR SUMMARY JUDGMENT

The above-entitled matter came on before the Honorable Erin Johnson on January 1, 2010 pursuant to Plaintiff's Motion for Summary Judgment. Jacob Johnson, Esq., appeared on behalf of Plaintiff. Brandon Fuller, Esq., appeared on behalf of Defendant.

Based upon all the files, records, and proceedings herein, the Court makes the following:

ORDER

Plaintiff's Motion for Summary Judgment is denied for failure to follow the requirements of Minn. Stat. §565.23.

The attached Memorandum of Law is hereby incorporated.

MEMORANDUM OF LAW

This dispute centers around a Shiba Inu dog named Millie. On January 21, 2008, Plaintiff Andy Anderson ("Anderson") traveled to Alexandria, Minnesota and chose Millie out of a litter. He paid $500.00 for Millie. Anderson used only his money for Millie's purchase and the breeder of Millie, Alex Gustafson, confirmed that Anderson is the sole owner of Millie. (Gustafson Aff.) Anderson received a document entitled the American Kennel Club Litter Record which included a puppy number for Millie, Millie's name, and new owner information. Anderson is listed as the "new owner" in the document. (Id.)

After purchasing Millie, the dog lived with Anderson at his apartment in Wilco, Minnesota. To comply with the pet policy at his apartment, Anderson was required to complete the pet policy agreement and pay an additional damage deposit of $300.00. (Anderson Aff.) Anderson also submitted a one-year Dog License Application with the City of Wilco in 2008 which indicated that Anderson was the owner of Millie. (Id.) Anderson further attended dog obedience training school with Millie. (Id.)

Anderson moved in with Defendant Nicole Davis ("Davis") and into Davis' residence on July 1, 2008. The parties shared Davis' property as a co-residence. Both Anderson and Davis took care of Millie. Sometime thereafter, Anderson moved out of Davis' residence. Anderson has demanded the safe return of Millie but Davis refused to give Millie back to Anderson. Anderson did not renew Millie's license after it expired. Davis purchased a new license for Millie in 2009, after realizing Millie did not have a valid license.

Anderson moved for summary judgment on his replevin cause of action. The common law claim of replevin was replaced by Minnesota statutes with an action for claim and delivery of personal property. *A&A Credit Co. v. Berquist*, 41 N.W.2d 582, 583-84 (Minn. 1950) (discussing history of replevin actions). "The gist of the action of replevin under the code is 'to determine the right of possession of personal property or the title thereto.'" (Id.) (citation omitted). In order to recover possession of property under replevin, Anderson must follow Minn. Stat. §565.23 which explicitly states that a claimant must proceed by a motion that is accompanied by an affidavit. The requirements for said affidavit are found in Minn. Stat. §565.23, subd. 1. Both the notice of hearing, and the claimant's affidavit, must be served upon the respondent pursuant to Minn. Stat. §565.23, subd. 2. Here, Anderson has failed to follow the requirements set forth in Minn. Stat. §565. There is no indication that any affidavit as required by Minn. Stat. §565.23, subd. 1 was ever served on Davis. Consequently, Plaintiff's Motion for Summary Judgment on his replevin claim is denied.[150]

150. If the plaintiff now filed the required affidavit, would the plaintiff get "two bites" of the summary judgment apple? Once a lawyer loses, his or her client may no longer wish to return to court.

Appendix 13

Order Regarding Motion to Dissolve Ex Parte Writ of Replevin

The following is an actual Decision and Order Regarding Motion to Dissolve Ex Parte Writ of Replevin and Motion to Dismiss that will help you better understand how complex a pet custody dispute can be. In this case, a rescue group claimed that there was a wrongful transfer of a dog by the adopter to another family member.

The key to the court's ruling is a concept that should not be forgotten: contracts are subject to an implied covenant in good faith and fair dealing. This is an idea rooted in the *Restatement (Second) of Contracts* section 205 comment a (1981). The decision also reminds us that the Federal Arbitration Act 9 U.S.C. § 1 *et seq.* applies when interstate commerce is involved. Lawyers and jurists will appreciate the quality of this Order.

STATE OF VERMONT

SUPERIOR COURT | CIVIL DIVISION
ADDISON UNIT | Docket No. 185-8-13 Ancv

HEIDI'S HAVEN RESCUE, INC.,

Plaintiff,

v.

JEANNETTE MYERS, a/k/a JEANNETTER RINGER, GORDON MYERS and TAMARA CLARKE,[1]

Defendants.

DECISION AND ORDER RE: MOTION TO DISSOLVE EX PARTE WRIT OF REPLEVIN AND MOTION TO DISMISS

This matter came before the Court for a hearing on December 20, 2013 regarding Defendant's Motion to Dissolve Ex Parte Writ of Replevin, filed November 15, 2013, Hon. Robert A. Mello, Superior Judge, presiding. Defendant's Motion to Dismiss, filed September 18, 2013 is also before the Court. Plaintiff, Heidi's Haven Rescue, Inc., is represented by Pamela Marsh, Esq. Defendants, Jeannette Myers (also known as Jeannette Ringer), Tamara Clarke, and Gordon Myers, are represented by Richard Cassidy, Esq.

BACKGROUND/PROCEDURAL HISTORY

On May 12, 2013, Plaintiff entered into a dog adoption agreement with Defendant Jeannette Ringer which contemplates the adoption of a dog named Sunday, which originally came from Louisiana. Defendants later renamed the dog Paisley. Heidi's Haven Rescue Adoption Agreement (admitted Dec. 20, 2013) [hereinafter Agreement]. The Agreement provides in relevant part:

> 2.2 RETURN. HEIDI'S HAVEN RESCUE retains the right to recover the adopted dog from Adopter if:
>
> - the adoption is not satisfactory to the Adopter.
> - in HEIDI'S HAVEN RESCUE's sole judgment, recovery would be in the best interest of the adopted dog,
> - Adopter fails to comply with the provisions of this agreement,

1. It is of note that the defense was helped by Richard Cassidy, who is the president of the Uniform Law Commission.

- Adopter at any time misrepresents to HEIDI'S HAVEN RESCUE matters which are material to the welfare of the adopted dog,
- the adopted dog is found, in HEIDI'S HAVEN RESCUE's sole judgment, to be unsuitable for this placement, or
- HEIDI'S HAVEN RESCUE is legally obliged to recover the adopted dog from this placement . . .

2.4 TRANSFER OF OWNERSHIP. The adopted dog may not be transferred to any other person, firm, corporation, or organization for any reason whatsoever. Dog must be returned to Heidi's Haven if, for any reason, the adopter cannot keep him/her.

The contract also provides the following arbitration clause, "Any controversy or claim arising out of or relating to this agreement or the adopted dog shall be submitted to arbitration under the Commercial Arbitration Rules of the American Arbitration Association." *Id.*

The following facts are also relevant to the present dispute. Defendant Clarke is dating Jeannette Ringer/Myers and Gordon Myers' son Aaron. Sheila McGregor, agent for Heidi's Rescue, has seen the dog with Ms. Clarke since its adoption in May 2013. Ms. McGregor also looked on Ms. Clarke's Facebook page and noticed a picture of a dog with a tag that reads "Paisley." The picture has been admitted into evidence and the Court finds that it is a true and accurate picture of the dog once known as Sunday and referred to, by the Myers, as Paisley.

Evidence was also presented at the December 20th hearing that indicates Ms. Clarke and Ms. McGregor once worked together at a company where Ms. Clarke is a manager. At some point, Ms. Clarke reported to her superiors that Ms. McGregor was not performing well. Although the parties dispute terms upon which Ms. McGregor's employment thereafter ended, Ms. McGregor was either fired or agreed to leave after Ms. Clarke's performance report. During the time that Ms. Clarke and Ms. McGregor worked together, Ms. McGregor allowed Ms. Clarke to take rescue dogs from Heidi's Haven home with her for the weekend. That ended when Ms. McGregor no longer worked at the company.

On August 14, 2013, this Court, the Hon. Helen Toor presiding, issued an Ex Parte Order of Approval, based on Plaintiff's Ex Parte Motion for a Writ of Replevin, filed along with Plaintiff's Verified Complaint on August 14, 2013. Shortly thereafter, a constable attempted to execute the writ, but Ms. Myers would not voluntarily turn over the dog. On August 18, 2013 Plaintiff filed a Motion for Contempt regarding Mr. Myers' failure to abide by the writ. On September 16, 2013, Defendants filed a Motion for an Immediate Stay and to Dissolve Ex Parte Writ of Replevin. The Court addressed these two motions at a hearing held on November 8, 2013, and found Mr. Myers in contempt of Court for failing to comply with the writ. The Court denied Defendants' motion to dissolve the writ as it had not been complied with. The Myers subsequently turned the dog over to Heidi's Rescue, purging Mr. Myers' contempt.

Litigation over the dog continued in late November and early December as Defendants renewed their Motion to Dissolve pursuant to Vermont Rule of Civil Procedure 64. The Court held a hearing on December 20, 2013. Having heard the evidence and considered the arguments of the parties, the Court makes the following conclusions of law.

DISCUSSION

There are two issues before the Court, (1) whether the Ex Parte Writ should remain in place while this lawsuit is pending, and (2) whether the Court must dismiss Plaintiff's contract claim because the above quoted arbitration clause requires disputes under this contract to be submitted to binding arbitration.

I.

The first issue is whether the Ex Parte Writ should stand or whether the dog should be returned to the Myers while this litigation is pending. The December 20, 2013 hearing was held pursuant to V.R.C.P. 64, which provides the parties a timely opportunity to dispute the merits of an Ex Parte Writ while litigation is still pending. Rule 64(i) provides that during such a hearing:

> [T]he plaintiff shall have the burden of justifying the continuance of the replevin. Unless the judge finds that there is a reasonable likelihood that the plaintiff will prevail in the replevin action, that the bond required by law has been given by plaintiff, that the amount of the bond is based upon a reasonable valuation of the property replevied, and that the amount of the valuation is within the jurisdiction of the superior court, the judge shall order return of the property to the defendant.

V.R.C.P. 64(i). The writ will only continue if the Plaintiff is able to demonstrate that she is likely to prevail on the merits. In this case, the merits of Plaintiff's claim turns on the language of the parties' contract.

A contract is governed by its own terms and the Court is required to give effect to the intentions of the parties. As stated by the Vermont Supreme Court:

> [A contract] must be construed to give effect to the intention of the parties as stated in their writing. And the language used must be interpreted with reference to the purpose sought to be accomplished and the conditions prevailing at the time the instrument was executed. Where the language is clear, the intention and understanding of the parties must be taken to be that which their agreement declares.

H. P. Hood and Sons v. Heins, 124 Vt. 331, 336 (1964). Because Plaintiff has not demonstrated that she is likely to prevail on the merits of her contract claim in this case, the Court must dissolve the writ and order that Heidi's Haven return the dog to the Myers while litigation over the contract continues.

Plaintiff makes three arguments on the merits: (1) Heidi's Rescue is entitled to return of the dog because the Adopter under the Agreement, Jeannette Ringer/Myers, has transferred the dog to Ms. Clarke in violation of Section 2.4 of the Agreement, (2) Jeannette Ringer/Myers misrepresented herself in the contract by signing as Jeannette Ringer rather than Jeannette Myers, in violation of Section 2.2 of the Agreement, and (3) the Myers have breached the contract by failing to return the dog upon request, also a violation of 2.2.

Plaintiff's first claim is based on Section 2.4 of the Agreement, which provides, "The adopted dog may not be transferred to any other person, firm, corporation, or organization for any reason whatsoever. Dog must be returned to Heidi's Haven if, for any reason, the adopter cannot keep him/her." Agreement at 1 (admitted Dec. 20, 2013). The Myers did not transfer ownership of the dog to anyone else. Therefore, Plaintiff is not likely to succeed on this claim.

Plaintiff's evidence of transfer merely shows the Myers have entrusted their dog to Ms. Clarke when the Myers were out of town or otherwise engaged. Neither Ms. Clarke's temporary care of the dog nor her affection for the dog, as evidenced by her online photographic display of Paisley's dog tag, establish that a transfer has occurred. Nothing in the Agreement prohibits the Myers from temporarily entrusting the dog to a family friend. Furthermore, the credibility of Plaintiff's evidence suggesting a transfer of ownership to Ms. Clarke is undermined by Plaintiff's personal animus toward Ms. Clarke as a result of their failed professional relationship. Therefore, the Court concludes that Plaintiff is not likely to prevail on her claim that Defendants transferred ownership of the dog to another party in violation of Section 2.4 of the Agreement.

Plaintiff's second claim alleges misrepresentation by the Myers in violation of Section 2.2 of the Agreement. The contract provides the dog shall be returned to Heidi's Rescue if the "[a]dopter at any time misrepresents to HEIDI'S HAVEN RESCUE matters which are material to the welfare of the adopted dog." Because Plaintiff was not able to present any evidence that supports a misrepresentation material to the welfare of the dog, the Court concludes that Plaintiff is not likely to prevail on her misrepresentation claim.

Plaintiff argues that Jeannette Myers misrepresented herself by signing the contract as Jeannette Ringer, which is Jeannette's maiden name. Plaintiff claims this was "material to the welfare of the adopted dog" because signing the contract as Myers rather than Ringer would have tipped Plaintiff off to the fact that Ms. Clarke, Aaron Myers' girlfriend, would be involved with the dog. Plaintiff testified that, having worked with Ms. Clarke, she found her destructive, dishonest, and unstable. Thus, the argument goes, Jeannette's so-called misrepresentation was material to the welfare of the dog because it resulted in a placement that would expose the dog to a destructive, dishonest, and unstable person.

To the contrary, the evidence indicates that Ringer is Jeannette's maiden name. Jeannette is known as Jeannette Ringer and sometimes uses the name Ringer instead of Myers. Jeannette also provided references to Plaintiff, participated in a home visit and introduced Plaintiff to her husband, "Gordy." Therefore, Jeannette did not misrepresent herself. Furthermore, even if Jeannette used the name Ringer to evade detection as a Myers, there is no reliable indication that the misrepresentation was material to the welfare of the dog. Plaintiff's concern over Ms. Clarke's so-called destructive, dishonest, and unstable behavior is belied by the fact that Plaintiff herself frequently entrusted dogs from Heidi's Haven to Ms. Clarke and there is no evidence, or claim, that Ms. Clarke mistreated the dogs in any way. Plaintiff's evidence is further undermined by evidence suggesting Plaintiff holds a grudge against Ms. Clarke as a result of their failed professional relationship. Therefore, the Court concludes that Plaintiff is not likely to prevail on her misrepresentation claim.

Plaintiff's third claim is that Defendants were obligated under the Agreement to turn over the dog by request because the contract provides the dog shall be returned to Heidi's Rescue if, "in HEIDI'S HAVEN RESCUE's sole judgment, recovery would be in the best interest of the adopted dog." Because Plaintiff has not presented any credible evidence that the Myers or Ms. Clarke posed a threat to the dog's "best interest," the issue before the Court regarding Plaintiff's third claim is whether this provision may be enforced without any explanation or rationale on the part of Heidi's Rescue.

Resolution of this issue is a matter of contract law, which provides, "[T]he law of contract formation requires some sort of consideration . . . " *In re Spring Brook Farm Foundation, Inc.*, 164 Vt. 282, 288 (1995). "Either a benefit to the promisor or a detriment to the promisee is sufficient consideration for a contract." *Bergeron v. Boyle*, 176 Vt. 78, 86-87 (2003) (quoting *Lloyd's Credit Corp. v. Marlin Mgmt. Servs., Inc.*, 158 Vt. 594, 598-99 (1992). A contract does not fail for lack of mutuality merely because one party has discretion to make a unilateral decision. *Century Partners, LP v. Lesser Goldsmith Enterprises, Ltd.*, 184 Vt. 215, 227 (2008). Such provisions—which would otherwise be illusory—are saved by the implied covenant of good faith and fair dealing. *Id.* (finding landlord's unilateral power to consent to renovations enforceable because exercise of the power was subject to covenant of good faith and fair dealing); *see also Carmichael v. Adirondack Bottled Gas Corp. of Vermont*, 161 Vt. 200, 208 (1993) (quoting *deTreville v. Outboard Marine Corp.*, 439 F.2d 1099, 1100 (4th Cir. 1971) ("[R]egardless of broad unilateral termination powers, the party who terminates a contract commits an actionable wrong if the manner of termination is contrary to equity and good conscience.")).

Here, the Court cannot enforce a provision empowering Plaintiff to recover the dog based on her "sole judgment" unless Plaintiff's discretion under the provision is exercised in good faith. The covenant of good faith prohibits either party from "undermin[ing] or destroy[ing] the other's rights to receive the benefits of the agreement." *Id.* at 208. "The implied covenant of good faith and fair dealing exists to ensure that parties to a contract act with 'faithfulness to an agreed common purpose and consistency with the justified expectations of the other party.'" *Id.* (quoting Restatement (Second) of Contracts § 205 comment a (1981)).

Here, Plaintiff provides no evidence that her attempt to recover the dog was based on a good faith belief that recovery was in the best interest of the dog. Plaintiff presented no evidence that the Myers have mistreated the dog or otherwise acted contrary to the parties' expectations under the contract. Plaintiff's motivation here can only be explained by her personal distaste for Ms. Clarke, who is not a party to the contract. Because Plaintiff has provided no objective basis upon which a jury might conclude that she exercised her "sole judgment" in good faith, and Plaintiff is barred, as a matter of law from exercising her judgment arbitrarily, she is not likely to prevail on her third contract claim.

The conclusion that Plaintiff must exercise her discretion under Section 2.2 of the Agreement in good faith comports with Vermont precedent addressing a party's exercise of unilateral power under a bilateral contract. Although this principle has not been applied to any Vermont dog replevin cases,[2] the Vermont Supreme Court has required good faith and fair dealing where one party is granted unilateral discretion under a contract. In *Century Partners*, a lease agreement required commercial tenants to obtain landlord's consent prior to making any alterations, additions or modifications to the rented space. *Century Partners*, 184 Vt. at 227. The Court held that "landlord's ability to withhold consent was 'subject to the implied covenant of good faith and fair dealing, present in every contract.'" *Id.* Also, in *deTreville v. Outboard Marine Corp.*, a case quoted by the Vermont Supreme Court in *Carmichael v. Adirondack Bottled Gas Corp. of Vermont*, the Fourth Circuit Court of Appeals held that "unilateral termination powers" could not be exercised arbitrarily.

Moreover, Plaintiff's cause of action here is distinct from *McClure v. Briggs*, and other similar cases, where courts have upheld so-called "satisfaction" contracts. 2 A. 583, 586 (1886) (upholding a contract for the sale of an organ that turned on buyers' sole satisfaction). Courts will enforce a unilateral power in contracts

2. *See Lamare v. North Country Animal League*, 170 Vt. 115, 125 (1999) (denying due process claims of owners who were deprived of dog through town ordinance); and *Morgan v. Kroupa*, 167 Vt. 99, 105 (1997) ("Where . . . the finder of a lost domestic animal diligently attempts to locate its owner and provides care, shelter and companionship to the animal for over a year, a trial court does not abuse its discretion in awarding possession to the finder.")

which inherently "involve the feelings, taste, or sensibility of the promisor." *Id.* But as the Restatement (Second) of Contracts states;

> When it is a condition of an obligor's duty that he be satisfied with respect to the obligee's performance or with respect to something else, and it is practicable to determine whether a reasonable person in the position of the obligor would be satisfied, an interpretation is preferred under which the condition occurs if such a reasonable person in the position of the obligor would be satisfied.

Restatement (Second) Contracts § 228. Thus, even if the Court were to construe the present contract as a "satisfaction" contract, such that Heidi's Haven essentially retains the absolute right to rescind if Plaintiff is not satisfied with the placement, the test of Plaintiff's satisfaction would be an objective test where "it is practicable to determine whether a reasonable person" would be satisfied.

Here, it is practicable to determine reasonable satisfaction because the contract itself contemplates recovery when it is in the "best interest of the dog" and or the placement is not 'suitable.' Although Plaintiff is free to make these determinations in her "sole judgment," that freedom is limited to rational decisions based on the Agreement of the parties. Plaintiff has not articulated any basis, let alone a rational one, that pegs recovery of the dog to the dog's welfare. Because Plaintiff has failed to present evidence that would give a reasonable person concern over the welfare of the dog, the Court concludes that she is not likely to prevail on any of her contract claims.

II.

The next issue is whether the Court must dismiss this action pursuant to the Agreement's arbitration clause, which provides, "Any controversy or claim arising out of or relating to this agreement or the adopted dog shall be submitted to arbitration." Heidi's Haven Rescue Adoption Agreement (admitted Dec. 20, 2013).

Because this contract dispute is governed by the language of the contract which requires "any controversy or claim" be submitted to arbitration, the Court must dismiss this action if the parties' claim relates to the Agreement. Here, the dispute arises directly under the Agreement as a breach of contract claim. Therefore, the Court must dismiss the case as the contract itself requires the parties to arbitrate this dispute.

Plaintiff argues the arbitration clause in Heidi's Haven's own contract is not enforceable because it does not meet the requirements of 12 V.S.A. § 5652. *See Joder Bldg. Corp. v. Lewis*, 153 Vt. 115, 119 (1989) (finding clause in small type didn't meet the "display requirement" of the statute where no part of the statement was bold face or underlined). The Court need not address whether this arbitration clause is valid under Section 5652 because this case is governed by the Federal

Arbitration Act (FAA). *See David L. Threlkeld & Co., Inc. v. Metallgesellschaft Ltd.*, 923 F.2d 245, 249 (2nd Cir. 1991) (preempting Vermont's 12 V.S.A. § 5652 where the transaction concerns interstate or international commerce). The Arbitration Act applies to all "contract[s] evidencing a transaction involving commerce . . . " *Id.* (quoting 9 U.S.C. § 2).

Here, Heidi's Haven facilitated the placement of a dog from Louisiana with a family in Vermont. Therefore, the contract involves a transaction involving interstate commerce. As such it is governed by the FAA, which provides, "A written provision in any . . . contract evidencing a transaction involving commerce to settle by arbitration a controversy thereafter arising out of such contract or transaction . . . shall be valid, irrevocable, and enforceable." 9 U.S.C. § 2.

Because the contract in this case provides that all disputes "shall be submitted to arbitration under the Commercial Arbitration Rules of the American Arbitration Association," this dispute is committed to arbitration and the Court must dismiss this case.

ORDER

The Ex Parte Writ of Replevin, issued August 14, 2013, is hereby dissolved and the Plaintiff, Heidi's Haven, is ordered to place the dog known interchangeably as "Sunday" and/or "Paisley" in the possession of Jeannette Myers or her husband within three business days. Plaintiff's Complaint is also dismissed as this dispute is subject to arbitration pursuant to Section 5 of the parties' Agreement.

SO ORDERED this 27th day of December, 2013.
Robert A. Mello, Superior Judge
Margaret E. Gossens, Assistant Judge

Appendix 14

Proposed Dangerous Dog Determination and Order

Below is a proposed dangerous dog determination and order prepared pursuant to the hearing officer's request to incorporate both the state statute and the local ordinance language in an order following a death row dog hearing. In the underlying case, part of a child's ear was bit off by a one-year-old Akita. Personal identifiers, other than the author's and breed of dog, have been changed in this appendix. The destruct order was eventually vacated, following another favorable behavioral assessment of the dog by a veterinarian with behavioral expertise from the University of Minnesota.

The following proposed order may help the family lawyer learn about dangerous dog proceedings. This is why parties seeking to have any type of shared arrangement with a dog should be vigilant about potential perils. It is also important to realize that dangerous dog proceedings reflect the government exercising its police powers against what the U.S. Supreme Court, in *Sentell v. New Orleans Carrollton Railroad Co.*,[1] classified as quasi-property.

1. 166 U.S. 698, 17 S. Ct. 693, 41 L. Ed. 1169 (1897).

STATE OF MINNESOTA
CITY OF MINNEAPOLIS

HENNEPIN COUNTY

Superb Animal Care and Control,

vs.

Craig Cooper.

DANGEROUS DOG DETERMINATION AND ORDER

This matter first came on before Administrative Hearing Officer Frank Franklin on January 1, 2010 at Superb Animal Care and Control, which is an animal control authority located at 123 Street, Minneapolis, MN 55408.

Sarah Nelson appeared on behalf of Superb Animal Care and Control. Barbara J. Gislason appeared as the attorney for Craig Cooper, the owner of a dog named Spirit. Others present at this first scheduled hearing were Sam and Stacy Thompson, Craig Cooper, Nancy Cooper, Mallory Swanson, Penelope Potter, and Betsy Winter.

At the time of this first hearing, notwithstanding a written request, animal expert Penelope Potter was not afforded the opportunity to perform an assessment on Spirit. It was for this reason that the court granted the request of attorney Barbara J. Gislason for a continuance so that an evaluation by Potter could be performed.

Accordingly, the hearing was continued to January 16, 2010. Appearing at the second hearing were Steven Baker for the City of Minneapolis and Craig Cooper's attorney, Barbara J. Gislason. Also appearing were Craig Cooper, Nancy Cooper, Mallory Swanson, Officer Eric Hanson, and Penelope Potter.

After having been fully advised in the premises and upon all the files and records herein, the hearing officer makes the following:

FINDINGS OF FACT

1. Based upon an incident on December 15, 2009 wherein a child suffered substantial bodily harm, without provocation, on public property, the City of Minneapolis issued Destruct Order #DES123 for a dog named Spirit on December 20, 2009.

2. Once the declaration with regard to Spirit was issued by citation on December 20, 2009, Superb Animal Care and Control properly seized Spirit.

3. Pursuant to Minneapolis appeal hearing procedures, Craig Cooper timely submitted his request in writing for a hearing. After said request, a hearing was promptly scheduled. The hearing was then rescheduled based upon the request of Barbara J. Gislason after the required time period was waived on the record. The proceeding was properly heard before Hearing Officer Frank Franklin.

4. At the hearing on January 16, 2010, the City of Minneapolis offered into evidence the following: Administrative Citation, Notice of Rabies Quarantine, Notification of Destruct Order, Destruct Order Hearing Request, Owner Notification of Declaration Appeal Hearing, Minneapolis Police Department Case Report with Supplements, Report of Animal Bite or Incident, and Superb Animal Care and Control Narrative and Supplemental Report, together with photographs of minor David Thompson's injuries.

5. Barbara J. Gislason objected to the introduction of the reports based upon *In Re Molly,* 712 N.W.2d 567 (Minn.App.2006), an opinion that addressed evidentiary standards. This Hearing Officer agreed that this was a valid objection.

6. Barbara J. Gislason also objected to the administrative process as there was no information available about what procedures would be used for the hearing in advance of the hearing. This Hearing Officer agreed that this was a valid objection.

7. Craig Cooper first called Nancy Cooper as a witness. She testified about how she and her brother had selected Spirit from a breeder and communicated with the breeder about proper care of Spirit, who was purchased by her brother. She described both of their ongoing efforts to properly socialize and train Spirit. She indicated Spirit had a history of good behavior, including taking treats directly from people's hands, especially 12 young children from a school program where she volunteered in March 2009. She expressed her willingness to help her brother with regard to the rehabilitation of Spirit.

Nancy Cooper stated that following the incident on December 15, 2009, she joined her brother, his significant other, and Spirit, and they all waited near the corner of 12th and 13th Avenue South for two hours for Superb Animal Care and Control to pick Spirit up.

8. Next, Officer Eric Hanson testified that following the incident on December 15, 2009, he and another officer went to the intersection of 12th and 13th Avenue South, met Craig Cooper, Nancy Cooper, and Mallory Swanson, and that he observed that Spirit was well-behaved for the two hours that they waited for Superb Animal Care and Control to arrive, including when pedestrian traffic

passed Spirit. Upon cross-examination, Officer Eric Hanson testified that he neither wrote the report about the incident nor interviewed Sam Thompson.

9. Craig Cooper then testified about his efforts to be a responsible owner. One of these efforts was that he had Spirit attend a four-week training class at Twin Cities Obedience Training Club. Spirit graduated and earned a Certificate.

Craig Cooper offered 18 notarized statements by individuals who were familiar with Spirit and Spirit's interactions with others, including Spirit's past positive history of interactions with children and other dogs. He also offered a notarized statement from his veterinarian at Caring Animal Hospital that indicated a history of positive interactions between the veterinarian and Spirit and also provided copies of Spirit's veterinary records that showed Spirit's vaccine history, including his rabies vaccination. The Hearing Officer received these notarized statements.

Craig Cooper also offered photographs of a variety of individuals interacting with Spirit. The Hearing Officer received these records. In addition, Craig Cooper brought videos on a USB drive of Spirit interacting with others, including children, which the Hearing Officer declined to receive.

Craig Cooper testified that Sam and Stacy Thompson's two children, including David Thompson, had met Spirit prior to the incident on December 15, 2009. On this earlier occasion, both children were with their mother. On December 15, 2009, the children, now in the company of their father and not their mother, recognized Spirit from across the street. Spirit turned around from the direction he was going and lay down on the sidewalk; he was facing the direction of the children across the street.

The children then crossed the street with their father to meet Spirit and waited on the corner. With the permission of Sam Thompson, Craig Cooper then approached Sam Thompson and his two children at the corner and offered each boy one treat to give to Spirit. Craig Cooper testified that when the older boy, David, offered Spirit a treat, Spirit took it gently from his hand and David pet him. At that point, Craig Cooper testified that he was making eye contact with Sam Thompson, the childrens' father.

Craig Cooper than noticed through his peripheral vision that the remaining treat in David's brother's hand was thrown to the ground and David, who was near Craig Cooper, bent down to reach for it right in front of Spirit's head. It was unknown whether David had already picked up the treat off the ground or whether he was simply reaching down for the treat at the moment his ear was bit.

10. Craig Cooper has paid the City of Minneapolis all fees with regard to the hearing and for the boarding of Spirit, as well as related costs, per the direction of Superb Animal Care and Control Manager, Steven Baker. Accordingly, Craig Cooper

has complied with his financial obligations under the Minneapolis Ordinance. In the event that the declaration is overturned, the fees described above are subject to review by the Hearing Officer or the Manager of Superb Animal Care and Control.

11. The next witness was Penelope Potter, an animal expert who did an assessment of Spirit at the Superb Animal Care and Control animal shelter on January 5, 2010 in the presence of Sarah Nelson. In her report, Penelope Potter described her assessment as follows:

> My assessment of Spirit took place at the Superb Animal Care and Control on January 5th around 3:15 p.m. I was in the company of Sarah Nelson, Assistant Manager. Spirit had been at Superb Animal Care and Control for 19 days. It was done inside his kennel with the kennel divider up for more space.
>
> Upon first arriving at Spirit's kennel, he barked in an alert manner. While I have done many evaluations, I have never done an evaluation inside a kennel so it took me a minute to determine how to proceed safely. I offered Spirit a couple of treats through the fence. When Spirit did not take them out of my hand, I tossed them on the floor to see if he would take them. He ate one but left two on the ground.
>
> When I first entered Spirit's kennel, I walked towards the back and let him sniff me before I interacted with him. I immediately put a basket muzzle on him. He moved his head quite a bit while I put it on. I had some trouble adjusting the straps, especially with his head movements and long hair, but he did not show any signs of aggression. Sarah Nelson took notes for me as I spoke.
>
> I left the kennel and came back in. Spirit seemed more concerned with the muzzle than he was with me re-entering the kennel. I proceeded with basic handling as follows:
>
> 1. Pet him head to tail three times. Spirit responded by stiffening up and his tail was down, not tucked. He panted.
> 2. Hold his tail firmly (not pulling) for one second, two seconds, then three seconds. Spirit responded by orienting towards me but did not seem to care. (He was sitting).
> 3. Grab and hold each paw for two seconds. Spirit responded by orienting towards me when I picked up the first paw. He managed to get the muzzle off and started chewing it. I reached behind (bent over his back) to put the muzzle back on. He allowed me to do it but did move his head a bit. As I continued to grab his paws, he gave no reaction. (Still sitting)
> 4. Hold and examine each ear. Spirit responded with no reaction. (Still sitting)
> 5. Hug from the side, with one hand around the neck and other hand on body. Spirit responded with no reaction. Continued to pant. (Still sitting)
> 6. Scruff: grab handful of skin at the neck and hindquarters. Spirit oriented towards me with the neck scruff. He looked away when I scruffed his hindquarters. (Still sitting)
>
> Startle Assessment: I used an umbrella that made a noise, opened up and got bigger. Spirit responded by sniffing the umbrella and lifted one of his paws.

Child Assessment: Since there was not a child, I jumped around and behaved like a child. I squealed, touched Spirit on the back, and jumped back and said: "Do you want to play," waved my arms in the air, squealed, touched Spirit on the head, and then jumped back. Spirit responded by playfully reaching towards me with one paw and then dropped down to the ground in a playbow stance (rear in the air) and then lay down.

For the rest of the assessment, I tethered Spirit to the fence and took off his muzzle. Sarah Nelson gave me a bowl of food, handed me a toy with treats in it and a metal grabbing tool (to act as my hand).

Food Assessment: I placed the food bowl inside Spirit's portion of the kennel while I was on the other side of the kennel. I first touched Spirit with the tool, put the tool on the food bowl, and used the tool to take the bowl away. Spirit responded by sniffing the tool, grabbing some food, looking away while chewing and dropping some food on the ground.

When I took the bowl away, he licked his lips and continued eating the food on the ground. He did not accelerate or decelerate his eating. He did not seem to care that I took the food bowl away but he did look for it. No aggression seen. No guarding seen.

High value item: treats inside toy. When I gave him the toy, he licked his lips when I touched him with the tool. He backed away when I touched the toy with the tool. Then he started licking the toy but gave no reaction when I took the toy away with the tool.

I finished the handling portion with muzzle off:

1. Lift dog's lips and look at teeth. Spirit responded by yawning and lip licking.
2. Open jaws and look into mouth. Spirit responded by yawning and lip licking.

After the assessment, I spoke with Sarah Nelson about a few things. She told me she has not had any negative interactions with Spirit. There was a female employee who did report that Spirit lunged at the kennel door when she brought his owner, Craig Cooper, back to visit. Spirit is fed once per day.

Craig Cooper comes almost every day when there is a visitation opportunity and often comes early, before the visitation hours actually begin and the visits last between five and ten minutes. Craig would visit Spirit for the entire hour, but there is limited staff and other people who want to visit their animals. Spirit has not left his kennel since his arrival at Superb Animal Care and Control.

Given the fact that Spirit has been in a stressful environment for almost three weeks, with no opportunity to exercise or get out of his kennel, with only a few minutes each day to interact with his owner, it is difficult for me to draw definite conclusions from the assessment. With the exception of when I was acting like a child, Spirit was somewhat shut down and non-responsive which was not a surprise to me given my experience working in a shelter environment.

Other than the barking when we arrived, there was nothing about his behavior that caused me any concern for my safety. His muzzle came off a few times during the assessment because he was not wearing a collar to secure the bottom portion and he never got upset with me putting it back on. In reference to his behavior

> with the female employee, it is not uncommon for a dog to behave out of character under Spirit's circumstances and depending on a person's approach to Spirit's kennel. Spirit's behavior was consistent with his owner's accounts as well as the many notarized witness statements I have reviewed.

12. Based on Penelope Potter's assessment, together with her review of the exhibits offered by the City of Minneapolis and the exhibits offered on behalf of Craig Cooper, and Penelope Potter's opportunity to interview Spirit's veterinarian and review the 18 notarized witness statements offered by Craig Cooper, she made a variety of recommendations. This Hearing Officer notes the high quality of Penelope Potter's report and stated that her report influenced his determination to give Spirit one more chance.

13. Soon after the hearing on January 16, 2010, and shortly after leaving the Superb Animal Care and Control facility on January 18, 2010, Spirit was neutered and implanted with a microchip. Furthermore, based upon veterinary records presented at the hearing on January 16, 2010, Spirit is current on his rabies vaccine.

14. Soon after the hearing on January 16, 2010, Craig Cooper contacted Dr. Johnson at the University of Minnesota Veterinary School and scheduled an appointment with her. Craig Cooper has agreed to follow her recommendations, including for further training, and to pay for the preparation of her assessment of Spirit and report.

15. Craig Cooper shall maintain secured areas inside his home for Spirit when persons, other than family members, are present. For the purpose of this Order, both Nancy Cooper and Mallory Swanson are Craig Cooper's family members. The secured areas in Craig Cooper's home are Craig Cooper's bedroom and Spirit's kennel. Craig Cooper has provided Superb Animal Care and Control with a photograph of each area.

16. If Craig Cooper plans to take Spirit to another location, or wants to establish another secure area, he agrees to obtain advanced approval from Superb Animal Care and Control and provide Superb Animal Care and Control with a photograph.

17. Craig Cooper shall license and pay for Spirit's annual registration fee for having a Dangerous Dog as long as this designation is in effect. Any future owner or custodian of Spirit may not be a minor under age 18. Payment for the current year is acknowledged.

18. Spirit shall not be subjected to neglect, suffering, cruelty, or abuse.

19. Spirit's living quarters shall be kept clean and sanitary with proper and adequate food, water, ventilation, shelter, and care.

20. If requested by Superb Animal Care and Control, Craig Cooper shall work with Spirit to complete an approved obedience class.

21. If Craig Cooper plans to move, he must provide written notification to the Manager of Superb Animal Care and Control ten business days prior to relocation.

22. The Manager of Superb Animal Care and Control, or the Manager's designee, shall be allowed at any reasonable time to inspect Spirit, Spirit's muzzle and leash, and the place where Spirit is located.

23. Craig Cooper, or any of his successor owners, shall fully comply with the following requirements within 14 calendar days following the signature of this Order by the Hearing Officer:

a. Spirit shall be immediately neutered at Craig Cooper's expense and evidence of said sterilization shall be submitted to Superb Animal Care and Control. (Said sterilization has already occurred to Superb Animal Care and Control's satisfaction.)
b. Craig Cooper shall obtain and maintain an insurance policy or surety bond in the amount of at least three hundred thousand dollars ($300,000.00) to cover any future personal injuries inflicted by Spirit payable to the injured party or parties. (Said insurance has already been secured to Superb Animal Care and Control's satisfaction.)
c. Craig Cooper shall post a clearly visible sign in the front and rear of his property indicating that a "dangerous animal" is on or in the premises. (Said sign has already been approved by Superb Animal Care and Control and said posting has already occurred to Superb Animal Care and Control's satisfaction.)

24. Craig Cooper was cautioned that failure to comply with the provisions of this Order may result in seizure of Spirit by Superb Animal Care and Control and Spirit's disposition pursuant to the Minneapolis Ordinance.

25. Craig Cooper must notify Superb Animal Care and Control in writing of the death of Spirit within 14 days of Spirit's death and, if requested, will provide a sworn Affidavit setting forth the circumstances of Spirit's death and disposition.

26. If Spirit becomes lost or runs away, Craig Cooper shall promptly provide written notification to the Manager of Superb Animal Care and Control.

27. The state has met its burden of proof with regard to the City's Destruct Order and for the determination that Spirit is a Dangerous Dog.

28. The injury suffered by the child was not caused or contributed to by the actions of the child. Spirit's bite was not provoked.

29. Craig Cooper is Spirit's owner.

30. The Hearing Officer announced his decision at the hearing on January 16, 2010 and his decision took effect on January 16, 2010, except as otherwise set forth herein. Said Hearing Officer's decision may be appealed to the Minnesota Court of Appeals.

NOW THEREFORE, IT IS HEREBY ORDERED:

1. Superb Animal Care and Control's Order for Destruct shall be on hold for six months from January 16, 2010, during which time Craig Cooper will comply with his above-stated responsibilities.

2. Within three months of the hearing, which took place on January 16, 2010, Craig Cooper shall provide Superb Animal Care and Control with an update with regard to Spirit receiving an assessment from an expert on the list provided by the Superb Animal Care and Control Manager, Steven Baker. If, because of scheduling delays, the assessment cannot be completed within three months, the approved assessor shall be asked to update the Hearing Officer of Craig Cooper's good faith efforts to comply with this provision. Following said assessment, and the receipt of the accompanying report, Craig Cooper will comply with said assessor's recommendations.

3. Frank Franklin shall be the same Hearing Officer to preside over the next hearing in this matter, which shall take place on or after January 16, 2012.

4. Superb Animal Care and Control shall hold another hearing in six months to determine if the status of Spirit may be changed from a Destruct Order and Dangerous Dog to Dangerous Dog if Craig Cooper fulfills his obligations under this Order with regard to Spirit.

5. If Craig Cooper fails to comply with the express terms of this Order, Superb Animal Care and Control may destroy Spirit within the next six months.

6. If not already done, Craig Cooper shall immediately have Spirit neutered.

7. If questions arise in the next six months about fulfillment of his obligations, Craig Cooper shall discuss this with the Superb Animal Care and Control Manager, Steven Baker, or his designee, with regard to expectations, particularly with how to timely meet Dr. Johnson's or other approved Superb Animal Care and Control assessors' recommendations.

8. Craig Cooper may not secure an off leash permit for Spirit in the City of Minneapolis.

9. Spirit shall be confined so as not to interfere with the peaceful and lawful duties of postal carriers or police officers and others lawfully on Craig Cooper's real property.

10. Craig Cooper shall annually pay for a license and registration for Spirit, if not already done.

11. There is no requirement here for a proper enclosure for Spirit under the Minneapolis Ordinance as Spirit will be both properly leashed and muzzled while outside.

12. While outdoors, Spirit shall wear a basket muzzle and be on a three-foot leash held by an adult, unless he is in a proper enclosure. While inside, Spirit will be in a secured area when people other than Nancy Cooper and Mallory Swanson are in Craig Cooper's living quarters.

13. Pursuant to Minneapolis Ordinance 64.110, Craig Cooper may not request an annual review of this Order before January 16, 2012.

Dated: ______________________________ ______________________________

Hearing Officer

Appendix 15

Animal Law Books Published by the American Bar Association

Yolanda Eisenstein, *Concerns in Animal Law: Welfare, Protection, and Advocacy* (2013)

Yolanda Eisenstein, *Legal Guide for Dog Owners* (2015)

Raj Panjwani, *Wildlife Law: A Global Perspective* (2008)

Joan Schaffner, *A Lawyer's Guide to Dangerous Dog Issues* (2009)

Joan Schaffner & Julie Fershtman, *Litigating Animal Law Disputes: A Complete Guide for Lawyers* (2009)

Table of Cases

184 West 10th Street Corp. v. Marvits, 59 A.D.3d 287, 874 N.Y.S.2d 403, 2009 N.Y. Slip Op. 01327, 230

Aguillard v. Madura, 257 S.W.3d 494 (Tex. App. 2008), 372, 379–381
Aho v. Aho, 2012 WL 5235982 (Mich. Ct. App. Oct. 23, 2012), Not reported in N.W.2d (2012), 64
Akers v. Sellers, 54 N.E.2d 779, 114 Ind. App. 660 (Ind. App. 1944), 11–12, 24–25, 377, 381
Albemarle Theatre Inc. v. BayBerry Realty Corp., 27 A.D.2d 172, 277 N.Y.S.2d 505 (1st Dept. 1967), 182
Allied-Bruce Terminix Companies, Inc. v. Dobson, 513 U.S. 265, 115 S. Ct. 834, 130 L. Ed. 2d 753 (1995), 119–120
American Canine Foundation v. Sun, No. C-06-4713 MMC, March 21, 2007, 415–417
American Dog Owners Ass'n, Inc. v. City of Minneapolis, 453 N.W.2d 69 (Minn. App. 1990), 408, 420
Ammon v. Welty, 64 F.3d 662 (C.A. 6 Ky. 1995), 221–222
Andersen v. Koss, 527 N.E.2d 1098, 173 Ill. App. 3d 872 (Ill. App. 1st Dist. 1988), 154, 177–178
Anderson v. Farmers Hybrid Companies, Inc., 408 N.E.2d, 1194 87 Ill. App. 3d 493, 42 Ill. Dec. 485 (1980), 275
Anderson v. Gouldberg, 53 N.W. 636 (Minn. 1982), 606
Andrus v. Allard, 444 U.S. 51, 100 S. Ct. 318, 62 L. Ed. 2d 210 (1979), 148
Animal Legal Defense Fund v. Glickman, 154 F.3d 426 (C.A.D.C. 1998), 337, 338–339
Animal Welfare Institute v. Kreps, 561 F.2d 1002, 183 U.S. App. D.C. 109 (C.A.D.C. 1977), 337
Appell v. Rodriguez, 2007 N.Y. Slip Op. 50051 (U) (N.Y. App. Term 1/8/2007), 156, 190–191
Arguello v. Behmke, 2006 WL 205097 (N.J. Super. Ch. 2006), 249 n.19, 371–372, 376–379
Aronson v. Aronson, 2013 Ill. App. (3d) 120715-U, not reported in N.E.2d (2013), 69 n.143
Arrington v. Arrington, 613 S.W.2d 565 (Tex. Civ. App. Fort Worth 1981), 13, 27–28, 296
Ashcroft v. American Civil Liberties Union, 535 U.S. 564 (S. Ct. 2002), 348
Association for Molecular Pathology v. Myriad Genetics, Inc. et al., 569 U.S. ___, 133 S. Ct. 2107 (2013), 437

Bachman v. Artinger, 426 A.2d 702, 285 Pa. Super. 57 (Pa. Super. 1981), 172
Baggett v. Baggett, 2013 WL 4606383 (Tenn. App. 2013), 70
Bakay v. Yarnes, 431 F. Supp. 2d 1103 (W.D. Wash. 2006), 345–346
Ballas v. Ballas, 3 Cal. Rptr. 11, 178 Cal. App. 2d 570 (Cal. App. 2d Dist. 1960), 25–26
Banasczek v. Kowalski, 10 Pa. D. & C. 3rd 94 (Luzerne Cnty. 1979), 270
Banken v. Banken, State of Minnesota in Court of Appeals, A11-2156, Minn. App. 2013, 70 n.146
Baram v. Farugia, 606 F.2d 42 (1979), 263–264
Bartanus v. Lis, 332 Pa. Super. 61, 480 A.2d 1185 (1984), 269
Bazzini v. Garrant, 116 Misc. 2d 119, 455 N.Y.S.2d 77, 54 N.Y.2d 207 (N.Y. Dist. Ct. 1982), 173–174
Beardsley v. Garcia, 753 N.W.2d 735 (Minn. 2008), 52–53
Beard v. Mossman, 19 A.2d 850 (Pa. Super. Ct. 1941), 66 n.138
Behnke v. Green-Behnke, 2004 WL 376984 (Minn. Ct. App. Mar. 2, 2004), 609
Bennett v. Bennett, 655 So. 2d 109 (Fla. App. 1st Dist. 1995), 12, 37
Berry v. Heinel Motors, Inc., 162 Pa. Super. 52, 56 A.2d 374 (1948), 263 n.70
Beyer v. Aquarium Supply Co., 404 N.Y.S.2d 778, 94 Misc. 2d 336 (N.Y. Sup. Ct. 1977), 158 n.17, 254, 262–263, 273 n.92, 275, 292
Blaha v. Stuard, 2002 S.D. 19, 640 N.W.2d 85 (S.D. 2002), 292–293
Board of Regents of State Colleges v. Roth, 408 U.S. 564 (1972), 423
Bolan v. Bolan, 796 S.W.2d 358, 32 Ark. App. 65 (Ark. App. 1990), 36
Borderlon v. Peck, 661 S.W.2d 907 (Tex. 1983), 278–279
Bovsun v. Sanperi, 61 N.Y.2d 219 (1984), 289–290
Bowman v. Brooklyn Pet Hospital, 247 N.W.2d 424 (Minn. 1976), 112 n.90
Brooks v. Commissioner of Public Safety, 584 N.W.2d 15 (Minn. App. 1998), *review denied* (Minn. Nov. 24, 1998), 422
Brousseau v. Rosenthal, 443 N.Y.S.2d 285, 110 Misc. 2d 1054 (N.Y. City Civ. Ct. 1980), 213–214, 247, 268 n.81
Brown v. Frontier Theatres, Inc., 369 S.W.2d 299 (Tex. 1963), 317–318
Brown v. Muhlenberg Township, 269 F.3d 205 (3d Cir. 2001), 339–341
Buczkowicz v. Lubin, 399 N.E.2d 680 (Ill. Ct. App. 1980), 66 n.138
Bueckner v. Hamel, 886 S.W.2d 368 (Tex. App. 1994), 275–276, 580, 583
Burgess v. Taylor, 44 S.W.3d 806 (Ky. App. 2001), 248 n.12, 285–287, 346 n.108

Cahill v. Blume, 801 N.Y.S.2d 776, 8 Misc. 3d 1004 (A) (N.Y. City Civ. Ct. 2005), 166 n.29, 187–188
Calhoon v. Neely, 201 Pa. 97, 50 A. 967 (1902), 510
Campbell v. Animal Quarantine Station, 632 P.2d 1066, 63 Haw. 557 (Haw. 1981), 249, 266
Carmania Corp., N.V. v. Hambrecht Terrell Int'l, 705 F. Supp. 936 (S.D.N.Y. 1989), 182
Carmichael v. Adirondack Bottled Gas Corp. of Vermont, 635 A.2d 1211, 161 Vt. 200 (1993), 634, 635
Century Partners, LP v. Lesser Goldsmith Enterprises, Ltd., 958 A.2d 627, 184 Vt. 215 (2008), 634, 635

Chang v. Siu, 323 P.3d 725, 234 Ariz. 442, 685 Ariz. Adv. Rep. 18 (Ariz. App. 2014), 134–136
Chapman v. Decrow, 45 A. 295 (Me. 1899), 583
Cincinnati, New Orleans & Texas Pacific Railway Co. v. Rankin, 156 S.W. 400, 153 Ky. 730 (1913), 287
City of Garland v. White, 368 S.W.2d 12 (Tex. Civ. App.–Eastland 1963, *writ ref'd n.r.e.*), 296
City of Minneapolis v. Police Officers' Fed'n, 566 N.W.2d 83 (Minn. App. 1997), 122 n.119
City of Toledo v. Tellings, No. L-04-1224 2006 WL 513946 (Mar. 3, 2006), 385, 388, 411–413
City of Toledo v. Tellings, 114 Ohio St. 3d 278, 2007-Ohio-3724, 871 N.E.2d 1152 (Ohio 2007), 385, 388, 411–413
City of Tyler v. Likes, 962 S.W.2d 489 (Tex. 1998), 319
Clark-Fitzpatrick, Inc. v. Long Island R. Col., 70 N.Y.2d 382, 521 N.Y.S.2d 653 (1987), 182
Clark v. McGinnis, 298 P.3d 1137 (Kan. Ct. App. 2013), 71
Clauson v. Clauson, 831 P.2d 1257 (Alaska 1992), 50 n.104
Cleveland Board of Education v. Loudermill, 470 U.S. 532, 105 S. Ct. 1487, 84 L. Ed. 2d 494 (1984), 513
Coballes v. Spokane County, 274 P.3d 1102 (Wash. App. 2012), 386–387, 419
Commonwealth Coatings Corp. v. Continental Casualty Co., 393 U.S. 145, 89 S. Ct. 337, 21 L. Ed. 2d 301 (1968), 138
Commonwealth of Pennsylvania v. Clayton, 684 A.2d 1060, 546 Pa. 342 (1996), 513
Commonwealth of Pennsylvania v. Wright, 961 A.2d 119, 599 Pa. 270 (2008), 513
Commonwealth v. Barnes, 629 A.2d 123, 427 Pa. Super. 326 (1993), 513
Commonwealth v. Gonzalez, 403 Pa. Super. 157, 588 A.2d 528 (1991), 513
Commonwealth v. Wetmore, 301 Pa. Super. 370, 447 A.2d 1012 (Pa. Super. 1982), 510
Conahan-Baltzelle v. Baltzelle, 2004 WL 1959489 (Va. Ct. App. Sept. 7, 2004), 51
Connor v. Bogrett, 596 P.2d 683 (Wyo. 1979), 170–171
Conte v. Fossett, 2013 WL 1143329 (Del. Super. Ct.), not reported in A.3d (2013), 17, 72
Corn v. Sheppard, 229 N.W. 869 (Minn. 1930), 583
Corso v. Crawford Dog & Cat Hosp., Inc., 415 N.Y.S.2d 182, 97 Misc. 2d 530 (City Civ. Ct. 1979), 2 n.6, 19, 74, 223, 249 n.18, 250, 255, 264–265, 291
County of Pasco v. Riehl, 620 So. 2d 229 (Fla. App. 2d Dist. 1993), 386, 409–410
C.R.S. v. T.K.S., 746 N.Y.S.2d 568, 192 Misc. 2d 547 (2002), 2002 N.Y. Slip Op. 22625, 46, 74

Damiano v. Lind, 163 Wash. App. 1017, not reported in P.3d (2011), 305–306
Daughen v. Fox, 539 A.2d 858, 372 Pa. Super. 405 (Pa. Super. 1988), 248, 269–270
David L. Threlkeld & Co., Inc. v. Metallgesellschaft Ltd., 923 F.2d 245 (2nd Cir. 1991), 637

Davis v. Davis, 842 S.W.2d 588 (Tenn. 1992), 433
DeBlasio v. Zoning Board of Adjustment, 53 F.3d 592 (3rd Cir. 1995), 341 n.98
Decorso v. Saksa, No. HHBCV1150153095, 2011 WL 2611801 (Conn. Super. Ct. June 1, 2011), not reported in A.3d (2011), 59
Dempsey v. Rosenthal, 468 N.Y.S.2d 441, 121 Misc. 2d 612 (N.Y. City Civ. Ct. 1983), 166 n.29, 174–175
Desanctis v. Pritchard, 803 A.2d 230, 2002 Pa. Super. 221 (Pa. Super. Ct. 2002), 12 n.9, 47–48, 54
deTreville v. Outboard Marine Corp., 439 F.2d 1099 (4th Cir. 1971), 634, 635
Diamond v. Chakrabarty, 447 U.S. 303, 100 S. Ct. 2204, 65 L. Ed. 2d 144 (1980), 437
Dietz v. Dodge County, 487 N.W.2d 237 (Minn. 1992), 422
DiGrazia v. Old, 900 S.W.2d 499 (Tex. App. 1995), 277–278
Dimario v. Coppola, 10 F. Supp. 2d 213 (E.D.N.Y. 1998), 185–187
DLH, Inc. v. Russ, 566 N.W.2d 60 (Minn. 1997), 601, 618
Downey v. Pierce County, 267 P.3d 445, 165 Wash. App. 152 (2011), 417–418
Downing v. Gully, D.V.M, P.C., 915 S.W.2d 181 (Tex. App. 1996), 252 n.38
Dubin v. Pelletier, No. WL 10-0825, 2012 WL 5983184 (R.I. Super. Ct. 2012), 65–68

Economou v. Carpenter, 207 A.2d 241, 124 Vt. 451 (1965), 303
Edward Elec. Co. v. Automation, Inc., 593 N.E.2d 833, 229 Ill. App. 3d 89, 171 Ill. Dec. 13 (Ill. App. 1st Dist. 1992), 117–119
Eljer Mfg. Inc. v. Kowin Development Corp., 14 F.3d 1250 (7th Cir.), *cert. denied,* 512 U.S. 1205, 114 S. Ct. 2675, 129 L. Ed. 2d 810 (1994), 120 n.116
Ellington Constr. Corp. v. Zoning Bd. of Appeals, 566 N.E.2d 128, 77 N.Y.2d 114, 564 N.Y.S.2d 1001 (1990), 149 n.26
Erie Railroad Co. v. Tompkins, 304 U.S. 64, 58 S. Ct. 817, 82 L. Ed. 1188 (1938), 186
In re Estate of Russell, 444 P.2d 353, 69 Cal. 2d 200, 70 Cal. Rptr. 561 (Cal. 1968), 143

Fairfax County Sch. Bd. v. Rose, 509 S.E.2d 525, 29 Va. App. 32 (Va. Ct. App. 1999) (en banc), 64 n.135
Faul v. Trahan, 98-488 (La. App. 3d Cir. 10/7/98), 718 So. 2d 1081 (La. Ct. App. 1998), 280–282
Feger v. Warwick Animal Shelter, 870 N.Y.2d 1124, 2008 N.Y. Slip Op. 10122, 59 A.D.3d 68 (2d Dept. 2008), 74, 149, 230–231, 241
First Options of Chicago, Inc. v. Kaplan, 514 U.S. 938, 115 S. Ct. 1920, 131 L. Ed. 2d 985 (1995), 119
Fitch v. Eiseman, 2000 WL 34545801 (Alaska Apr. 19, 2000), 45–46
Fitzgerald v. State, 864 A.2d 1006 (Md. 2004), 333, 341–343, 580, 584
Flexible Mfg. Systems Pty. Ltd. v. Super Products Corp., 86 F.3d 96 (C.A. 7 (Wis.) 1996), 119–120
In re Fouts, 677 N.Y.S.2d 699, 176 Misc. 2d 521 (N.Y. Sur. Ct. 1998), 149 n.28
Frauenshuh v. Giese, 599 N.W.2d 153 (Minn. 1999), 42–43
Fuller v. Vines, 36 F.3d 65 (C.A. 9 (Cal.) 1994), 337–338
Furlan v. Rayan Photo Works, Inc., 12 N.Y.S.2d 921, 171 Misc. 839 (N.Y. Mun. Ct. 1939), 268 n.80

Garcia v. Albuquerque Public Schools Board of Education, 622 P.2d 699, 95 N.M. 391 (Ct. App. 1980), 407
Garcia v. Village of Tijeras, 767 P.2d 355, 108 N.M. 116 (N.M. App. 1988), 384, 406–408
Gebbia v. Schulder, 2011 N.Y. Slip Op. 51725 (N.Y. App. Term 2011), 196
Gehrts v. Batteen, 620 N.W.2d 775 (S.D. 2001), 292
Gluckman v. American Airlines, Inc., 844 F. Supp. 151 (S.D.N.Y. 1994), 169, 184
In re G.M.P. Land Company, 33 B.R. 729 (Bankr. E.D. Pa. 1983), 511
Goodby v. Vetpharm, Inc., 182 Vt. 648, 927 A.2d 792 (2007), 74, 301–302, 303
Gossman v. Gossman, 847 N.W.2d 718 (Minn. App. 2014), 136–137
Gradjelick v. Hance, 646 N.W.2d 225 (Minn. 2002), 601
Graham v. Notti, 196 P.3d 1070, 147 Wash. App. 629 (Wash. Ct. App. 2008), 205–206, 231–233
Gramercy Equities Corp. v. Dumont, 72 N.Y.2d 560, 534 N.Y.S.2d 908 (1988), 182
Greater Houston German Shepherd Dog Rescue, Inc. v. Lydia Lira and Alfonso Lira, No. 14-13-00240-CV, Trial Court Case No. 2013-03944 (Tex. App. 2014), 241–242

Hall Street Associates, LLC v. Mattel, Inc., 552 U.S. 576 (2008), 135
Hament v. Baker, 97 A.3d 461 (Vt. 2014), 18, 75–77
Hannan v. City of Minneapolis, 623 N.W.2d 281 (Minn. App. 2001), 384, 410–411, 414
Hans Hagen Homes, Inc. v. City of Minnetrista, 728 N.W.2d 536 (Minn. 2007), 425
Hanson v. Belveal, 2012 WY 98, 280 P.3d 1186 (Wyo. 2012), 130–131
Harabes v. The Barkery, Inc., 348 N.J. Super. 366, 791 A.2d 1142 (N.J. Super. Ct. 2001), 288–289
Hardenbergh v. Schulder, 25 Misc. 3d 141 (A), 2009 N.Y. Slip Op. 52454 (U) (N.Y. App. Term 12/1/2009), 194
Harlan v. Lovett, 1996 WL 97590 (Tenn. App. March 6, 1996), 278–279
Heiligmann v. Rose, 81 Tex. 222, 16 S.W. 931 (1891), 296, 317, 318
Matter of Helmsley, 31 Misc. 3d 1233 (A) (Sur. Ct. N.Y. Cnty., Feb. 18, 2009), 2009 N.Y. Slip Op. 52802 (U), 146
Hennet v. Allan, 43 Misc. 3d 542 (2014), 243
Hidden Harbour Estates, Inc. v. Norman, 309 So. 2d 180 (Fla. Dist. Ct. App. 1975), 215
Hohenstein v. Dodds, 10 N.W.2d 236 (Minn. 1943), 252 n.43
Hotel & Motel Association of Oakland v. City of Oakland, 344 F.3d 959 (9th Cir. 2003), 416–417
Houseman v. Dare, 966 A.2d 24 (N.J. Super. Ct. App. Div. 2009), 12, 54–57, 289 n.129, 601 n.52
H. P. Hood and Sons v. Heins, 124 Vt. 331 (1964), 632–633
Hunt v. IBM Mid Am. Employees Fed. Credit Union, 384 N.W.2d 853 (Minn. 1986), 618
Hyland v. Borras, 719 A.2d 662, 316 N.J. Super. 22 (N.J. Super. 1998), 282, 288

Jacobellis v. Ohio, 378 U.S. 184, 84 S. Ct. 1676, 12 L. Ed. 2d 793 (1964), 4
Jankoski v. Preiser Animal Hospital, Ltd., 510 N.E.2d 1084, 157 Ill. App. 3d 818 (Ill. App. 1st Dist. 1987), 248, 268–269

Jersey City Management v. Garcia, 729 A.2d 521, 321 N.J. Super. 543 (N.J. Super. 1999), 223–224
Jijon v. Custodio, 251 N.J. Super. 370, 598 A.2d 251 (Law Div. 1991), 223 n.48
JKG v. SG, 2011 N.Y. Slip Op. 21073, 31 Misc. 3d 639, 922 N.Y.S.2d 742 (N.Y. Civ. Ct. 2011), 236–327
Joder Bldg. Corp. v. Lewis, 153 Vt. 115 (1989), 636
Johnson v. Atlanta Humane Society, 173 Ga. App. 416, 326 S.E.2d 585 (1985), 225
Johnson v. Douglas, 723 N.Y.S.2d 627, 187 Misc. 2d 509 (N.Y. Sup. Ct. 2001), 289–290
Jones v. Office of Fin. of Baltimore County, 451 A.2d 926 (Md. 1982), 66 n.138
Juelfs v. Gough, 41 P.3d 593 (Alaska 2002), 2 n.6, 18, 49–50

Kazatsky v. King David Memorial Park, 515 Pa. 183, 527 A.2d 988 (1987), 269–270
In re Kellogg Brown & Root, Inc., 166 S.W.3d 732 (Tex. 2005), 129 n.125
Kemp, State *ex rel.,* v. City of Baton Rouge, 215 La. 315, 40 So. 2d 477 (1949), 281 n.109
Kloepfel v. Bokor, 149 Wash. 2d 192, 66 P.3d 630 (2003), 300
Koester v. VCA Animal Hospital, 244 Mich. App. 173, 624 N.W.2d 209 (Mich. App. 2001), 290–291
Krasnecky v. Meffen, 777 N.E.2d 1286, 56 Mass. App. Ct. 418 (Mass. App. 2002), 293–295
Kyllo v. United States, 533 U.S. 27, 121 S. Ct. 2038, 150 L. Ed. 2d 94 (2001), 342

Ladnier v. Norwood, D.V.M., 781 F.2d 490 (5th Cir. 1986), 252 n.38
Lamare v. North Country Animal League, 743 A.2d 598 (Vt. 1999), 224–226, 301, 635 n.2
Landers v. Municipality of Anchorage, 915 P.2d 614 (Alaska 1996), 291
LaPorte v. Associated Independents, Inc.,163 So. 2d 267 (Fla. 1964), 248, 258–259, 288
Latham v. Wal-Mart Stores, Inc., 818 S.W.2d 673 (Mo. App. E.D. 1991), 254, 274–275
LeConte v. Lee, 935 N.Y.S.2d 842, 35 Misc. 3d 286, 2011 N.Y. Slip Op. 21452 (N.Y. Civ. Ct. 2011), 60–61
Levine v. Knowles, 197 So. 2d 329 (Fla. 3d Dist. App. 1967), 250 n.25
Linceum v. Smith, 287 So. 2d 625 (La. App. 3rd Cir. 1973), 259–260, 305–306
Lipnick v. Reisinger, 859 N.E.2d 600, 168 Ohio App. 3d 253, 2006 Ohio 3878 (Ohio App. 2006), 189–190
Litowitz v. Litowitz, 48 P.2d 261, 146 Wash. 2d 514 (Wash. 2002), 18 n.31, 433
Lloyd's Credit Corp. v. Marlin Mgmt. Servs., Inc., 158 Vt. 594, 614 A.2d 812 (1992), 634
Loman v. Freeman, 890 N.E.2d 446, 229 Ill. 2d 104 (2008), 69 n.144
Lubbers v. Anderson, 539 N.W.2d 398 (Minn. 1995), 601

In re Mabray, 355 S.W.3d 16 (2010), 125–128
Maguire v. Mohrmann, 935 A.2d 1259, 397 N.J. Super. 103 (N.J. Super. 2007), 191–192
Maloney v. Conroy, 545 A.2d 1059, 208 Conn. 392 (1988), 308
Manning v. Mitcherson, 69 Ga. 447, 69 Am. Rep. 764 (Ga. 1882), 23
Mansour v. King County, 131 Wash. App. 255, 128 P.3d 1241 (2006), 418

Marbury v. Madison, 5 U.S. (1 Cranch) 137, 2 L. Ed. 60 (1803), 6
Marose v. Hennameyer, 347 N.W.2d 509 (Minn. Ct. App. 1984), 601
In re Marriage of Bereznak and Heminger, 2 Cal. Rptr. 3d 351, 110 Cal. App. 4th 1062 (Cal. App. 2003), 121
In re Marriage of Enders and Baker, 2015 Ill. App. (1st) 142435 (Ill. App. 2015), 78–79
In re Marriage of Golden and Friedman, 974 N.E.2d 927, 363 Ill. Dec. 130, 2012 Ill. App (2d) 120513 (2012), 131–132
Martinelli v. Petland, 2009 WL 2424655 (D. Ariz. 2009), 197–198
Marvin v. Marvin, 176 Cal. Rptr. 555, 122 Cal. App. 3d 871 (Cal. App. 2d Dist. 1981), 21–22, 28–32, 129, 155 n.8, 596 n.36, 622 n.137
Mastrobuono v. Shearson Lehman Hutton, Inc., 514 U.S. 52, 115 S. Ct. 1212, 131 L. Ed. 2d 76 (1995), 119
Mathews v. Eldridge, 424 U.S. 319, 96 S. Ct. 893, 47 L. Ed. 2d 18 (1976), 225, 386, 387, 388, 407, 408, 409, 417, 422, 423
Matthews v. Amberwood Associates Ltd. P'ships, Inc., 719 A.2d 119, 351 Md. 544 (1998), 310 n.202, 311
Mayo Collaborative Services v. Prometheus Laboratories, 566 U.S. ___, 132 S. Ct. 1289 (2012), 437
Mayor & City Council of Baltimore, et al. v. Clark, 944 A.2d 1122, 404 Md. 13 (2008), 311
McClure v. Briggs, 2 A. 583 (1886), 635
McCoy v. Lucius, 36,894 (La. App. 2d Cir. 3/5/03), 839 So. 2d 1050, *writ denied,* 03-1217 (La. 3/26/04), 299 n.168
McDonald v. Burgess, 255 A.2d 299, 254 Md. 452 (1969), 313
McDonald v. Ohio State Univ. Veterinary Hosp., 644 N.E.2d 750 (Ohio Ct. Cl. 1994), 249 n.21, 276–277
McGee v. Smith, 107 S.W.3d 725 (Tex. App. 2003), 252 n.41
Medura v. Town & Country Veterinary Associates, P.C., 2012 WL 3871953 (Conn. Super.), 54 Conn. L. Rptr. 483, 307–309
Metge v. Cent. Neighborhood Improvement Ass'n, 649 N.W.2d 488 (Minn. Ct. App. 2002), 601
Miller v. California, 413 U.S. 15, 93 S. Ct. 2607, 37 L. Ed. 2d 419 (U.S. 1973), 349–350
Mitchell v. Heinrichs, 27 P.3d 309 (Alaska 2001), 291–292
Mittasch v. Reviczky, 2013 WL 2948344, not reported in F. Supp. 2d (Conn. 2013), 147–149
Miuccio v. Puppy City, Inc., 2009 N.Y. Slip Op. 50404 (U) (N.Y. Civ. Ct. 2009), 194–195
Mizan Arabians v. Pyramid Society, 821 F.2d 357 (1987), 176–177
In re Molly, 712 N.W.2d 567 (Minn. App. 2006), 410 n.67
Mongelli v. Cabral, 632 N.Y.S.2d 927, 166 Misc. 2d 240 (N.Y. City Ct. 1995), 38
Moore v. Regents of the University of California, 793 P.2d 479, 51 Cal. 3d 120, 271 Cal. Rptr. 146 (1990), 446, 467
Moore v. RLCC Technologies, Inc., 95 2621 (La. 2/28/96), 668 So. 2d 1135, 281 n.109
Moreno v. Sterling Drug, Inc., 787 S.W.2d 348 (Tex. 1990), 278
Morgan v. Kroupa, 167 Vt. 99, 702 A.2d 630 (Vt. 1997), 2 n.6, 18 n.31, 222–223, 225, 301, 303, 635 n.2

Morrissey v. Brewer, 408 U.S. 471, 92 S. Ct. 2593, 33 L. Ed. 2d 484 (1972), 408 n.61
Mullaly v. People, 86 N.Y. 365 (1881), 243
Murphy v. Buonato, 42 Conn. App. 239, 679 A.2d 411 (1996), 148 n.24
Murphy v. Country House, Inc., 240 N.W.2d 507 (Minn. 1976), 601
Musicland Group v. Ceridian Corp., 508 N.W.2d 524 (Minn. Ct. App. 1993), 610
Myers v. City of Hartford, 859 A.2d 582, 84 Conn. App. 395, 853 A.2d 621, *cert. denied,* 271 Conn. 927 (Conn. App. Ct. 2004), 307, 344

Nahrstedt v. Lakeside Village Condominium Association, 878 P.2d 1275, 33 Cal. Rptr. 2d 63, 8 Cal. 4th 361 (Cal. 1994), 21, 207, 214–221, 227, 230 n.62, 234, 429 n.1, 446 n.25
Neefe v. Neefe, 16 Just. 16 (1900), 510
New Jersey Power & Light Co. v. Mabee, 197 A.2d 194, 41 N.J. 439 (1964), 282
New York v. Ferber, 458 U.S. 747, 102 S. Ct. 3348, 73 L. Ed. 2d 1113 (U.S. 1982), 349, 351
Nichols v. Sukaro Kennels, 555 N.W.2d 689 (Iowa 1996), 288, 289 n.128
Nicollet Restoration, Inc. v. City of St. Paul, 533 N.W.2d 845 (Minn. 1995), 601
Nollan v. California Coastal Commission, 483 U.S. 825, 107 S. Ct. 3141, 97 L. Ed. 2d 677 (1987), 239
Nord v. Herreid, 305 N.W.2d 337 (Minn. Ct. App. 1981), 601
Northgate Cooperative v. Donaldson, 54 A.D.3d 414, 863 N.Y.S.2d 469, 2008 N.Y. Slip Op. 6646 (N.Y. App. Div. 2008), 234
North Shore Bottling Co. v. C. Schmidt and Sons, Inc., 22 N.Y.2d 171, 292 N.Y.S.2d 86, 182
Northwest Animal Rights Network v. State of Washington, 242 P.3d 891, 158 Wash. App. 237 (2010), 346–347
Northwest Greyhound Kennel Association, Inc. v. State, 506 P.2d 878, 8 Wash. App. 314 (1973), 347
Nuijens v. Novy, 543 N.Y.S.2d 887, 144 Misc. 2d 453 (N.Y. Just. Ct. 1989), 156, 178–179
Nuzzaci v. Nuzzaci, No. CN194-10771, 1995 WL 783006 (Del. Fam. Ct. Apr. 19, 1995), 13, 39–40

Oats v. Whittaker, 18 Mass. L. Rptr. No. 29, 637 (MA 1/3/2005), 18 Mass. L. Rptr. No. 29, 637 (Mass. 2005), 188–189
Obergefell v. Hodges, 576 U.S. ___, 35 S. Ct. 2584 (2015), 352 n.127
Oberschlake v. Veterinary Assocs. Animal Hosp., 785 N.E.2d 811 (Ohio Ct. App. 2003), 249 n.18
O'Brien v. Wade, 540 S.W.2d 603 (Mo. App. 1976), 166, 169–170
O'Keefe v. Gist, 908 F. Supp. 2d 946 (2012), 237–238

Parker v. Kensington Hospital, 483 Pa. 106, 394 A.2d 932 (1978), 513
Parker v. Levy, 417 U.S. 733, 94 S. Ct. 2547, 41 L. Ed. 2d 439 (1974), 407
Pasado's Safe Haven v. State, 162 Wash. App. 746 (2011), 353
Patchett v. Patchett, 964 P.2d 1114, 156 Or. App. 69 (Or. App. 1998), 41–42
Patterson v. City of Bellmead, 2013 WL 1188929 (Tex. App. 2013), 238–240

Peloquin v. Calcasieu Parish Police Jury, 378 So. 2d 560 (La. App. 3rd Cir. 1979), 265–266, 377
Pelzel v. St. Paul Office of License, Inspections and Environmental Protection, No. A05-2534 (Minn. App. 2006), 386, 413–415
People v. Gutkaiss, 614 N.Y.S.2d 599, 206 A.D.2d 628 (N.Y. A.D. 3rd Dept. 1994), 355
People v. Haynes Michigan, 760 N.W.2d 283 (Mich. App. 2008), 325 n.11
People v. Spence, 212 Cal. App. 4th 478, 151 Cal. Rptr. 3d 374 (Cal. App. 2012), 355
People v. Tohom, 2013 N.Y. Slip Op. 5234 (N.Y. App. Div. 2013), 354–356
Petco Animal Supplies, Inc. v. Schuster, 144 S.W.3d 554 (Tex. App. 2004), 249 n.21, 295–298
Pickford v. Mason, 98 P.3d 1232, 124 Wash. App. 257 (2004), 300
Placey v. Placey, 51 So. 3d 374 (Ala. Civ. App. 2010), 235–236
Polakoff v. Turner, 869 A.2d 837, 385 Md. 467 (2005), 312
Polk v. Edwards, 626 So. 2d 1128 (La. 1993), 281 n.109
Pollard v. Southdale Gardens of Edina Condominium Association, Inc., 698 N.W.2d 449 (Minn. App. 2005), 228–229
Porras v. Craig, 675 S.W.2d 503 (Tex. 1984), 297, 318
Porter v. DiBlasio, 93 F.3d 301 (7th Cir. 1996), 225
Pratt v. Pratt, 1988 WL 120251 (Minn. Ct. App.), 8 n.34, 18, 33–34, 328, 420, 588, 606 n.77, 623
Preston v. Dyer, 2012 WL 5960193 (Tex. App. 2012), 132–133
Price v. Brown, 680 A.2d 1149 (Pa. 1996), 250, 279–280
Prim v. Fisher, No. S1464-09 CnC WL 6465236 (Vt. Super. Ct. 2009) (Toor, J., Dec. 22, 2009), 58
Prisco v. Forest Villas Condominium Apartments, 847 So. 2d 1012 (Fla. App. 2003), 226–227
Propes v. Griffith, 25 S.W.3d 544 (Mo. App. W.D. 2000), 248 n.12

Rabideau v. City of Racine, 627 N.W.2d 795 (Wis. 2001), 1 n.4, 4, 9, 14, 208 n.13, 250 n.26, 251 n.37, 283–285, 288–289, 290 n.136, 304 n.184, 352 n.126, 360, 360 n.152, 580, 583, 584
Rachal v. Reitz, 403 S.W.3d 840 (Tex. 2013), 128–129
Ramirez v. Goldberg, 439 N.Y.S.2d 959, 82 A.D.2d 850 (2d Dept. 1981), 180
Ramseur v. Askins, 44 Misc. 3d 1209 (A), 2014 N.Y. Slip Op. 51068 (U), 17, 77
Raymond v. Lachmann, 695 N.Y.S.2d 308 (N.Y.A.D. 1st Dept. 1999), 12, 16, 43–44, 60, 74 n.156
Reid v. Pierce County, 961 P.2d 333, 136 Wash. 2d 195 (1998), 306 n.192
Richardson v. Fairbanks North Star Borough, 705 P.2d 454 (Alaska 1985), 267–268
Rich v. New York Cent. & Hudson Riv. R.R. Co., 87 N.Y. 382 (1882), 182
Rivercenter Assocs. v. Rivera, 858 S.W.2d 366 (Tex. 1993), 125 n.123
Rizzo v. Puppy Boutique, 2010 N.Y. Slip Op. 50926 (U) (N.Y. Civ. Ct. 2010), 195–196
Rodrigues v. State, 472 P.2d 509, 52 Haw. 156 (1970), 266
Romero v. County of Santa Clara, 3 Cal. App. 3d 700, 83 Cal. Rptr. 758 (Cal. App. 1st Dist. 1970), 211–213
Rousso v. State, 239 P.3d 1084, 170 Wash. 2d 70 (2010), 347

Sacco v. Tate, 672 N.Y.2d 618, 175 Misc. 2d 901 (App. Term. 1998), 166 n.29
Sandefur v. Jeansonne, 9 So. 2d 80 (La. Ct. App. 1942), 67 n.141, 211
Sawh v. City of Lino Lakes, 800 N.W.2d 663 (Minn. App. 2011), 12, 385 n.8, 387, 420–426
Sawh v. City of Lino Lakes, 823 N.W.2d 627 (Minn. 2012), 385 n.8, 387, 420–426
Scheele v. Dustin, 2010 Vt. 45, 998 A.2d 697 (Vt. 2010), 302–304, 423 n.106
Schneider v. Green, 1990 WL 151142 (S.D.N.Y.), 162, 179–183
Schutzman v. Munson, 51 So. 2d 125 (La. Ct. App. 1951), 67 n.141
Scruggs v. Caba, 2007 WL 866068 (Conn. Super.), 154, 192–193
Sentell v. New Orleans Carrollton Railroad Co., 166 U.S. 698, 17 S. Ct. 693, 41 L. Ed. 1169 (1897), 5, 9, 203, 207–209, 225 n.52, 233, 245, 376, 383, 385, 387, 407 n.55, 409, 411, 413, 416, 420, 446, 467
Servel v. Corbett, 290 P. 200 (Idaho 1930), 66 n.139
Sherrier v. Richard, 564 F. Supp. 448 (S.D.N.Y. 1983), 181
Shields v. Wagman, 714 A.2d 881, 350 Md. 666 (1998), 311
Shirk v. Shirk, 561 N.W.2d 519 (Minn. 1997), 112 n.93
S.L.J. v. R.J. v. Kahn, 778 S.W.2d 239 (Mo. App. E.D. 1989), 33–35
Smalich v. Westfall, 440 Pa. 409 (1970), 280 n.107
Smith v. Palace Transportation Co., 253 N.Y.S. 87, 142 Misc. 93 (Mun. Ct. 1931), 271 n.88
Soucek v. Barnham, 524 N.W.2d 478 (Minn. Ct. App. 1995), 288
Southall v. Gabel, 277 N.E.2d 230 (Ohio Ct. App. 1971), 248 n.15
In re Spring Brook Farm Foundation, Inc., 164 Vt. 282 (1995), 634
State of Ohio v. Anderson, 566 N.E. 1224 (Ohio 1991), 413, 580, 584
State of Ohio v. McColor, 2013 Ohio 1279 (Ohio App. 2013), 426–427
State of Washington v. Peterson, 301 P.3d 1060 (Wash. App. 2013), 356–358
State v. Baker, 350 Or. 641, 260 P.3d 476 (2011), 358
State v. Buchanan, 5 H. & J. 317 (1821), 311
State v. Dye, 283 P.3d 1130 (Wash. App. 2012), 355
State v. Fessenden, 354 Or. 597, 318 P.3d 749 (2013), *aff'd*, 355 Or. 759 (2014), 19 n.36, 50, 325 n.13, 327, 358–361
State v. Hess, 359 P.3d 288 (Or. Ct. App. 2015), 19 n.36, 96 n.44, 325, 327, 361, 363
State v. Newcomb, 359 Or. 756 (2016), 363–364
State v. Nix, 355 Or. 777, 334 P.3d 437 (2014), *vacated,* 356 Or. 768, 345 P.3d 416 (2015), 19 n.36, 50, 96 n.44, 294 n.148, 325, 327, 358 n.147, 360, 361–362, 363
Stettner v. Graubard, 82 Misc. 2d 132, 368 N.Y.S.2d 132 (Town Ct. 1975), 271 n.88
Stewart v. Wilson, 356 N.W.2d 611 (Iowa App. 1984), 32–33
Stoddard v. VanZandt, 975 N.Y.S.2d 712, 2013 N.Y. Slip Op. 51175(U), 40 Misc. 3d 1213(A) (2013), 240–241
Strickland v. Medlen, 397 S.W.3d 184 (Tex. 2013), 12, 87 n.20, 242, 247 n.7, 253 n.45, 315–321, 385 n.8, 388, 423 n.106
Sullivan v. Ringland, 376 A.2d 130, 117 N.H. 596 (N.H. 1977), 26
Supchak v. Pruitt, 503 S.E.2d 581 (Ga. Ct. App. 1998), 283

Take Me Home Rescue v. Luri, 208 Cal. App. 4th 1342, 146 Cal. Rptr. 3d 461 (Cal. App. 2012), 161, 199–201
Taylor v. Welsh, 138 Ill. App. 190 (Pa. Super. Ct. 1909), 257–258
Tenaska Energy, Inc. v. Ponderosa PineEnergy, LLC, 437 S.W.3d 518 (Tex. 2014), 137–139
Terral v. La. Farm Bureau Cas. Ins. Co., 892 So. 2d 732 (La. Ct. App. 2005), 67 n.141, 78 n.163
Terral v. Louisiana Farm Bureau Casualty Insurance Co., 892 So. 2d 732 (La. 2005), 298–299
Tevis-Bleich v. Bleich, 939 P.2d 966, 23 Kan. App. 2d 982 (Kan. App. 1997), 40–41
Thiele v. Stich, 425 N.W.2d 580 (Minn. 1988), 602
Thompson v. Sicard, 385 So. 2d 334 (La. App. 1st Cir. 1980), *writ refused,* 386 So. 2d 355 (La. 1980), 299 n.168
Tillman v. Cook, 3 So. 2d 230 (La. App. Orleans 1941), 299 n.168
Toledo v. Tellings, 114 Ohio St. 3d 278, 871 N.E.2d 1152 (2007), 312 n.210, 426 n.114
Tracey v. Solesky, 50 A.3d 1075, 2012 WL 1432263 (Md. 2012), 309–314, 309 n.200, 311 n.206, 335 n.73, 385, 386
Travis v. Murray, 2013 N.Y. Slip Op. 23405 (N.Y. Sup. Ct. 2013), 17, 23, 40 n.83, 73–74, 83 n.9, 104 n.73, 243, 255, 466

United States v. Jacobsen, 466 U.S. 109 (1984), 340
United States v. Place, 462 U.S. 696, 103 S. Ct. 2637, 77 L. Ed. 2d 110 (1983), 340, 342
United States v. Six Hundred Thirty-Nine Thousand Five Hundred and Fifty-Eight Dollars ($639,558) in U.S. Currency, 955 F.2d 712 (D.C. Cir. 1992), 343 n.102
United States v. Stevens, 130 S. Ct. 1577 (2010), 332, 347–353
United States v. Windsor, 570 U.S. ___ (2013), 133 S. Ct. 2675, 186 L. Ed. 2d 808 (2013), 353

Vacura v. Haar's Equipment, Inc., 364 N.W.2d 387 (Minn. 1985), 618, 621
Valenza v. Valenza, 67 A.D.2d 879, 413 N.Y.S.2d 680 (1st Dept. 1979), 60 n.130
Van Arsdale v. Van Arsdale, 2013 WL 1365358, not reported in A.3d (2013), 75
Vargas v. Vargas, 1999 WL 1244248 (Conn. Super. Ct. Dec. 1, 1999), 18, 44–45
Vaughn v. Nelson, 62 S.E. 708 (Ga. Ct. App. 1908), 583
V.C. v. M.J.B., 748 A.2d 539 (N.J. 2000), 435 n.29
Villa de Las Palmas Homeowners Association v. Terifaj, 14 Cal. Rptr. 3d 67, 33 Cal. 4th 73, 90 P.3d 1223 (Cal. 2004), 227–228
Vimar Seguros y Reaseguros, S.A. v. M/V Sky Reefer, 515 U.S. 528, 115 S. Ct. 2322, 132 L. Ed. 2d 462 (1995), 119
Vue v. Vue, No. A05-728 (Minn. Feb. 7, 2006), 122–123

Walash v. Kilgour, 32 Misc. 3d 1244(A) (2011), 938 N.Y.S.2d 230, 2011 N.Y. Slip Op. 51700(U), 61–62
Warren v. Driscoll, 227 N.W. 199 (Minn. 1929), 606
Washburn v. Cutter, 17 Minn. 335 (Minn. 1872), 606
Webb's Fabulous Pharmacies, Inc. v. Beckwith, 449 U.S. 155 (1980), 407 n.56

Werronen v. Taylor, 589 N.Y.S.2d 666, 187 A.D.2d 774 (N.Y. A.D. 3rd Dept. 1992), 183
Western Horizontal Drilling, Inc. v. Jonnet Energy Corp., 11 F.3d 65 (5th Cir. 1994), 609
Whitmer v. Schneble, 29 Ill. App. 3d 651, 331 N.E. 115 (1975), 171, 254, 261–262, 262 n.68, 274–275
Whitmore v. Whitmore, Record No. 1644-10-4 (Va. App. 2011), 13, 62–64
Wilkinson v. Austin, 545 U.S. 209 (2005), 416
Williamson v. Prida, 89 Cal. Rptr. 2d 868 (Ct. App. 1999), 250 n.29
Williams v. Tam, 131 Cal. 64 (Cal. 1900), 209–210
Wilson v. City of Eagan, 297 N.W.2d 146 (Minn. 1980), 248 n.12
Wolf v. Taylor, 627 N.W.2d 795 (Wis. 2001), 53–54
Womack v. Von Rardon, 135 P.3d 542 (Wash. 2006), 300–301, 305 n.188, 305 n.189
Worrell v. Sachs, 41 Conn. Supp. 179, 563 A.2d 1387 (Conn. Super. 1989), 273–274

Zager v. Dimilia, 524 N.Y.S.2d 968, 138 Misc. 2d 448 (N.Y. Vill. Ct. 1988), 271–273
Zappa v. Fahey, 245 N.W.2d 258 (Minn. 1976), 602
Zeid v. Pearce, 953 S.W.2d 368 (Tex. App. 1997), 288

Index

AAA. *See* American Arbitration Association (AAA)
ABA. *See* American Bar Association (ABA)
Abandonment, seizure and, 507–513
Absolute rights, 5–6
Abuse. *See* Animal abuse and cruelty; Domestic abuse
Abuse reports, 108
Access contracts, 167–168. *See also* Visitation; Pet time
Adoption contracts, rescue group, 159–161, 199–201, 531–538
ADR. *See* Alternative dispute resolution (ADR)
Advertising, of mediation services, 101
AETA. *See* Animal Enterprise Terrorism Act (AETA)
AFFT. *See* Animal-focused facilitation team (AFFT)
Airlines, 169, 184
Alaska, 517
ALC. *See* Animal Law Committee (ALC)
ALI. *See* American Law Institute (ALI)
Alternative dispute resolution (ADR), 81
  alternatives, 464
  case law, 117–139
  interest-based, 86–87
  positional, 86–87
  See also Arbitration; Mediation; Collaborative law
American Arbitration Association (AAA), 116
American Bar Association (ABA), 451–452
American Law Institute (ALI)
  Restatement (Second) of Contracts, 158, 161, 186, 629, 636
  Restatement (First) of Torts, 269
  Restatement (Second) of Torts, 58, 158, 254, 261, 263, 267, 269, 273, 274, 286, 293
  Restatement (Third) of Torts, 158, 319
  Restatement of Trusts, 144
American Pet Products Association (APPA), 3–4
American Red Cross (ARC), 375
American Society for the Prevention of Cruelty to Animals (ASPCA), 2
Animal abuse and cruelty
  animal control officers and, 335
  bestiality and, 326
  case law, 337–364
  Constitution and, 332–335
  criminal forfeitures and, 336
  crush videos and, 332
  federal laws and, 331
  as felony vs. misdemeanor, 326
  Fifth Amendment and, 333–334
  First Amendment and, 332–333, 347–353
  forfeitures and, 335–336
  Fourteenth Amendment and, 334–335
  Fourth Amendment and, 333
  hoarders and, 330–331
  horse permits and, 331
  horses and, 330
  human abuse and, 324–325
  Louis Vuitton, 328
  personhood and, 327
  pit bulls and, 328–329
  sex offenders and, 325
  state regulations and, 325
  tracking of, 323–324
  victim concept in, 327
Animal/animal bonds, 14
Animal-centered mediation, 83–84
Animal classifications, mediation and, 87
Animal control, 398
Animal control officers, 335
Animal Cruelty Violence Act, 332
Animal Disaster Relief Network (ADRN), 373–374

Animal Disease Traceability Program, 331
Animal Enterprise Terrorism Act (AETA), 7, 331, 332–333
Animal-focused facilitation team (AFFT), 106
Animal/human bonds, 13–14, 75–77
Animal Law Committee (ALC), 451, 451 n.47
Animal lawyers, 450
Animals. *See* Pets; Companion animals; specific animals
Animal seizure memorandum of law, 507–513
Animal Welfare Act (AWA), 6–7, 220 n.40, 254 n.48, 331, 339, 461
Antenuptial agreements, 164–166
APPA. *See* American Pet Products Association
Arabian, Armand, 207, 218–221, 446 n.25, 466
Arbitration
  American Arbitration Association, 116
  benefits of, 109
  and best-interest factors, 123–124
  binding, 111
  child support and, 121
  controversy, 113–114
  co-ownership and, 113
  direct benefits estoppel and, 128–129
  drafting of agreements in, 114–116
  and Family Law Arbitration Act, 109–111, 115
  finality requirement in, 112–113
  frivolous appeal of, 119–120
  judicial, 115
  jurisdiction and, 112
  justice in, 116–117
  liability coverage and, 110 n.87
  mediation and, 85–86 (*See also* Mediation)
  partiality in, 137–139
  perception of case in, 113
  and pre-arbitration agreements, 134–136
  premarital contract and, 132–133
  private agreements and, 114, 125–128
  private justice and, 116–117
  public justice and, 116–117
  single-issue, 111–112
  types of, 108–109
  vacation of award, 111, 117–119, 122–123, 137–139
  waivers in, 112, 136–137
ARC. *See* American Red Cross (ARC)
ART. *See* Assisted reproductive technology (ART)
ASPCA. *See* American Society for the Prevention of Cruelty to Animals
Assisted reproductive technology (ART), 432–435
AWA. *See* Animal Welfare Act (AWA)

Bad actors, 78, 179–183
Bailments, 163, 169, 184, 213–214, 241, 242, 279–280, 280 n.107, 371–372, 376–377, 378 n.42
BDL. *See* Breed-discriminatory legislation (BDL)
Benefits, of pet ownership, 21
Bentham, Jeremy, 447
Bestiality, 326
Best-interest factors, 15–19, 73–74, 91–93, 104, 123–124, 463
Bias
  cognitive, of mediator, 88
  implicit, 87
Binding arbitration, 111. *See also* Arbitration
Bioethics, 432–435
Blackstone, William, 5–6
Blessing animals, 375
Body language, dangerous dogs and, 399–400
"Body of Liberties," 323
Bonds
  animal/animal, 14
  animal/human, 13–14
Books, animal law, 649
Brain Research through Advancing Innovative Neurotechnologies (BRAIN), 442
Breed-discriminatory legislation (BDL), 389–390
Breeder contracts, 161–162, 539–548
Breeder reputation, 162–163
Breed identification, 309–314
Breeding conformation standards, 430–431

Canine Health Information Center (CHIC), 429–430
Carson, Rachel, 447
Cats, 16, 43–44, 162, 257, 363
CFFT. *See* Child-focused facilitation team (CFFT)
CHIC. *See* Canine Health Information Center (CHIC)

Child-focused considerations, 99–100
Child-focused facilitation team (CFFT), 106
Children, best-interest decisions and, 463
Child support, arbitration and, 121
Chimpanzee Protection Act, 254
Choice of law, 222–223
Civil forfeitures, 336
Client, in mediation
  perceptions of, 88
  preparation of, 102, 104
Cloning, 431–432
Cognition, 443, 445
Cognitive bias, of mediator, 88
Collaborative law, alternative dispute resolution and, 106–108. *See also* Mediation
Collateral, animals as, 211
Commentaries on the Laws of England (Blackstone), 5–6
Community property, 209–210
Companion animals
  contracts and, 158
  custody and ownership statute amendment, model language for, 515
  defining, 2–4
  estate planning for, 141–142, 150
  in family, 463–464
  fundamental rights and, 238–240
  love by, 4, 8, 14, 16–17, 21, 24–25, 27–28, 31, 34, 38, 43, 44, 48, 59–60, 63, 72–74, 77, 94
  love for, 4, 14, 16, 31, 43, 44, 59, 63, 73, 77, 220, 285, 286, 466
  and old conceptions of animals, 245
  from pet stores, 187–188
  prohibited types of, 84 n.11
  sentencing, 19 n.36, 50, 96 n.44, 294 n.148, 325, 327, 358 n.147, 360, 361–362, 363
  veterinary college care of, in estate planning, 150
  See also Pets
Companionship, loss of, 20–21
Compensation, of mediator, 97
Conformation standards, 430–431
Consciousness, 444
Constitution
  animal abuse and, 332–335
  dangerous dogs and, 388–389
  Fifth Amendment and, 333–334
  First Amendment and, 332–333, 347–353
  Fourteenth Amendment and, 334–335
  Fourth Amendment and, 333
  See also Animal abuse and cruelty
Continuum, The, 1, 8, 19, 87, 112, 112 n.92, 285, 327, 336, 423, 434, 441, 445, 465
Contract law
  and animal transport by air, 169, 184
  case law, 169–201
  concepts in, 153–155
  contract analyses in, 156–157
  custody disputes and, 158–164, 167–168
  drafting in, 157
  equitable principles and, 154–155
  hearsay rule and, 172
  lemon laws and, 157, 157 n.14
  and liability releases, 158
  liens and, 158
  oral agreements and, 185–187
  practice pointers, 156–158
  and prestige of state, 176–177
  replevin in, 155–156
  severability clause, 162
  state laws and, 157
  and statute of frauds, 154
  summary judgment and, 177–178
  and Uniform Commercial Code, 157, 166–167, 169–170, 173–174, 174–175, 178–179
  veterinarians and, 164
  warranties and, 169–170, 173–174, 174–175
Contracts
  access, 167–168
  antenuptial, 164–166
  breeder, 161–162, 539–548
  foster, 163
  premarital, 132–133
  prenuptial, 164–166
  rescue group, 159–161, 199–201, 531–538
  severability clauses in, 162
  void, 159
  voidable, 159
Conversion claim, 58, 59, 69
Co-ownership, 85 n.12, 113, 192–193. *See also* Joint ownership agreement
Copyrights, 438–440
Council of State Governments, 449–450
Courage, 461
Courts
  mediation and, 105, 107
  offense of, awards and, 194

Courts, *continued*
role of, 464
as siding with law enforcement, 265–266
small claims, 190–191
Criminal forfeitures, 336
Criminal law, 19 n.36, 50, 96 n.44, 294 n.148, 325, 327, 358 n.147, 360, 361–362, 363. *See also* Constitutional law; First Amendment; Fourth Amendment; Fifth Amendment; Fourteenth Amendment
Cruelty. *See* Animal abuse and cruelty; Mistreatment
Crush videos, 332
Culture, law and, 8–9
Custody disputes, 8, 45–46, 464–465
contracts and, 158–164, 167–168
discovery in, 549–578
See also Family law; Replevin; Gift; Joint custody; Lost animals
Custody model statutory provisions, 517–523
Custody questionnaire, 473–478

Damages, in tort law, 247–250
economic damages, 247
noneconomic damages, 247–248
punitive damages, 21 n.41, 117–119, 170, 177, 250, 255, 256, 258–259, 272, 287 n.118, 302–304
Dangerous dogs
animal control and, 398
body language and, 399–400
and breed-discriminatory legislation, 389–390
case law, 384–388, 406–427
declaration consequences, 391
determination order for, 639–648
divorce and, 403
due process and, 388–389
evidence with, 395
experts and, 399
hearing officers, 397–398
insurance and, 393–394
lawyer strategy with, 397
legal arguments with, 400
mistaken identity with, 400–401
nature vs. nurture argument with, 402–403
ordinances, 395–396
ownership of, 404–406
pleadings with, 396
potentially, labels for, 390
proceeding consultation, 391–393
provocation of, 401–402
records with, 395
statutes, 395–396
strict compliance and, 390
travel risks and, 384
witnesses with, 399
Darwin, Charles, 441–442
Defendants, animals as, 444–445
Direct benefits estoppel, 128–129
Disaster Relief Act, 373
Discovery
custody, 549–578
in mediation, 103–104
sample interrogatory, 550–555
sample request for production of documents, 556–560
Divorce, 26, 40–41, 47–48, 94–102, 403. *See also* Family law
Documentation. *See* Records
Dogs
breeder agreements for, 539–548
breed identification in, 309–314
death, 12, 20, 92, 95, 146
as family members, 1, 6, 13–14, 17, 22, 29, 31, 40, 48, 60, 62–63, 73–74, 87, 96, 131, 144
as gift, 72
military, 1 n.3
with monetary value, 179–183
from pet stores, 187–188
police, 1 n.1, 1 n.2
as property, 207–209
from puppy mills, 188 n.69
registries for, 161 n.23
show, 65–68, 162
splitting up, 71
toy, 189–190
valuation of, 11–14, 246, 267, 268, 282, 291, 292, 297, 318
worth of, 213–214
See also Companion animals; Dangerous dogs; Pets
Domestic abuse
animal abuse and, 324–325
child-focused considerations in, 99–100
family law and, 18–19, 52–53
mediation in, 98–101
Due process, 237–238, 388–389

Durable powers of attorney, in estate planning, 149–150
Duress, 108

Economic damages, in tort law, 247
Education, mediator, 94–95
Emotions
animal, 443
sentience, 47, 63, 96, 96 n.44, 317, 359, 362, 444, 583
somatic marker hypothesis, 444
Equitable principles, 21–22, 28–32
Estate planning
case, 147–149
companion animals and, 141–142, 150
durable powers of attorney in, 149–150
euthanasia and, 142
Loved for Life program and, 150–151
oral communications and, 142
trusts in, 143–146
wills in, 143
Estoppel, arbitration and, 128–129
Ethics, 432–435
Euthanasia, estate planning and, 142
Evaluative mediation, 82–83
Evolution, 441–442
Exercise, for values clarification, 479–486
Expertise, in mediation, 93
Experts, dangerous dogs and, 399

FAA. *See* Federal Arbitration Act (FAA)
Facilitation team, in mediation, 106
Facilitative mediation, 82
Fair Housing Act (FHA), 150 n.29
Family, 463–464
Family law
and animal/animal bonds, 14
and animal/human bonds, 75–77
and benefits of pet ownership, 21
and best-interest factors, 15–19, 73–74
case law, 23–79
and criteria for record, 12
and determination of family members, 14
and domestic abuse, 18–19, 52–53
and equitable principles, 21–22, 28–32
and fictitious standard of value, 11–14
and human/animal bonds, 13–14
and joint custody, 12–13, 54–57, 62–64, 75–77
and loss of companionship, 20–21
and replevin, 14–15, 26, 59, 60–61, 61–62
tort law and, 255–256
and visitation, 12–13, 27, 37, 40–41, 45–46, 47–48, 52–53, 53–54
Family Law Arbitration Act, 109–111, 115
Family members, 14
Family values, 435
Favre, David, 207, 253–254, 253 n.47, 374 n.30, 451 n.47
Federal Arbitration Act (FAA), 636–637
Federal Civil Defense Act, 373
Federal law
aesthetic injury, 338–339, 339 n.88
Animal Enterprise Terrorism Act, 7, 331, 332–333
Animal Welfare Act, 6–7, 220 n.40, 254 n.48, 331, 339, 461
Fair Housing Act, 150 n.29
Section 1983 actions, 333
Ferrets, 84 n.11
FHA. *See* Fair Housing Act (FHA)
Fictitious standard of value, 11–14
Fifth Amendment, 333–334
First Amendment, 332–333, 347–353
Forfeitures, 335–336
Foster contracts, 163
Fostering, 20
Fourteenth Amendment, 334–335
Fourth Amendment, 333
Fraud, contract law and, 154
Freud, Sigmund, 442
Fundamental interest tort, 253–254
"Furniture approach," 17

Gendered communication, mediation and, 88–90
Genetic propensity, 95–96
Genetic testing, 429–430
Gift, 26, 31, 32, 35, 38, 45, 46, 62, 66, 69, 72, 73, 74, 91, 102, 161, 163, 164, 209–210, 236, 475
Goodall, Jane, 443, 461
Grandin, Temple, 447, 461
Guardians, 448–449

Hearsay rule, 172
HeLa cells, 446, 462
Helmsley, Leona, 146
Hoarders, animal, 330–331

Hold periods, 369
Horizontal intersection of practice areas, 20, 22
Horizontal property rights, 12
Horizontal real property, 214–221
Horses, 3, 5, 47, 88, 92, 101, 113–114, 145, 158, 176, 177, 183, 185–186, 285–287, 330, 331
Human abuse, animal abuse and, 324–325. *See also* Domestic abuse
Human property, 446
Hurricane Katrina, 365–376, 379–381
Huss, Rebecca, 329, 448
Hydrophobic madness, 5, 9, 208–209, 385, 387 n.16, 411, 424, 467. *See also* Rabies

Illinois goods-based doctrine, 48, 158, 171, 254, 262, 273 n.92, 274, 275, 293
Implicit bias, 87
Indicia of ownership, 163–164
Insurance, dangerous dogs and, 393–394
Intellectual property. *See* Copyrights; Patents
Interest-based alternative dispute resolution, 86–87
Interim category, 18 n.31, 19, 43, 82 n.4, 87, 96, 101, 107, 110 n.85, 111, 121, 161, 254, 298, 304 n.181, 311 n.207, 314, 319 n.227, 327 n.26, 336, 361, 433, 434, 465, 488 n.1
Interrogatories, 550–555, 563–572

JAMS. *See* Judicial Arbitration and Mediation Services (JAMS)
Joint custody, 12–13, 54–57, 62–64, 75–77. *See also* Custody disputes
Joint custody agreement, 525–530
Joint ownership agreement, 525–530
Joint tenancy, 209–210
Judicial Arbitration and Mediation Services (JAMS), 115. *See also* Arbitration
Jung, Carl, 442
Jurisdiction, in arbitration, 112
Justice, private vs. public, in arbitration, 116–117

Karp, Adam, 205, 335, 386–387

Lacks, Henrietta, 446, 467
Large confinement operations. *See* Puppy mills
Law
  choice of, 222–223
  culture and, 8–9
  model language, 515–523
  rule of, 461–462
Law enforcement, courts siding with, 265–266
Lawyers, animal, 450
Lemon laws, 157, 157 n.14
Liability, veterinary, 251–253
Liens, 158, 278–279
Life expectancy, 43–44
London, Jack, 271
Loss of companionship, 20–21
Lost animals
  Animal Welfare Act and, 7
  case law, 207–243
  found, 205
  Hurricane Katrina and, 370–371
  importance of time with, 221–222
  legal questions with, 205–206
  microchips in, 206, 206 n.8
  owners of, 204
  pleadings, 487–506
  property law and, 203–205
  replevin and, 240–241
  tort law and, 259–260
  unsterilized, 241–242
Loved for Life program, 150–151, 151 n.31

Malpractice, 251–253
Maltreatment, 8 n.34, 18, 33–34, 328, 420, 588, 606 n.77, 623. *See also* Mistreatment; Animal abuse and cruelty
Mediation
  animal best-interest topics in, 92–93
  animal-centered, 83–84
  animal classifications and, 87
  animal expertise of mediator in, 93
  and arbitration, 85–86
  attorney awareness during, 105
  attorney expertise and, 93
  best-interest factors in, 104
  bias in, 87–88
  child-focused considerations in, 99–100
  choice of mediator in, 85
  choosing type of, 84–85
  client perception and, 88
  client preparation for, 102, 104
  cognitive bias and, 88

court action and, 105, 107
deals in, 102–104
in domestic abuse, 98–101
evaluative, 82–83
facilitation team in, 106
facilitative, 82
final disposition in, 86
gendered communication and, 88–90
human best-interest topics, 91–92
impartiality in, 96
informed decision-making in, 97
mediator approaches in, 85
mediator compensation in, 97
mediator competence in, 102
mediator education in, 94–95
mediator legal perspective in, 96
mediator self-promotion and, 101
mediator training in, 94–95
mediator values and, 96
moral standards in, 94–102
negotiation dynamics in, 103
objectivity and, 87–90, 96
and parties' capacity to mediate, 95
party disclosures in, 107
positional-based questions in, 91
preparation for, 102
questions, 91–93
records for, 90
record sharing in, 103–104
self-determination in, 94
transformative, 84
types of, 81–84
and Uniform Collaborative Law Rules Act, 106–108
values in, 96

Merchants, rescue groups as, 160
Microchips, 206, 206 n.8
Military dogs, 1 n.3
Minnesota, 7–8, 328, 330, 330 n.41, 387, 413–414, 420–426, 469, 487, 488
Mistreatment, 18–19, 327–328. *See also* Animal abuse and cruelty; Maltreatment
Morals and ethics, 11, 24, 25, 29, 32, 122
Moral standards, in mediation, 94–102

Negotiation dynamics, in mediation, 103
Neuroscience, 442–443
New York products-based doctrine, 158, 254, 262, 273, 275, 292
Noneconomic damages in tort, 247–248
No-pets provisions, 223–224, 226–227, 227–228, 228–229, 230

Objectivity, in mediation, 87–90, 96
Old Yeller, 315, 317
Oral agreements, 185–187
Ordinances, 7–8
Ownership
of companion animals, statute amendment model language for, 515
co-ownership, 85 n.12, 113, 192–193
of dangerous dogs, 404–406
Hurricane Katrina and, 369
indicia of, 163–164
and lost and found pleadings, 487–506
See also Joint ownership agreement; Lost animals; Property

Partnership law, 183
Patents, 435–438
Personhood, 19 n.36, 50, 96 n.44, 294 n.148, 325, 325 n.13, 327, 358–361, 358 n.147, 361–362, 363, 445
Pets
defining, 2–4
estate planning for, 141–142
in Hurricane Katrina, 365–376, 379–381
in legal system, 4–8
lost, 7, 487–506
old conceptions of, 245
as property, 4, 18, 49–50, 77, 78, 207–209
See also Dogs
Pet stores, dogs from, 187–188
Pet time, 13, 15, 37, 82, 89, 107, 116, 167–168, 466, 520. *See also* Visitation
Pit bulls, 309–314, 328–329, 402 n.44. *See also* Dangerous dogs
Pleadings, lost and found dog, 487–506. *See also* Replevin
Police dogs, 1 n.1, 1 n.2
Positional alternative dispute resolution, 86–87
Powers of attorney, in estate planning, 149–150
Premarital contract, 132–133
Prenuptial agreements, 164–166
Prestige of state, 176–177
Private justice, public vs., in arbitration, 116–117

Promotion, of mediation services, 101
Property
  community, 209–210
  horizontal real, 214–221
  human, 446
  pets as, 4, 18, 49–50, 77, 78, 207–209
Property law
  case law, 207–243
  lost animals and, 203–205
Protection order, 18 n.33
Provocation, of dangerous dogs, 401–402
Public justice, private vs., in arbitration, 116–117
Punitive damages, 21 n.41, 117–119, 170, 177, 250, 255, 256, 258–259, 272, 287 n.118, 302–304
Puppy mills, 188 n.69, 197–198

Questionnaire, custody, 473–478

Rabies, 5, 9, 208–209, 385, 387 n.16, 411, 424, 467. *See also* Hydrophobic madness
Records, for mediation, 90, 103–104
  dangerous dogs, 395
Regan, Thomas, 447
Registries, 161 n.23
Relocation, custody and, 130–131
Renters, 228–229
Replevin, 23, 24–25, 26, 38, 54–57, 59, 60–61, 61–62, 65–68, 72, 73–74, 77, 177–178, 581–585
  in contract law, 155–156
  in family law, 14–15, 26, 59, 60–61, 61–62
  lost animals and, 240–241
  motion to dissolve ex parte writ of, 629–637
  order denying, 579–585
  order deciding, 630–637
  pleadings and analysis, 587–628
Request for production of documents, 556–560
Rescue group
  adoption contracts, 159–161, 199–201, 531–538
  in lost and found pleadings, 487–506
Restatement (Second) of Contracts, 158, 161, 186, 629, 636
Restatement (First) of Torts, 269
Restatement (Second) of Torts, 58, 158, 254, 261, 263, 267, 269, 273, 274, 286, 293
Restatement (Third) of Torts, 158, 319
Restatement of Trusts, 144
Rights, absolute, 5–6
Robert T. Stafford Disaster Relief and Emergency Assistance Act, 331, 373
Rollin, Bernard, 461
Rule of law, 461–462

Science, 462–463. *See also* Assisted reproductive technology (ART); Cloning; Genetic testing; Neuroscience; Patents
Section 1983 actions, 333
Seizure, 7, 206, 233, 327, 338, 340, 342, 359, 360, 451
Seizure memorandum of law, 507–513
Self-determination, in mediation, 94
Sentience, 47, 63, 96, 96 n.44, 317, 359, 362, 444, 583
Severability clause, 162
Sex offenders, 325
Shall/may dichotomy, 12, 385 n.8, 387, 389, 420–426
Shared custody. *See* Joint custody
Show cats, 162, 257
Show dogs, 65–68, 162
Singer, Peter, 447
Single-issue arbitration, 111–112. *See also* Arbitration
Skinner, B. F., 442
Small claims courts, 190–191
Solicitation, by mediator, 101
Spay and neuter adoption terms, 199–201
Standards, breed conformation, 430–431
Statute of frauds, contract law and, 154
Statute of limitations, 261–262
Statutes, 7–8
Stores, dogs from, 187–188
Summary judgment, 171, 177–178, 185–187, 205, 210, 223–224, 226–227, 240–241, 587, 601–602, 609–610, 618–619, 626 n.150

Teacup-sized pets, 189–190
Technology. *See* Assisted reproductive technology (ART); Cloning; Genetic testing; Patents
Tech transfer, 438
Tenants in common, 209–210
Terminology, for animals, 1–2

Third-party rights
  breeder contracts and, 161–162, 539–548
  rescue groups and, 160–161
TIPS. *See* Tort Trial & Insurance Practice Section (TIPS)
Title
  not passing through operation of law, 204
  passing of, 231–233
  passing through operation of law, 204
  rescue groups and, 160
Tort law
  case law, 257–321
  claims in, 246–250
  economic damages in, 247
  family law and, 255–256
  and fundamental interest torts, 253–254
  lost animals and, 259–260
  malpractice and, 251–253
  noneconomic damages in, 247–248
  and old conceptions of animals, 245
  punitive damages in, 250
  tort transformation and, 250
  and valuation of animals, 246
  veterinary liability and, 251–253
Tort Trial & Insurance Practice Section (TIPS), 374, 451, 451 n.47. *See also* Animal Law Committee
Toy-sized pets, 189–190
Training, mediator, 94–95
Transformative mediation, 84
Transport, by airline, 169, 184
Trespass, 14
Trespass to chattel, 300 n.171, 305–306, 369
Trusts
  basics with, 145–156
  conditional, 144
  in estate planning, 143–146
  honorary, 144
  traditional, 143–144
  and Uniform Probate Code, 144–145
  and Uniform Statutory Rule Against Perpetuities, 145
  and Uniform Trust Code, 145

UCC. *See* Uniform Commercial Code (UCC)
UCLRA. *See* Uniform Collaborative Law Rules Act (UCLRA)
Uniform Code of Military Justice, 1 n.3
Uniform Collaborative Law Rules Act (UCLRA), 106–108
Uniform Commercial Code (UCC), contracts and, 157, 166–167, 169–170, 173–174, 174–175, 178–179. *See also* Warranties
Uniform Emergency Volunteer Health Protection Act (UEVHPA), 374
Uniform Law Commission Family Law Arbitration Act, 109–111
Uniform Probate Code (UPC), 144–145
Uniform Statutory Rule Against Perpetuities (USRAP), 145
Uniform Trust Code (UTC), 145
UPC. *See* Uniform Probate Code (UPC)
USRAP. *See* Uniform Statutory Rule Against Perpetuities (USRAP)
UTC. *See* Uniform Trust Code (UTC)
Utilitarianism, 447

Valuation, of animals, 11–14, 246, 267, 268, 282, 291, 292, 318
Values
  family, 435
  in mediation, 96
Values clarification exercise, 479–486
Veterinarians, contract law and, 164
Veterinary colleges, companion animal care through, 150
Veterinary liability, 251–253
Vick, Michael, 328–329
Victims, animals as, 19 n.36, 50, 96 n.44, 294 n.148, 325, 327, 358 n.147, 360, 361–362, 363
Violence. *See* Domestic abuse
Visitation, 12–13, 27, 37, 40–41, 45–46, 47–48, 52–53, 53–54, 82. *See also* Pet time
Voidable contracts, 159
Void contracts, 159

Waivers, in arbitration, 112, 136–137
Warranties, 169–170, 173–174, 174–175
Wills, 143
Witnesses, of dangerous dog behavior, 399
Women, and gendered communication in mediation, 88–90